The Essential Guide to Prescription Drugs

JAMES W. LONG, M.D.

The Essential Guide
to Prescription Drugs

*What You Need to Know
for Safe Drug Use*

HARPER & ROW, PUBLISHERS
New York, Hagerstown, San Francisco, London

for Alice
who understood so well
and helped so much

Designed by C. Linda Dingler

Library of Congress Cataloging in Publication Data

Long, James W
   The essential guide to prescription drugs.
   Includes bibliographical references and index.
   1. Drugs. I. Title.
RM300.L64   615'.1   76–5141
ISBN 0–06–012676–0
ISBN 0–06–012677–9 pbk.

79 80 10 9 8 7 6 5

CONTENTS

Author's Note

The information in this book has been derived from a wide variety of authoritative publications of drug information, as well as from appropriate unpublished data. Obviously no claim can be made that the information presented for any one drug includes *all* known side-effects, adverse effects, or interactions possibly related to the use of that drug. While diligent care has been taken to ensure the accuracy of the book's contents at the time it went to press, the continued accuracy, currency, and completeness of the information presented is dependent on changing observations and developments in the field.

Information has been obtained only from professional sources widely accepted as reliable. However, there is controversy even among experts about the interpretation of certain drug actions, the nature of the relationship between drug use and certain adverse effects, and the precautions to be observed in the use of certain drugs. Where appropriate, the reader is alerted to areas of special uncertainty, disagreement, or concern.

More than 1370 brand names are given for generic drugs marketed in the United States and Canada. Canadian readers are advised that some categories of information may include statements that are at variance with those contained in official drug product monographs issued by the Canadian Government. Differences may be found in categories dealing with prescription requirement, drug schedule classification, intended therapeutic effects, recognized contraindications, precautions in use, adverse reactions, and others. Canadian readers are advised to consult official Canadian sources of drug information to supplement the information contained in this book.

Commonly used and recognized brand names of drug products included in the Cross-Index, Profiles, and Tables appear for purposes of identification; the listings are not to be interpreted as endorsements of the brands named. In many instances, the number of available brands of a generic drug was too great to allow a complete listing of all brand names. The omission of a particular brand name does not indicate that the unnamed product is in any way unsatisfactory or inferior to those listed. In the category in each Profile that lists possible interactions with other drugs, the inclusion of any brand names following the generic name of the interactant is for purposes of illustration only. It is not intended to mean that the particular brand(s) named have interactions which are different from other brands of the same generic drug. Readers are reminded that the generic drug, and *all* brand names under which it is marketed, are to be considered as possible interactants.

Acknowledgments

Many individuals in diverse professional settings have contributed in a variety of ways to the creation of this book. I wish to acknowledge with particular gratitude the helpful suggestions and tangible assistance provided by the following individuals:

Graeme S. Avery, Editor-in-Chief, Australasian Drug Information Services, ADIS Press Australasia Pty Limited, Auckland, New Zealand.

James A. Donahue, Jr., Group Vice President, Health Care Services, IMS America Ltd., Ambler, Pennsylvania.

J. Donald Harper, President, The Proprietary Association of Canada, Ottawa, Ontario, Canada.

Nelson S. Irey, M.D., Chief, Division of Tissue Reactions to Drugs, Armed Forces Institute of Pathology, Washington, D.C.

Hershel Jick, M.D., Boston University Medical Center, Boston Collaborative Drug Surveillance Program, Waltham, Massachusetts.

Don Harper Mills, M.D., J.D., Clinical Professor of Pathology, University of Southern California School of Medicine, Los Angeles, California.

Gerald N. Rotenberg, B.Sc.Phm., Editor, *Compendium of Pharmaceuticals and Specialties*, Canadian Pharmaceutical Association, Toronto, Ontario, Canada.

John. E. Steinhaus, M.D., Ph.D., Chairman, Department of Anesthesiology, Emory University School of Medicine, Atlanta, Georgia.

Christopher Tietze, M.D., Senior Fellow, The Population Council, New York, New York.

Professor Owen L. Wade, M.A., M.D., F.R.C.P. (London), Hon. F.R.C.P.I., Department of Therapeutics and Clinical Pharmacology, The Medical School, The University of Birmingham, Birmingham, England.

The helpful cooperation of many pharmaceutical manufacturers is greatly appreciated. In response to numerous inquiries they provided much detailed and hard-to-find information needed to complete the Drug Profiles in Section Three.

In addition, I wish to express my thanks to Lana Skirboll, Predoctoral Fellow in the Department of Pharmacology, Georgetown University School of Medicine, for assistance in researching appropriate medical literature; and to Carol Stiles and Linda Porter for the skill, patience, and cheerfulness with which they carried out the voluminous typing of a much revised and difficult manuscript.

Finally, I acknowledge with special gratitude and appreciation the masterful stewardship of Ann Harris, my editor at Harper & Row. It was she who perceived the timeliness and need for this unorthodox book and provided the constructive guidance, the painstaking attention to detail, and the diplomacy so essential to its development. My thanks go also to Ann's assistant, Maria Guarnaschelli, for her competent, enthusiastic, and genuinely helpful liaison in my behalf.

Preface

This book is the outgrowth of three recurring observations. First, many people request—and need—more information about the drugs prescribed for them than they have been given. Second, many patients encounter unexpected, and sometimes unrecognized, difficulties that are related to the drugs they are taking. Third, there is no single comprehensive source of drug information written for the patient.

Before the introduction of sulfa drugs in 1936, the number of available prescription drugs was relatively small. Most of them had been in general use for a long time, and their actions were comparatively simple and reasonably well understood. It took the physician little time and effort to give his patients all the information considered necessary for them to use their medicines with safety.

But as new and more powerful drugs were developed, it was discovered that the full range of effects a drug could have on the body was not always immediately apparent or predictable. We now know that most drugs require wide use for many years before *all* their possible effects can be recognized. New drugs reach the market regularly in this country and abroad. Many of them possess greater potency or more complex actions than those they replace. The abundance of prescription drugs now available has therefore generated an enormous volume of new drug information. Some of this information both the physician and the patient must know if a drug is to be used wisely.

Every prescription drug marketed in the United States today is accompanied by a package insert—the official literature which the manufacturer is required by law to provide as guidance *for the physician*. This package insert is enclosed in each drug package purchased by the pharmacist from the manufacturer. The pharmacist may or may not pass it along to the physician, but it is never given to the patient; neither the information nor the language used in the insert is designed for the layman.

Yet the package inserts of approximately 60 percent of the most commonly prescribed drugs contain necessary information about possible adverse effects of a serious nature. The package inserts of another 25 percent describe significant but less serious adverse effects. The patient's need to be informed—as well as the recognition of his right to be informed—grows greater all the time.

Though copious drug information is available to the health professions, it has been recognized for many years that only a small portion of it reaches the public. There are understandable reasons for this. The busy physician finds it difficult to devote the time he or she would require to keep fully informed on all aspects of drug therapy. The same constraints of time limit the amount of information the physician can convey to each patient who must be treated. It is also unrealistic to expect that the patient can retain all the significant information he or she needs for the proper use of certain modern drugs. The frequent prescribing of two or more drugs simultaneously makes the problem even more difficult to manage. Often the patient is understandably preoccupied by concerns about his illness, his future, or his absence from work, and he may not comprehend fully the details or the importance of the physician's instructions. He may hesitate to ask for clarification of technically complicated, confusing, or incomplete directions out of embarrassment or reluctance to infringe on a busy doctor's time. Frequently, therefore, whether as a result of misunderstanding or the lack of adequate information, the patient may use the drug improperly or abandon it altogether.

But if the goals of drug treatment are to be achieved, adequate information and its proper use by all concerned are indispensable. We have now reached the point where the use of prescription drugs must become a *shared* responsibility, a collaboration between physician and patient.

There is precedent for this. An early model for such joint participation followed the introduction in the 1920s of insulin in the treatment of diabetes. In the management of this disease it is imperative that the physician have a thorough knowledge of the drug he or she selects (there are now many forms of insulin) *and* that the patient understand the detailed instructions which he or she must follow if the drug is to be used correctly. Here the medical professions and interested lay organizations have collaborated admirably in the creation of teaching aids (pamphlets, books, films) designed to inform the diabetic patient as fully as possible.

Unfortunately, this principle of educating the patient to recognize and accept his rightful share of responsibility has not been applied to drug therapy in general. Although most illnesses requiring drug treatment do not include the sudden and dramatic events seen with diabetes, the principle of informed responsibility on the part of the patient is no less valid in their management.

New drugs, and the problems they create, have outdistanced our nascent realization that some drug information is as essential to the patient as it is to the physician. It is now obvious that the traditionally paternalistic and uninformative attitudes of some physicians have no place in the context of today's powerful and complex drugs. At the same time, the patient has become increasingly aware of how dangerous it can be to continue in the passive role of unquestioning drug consumer.

The mutual but distinct responsibilities of patient and physician follow an obvious and logical pattern. There are three key points in the physician-patient relationship at which dual responsibility for the exchange of information is of vital importance to the patient's welfare. The first is when the patient, experiencing an illness which he feels he cannot evaluate properly or treat without professional help, consults the physician. Using information provided by the patient, as well as his or her own findings on examination, the physician makes a diagnosis and establishes the goals of treatment. Then he considers the advisability of using drugs in the treatment plan. If he decides that treatment should include drug therapy, he selects the most appropriate drug(s) to use. This is the second point of dual responsibility: Both physician and patient should play a part in the selection of the most appropriate drug. The physician's knowledge and judgment can be fully utilized only if the patient has provided the information he or she possesses that is essential to that proper choice, either by volunteering it or in responding to the physician's questions. In this way, physician and patient together determine that the chosen drug will not be one to which the patient is known to be allergic, or one that will interact unfavorably with a drug already being taken, or one that the patient cannot tolerate because of an unusual sensitivity, reduced kidney function, or one of many other possible conditions.

Having selected the correct drug, physician and patient undertake a third exercise of dual responsibility: the proper use of the drug. Acting in his own behalf, the patient makes certain that he knows the name of the drug, the correct dosage schedule, and any precautions he should observe while taking it. A patient complies with a doctor's instructions far better when he is sufficiently informed to recognize and interpret anticipated drug effects and to know when he should consult the doctor about the possible need to modify therapy. Satisfaction in treatment is greatest when patient and physician keep each other fully informed throughout the course of therapy.

This book is meant to be a source of basic information about the most commonly used drugs—the equivalent of a "patient package insert"—presented in an accessible form for you and your family. It is *not* a do-it-yourself manual that can substitute for the professional judgment and direction of the physician. It will not tell you what drug to take, in what dosage, or for how long. It will tell you the kind of information you should share with your physician as he determines the drugs you are to take and the kind of information you should report to him while you are taking them. Properly used, this book will provide you with enough information to enable you to obtain the greatest benefit, with the least risk, from the drugs you are taking.

JAMES W. LONG, M.D.

1

Drug Actions and Reactions in Perspective

Approximately two-thirds of the population of the United States use prescription drugs at one time or another. At present, an estimated 75 million Americans are taking one or more drugs on a regular basis. The annual volume of prescriptions and drug orders written in this country now approaches three billion—almost double the volume of ten years ago—and market analysts predict that drug sales will double again by the early 1980s. From 70 to 80 percent of the prescriptions written by private physicians are for drugs used by non-hospitalized patients—drugs that are self-administered, usually without direct supervision. Huge quantities of non-prescription drugs are consumed daily. Over 15 million people take aspirin or combination drugs containing aspirin regularly; more than 10 million people are taking drugs for high blood pressure; 10 million women are using oral contraceptives; and another 5 million citizens are taking mild tranquilizers. The magnitude of drug consumption in most western cultures has become a major scientific, social, and economic concern.

Increasing public debate repeatedly exposes the consumer to claims and counterclaims regarding the virtues and evils of drugs, both those prescribed in medical practice and the numerous over-the-counter drugs often taken without the physician's knowledge or approval. Spokesmen for the drug industry, medical professions and government agencies, lawmakers, consumer advocates, and even the world of entertainment have all provided us with distorted and conflicting accounts of the role of drugs in modern society. Understandably, many citizens are confused and frustrated about safety in drug therapy. To comprehend the full potential for benefit and for harm which today's medicines have to offer, we must sort fact from fiction and put the picture of rational drug use in reasonable perspective.

The Wanted and Intended Actions of Drugs

The human body is an intricate chemical system. Most medicinal drugs are chemicals which are alien to the natural body chemistry. They are useful in treatment, however, because a particular aspect of their chemical interactions within the body favorably modifies some tissue structure or function. This, in turn, assists natural mechanisms that heal and restore. Drug actions alone do not "cure" disease. They benefit the patient by making a significant contribution to the total scheme of processes needed to restore health. Many illnesses are normally self-limiting; recovery often occurs as a result of natural recuperative forces, without the use of drugs.

When drugs are advisable, the "drug of choice" is the one which, in the judgment of the physician, is most likely to produce those effects most desired in a given treatment situation. This selection—the best drug, in the right dose, for the right person, at the right time—is the crucial first step in the successful use of drugs. But this decision can never be made with complete assurance that the interactions of drug, patient, and disease will be exactly as intended or predicted. When a patient takes any prescribed drug for the first time, he or she is in fact participating in an experiment under the physician's direction. While the physician's knowledge of the patient's general condition, his current illness, and the actions of the drug make it possible to predict the probable (and certainly the desirable) course of the experiment, the full consequences can never be foreseen. There is always an inescapable element of uncertainty.

The reasons for this are clear. The first relates to the drug itself: All drugs have multiple actions. There is no such thing as a drug with a single action. If a drug is to have any usefulness in treatment, it must be active enough to alter body chemistry and function in a beneficial way and to a sufficient degree. The complex nature of the human body makes it impossible to design a drug that can selectively limit its action to produce *only* one desired effect at a precise location. In actual use, a drug is selected because of its *principal* action—that particular one of its several effects which is wanted and intended. Simultaneously, however, its other actions ("side-effects") will occur, some of them trivial and unimportant, others more significant and even serious, but all quite natural and unavoidable.

The second reason for unpredictability relates to the patient: All patients experience multiple responses, some of which may not be readily apparent. The body's reaction to a drug varies widely from person to person, and in the same person at different times and under different circumstances. Personal characteristics due to inherited sensitivities, allergies, variations in metabolism, etc., all influence the total drug experience. At the outset of drug therapy, individual variation in response to both the intended effects and the side-effects of a drug is always unknown.

A third factor in the unpredictability of drug therapy is encountered in treating the chronically ill and the elderly. In these situations vital body functions are often impaired, and a new and urgent illness of immediate concern may be superimposed on a state of chronic illness or general deterioration. All hazards of drug treatment are usually increased in the elderly, and it is difficult to predict either the favorable or the unfavorable consequences of drug action in such situations.

When one understands all of the possible variables that must be considered, one realizes how truly remarkable it is that modern medical practice has achieved a reasonable standardization in drug selection and use.

The Unwanted and Unintended Actions of Drugs

All drugs can produce both wanted and unwanted effects. Unwanted drug responses are of two kinds. The first is the "side-effect," a natural, expected, and predictable action of the drug, which accompanies its principal and intended action; it occurs *on the side*. Many patients experience side-effects in one form or another. When the antihistamine Benadryl (a brand of diphenhydramine) is given to reduce the nasal congestion and excessive flow of mucus caused by seasonal hayfever, the drying effect on the lining of the nose is its principal (wanted and intended) action. The drowsiness it produces is one of its side-effects. When the same drug is given to treat insomnia, drowsiness is its principal action, and dryness of the nose and throat are side-effects. And so it is with many drugs in common use; while the obvious goal of drug therapy is to obtain the greatest relief possible with the least unpleasantness, in many treatment situations it is necessary to accept the minor annoyance of side-effects in order to obtain the more important therapeutic effect. Many side-effects are transient, gradually disappearing as the body adjusts to the continued use of the drug. In many instances the intensity of side-effects can be reduced by adjusting the dosage schedule or by substituting another drug from the same drug family. The wide variation in the frequency and nature of side-effects is responsible, in part, for the large number of similar drugs available to treat the same condition; this sometimes enables the physician to choose a drug which will produce fewer side-effects in a particular patient.

A second kind of unwanted drug response is the "adverse reaction," an unusual, unexpected, and infrequent response that is clearly undesirable and potentially harmful. Adverse reactions can and do occur when the best drug is being used in the correct dosage to treat the right patient for the right condition. Most adverse reactions are unpredictable; some can be prevented (as described at length later in this chapter).

Many sources of drug information use the terms "side-effect," "adverse reaction," and "untoward effect" interchangeably. The failure to draw a distinction between an understandable and acceptable drug action (a side-effect) and an unexpected and unacceptable toxic response (an adverse reaction) is one reason for widespread popular apprehension and misunderstanding about drug effects and their proper management.

Over the past ten years both professional and lay publications have given increasing attention to adverse drug reactions, often referring to them as "drug-induced illnesses." These are now generally accepted as a major health problem. The magnitude and seriousness of the problem justify concern and appropriate action, but it is important to remember that its true dimensions have not yet been established. Statistics of illness and death attributed to the adverse effects of drugs have been widely publicized, but these figures are crudely drawn estimates projected improperly from the results of a few studies limited in size and scope. When we analyze the studies, we find significant discrepancies of interpretation and representation. Some studies which collected "adverse reaction" data ignored the distinction between the natural consequences of overdose, which is a misuse of a drug, and truly unavoidable toxic effects. Reports of other studies have failed to include balanced consideration of the roles of advanced disease and fatal illness in cases of "drug-related" death. To attribute death in such cases primarily to drug effects is clearly inaccurate and misleading.

Another aspect of the problem which publicized reports have failed to explain is that the majority of drug-related illnesses and deaths involve *a small number* of highly potent drugs which are known to have narrow margins of safety. In most such instances, the life-threatening nature of the illness clearly justifies the hazards of treatment, even though the nature and severity of the underlying disease often render the patient more vulnerable to possible adverse effects of drugs, some of which are quite toxic by nature.

The distorted and exaggerated picture of drug-induced illness in this and other countries is a disservice to the best interests of the public. (Unfortunately, this critical field of public health lends itself to exploitation as "sensational" news.) Misrepresentation of the actual situation has a negative influence on both the health professional and the health consumer. A growing number of physicians are now more inclined to prescribe defensively, using a less effective drug which is "safer" rather than a more effective one reputed to be "less safe." Surveys of physicians have verified that fear of an adverse reaction (with the possibility of a resulting malpractice suit) is a major reason for not prescribing a particular drug. Many studies have also documented the frequency with which wary patients underutilize drugs prescribed for them. An example of this is the unusually high incidence of omitted doses and discontinued medications by individuals on drug treatment for high blood pressure. Thus fear deprives them of the best available treatment. This problem of patient noncompliance, already serious, can only worsen as public uncertainty and concern grow in response to heated debate that is lacking in balance and perspective.

Studies published to date have not been large enough, or adequately enough designed, to obtain an accurate assessment of the overall incidence of adverse drug reactions or the causative factors which characterize them. However, the few sober reviews available to this author support the following realistic conclusions

- Considered in the context of national drug consumption, serious adverse reactions are relatively uncommon.
- Most adverse reactions are transient and of a minor nature.
- The majority of life-threatening drug reactions occur in people who are already severely ill with advanced or known fatal disease.
- Most serious adverse reactions are caused by a small number of drugs which are quite hazardous by nature.
- The number of deaths properly attributed to drugs is quite small in relation to the number of lives saved by these same drugs.
- The reported high incidence of drug-induced illness and death reflects primarily the magnitude and extent of drug use rather than the inherent toxicity of drugs in general.

While this analysis suggests a positive and optimistic perspective of drug therapy, the individual who is about to begin a course of medication may be apprehensive about his or her chances of experiencing an unfavorable drug response. He or she is now aware of dual needs: the benefit to be derived from the proper drug *and* the protection to be sought through appropriate safeguards. Fortunately, both the health professions and spokesmen for the general public are devoting increased attention to meeting these needs more effectively.

The Balance of Benefit and Risk

The drug of choice in any treatment situation is the one that produces the most desirable combination of effects—the net worth of the drug's benefits, allowing for its hazards. This decision must be made in the context of the patient's overall condition and the natural history of his disease. The variables which require evaluation are many, and their possible interactions are often extremely complex. Rational drug therapy is not a simple exercise. The physician's responsibility is to devise a plan of treatment that tips the balance as far as possible in the direction of recovery and cure. He or she must ask simultaneously, How ill is the patient? How threatening is the disease? How dangerous is the drug? The more threatening the illness, the greater the potency (and consequently the toxic potential) of the drugs required to treat it. In serious illnesses, *every* appropriate drug may have some relative contraindication (see Glossary). Drug selection in these circumstances requires the most careful consideration of *all* pertinent factors—patient profile, disease profile, and drug profile.

Whenever possible the drug selected will have a wide margin of safety—a sizable spread between the helpful dose and the harmful dose. Fortunately, most drugs in general use today have a reasonable safety margin. However, a few drugs with uncomfortably narrow margins of safety are also in wide use. This is because they are often the only appropriate drugs available, they are highly effective, and the conditions requiring them are very common. The use of these drugs calls for an extra measure of vigilance by *both physician and patient* to maintain the delicate balance between benefit and harm. The patient should be sure that he fully understands the amount of variation in dosage he is permitted when he assumes the management of his medication. It is important that he realize that fluctuations in his living routines can temporarily alter his drug requirement and that from time to time he may experience indications of too much or too little of the drug. The well-informed patient will know what adjustments to make until he is able to consult his physician. He will also understand that the occasional annoyance and discomfort of incorrect dosage is a small price to pay for the long-run benefits which sustain his health and performance.

The use of highly potent and potentially toxic drugs in the treatment of life-threatening disease is another area which requires the closest cooperation between patient and physician. Here the trade-off between highly undesirable reactions and possible cure or control of the illness calls for much greater understanding and tolerance on the part of the patient. Close observation and periodic examinations to monitor the course of the disease and the effects of drugs on body functions are of utmost importance in achieving the best possible balance of benefit and risk.

Considered within the context of their proper use, the vast majority of drugs in use today offer benefits which significantly outweigh their hazards.

Preventing Adverse Drug Reactions

Our knowledge of the mechanisms of adverse reactions is very limited. For the most part, we cannot identify with certainty the person who is at greater risk of experiencing a true adverse effect. Available tests for the early detection of toxicity are of definite value, but they do not provide as full a measure of protection as we could wish.

As our understanding of drug actions and reactions expands, it becomes more apparent that there *is* a sizable proportion of adverse effects that are, to some extent, predictable and preventable. The exact percentage of preventable reactions is yet to be determined, but several contributing factors are now well recognized, and specific recommendations are available to guide both physician and patient. These fall into eleven categories of consideration.

PREVIOUS ADVERSE REACTION TO A DRUG

There is evidence to indicate that an individual who has experienced an adverse drug reaction in the past is more likely to have adverse reactions to other drugs, even though the drugs are unrelated. This suggests that some individuals may have a genetic (inborn) predisposition to unusual and abnormal drug responses. *The patient should inform the physician of any history of prior adverse drug experiences.*

ALLERGIES

Individuals who are allergic by nature (hayfever, asthma, eczema, hives) are more likely to develop allergies to drugs than are nonallergic individuals. The allergic patient must be observed very closely for the earliest indication of a developing hypersensitivity to any drug. Known drug allergies must be noted in the medical record. The patient must inform every physician and dentist he consults that he is allergic by nature and is allergic to specific drugs by name. *The patient should provide this information without waiting to be asked.* The physician will then be able to avoid those drugs which could provoke an allergic reaction, as well as those related drugs to which the patient may have developed a cross-sensitivity.

CONTRAINDICATIONS

Both patient and physician must strictly observe all known contraindications to any drug under consideration. *Absolute contraindica-*

tions include those conditions and situations which prohibit the use of the drug for any reason. *Relative contraindications* include those conditions which, in the judgment of the physician, do not preclude the use of the drug altogether, but make it essential that special considerations be given to its use to prevent the intensification of preexisting disease or the development of new disease. Such conditions and situations usually require adjustment of dosage, additional supportive measures, and close supervision.

PRECAUTIONS IN USE

The patient should know about any special precautions to observe while taking the drug. This includes the advisability of use during pregnancy or while nursing an infant; precautions regarding exposure to the sun (or ultraviolet lamps); the avoidance of extreme heat or cold, heavy physical exertion, etc.

DOSAGE

The patient must adhere to the prescribed dosage schedule as closely as possible. *This is most important with those drugs that have narrow margins of safety.* Circumstances which interfere with taking the drug as prescribed (nausea, vomiting, diarrhea) must be reported to the physician so that appropriate adjustments can be made.

INTERACTIONS

Much is known today about how some drugs can interact unfavorably with certain foods, alcohol, and other drugs to produce serious adverse effects. *The patient must be informed regarding all likely interactants* that could alter the action of the drug he is using. If, during the course of treatment, the patient has reason to feel he has discovered a new interaction of importance, he should inform the physician so that its full significance can be determined. (It is through such observations that much of our understanding of drug interactions has come.)

WARNING SYMPTOMS

Experience has shown that many drugs will produce symptoms that are actually early indications of a developing adverse effect. Examples include the appearance of severe headaches and visual disturbances *before* the onset of a stroke in a woman taking oral contraceptives; the development of acid indigestion and stomach distress *before* the activation of a bleeding peptic ulcer in a man taking phenylbutazone (Butazolidin) for shoulder bursitis. *It is imperative that the patient be familiar with those symptoms and signs that could be early indicators of impending adverse reactions.* With this knowledge he can act in his own behalf by discontinuing the drug and consulting the physician for additional guidance.

EXAMINATIONS TO MONITOR DRUG EFFECTS

Certain drugs (less than half of those in common use) are capable of damaging vital body tissues (bone marrow, liver, kidney, eye structures, etc.)—especially when these drugs are used over an extended period. Such adverse effects are relatively rare, and many of them are not discovered until the drug has been in wide use for a long time. As our knowledge of such effects accumulates, we learn which kinds of drugs (that is, which chemical structures) are most likely to produce such tissue reactions. Hence, we know those drugs which should be monitored periodically to detect as early as possible any evidence of tissue injury resulting from their use. *The patient should cooperate fully with the physician in the performance of periodic examinations for evidence of adverse drug effects.*

ADVANCED AGE AND DEBILITY

The altered functional capacity of vital organs that accompanies advancing age and debilitating disease can greatly influence the body's response to drugs. Such patients tend not to tolerate drugs with inherent toxic potential well; it is usually necessary for them to use smaller doses at longer intervals. *The effects of drugs on the elderly and severely ill are often unpredictable.* The frequent need for dosage adjustments or change in drug selection requires continuous observation of these patients if adverse effects are to be prevented or minimized.

POLYPHARMACY

This term refers to the concurrent use of many drugs during the course of treatment for a particular illness or condition. Several studies have demonstrated that the frequency of adverse reactions for any individual increases in proportion to the number of drugs he is taking. *In any situation requiring drug therapy, it is always best to use the fewest drugs possible.* The smaller the number of drugs in use, the smaller the chance for adverse reactions.

APPROPRIATE DRUG CHOICE

The drug(s) selected to treat any condition should be the most appropriate of those available. Many adverse reactions can be prevented if both physician and patient exercise good judgment and restraint. *The wise patient will not demand overtreatment.* He or she will cooperate with the physician's attempt to balance properly the seriousness of the illness and the hazard of the drug.

The Relativity of Risk

When we reflect on the changes in patterns of major disease that have been brought about over the past 60 years, we see that the remarkable contribution of modern drugs to our present health and well-being is most impressive. No one can reasonably deny the magnificent benefits that society derives from the intelligent use of today's medicines. Many serious illnesses regarded as incapacitating or fatal before the development of effective drugs now lend themselves to "routine" therapy and easy cure or control. Today we take for granted the large array of anti-infective drugs that change the course of many infectious diseases so dramatically that we refer to them as "miracle drugs." It is now the rule rather than the exception that, with appropriate drug therapy, we recover from typhoid fever, pneumonia, meningitis, and "blood poisoning" (septicemia). Families no longer experience the trauma and disruption of prolonged separation when a member contracts tuberculosis. The child with diabetes now grows to adulthood and often leads a full and vigorous life.

Such gains, however, have extracted their price, for there can be no progress without risk. Our present abundance of effective drugs has brought with it an increased potential for serious harm. This is a reasonable and unavoidable consequence and, indeed, not greatly different from any other of man's major endeavors. This year, for example, each of us has a greater than 2-in-10,000 chance of dying in an automobile accident, and a 1-in-500 chance of being seriously injured. Estimates of fatal reactions to the use of penicillin are 2 in 100,000, to mono-amine oxidase inhibitor drugs (antidepressants) from 1 in 10,000 to 1 in 100,000. The most carefully designed and evaluated study published to date found the rate of drug-attributed deaths per course of drug treatment in hospitals to be about 3 in 10,000. And over two-thirds of these drug-related deaths occurred in patients who were terminally ill or whose illness was judged to be fatal in the absence of drug therapy.

The concept of maximal benefit with minimal risk is the accepted basis for all rational drug use. The seriousness of the illness and the benefit sought must always justify the known risks of any drug to be used. A drug which is "completely safe for everyone" must also be weak and ineffective, for such a goal is not only unrealistic but unobtainable.

To demand absolute protection against all possible injury from drugs is to ensure the unavailability of useful drugs for all.

The inherent complexities of drug development, regulation, and utilization in this country promote contention and unrest. Not until the health professions and the general public jointly acknowledge their *obligations* to communicate can we hope to achieve a system of drug therapy that provides the greatest possible benefit at the lowest cost in unavoidable injury and death. The process begins when patient and physician collaborate with candor, reason, and mutual concern—in shared responsibility.

2

The Patient's Guidelines for Safe Drug Use

DO NOT

- pressure your physician to prescribe drugs which, in his or her judgment, you do not need.
- take prescription drugs on your own or on the advice of friends and neighbors because your symptoms are "just like theirs."
- offer drugs prescribed for you to anyone else without a physician's guidance.
- change the dose or timing of any drug without the advice of your physician (except when the drug appears to be causing adverse effects).
- continue to take a drug which you feel is causing adverse effects, until you are able to reach your physician for clarification.
- take *any* drug (prescription or non-prescription) while pregnant or nursing an infant until you are assured by your physician that no harmful effects will occur to either mother or child.
- take any more medicines than are absolutely necessary. (The greater the number of drugs taken simultaneously, the greater the likelihood of adverse effects.)
- withhold from your physician important information about previous drug experiences. He or she will want to know both beneficial and undesirable drug effects you have experienced in the past.
- take any drug in the dark. Identify every dose of medicine carefully in adequate light to be certain you are taking the drug intended.
- keep drugs on a bedside table. Drugs for emergency use, such as nitroglycerin, are an exception. It is advisable to have only one such drug at the bedside for use during the night.

DO

- know the name (and correct spelling) of the drug(s) you are taking. It is advisable to know both the brand name and the generic name.
- read the package labels of all non-prescription drugs to become familiar with the contents of the product.
- follow your physician's instructions regarding dosage schedules as closely as possible. Notify him if it becomes necessary to make major changes in your treatment routine.
- thoroughly shake all liquid suspensions of drugs to ensure uniform distribution of ingredients.
- use a standardized measuring device for giving liquid medications by mouth. The household "teaspoon" varies greatly in size.
- follow your physician's instruction on dietary and other treatment measures designed to augment the actions of the drugs prescribed. This makes it possible to achieve desired drug effects with smaller doses. (A familiar example is the reduction of salt intake during drug treatment for high blood pressure.)
- keep your personal physician informed of all drugs prescribed for you by someone else. Consult him regarding non-prescription drugs you intend to take on your own initiative at the same time that you are taking drugs prescribed by him.
- inform your anesthesiologist, surgeon, and dentist of *all* drugs you are taking, prior to any surgery.
- inform your physician if you become pregnant while you are taking any drugs from any source.
- keep a written record of *all* drugs (and vaccines) you take during your entire pregnancy—name, dose, dates taken, and reasons for use (see Section Seven).
- keep a written record of *all* drugs (and vaccines) to which you become allergic or experience an adverse reaction. This should be done for each member of the family, especially the elderly and infirm (see Section Seven).
- keep a written record of *all* drugs (and vaccines) to which *your children* become allergic or experience an adverse reaction (see Section Seven).
- inform your physician of all known or suspected allergies, especially allergies to drugs. Be certain that this information is included in your medical record. (Allergic individuals are four times more prone to drug reactions than those who are free of allergy).
- inform your physician promptly if you think you are experiencing an overdose, a side-effect, or an adverse effect from a drug.
- determine if it is safe to drive a car, operate machinery, or engage

in other hazardous activities while taking the drug(s) prescribed.

- determine if it is safe to drink alcoholic beverages while taking the drug(s) prescribed.
- determine if any particular foods, beverages, or other drugs should be avoided while taking the drug(s) prescribed.
- keep all appointments for follow-up examinations to determine the effects of the drugs and the course of your illness.
- ask for clarification of any point that is confusing or difficult to understand, at the time the drug(s) are prescribed or later if you have forgotten. Request information in writing if circumstances justify it.
- discard all outdated prescription drugs. This will prevent the use of drugs which have deteriorated with time.
- store all drugs to be retained for intermittent use out of the reach of children to prevent accidental poisoning.

3

How to Use This Book

Your physician has advised you to take a drug (or drugs), or you have been directed to administer a drug (or drugs) to someone under your care. The kind and amount of information you have been given about how to use these drugs, and what to expect from them, will vary tremendously. In many instances it will not be practical or possible for the physician to provide you with *all* the information that could be considered appropriate and useful, or it will be difficult for you to remember it. From time to time you will find it desirable—even necessary—to seek clarification and guidance about some aspect of drug action or drug use. The aim of this book is to give you the kind of information you may need to supplement the direction and guidance you receive from your physician.

The book consists of seven sections. The first section will give you the orientation and insight necessary to appreciate the complexities of modern drug therapy and help you to make the best use of the information contained in Sections Three through Seven.

Section Two is an alphabetical cross-index that translates brand names into generic drug names. A brand name is the trade name given to a drug product by its manufacturer. A generic name is the common or public name officially assigned to a drug by a governmental authority. (Any generic drug may be marketed under many brand names.) The cross-index will enable you to look up the brand name of a drug prescribed for you and match it to the drug's generic name so that you can locate the appropriate Profile in Section Three. If you do not find the brand name of your drug listed in the cross-index, ask your pharmacist or physician for the generic name of the product. (The large number of brand names in use for some drugs makes it impractical to list them all.) Then consult the generic name index at the back of the book to see if a Profile is provided. Brand names of combination drug products (those containing a mixture of two or more active ingredients) are cross-indexed to the generic name of *each* of the active drugs in the combination. In order to learn the full spectrum of possible effects of the combination products, you will want to look up the Drug Profile of each designated generic drug.

Section Three is a compilation of Drug Profiles covering more than 200 prescription (and several non-prescription) drugs used widely in the United States and Canada. The selection of each drug was based upon three considerations: the extent of its use; the urgency of the conditions for which it is prescribed; the volume and complexity of the information essential to its proper utilization. The Drug Profiles are arranged alphabetically by generic name. (Some generic names have spellings similar to other generic names; be careful not to confuse one with another.)

The Profile of each drug is presented in a uniform sequence of information categories. (When you become familiar with the format, you will be able to find quickly specific items of information on any drug, without having to read the entire Profile.)

YEAR INTRODUCED

This tells you how long the drug has been in general use. The older the drug, the more likely its full spectrum of actions is known and the less likely its continued use will produce new surprises. Most dates represent the year the drug was introduced in the United States. Where a drug had been used widely in other countries for a significant time before it was marketed in the United States, the date of its earlier foreign introduction is given.

BRAND NAMES

These are provided to confirm that you are consulting the correct Drug Profile. They may also help you to recognize a brand name that identifies this drug as one that produced in you an unfavorable reaction on previous use. Brand names and their manufacturers are listed for the United States and for Canada. A combination drug (a drug product with more than one active ingredient) is identified by [CD] following the brand name.

DRUG FAMILY

This identifies the therapeutic and/or chemical class to which the drug belongs. Designations in parentheses and/or brackets are professional terms used in established classifications and appearing in standard reference books. You will find it helpful to recognize the family (class) of the drugs you are taking because many actions, side-effects, adverse effects, and interactions with other drugs are usually shared by drugs of the same chemical family. Throughout this book (and in most literature on drug information) you will find reference to drugs by their family designation. (Section Four provides alphabetically arranged listings of the chemical and therapeutic families of drugs referred to in this guide.)

PRESCRIPTION REQUIRED

This indicates whether a drug is a prescription or a non-prescription (over-the-counter) purchase. Drugs subject to regulation under the Controlled Substances Act of 1970 (those with potential for abuse) are so designated in parentheses, and the particular schedule that governs their dispensing in the United States is cited.

AVAILABLE DOSAGE FORMS AND STRENGTHS

This represents a composite of available manufacturers' dosage forms (tablets, capsules, elixirs, etc.) and strengths, without company identification. Included are those dosage forms appropriate for use by outpatients and in extended care facilities and nursing homes. Dosage forms limited to hospital use are not included. Refer to Dosage Forms and Strengths in the Glossary (Section Five) for an explanation of those few abbreviations used to designate the strengths of each dosage form.

HOW THIS DRUG WORKS

This simplified explanation is limited to consideration of where and how the drug acts to produce its principal (intended) therapeutic effect(s).

THIS DRUG SHOULD NOT BE TAKEN IF

This category consists of the *absolute* contraindications to the use of the drug (see Contraindications in Glossary). It is most important that you alert your physician or dentist if any information in this category applies to you.

INFORM YOUR PHYSICIAN BEFORE TAKING THIS DRUG IF

This category lists the *relative* contraindications to the use of the drug. Here again, it is important that you communicate all relevant information to your physician or dentist.

TIME REQUIRED FOR APPARENT BENEFIT

The time stated represents a range that covers the shortest to the longest estimates that are generally recognized. Many factors influence the period of time required for any drug to exert beneficial effects. Among them are the nature and severity of the symptoms being treated, the formulation and strength of the drug, the presence or absence of food in the stomach, the ability of the patient to respond, and the concurrent use of other drugs. The information in this category is helpful in preventing premature termination of medication in treatment situations where improvement may seem to you to be unreasonably delayed.

POSSIBLE SIDE-EFFECTS

This category describes the natural, expected, and usually unavoidable actions of the drug—the normal and anticipated consequences of taking it. It is important that you maintain a realistic perspective that balances properly the occurrence of side-effects and the goals of treatment. Consult your physician for guidance whenever side-effects are troublesome or distressing, so that appropriate adjustments of your treatment program can be made.

POSSIBLE ADVERSE EFFECTS

This category includes those unusual, unexpected, and infrequent drug effects which are commonly referred to as adverse drug reactions. For the sake of evaluation, adverse effects are classified as mild or serious in nature. It is always wise to inform your physician as soon as you have reason to suspect you may be experiencing an adverse drug effect. Serious adverse reactions usually announce their development initially in the form of mild, unthreatening symptoms. It is important that you remain alert to significant changes in your well-being when you are taking a drug that is known to be capable of producing a serious adverse effect. It is also possible to experience an adverse reaction that has not yet been reported. Do not discount the possibility of an adverse effect just because it is not listed in this category. Following standard practice, some adverse reactions (and interactions) of certain drugs are listed, as a precaution, because these reactions are associated with the use of a particular family (or class) of drugs. Although the literature may not document such reactions in connection with the use of an individual drug within that family, the possibility of their occurence must be considered.

A word of caution is appropriate here. You have consulted your physician for medical evaluation and management. He or she has advised you to take a drug (or administer it to someone else). It is important that you recognize and understand that *in the vast majority of instances a properly selected drug has a comparatively small chance of producing serious harm.* Most of the drugs included in this book produce serious adverse effects rarely. Knowledge that a drug is capable of causing a serious adverse reaction should not deter you from using it when it has been properly selected and its use will be carefully supervised.

Occasionally a dagger (†) will precede a serious adverse effect. It serves as a warning flag of an especially hazardous or frequent reaction.

RECOMMENDED PERIODIC EXAMINATIONS WHILE TAKING THIS DRUG

This category lists those examinations your physician may recommend you undergo while taking the drug(s) he or she has prescribed, in order to monitor your reaction to them and the course of your condition. You should remember that the advisability of performing such examinations varies greatly from one situation to another, and is best left to the judgment of your physician. The selection and timing of examinations are based on many variables, including your past and present medical history, the nature of the condition under treatment, the dosage and anticipated duration of drug use, and your physician's observations of your response to treatment. There may be many occasions when he or she will feel no examinations are necessary.

To assure optimal results from drug treatment, it is important that you keep your physician informed of all developments you think may be drug-related.

WHILE TAKING THIS DRUG, OBSERVE THE FOLLOWING: OTHER DRUGS

For clarification of this confusing and often controversial area of drug information, this category is divided into five subcategories of possible interactions between drugs. Observe carefully the wording of each subcategory heading (see also Interaction in Glossary). Some of the drugs listed as possible interactants do not have a representative Profile in Section Three. If you are using one of these drugs, consult your physician for guidance regarding potential interactions. A brand name or names that follows the generic name of an interacting drug is given for purposes of illustration only. It is not intended to mean that the particular brand(s) named have interactions which are different from other brands of the same generic drug. If you are taking the generic drug, *all* brand names under which it is marketed are to be considered as possible interactants.

DRIVING A VEHICLE, PILOTING A PLANE, OPERATING MACHINERY

In addition to these specific activities, the information in this category applies to any activity of a hazardous nature such as working on ladders, using power tools, and handling weapons.

OCCURRENCE OF UNRELATED ILLNESS

This category relates to those drugs which require careful regulation of daily doses to maintain a constant drug effect within critical limits. Anticoagulants, anti-diabetic medication, and digitalis are examples of such drugs. Emphasis is given to those interim illnesses, separate from the condition for which the drug has been prescribed, that might interrupt the established schedule of drug use.

Other information categories in the Drug Profile are self-explanatory.

Section Four is a presentation of Drug Families arranged alphabetically according to their chemical or therapeutic class designation. The drugs within each family are listed alphabetically by their brand and generic names. Because of their chemical composition and biological activities, some drugs will appear in two or more families. For example, the drug product with the brand name Diuril will be represented by its generic name, chlorothiazide, in three drug families: the Thiazides (a chemical classification), the Diuretics (a drug action classification), and the Anti-hypertensives (a disease-oriented classification).

Frequently in the Drug Profiles in Section Three you are advised to "See (a particular) Drug Family." This alerts you to a possible contraindication for drug use, or to possible interactions with certain foods, alcohol, or other drugs. In each case, you can determine the more readily recognized brand names for each drug listed generically within a drug family by consulting the appropriate Drug Profile. Timely use of these references will enable you to avoid many possible hazards of medication.

Section Five is a glossary of drug-related terms used throughout the book. Each term is explained, and in most instances an example is provided to illustrate the preferred use of the term. Frequent references to the glossary are made in the Drug Profiles. Use of the glossary will increase your understanding of how to recognize and interpret significant drug effects.

Section Six consists of tables of drug information. The title and introductory material explain the content and purpose of each table. The information in the tables is drawn from certain information categories in the Profiles and is rearranged to emphasize pertinent aspects of drug behavior. The tables are intended to provide another source of ready reference.

Section Seven offers a method of recording personal histories of drug use for each member of the family. Model forms are provided for keeping records of drug intake during pregnancy, drug administration to the infant and child, and drug use by adults. In addition, there is a Medical Alert form suitable for carrying in your wallet or purse which can serve as an immediate source of information regarding (1) your current use of certain critical drugs and (2) the names of drugs to which you are allergic. Table 14 in Section Six lists the names of those drugs which should be entered on your personal identification card and carried with you at all times. This information can be of vital importance in the event of accident or serious illness, especially if you are unable to communicate with those providing you with medical care.

Cross-Index of Brand and Generic (Official) Names

Cross-Index
of Brand and Generic Names

If you know only the brand name of a drug product, use this cross-index to identify the corresponding generic name of the drug so that you may look up its Profile in Section Three.

The designation [CD] following a brand name identifies a combination drug product, that is, one that combines two or more active ingredients. Combination drugs that contain significantly different components are cross-indexed to all those generic drugs whose Profiles you should consult.

A generic name in parentheses indicates an active component of a combination drug for which there is no Profile in Section Three. It is included to alert you to its presence, should you wish to consult your physician regarding its significance.

Brand Name	Generic Name
A	
Aarane	cromolyn
Abbocillin	penicillin G
Acetal	aspirin
Acet-Am [CD]	ephedrine theophylline
Acetophen	aspirin
Acetyl-Sal	aspirin
Achromycin	tetracycline
Achromycin V	tetracycline
Achrostatin V [CD]	nystatin tetracycline
Acillin	ampicillin
Actidil	triprolidine
Actifed [CD]	pseudoephedrine tripolidine
Actifed-A [CD]	acetaminophen pseudoephedrine triprolidine

Brand Name   Generic Name

Brand Name	Generic Name
Actifed-C [CD]	codeine pseudoephedrine triprolidine
Actifed-Plus [CD]	pseudoephedrine triprolidine (noscapine)
Adapin	doxepin
Adenex	Vitamin C
Afrin	oxymetazoline
A-H Gel	antacids
Akineton	biperiden
Alcon-Efrim	phenylephrine
Aldactazide [CD]	hydrochlorothiazide spironolactone
Aldactone	spironolactone
Aldoclor [CD]	chlorothiazide methyldopa
Aldomet	methyldopa
Aldoril [CD]	hydrochlorothiazide methyldopa
Algoverine	phenylbutazone
Alka-Citrate Compound	antacids
Alkarau	reserpine
Alka-Seltzer Antacid	antacids
Alka-Seltzer (original) [CD]	antacids aspirin
Alka-2	antacids
Alkets	antacids
Allerest [CD]	chlorpheniramine phenylpropanolamine
Almocarpine	pilocarpine
Alpen	ampicillin
Alsimox	antacids
Altacite	antacids
Aludrox	antacids
Aluminum Aspirin	aspirin
Alu-Tab	antacids
Ambenyl [CD]	codeine diphenhydramine
Ambodryl	diphenhydramine
Amcill	ampicillin
Amen	medroxyprogesterone
Ameril	ampicillin
Amesec [CD]	amobarbital ephedrine theophylline
A.M.H. Suspension	antacids

Brand Name	Generic Name
Aminodur	theophylline
Aminophyl	theophylline
Aminophylline	theophylline
Aminophylline + Amytal [CD]	⎰ amobarbital ⎱ theophylline
Amitone	antacids
Amnestrogen	estrogen
Amodrine [CD]	⎰ phenobarbital ⎱ theophylline
Amosene	meprobamate
Amoxil	amoxicillin
Ampen	ampicillin
Amphicol	chloramphenicol
Amphojel	antacids
Amphojel 65	antacids
Ampicin	ampicillin
Ampi-Co	ampicillin
Ampilean	ampicillin
Amsebarb	amobarbital
A.M.T.	antacids
Amtet	tetracycline
Amytal	amobarbital
Anacin [CD]	⎰ aspirin ⎱ caffeine
Ancasal	aspirin
Anevral	phenylbutazone
Angidil	isosorbide dinitrate ·
Anginar	erythrityl tetranitrate
Anoryol	oral contraceptives
Anspor	cephradine
Antabuse	disulfiram
Antamel	antacids
Antibiopto	chloramphenicol
Anti-B Nasal Spray	phenylephrine
Antivert	meclizine
Antivert [CD]	⎰ meclizine ⎱ nicotinic acid
Anxium-5	diazepam
Aparkane	trihexyphenidyl
A.P.C. Tablets [CD]	⎧ aspirin ⎨ caffeine ⎩ phenacetin
Apresazide [CD]	⎰ hydralazine ⎱ hydrochlorothiazide
Apresoline	hydralazine
Apresoline-Esidrix [CD]	⎰ hydralazine ⎱ hydrochlorothiazide

Brand Name	Generic Name
Aquachloral	chloral hydrate
Arcoban	meprobamate
Arcocillin	penicillin G
Arcum R-S	reserpine
Aristocort	triamcinolone
Armour Thyroid	thyroid
Artane	trihexyphenidyl
Arthralgen [CD]	acetaminophen (salicylamide)
A.S.A. Preparations	aspirin
Ascorbajen	Vitamin C
Ascorbicap	Vitamin C
Ascriptin [CD]	antacids (aluminum hydroxide + magnesium hydroxide) aspirin
Aspergum	aspirin
Aspirjen Jr.	aspirin
Asthmophylline	theophylline
Astrin	aspirin
Atarax	hydroxyzine
Ataraxoid [CD]	hydroxyzine prednisolone
Atasol	acetaminophen
Atasol Forte	acetaminophen
Athrombin-K	warfarin
Atrobarb [CD]	atropine phenobarbital
Atrobarbital [CD]	atropine phenobarbital
Atromid-S	clofibrate
Atrosed [CD]	atropine phenobarbital
Aureomycin	chlortetracycline
Aventyl	nortriptyline
Azo Gantanol [CD]	phenazopyridine sulfamethoxazole
Azo Gantrisin [CD]	phenazopyridine sulfisoxazole
Azolid	phenylbutazone
Azo-Mandelamine [CD]	phenazopyridine (methenamine)
Azotrex [CD]	phenazopyridine (sulfamethizole) tetracycline
Azulfidine	sulfasalazine

Brand Name   Generic Name

B

Brand Name	Generic Name
Bactocill	oxacillin
Bactrim [CD]	sulfamethoxazole trimethoprim
Bamadex [CD]	dextroamphetamine meprobamate
Bamate	meprobamate
Bamo 400	meprobamate
Banlin	propantheline
Barazole	sulfisoxazole
Barbidonna [CD]	atropine phenobarbital
Barbipil	phenobarbital
Barbita	phenobarbital
Bardase [CD]	atropine phenobarbital
Bardona [CD]	atropine pentobarbital
Bar-15, -25, -100	phenobarbital
Bayer Aspirin	aspirin
Bayer Children's Aspirin	aspirin
BBS	butabarbital
Belbarb [CD]	atropine phenobarbital
Bellabarb [CD]	atropine phenobarbital
Belladenal [CD]	atropine phenobarbital
Bell-Ans	antacids
Bella-Probal [CD]	atropine meprobamate
Bellergal [CD]	atropine ergotamine phenobarbital
Benacen	probenecid
Benadryl	diphenhydramine
Bendectin [CD]	dicyclomine doxylamine
Bendopa	levodopa
Benemid	probenecid
Benhydramil	diphenhydramine
Bentyl	dicyclomine
Bentyl with Phenobarbital [CD]	dicyclomine phenobarbital
Bentylol	dicyclomine

Brand Name	Generic Name
Benuryl	probenecid
Benylin [CD]	diphenhydramine (ammonium chloride)
Betapen VK	penicillin V
Bicycline	tetracycline
Biotic-T-500	penicillin G
Biphetamine [CD]	dextroamphetamine (amphetamine)
Biquin Durules	quinidine
Bismocal	antacids
BiSoDol Powder	antacids
BiSoDol Tablets	antacids
Bonadoxin [CD]	meclizine (pyridoxine)
Bonamine	meclizine
Bonapene	reserpine
Bonine	meclizine
Brioschi	antacids
Bristacycline	tetracycline
Bristamycin	erythromycin
Bromo-Seltzer [CD]	acetaminophen antacids (sodium bicarbonate)
Brondecon [CD]	theophylline (quaifenesin)
Brondilate [CD]	butabarbital ephedrine isoproterenol theophylline
Bronkaid [CD]	ephedrine theophylline
Bronkolixir [CD]	ephedrine phenobarbital theophylline
Bronkotabs [CD]	ephedrine phenobarbital theophylline
Broserpine	reserpine
Brown Mixture [CD]	paregoric (glycyrrhiza)
Bubartal TT	butabarbital
Bufferin [CD]	antacids (magnesium carbonate) aspirin
Buffonamide	trisulfapyramidines
Buta-Barb	butabarbital

Brand Name	Generic Name
Butadyne	phenylbutazone
Butagesic	phenylbutazone
Butal	butabarbital
Butazem	butabarbital
Butazolidin	phenylbutazone
Butazolidin alka [CD]	antacids (aluminum hydroxide + magnesium trisilicate) phenylbutazone
Butibel [CD]	atropine butabarbital
Buticaps	butabarbital
Butisol	butabarbital
Butte	butabarbital
Butylone	pentobarbital

C

Cafecetin [CD]	aspirin caffeine phenacetin
Cafecon	caffeine
Cafeine	caffeine
Cafergot [CD]	caffeine ergotamine
Cafermine [CD]	caffeine ergotamine
Calcidrine [CD]	codeine ephedrine
Cama [CD]	antacids (aluminum hydroxide + magnesium hydroxide) aspirin
Camalox	antacids
Campain	acetaminophen
Canazepam	diazepam
Cap-O-Tran	meprobamate
Carbolith	lithium
Carbrital [CD]	carbromal pentobarbital
Carbromal	carbromal
Cardilate	erythrityl tetranitrate
Cardioquin	quinidine
Cartrax [CD]	hydroxyzine pentaerythritol tetranitrate
Catapres	clonidine

Brand Name	Generic Name
Cefracycline	tetracycline
Cenafed	pseudoephedrine
Centet	tetracycline
Ceporex	cephalexin
Cerespan	papaverine
Cetane	Vitamin C
Cetasal	aspirin
Cevalin	Vitamin C
Cevi-Bid	Vitamin C
Chardonna [CD]	{ atropine phenobarbital
Chembicarb	antacids
Chembutamide	tolbutamide
Chembutazone	phenylbutazone
Chem C	Vitamin C
Chemcetaphen	acetaminophen
Chemcycline	tetracycline
Chemdigtal	digitalis
Chemdipoxide	chlordiazepoxide
Chemflurazine	trifluoperazine
Chemgel	antacids
Chemgoxin	digoxin
Chemhydrazide	hydrochlorothiazide
Chemipramine	imipramine
Chemovag	sulfisoxazole
Chemthromycin	erythromycin
Chemthyroid	thyroid
Chloralex	chloral hydrate
Chloralixir	chloral hydrate
Chloralvan	chloral hydrate
Chloromide	chlorpropamide
Chloromycetin	chloramphenicol
Chloronase	chlorpropamide
Chloroptic	chloramphenicol
Chlor-Promanyl	chlorpromazine
Chlorprom-Ez-Ets	chlorpromazine
Chlor-PZ	chlorpromazine
Chlor-Trimeton	chlorpheniramine
Chlor-Trimeton Expectorant [CD]	{ chlorpheniramine phenylephrine
Chlor-Tripolon	chlorpheniramine
Chlortrone	chlorpheniramine
Choledyl	{ theophylline (oxtriphylline)
Cin-Quin	quinidine
Cleocin	clindamycin

Brand Name   Generic Name

Climestrone   estrogen
Clinazine   trifluoperazine
Clistin-D [CD]   { acetaminophen
                                    { phenylephrine
C-Long   Vitamin C
CM with Paregoric [CD]   { paregoric
                                    { (bismuth subsalicylate)
Cogentin   benztropine
Cohidrate   chloral hydrate
Colbenemid [CD]   { probenecid
                                    { (colchicine)
Colisone   prednisone
Coly-Mycin S   colistin
Combid [CD]   { isopropamide
                                    { prochlorperazine
Combipres [CD]   { chlorthalidone
                                    { clonidine
Compazine   prochlorperazine
Compocillin V & VK   penicillin V
Comycin [CD]   { nystatin
                                    { tetracycline
Conestrone   estrogen
Conjugated Estrogens   estrogen
                                    { atropine
Contac [CD]   { chlorpheniramine
                                    { phenylpropanolamine
Copavin [CD]   { codeine
                                    { papaverine
Cope [CD]   { aspirin
                                    { caffeine
Coprobate   meprobamate
Corax   chlordiazepoxide
Corivin   theophylline
Coronex   isosorbide dinitrate
Corophyllin   theophylline
Cortef   hydrocortisone
Cortenema   hydrocortisone
Cortril   hydrocortisone
                                    { acetaminophen
Co-Tylenol [CD]   { chlorpheniramine
                                    { phenylephrine
Coumadin   warfarin
Creamalin   antacids
Crestanil   meprobamate
Cryspen 400   penicillin G
Crystapen   penicillin G

Brand Name	Generic Name
Crystodigin	digitoxin
C-Tran	chlordiazepoxide
C-Vita	Vitamin C
C-Vite	Vitamin C
Cycline-250	tetracycline
Cyclobec	dicyclomine
Cyclopar	tetracycline
Cyclospasmol	cyclandelate
Cytolen	thyroxine
Cytomel	liothyronine

D

Brand Name	Generic Name
Dalacin C	clindamycin
Dalimycin	oxytetracycline
Dalmane	flurazepam
Dantoin	phenytoin
Darbid	isopropamide
Darvocet-N [CD]	acetaminophen propoxyphene
Darvon	propoxyphene
Darvon Compound [CD]	aspirin caffeine phenacetin propoxyphene
Darvon-N	propoxyphene
Darvon With A.S.A. [CD]	aspirin propoxyphene
Da-Sed	butabarbital
Datril	acetaminophen
Davoxin	digoxin
Day-Barb	butabarbital
DBI	phenformin
DBI-TD	phenformin
Deapril-ST	dihydroergotoxine
Decadron	dexamethasone
Decagesic [CD]	aspirin dexamethasone
Decapryn	doxylamine
Declomycin	demeclocycline
Declostatin [CD]	demeclocycline nystatin
Decycline	tetracycline
Degest	phenylephrine
Delcid	antacids
Delta-Cortef	prednisolone
Deltapen	penicillin G

Brand Name   Generic Name

Deltasone	prednisone
Deltra	prednisone
Demazin [CD]	{ chlorpheniramine { phenylephrine
Demer-Idine	meperidine
Demerol	meperidine
Demulen	oral contraceptives
Deprex	amitriptyline
Depronal-SA	propoxyphene
Deronil	dexamethasone
Desamycin	tetracycline
DeSerpa	reserpine
Dexameth	dexamethasone
Dexamethadrone	dexamethasone
Dexamyl [CD]	{ amobarbital { dextroamphetamine
Dexasone	dexamethasone
Dexedrine	dextroamphetamine
Dezone	dexamethasone
D-Feda	pseudoephedrine
Diabeta	glyburide
Diabinese	chlorpropamide
Diamox	acetazolamide
Diapax	chlordiazepoxide
Diban [CD]	{ atropine { paregoric
Dibenzyline	phenoxybenzamine
Dicarbosil	antacids
Dicumarol	dicumarol
Didan-TDC-250	phenytoin
Dietec	diethylpropion
Di-Gel Liquid	antacids
Di-Gel Tablets	antacids
Digifortis	digitalis
Digiglusin	digitalis
Digitaline Nativelle	digitoxin
Digitalis	digitalis
Digitora	digitalis
Dihycon	phenytoin
Dilanca	{ pentaerythritol { tetranitrate
Dilantin	phenytoin
Dimacol [CD]	{ pheniramine { pseudoephedrine
Dimelor	acetohexamide
Dimetane	brompheniramine

Brand Name	Generic Name
Dimetapp [CD]	brompheniramine phenylephrine phenylpropanolamine
Diovol	antacids
D.I.P.	diethylpropion
Di-Phen	phenytoin
Diphentyn	phenytoin
Diphenyl	phenytoin
Diphenylan	phenytoin
Disipal	orphenadrine
Dispas	dicyclomine
Diucardin	hydroflumethiazide
Diuchlor H	hydrochlorothiazide
Diupres [CD]	chlorothiazide reserpine
Diuril	chlorothiazide
Diutensen [CD]	methyclothiazide (cryptenamine)
Diutensen-R [CD]	methyclothiazide reserpine (cryptenamine)
Divercillin	ampicillin
Divulsan	phenytoin
Dolophine	methadone
Donna Extendtabs	atropine
Donnagel [CD]	atropine (kaolin) (pectin)
Donnagel-PG [CD]	atropine paregoric (kaolin) (pectin)
Donnatal [CD]	atropine phenobarbital
Dopamet	methyldopa
Dopar	levodopa
Doriden	glutethimide
Dorimide	glutethimide
Dormal	chloral hydrate
Dowmycin-E	erythromycin
Dowpen VK	penicillin V
Doxychel	doxycycline
Doxy-II	doxycycline
Dralserp [CD]	hydralazine reserpine
Dralzine	hydralazine

Brand Name   Generic Name

Dramamine   dimenhydrinate
Dramavol   dimenhydrinate
Drixoral [CD]   { brompheniramine
                                    { pseudoephedrine
D-Tran   diazepam
Duatrol   antacids
Ducon   antacids
Dufalone   dicumarol
Duohaler [CD]   { isoproterenol
                                    { phenylephrine
Duo-Medihaler [CD]   { isoproterenol
                                    { phenylephrine
                                    { ephedrine
Duovent [CD]   { phenobarbital
                                    { theophylline
Duratet   tetracycline
Duretic   methyclothiazide
Dyazide [CD]   { hydrochlorothiazide
                                    { triamterene
Dymelor   acetohexamide
Dymenol   dimenhydrinate
Dymocillin   penicillin G
Dymoperazine   trifluoperazine
Dymopoxide   chlordiazepoxide
Dymopoxyphene-65   propoxyphene
Dynapen   dicloxacillin
Dyrenium   triamterene
Dyspas   dicyclomine

E

E-Biotic   erythromycin
Ecotrin   aspirin
Ekko   phenytoin
Elavil   amitriptyline
Elixophyllin   theophylline
Elserpine   reserpine
Eltroxin   thryoxine
Emcinka   erythromycin
                                    { aspirin
Empirin Compound [CD]   { caffeine
                                    { phenacetin
                                    { aspirin
Empirin Compound with   { caffeine
   Codeine [CD]   { codeine
                                    { phenacetin

Brand Name	Generic Name
Emprazil [CD]	aspirin caffeine phenacetin pseudoephedrine
E-Mycin	erythromycin
Enarax [CD]	hydroxyzine (oxyphencyclimine)
Endep	amitriptyline
Enduron	methyclothiazide
Enduronyl [CD]	methyclothiazide (deserpidine)
Eno	antacids
Enovid	oral contraceptives
Enovid-E	oral contraceptives
Enovid 5 mg.	oral contraceptives
Enovid 10 mg.	oral contraceptives
Entrophen	aspirin
E-Pam	diazepam
Epilol	phenobarbital
Epragen [CD]	amobarbital ephedrine phenacetin
Epsylone	phenobarbital
Equagesic [CD]	aspirin meprobamate (ethoheprazine)
Equanil	meprobamate
Equanitrate [CD]	meprobamate pentaerythritol tetranitrate
Ergomar	ergotamine
Eributazone	phenylbutazone
Erital	diazepam
Erivit C	Vitamin C
Erymycin	erythromycin
Erypar	erythromycin
Erythrocin	erythromycin
Erythromid	erythromycin
Erythromyctine	erythromycin
Esbaloid	bethanidine
Esidrix	hydrochlorothiazide
Esimil [CD]	guanethidine hydrochlorothiazide
Eskabarb	phenobarbital
Eskalith	lithium
Eskatrol [CD]	dextroamphetamine prochlorperazine
Ethril	erythromycin

Brand Name   Generic Name

Etrafon [CD]   ⎰ amitriptyline
                        ⎱ perphenazine
Euglucon   glyburide
Euthroid [CD]   ⎰ liothyronine
                        ⎱ thyroxine
Evex   estrogen
                        ⎧ acetaminophen
Excedrin [CD]   ⎨ aspirin
                        ⎩ caffeine
Expansatol   butabarbital

F

Falapen   penicillin G
Fastin   phentermine
Fedahist [CD]   ⎰ chlorpheniramine
                        ⎱ pseudoephedrine
Fed-Mycin   tetracycline
Fedrazil [CD]   ⎰ pseudoephedrine
                        ⎱ (chlorcyclizine)
Fellozine   promethazine
Felsules   chloral hydrate
Femogen   estrogen
Fenicol   chloramphenicol
Fenosed   phenobarbital
Fernisolone   prednisolone
                        ⎧ aspirin
Fiorinal [CD]   ⎪ butalbital
                        ⎨ caffeine
                        ⎩ phenacetin
                        ⎧ aspirin
                        ⎪ butalbital
Fiorinal-C [CD]   ⎨ caffeine
                        ⎪ codeine
                        ⎩ phenacetin
                        ⎧ aspirin
                        ⎪ butalbital
Fiorinal with Codeine [CD] ⎨ caffeine
                        ⎪ codeine
                        ⎩ phenacetin
Fizrin   antacids
Flagyl   metronidazole
Floramine   phenobarbital
                        ⎧ estrogen
Formatrix [CD]   ⎨ Vitamin C
                        ⎩ (methyltestosterone)

Brand Name   Generic Name

4-Way Cold Tabs [CD]
{ antacids (magnesium
   hydroxide)
aspirin
phenylephrine
(phenolphthalein) }

4-Way Nasal Spray [CD]
{ phenylephrine
phenylpropanolamine
pyrilamine
(naphazoline) }

Brand Name	Generic Name
Fulvicin P/G	griseofulvin
Fulvicin-U/F	griseofulvin
Furachel	nitrofurantoin
Furadantin	nitrofurantoin
Furalan	nitrofurantoin
Furaloid	nitrofurantoin
Furanex	nitrofurantoin
Furanite	nitrofurantoin
Furantoin	nitrofurantoin
Furatine	nitrofurantoin
Furoside	furosemide
Furoxone	furazolidone

G

Brand Name	Generic Name
Gammacorten	dexamethasone
Ganphen	promethazine
Gantanol	sulfamethoxazole
Gantrisin	sulfisoxazole
Gardenal	phenobarbital
Gelusil	antacids
Gene-Cycline	tetracycline
Gene-Poxide	chlordiazepoxide
Genisis	estrogen
Geocillin	carbenicillin
Geopen	carbenicillin
Globin Zinc Insulin	insulin

Gluco-Fedrin [CD]
{ ephedrine
(dextrose) }

Brand Name	Generic Name
Glucophage	metformin
G-Mycin	tetracycline
Gravol	dimenhydrinate
G-Recillin-T	penicillin G
Grifulvin V	griseofulvin
Grisactin	griseofulvin
Grisovin-FP	griseofulvin
Grisowen	griseofulvin

Brand Name	Generic Name
G-Sox	sulfisoxazole
GT-250	tetracycline
GT-500	tetracycline
Gustalac	antacids
Gynergen	ergotamine

H

Brand Name	Generic Name
Haldol	haloperidol
Harmar	propoxyphene
Henomint	phenobarbital
Hexadrol	dexamethasone
Hi-Pen	penicillin V
Hiserpia	reserpine
Histalon	chlorpheniramine
Histanil	promethazine
Histaspan	chlorpheniramine
H.S. Need	chloral hydrate
Hyasorb	penicillin G
Hydeltra	prednisolone
Hydergine	dihydroergotoxine
Hydrazide	hydrochlorothiazide
Hydrid	hydrochlorothiazide
Hydro-Aquil	hydrochlorothiazide
Hydrocortone	hydrocortisone
Hydrodiuretex	hydrochlorothiazide
HydroDiuril	hydrochlorothiazide
Hydropres [CD]	hydrochlorothiazide reserpine
Hydrosaluret	hydrochlorothiazide
Hydrozide	hydrochlorothiazide
Hydrozide-50	hydrochlorothiazide
Hygroton	chlorthalidone
Hylenta	penicillin G
Hyperetic	hydrochlorothiazide
Hyperine	reserpine
Hypnette	phenobarbital
Hypnol	pentobarbital
Hypnolone	phenobarbital
Hypnotal	pentobarbital
Hyptor	methaqualone
Hyserpia	reserpine
Hyzyd	isoniazid

Brand Name	Generic Name

I

Brand Name	Generic Name
Ibatal	pentobarbital
Iletin Preparations	insulin
Ilosone	erythromycin
Ilotycin	erythromycin
Impranil	imipramine
Impril	imipramine
Inderal	propranolol
Indocid	indomethacin
Indocin	indomethacin
Inflamase	prednisolone
Infrocin	indomethacin
INH	isoniazid
Inhiston	pheniramine
Insulin Preparations	insulin
Intal	cromolyn
Intasedol	butabarbital
Interbarb	butabarbital
Intrabutazone	phenylbutazone
Intrazine	promazine
Ionamin	phentermine
I-Sedrin [CD]	ephedrine (gluconic acid)
Ismelin	guanethidine
Ismelin-Esidrix [CD]	guanethidine hydrochlorothiazide
Iso-Asminyl [CD]	ephedrine isoproterenol phenobarbital theophylline
Iso-Autohaler	isoproterenol
Isobec	amobarbital
Isonal	amobarbital
Isophrin	phenylephrine
Isopto Carpine	pilocarpine
Isopto Fenicol	chloramphenicol
Isopto Frin	phenylephrine
Isopto Prednisolone	prednisolone
Isordil	isosorbide dinitrate
Isotamine	isoniazid
Isuprel	isoproterenol
Isuprel Compound [CD]	ephedrine isoproterenol phenobarbital theophylline (potassium iodide)

Brand Name   Generic Name

Isuprel-Neo [CD]   ⎰ isoproterenol
                                ⎱ phenylephrine

K

Kalmm   meprobamate
Kaochlor   potassium
Kaon   potassium
Kaoparin [CD]   ⎰ paregoric
                                ⎱ (kaolin)
Ka-Pen   penicillin G
Kay Ciel   potassium
K-Cillin   penicillin G
KCl Rougier   potassium
Keflex   cephalexin
Kemadrin   procyclidine
Kenacort   triamcinolone
Kesso-Bamate   meprobamate
Kessodanten   phenytoin
Kessodrate   chloral hydrate
Kesso-Mycin   erythromycin
Kesso-Pen   penicillin G
Kesso-Pen V & VK   penicillin V
Kesso-Tetra   tetracycline
Key-Serpine   reserpine
Kiophyllin [CD]   ⎰ phenobarbital
                                ⎱ theophylline
K-Lor   potassium
Klorazine   chlorpromazine
Klort   meprobamate
Klorvess   potassium
K-Lyte   potassium
Kolantyl   antacids
K-Pen   penicillin G
K-Phen   promethazine
K-10   potassium

L

Lanacillin   penicillin G
Lan-Dol   meprobamate
Laniazid   isoniazid
Lanoxin   digoxin
Largactil   chlorpromazine
Larodopa   levodopa
Larotid   amoxicillin
Laserdil   isosorbide dinitrate

Brand Name	Generic Name
Lasix	furosemide
Ledercillin VK	penicillin V
Lemiserp	reserpine
Lemiserp TY-Med	reserpine
Lente Insulin	insulin
Letter	thyroxine
Levate	amitriptyline
Levoid	thyroxine
Levopa	levodopa
Librax [CD]	chlordiazepoxide clidinium
Libritabs	chlordiazepoxide
Librium	chlordiazepoxide
Lincocin	lincomycin
Liomel	liothyronine
Liquamar	warfarin
Lithane	lithium
Lithonate	lithium
Lithotabs	lithium
Loestrin 1/20	oral contraceptives
Loestrin 1.5/30	oral contraceptives
Logest 1/50	oral contraceptives
Logest 1.5/30	oral contraceptives
Lomotil [CD]	atropine diphenoxylate
Lo/Ovral	oral contraceptives
Lopress	hydralazine
Lotusate	butalbital
Luminal	phenobarbital
Lyndiol-22	oral contraceptives

M

Brand Name	Generic Name
Maalox	antacids
Macrodantin	nitrofurantoin
Magaldrate	antacids
Magnatril	antacids
Magnesed	antacids
Malcogel	antacids
Malgesic	phenylbutazone
Mandrax [CD]	diphenydramine methaqualone
Marax [CD]	ephedrine hydroxyzine theophylline
Mareline	amitriptyline

Brand Name	Generic Name
Marezine	cyclizine
Marzine	cyclizine
Maso-Bamate	meprobamate
Maxamag Suspension	antacids
Maxidex	dexamethasone
Maytrex	tetracycline
Measurin	aspirin
Mecazine	meclizine
Medarsed	butabarbital
Medicycline	tetracycline
Medihaler-Ergotamine	ergotamine
Medihaler-Iso	isoproterenol
Medilium	chlordiazepoxide
Mediphen	phenobarbital
Meditran	meprobamate
Medrol	methylprednisolone
Megacillin	penicillin G
Mellaril	thioridazine
Mellitol	tolbutamide
Meltrol	phenformin
Menest	estrogen
Menospasm	dicyclomine
Menotabs	estrogen
Menotrol	estrogen
Menrium [CD]	{ chlordiazepoxide / estrogen
Meprocon	meprobamate
Meprospan	meprobamate
Meprospan-400	meprobamate
Meprotab	meprobamate
Mequelon	methaqualone
Meribam	meprobamate
Mericycline	tetracycline
Methadorm	methaqualone
Meth-Dia-Mer Sulfonamides	trisulfapyrimidines
Methidate	methylphenidate
Meticorten	prednisone
Meval	diazepam
Micronor 0.35 mg.	oral contraceptives
Midol [CD]	{ aspirin / caffeine / (cinnamedrine)
Migral [CD]	{ caffeine / cyclizine / ergotamine

Brand Name	Generic Name
Milk of Magnesia	antacids
Milpath [CD]	{ meprobamate tridihexethyl
Milprem [CD]	{ estrogen meprobamate
Miltown	meprobamate
Miltrate [CD]	{ meprobamate pentaerythritol tetranitrate
Minocin	minocycline
Min-Ovral	oral contraceptives
Miocarpine	pilocarpine
Mi-Pilo	pilocarpine
Miradon	anisindione
Mobenol	tolbutamide
Moditen	fluphenazine
Motrin	ibuprofen
Mucotin	antacids
Mudrane [CD]	{ ephedrine phenobarbital theophylline
Muracine	tetracycline
Mychel	chloramphenicol
Mycinol	chloramphenicol
Mycolog [CD]	{ nystatin triamcinolone
Mycostatin	nystatin
Mylanta	antacids
Mysoline	primidone
Mysteclin-F [CD]	{ tetracycline (amphotericin B)

N

Nack	chlordiazepoxide
Nadopen-V	penicillin V
Nadostine	nystatin
Nadozone	phenylbutazone
Nafrine	oxymetazoline
Naldecol [CD]	{ phenylephrine phenylpropanolamine
Naldecon [CD]	{ chlorpheniramine phenylephrine phenylpropanolamine
Naprosyn	naproxen
Naturetin	bendroflumethiazide
Naturetin-K [CD]	{ bendroflumethiazide potassium

Brand Name	Generic Name
Nauseal	dimenhydrinate
Nauseatol	dimenhydrinate
Navane	thiothixene
Nebs	acetaminophen
NegGram	nalidixic acid
Nemasol	para-aminosalicylic acid
Nembu-donna [CD]	{ atropine { pentobarbital
Nembutal	pentobarbital
Neo-Antergan	pyrilamine
Neo-Barb	butabarbital
Neo-Calme	diazepam
Neo-Codema	hydrochlorothiazide
Neo-Corodil	pentaerythritol tetranitrate
Neo-Corovas-80	isosorbide dinitrate
Neo-Dibetic	tolbutamide
Neo-Mal	propoxyphene
Neopirine-25	aspirin
Neo-Serp	reserpine
Neo-Synephrine	phenylephrine
Neo-Tetrine	tetracycline
Neo-Tran	meprobamate
Neo-Tric	metronidazole
Neotrizine	trisulfapyrimidines
Neo-Zoline	phenylbutazone
Nephronex	nitrofurantoin
Neutralca-S	antacids
Neutral Insulin	insulin
Niacin	nicotinic acid
Nicalex	nicotinic acid
Nicobid	nicotinic acid
Nicolar	nicotinic acid
Nico-Metrazol [CD]	{ nicotinic acid { (pentylenetetrazol)
Niconyl	isoniazid
Nico-Span	nicotinic acid
Nicotinex Elixir	nicotinic acid
Nifuran	nitrofurantoin
Night-Caps	pentobarbital
Nigracap	chloral hydrate
Nilstat	nystatin
Niritol	pentaerythritol tetranitrate
Nitrex	nitrofurantoin
Nitrobid	nitroglycerin
Nitrodan	nitrofurantoin
Nitrol	nitroglycerin
Nitrong	nitroglycerin

Brand Name	Generic Name
Nitro-Span	nitroglycerin
Nitrostabilin	nitroglycerin
Nitrostat	nitroglycerin
Nobesine-25	diethylpropion
Noctec	chloral hydrate
Nodoz	caffeine
Noludar	methyprylon
Norasen	aspirin
Norflex	orphenadrine
Norgesic [CD]	{ aspirin caffeine orphenadrine phenacetin
Noriday	oral contraceptives
Norinyl-1	oral contraceptives
Norinyl 1+50	oral contraceptives
Norinyl 1+80	oral contraceptives
Norinyl-2	oral contraceptives
Norinyl 2 mg.	oral contraceptives
Norisodrine	isoproterenol
Norlestrin 1.0 mg.	oral contraceptives
Norlestrin 1/50	oral contraceptives
Norlestrin 2.5 mg.	oral contraceptives
Norlestrin 2.5/50	oral contraceptives
Norlestrin Fe 1/50	oral contraceptives
Norlestrin Fe 2.5/50	oral contraceptives
Norpanth	propantheline
Norpramin	desipramine
Nor-Q.D.	oral contraceptives
Nor-Tet	tetracycline
Nospaz	dicyclomine
Nova-Carpine	pilocarpine
Novadex	dexamethasone
Novafed	pseudoephedrine
Novahistine [CD] (Canada)	{ phenylephrine (diphenylpyraline)
Novahistine DH [CD] (Canada)	{ phenylephrine (diphenylpyraline) (hydrocodone)
Novahistine DH [CD] (USA)	{ chlorpheniramine codeine phenylephrine
Novahistine Expectorant [CD] (Canada)	{ phenylephrine (diphenylpyraline) (hydrocodone)

Brand Name	Generic Name
Novahistine Expectorant [CD] (USA)	chlorpheniramine codeine phenylephrine
Novahistine Melet [CD]	chlorpheniramine phenylephrine
Nova-Phase	aspirin
Nova-Pheno	phenobarbital
Nova-Pred	prednisolone
Nova-Rectal	pentobarbital
Novinol	oral contraceptives
Novobutamide	tolbutamide
Novochlorhydrate	chloral hydrate
Novochlorocap	chloramphenicol
Novodigoxin	digoxin
Novodimenate	dimenhydrinate
Novodipam	diazepam
Novodiphenyl	phenytoin
Novoflurazine	trifluoperazine
Novofuran	nitrofurantoin
Novohexidyl	trihexyphenidyl
Novohydrazide	hydrochlorothiazide
Novomedopa	methyldopa
Novomepro	meprobamate
Novoniacin	nicotinic acid
Novonidazol	metronidazole
Novopen G	penicillin G
Novopen-V-500	penicillin V
Novopheniram	chlorpheniramine
Novophenyl	phenylbutazone
Novopoxide	chlordiazepoxide
Novopramine	imipramine
Novopropamide	chlorpropamide
Novopropanthil	propantheline
Novoridazine	thioridazine
Novorythro	erythromycin
Novosoxazole	sulfisoxazole
Novotetra	tetracycline
Novothalidone	chlorthalidone
Novotriptyn	amitriptyline
NPH Insulin	insulin
Nydrazid	isoniazid
Nyquil [CD]	acetaminophen doxylamine ephedrine

Brand Name   Generic Name

O

Brand Name	Generic Name
Ocusert Pilo-20 and 40	pilocarpine
Oestrilin	estrogen
Omnipen	ampicillin
Ophthochlor	chloramphenicol
Op-Isophrin	phenylephrine
Oprine	phenobarbital
Oradrate	chloral hydrate
Oramide	tolbutamide
Orbenin	cloxacillin
Oretic	hydrochlorothiazide
Orinase	tolbutamide
Ornacol [CD]	phenylpropanolamine (dextromethorphan)
Ornade [CD]	chlorpheniramine isopropamide phenylpropanolamine
Ornex [CD]	acetaminophen phenylpropanolamine
Ortho-Novum 0.5 mg.	oral contraceptives
Ortho-Novum 1/50	oral contraceptives
Ortho-Novum 1/80	oral contraceptives
Ortho-Novum 2 mg.	oral contraceptives
Ortho-Novum 5 mg.	oral contraceptives
Ortho-Novum 10 mg.	oral contraceptives
Ovral	oral contraceptives
Ovrette	oral contraceptives
O-V Statin	nystatin
Ovulen	oral contraceptives
Ovulen 0.5 mg.	oral contraceptives
Ovulen 1 mg.	oral ontraceptives
Oxalid	oxyphenbutazone
Oxlopar	oxytetracycline
Oxy-Kesso-Tetra	oxytetracycline
Oxy-Tetrachel	oxytetracycline

P

Brand Name	Generic Name
P.A.C. Compound [CD]	aspirin caffeine phenacetin
Palocillin	penicillin G
Paltet	tetracycline
Pamine	methscopolamine

Brand Name	Generic Name
Pamine PB [CD]	methscopolamine phenobarbital
Pamiphen [CD]	methscopolamine phenobarbital
Pamisyl	para-aminosalicyclic acid
Pamisyl Sodium	para-aminosalicylic acid
Panectyl	trimeprazine
Panmycin	tetracycline
Panwarfin	warfarin
Papaverine	papaverine
Paracort	prednisone
Paraflex	chlorzoxazone
Parafon Forte [CD]	acetaminophen chlorzoxazone
Paralgin	acetaminophen
Parasal	para-aminosalicyclic acid
Parasal Calcium	para-aminosalicyclic acid
Parasal Sodium	para-aminosalicylic acid
Parasal S.A.	para-aminosalicylic acid
Parda	levodopa
Parepectolin [CD]	paregoric (kaolin) (pectin)
Parest	methaqualone
Parfuran	nitrofurantoin
P.A.S.	para-aminosalicylic acid
P.A.S. Acid	para-aminosalicylic acid
Pasna	para-aminosalicylic acid
Pathibamate [CD]	meprobamate tridihexethyl
Pathilon	tridihexethyl
Pathocil	dicloxacillin
Pavabid	papaverine
Paveral	codeine
Paxel	diazepam
Pax-400	meprobamate
PEBA	phenobarbital
Pen-A	ampicillin
Penapar VK	penicillin V
Penbec-V	penicillin V
Penbritin	ampicillin
Pencitabs	penicillin G
Penioral 500	penicillin G
Penital	pentobarbital
Pensyn	ampicillin

Brand Name	Generic Name
Penta	pentobarbital
Pentacarpine	pilocarpine
Pental	pentobarbital
Pentamycetin	chloramphenicol
Pentanca	pentobarbital
Pentazine (Canada)	trifluoperazine
Pentazine (USA)	promethazine
Pentids	penicillin G
Pentogen	pentobarbital
Pen-Vee	penicillin V
Pen-Vee K	penicillin V
Pepsogel	antacids
Pepto-Bismol Tablets	antacids
Percobarb [CD]	aspirin caffeine oxycodone phenacetin (hexobarbital)
Percocet-5 [CD]	acetaminophen oxycodone
Percodan [CD]	aspirin caffeine oxycodone phenacetin
Periactin	cyproheptadine
Perispan	pentaerythritol tetranitrate
Peritrate	pentaerythritol tetranitrate
Permitil	fluphenazine
Pertofrane	desipramine
Perynitrate	pentaerythritol tetranitrate
P.E.T.N.	pentaerythritol tetranitrate
Pexobiotic	tetracycline
P-50	penicillin G
Pfiklor	potassium
Pfizer-E	erythromycin
Pfizerpen G	penicillin G
Pfizerpen VK	penicillin V
P.G.A.	penicillin G
Phenaphen [CD] (Canada)	aspirin phenobarbital
Phenaphen (USA)	acetaminophen
Phenaphen Plus [CD]	acetaminophen phenylpropanolamine
Phenaphen with Codeine [CD] (Canada)	aspirin codeine phenobarbital

Brand Name	Generic Name
Phenaphen with Codeine [CD] (USA)	acetaminophen codeine
Phenazine	perphenazine
Phenazo	phenazopyridine
Phen Bar	phenobarbital
Phenbutazone	phenylbutazone
Phenergan	promethazine
Phenergan Compound [CD]	aspirin promethazine pseudoephedrine
Phenergan Expectorant with Codeine [CD]	codeine promethazine
Phenergan VC Expectorant [CD]	phenylephrine promethazine
Phenergan VC Expectorant with Codeine [CD]	codeine phenylephrine promethazine
Phenerhist	promethazine
Phenylbetazone	phenylbutazone
Phenylone	phenylbutazone
Phillips' Milk of Magnesia	antacids
Pil-Digis	digitalis
Pilocar	pilocarpine
Pilocel	pilocarpine
Pilomiotin	pilocarpine
Pipanol	trihexyphenidyl
Piracaps	tetracycline
Placidyl	ethchlorvynol
PMB-200, PMB-400 [CD]	estrogen meprobamate
Polaramine	chlorpheniramine
Polycillin	ampicillin
Polymox	amoxicillin
Pomalin [CD]	paregoric (kaolin) (pectin) (sulfaguanidine)
Potassium-Rougier	potassium
Potassium-Sandoz	potassium
Potassium Triplex	potassium
Prednis	prednisolone
Prefrin	phenylephrine
Premarin	estrogen
Presamine	imipramine
Principen	ampicillin
Probal	meprobamate

Brand Name	Generic Name
Probalan	probenecid
Pro-Banthine	propantheline
Probanthrax [CD]	{ promazine propantheline
Probital [CD]	{ phenobarbital propantheline
Procyclid	procyclidine
Prodecadron [CD]	{ dexamethasone isoproterenol
Progesic	propoxyphene
Prolixin	fluphenazine
Proloid	thyroid
Promabec	promazine
Promachlor	chlorpromazine
Promanyl	promazine
Promapar	chlorpromazine
Promate	meprobamate
Promazettes	promazine
Promezerine	promazine
Pronalgic	propoxyphene
Pronestyl	procainamide
Propadrine	phenylpropanolamine
Propanthel	propantheline
Proproxychel	propoxyphene
Prorex	promethazine
Prosedin	promethazine
Pro-65	propoxyphene
Prostaphlin	oxacillin
Protamine Zinc Insulin	insulin
Protensin	chlordiazepoxide
Proval	acetaminophen
Provera	medroxyprogesterone
Provigan	promethazine
Prydon	atropine
Prydonnal [CD]	{ atropine phenobarbital
P-T	pentaerythritol tetranitrate
Purodigin	digitoxin
P.V. Carpine	pilocarpine
"PVF" K	penicillin V
Pyma [CD]	{ chlorpheniramine pheniramine phenylephrine pyrilamine
Pyribenzamine	tripelennamine

Brand Name   Generic Name

Pyridium   phenazopyridine

Pyristan [CD]
- chlorpheniramine
- phenylephrine
- phenylpropanolamine
- pyrilamine

Q

QIDamp   ampicillin
QIDbamate   meprobamate
QIDmycin   erythromycin
QIDpen G   penicillin G
QIDpen VK   penicillin V
QIDtet   tetracycline
Quaalude   methaqualone

Quadrinal [CD]
- ephedrine
- phenobarbital
- theophylline
- (potassium iodide)

Quelidrine [CD]
- chlorpheniramine
- ephedrine
- phenylephrine

Quibron [CD]
- theophylline
- (glyceryl guaiacolate)

Quibron Plus [CD]
- butabarbital
- ephedrine
- theophylline
- (glyceryl guaiacolate)

Quiebar   butabarbital
Quietal   meprobamate
Quinaglute   quinidine
Quinate   quinidine
Quinidate   quinidine
Quinidex   quinidine

Quinidine M.B. [CD]
- quinidine
- (mephobarbital)

Quinobarb [CD]
- quinidine
- (phenylethylbarbiturate)

Quinora   quinidine

R

Ratio   antacids
Rauloydin   reserpine
Raurine   reserpine
Rau-Sed   reserpine

Brand Name	Generic Name
Rauserpine	reserpine
Rautractyl [CD]	{ bendroflumethiazide reserpine
Rautrax-N [CD]	{ bendroflumethiazide reserpine
Rauzide [CD]	{ bendroflumethiazide reserpine
Rectules	chloral hydrate
Redoxon	Vitamin C
Regibon	diethylpropion
Regroton [CD]	{ chlorthalidone reserpine
Regular Insulin	insulin
Rela	carisoprodol
Relaxil	chlordiazepoxide
Remsed	promethazine
Renbu	butabarbital
Repen VK	penicillin V
Resercen	reserpine
Resercrine	reserpine
Reserfia	reserpine
Reserjen	reserpine
Reserpanca	reserpine
Reserpaneed	reserpine
Reserpoid	reserpine
Retet	tetracycline
Retet-S	tetracycline
Rezipas	para-aminosalicylic acid
Rhonal	aspirin
Rifadin	rifampin
Rifomycin	rifampin
Rimactane	rifampin
Rimifon	isoniazid
Riopan	antacids
Rioplus	antacids
Ritalin	methylphenidate
Robalate	antacids
Robamate	meprobamate
Robicillin-VK	penicillin V
Robimycin	erythromycin
Robitet	tetracycline
Robitussin-AC [CD]	{ codeine pheniramine
Ro-Cillin-VK	penicillin V
Ro-Cycline	tetracycline
Ro-Fedrin	pseudoephedrine

Brand Name	Generic Name
Ro-Hist	tripelennamine
Rolaids	antacids
Rondomycin	methacycline
Ropanth	propantheline
Ro-Sulfa	trisulfapyrimidines
Ro-Sulfa-A [CD]	phenazopyridine trisulfapyrimidines
Rougoxin	digoxin
Rounox	acetaminophen
RP-Mycin	erythromycin
Rynacrom	cromolyn

S

Sal-Adult	aspirin
Salazopyrin	sulfasalazine
Sal-Infant	aspirin
Salutensin [CD]	hydroflumethiazide reserpine
Sandoptal	butalbital
Sandril	reserpine
Sansert	methysergide
Saramp	ampicillin
Sarocycline	tetracycline
Sarodant	nitrofurantoin
Saronil	meprobamate
SAS-500	sulfasalazine
Scoline	methscopolamine
Scotrex	tetracycline
SDPH	phenytoin
Seco-8	secobarbital
Secogen	secobarbital
Seconal	secobarbital
Secotabs	secobarbital
Sedabar	phenobarbital
Sedalone	methaqualone
Seidlitz Powder	antacids
Semilente Insulin	insulin
Septra [CD]	sulfamethoxazole trimethoprim
Seral	secobarbital
Ser-Ap-Es [CD]	hydralazine hydrochlorothiazide reserpine
Serax	oxazepam

Brand Name	Generic Name
Serenack	diazepam ·
Serentil	mesoridazine
Serp	reserpine
Serpalan	reserpine
Serpaloid	reserpine
Serpanray	reserpine
Serpasil	reserpine
Serpasil-Apresoline [CD]	{ hydralazine { reserpine
Serpate	reserpine
Serpax	reserpine
Serpena	reserpine
Sertabs	reserpine
Sertina	reserpine
Servisone	prednisone
Sigazine	promethazine
Sigmavin	penicillin V
Sinarest [CD]	⌈ acetaminophen | caffeine | chlorpheniramine ⌊ phenylephrine
Sinarest Nasal Spray	phenylephrine
Sinemet [CD]	{ levodopa { (carbidopa)
Sinequan	doxepin
Sinex [CD]	{ phenylephrine { (methapyrilene)
Sintrom	acenocoumarol
Sinubid [CD]	⌈ acetaminophen { phenacetin ⌊ phenylpropanolamine
Sinutab [CD]	⌈ acetaminophen { phenylpropanolamine ⌊ (phenyltoloxamine)
65P	propoxyphene
642	propoxyphene
SK-Ampicillin	ampicillin
SK-APAP	acetaminophen
SK-Bamate	meprobamate
SK-Erythromycin	erythromycin
SK-Estrogens	estrogen
SK-Penicillin VK	penicillin V
SK-Petn	pentaerythritol tetranitrate
SK-65	propoxyphene
SK-Soxazole	sulfisoxazole
SK-Tetracycline	tetracycline
Slo-Phyllin	theophylline

Brand Name	Generic Name
Slow-K	potassium
Soda Mint	antacids
Sodizole	sulfisoxazole
Soduben	butabarbital
Solacen	tybamate
Solazine	trifluoperazine
Solium	chlordiazepoxide
Solu-barb	phenobarbital
Soma	carisoprodol
Soma Compound [CD]	caffeine carisoprodol phenacetin
Somnafac	methaqualone
Somnos	chloral hydrate
Somophyllin	theophylline
Sonazine	chlorpromazine
Sopor	methaqualone
Sorbitrate	isosorbide dinitrate
Sorquad	isosorbide dinitrate
Sosol	sulfisoxazole
Soxa	sulfisoxazole
Soxomide	sulfisoxazole
S-Pain-65	propoxyphene
Sparine	promazine
S-P-T	thyroid
Stabinol	chlorpropamide
Stanback [CD]	aspirin caffeine
Stelazine	trifluoperazine
Stemetil	prochlorperazine
Stental	phenobarbital
Sterane	prednisolone

Sterazolidin [CD]	antacids (aluminum
	  hydroxide + magnesium
	  trisilicate)
	phenylbutazone
	prednisone

Sterium	chlordiazepoxide
St. Joseph's Children's Aspirin	aspirin
Sub-Quin	procainamide
Sudafed	pseudoephedrine
Sugracillin	penicillin G
Sulcolon	sulfasalazine
Sulfagen	sulfisoxazole
Sulfalar	sulfisoxazole
Sulfium	sulfisoxazole

Brand Name	Generic Name
Sulfizin	sulfisoxazole
Sulfizole	sulfisoxazole
Sulphated Insulin	insulin
Sumycin	tetracycline
Supasa	aspirin
Supen	ampicillin
Synalgos [CD]	{ aspirin caffeine phenacetin promethazine
Synalgos-DC [CD]	{ aspirin caffeine codeine phenacetin promethazine
Synasal Spray	phenylephrine
Synchro-C	Vitamin C
Synthroid	thyroxine
Synt-PB [CD]	{ methscopolamine phenobarbital
Syráprim	trimethoprim

T

Talwin	pentazocine
Tandearil	oxyphenbutazone
Taper	acetaminophen
Tazone	phenylbutazone
T-Caps	tetracycline
Tedral [CD]	{ ephedrine phenobarbital theophylline
Teebaconin	isoniazid
Tegopen	cloxacillin
Teldrin	chlorpheniramine
Temaril	trimeprazine
Tempra	acetaminophen
Tensin	reserpine
Tenuate	diethylpropion
Tepanil	diethylpropion
Terfluzine	trifluoperazine
Terfonyl	trisulfapyrimidines
Terramycin	oxytetracycline
Terrastatin [CD]	{ nystatin oxytetracycline
Tertroxin	liothyronine

Brand Name   Generic Name

Tet-Cy	tetracycline
Tetrabiotic	tetracycline
Tetra-C	tetracycline
Tetracaps	tetracycline
Tetrachel	tetracycline
Tetrachlor	tetracycline
Tetra-Co	tetracycline
Tetracrine	tetracycline
Tetracyn	tetracycline
Tetra-500	tetracycline
Tetral	tetracycline
Tetralan	tetracycline
Tetralean	tetracycline
Tetram	tetracycline
Tetramax	tetracycline
Tetranite Bitab	pentaerythritol tetranitrate
Tetrastatin [CD]	{ nystatin tetracycline
Tetrex	tetracycline
Tetrosol	tetracycline
Thegitoxin	digoxin
Theocyne	theophylline
Theogen	estrogen
Theolixir	theophylline
Therapen K	penicillin G
Therapen V	penicillin V
Thioril	thioridazine
Thiosulfil-A[CD]	{ phenazopyridine (sulfamethizole)
Thiuretic	hydrochlorothiazide
Thorazine	chlorpromazine
Thyrobrom	thyroid
Thyrolar [CD]	{ liothyronine thyroxine
Tigan	trimethobenzamide
Titralac	antacids
T-Liquid	tetracycline
Tofranil	imipramine
Tolbutone	tolbutamide
Tolinase	tolazamide
T-125, T-250	tetracycline
Tora	phentermine
Totacillin	ampicillin
Tranmep	meprobamate
Tranquilsin	reserpine
Trantoin	nitrofurantoin

Brand Name   Generic Name

Brand Name	Generic Name
Tranxene	clorazepate
Travamine	dimenhydrinate
Trelmar	meprobamate
Tremin	trihexyphenidyl
Trexin	tetracycline
Triactin [CD]	antacids (aluminum hydroxide + magnesium hydroxide) dicyclomine
Triacycline	tetracycline
Triador	methaqualone
Triaminic [CD]	pheniramine phenylpropanolamine pyrilamine
Triaminicin [CD]	acetaminophen aspirin caffeine pheniramine phenylpropanolomine pyrilamine
Triaminicol [CD]	pheniramine phenylpropanolamine pyrilamine
Triaphen-10	aspirin
Tri-A-Tab	trisulfapyrimidines
Triavil [CD]	amitriptyline perphenazine
Trifluoper-Ez-Ets	trifluoperazine
Triflurin	trifluoperazine
Trihexy	trihexyphenidyl
Trikacide	metronidazole
Trikamon	metronidazole
Trilafon	perphenazine
Trilium	chlordiazepoxide
Triniad	isoniazid
Triple Sulfa	trisulfapyrimidines
Triptil	protriptyline
Trisogel	antacids
Tri-Sulfa	trisulfapyrimidines
Trisulfazine	trisulfapyrimidines
Trisureid	trisulfapyrimidines
Trixyl	trihexyphenidyl
Tromexan	warfarin
T-Serp	reserpine
T-Tabs	tetracycline
T-250	tetracycline

Brand Name	Generic Name
Tualone	methaqualone
Tuinal [CD]	⌈ amobarbital ⌊ secobarbital
Tums	antacids
Tussagesic [CD]	⌈ acetaminophen pheniramine phenylpropanolamine pyrilamine ⌊ (dextromethorphan)
Tussaminic [CD]	⌈ pheniramine phenylpropanolamine pyrilamine ⌊ (dextromethorphan)
Tuss-Ornade [CD]	⌈ chlorpheniramine isopropamide ⌊ phenylpropanolamine
Tybatran	tybamate
Tylenol	acetaminophen
Tylenol with Codeine [CD]	⌈ acetaminophen ⌊ codeine

U

Ultralente Insulin	insulin
Ultramycin	minocycline
Uniad	isoniazid
Unipen	nafcillin
Univol	antacids
Uridon	chlorthalidone
Urised [CD]	⌈ atropine (methenamine) ⌊ (methylene blue)
Urisede [CD]	⌈ atropine (methenamine) ⌊ (methylene blue)
Urisoxin	sulfisoxazole
Uri-Tet	oxytetracycline
Urobiotic [CD]	⌈ oxytetracycline phenazopyridine ⌊ (sulfamethizole)
Urotoin	nitrofurantoin
Urozide	hydrochlorothiazide
Ursinus [CD]	⌈ aspirin pheniramine phenylpropanolamine ⌊ pyrilamine

Brand Name	Generic Name
U.S.-67	sulfisoxazole
Uticillin VK	penicillin V

V

Brand Name	Generic Name
Valadol	acetaminophen
Valium	diazepam
Valmid	ethinamate
Valpin	anisotropine
Valpin-PB [CD]	anisotropine phenobarbital
Vanquish [CD]	acetaminophen aspirin caffeine
Vasodilan	isoxsuprine
Vasospan	papaverine
V-Cillin	penicillin V
V-Cillin K	penicillin V
VC-K 500	penicillin V
Vectrin	minocycline
Veetids	penicillin V
Velosef	cephradine
Veltane	brompheniramine
Veracillin	dicloxacillin
Verequad [CD]	ephedrine phenobarbital theophylline
Vertrol	meclizine
Via-Quil	chlordiazepoxide
Vibramycin	doxycycline
Vimicon	cyproheptadine
Vio-Serpine	reserpine
Viscerol	dicyclomine
Vistaril	hydroxyzine
Vistrax [CD]	hydroxyzine (oxyphencyclimine)
Vivactil	protriptyline
Vivol	diazepam

W

Brand Name	Generic Name
Warfilone	warfarin
Warnerin	warfarin
Wescomep	meprobamate
Wescopen	penicillin G

Brand Name	Generic Name
Wescopred	prednisone
Wescotol	tolbutamide
Wescozone	phenylbutazone
Wigraine [CD]	{ atropine caffeine ergotamine phenacetin
Wilpo	phentermine
WinGel	antacids
Wintracin	tetracycline
Win-V-K	penicillin V
Wygesic [CD]	{ acetaminophen propoxyphene

Z

Zide	hydrochlorothiazide
ZiPan	promethazine
Zorane	oral contraceptives
Zyloprim	allopurinol

Drug Profiles

NOTE

A dagger (†) that occasionally precedes an adverse effect, or an effect of extended use, signifies an especially hazardous or frequent reaction.

The designation [CD] following the brand names of any drugs in these Profiles indicates a combination drug (a drug product with more than one active ingredient).

ACENOCOUMAROL

Year Introduced: 1957

Brand Names

USA	Canada
Sintrom (Geigy)	Sintrom (Geigy)

Drug Family: Anticoagulant [Coumarins]

Prescription Required: Yes

Available Dosage Forms and Strengths

Tablets — 4 mg.

How This Drug Works

Intended Therapeutic Effect(s): A deliberate reduction in the ability of the blood to clot. This effect is often beneficial in the management of stroke, heart attack, abnormal clotting in arteries and veins (thrombosis), and the movement of a blood clot from vein to lung (pulmonary embolism).

Location of Drug Action(s): Those tissues in the liver that use Vitamin K to produce prothrombin (and other factors) essential to the clotting of the blood.

Method of Drug Action(s): The oral anticoagulants interfere with the production of four essential blood-clotting factors by blocking the action of Vitamin K. This leads to a deficiency of these clotting factors in circulating blood and inhibits blood-clotting mechanisms.

THIS DRUG SHOULD NOT BE TAKEN IF

—you have had an allergic reaction to any dosage form of it previously.
—you have a history of a bleeding disorder.
—you have an active peptic ulcer.
—you have ulcerative colitis.

INFORM YOUR PHYSICIAN BEFORE TAKING THIS DRUG IF

—you are now taking *any other drugs*—either drugs prescribed by another physician or non-prescription drugs you purchased over-the-counter (see OTC drugs in Glossary).
—you have high blood pressure.
—you have abnormally heavy or prolonged menstrual bleeding.
—you have diabetes.
—you are using an indwelling catheter.

—you have a history of serious liver or kidney disease, or impaired liver or kidney function.

—you plan to have a surgical or dental procedure in the near future.

Time Required for Apparent Benefit

Drug action begins in 24 to 36 hours, produces desired effects within 36 to 48 hours, and persists for 36 to 48 hours. Continuous use on a regular schedule for up to 10 days (with daily prothrombin testing and dosage adjustment) is needed to determine the correct maintenance dose for each individual.

Possible Side-Effects *(natural, expected, and unavoidable drug actions)*

Minor episodes of bleeding may occur even when dosage is well within the recommended range. If in doubt regarding its significance, consult your physician regarding the need for prothrombin testing.

CAUTION

1. Always carry with you a card of personal identification that includes a statement indicating that *you are using an anticoagulant* (see Table 14 and Section Seven).
2. While you are taking an anticoagulant drug, always consult your physician *before* starting any new drug, changing the dosage schedule of any drug, or discontinuing any drug.

Possible Adverse Effects *(unusual, unexpected, and infrequent reactions)*

IF ANY OF THE FOLLOWING DEVELOP, DISCONTINUE DRUG AND NOTIFY YOUR PHYSICIAN AS SOON AS POSSIBLE

Mild Adverse Effects

Allergic Reactions: Skin rash, hives, loss of scalp hair, drug fever. Nausea, vomiting, diarrhea.

Serious Adverse Effects

Abnormal bruising, major bleeding or hemorrhage. Notify physician of nosebleeds, bleeding gums, bloody sputum, blood-tinged urine, bloody or tarry stools. (The incidence of significant bleeding is 2% to 4%.)

Advisability of Use During Pregnancy

This drug can cause hemorrhage in the fetus. Avoid use completely if possible.

Advisability of Use While Nursing Infant

This drug is present in milk and may cause bleeding or hemorrhage in the nursing infant. Avoid drug or avoid nursing. Ask physician for guidance.

Habit-Forming Potential

None.

Effects of Overdosage

With Moderate Overdose: Episodes of minor bleeding: blood spots in white portion of eye, nosebleeds, gum bleeding, small bruises, prolonged bleeding from minor cuts received while shaving or from other small lacerations.

With Large Overdose: Episodes of major internal bleeding: vomiting of blood, grossly bloody urine or stools.

Possible Effects of Extended Use
None reported.

Recommended Periodic Examinations While Taking This Drug
Regular determination of prothrombin time is essential to safe dosage and proper control. Occasional urine analysis for red blood cells.

While Taking This Drug, Observe the Following
Foods: A larger intake than usual of foods high in Vitamin K may reduce the effectiveness of this drug and make larger doses necessary. Foods rich in Vitamin K include: cabbage, cauliflower, fish, kale, liver, spinach.
Beverages: No restrictions.
Alcohol: Use with caution until combined effect has been determined. Alcohol may either increase or decrease the effect of this drug. It is advisable to use alcohol sparingly while taking anticoagulants.
(*Note:* Heavy users of alcohol with liver damage may be very sensitive to anticoagulants and require smaller than usual doses.)
Tobacco Smoking: No interactions expected with this drug. Follow physician's advice regarding smoking (based upon condition under treatment).
Other Drugs: See WARFARIN Drug Profile. Drug interactions for acenocoumarol are essentially the same as for warfarin.
Driving a Vehicle, Piloting a Plane, Operating Machinery: No restrictions. Avoid unnecessary hazardous activities that could cause injury and result in excessive bleeding.
Exposure to Sun: No restrictions.
Exposure to Heat: Prolonged hot weather may increase the prothrombin time and make it advisable to reduce anticoagulant dosage. Ask physician for guidance.
Occurrence of Unrelated Illness: Any acute illness that causes fever, vomiting, or diarrhea can alter your response to this drug. Notify your physician so corrective action can be taken.
Discontinuation: Do not discontinue this drug abruptly unless abnormal bleeding occurs. Ask physician for guidance regarding gradual reduction of dosage over a period of 3 to 4 weeks.

Special Storage Instructions
Keep in a dry, tightly closed container. Protect from light.

ACETAMINOPHEN
(Paracetamol)

Year Introduced: 1893

Brand Names

USA		Canada
Datril (Bristol-Myers)	Excedrin [CD]	Atasol (Horner)
Nebs (Eaton)	(Bristol-Myers)	Atasol Forte (Horner)
Phenaphen (Robins)	Parafon-Forte [CD]	Campain (Winthrop)
Proval (Reid-	(McNeil)	Chemcetaphen
Provident)	Percocet-5 [CD]	(Chemo)
SK-APAP (Smith	(Endo)	Paralgin (ICN)
Kline & French)	Sinarest [CD]	Rounox (Rougier)
Taper (Parke-Davis)	(Pharmacraft)	Tempra (Mead
Tempra (Mead	Sinutab [CD]	Johnson)
Johnson)	(Warner/Chilcott)	Tylenol (McNeil)
Tylenol (McNeil)	Triaminicin [CD]	
Valadol (Squibb)	(Dorsey)	
Arthralgen [CD]	(Numerous other	
(Robins)	brand and	
Co-Tylenol [CD]	combination brand	
(McNeil)	names)	

Drug Family: Analgesic, Mild; Fever Reducer (Antipyretic)

Prescription Required: No (some combinations require prescription)

Available Dosage Forms and Strengths
>   Tablets — 300 mg., 325 mg., 500 mg.
> Chewable Tablets — 120 mg.
>   Capsules — 500 mg.
>   Elixir — 100 mg. per ml., 120 mg. per teaspoonful
>   Drops — 60 mg. per 0.6 ml.
> Suppositories — 300 mg.

How This Drug Works
Intended Therapeutic Effect(s)
- relief of mild to moderate pain.
- reduction of high fever.

Location of Drug Action(s):   Principal actions occur in
- areas of injury, muscle spasm, or inflammation in many body tissues.
- the heat-regulating center, located in the hypothalamus of the brain.

Method of Drug Action(s):   Not fully established. It is thought that this drug relieves both pain and fever by reducing the tissue concentration of prostaglandins, chemicals involved in the production of pain, fever, and inflammation.

THIS DRUG SHOULD NOT BE TAKEN IF
—you have had an allergic reaction to any dosage form of it previously.

INFORM YOUR PHYSICIAN BEFORE TAKING THIS DRUG IF
—you have impaired liver or kidney function.

Time Required for Apparent Benefit
Drug action begins in 15 to 30 minutes and persists for 3 to 4 hours.

Possible Side-Effects *(natural, expected, and unavoidable drug actions)*
Drowsiness (in sensitive individuals).

CAUTION
Do not exceed 2.6 grams (up to 8 tablets) in 24 hours.

Possible Adverse Effects *(unusual, unexpected, and infrequent reactions)*

IF ANY OF THE FOLLOWING DEVELOP, DISCONTINUE DRUG AND NOTIFY YOUR PHYSICIAN AS SOON AS POSSIBLE

Mild Adverse Effects
Allergic Reactions: Skin rash, hives (rare).
Impaired thinking and concentration.

Serious Adverse Effects
Allergic Reactions: Swelling of the vocal cords, resulting in difficult breathing, anaphylactic reaction (see Glossary).
Abnormally low white blood cells.
Abnormal bruising or bleeding due to reduced blood platelets (see Glossary).

Advisability of Use During Pregnancy
No adverse effects on fetus reported. Limit use to small doses and for short periods of time.

Advisability of Use While Nursing Infant
This drug is known to be present in milk. Ask physician for guidance.

Habit-Forming Potential
None.

Effects of Overdosage
With Moderate Overdose: Nausea, vomiting, abdominal pain, chills, drowsiness.
With Large Overdose: Nervous irritability followed by stupor and convulsions. Coma may develop due to damage to liver and kidney tissues. Jaundice may occur in 2 to 5 days.

Possible Effects of Extended Use
Formation of abnormal hemoglobin (methemoglobin).
Development of anemia.

Recommended Periodic Examinations While Taking This Drug
None required for short-term use.
During long-term use, examination for abnormal hemoglobin (methemoglobin), anemia, and reduced white blood cells or platelets is advisable.

While Taking This Drug, Observe the Following
Foods: No restrictions.
Beverages: No restrictions.
Alcohol: No interactions expected.
Tobacco Smoking: No interactions expected.
Other Drugs
   Acetaminophen may *increase* the effects of
   • oral anticoagulants. Use with caution and monitor prothrombin times until combined effect has been determined.

   The following drugs may *decrease* the effects of acetaminophen:
   • phenobarbital may hasten its elimination from the body.
Driving a Vehicle, Piloting a Plane, Operating Machinery: No restrictions.
Exposure to Sun: No restrictions.

Special Storage Instructions
Keep in a tightly closed container. Protect from light.

ACETAZOLAMIDE
Year Introduced: 1953

Brand Names

USA	Canada
Diamox (Lederle)	Diamox (Lederle)

Drug Family: Anti-glaucoma; Diuretic [Carbonic Anhydrase Inhibitors] [Sulfonamides]

Prescription Required: Yes

Available Dosage Forms and Strengths
   Tablets — 125 mg., 250 mg.
   Prolonged Action Capsules — 500 mg.

How This Drug Works
Intended Therapeutic Effect(s)
   • reduction of elevated internal eye pressure, of benefit in the management of glaucoma.
   • reduction of excessive fluid retention (edema) in the body.
Location of Drug Action(s)
   • the ciliary processes of the eye, the source of fluid in the anterior chamber.
   • the tubular systems of the kidney that determine the final composition of the urine.

Method of Drug Action(s):   By inhibiting the action of the enzyme carbonic anhydrase, this drug:
- decreases the formation of fluid (the aqueous humor) in the eye, thus lowering the internal eye pressure.
- increases the sodium content of the urine, resulting in an associated increase in the excretion of water (increased urine volume).

THIS DRUG SHOULD NOT BE TAKEN IF
—you have had an allergic reaction to any dosage form of it previously.
—you have serious liver or kidney disease.
—you have Addison's disease.

INFORM YOUR PHYSICIAN BEFORE TAKING THIS DRUG IF
—you have had an allergic reaction to any "sulfa" drug in the past.
—you have lupus erythematosus.
—you have gout.

Time Required for Apparent Benefit
Drug action begins in approximately 2 hours and persists for 8 to 12 hours. The maximal fall in internal eye pressure occurs in 4 hours and may persist for 12 to 24 hours.

Possible Side-Effects *(natural, expected, and unavoidable drug actions)*
Drowsiness, temporary nearsightedness.

Possible Adverse Effects *(unusual, unexpected, and infrequent reactions)*

IF ANY OF THE FOLLOWING DEVELOP, DISCONTINUE DRUG AND NOTIFY YOUR PHYSICIAN AS SOON AS POSSIBLE

Mild Adverse Effects
   Allergic Reactions: Skin rash, hives, drug fever.
   Reduced appetite, indigestion, nausea.
   Fatigue, weakness, tingling of face, arms, or legs, dizziness.

Serious Adverse Effects
   Allergic Reactions: Hemolytic anemia (see Glossary), spontaneous bruising (not due to injury).
   Bone marrow depression (see Glossary)—fatigue, weakness, fever, sore throat, abnormal bleeding or bruising.
   Hepatitis with jaundice (see Glossary)—yellow eyes and skin, dark-colored urine, light-colored stools.

Advisability of Use During Pregnancy
Safety not established. Avoid completely during first 3 months. If use during last 6 months is considered necessary, limit dosage to the smallest effective amount and use in short, interrupted courses.

Advisability of Use While Nursing Infant
Safety not established for infant. Avoid use or avoid nursing. Ask physician for guidance.

Habit-Forming Potential
None.

Effects of Overdosage
With Moderate Overdose: Drowsiness, numbness and tingling, thirst, nausea, vomiting.
With Large Overdose: Confusion, excitement, convulsions, coma.

Possible Effects of Extended Use
Formation of kidney stones.

Recommended Periodic Examinations While Taking This Drug
Complete blood cell counts.
Measurements of blood sodium and potassium levels.
Liver function tests.

While Taking This Drug, Observe the Following
Foods: It is recommended that you include in your daily diet liberal servings of foods rich in potassium (unless directed otherwise by your physician). The following foods have a high potassium content:

All-bran cereals	Fish, fresh
Almonds	Lentils
Apricots (dried)	Liver, beef
Bananas, fresh	Lonalac
Beans (navy and lima)	Milk
Beef	Peaches
Carrots (raw)	Peanut butter
Chicken	Peas
Citrus fruits	Pork
Coconut	Potato chips
Coffee	Prunes (dried)
Crackers (rye)	Raisins
Dates and figs (dried)	Tomato Juice

Beverages: No restrictions.
Alcohol: No interactions expected.
Tobacco Smoking: No interactions expected.
Other Drugs
Acetazolamide may *increase* the effects of
• amphetamines and related drugs, by delaying their elimination from the body.
• tricyclic antidepressants, by delaying their elimination from the body.

Acetazolamide may *decrease* the effects of
• aspirin, by hastening its elimination from the body.
• lithium, by hastening its elimination from the body. Consult physician regarding dosage adjustment.
Driving a Vehicle, Piloting a Plane, Operating Machinery: Usually no restrictions. Be alert to the possible occurrence of drowsiness or dizziness.
Exposure to Sun: No restrictions.

Special Storage Instructions
Keep in a dry, tightly closed container.

ACETOHEXAMIDE

Year Introduced: 1963

Brand Names

USA	Canada
Dymelor (Lilly)	Dimelor (Lilly)

Drug Family: Anti-diabetic, Oral (Hypoglycemic) [Sulfonylureas]

Prescription Required: Yes

Available Dosage Forms and Strengths
Tablets — 250 mg., 500 mg.

How This Drug Works
Intended Therapeutic Effect(s):   The correction of insulin deficiency in
adult (maturity-onset) diabetes of moderate severity.
Location of Drug Action(s):   The insulin-producing tissues of the pancreas.
Method of Drug Action(s):   It is well established that sulfonylurea drugs
stimulate the secretion of insulin (by a pancreas capable of responding to
stimulation). Therapeutic doses may increase the amount of available insulin.

THIS DRUG SHOULD NOT BE TAKEN IF
—you have had an allergic reaction to any dosage form of it previously.
—you have a history of impaired liver function or kidney function.

INFORM YOUR PHYSICIAN BEFORE TAKING THIS DRUG IF
—your diabetes has been difficult to control in the past ("brittle type").
—you have a history of peptic ulcer of the stomach or duodenum.
—you have a history of porphyria.
—you do not know how to recognize or treat hypoglycemia (see Glossary).

Time Required for Apparent Benefit:
A single dose may lower the blood sugar within 2 to 4 hours. Regular use for
1 to 2 weeks may be needed to determine this drug's effectiveness in controlling your diabetes.

Possible Side-Effects *(natural, expected, and unavoidable drug actions)*
Usually none. If drug dosage is excessive or food intake is inadequate, abnormally low blood sugar (hypoglycemia) will occur as a predictable drug effect
(see hypoglycemia in Glossary).

CAUTION
The elderly (over 60 years of age) require smaller doses and are more likely
to experience episodes of prolonged hypoglycemia when taking this drug.

Possible Adverse Effects *(unusual, unexpected, and infrequent reactions)*

IF ANY OF THE FOLLOWING DEVELOP, DISCONTINUE DRUG AND NOTIFY YOUR PHYSICIAN AS SOON AS POSSIBLE

Mild Adverse Effects

Allergic Reactions: Skin rashes (various kinds), hives, itching, drug fever. Headache, ringing in ears.

Indigestion, heartburn, nausea, diarrhea.

Serious Adverse Effects

Allergic Reactions: Hepatitis with jaundice (see Glossary).

Idiosyncratic Reactions: Hemolytic anemia in susceptible individuals (see Glossary).

Bone marrow depression (see Glossary)—fatigue, weakness, fever, sore throat, unusual bleeding or bruising.

Advisability of Use During Pregnancy

Safety not established. Prudent use is best determined by the physician's evaluation.

Advisability of Use While Nursing Infant

Drug is known to be present in milk. Ask physician for guidance.

Habit-Forming Potential

None.

Effects of Overdosage

With Moderate Overdose: Symptoms of mild to moderate hypoglycemia: headache, lightheadedness, faintness, nervousness, confusion, tremor, sweating, heart palpitation, weakness, and hunger.

With Large Overdose: Hypoglycemic coma (see Glossary).

Possible Effects of Extended Use

Reduced function of the thyroid gland (hypothyroidism) resulting in lowered metabolism.

Reports of increased frequency and severity of heart and blood vessel diseases associated with long-term use of the members of this drug family are highly controversial and inconclusive. A direct cause-and-effect relationship (see Glossary) has not been established to date. Ask your physician for guidance regarding extended use.

Recommended Periodic Examinations While Taking This Drug

Complete blood cell counts.

Liver function tests.

Thyroid function tests.

Periodic evaluation of heart and circulatory system.

While Taking This Drug, Observe the Following

Foods: Follow the diabetic diet prescribed by your physician.

Beverages: As directed in the diabetic diet prescribed by your physician.

Alcohol: Use with extreme caution until the combined effect has been determined. This drug can cause a marked intolerance to alcohol resulting in a disulfiram-like reaction (see Glossary).

Tobacco Smoking: No restrictions unless imposed as part of your overall treatment program. Ask physician for guidance.

Other Drugs

Acetohexamide may *increase* the effects of

• sedatives and sleep-inducing drugs, by slowing their elimination from the body.
• "sulfa" drugs, by slowing their elimination from the body.

Acetohexamide *taken concurrently* with

• oral anticoagulants, may cause unpredictable changes in anticoagulant drug actions. Ask physician for guidance regarding prothrombin blood tests and dosage adjustment.
• propranolol (Inderal), may allow hypoglycemia to develop without adequate warning. Follow diet and dosage schedules very carefully.

The following drugs may *increase* the effects of acetohexamide:

• bishydroxycoumarin (Dicumarol, Dufalone)
• chloramphenicol (Chloromycetin, etc.)
• clofibrate (Atromid-S)
• mono-amine oxidase (MAO) inhibitors (see Drug Family, Section Four)
• oxyphenbutazone (Oxalid, Tandearil)
• phenformin (DBI)
• phenylbutazone (Azolid, Butazolidin, etc.)
• phenyramidol (Analexin)
• probenecid (Benemid)
• propranolol (Inderal)
• salicylates (aspirin, sodium salicylate)
• sulfaphenazole (Orisul, Sulfabid)
• sulfisoxazole (Gantrisin, Novosoxazole, etc.)

The following drugs may *decrease* the effects of acetohexamide:

• chlorpromazine (Thorazine, Largactil, etc.)
• cortisone and related drugs (see Drug Family, Section Four)
• estrogens (Premarin, Menotrol, Ogen, etc.)
• isoniazid (INH, Isozide, etc.)
• nicotinic acid (Niacin, etc.)
• oral contraceptives (see Drug Profile)
• pyrazinamide (Aldinamide)
• thiazide diuretics (see Drug Family, Section Four)
• thyroid preparations (see Drug Family, Section Four)

Driving a Vehicle, Piloting a Plane, Operating Machinery: Regulate your dosage schedule, eating schedule, and physical activities very carefully to prevent hypoglycemia. Be able to recognize the early symptoms of hypoglycemia and avoid hazardous activities if you suspect that hypoglycemia is developing.

Exposure to Sun: Use caution until sensitivity has been determined. This drug can cause photosensitivity (see Glossary).

Heavy Exercise or Exertion: Use caution. Excessive exercise may result in hypoglycemia.

Occurrence of Unrelated Illness: Acute infections, illnesses causing vomiting or diarrhea, serious injuries, and the need for surgery can interfere with diabetic control and may require a change in medication. If any of these conditions occur, ask your physician for guidance regarding the continued use of this drug.

Discontinuation: If you find it necessary to discontinue this drug for any reason, notify your physician and ask for guidance regarding necessary changes in your treatment program for diabetic control.

Special Storage Instructions
Keep in a dry, tightly closed container.

ALLOPURINOL

Year Introduced: 1963

Brand Names

USA	Canada
Zyloprim (Burroughs Wellcome)	Zyloprim (B.W. Ltd.)

Drug Family: Anti-gout [Xanthine Oxidase Inhibitors]

Prescription Required: Yes

Available Dosage Forms and Strengths
Tablets — 100 mg., 300 mg.

How This Drug Works
Intended Therapeutic Effect(s):   Prevention of acute episodes of gout through maintenance of normal uric acid blood levels.

Location of Drug Action(s):   Tissues throughout the body in which sufficient concentration of the drug can be achieved to reduce the production of uric acid.

Method of Drug Action(s):   By inhibiting the action of the tissue enzyme xanthine oxidase, this drug decreases the conversion of purines (protein nutrients) to uric acid.

THIS DRUG SHOULD NOT BE TAKEN IF
—you have had an allergic reaction to any dosage form of it previously.
—you are experiencing an attack of acute gout at the present time.

INFORM YOUR PHYSICIAN BEFORE TAKING THIS DRUG IF
—you have a history of liver or kidney disease, or impaired function of the liver or kidneys.

Time Required for Apparent Benefit
Blood uric acid levels usually begin to decrease in 48 to 72 hours and reach a normal range in 1 to 3 weeks. However, regular use for several months may be necessary to prevent attacks of acute gout.

Possible Side-Effects *(natural, expected, and unavoidable drug actions)*
An increase in the frequency and severity of episodes of acute gout may occur during the first several weeks of drug use. Consult physician regarding use of colchicine during this period.

Possible Adverse Effects *(unusual, unexpected, and infrequent reactions)*
IF ANY OF THE FOLLOWING DEVELOP, DISCONTINUE DRUG AND NOTIFY YOUR PHYSICIAN AS SOON AS POSSIBLE

Mild Adverse Effects
Allergic Reactions: Skin rash (various kinds), hives, itching, drug fever.
Nausea, vomiting, diarrhea, abdominal cramping.
Drowsiness, headache, dizziness.
Loss of scalp hair.

Serious Adverse Effects
Allergic Reactions: Severe skin reactions, high fever, chills, joint pains, swollen glands, kidney damage.
Hepatitis with or without jaundice (see Glossary)—yellow coloration of eyes and skin, dark colored urine, light colored stools.
Bone marrow depression (see Glossary).

Advisability of Use During Pregnancy
Safety not established. Prudent use is best determined by the physician's evaluation.

Advisability of Use While Nursing Infant
Safety for infant not established. Ask physician for guidance.

Habit-Forming Potential
None.

Effects of Overdosage
With Moderate Overdose: No significant symptoms reported in non-sensitive individuals. Nausea, vomiting, or diarrhea may occur as a result of individual sensitivity.
With Large Overdose: No serious toxic effects known and none anticipated in the presence of normal kidney function.

Possible Effects of Extended Use
No serious effects reported.

Recommended Periodic Examinations While Taking This Drug
Liver and kidney function tests.
Complete blood cell counts.
Complete examination of the eyes for the development of cataract. (A cause-and-effect relationship [see Glossary] between this drug and the development of cataracts has not been established.)

While Taking This Drug, Observe the Following

Foods: Follow physician's advice regarding the need for a low purine diet. Drug may be taken after eating to reduce stomach irritation or nausea.

Beverages: A large intake of coffee, tea, or cola beverages may reduce the effectiveness of treatment. It is advisable to drink no less than 5 to 6 pints of liquid every 24 hours.

Alcohol: No interactions expected with this drug, but alcohol may impair successful management of gout.

Tobacco Smoking: No interactions expected.

Other Drugs

Allopurinol may *increase* the effects of

- azathioprine (Imuran) and mercaptopurine (Purinethol), making it necessary to reduce their dosages to one-third or one-quarter the usual amount.
- oral anticoagulants (see Drug Family, Section Four), in some individuals. Ask physician for guidance regarding prothrombin time testing and dosage adjustment to prevent abnormal bleeding.

Allopurinol *taken concurrently* with

- iron preparations, may cause excessive accumulation of iron in body tissues. Avoid iron while taking this drug unless advised otherwise by your physician.

The following drugs may *increase* the effects of allopurinol

- acetohexamide (Dymelor) may increase its effectiveness in eliminating uric acid.
- probenecid (Benemid) adds to the elimination of uric acid.

The following drugs may *decrease* the effects of allopurinol

- thiazide diuretics (see Drug Family, Section Four) may reduce its effectiveness in controlling gout.
- ethacrynic acid (Edecrin) may reduce its effectiveness in controlling gout.

Driving a Vehicle, Piloting a Plane, Operating Machinery: Drowsiness may occur in some individuals. Determine sensitivity before engaging in hazardous activities.

Exposure to Sun: No restrictions.

Special Storage Instructions

Keep in a dry, tightly closed container.

AMITRIPTYLINE

Year Introduced: 1961

Brand Names

USA	Canada
Elavil (Merck Sharp & Dohme)	Deprex (M & M)
Endep (Roche)	Elavil (MSD)
Etrafon [CD] (Schering)	Levate (ICN)
Triavil [CD] (Merck Sharp & Dohme)	Mareline (Elliott-Marion)
	Novotriptyn (Novopharm)
	Etrafon [CD] (Schering)
	Triavil [CD] (MSD)

Drug Family: Antidepressant, Tricyclic (Anti-psychotic)

Prescription Required: Yes

Available Dosage Forms and Strengths
Tablets — 10 mg., 25 mg., 50 mg., 75 mg., 100 mg., 150 mg.
Injection — 10 mg. per ml.

How This Drug Works
Intended Therapeutic Effect(s):   Gradual improvement of mood and relief of emotional depression.

Location of Drug Action(s):   Those areas of the brain that determine mood and emotional stability.

Method of Drug Action(s):   Not established. Present thinking is that this drug slowly restores to normal levels certain constituents of brain tissue (such as norepinephrine) that transmit nerve impulses.

THIS DRUG SHOULD NOT BE TAKEN IF
—you are allergic to any of the drugs bearing the brand names listed above.
—you are taking or have taken within the past 14 days any mono-amine oxidase (MAO) inhibitor drug (see Drug Family, Section Four).
—you are recovering from a recent heart attack.
—you have glaucoma (narrow-angle type).
—it is prescribed for a child under 12 years of age.

INFORM YOUR PHYSICIAN BEFORE TAKING THIS DRUG IF
—you are allergic or sensitive to any other tricyclic antidepressant (see Drug Family, Section Four).
—you have a history of any of the following: diabetes, epilepsy, glaucoma, heart disease, prostate gland enlargement, or overactive thyroid function.
—you plan to have surgery under general anesthesia in the near future.

Time Required for Apparent Benefit
Some benefit may be apparent within 1 to 2 weeks. Adequate response may require continuous treatment for 4 to 6 weeks or longer.

Possible Side-Effects *(natural, expected, and unavoidable drug actions)*
Drowsiness, blurring of vision, dryness of mouth, constipation, impaired urination.

CAUTION
The elderly (over 60 years of age) are more likely to experience adverse effects from this drug. Small doses are advisable until tolerance has been determined.

Possible Adverse Effects *(unusual, unexpected, and infrequent reactions)*

IF ANY OF THE FOLLOWING DEVELOP, DISCONTINUE DRUG AND NOTIFY YOUR PHYSICIAN AS SOON AS POSSIBLE

Mild Adverse Effects
Allergic Reactions: Skin rash, hives, swelling of face or tongue, drug fever (see Glossary).
Nausea, indigestion, irritation of tongue or mouth, peculiar taste.
Headache, dizziness, weakness, fainting, unsteady gait, tremors.
Swelling of testicles, breast enlargement, milk formation.
Fluctuation of blood sugar levels.

Serious Adverse Effects
Allergic Reactions: Hepatitis with jaundice (see Glossary).
Confusion (especially in the elderly), hallucinations, agitation, restlessness, nightmares.
Heart palpitation and irregular rhythm.
Bone marrow depression (see Glossary)—fatigue, weakness, fever, sore throat, unusual bleeding or bruising.
Peripheral neuritis (see Glossary)—numbness, tingling, pain, loss of strength in arms and legs.
Parkinson-like disorders (see Glossary)—usually mild and infrequent; more likely to occur in the elderly (over 60 years of age).

Advisability of Use During Pregnancy
Safety not established. Prudent use is best determined by the physician's evaluation.

Advisability of Use While Nursing Infant
This drug may be present in milk in small quantities. Ask physician for guidance.

Habit-Forming Potential
Psychological or physical dependence is rare and unexpected.

Effects of Overdosage
With Moderate Overdose: Confusion, hallucinations, extreme drowsiness, drop in body temperature, heart palpitation, dilated pupils, tremors.
With Large Overdose: Stupor, deep sleep, coma, convulsions.

Possible Effects of Extended Use
None reported.

Recommended Periodic Examinations While Taking This Drug
Complete blood cell counts.
Liver function tests.
Serial blood pressure readings and electrocardiograms.

While Taking This Drug, Observe the Following
Foods: No restrictions.

Beverages: No restrictions.

Alcohol: Avoid completely. This drug can increase markedly the intoxicating effects of alcohol and accentuate its depressant action on brain function.

Tobacco Smoking: No interactions expected.

Other Drugs
Amitriptyline may *increase* the effects of
- amphetamine-like drugs (see Drug Family, Section Four).
- atropine-like drugs (see Drug Family, Section Four).
- levodopa (Dopar, Larodopa, etc.), in its control of Parkinson's disease.
- oral anticoagulants of the coumarin family (see Drug Family, Section Four).
- sedatives, sleep-inducing drugs, tranquilizers, anthihistamines, and narcotic drugs, and cause oversedation. Dosage adjustments may be necessary.

Amitriptyline may *decrease* the effects of
- clonidine (Catapres).
- guanethidine (Ismelin).
- other commonly used anti-hypertensive drugs. Ask physician for guidance regarding the need to monitor blood pressure readings and to adjust dosage of anti-hypertensive medications. (The action of methyldopa (Aldomet) is not decreased by amitriptyline or other tricyclic antidepressants.)
- phenytoin (Dantoin, Dilantin, etc.).

Amitriptyline *taken concurrently* with
- ethchlorvynol (Placidyl), may cause delirium.
- mono-amine oxidase (MAO) inhibitor drugs, may cause high fever, delirium, and convulsions (see Drug Family, Section Four).
- quinidine, may impair heart rhythm and function. Avoid the concurrent use of these two drugs.
- thyroid preparations, may impair heart rhythm and function. Ask physician for guidance regarding thyroid dosage adjustment.

The following drugs may *increase* the effects of amitriptyline
- thiazide diuretics (see Drug Family, Section Four) may slow its elimination from the body. Overdosage may occur.

Driving a Vehicle, Piloting a Plane, Operating Machinery: This drug may impair mental alertness, judgment, physical coordination, and reaction time. Avoid hazardous activities.

Exposure to Sun: Use caution until sensitivity to sun has been determined. This drug may cause photosensitivity (see Glossary).

Discontinuation: If it has been necessary to use this drug for an extended period of time, do not discontinue it abruptly. Ask physician for guidance regarding dosage reduction and withdrawal. It may be necessary to adjust the dosage of other drugs taken concurrently with amitriptyline.

Special Storage Instructions
Keep in a dry, tightly closed container.

AMOBARBITAL

Year Introduced: 1925

Brand Names

USA	Canada
Amytal (Lilly)	Amsebarb (Maney)
Tuinal [CD] (Lilly)	Amytal (Lilly)
(Numerous other	Isobec (Pharbec)
combination brand	Isonal (ICN)
names)	

Drug Family: Sedative, Mild; Sleep Inducer (Hypnotic) [Barbiturates]

Prescription Required: Yes (Controlled Drug, U.S. Schedule 3)

Available Dosage Forms and Strengths
Tablets — 15 mg., 30 mg., 50 mg., 100 mg.
Capsules — 65 mg., 200 mg.
Elixirs — 22 mg. per teaspoonful
— 44 mg. per teaspoonful

How This Drug Works
Intended Therapeutic Effect(s)
• with low dosage, relief of mild to moderate anxiety or tension (sedative effect).
• with higher dosage taken at bedtime, sedation sufficient to induce sleep (hypnotic effect).
Location of Drug Action(s):   The connecting points (synapses) in the nerve pathways that transmit impulses between the wake-sleep centers of the brain.
Method of Drug Action(s):   Not completely established. Present thinking is that this drug selectively blocks the transmission of nerve impulses by reducing the amount of available norepinephrine, one of the chemicals responsible for impulse transmission.

THIS DRUG SHOULD NOT BE TAKEN IF
—you have had an allergic reaction to any dosage form of it previously.
—you have a history of porphyria.

INFORM YOUR PHYSICIAN BEFORE TAKING THIS DRUG IF
—you are allergic or sensitive to any barbiturate drug.
—you are taking sedatives, sleep-inducing drugs, tranquilizers, antihistamines, pain relievers, or narcotic drugs of any kind.
—you have epilepsy.

—you have a history of liver or kidney disease.

—you plan to have surgery under general anesthesia in the near future.

Time Required for Apparent Benefit
Approximately 1 hour.

Possible Side-Effects *(natural, expected, and unavoidable drug actions)*
Drowsiness, lethargy, and sense of mental and physical sluggishness as "hangover" effect.

CAUTION
The elderly (over 60 years of age) and the debilitated may experience agitation, excitement, confusion, and delirium with standard doses. Caution and small doses are advisable until tolerance has been determined.

Possible Adverse Effects *(unusual, unexpected, and infrequent reactions)*

IF ANY OF THE FOLLOWING DEVELOP, DISCONTINUE DRUG AND NOTIFY YOUR PHYSICIAN AS SOON AS POSSIBLE

Mild Adverse Effects
Allergic Reactions: Skin rash (various kinds), hives, localized swelling of eyelids, face, or lips, drug fever.
"Hangover" effect, dizziness, unsteadiness.
Nausea, vomiting, diarrhea.
Joint and muscle pains, most often in the neck, shoulders, and arms.

Serious Adverse Effects
Allergic Reactions: Hepatitis with jaundice (see Glossary). Severe skin reactions.
Idiosyncratic Reactions: Paradoxical excitement and delirium (rather than sedation).
Anemia—weakness and fatigue.
Abnormally low blood platelets (see Glossary)—unusual bleeding or bruising.

Advisability of Use During Pregnancy
Safety not established. Prudent use is best determined by the physician's evaluation.

Advisability of Use While Nursing Infant
Drug is known to be present in milk. Avoid use if possible. Ask physician for guidance.

Habit-Forming Potential
This drug can cause both psychological and physical dependence (see Glossary).

Effects of Overdosage
With Moderate Overdose: Behavior similar to alcoholic intoxication: confusion, slurred speech, physical incoordination, staggering gait, drowsiness.
With Large Overdose: Deepening sleep, coma, slow and shallow breathing, weak and rapid pulse, cold and sweaty skin.

Possible Effects of Extended Use
Psychological and/or physical dependence.
Anemia.
If dose is excessive, a form of chronic intoxication can occur—headache, impaired vision, slurred speech, and depression.

Recommended Periodic Examinations While Taking This Drug
Complete blood cell counts.
Liver function tests.

While Taking This Drug, Observe the Following
Foods: No restrictions.
Beverages: No restrictions.
Alcohol: Avoid completely. Alcohol can increase greatly the sedative and depressant actions of this drug on brain function.
Tobacco Smoking: No interactions expected.
Other Drugs
Amobarbital may *increase* the effects of
• other sedatives, sleep-inducing drugs, tranquilizers, antihistamines, pain relievers, and narcotic drugs, and cause oversedation. Ask your physician for guidance regarding dosage adjustments.

Amobarbital may *decrease* the effects of
• oral anticoagulants of the coumarin family (see Drug Family, Section Four). Ask physician for guidance regarding prothrombin time testing and adjustment of the anticoagulant dosage.
• aspirin, and reduce its pain-relieving action.
• cortisone and related drugs, by hastening their elimination from the body.
• oral contraceptives, by hastening their elimination from the body.
• griseofulvin (Fulvicin, Grisactin, etc.), and reduce its effectiveness in treating fungus infections.
• phenylbutazone (Azolid, Butazolidin, etc.), and reduce its effectiveness in treating inflammation and pain.

Amobarbital *taken concurrently* with
• anti-convulsants, may cause a change in the pattern of epileptic seizures. Careful dosage adjustments are necessary to achieve a balance of actions that will give the best protection from seizures.

The following drugs may *increase* the effects of amobarbital:
• both mild and strong tranquilizers may increase the sedative and sleep-inducing actions and cause oversedation.
• isoniazid (INH, Isozide, etc.) may prolong the action of barbiturate drugs.
• antihistamines may increase the sedative effects of barbiturate drugs.
• oral anti-diabetic drugs of the sulfonylurea type may prolong the sedative effect of barbiturate drugs.

Driving a Vehicle, Piloting a Plane, Operating Machinery: This drug can produce drowsiness and can impair mental alertness, judgment, physical coordination, and reaction time. Avoid hazardous activities.

Exposure to Sun: Use caution until sensitivity has been determined. Some barbiturates can cause photosensitivity (see Glossary).

Exposure to Heat: No restrictions.

Exposure to Cold: The elderly (over 60 years of age) may experience excessive lowering of body temperature while taking this drug. Keep dosage to a minimum during winter and dress warmly.

Heavy Exercise or Exertion: No restrictions.

Discontinuation: If it has been necessary to use this drug for an extended period of time, do not discontinue it abruptly. Ask physician for guidance regarding dosage adjustment and withdrawal. It may also be necessary to adjust the doses of other drugs taken concurrently with it.

Special Storage Instructions

Keep tablets and capsules in a dry, tightly closed container. Keep the elixir in a tightly closed, amber glass bottle.

AMOXICILLIN

Year Introduced: 1969

Brand Names

USA	Canada
Amoxil (Beecham)	Amoxil (Ayerst)
Larotid (Roche)	
Polymox (Bristol)	

Drug Family: Antibiotic (Anti-infective) [Penicillins]

Prescription Required: Yes

Available Dosage Forms and Strengths

Capsules — 250 mg., 500 mg.
Oral Suspension — 125 mg., 250 mg. per teaspoonful
Pediatric Drops — 50 mg. per ml.

How This Drug Works

Intended Therapeutic Effect(s):   The elimination of infections responsive to the action of this drug.

Location of Drug Action(s):   Any body tissue or fluid in which sufficient concentration of the drug can be achieved.

Method of Drug Action(s):   This drug destroys susceptible infecting bacteria by interfering with their ability to produce new protective cell walls as they multiply and grow.

THIS DRUG SHOULD NOT BE TAKEN IF

—you have had an allergic reaction to any dosage form of it previously.
—you are certain you are allergic to *any* form of penicillin.

INFORM YOUR PHYSICIAN BEFORE TAKING THIS DRUG IF

—you suspect you may be allergic to penicillin or you have a history of a previous "reaction" to penicillin.

—you are allergic to cephalosporin antibiotics (Ancef, Ceporan, Ceporex, Kafocin, Keflex, Keflin, Kefzol, Loridine).

—you are allergic by nature (hayfever, asthma, hives, eczema).

Time Required for Apparent Benefit

Varies with the nature of the infection under treatment; usually from 2 to 5 days.

Possible Side-Effects *(natural, expected, and unavoidable drug actions)*

Superinfections (see Glossary).

Possible Adverse Effects *(unusual, unexpected, and infrequent reactions)*

IF ANY OF THE FOLLOWING DEVELOP, DISCONTINUE DRUG AND NOTIFY YOUR PHYSICIAN AS SOON AS POSSIBLE

Mild Adverse Effects

Allergic Reactions: Skin rashes (various kinds).

Irritations of mouth or tongue, "black tongue," nausea, vomiting, diarrhea, dizziness (rare).

Serious Adverse Effects

Allergic Reactions: †Anaphylactic reaction (see Glossary), severe skin reactions, high fever, swollen painful joints, sore throat, unusual bleeding or bruising.

Advisability of Use During Pregnancy

Safety not established. Prudent use is best determined by the physician's evaluation.

Advisability of Use While Nursing Infant

Drug may be present in milk and may sensitize infant to penicillin. Ask physician for guidance.

Habit-Forming Potential

None.

Effects of Overdosage

Possible nausea, vomiting, and/or diarrhea.

Possible Effects of Extended Use

Superinfections (see Glossary).

Recommended Periodic Examinations While Taking This Drug

Complete blood cell counts.

Liver and kidney function tests.

While Taking This Drug, Observe the Following

Foods: No restrictions of food selection. Drug is absorbed better if taken 1 hour before eating or 2 hours after eating.

---

†A rare but potentially dangerous reaction characteristic of penicillins.

Beverages: No restrictions.

Alcohol: No interactions expected.

Tobacco Smoking: No interactions expected.

Other Drugs

The following drugs may *decrease* the effects of amoxicillin

• antacids reduce absorption of amoxicillin.

• chloramphenicol (Chloromycetin)

• erythromycin (Erythrocin, E-Mycin, etc.)

• tetracyclines (Achromycin, Aureomycin, Declomycin, Minocin, etc.; see Drug Family, Section Four)

Driving a Vehicle, Piloting a Plane, Operating Machinery: No restrictions.

Exposure to Sun: No restrictions.

Discontinuation: When used to treat infections that predispose to rheumatic fever or kidney disease, take continuously in full dosage for no less than 10 days. Ask physician for guidance regarding recommended duration of therapy.

Special Storage Instructions

Capsules should be kept in a tightly closed container at room temperature. Oral suspension and pediatric drops should be refrigerated.

Do Not Take the Oral Suspension or Drops of This Drug If It Is Older Than

7 days—when kept at room temperature.

14 days—when kept refrigerated.

AMPICILLIN

Year Introduced: 1961

Brand Names

USA		Canada
Acillin (ICN)	Polycillin (Bristol)	Amcill (P.D. & Co.)
Alpen (Lederle)	Principen (Squibb)	Ampen (ICN)
Amcill (Parke-Davis)	QIDamp	Ampicin (Bristol)
Ameril (Geneva)	(Mallinckrodt)	Ampilean (Harris)
Ampi-Co (Coastal)	Saramp (Saron)	Penbritin (Ayerst)
Divercillin (B.F.	SK-Ampicillin (Smith	Polycillin (Will)
Ascher)	Kline & French)	
Omnipen (Wyeth)	Supen	
Pen-A (Pfizer)	(Reid-Provident)	
Penbritin (Ayerst)	Totacillin (Beecham)	
Pensyn (Upjohn)		

Drug Family: Antibiotic (Anti-infective) [Penicillins]

Prescription Required: Yes

Available Dosage Forms and Strengths
Chewable Tablets — 125 mg.
    Capsules — 250 mg., 500 mg.
Oral Suspension — 125 mg., 250 mg., 500 mg. per teaspoonful
Pediatric Drops — 100 mg. per ml.

How This Drug Works
Intended Therapeutic Effect(s):   The elimination of infections responsive to the action of this drug.
Location of Drug Action(s):   Any body tissue or fluid in which sufficient concentration of the drug can be achieved.
Method of Drug Action(s):   This drug destroys susceptible infecting bacteria by interfering with their ability to produce new protective cell walls as they multiply and grow.

THIS DRUG SHOULD NOT BE TAKEN IF
—you are allergic to any of the drugs bearing the brand names listed above.
—you are certain you are allergic to any form of penicillin.
—you have infectious mononucleosis (glandular fever).

INFORM YOUR PHYSICIAN BEFORE TAKING THIS DRUG IF
—you suspect you may be allergic to penicillin or you have a history of a previous "reaction" to penicillin.
—you are allergic to cephalosporin antibiotics (Ancef, Ceporan, Ceporex, Kafocin, Keflex, Keflin, Kefzol, Loridine).
—you are allergic by nature (hayfever, asthma, hives, eczema).

Time Required for Apparent Benefit
Varies with the nature of the infection under treatment; usually 2 to 5 days.

Possible Side-Effects *(natural, expected, and unavoidable drug actions)*
Superinfections (see Glossary).

Possible Adverse Effects *(unusual, unexpected, and infrequent reactions)*
IF ANY OF THE FOLLOWING DEVELOP, DISCONTINUE DRUG AND NOTIFY YOUR PHYSICIAN AS SOON AS POSSIBLE
Mild Adverse Effects
    Allergic Reactions: Skin rashes (various kinds).
    Irritations of mouth and tongue, "black tongue," nausea, vomiting, diarrhea, dizziness (rare).
    Note: A generalized rash occurs commonly (approximately 90% of the time) when ampicillin is taken in the presence of infectious mononucleosis.
Serious Adverse Effects
    Allergic Reactions: †Anaphylactic reaction (see Glossary), severe skin reactions, high fever, swollen painful joints, sore throat, unusual bleeding or bruising.

---

†A rare but potentially dangerous reaction characteristic of penicillins.

Advisability of Use During Pregnancy
Safety not established. Prudent use is best determined by the physician's evaluation.

Advisability of Use While Nursing Infant
Drug may be present in milk and could sensitize infant to penicillin. Ask physician for guidance.

Habit-Forming Potential
None.

Effects of Overdosage
Possible nausea, vomiting, and/or diarrhea.

Possible Effects of Extended Use
Superinfections (see Glossary).

Recommended Periodic Examinations While Taking This Drug
Complete blood cell counts
Liver and kidney function tests.

While Taking This Drug, Observe the Following
Foods: No restrictions of food selection. Drug is absorbed better if taken 1 hour before or 2 hours after eating.
Beverages: No restrictions.
Alcohol: No interactions expected.
Tobacco Smoking: No interactions expected.
Other Drugs
  The following drugs may *decreàse* the effects of ampicillin
  • antacids may reduce its absorption.
  • chloramphenicol (Chloromycetin)
  • erythromycin (Erythrocin, E-Mycin, etc.)
  • tetracyclines (Achromycin, Aureomycin, Declomycin, Minocin, etc.; see Drug Family, Section Four)
Driving a Vehicle, Piloting a Plane, Operating Machinery: No restrictions.
Exposure to Sun: No restrictions.
Discontinuation: When used to treat infections that predispose to rheumatic fever or kidney disease, take continuously in full dosage for no less than 10 days. Ask physician for guidance regarding recommended duration of therapy.

Special Storage Instructions
Tablets and capsules should be kept in tightly closed containers. Oral suspension and pediatric drops should be refrigerated. Keep bottles tightly closed.

Do Not Take the Oral Suspension or Drops of This Drug If It Is Older Than
7 days—when kept at room temperature: 70°F. (21°C.).
14 days—when kept refrigerated: 40°F. (4°C.).

ANISINDIONE

Year Introduced: 1960

Brand Names

USA	Canada
Miradon (Schering)	None

Drug Family: Anticoagulant [Indandiones]

Prescription Required: Yes

Available Dosage Forms and Strengths
Tablets — 50 mg.

How This Drug Works

Intended Therapeutic Effect(s):   A deliberate reduction in the ability of the blood to clot. This effect is often beneficial in the management of stroke, heart attack, abnormal clotting in arteries and veins (thrombosis), and the movement of a blood clot from vein to lung (pulmonary embolism).

Location of Drug Action(s):   Those tissues in the liver that use Vitamin K to produce prothrombin (and other factors) essential to the clotting of the blood.

Method of Drug Action(s):   The oral anticoagulants interfere with the production of four essential blood-clotting factors by blocking the action of Vitamin K. This leads to a deficiency of these clotting factors in circulating blood and inhibits blood-clotting mechanisms.

THIS DRUG SHOULD NOT BE TAKEN IF

—you have had an allergic reaction to it or an unfavorable response to any indandione drug (Danilone, Dipaxin, Eridione, Hedulin).
—you have a history of a bleeding disorder.
—you have an active peptic ulcer.
—you have ulcerative colitis.

INFORM YOUR PHYSICIAN BEFORE TAKING THIS DRUG IF

—you are now taking *any other drugs*—either drugs prescribed by another physician or non-prescription drugs you purchased over-the-counter (see OTC drugs in Glossary).
—you have high blood pressure.
—you have abnormally heavy or prolonged menstrual bleeding.
—you have diabetes.
—you are using an indwelling catheter.
—you have a history of serious liver or kidney disease, or impaired liver or kidney function
—you plan to have a surgical or dental procedure in the near future.

Time Required for Apparent Benefit

Drug action begins within 24 hours, produces desired effects in 24 to 72 hours, and persists for 1 and one-half to 3 days. Continuous use on a regular schedule for up to 10 days (with daily prothrombin testing and dosage adjustment) is needed to determine the correct maintenance dose for each individual.

Possible Side-Effects *(natural, expected, and unavoidable drug actions)*

A red-orange discoloration of the urine may occur from time to time. This is a normal side-effect and does not indicate bleeding. However, minor episodes of bleeding (nose, gums) may occur even when dosage is well within the recommended range. If in doubt regarding its significance, consult your physician regarding the need for prothrombin testing.

CAUTION

1. Always carry with you a card of personal identification that includes a statement indicating that you are using an anticoagulant (see Table 14 and Section Seven).
2. While you are taking an anticoagulant drug, always consult your physician before starting any new drug, changing the dosage schedule of any drug, or discontinuing any drug.

Possible Adverse Effects *(unusual, unexpected, and infrequent reactions)*

IF ANY OF THE FOLLOWING DEVELOP, DISCONTINUE DRUG AND NOTIFY YOUR PHYSICIAN AS SOON AS POSSIBLE

Mild Adverse Effects

Allergic Reactions: Skin rash, itching, drug fever.

Blurred vision (impairment of focus).

Mouth ulceration, diarrhea.

Serious Adverse Effects

Episodes of major bleeding or hemorrhage. Notify physician of abnormal bruising, nosebleeds, heavy gum bleeding, bloody sputum, bloody urine, bloody or tarry stools.

Abnormally low white blood cell counts, reducing natural resistance to infection. Report any fever or sore throat.

Hepatitis with or without jaundice (see Glossary). Report yellow discoloration of eyes or skin, dark-colored urine, or light-colored stools.

Kidney damage.

Advisability of Use During Pregnancy

This drug can cause hemorrhage in the fetus. Avoid use completely if possible.

Advisability of Use While Nursing Infant

This drug is present in milk and may cause bleeding or hemorrhage in the nursing infant. Avoid drug or avoid nursing. Ask physician for guidance.

Habit-Forming Potential

None.

Effects of Overdosage
With Moderate Overdose: Episodes of minor bleeding: blood spots in white portion of eye, nosebleeds, gum bleeding, small bruises, prolonged bleeding from minor cuts received while shaving or from other small lacerations.

With Large Overdose: Episodes of major internal bleeding: vomiting of blood, grossly bloody urine or stools.

Possible Effects of Extended Use
None reported.

Recommended Periodic Examinations While Taking This Drug
Regular determination of prothrombin time is essential to safe dosage and proper control.

Complete blood cell counts.

Liver function tests.

Kidney function tests.

While Taking This Drug, Observe the Following
Foods: A larger intake than usual of foods high in Vitamin K may reduce the effectiveness of this drug and make larger doses necessary. Foods rich in Vitamin K include: cabbage, cauliflower, fish, kale, liver, spinach.

Beverages: No restrictions.

Alcohol: Use with caution until combined effect has been determined. Alcohol may either increase or decrease the effect of this drug. It is advisable to use alcohol sparingly while taking anticoagulants.

(Note: Heavy users of alcohol with liver damage may be very sensitive to anticoagulants and require smaller than usual doses.)

Tobacco Smoking: No interactions expected. Follow physician's advice regarding smoking (based upon condition under treatment).

Other Drugs: See WARFARIN Drug Profile. Drug interactions for anisindione are essentially the same as for warfarin.

Driving a Vehicle, Piloting a Plane, Operating Machinery: No restrictions. Avoid unnecessary hazardous activities that could cause injury and result in excessive bleeding.

Exposure to Sun: No restrictions.

Exposure to Heat: Prolonged hot weather may increase the prothrombin time and make it advisable to reduce anticoagulant dosage. Ask physician for guidance.

Occurrence of Unrelated Illness: Any acute illness that causes fever, vomiting, or diarrhea can alter your response to this drug. Notify your physician so corrective action can be taken.

Discontinuation: Do not discontinue this drug abruptly unless abnormal bleeding occurs. Ask physician for guidance regarding gradual reduction of dosage over a period of 3 to 4 weeks.

Special Storage Instructions
Keep in a dry, tightly closed container. Protect from light.

ANISOTROPINE

Year Introduced: 1962

Brand Names

USA	Canada
Valpin (Endo)	Valpin (Endo)
Valpin-PB [CD] (Endo)	Valpin-PB [CD] (Endo)

Drug Family: Antispasmodic; Atropine-like Drug [Anticholinergics]

Prescription Required: Yes

Available Dosage Forms and Strengths
Tablets — 10 mg.
Elixir — 10 mg. per teaspoonful

How This Drug Works
Intended Therapeutic Effect(s):   Relief of discomfort resulting from excessive activity and spasm of the digestive tract (esophagus, stomach, intestine, and colon).

Location of Drug Action(s):   The terminal nerve fibers of the parasympathetic nervous system that control the activity of the gastrointestinal tract.

Method of Drug Action(s):   By blocking the action of the chemical (acetylcholine) that transmits impulses at parasympathetic nerve endings, this drug prevents stimulation of muscular contraction and glandular secretion within the organ involved. This results in reduced overall activity, including the prevention or relief of muscle spasm.

THIS DRUG SHOULD NOT BE TAKEN IF
—you have had an allergic reaction to any dosage form of it previously.
—your stomach cannot empty properly into the intestine (pyloric obstruction).
—you are unable to empty the urinary bladder completely.
—you have glaucoma (narrow-angle type).
—you have severe ulcerative colitis.

INFORM YOUR PHYSICIAN BEFORE TAKING THIS DRUG IF
—you have glaucoma (open-angle type).
—you have angina or coronary heart disease.
—you have chronic bronchitis.
—you have a hiatal hernia.
—you have enlargement of the prostate gland.
—you have myasthenia gravis.
—you have a history of peptic ulcer disease.
—you plan to have surgery under general anesthesia in the near future.

Time Required for Apparent Benefit
Drug action begins in 1 to 2 hours and persists for approximately 4 hours.

Possible Side-Effects *(natural, expected, and unavoidable drug actions)*
Blurring of vision (impairment of focus), dryness of the mouth and throat, constipation, hesitancy in urination. (Nature and degree of side-effects depend upon individual susceptibility and drug dosage.)

CAUTION
The elderly (over 60 years of age) may be more susceptible to all of the actions of this drug. Small doses are advisable until response has been determined.

Possible Adverse Effects *(unusual, unexpected, and infrequent reactions)*

IF ANY OF THE FOLLOWING DEVELOP, DISCONTINUE DRUG AND NOTIFY YOUR PHYSICIAN AS SOON AS POSSIBLE

Mild Adverse Effects
Allergic Reactions: Skin rash, hives.
Dilation of pupils, causing sensitivity to light.
Flushing and dryness of the skin (reduced sweating).
Rapid heart action.
Lightheadedness, dizziness, unsteady gait.

Serious Adverse Effects
Idiosyncratic Reactions: Acute confusion, delirium, and behavioral abnormalities.
Development of acute glaucoma (in susceptible individuals).

Advisability of Use During Pregnancy
Safety not established. Prudent use is best determined by the physician's evaluation.

Advisability of Use While Nursing Infant
This drug may impair the formation of milk and make nursing difficult. Safety for infant not established. Avoid drug or avoid nursing. Ask physician for guidance.

Habit-Forming Potential
None.

Effects of Overdosage
With Moderate Overdose: Marked dryness of the mouth, dilated pupils, blurring of near vision, rapid pulse, heart palpitation, headache, difficulty in urination.
With Large Overdose: Extremely dilated pupils, rapid pulse and breathing, hot skin, high fever, excitement, confusion, hallucinations, delirium, eventual loss of consciousness, convulsions, and coma.

Possible Effects of Extended Use
Chronic constipation, severe enough to result in fecal impaction. (Constipation should be treated promptly with effective laxatives.)

Recommended Periodic Examinations While Taking This Drug
Measurement of internal eye pressure to detect any significant increase that could indicate developing glaucoma.

While Taking This Drug, Observe the Following

Foods:　No interaction with drug. Effectiveness is greater if drug is taken one-half to 1 hour before eating. Follow diet prescribed for condition under treatment.

Beverages:　No interactions. Follow prescribed diet.

Alcohol:　No interactions expected with this drug. Follow physician's advice regarding use of alcohol (based upon its effect on the condition under treatment).

Tobacco Smoking:　No interactions expected. Follow physician's advice regarding smoking.

Other Drugs

Anisotropine may *increase* the effects of

- all other drugs having atropine-like actions (see Drug Family, Section Four).

Anisotropine may *decrease* the effects of

- pilocarpine eye drops, and reduce their effectiveness in lowering internal eye pressure in the treatment of glaucoma.

Anisotropine *taken concurrently* with

- mono-amine oxidase (MAO) inhibitor drugs, may cause an exaggerated response to normal doses of atropine-like drugs. It is best to avoid atropine-like drugs for 2 weeks after the last dose of any MAO inhibitor drug (see Drug Family, Section Four).
- haloperidol (Haldol), may significantly increase internal eye pressure (dangerous in glaucoma).

The following drugs may *increase* the effects of anisotropine:

- tricyclic antidepressants
- those antihistamines that have an atropine-like action
- meperidine (Demerol, pethidine)
- methylphenidate (Ritalin)
- orphenadrine (Disipal, Norflex)
- those phenothiazines that have an atropine-like action (see Drug Family, Section Four)

Driving a Vehicle, Piloting a Plane, Operating Machinery:　Usually no restrictions. However, if blurred vision, drowsiness, or lightheadedness occurs, avoid hazardous activities.

Exposure to Sun:　No restrictions.

Exposure to Heat:　Use extreme caution. The use of this drug in hot environments may significantly increase the risk of heat stroke.

Heavy Exercise or Exertion:　Use caution in warm or hot environments. This drug may impair normal perspiration (heat loss) and interfere with the regulation of body temperature.

Special Storage Instructions

Keep in a tightly closed container. Protect from light.

ANTACIDS

Aluminum hydroxide	**Magnesium hydroxide**
Calcium carbonate	**Magnesium trisilicate**
Magaldrate	**Sodium bicarbonate**
Magnesium carbonate	**Sodium carbonate**

Year Introduced: Aluminum hydroxide, 1936
Calcium carbonate, 1825
Magaldrate, 1960
Magnesium hydroxide, 1873
Magnesium trisilicate, 1936
Sodium bicarbonate, 1886

Brand Names

USA	Canada**
Absorbable Antacids:	Absorbable Antacids:
Sodium bicarbonate*:	Sodium bicarbonate*:
Alka-Seltzer Antacid (Miles)	Alka-Citrate Compound (I&B)
Bell-Ans (C. S. Dent)	Alka-Seltzer (Miles)
BiSoDol Powder (Whitehall)	Bismocal (C & C)
Brioschi (Brioschi, Inc.)	BiSoDol Powder (Whitehall)
Bromo-Seltzer (Warner-Lambert)	Brioschi (Brioschi, Inc.)
Eno's Antacid (Beecham)	Bromo-Seltzer (Warner-Lambert)
Fizrin (Glenbrook)	Chembicarb (Chemo)
Seidlitz Powder (Garfield)	Eno's Antacid (Beecham)
Soda Mint (Numerous mfrs.)	Soda Mint (Numerous mfrs.)
Less Absorbable Antacids:	Less Absorbable Antacids:
Aluminum hydroxide:	Aluminum hydroxide:
Amphojel (Wyeth)	A-H Gel (Dymond)
Calcium carbonate*:	Alu-Tab (Riker)
Alka-2 (Miles)	Amphojel (Wyeth)
Amitone (Mitchum-Thayer)	Chemgel (Chemo)
	Pepsogel (C & C)
	Robalate (Robins)

*The principal antacid component.
**At press time, complete and accurate information regarding the content of some antacids marketed in Canada was unavailable. Recent enactment of new Canadian laws governing over-the-counter drug products may lead to changes in the formulation of some antacid preparations beginning in 1976. It is advisable to read the package label to ascertain the current composition of any over-the-counter drug product you intend to use.

Dicarbosil (Lewis-Howe)
Gustalac (Geriatric)
Pepto-Bismol Tablets (Norwich)
Ratio (Warren-Teed)
Titralac (Riker)
Tums (Lewis-Howe)
Magnesium hydroxide:
Milk of Magnesia (Numerous mfrs.)

Antacid Combinations:
Aluminum hydroxide +
Magnesium hydroxide:
Aludrox (Wyeth)
Creamalin (Winthrop)
Delcid (Merrell-National)
Di-Gel Liquid (Plough)
Kolantyl (Merrell-National)
Maalox (Rorer)
Maxamag (Vitarine)
Mylanta (Stuart)
Win-Gel (Winthrop)
Aluminum hydroxide +
Magnesium trisilicate:
A-M-T (Wyeth)
Gelusil (Warner/Chilcott)
Malcogel (Upjohn)
Trisogel (Lilly)
Aluminum hydroxide + Sodium
carbonate:
Rolaids (American Chicle)
Aluminum hydroxide +
Calcium carbonate +
Magnesium hydroxide:
Camalox (Rorer)
Ducon (Smith Kline & French)
Aluminum hydroxide +
Magnesium carbonate +
Magnesium hydroxide:
Di-Gel Tablets (Plough)
Aluminum hydroxide +
Magnesium hydroxide +
Magnesium trisilicate:
Magnatril (Lannett)
Mucotin (Warner/Chilcott)
Calcium carbonate +
Magnesium carbonate +
Magnesium oxide:
Alkets (Upjohn)

Calcium carbonate*:
Pepto-Bismol Tablets (Norwich)
Titralac (Riker)
Tums (Lewis-Howe)
Magnesium hydroxide:
Milk of Magnesia (Numerous mfrs.)

Antacid Combinations:
Aluminum hydroxide +
Calcium carbonate:
Duatrol (SK&F)
Aluminum hydroxide +
Magnesium carbonate:
Antamel (Elliott-Marion)
Magnesed (M & M)
Aluminum hydroxide +
Magnesium hydroxide:
Alsimox (ICI)
A.M.H. Suspension (M & M)
Creamalin (Winthrop)
Di-Gel Liquid (Plough)
Diovol (Horner)
Kolantyl (Merrell)
Maalox (Rorer)
Mylanta (P.D. & Co.)
Neutralca-S (Desbergers)
Univol (Horner)
Aluminum hydroxide +
Magnesium trisilicate:
Gelusil (Warner/Chilcott)
Aluminum hydroxide + Sodium
carbonate:
Rolaids (Adams)
Aluminum hydroxide +
Calcium carbonate +
Magnesium hydroxide:
Camalox (Rorer)
Aluminum hydroxide +
Magnesium carbonate +
Magnesium hydroxide:
Amphojel 65 (Wyeth)
Di-Gel Tablets (Plough)
Calcium carbonate +
Magnesium hydroxide:
BiSoDol Tablets (Whitehall)
Hydrotalcite:
Altacite (Roussel)
Magaldrate:
Riopan (Ayerst)

*The principal antacid component.

Calcium carbonate +
Magnesium hydroxide:
BiSoDol Tablets (Whitehall)
Magaldrate: Riopan (Ayerst)

Drug Family: Antacids, Stomach

Prescription Required: No

Available Dosage Forms and Strengths
Tablets
Chewable Tablets
Wafers
Granules
Powders
Liquid Suspensions
Available in a large variety of formulations and strengths. See package label
for product composition and individual component strengths.

How This Drug Works
Intended Therapeutic Effect(s)
- Relief of heartburn, sour stomach, and acid indigestion.
- Relief of discomfort associated with peptic ulcer, gastritis, esophagitis,
and hiatal hernia.

Location of Drug Action(s):   Within the digestive juices of the stomach.

Method of Drug Action(s)
By neutralizing some of the hydrochloric acid in the stomach, these drugs
reduce the degree of acidity and thus lessen the irritant effect of digestive juices on inflamed and ulcerated tissues.
By reducing the action of the digestive enzyme pepsin, these drugs are
thought to create a more favorable environment for the healing of peptic
ulcer.

THIS DRUG SHOULD NOT BE TAKEN IF
—you have a known allergy or sensitivity to any of its components. (Brand
names listed above are arranged according to generic components.)
—it contains a calcium compound, and you are known to have a high blood
calcium level.

INFORM YOUR PHYSICIAN BEFORE TAKING THIS DRUG IF
—you have a history of chronic kidney disease or reduced kidney function.
—you have a history of kidney stones.
—you have chronic constipation or chronic diarrhea.
—you have any disorder that causes fluid retention.
—you have high blood pressure.
—you have a history of congestive heart failure.

Time Required for Apparent Benefit
Depending upon the composition and dose of the antacid, relief can begin in 5 to 15 minutes and persist for 45 minutes to 3 hours. Liquid preparations give relief more rapidly than tablets.

Possible Side-Effects *(natural, expected, and unavoidable drug actions)*
Aluminum preparations may cause constipation. Calcium carbonate may cause belching and constipation. Magnesium carbonate may cause belching and diarrhea. Magnesium preparations may cause diarrhea. Sodium bicarbonate may cause belching and weight gain.

CAUTION
1. Do not use any antacid regularly for more than 2 weeks without your physician's guidance.
2. If symptoms requiring the use of antacids persist, consult your physician for definitive diagnosis and appropriate treatment.
3. If frequent and continuous use of antacids is necessary, it is advisable to use aluminum and/or magnesium preparations.
4. Calcium carbonate and sodium bicarbonate preparations should be limited to occasional use by healthy individuals. Their frequent or continuous use should be avoided.
5. The elderly (over 60 years of age) and individuals with high blood pressure, fluid retention, or a history of congestive heart failure should avoid antacids with a high sodium content. These include:

Alka-Seltzer   Fizrin
Bell-Ans   Rolaids
BiSoDol Powder   Seidlitz Powder
Brioschi   Soda Mints
Bromo-Seltzer   Trisogel
Eno's Antacid

6. Do not exceed the maximal daily dose stated on the product label.
7. Do not swallow chewable tablets and wafers whole. These preparations must be thoroughly sucked or chewed before swallowing, and preferably followed by a small amount of water or milk. (Antacid tablets designed for chewing can cause intestinal obstruction if swallowed whole.)
8. Shake all liquid suspensions of antacids well before measuring dose.
9. In the presence of reduced kidney function: (1) antacids may accumulate in the blood and cause an excessive shift in the acid-alkaline balance of body chemistry to the alkaline side (alkalosis); (2) antacids containing magnesium may lead to excessive retention of magnesium and resulting toxicity.
10. Individuals sensitive to aspirin should note that these antacids contain aspirin: Alka-Seltzer (original formulation; see label), Cama Inlay-Tabs, and Fizrin.
11. Bromo-Seltzer also contains acetaminophen.

Possible Adverse Effects *(unusual, unexpected, and infrequent reactions)*

IF ANY OF THE FOLLOWING DEVELOP, DISCONTINUE DRUG AND NOTIFY YOUR PHYSICIAN AS SOON AS POSSIBLE

Mild Adverse Effects

Aluminum hydroxide may cause nausea and/or vomiting.

Calcium carbonate may cause nausea.

Serious Adverse Effects

Aluminum hydroxide taken in large doses and with inadequate fluids can cause intestinal obstruction.

Calcium carbonate taken in large doses can cause abnormally high calcium levels in the blood; chronic use can lead to kidney stones and impaired kidney function.

Sodium bicarbonate taken in large doses or on a regular basis can cause elevation of the blood pressure, fluid retention (edema), and serious disturbance of the acid-alkaline balance of body chemistry (alkalosis).

Advisability of Use During Pregnancy

Select antacid preparations with contents limited to aluminum and magnesium compounds. Avoid antacid preparations containing sodium compounds and aspirin. If you have impaired kidney function, ask your physician for guidance in selecting an antacid.

Advisability of Use While Nursing Infant

As for pregnancy.

Habit-Forming Potential

None. However, frequent use of sodium bicarbonate, and large doses of calcium carbonate or magnesium hydroxide, may cause "acid rebound," which requires repeated use of the antacid to sustain relief from recurring hyperacidity.

Effects of Overdosage

With Moderate Overdose: Aluminum hydroxide may cause nausea, vomiting, and/or severe constipation. Magnesium compounds may cause severe diarrhea.

With Large Overdose: Moderate alkalosis, manifested by loss of appetite, weakness, fatigue, and dizziness. Severe alkalosis, manifested by nervous irritability, restlessness, and muscle spasms. Magnesium overdose may cause dryness of the mouth, stupor, and slow, shallow breathing.

Possible Effects of Extended Use

Aluminum hydroxide may cause decreased levels of blood phosphates, resulting in loss of calcium and phosphate from bone with weakening of bone structure (osteomalacia).

Calcium carbonate may cause an abnormally high blood level of calcium, disturbance of the acid-alkaline balance of body chemistry (alkalosis), impaired kidney function, and the formation of kidney stones.

Magnesium hydroxide may cause toxic effects on the nervous system (if used in the presence of reduced kidney function).

Magnesium trisilicate may cause the formation of kidney stones.
Sodium bicarbonate may predispose to recurrent urinary tract infections, kidney stones, excessive retention of sodium leading to elevated blood pressure, and fluid retention.

Recommended Periodic Examinations While Taking This Drug
Measurements of blood calcium and phosphorus levels.
Measurements of blood acid-alkaline status.
Kidney function tests and urine analyses.

While Taking This Drug, Observe the Following
Foods: Follow the diet prescribed by your physician. Maintain regular intake of high phosphate foods such as meats, poultry, fish, eggs, dairy products, and cereals. When used on a regular basis for continuous effect, antacids are most effective when taken 1 hour after eating.
Beverages: As directed by your physician.
Alcohol: No interactions with antacids. However, alcoholic beverages may increase stomach acidity and thus increase antacid requirements.
Tobacco Smoking: No interactions with antacids. However, nicotine may increase stomach acidity and thus increase antacid requirements.
Other Drugs

Aluminum hydroxide may *increase* the effects of
• meperidine (pethidine, Demerol).
• pseudoephedrine (Sudafed).

Magnesium hydroxide may *increase* the effects of
• dicumarol.

Sodium bicarbonate may *increase* the effects of
• quinidine.

Antacids may *decrease* the effects of
• chlorpromazine.
• digitalis preparations.
• iron preparations.
• isoniazid.
• nalidixic acid.
• para-aminosalicylic acid.
• penicillins.
• pentobarbital.
• phenylbutazone.
• sulfonamides ("sulfa" drugs).
• tetracyclines.
• Vitamins A and C.

Antacids *taken concurrently* with
• anticoagulants, may cause impaired absorption and reduced effectiveness of the anticoagulant. Consult physician regarding need for prothrombin time determinations.
Driving a Vehicle, Piloting a Plane, Operating Machinery: No precautions or restrictions.

Special Storage Instructions
Keep all antacids in tightly closed containers. Store liquid suspensions in a
cool place; avoid freezing.

ASPIRIN*
(Acetylsalicylic Acid)

Year Introduced: 1899

Brand Names

USA	Canada
A.S.A. Preparations (Lilly)	Acetal (Dymond)
Aluminum Aspirin	Acetophen (Frosst)
(Abbott)	Acetyl-Sal (Hartz)
Aspirjen Jr. (Jenkins)	Ancasal (Anca)
Bayer Aspirin	Astrin (Medic)
(Glenbrook)	Bayer Aspirin* (Sterling)
Bayer Children's Aspirin	Cetasal (I&B)
(Glenbrook)	Ecotrin (SK&F)
Ecotrin (Smith Kline &	Entrophen (Frosst)
French)	Neopirine-25 (C & C)
Measurin (Breon)	Norasen (Novopharm)
St. Joseph Children's	Nova-Phase (Nova)
Aspirin (Plough)	Phonal (Poulenc)
	Sal-Adult (M & M)
	Sal-Infant (M & M)
	Supasa (Nordic)
	Triaphen-10 (Trianon)

OTC Preparations containing Aspirin

Alka-Seltzer [CD] (Miles)
Anacin [CD] (Whitehall)
A.P.C. Tablets [CD]
(Various
Manufacturers)
Ascriptin [CD] (Rorer)
Aspergum [CD] (Plough)
Bufferin [CD]
(Bristol-Myers)
Cama [CD] (Dorsey)
Cope [CD] (Glenbrook)

Empirin Compound [CD]
(Burroughs Wellcome)
Excedrin [CD]
(Bristol-Myers)
4-Way Tablets [CD]
(Bristol-Myers)
Midol [CD] (Glenbrook)
Stanback [CD] (Stanback)
Vanquish [CD]
(Glenbrook)
(Numerous others)

*In the United States *aspirin* is an official generic designation. In Canada *Aspirin* is the
Registered Trade Mark of the Bayer Company Division of Sterling Drug Ltd.

Drug Family: Analgesic, Mild; Anti-inflammatory; Fever Reducer (Antipyretic) [Salicylates]

Prescription Required: No

Available Dosage Forms and Strengths
> Tablets — 60 mg. (1 gr.), 75 mg. (1.2 gr.), 300 mg. (5 gr.), 600 mg. (10 gr.)
> Chewable Tablets
> (Orange Flavored) — 81 mg. (1.25 gr.) (child's dosage form)
> Capsules — 300 mg. (5 gr.), 600 mg. (10 gr.)
> Suppositories — 60 mg. (1 gr.), 150 mg. (2.5 gr.) 200 mg. (3.33 gr.), 300 mg. (5 gr.) 600 mg. (10 gr.)

How This Drug Works
Intended Therapeutic Effect(s)
- reduction of high fever.
- relief of mild to moderate pain and inflammation.
- prevention of blood clots (as in phlebitis, heart attack, and stroke).

Location of Drug Action(s):   Principal actions occur in:
- a major control center of the brain known as the hypothalamus.
- areas of injury, inflammation, or spasm, in many body tissues.
- blood platelets (see Glossary).

Method of Drug Action(s)
Aspirin, by indirect action on the hypothalamus, reduces fever by dilating blood vessels in the skin. This hastens the loss of body heat.
Aspirin reduces the tissue concentration of prostaglandins, chemicals involved in the production of inflammation and pain.
Aspirin interferes with the blood clotting mechanism by its action on blood platelets.

THIS DRUG SHOULD NOT BE TAKEN IF
—you have had an allergic reaction or an unfavorable response to it previously.
—you have any type of bleeding disorder (such as hemophilia).
—you are taking anticoagulant drugs.
—you have an active peptic ulcer (stomach or duodenum).

INFORM YOUR PHYSICIAN BEFORE TAKING THIS DRUG IF
—you have a history of peptic ulcer disease.
—you have a history of gout.
—you are taking oral anti-diabetic drugs.
—you are pregnant or planning pregnancy.
—you plan to have surgery of any kind in the near future.

Time Required for Apparent Benefit
Drug action begins in 15 to 20 minutes, reaches a maximum in approximately 1 to 2 hours, and persists for 3 to 4 hours.

Possible Side-Effects *(natural, expected, and unavoidable drug actions)*
Mild drowsiness in sensitive individuals.

CAUTION

1. It is most important to understand that aspirin is a drug. While it is one of our most useful drugs, we have an unrealistic sense of safety and unconcern regarding its actions within the body and its potential for adverse effects. This is due to its unlimited availability in over 400 products and its extremely wide use (100 million aspirin tablets taken daily in the United States).

2. In order to know if you are taking aspirin, make it a point to learn the contents of all drugs you take—those prescribed by your physician and those you purchase over-the-counter (OTC) without prescription.

3. Limit the dosage of aspirin to no more than 3 tablets (15 grs.) at one time, allow at least 4 hours between doses, and take no more than 10 tablets (50 grs.) in 24 hours.

4. Remember that aspirin can
   • cause new illnesses
   • complicate existing illnesses
   • complicate pregnancy
   • complicate surgery
   • interact unfavorably with many other drugs

5. When your physician asks "Are you taking any drugs?", the answer is yes if you are taking aspirin. This also applies to any non-prescription drug you are taking (see OTC drugs in Glossary).

Possible Adverse Effects *(unusual, unexpected, and infrequent reactions)*

IF ANY OF THE FOLLOWING DEVELOP, DISCONTINUE DRUG AND NOTIFY YOUR PHYSICIAN AS SOON AS POSSIBLE

Mild Adverse Effects
   Allergic Reactions: Skin rash, hives, nasal discharge (resembling hay fever), nasal polyps.
   Stomach irritation, heartburn, nausea, vomiting.

Serious Adverse Effects
   Allergic Reactions: Acute anaphylactic reaction (see Glossary), asthma, unusual bruising due to allergic destruction of blood platelets (see Glossary).
   Idiosyncratic Reactions: Hemolytic anemia (see Glossary).
   Erosion of stomach lining, with silent bleeding.
   Activation of peptic ulcer, with and without hemorrhage.
   Bone marrow depression (see Glossary)—fatigue, weakness, fever, sore throat, abnormal bruising or bleeding.
   Hepatitis with jaundice (see Glossary)—yellow skin and eyes, dark-colored urine, light-colored stools.
   Kidney damage, if used in large doses or for a prolonged time.

Advisability of Use During Pregnancy
Studies indicate that the regular use of salicylates during pregnancy is often detrimental to the health of the mother and to the welfare of the infant. Excessive use of salicylate drugs can cause anemia, hemorrhage before and after delivery, and an increased incidence of still births. It is advisable to limit the use of aspirin during pregnancy to small doses and to brief periods of time, and to avoid aspirin altogether during the last month of pregnancy.

Advisability of Use While Nursing Infant
This drug is present in milk and may cause adverse effects in the nursing infant. It is advisable to avoid use if nursing.

Habit-Forming Potential
Use of this drug in large doses for a prolonged period of time may cause a form of psychological dependence (see Glossary).

Effects of Overdosage
With Moderate Overdose: Stomach distress, nausea, vomiting, ringing in the ears, dizziness, impaired hearing, drowsiness, sweating.

With Large Overdose: Stupor, warm and dry skin, fever, deep and rapid breathing, fast pulse, muscular twitching, delirium, hallucinations, convulsions.

Possible Effects of Extended Use
A form of psychological dependence (see Glossary).
Anemia due to chronic blood loss from erosion of stomach lining.
The development of stomach ulcer.
The development of "aspirin allergy"—nasal discharge, nasal polyps, asthma.
Kidney damage.
Excessive prolongation of bleeding time, of major importance in the event of injury or surgical procedure.

Recommended Periodic Examinations While Taking This Drug
Complete blood cell counts.
Kidney function tests and urine analysis.
Liver function tests.

While Taking This Drug, Observe the Following
Foods: No restrictions. Stomach irritation can be reduced by taking aspirin with milk or after food. Supplement diet, if necessary, with no more than the recommended daily allowance of Vitamin C. Do not take large doses of Vitamin C while taking aspirin on a regular basis.

Beverages: No restrictions. It is advisable to drink a full glass of water with each dose of aspirin to reduce its irritant effect on the stomach lining.

Alcohol: No interactions expected. However, the concurrent use of alcohol and aspirin may significantly increase the possibility of erosion and ulceration of the stomach lining and result in bleeding.

Tobacco Smoking: No interactions expected.

Other Drugs
Aspirin may *increase* the effects of
• oral anticoagulants, and cause abnormal bleeding. Dosage adjustment is often necessary.

- oral anti-diabetic drugs and insulin, and cause hypoglycemia (see Glossary). Dosage adjustment is often necessary.
- cortisone-like drugs, by raising their blood levels. Monitor cortisone effects to determine the need for dosage adjustment. Withdrawal of cortisone drugs may cause aspirin toxicity and require a reduction of aspirin dosage.
- methotrexate, and increase its toxicity on the bone marrow.
- penicillin drugs, by raising their blood levels.
- phenytoin (Dantoin, Dilantin, etc.), by raising its blood level.
- "sulfa" drugs, by raising their blood levels.

Aspirin may *decrease* the effects of
- probenecid (Benemid), and reduce its effectiveness in the treatment of gout.
- spironolactone (Aldactone), and impair its ability to lower the blood pressure.
- sulfinpyrazone (Anturane), and reduce its effectiveness in the treatment of gout.

Aspirin *taken concurrently* with
- para-aminosalicylic acid (PAS), may cause salicylate toxicity. Dosage reduction may be necessary.
- cortisone-like drugs, may increase the risk of stomach ulceration and bleeding. Monitor stomach reaction carefully.
- furosemide (Lasix), may cause aspirin toxicity.
- indomethacin (Indocin), may increase the risk of stomach ulceration and bleeding.
- phenylbutazone (Azolid, Butazolidin, etc.), may increase the risk of stomach ulceration and bleeding.

The following drugs may *increase* the effects of aspirin
- Vitamin C in large doses may cause aspirin accumulation and toxicity.

The following drugs may *decrease* the effects of aspirin
- antacid preparations may reduce the absorption of aspirin.
- phenobarbital may hasten the elimination of aspirin.
- propranolol (Inderal) may abolish aspirin's ability to reduce inflammation.
- reserpine and related drugs may reduce aspirin's ability to relieve pain.

Driving a Vehicle, Piloting a Plane, Operating Machinery: No restrictions or precautions.

Exposure to Sun: No restrictions.

Discontinuation: The use of aspirin should be discontinued completely at least 1 week before surgery of any kind.

Special Storage Instructions
Keep in a dry, tightly closed container. Keep suppositories in a cool place.

Do Not Take This Drug If
it has an odor resembling vinegar. This is due to the presence of acetic acid and indicates the decomposition of aspirin.

ATROPINE
(Belladonna, Hyoscyamine)

Year Introduced: 1831 (Belladonna preparations have been in use for many centuries)

Brand Names

USA	Canada
Donna Extendtabs (Robins)	Donna Extendtabs (Robins)
Prydon (Smith Kline & French)	Atrobarb [CD] (Powell)
Barbidonna [CD] (Mallinckrodt)	Atrobarbital [CD] (Dymond)
Belbarb [CD] (Arnar-Stone)	Atrosed [CD] (Anca)
Belladenal [CD] (Sandoz)	Bardase [CD] (P.D. & Co.)
Bellergal [CD] (Sandoz)	Bardona [CD] (Will)
Butibel [CD] (McNeil)	Bellabarb [CD] (Dymond)
Chardonna [CD] (Rorer)	Belladenal [CD] (Sandoz)
Donnagel [CD] (Robins)	Bella-Probal [CD] (Nadeau)
Donnagel-PG [CD] (Robins)	Bellergal [CD] (Sandoz)
Donnatal [CD] (Robins)	Donnagel [CD] (Robins)
Nembu-donna [CD] (Abbott)	Donnagel-PG [CD] (Robins)
Prydonnal [CD] (Smith Kline & French)	Donnatal [CD] (Robins)
Urised [CD] (Webcon)	Prydonnal [CD] (SK&F)
(Numerous other combination brand names)	Urisede [CD] (Barlowe Cote)
	(Numerous other combination brand names)

Drug Family: Antispasmodic; Atropine-like Drug [Anticholinergics]

Prescription Required: For low-strength formulations—No
For high-strength formulations—Yes

Available Dosage Forms and Strengths
Numerous combination drugs are available in a wide variety of dosage forms and strengths including tablets, capsules, prolonged-action forms, elixirs, suspensions, eye drops, etc.

How This Drug Works
Intended Therapeutic Effect(s):   Relief of discomfort associated with
- excessive activity and spasm of the digestive tract (esophagus, stomach, intestine, colon and gall bladder).
- irritation and spasm of the lower urinary tract (bladder and urethra).
- painful menstruation (cramping of the uterus).

Location of Drug Action(s):   The terminal nerve fibers of the parasympathetic nervous system that control the activity of the gastrointestinal tract and the genitourinary tract.

Method of Drug Action(s):   By blocking the action of the chemical (acetylcholine) that transmits impulses at parasympathetic nerve endings, this drug prevents stimulation of muscular contraction and glandular secretion within the organs involved. This results in reduced overall activity, including the prevention or relief of muscle spasm.

THIS DRUG SHOULD NOT BE TAKEN IF

—you have had an allergic reaction or unfavorable response to any atropine or belladonna preparation in the past.

—your stomach cannot empty properly into the intestine (pyloric obstruction).

—you are unable to empty the urinary bladder completely.

—you have glaucoma (narrow-angle type).

—you have severe ulcerative colitis.

INFORM YOUR PHYSICIAN BEFORE TAKING THIS DRUG IF

—you have glaucoma (open-angle type).

—you have angina or coronary heart disease.

—you have chronic bronchitis.

—you have a hiatal hernia.

—you have enlargement of the prostate gland.

—you have myasthenia gravis.

—you have a history of peptic ulcer disease.

—you plan to have surgery under general anesthesia in the near future.

Time Required for Apparent Benefit

Drug action begins in 1 to 2 hours and persists for approximately 4 hours.

Possible Side-Effects *(natural, expected, and unavoidable drug actions)*

Blurring of vision (impairment of focus), dryness of the mouth and throat, constipation, hesitancy in urination. (Nature and degree of side effects depend upon individual susceptibility and drug dosage.)

CAUTION

The elderly (over 60 years of age) may be more susceptible to all of the actions of this drug. Small doses are advisable until response has been determined.

Possible Adverse Effects *(unusual, unexpected, and infrequent reactions)*

IF ANY OF THE FOLLOWING DEVELOP, DISCONTINUE DRUG AND NOTIFY YOUR PHYSICIAN AS SOON AS POSSIBLE

Mild Adverse Effects

Allergic Reactions:—Skin rash, hives.

Dilation of pupils, causing sensitivity to light.

Flushing and dryness of the skin (reduced sweating).

Rapid heart action.

Lightheadedness, dizziness, unsteady gait.

Serious Adverse Effects

Idiosyncratic Reactions: Acute confusion, delirium, and behavioral abnormalities.

Development of acute glaucoma (in susceptible individuals).

Advisability of Use During Pregnancy

This drug enters the blood stream of the fetus. Complete safety has not been established. If use is necessary, limit dosage to the smallest effective amount and for short, interrupted periods. Prudent use is best determined by the physician's evaluation.

Advisability of Use While Nursing Infant

This drug may impair the formation of milk and make nursing difficult. Sufficient quantities of drug may be present in the milk to affect the infant. Avoid drug or avoid nursing as directed by your physician.

Habit-Forming Potential

None.

Effects of Overdosage

With Moderate Overdose: Marked dryness of the mouth, dilated pupils, blurring of near vision, rapid pulse, heart palpitation, headache, difficulty in urination.

With Large Overdose: Extremely dilated pupils, rapid pulse and breathing, hot skin, high fever, excitement, confusion, hallucinations, delirium, eventual loss of consciousness, convulsions, and coma.

Possible Effects of Extended Use

Chronic constipation, severe enough to result in fecal impaction. (Constipation should be treated promptly with effective laxatives.)

Recommended Periodic Examinations While Taking This Drug

Measurement of internal eye pressure to detect any significant increase that could indicate developing glaucoma.

While Taking This Drug, Observe the Following

Foods: No interaction with drug. Effectiveness is greater if drug is taken one-half to 1 hour before eating. Follow diet prescribed for condition under treatment.

Beverages: No interactions. Follow prescribed diet.

Alcohol: No interactions expected with this drug. Follow physician's advice regarding use of alcohol (based upon its effect on the condition under treatment).

Tobacco Smoking: No interactions expected. Follow physician's advice regarding smoking.

Other Drugs

Atropine may *increase* the effects of

• all other drugs having atropine-like actions (see Drug Family, Section Four).

Atropine may *decrease* the effects of
- pilocarpine eye drops, and reduce their effectiveness in lowering internal eye pressure in the treatment of glaucoma.

Atropine *taken concurrently* with
- mono-amine oxidase (MAO) inhibitor drugs, may cause an exaggerated response to normal doses of atropine-like drugs. It is best to avoid atropine-like drugs for 2 weeks after the last dose of any MAO inhibitor drug (see Drug Family, Section Four).
- haloperidol (Haldol), may significantly increase internal eye pressure (dangerous in glaucoma).

The following drugs may *increase* the effects of atropine
- tricyclic antidepressants
- those antihistamines that have an atropine-like action
- meperidine (Demerol, pethidine)
- methylphenidate (Ritalin)
- orphenadrine (Disipal, Norflex)
- those phenothiazines that have an atropine-like action (see Drug Family, Section Four).

The following drugs may *decrease* the effects of atropine
- Vitamin C reduces its effectiveness by hastening its elimination from the body. Avoid large doses of Vitamin C during treatment with this drug.

Driving a Vehicle, Piloting a Plane, Operating Machinery: This drug may produce blurred vision, drowsiness, or dizziness. Avoid hazardous activities if these drug effects occur.

Exposure to Sun: No restrictions.

Exposure to Heat: Use extreme caution. The use of this drug in hot environments may significantly increase the risk of heat stroke.

Heavy Exercise or Exertion: Use caution in warm or hot environments. This drug may impair normal perspiration (heat loss) and interfere with the regulation of body temperature.

Special Storage Instructions
Keep in a tightly closed container. Protect from light.

BENDROFLUMETHIAZIDE

Year Introduced: 1959

Brand Names

USA	Canada
Naturetin (Squibb)	Naturetin (Squibb)
Naturetin-K [CD]	Naturetin-K [CD]
(Squibb)	(Squibb)
Rautrax-N [CD] (Squibb)	Rautractyl [CD] (Squibb)
Rauzide [CD] (Squibb)	

Drug Family: Anti-hypertensive (Hypotensive); Diuretic [Thiazides]

Prescription Required: Yes

Available Dosage Forms and Strengths
Tablets — 2.5 mg., 5 mg., 10 mg.

How This Drug Works
Intended Therapeutic Effect(s)
- elimination of excessive fluid retention (edema).
- reduction of high blood pressure.

Location of Drug Action(s):   Principal actions occur in
- the tubular systems of the kidney that determine the final composition of the urine.
- the walls of the smaller arteries.

Method of Drug Action(s)
By increasing the elimination of salt and water from the body (through increased urine production), this drug reduces the volume of fluid in the blood and body tissues and lowers the sodium content throughout the body.

By relaxing the walls of the smaller arteries and allowing them to expand, this drug significantly increases the total capacity of the arterial system. The combined effect of these two actions (reduced blood volume in expanded space) results in lowering of the blood pressure.

THIS DRUG SHOULD NOT BE TAKEN IF
—you have had an allergic reaction to any dosage form of it previously.

INFORM YOUR PHYSICIAN BEFORE TAKING THIS DRUG IF
—you are allergic to any form of "sulfa" drug.
—you are pregnant and your physician does not know it.
—you have a history of kidney disease or liver disease, or impaired kidney or liver function.
—you have diabetes (or a tendency to diabetes).
—you have a history of gout.
—you have a history of lupus erythematosus.
—you are taking any form of cortisone, digitalis, oral anti-diabetic drugs, or insulin.
—you plan to have surgery under general anesthesia in the near future.

Time Required for Apparent Benefit
Increased urine volume begins in 2 hours, reaches a maximum in 4 to 6 hours, and subsides in 8 to 12 hours. Continuous use on a regular schedule will be necessary for 2 to 3 weeks to determine this drug's effectiveness in lowering your blood pressure.

Possible Side-Effects *(natural, expected, and unavoidable drug actions)*
Lightheadedness on arising from sitting or lying position (see orthostatic hypotension in Glossary).

Increase in level of blood sugar, affecting control of diabetes.

Increase in level of uric acid, affecting control of gout.

Decrease in level of blood potassium, resulting in muscle weakness and cramping.

CAUTION
The elderly (over 60 years of age) are frequently quite sensitive to the effects of standard doses. It is advisable to use this drug with caution until extent and duration of response have been determined.

Possible Adverse Effects *(unusual, unexpected, and infrequent reactions)*
IF ANY OF THE FOLLOWING DEVELOP, DISCONTINUE DRUG AND NOTIFY YOUR PHYSICIAN AS SOON AS POSSIBLE

Mild Adverse Effects
Allergic Reactions:—Skin rash (various kinds), hives, drug fever.

Reduced appetite, indigestion, nausea, vomiting, diarrhea.

Headache, dizziness, yellow vision, blurred vision.

Serious Adverse Effects
Allergic Reactions:—Hepatitis with jaundice (see Glossary), anaphylactic reaction (see Glossary), severe skin reactions.

Inflammation of the pancreas—severe abdominal pain, with nausea and vomiting.

Bone marrow depression (see Glossary)—fatigue, weakness, infection manifested by fever or sore throat, unusual bleeding or bruising.

Advisability of Use During Pregnancy
This drug should not be used during pregnancy unless a very serious complication of pregnancy occurs for which this drug is significantly beneficial. This type of diuretic can have adverse effects on the fetus.

Advisability of Use While Nursing Infant
This drug is known to be present in milk. Ask physician for guidance.

Habit-Forming Potential
None.

Effects of Overdosage
With Moderate Overdose: Dryness of mouth, thirst, lethargy, weakness, muscle pain and cramping, nausea, vomiting.

With Large Overdose: Drowsiness progressing to stupor and coma, weak and rapid pulse.

Possible Effects of Extended Use
Impaired balance of water, salt, and potassium in blood and body tissues.
Development of diabetes (in predisposed individuals).

Recommended Periodic Examinations While Taking This Drug
Complete blood cell counts.
Measurements of blood levels of sodium, potassium, chloride, sugar, and uric
acid.
Liver function tests.
Kidney function tests.

While Taking This Drug, Observe the Following
Foods: It is recommended that you include in your daily diet liberal servings of foods rich in potassium (unless directed otherwise by your physician). The following foods have a high potassium content:

All-bran cereals	Fish, fresh
Almonds	Lentils
Apricots (dried)	Liver, beef
Bananas, fresh	Lonalac
Beans (navy and lima)	Milk
Beef	Peaches
Carrots (raw)	Peanut butter
Chicken	Peas
Citrus fruits	Pork
Coconut	Potato chips
Coffee	Prunes, dried
Crackers (rye)	Raisins
Dates and figs (dried)	Tomato Juice

Note: Avoid licorice in large amounts while taking this drug. Follow your
physician's instructions regarding the use of salt.
Beverages: No restrictions unless directed by your physician.
Alcohol: Use with caution until the combined effect has been determined.
Alcohol can exaggerate the blood pressure-lowering effect of this drug and
cause orthostatic hypotension (see Glossary).
Tobacco Smoking: No interactions expected with this drug. Follow your
physician's advice regarding smoking.
Other Drugs
Bendroflumethiazide may *increase* the effects of
• other anti-hypertensive drugs. Careful adjustment of dosages is necessary
to prevent excessive lowering of the blood pressure.
• drugs of the phenothiazine family, and cause excessive lowering of the
blood pressure. (The thiazides and related drugs and the phenothiazines
may both cause orthostatic hypotension.)

Bendroflumethiazide may *decrease* the effects of
• oral anti-diabetic drugs and insulin, by raising the level of blood sugar.
Careful dosage adjustment is necessary to maintain proper control of
diabetes.

• allopurinol (Zyloprim), by raising the level of blood uric acid. Careful dosage adjustment is required to maintain proper control of gout.
• probenecid (Benemid), by raising the level of blood uric acid. Careful dosage adjustments are necessary to maintain control of gout.

Bendroflumethiazide *taken concurrently* with
• cortisone and cortisone-related drugs, may cause excessive loss of potassium from the body.
• digitalis and related drugs, requires very careful monitoring and dosage adjustments to prevent serious disturbances of heart rhythm.
• tricyclic antidepressants (Elavil, Sinequan, etc.), may cause excessive lowering of the blood pressure.

The following drugs may *increase* the effects of bendroflumethiazide:
• barbiturates may exaggerate its blood pressure-lowering action.
• mono-amine oxidase (MAO) inhibitor drugs (see Drug Family, Section Four) may increase urine volume by delaying this drug's elimination from the body.
• pain relievers (analgesics), both narcotic and non-narcotic, may exaggerate its blood pressure-lowering action.

The following drugs may *decrease* the effects of bendroflumethiazide
• cholestyramine (Cuemid, Questran) may interfere with its absorption. Take cholestyramine 30 to 60 minutes before any oral diuretic.

Driving a Vehicle, Piloting a Plane, Operating Machinery: Use caution until the possibility of orthostatic hypotension (lightheadedness, dizziness, incoordination) has been determined.

Exposure to Sun: Use caution until sensitivity has been determined. This drug can cause photosensitivity (see Glossary).

Exposure to Heat: Avoid excessive perspiring which could cause additional loss of water and salt from the body.

Heavy Exercise or Exertion: Avoid exertion that produces lightheadedness, excessive fatigue, or muscle cramping.

Occurrence of Unrelated Illness: Illnesses which cause vomiting or diarrhea can produce a serious imbalance of important body chemistry. Discontinue this drug and ask your physician for guidance.

Discontinuation: It may be advisable to discontinue this drug approximately 5 to 7 days before major surgery. Ask your physician, surgeon, and/or anesthesiologist for guidance regarding dosage reduction or withdrawal.

Special Storage Instructions
Keep in a dry, tightly closed container.

BENZTROPINE

Year Introduced: 1954

Brand Names

USA	Canada
Cogentin (Merck Sharp & Dohme)	Cogentin (MSD)

Drug Family: Anti-parkinsonism; Atropine-like Drug [Anticholinergics]

Prescription Required: Yes

Available Dosage Forms and Strengths
Tablets — 0.5 mg., 1 mg., 2 mg.

How This Drug Works
Intended Therapeutic Effect(s):   Relief of the rigidity, tremor, sluggish movement, and impaired gait associated with Parkinson's disease.

Location of Drug Action(s):   The principal site of the desired therapeutic action is the regulating center in the brain (the basal ganglia) which governs the coordination and efficiency of bodily movements.

Method of Drug Action(s):   The improvement in Parkinson's disease results from the restoration of a more normal balance of the chemical activities responsible for the transmission of nerve impulses within the basal ganglia.

THIS DRUG SHOULD NOT BE TAKEN IF
—you have had an allergic reaction to any dosage form of it previously.
—it is prescribed for a child under 3 years of age.

INFORM YOUR PHYSICIAN BEFORE TAKING THIS DRUG IF
—you have experienced an unfavorable response to atropine or atropine-like drugs in the past.
—you have glaucoma.
—you have high blood pressure or heart disease.
—you have a history of liver or kidney disease.
—you have difficulty emptying the urinary bladder.

Time Required for Apparent Benefit
Drug action begins in 1 to 2 hours and persists for approximately 24 hours. Daily dosage may be cumulative in some individuals. Regular use for 2 to 4 weeks may be needed to determine optimal dosage schedule.

Possible Side-Effects *(natural, expected, and unavoidable drug actions)*
Nervousness, blurring of vision, dryness of the mouth, constipation. (These often subside as drug use continues.)

CAUTION
The elderly (over 60 years of age) are often more sensitive to the actions of this drug. It is advisable to use small doses until tolerance has been determined.

Possible Adverse Effects *(unusual, unexpected, and infrequent reactions)*

IF ANY OF THE FOLLOWING DEVELOP, DISCONTINUE DRUG AND NOTIFY YOUR PHYSICIAN AS SOON AS POSSIBLE

Mild Adverse Effects

Allergic Reactions: Skin rashes.
Drowsiness, dizziness, headache.
Nausea, vomiting.
Urinary hesitancy, difficulty emptying bladder.

Serious Adverse Effects

Idiosyncratic Reactions: Confusion, delusions, hallucinations, agitation, abnormal behavior.

Advisability of Use During Pregnancy

Safety not established. Prudent use is best determined by the physician's evaluation.

Advisability of Use While Nursing Infant

Presence of drug in milk is not known. Safety for infant not established. Ask physician for guidance.

Habit-Forming Potential

None.

Effects of Overdosage

With Moderate Overdose: Drowsiness, stupor, weakness, impaired vision, rapid pulse.

With Large Overdose: Excitement, confusion, agitation, hallucinations, dry and hot skin, generalized skin rash, markedly dilated pupils.

Possible Effects of Extended Use

Increased internal eye pressure—possibly glaucoma.

Recommended Periodic Examinations While Taking This Drug

Measurement of internal eye pressure at regular intervals.

While Taking This Drug, Observe the Following

Foods: No restrictions. Drug may be taken after food if it causes indigestion.
Beverages: No restrictions.
Alcohol: No interactions expected.
Tobacco Smoking: No interactions expected.

Other Drugs

Benztropine may *increase* the effects of

• levodopa (Dopar, Larodopa, etc.), and improve its effectiveness in the treatment of parkinsonism.
• the mild and strong tranquilizers, and cause excessive sedation.

Benztropine *taken concurrently* with

• cortisone (and related drugs), on an extended basis, may cause an increase in internal eye pressure—possibly glaucoma.
• primidone (Mysoline), may cause excessive sedation.

• a phenothiazine drug, may cause (in sensitive individuals) severe behavioral disturbances (toxic psychosis).

The following drugs may *increase* the effects of benztropine:
• antihistamines may add to the dryness of mouth and throat.
• tricyclic antidepressants may add to the effects on the eye and further increase internal eye pressure (dangerous in glaucoma).
• mono-amine oxidase (MAO) inhibitor drugs may intensify all effects of this drug (see Drug Family, Section Four).
• meperidine (Demerol)
• methylphenidate (Ritalin)
• orphenadrine (Disipal, Norflex)
• quinidine

Driving a Vehicle, Piloting a Plane, Operating Machinery: Drowsiness and dizziness may occur in sensitive individuals. Avoid hazardous activities until full effects and tolerance have been determined.

Exposure to Sun: No restrictions.

Exposure to Heat: Use caution. This drug may reduce sweating, cause an increase in body temperature, and contribute to the development of heat stroke.

Heavy Exercise or Exertion: Avoid in hot environments.

Discontinuation: Do not discontinue this drug suddenly. Ask physician for guidance in reducing dose gradually.

Special Storage Instructions
Keep in a dry, tightly closed container. Protect from light.

BETHANIDINE
Year Introduced: 1968

Brand Names

USA	Canada
None	Esbaloid (B.W. Ltd.)

Drug Family: Anti-hypertensive (Hypotensive)

Prescription Required: Yes

Available Dosage Forms and Strengths
Tablets—10 mg., 25 mg.

How This Drug Works
Intended Therapeutic Effect(s):   Reduction of high blood pressure.

Location of Drug Action(s):   The storage sites of the nerve impulse transmitter norepinephrine in the terminal fibers of the sympathetic nervous system that activate the muscles in blood vessel walls.

Method of Drug Action(s): By displacing norepinephrine from its storage sites, this drug reduces the ability of the sympathetic nervous system to maintain the degree of blood vessel constriction responsible for elevation of the blood pressure. This depletion of norepinephrine results in relaxation of blood vessel walls and lowering of the blood pressure.

THIS DRUG SHOULD NOT BE TAKEN IF
—you have had an allergic reaction to any dosage form of it previously.
—you have an adrenalin-producing tumor (pheochromocytoma).
—you have a mild and uncomplicated case of high blood pressure.

INFORM YOUR PHYSICIAN BEFORE TAKING THIS DRUG IF
—you have a history of mental depression.
—you have a history of stroke or impaired circulation to the brain.
—you have a history of coronary heart disease, angina, or heart attack (myocardial infarction).
—you have a history of kidney disease or impaired kidney function.
—you plan to have surgery under general anesthesia in the near future.

Time Required for Apparent Benefit
Drug action begins in 2 hours, reaches a maximum in 4 to 5 hours, and subsides in 10 to 18 hours. Continuous use on a regular schedule for several weeks, with periodic dosage adjustment, may be necessary to determine optimal dosage.

Possible Side-Effects *(natural, expected, and unavoidable drug actions)*
Lightheadedness, dizziness, weakness, feeling of impending faint in upright position—postural or orthostatic hypotension (see Glossary).
Blurred vision, nasal congestion (stuffiness), dry mouth, water retention.

CAUTION
Orthostatic hypotension can occur frequently and unexpectedly while using this drug. Avoid sudden arising from a lying or sitting position; avoid prolonged standing and excessive physical exertion. At the onset of lightheadedness, dizziness, or weakness, promptly sit down or lie down to prevent fainting. Ask your physician for guidance in adjusting dosage schedules and activities to prevent orthostatic hypotension.

Possible Adverse Effects *(unusual, unexpected, and infrequent reactions)*
IF ANY OF THE FOLLOWING DEVELOP, DISCONTINUE DRUG AND NOTIFY YOUR PHYSICIAN AS SOON AS POSSIBLE
Mild Adverse Effects
  Allergic Reactions: Skin rash.
  Headache, faintness, weakness, fatigue.
  Impaired urination.
Serious Adverse Effects
  Mental depression.
  Impaired ejaculation.
  Possible decrease in blood platelets (see Glossary).

Advisability of Use During Pregnancy
Safety not established. Prudent use is best determined by the physician's evaluation.

Advisability of Use While Nursing Infant
The presence of this drug in milk is unknown. Avoid use if possible. Ask physician for guidance.

Habit-Forming Potential
None.

Effects of Overdosage
With Moderate Overdose: Marked drop in blood pressure, extreme weakness in upright position leading to falling and fainting, headache, nausea.
With Large Overdose: Drop in blood pressure to shock levels, loss of consciousness, slow and weak pulse, cold and sweaty skin.

Possible Effects of Extended Use
Due to this drug's accumulative action, careful dosage adjustment will be necessary to prevent wide fluctuations in blood pressure and unexpected episodes of sudden drop in blood pressure with fainting.

Recommended Periodic Examinations While Taking This Drug
Complete blood cell counts.

While Taking This Drug, Observe the Following
Foods: No restrictions with regard to drug interactions. Ask physician for guidance regarding salt intake. This drug is absorbed more rapidly if taken when the stomach is empty.
Beverages: No restrictions.
Alcohol: Use sparingly and with extreme caution until combined effect has been determined. Alcohol can increase the blood pressure-lowering action of this drug and cause the development of orthostatic hypotension.
Tobacco Smoking: Nicotine can cause an elevation of blood pressure in sensitive individuals. Follow your physician's advice regarding smoking.
Other Drugs
Bethanidine may *increase* the effects of
• other anti-hypertensives, and cause excessive lowering of the blood pressure.
• epinephrine (Adrenalin).

Bethanidine *taken concurrently* with
• digitalis preparations may cause reduction of heart rate. Careful monitoring is advisable.

The following drugs may *increase* the effects of bethanidine
• levodopa
• reserpine and related drugs
• thiazide diuretics (see Drug Family, Section Four)

The following drugs may *decrease* the effects of bethanidine
• amphetamines (Benzedrine, Dexedrine)
• antihistamines (some)

- chlorpromazine
- ephedrine
- methylphenidate
- oxyphenbutazone
- phenylbutazone
- phenylephrine
- phenylpropanolamine
- pseudoephedrine
- tricyclic antidepressants

Driving a Vehicle, Piloting a Plane, Operating Machinery: Be alert to the possibility of orthostatic hypotension developing while engaged in hazardous activities. This drug can also cause drowsiness and impair mental alertness, coordination, and reaction time.

Exposure to Sun: No restrictions.

Exposure to Heat: Hot weather and overheated environments favor the development of orthostatic hypotension. Avoid as much as possible.

Exposure to Cold: No restrictions.

Heavy Exercise or Exertion: Use caution until tolerance for physical activity and exercise is determined. Excessive exertion can induce orthostatic hypotension.

Occurrence of Unrelated Illness: The presence of high fever, such as may occur with an infectious disease, may increase the degree of orthostatic hypotension associated with the use of this drug.

Discontinuation: Upon stopping this drug, the dosage schedules of other drugs taken concurrently with it may require readjustment. Ask physician for guidance.

Special Storage Instructions:
Keep in a dry, tightly closed, light-resistant container.

BIPERIDEN

Year Introduced: 1960

Brand Names

USA	Canada
Akineton (Knoll)	Akineton (Pentagone)

Drug Family: Anti-parkinsonism; Atropine-like Drug [Anticholinergics]

Prescription Required: Yes

Available Dosage Forms and Strengths:
Tablets—2 mg.

How This Drug Works

Intended Therapeutic Effect(s):   Relief of the rigidity, tremor, sluggish movement, and impaired gait associated with Parkinson's disease.

Location of Drug Action(s):   The principal site of the desired therapeutic action is the regulating center in the brain (the basal ganglia) which governs the coordination and efficiency of bodily movements.

Method of Drug Action(s):   The improvement in Parkinson's disease results from the restoration of a more normal balance of the chemical activities responsible for the transmission of nerve impulses within the basal ganglia.

THIS DRUG SHOULD NOT BE TAKEN IF

—you have had an allergic reaction to any dosage form of it previously.

INFORM YOUR PHYSICIAN BEFORE TAKING THIS DRUG IF

—you have experienced an unfavorable response to atropine or atropine-like drugs in the past.

—you have glaucoma.

—you have high blood pressure or heart disease.

—you have a history of liver or kidney disease.

—you have difficulty emptying the urinary bladder.

Time Required for Apparent Benefit

Drug action may be apparent in first 48 hours. However, regular use with increasing dosage may be needed for several weeks to determine optimal dose and response.

Possible Side-Effects *(natural, expected, and unavoidable drug actions)*

Nervousness, blurring of vision, dryness of the mouth, constipation. (These often subside as drug use continues.)

CAUTION

The elderly (over 60 years of age) are often more sensitive to the actions of this drug. It is advisable to use small doses until tolerance has been determined.

Possible Adverse Effects *(unusual, unexpected, and infrequent reactions)*

IF ANY OF THE FOLLOWING DEVELOP, DISCONTINUE DRUG AND NOTIFY YOUR PHYSICIAN AS SOON AS POSSIBLE

Mild Adverse Effects

Allergic Reactions: Skin rashes.

Drowsiness, dizziness, headache.

Nausea, vomiting.

Urinary hesitancy, difficulty emptying bladder.

Serious Adverse Effects

Idiosyncratic Reactions: Confusion, delusions, hallucinations, agitation, abnormal behavior.

Advisability of Use During Pregnancy

Safety not established. Prudent use is best determined by the physician's evaluation.

Advisability of Use While Nursing Infant
Presence of drug in milk is not known. Safety for infant not established. Ask physician for guidance.

Habit-Forming Potential
None.

Effects of Overdosage
With Moderate Overdose: Drowsiness, stupor, weakness, impaired vision, rapid pulse.

With Large Overdose: Excitement, confusion, agitation, hallucinations, dry and hot skin, generalized skin rash, markedly dilated pupils.

Possible Effects of Extended Use
Increased internal eye pressure—possibly glaucoma.

Recommended Periodic Examinations While Taking This Drug
Measurement of internal eye pressure at regular intervals.

While Taking This Drug, Observe the Following
Foods: No restrictions. Drug may be taken after food if it causes indigestion.
Beverages: No restrictions.
Alcohol: No interactions expected.
Tobacco Smoking: No interactions expected.
Other Drugs

Biperiden may *increase* the effects of
- levodopa (Dopar, Larodopa, etc.), and improve its effectiveness in the treatment of parkinsonism.
- the mild and strong tranquilizers, and cause excessive sedation.

Biperiden *taken concurrently* with
- cortisone (and related drugs), on an extended basis, may cause an increase in internal eye pressure—possibly glaucoma.
- primidone (Mysoline), may cause excessive sedation.
- a phenothiazine drug, may cause (in sensitive individuals) severe behavioral disturbances (toxic psychosis).

The following drugs may *increase* the effects of biperiden
- antihistamines may add to the dryness of the mouth and throat.
- tricyclic antidepressants may add to the effects on the eye and further increase internal eye pressure (dangerous in glaucoma).
- mono-amine oxidase (MAO) inhibitor drugs may intensify all effects of this drug (see Drug Family, Section Four).
- meperidine (Demerol)
- methylphenidate (Ritalin)
- orphenadrine (Disipal, Norflex)
- quinidine

Driving a Vehicle, Piloting a Plane, Operating Machinery: Drowsiness and dizziness may occur in sensitive individuals. Avoid hazardous activities until full effects and tolerance have been determined.

Exposure to Sun: No restrictions.

Exposure to Heat: Use caution. This drug may reduce sweating, cause an increase in body temperature, and contribute to the development of heat stroke.

Heavy Exercise or Exertion: Avoid in hot environments.

Discontinuation: Do not discontinue this drug suddenly. Ask physician for guidance in reducing dose gradually.

Special Storage Instructions

Keep in a dry, tightly closed container. Protect from light.

BROMPHENIRAMINE

Year Introduced: 1957

Brand Names

USA	Canada
Dimetane (Robins)	Dimetane (Robins)
Veltane (Lannett)	Dimetapp [CD] (Robins)
Dimetapp [CD] (Robins)	
(Numerous other brand and combination brand names)	

Drug Family: Antihistamines

Prescription Required: Yes

Available Dosage Forms and Strengths

Tablets — 4 mg.

Prolonged Action Tablets — 8 mg., 12 mg.

Elixir — 2 mg. per teaspoonful

Injection — 10 mg. per ml., 100 mg. per ml.

How This Drug Works

Intended Therapeutic Effect(s): Relief of symptoms associated with hayfever (allergic rhinitis) and with allergic reactions in the skin, such as itching, swelling, hives, and rash.

Location of Drug Action(s): Those hypersensitive tissues that release excessive histamine as part of an allergic reaction. The principal tissue sites are the eyes, the nose, and the skin.

Method of Drug Action(s): This drug reduces the intensity of the allergic response by blocking the action of histamine after it has been released from sensitized tissue cells.

THIS DRUG SHOULD NOT BE TAKEN IF

—you have had an allergic reaction to any dosage form of it previously.

—it is prescribed for a newborn infant.

INFORM YOUR PHYSICIAN BEFORE TAKING THIS DRUG IF
—you have had any unfavorable reaction to previous use of antihistamines.
—you have glaucoma (narrow-angle type).
—you have difficulty in emptying the urinary bladder.
—you plan to have surgery under general anesthesia in the near future.

Time Required for Apparent Benefit
Drug action usually begins in 15 to 30 minutes, reaches maximal effect in 1 to 2 hours, and subsides in 3 to 6 hours.

Possible Side-Effects *(natural, expected, and unavoidable drug actions)*
Drowsiness, sense of weakness, dryness of the nose, mouth, and throat.

Possible Adverse Effects *(unusual, unexpected, and infrequent reactions)*
IF ANY OF THE FOLLOWING DEVELOP, DISCONTINUE DRUG AND NOTIFY YOUR PHYSICIAN AS SOON AS POSSIBLE

Mild Adverse Effects
  Allergic Reactions: Skin rash (rare).
  Headache, nervous agitation, dizziness, double vision, blurred vision, ringing in the ears, tremors.
  Reduced appetite, heartburn, nausea, vomiting, diarrhea.
  Reduced tolerance for contact lenses.
Serious Adverse Effects
  Reduced production of white blood cells possibly resulting in fever and/or sore throat.

Advisability of Use During Pregnancy
Safety not established. If necessary to use any antihistamine, limit use to small doses and for short periods of time. Prudent use is best determined by the physician's evaluation.

Advisability of Use While Nursing Infant
Drug is present in milk in small quantities. Avoid use or discontinue nursing. Ask physician for guidance.

Habit-Forming Potential
None.

Effects of Overdosage
With Moderate Overdose: Excitement, incoordination, staggering gait, hallucinations, muscular tremors and spasms.
With Large Overdose: Stupor progressing to coma, convulsions, dilated pupils, flushed face, fever, shallow respiration, weak and rapid pulse.

Possible Effects of Extended Use
Tardive dyskinesia (see Glossary).
Bone marrow depression (see Glossary).
(Note: Prolonged, continuous use of antihistamines should be avoided.)

Recommended Periodic Examinations While Taking This Drug
Complete blood cell counts.

While Taking This Drug, Observe the Following
Foods: No restrictions.

Beverages: Coffee and tea can help to offset the drowsiness produced by most antihistamines.

Alcohol: Use with extreme caution until combined effects have been determined. The combination of alcohol and antihistamine can produce rapid and marked sedation.

Tobacco Smoking: No interactions expected.

Other Drugs

Brompheniramine may *increase* the effects of

• all sedatives, sleep-inducing drugs, tranquilizers, analgesics, and narcotic drugs, and produce oversedation.

Brompheniramine may *decrease* the effects of

• oral anticoagulants, by hastening their elimination from the body. Consult physician regarding prothrombin time testing and dosage adjustment.

The following drugs may *increase* the effects of brompheniramine

• all sedatives, sleep-inducing drugs, tranquilizers, analgesics, and narcotic drugs exaggerate its sedative action.

• mono-amine oxidase (MAO) inhibitor drugs may prolong the action of antihistamines.

Driving a Vehicle, Piloting a Plane, Operating Machinery: This drug can impair mental alertness, judgment, coordination, and reaction time. Avoid hazardous activities until full sedative effects have been determined.

Exposure to Sun: No photosensitivity reactions reported.

Special Storage Instructions
Keep tablets and capsules in a dry, tightly closed container. Protect liquid drug preparations from light to prevent discoloration.

BUTABARBITAL
Year Introduced: 1939

Brand Names

USA		Canada
BBS (Reid-Provident)	Expansatol (Merit)	Buta-Barb (Dymond)
Bubartal TT (Philips	Intasedol (Elder)	Butisol (McNeil)
Roxane)	Medarsed (Medar)	Day-Barb (Anca)
Butal (Blaine)	Quiebar (Nevin)	Interbarb (M & M)
Butazem (Zemmer)	Renbu (Wren)	Neo-Barb (Neo)
Buticaps (McNeil)	Soduben (Arcum)	
Butisol (McNeil)	(Numerous	
Butte (Scrip)	combination brand	
Da-Sed (Sheryl)	names)	

Drug Family: Sedative, Mild: Sleep Inducer (Hypnotic) [Barbiturates]

Prescription Required: Yes (Controlled Drug, U.S. Schedule 3)

Available Dosage Forms and Strengths

Tablets — 15 mg., 30 mg., 50 mg., 100 mg.
Prolonged Action Tablets — 30 mg., 60 mg.
Capsules — 15 mg., 30 mg., 50 mg., 100 mg.
Elixir — 30 mg. per teaspoonful

How This Drug Works

Intended Therapeutic Effect(s)
- with low dosage, relief of mild to moderate anxiety or tension (sedative effect).
- with higher dosage taken at bedtime, sedation sufficient to induce sleep (hypnotic effect).

Location of Drug Action(s):   The connecting points (synapses) in the nerve pathways that transmit impulses between the wake-sleep centers of the brain.

Method of Drug Action(s):   Not completely established. Present thinking is that this drug selectively blocks the transmission of nerve impulses by reducing the amount of available norepinephrine, one of the chemicals responsible for impulse transmission.

THIS DRUG SHOULD NOT BE TAKEN IF

—you have had an allergic reaction to any dosage form of it previously.
—you have a history of porphyria.

INFORM YOUR PHYSICIAN BEFORE TAKING THIS DRUG IF

—you are sensitive or allergic to any barbiturate drug.
—you are taking any sedative, sleep-inducing drugs, tranquilizers, antihistamines, pain relievers, or narcotic drugs of any kind.
—you have epilepsy.
—you have a history of liver or kidney disease.
—you plan to have surgery under general anesthesia in the near future.

Time Required for Apparent Benefit

Approximately 30 minutes.

Possible Side-Effects *(natural, expected, and unavoidable drug actions)*

Drowsiness, lethargy, and sense of mental or physical sluggishness as "hangover" effect.

CAUTION

The elderly (over 60 years of age) and the debilitated may experience agitation, excitement, confusion, and delirium with standard doses. Caution and small doses are advisable until tolerance has been determined.

Possible Adverse Effects *(unusual, unexpected, and infrequent reactions)*

IF ANY OF THE FOLLOWING DEVELOP, DISCONTINUE DRUG AND NOTIFY YOUR PHYSICIAN AS SOON AS POSSIBLE

Mild Adverse Effects

Allergic Reactions: Skin rash (various kinds), hives, localized swelling of eyelids, face, or lips, drug fever.

"Hangover" effect, dizziness, unsteadiness.

Nausea, vomiting, diarrhea.

Joint and muscle pains, most often in the neck, shoulders, and arms.

Serious Adverse Effects

Allergic Reactions: Hepatitis with jaundice (see Glossary). Severe skin reactions.

Idiosyncratic Reactions: Paradoxical excitement and delirium (rather than sedation).

Anemia—weakness and fatigue.

Abnormally low blood platelets (see Glossary)—unusual bleeding or bruising.

Advisability of Use During Pregnancy

Safety not established. Prudent use is best determined by the physician's evaluation.

Advisability of Use While Nursing Infant

Drug is known to be present in milk. Ask physician for guidance.

Habit-Forming Potential

This drug can cause both psychological and physical dependence (see Glossary).

Effects of Overdosage

With Moderate Overdose: Behavior similar to alcoholic intoxication: confusion, slurred speech, physical incoordination, staggering gait, drowsiness.

With Large Overdose: Deepening sleep, coma, slow and shallow breathing, weak and rapid pulse, cold and sweaty skin.

Possible Effects of Extended Use

Psychological and/or physical dependence.

Anemia.

If dose is excessive, a form of chronic drug intoxication can occur: headache, impaired vision, slurred speech, and depression.

Recommended Periodic Examinations While Taking This Drug

Complete blood cell counts. Liver function tests.

While Taking This Drug, Observe the Following

Foods: No restrictions.

Beverages: No restrictions.

Alcohol: Avoid completely. Alcohol can increase greatly the sedative and depressant actions of this drug on brain function.

Tobacco Smoking: No interactions expected.

Other Drugs

Butabarbital may *increase* the effects of

• other sedatives, sleep-inducing drugs, tranquilizers, antihistamines, pain relievers, and narcotic drugs, and cause oversedation. Ask your physician for guidance regarding dosage adjustments.

Butabarbital may *decrease* the effects of

• oral anticoagulants of the coumarin drug family. Ask physician for guidance regarding prothrombin time testing and adjustment of the anticoagulant dosage.
• aspirin, and reduce its pain-relieving action.
• cortisone and related drugs, by hastening their elimination from the body.
• oral contraceptives, by hastening their elimination from the body.
• griseofulvin (Fulvicin, Grisactin, etc.), and reduce its effectiveness in treating fungus infections.
• phenylbutazone (Azolid, Butazolidin, etc.), and reduce its effectiveness in treating inflammation and pain.

Butabarbital *taken concurrently* with

• anti-convulsants, may cause a change in the pattern of epileptic seizures. Careful dosage adjustments are necessary to achieve a balance of actions that will give the best protection from seizures.

The following drugs may *increase* the effects of butabarbital

• both mild and strong tranquilizers may increase the sedative and sleep-inducing actions and cause oversedation.
• isoniazid (INH, Isozide, etc.) may prolong the action of barbiturate drugs.
• antihistamines may increase the sedative effects of barbiturate drugs.
• oral anti-diabetic drugs of the sulfonylurea type may prolong the sedative effect of barbiturate drugs.

Driving a Vehicle, Piloting a Plane, Operating Machinery: This drug can produce drowsiness and can impair mental alertness, judgment, physical coordination, and reaction time. Avoid hazardous activities.

Exposure to Sun: Use caution until sensitivity has been determined. Some barbiturates can cause photosensitivity (see Glossary).

Exposure to Heat: No restrictions.

Exposure to Cold: The elderly may experience excessive lowering of body temperature while taking this drug. Keep dosage to a minimum during winter and dress warmly.

Heavy Exercise or Exertion: No restrictions.

Discontinuation: If it has been necessary to use this drug for an extended period of time, do not discontinue it abruptly. Ask physician for guidance regarding dosage adjustment and withdrawal. It may also be necessary to adjust the doses of other drugs taken concurrently with it.

Special Storage Instructions

Keep tablets and capsules in a dry, tightly closed container. Keep the elixir in a tightly closed, amber glass bottle.

BUTALBITAL
(Talbutal)

Year Introduced: 1954

Brand Names

USA	Canada
Lotusate (Winthrop)	Fiorinal [CD] (Sandoz)
Sandoptal (Sandoz)	Fiorinal-C [CD] (Sandoz)
Fiorinal [CD] (Sandoz)	
Fiorinal with Codeine [CD] (Sandoz)	

Drug Family: Sedative, Mild; Sleep Inducer (Hypnotic) [Barbiturates]

Prescription Required: Yes (Controlled Drug, U.S. Schedule 3)

Available Dosage Forms and Strengths
Tablets — 50 mg. (in combination)
Capsules — 120 mg.; 50 mg. (in combination)

How This Drug Works
Intended Therapeutic Effect(s)
- with low dosage, relief of mild to moderate anxiety or tension (sedative effect).
- with higher dosage taken at bedtime, sedation sufficient to induce sleep (hypnotic effect).

Location of Drug Action(s):   The connecting points (synapses) in the nerve pathways that transmit impulses between the wake-sleep centers of the brain.

Method of Drug Action(s):   Not completely established. Present thinking is that this drug selectively blocks the transmission of nerve impulses by reducing the amount of available norepinephrine, one of the chemicals responsible for impulse transmission.

THIS DRUG SHOULD NOT BE TAKEN IF
—you have had an allergic reaction to any dosage form of it previously.
—you have a history of porphyria.

INFORM YOUR PHYSICIAN BEFORE TAKING THIS DRUG IF
—you are allergic or sensitive to any barbiturate drug.
—you are taking any sedative, sleep-inducing drugs, tranquilizers, antihistamines, pain relievers, or narcotic drugs of any kind.
—you have epilepsy.
—you have a history of liver or kidney disease.
—you plan to have surgery under general anesthesia in the near future.

Time Required for Apparent Benefit
Drug action begins in 15 to 30 minutes, reaches a maximum in approximately 1 hour, and subsides in 2 to 6 hours.

Possible Side-Effects *(natural, expected, and unavoidable drug actions)*
Drowsiness, lethargy, and sense of mental and physical sluggishness as "hangover" effect.

CAUTION
The elderly (over 60 years of age) and the debilitated may experience agitation, excitement, confusion, and delirium with standard doses. It is advisable to use with caution and in small doses until tolerance has been determined.

Possible Adverse Effects *(unusual, unexpected, and infrequent reactions)*
IF ANY OF THE FOLLOWING DEVELOP, DISCONTINUE DRUG AND NOTIFY YOUR PHYSICIAN AS SOON AS POSSIBLE

Mild Adverse Effects
  Allergic Reactions: Skin rash, hives, localized swellings of eyelids, face, or lips, drug fever.
  Nausea, vomiting, diarrhea.
  Headache, dizziness, mild "hangover" effect.
Serious Adverse Effects
  Idiosyncratic Reactions: Paradoxical excitement and delirium (rather than sedation). This is more likely to occur in the presence of pain and in the elderly (over 60 years of age).

Advisability of Use During Pregnancy
Safety not established. Prudent use is best determined by the physician's evaluation.

Advisability of Use While Nursing Infant
Drug is probably present in milk. Ask physician for guidance.

Habit-Forming Potential
If used for an extended period of time, this drug can cause both psychological and physical dependence (see Glossary).

Effects of Overdosage
  With Moderate Overdose: Behavior similar to alcoholic intoxication: confusion, slurred speech, physical incoordination, staggering gait, drowsiness.
  With Large Overdose: Deepening sleep, coma, slow and shallow breathing, weak and rapid pulse, cold and sweaty skin.

Possible Effects of Extended Use
Psychological and/or physical dependence. If dose is excessive, a form of chronic intoxication can occur: headache, impaired vision, slurred speech, and depression.

Recommended Periodic Examinations While Taking This Drug
With frequent or continual use, complete blood cell counts and liver function tests are desirable.

While Taking This Drug, Observe the Following
Foods: No restrictions.
Beverages: No restrictions.

Alcohol: Avoid completely. Alcohol can increase greatly the sedative and depressant actions of this drug on brain function.

Tobacco Smoking: No interactions expected.

Other Drugs

Butalbital may *increase* the effects of

• other sedatives, sleep-inducing drugs, tranquilizers, antihistamines, pain relievers, and narcotic drugs, and cause oversedation. Ask your physician for guidance regarding dosage adjustments.

Butalbital may *decrease* the effects of

• oral anticoagulants of the coumarin drug family. Ask physician for guidance regarding prothrombin time testing and adjustment of the anticoagulant dose.
• aspirin, and reduce its pain-relieving action.
• cortisone and related drugs, by hastening their elimination from the body.
• oral contraceptives, by hastening their elimination from the body.
• griseofulvin (Fulvicin, Grisactin, etc.), and reduce its effectiveness in treating fungus infections.
• phenylbutazone (Azolid, Butazolidin, etc.), and reduce its effectiveness in treating inflammation and pain.

Butalbital *taken concurrently* with

• anti-convulsants, may cause a change in the pattern of epileptic seizures. Careful dosage adjustments are necessary to achieve a balance of actions that will give the best protection from seizures.

The following drugs may *increase* the effects of butalbital:

• both mild and strong tranquilizers may increase its sedative and sleep-inducing actions and cause oversedation.
• isoniazid (INH, Isozide, etc.) may prolong the action of barbiturate drugs.
• antihistamines may increase the sedative effects of barbiturate drugs.
• oral anti-diabetic drugs of the sufonylurea type may prolong the sedative effect of barbiturate drugs.

Driving a Vehicle, Piloting a Plane, Operating Machinery: This drug can produce drowsiness and can impair mental alertness, judgment, physical coordination, and reaction time. Avoid hazardous activities.

Exposure to Sun: Use caution until sensitivity has been determined. Some barbiturates can cause photosensitivity (see Glossary).

Exposure to Heat: No restrictions.

Exposure to Cold: The elderly (over 60 years of age) may experience excessive lowering of body temperature while taking this drug. Keep dosage to a minimum during winter and dress warmly.

Heavy Exercise or Exertion: No restrictions.

Discontinuation: If it has been necessary to use this drug for an extended period of time, do not discontinue it abruptly. Ask physician for guidance regarding dosage adjustment and withdrawal. It may also be necessary to adjust the doses of other drugs taken concurrently with it.

Special Storage Instructions

Keep tablets and capsules in a dry, tightly closed container.

CAFFEINE

Year Introduced: In use for many centuries in the form of coffee, tea, and cocoa.

Brand Names

USA	Canada
Cafecon (Consol. Midland)	Cafeine (Welcker-Lyster)
Nodoz (Bristol-Myers)	Cafergot [CD] (Sandoz)
Cafacetin [CD] (Bowman)	
Cafergot [CD] (Sandoz)	
Cafermine [CD] (Spencer-Mead)	
(Numerous other combination brand names)	

Drug Family: Stimulant [Xanthines]

Prescription Required: Preparations without ergot—No
Preparations with ergot—Yes

Available Dosage Forms and Strengths
Tablets — 100 mg.
Capsules — 100 mg.
Granules — 100 mg. per teasponful

How This Drug Works
Intended Therapeutic Effect(s)
 • prevention and early relief of blood vessel (vascular) headaches, such as migraine and variations of migraine.
 • relief of drowsiness and mental fatigue (stimulant effect).
Location of Drug Action(s)
 • the walls of blood vessels in the head.
 • the wake-sleep centers and the thought-association areas of the brain.
Method of Drug Action(s)
 By constricting the walls of blood vessels, this drug corrects the excessive expansion (dilation) responsible for the pain of vascular headache.
 By increasing the energy level of the chemical systems responsible for nerve tissue activity, this drug induces wakefulness and improves alertness and mental acuity.

THIS DRUG SHOULD NOT BE TAKEN IF
—you have had an allergic reaction to any dosage form of it previously.
—you have severe heart disease.
—you have an active stomach ulcer.

INFORM YOUR PHYSICIAN BEFORE TAKING THIS DRUG IF
—you experience severe disturbances of heart rhythm.
—you have a history of peptic ulcer disease.

—you are subject to hypoglycemia.
—you have epilepsy.

Time Required for Apparent Benefit
Drug action begins in approximately 30 minutes and reaches a maximum in 50 to 75 minutes.

Possible Side-Effects *(natural, expected, and unavoidable drug actions)*
Sense of nervousness, insomnia, increased urine output.
(Nature and degree of side effects depend upon the dose of the drug and the susceptibility of the individual.)

CAUTION
Do not exceed 250 mg. per dose or 500 mg. per 24 hours.

Possible Adverse Effects *(unusual, unexpected, and infrequent reactions)*
IF ANY OF THE FOLLOWING DEVELOP, DISCONTINUE DRUG AND NOTIFY YOUR PHYSICIAN AS SOON AS POSSIBLE

Mild Adverse Effects
Headache, irritability, lightheadedness, feeling of drunkenness, impaired thinking.
Nausea, heartburn, indigestion, stomach irritation.
Serious Adverse Effects
Development of stomach ulcer.

Advisability of Use During Pregnancy
No reports that definitely establish adverse effects of caffeine on mother or fetus. One study, however, suggests that heavy coffee consumption (in excess of 5 cups daily) during pregnancy may increase the frequency of complications. Do not exceed recommended doses, including the use of caffeine beverages.

Advisability of Use While Nursing Infant
This drug is present in milk in very small amounts. The blood level in the nursing infant is too small to be significant, if the mother adheres to recommended dosage.

Habit-Forming Potential
Varying degrees of tolerance and psychological dependence may occur with prolonged use (see Glossary).

Effects of Overdosage
With Moderate Overdose: Nervousness, restlessness, insomnia (followed by depression in some individuals), tremor, sweating, ringing in the ears, spots before the eyes, heart palpitation, diarrhea.
With Large Overdose: Excitement, rapid and irregular pulse, rapid breathing, fever, delirium, hallucinations, convulsions.

Possible Effects of Extended Use
Development of tolerance and psychological dependence (see Glossary).
Development of stomach irritation (gastritis) and peptic ulcer in stomach or duodenum.

Recommended Periodic Examinations While Taking This Drug
None required.

While Taking This Drug, Observe the Following
Foods: No restrictions.

Beverages: Keep in mind that caffeine beverages (coffee, tea, and cola) will add to the total intake of caffeine used in medicinal form. Avoid possible overdosage. The approximate caffeine content of popular beverages is as follows:

Regular coffee	(average cup)	100–150 mg.
Instant coffee	(average cup)	80–100 mg.
Decaffeinated coffee	(average cup)	3–5 mg.
Tea	(average cup)	60–75 mg.
Regular cola	(6 ounces)	36 mg.
Diet cola	(6 ounces)	18 mg.

Alcohol: No harmful interactions expected. Caffeine can counteract the depressant action of alcohol on the brain.

Tobacco Smoking: Consult physician regarding possible adverse effects of combined nicotine and caffeine.

Other Drugs

Caffeine may *increase* the effects of

• thyroid preparations, by raising the body metabolism approximately 10%.

• amphetamines (and related drugs), and cause excessive nervousness. Dosage adjustment may be necessary.

Caffeine may *decrease* the effects of

• sedatives, tranquilizers, sleep-inducing drugs, pain relievers, and narcotic drugs.

Caffeine *taken concurrently* in large doses with

• mono-amine oxidase (MAO) inhibitor drugs (see Drug Family, Section Four), may cause an excessive rise in blood pressure. Use caffeine in small doses or discontinue the MAO inhibitor drug.

The following drugs may *increase* the effects of caffeine:

• isoniazid (INH, Isozide, etc.) may delay its elimination from the body.

• meprobamate (Equanil, Miltown) may increase the concentration of caffeine in the brain.

Driving a Vehicle, Piloting a Plane, Operating Machinery: No restrictions.

Exposure to Sun: No restrictions.

Discontinuation: Sudden discontinuation of this drug following extended use can produce a "caffeine-withdrawal" headache. This is readily relieved by coffee or caffeine in medicinal form.

Special Storage Instructions
Keep in a dry, tightly closed container.

CARBENICILLIN

Year Introduced: 1964

Brand Names

USA	Canada
Geocillin (Roerig)	Geopen (Pfizer)

Drug Family: Antibiotic (Anti-infective) [Penicillins]

Prescription Required: Yes

Available Dosage Forms and Strengths
Tablets—382 mg.

How This Drug Works

Intended Therapeutic Effect(s): The elimination of infections responsive to the action of this drug.

Location of Drug Action(s): Any body tissue or fluid in which sufficient concentration of the drug can be achieved.

Method of Drug Action(s): This drug destroys susceptible infecting bacteria by interfering with their ability to produce new protective cell walls as they multiply and grow.

THIS DRUG SHOULD NOT BE TAKEN IF

—you are certain you are allergic to any form of penicillin.

INFORM YOUR PHYSICIAN BEFORE TAKING THIS DRUG IF

—you suspect you may be allergic to penicillin, or you have a history of a previous "reaction" to penicillin.

—you are allergic to cephalosporin antibiotics (Ancef, Ceporan, Ceporex, Kafocin, Keflex, Keflin, Kefzol, Loridine).

—you are allergic by nature (hayfever, asthma, hives, eczema).

Time Required for Apparent Benefit

Varies with the nature of the infection under treatment; usually from 2 to 5 days.

Possible Side-Effects *(natural, expected, and unavoidable drug actions)*
Superinfections (see Glossary).

Possible Adverse Effects *(unusual, unexpected, and infrequent reactions)*

IF ANY OF THE FOLLOWING DEVELOP, DISCONTINUE DRUG AND NOTIFY YOUR PHYSICIAN AS SOON AS POSSIBLE

Mild Adverse Effects

Allergic Reactions: Skin rashes (various kinds).

Irritations of mouth or tongue, "black tongue," nausea, vomiting, diarrhea, dizziness (rare).

Serious Adverse Effects

Allergic Reactions: †Anaphylactic reaction (see Glossary), severe skin reactions, high fever, swollen painful joints, sore throat, unusual bleeding or bruising.

---

†A rare but potentially dangerous reaction characteristic of penicillins.

Advisability of Use During Pregnancy
Safety not established. Prudent use is best determined by the physician's evaluation.

Advisability of Use While Nursing Infant
Drug may be present in milk and may sensitize infant to penicillin. Ask physician for guidance.

Habit-Forming Potential
None.

Effects of Overdosage
Possible nausea, vomiting, and/or diarrhea.

Possible Effects of Extended Use
Superinfections (see Glossary).

Recommended Periodic Examinations While Taking This Drug
Complete blood cell counts.
Liver and kidney function tests.

While Taking This Drug, Observe the Following
Foods: No restrictions of food selection. Drug is absorbed better if taken 1 hour before or 2 hours after eating.
Beverages: No restrictions.
Alcohol: No interactions expected.
Tobacco Smoking: No interactions expected.
Other Drugs
The following drugs may *decrease* the effects of carbenicillin
• antacids reduce absorption of carbenicillin.
• chloramphenicol (Chloromycetin)
• erythromycin (Erythrocin, E-Mycin, etc.)
• tetracyclines (Achromycin, Aureomycin, Declomycin, Minocin, etc.; see Drug Family, Section Four)
Driving a Vehicle, Piloting a Plane, Operating Machinery: No restrictions.
Exposure to Sun: No restrictions.

Special Storage Instructions
Keep in a tightly closed container at room temperature.

CARBROMAL

Year Introduced: 1910

Brand Names

USA
Carbromal (Blue Line)
Carbrital [CD]
(Parke-Davis)

Canada
Carbrital [CD] (P.D. &
Co.)

Drug Family: Sedative, Mild; Sleep Inducer (Hypnotic)

Prescription Required: Yes (Controlled Drug, U.S. Schedule 3)

Available Dosage Forms and Strengths
Tablets — 325 mg.
Capsules [CD] — 125 mg. (+50 mg. pentobarbital)
— 250 mg. (+ 100 mg. pentobarbital)
Elixir [CD] — 375 mg. (+125 mg. pentobarbital) per 30 ml.

How This Drug Works
Intended Therapeutic Effect(s)
• with low dosage, relief of mild to moderate anxiety or tension (sedative effect).
• with higher dosage taken at bedtime, relief of insomnia (hypnotic effect).
Location of Drug Action(s):   Not completely established. Thought to be the wake-sleep centers of the brain, possibly the reticular activating system.
Method of Drug Action(s):   Not established.

THIS DRUG SHOULD NOT BE TAKEN IF
—you are allergic to bromides or to any of the drugs bearing the brand names listed above.

INFORM YOUR PHYSICIAN BEFORE TAKING THIS DRUG IF
—you are allergic to meprobamate (see Drug Profile for brand names).
—you are taking any sedative, sleep-inducing, tranquilizer, or antidepressant drugs.

Time Required for Apparent Benefit
Approximately 30 minutes.

Possible Side-Effects *(natural, expected, and unavoidable drug actions)*
Drowsiness (when used as daytime sedative).
"Hangover" drowsiness and lethargy (when used as sleep inducer).

Possible Adverse Effects *(unusual, unexpected, and infrequent reactions)*
IF ANY OF THE FOLLOWING DEVELOP, DISCONTINUE DRUG AND NOTIFY YOUR PHYSICIAN AS SOON AS POSSIBLE
Mild Adverse Effects
Skin rashes, unusual bruising.
Serious Adverse Effects
Reversible cataracts (rare), impaired vision.

Bromide intoxication—drowsiness, confusion, dizziness, delirium, hallucinations, skin eruptions.

Advisability of Use During Pregnancy
Safety not established. Prudent use is best determined by the physician's evaluation.

Advisability of Use While Nursing Infant
Safety not established. Ask physician for guidance.

Habit-Forming Potential
Can produce psychological and/or physical dependence if used in large doses for an extended period of time (see Glossary).

Effects of Overdosage
With Moderate Overdose: Confusion, delirium, agitation, slurred speech, staggering, incoordination.
With Large Overdose: Stupor progressing to deep sleep, coma.

Possible Effects of Extended Use
Psychological and/or physical dependence.
Reversible cataracts (rare).
Bromide intoxication.

Recommended Periodic Examinations While Taking This Drug
Careful eye examination during long-term use.

While Taking This Drug, Observe the Following
Foods: No restrictions.
Beverages: Large intake of coffee, tea, or cola drinks can reduce the sedative action of this drug.
Alcohol: Avoid completely. Alcohol can increase the sedative action of carbromal. Carbromal can increase the intoxicating effect of alcohol.
Tobacco Smoking: No interactions expected.
Other Drugs
Carbromal may *increase* the effects of
- all sedatives, sleep-inducing drugs, tranquilizers, antidepressants, and narcotic drugs, and cause oversedation. Ask physician for guidance regarding dosage adjustment.

Driving a Vehicle, Piloting a Plane, Operating Machinery: This drug can impair mental alertness, judgment, and physical coordination. Avoid hazardous activities.
Exposure to Sun: No restrictions.

Special Storage Instructions
Keep in a dry, tightly closed, light-resistant container.

CARISOPRODOL

Year Introduced: 1959

Brand Names

USA
Rela (Schering)
Soma (Wallace)
Soma Compound [CD]
(Wallace)

Canada
Rela (Schering)
Soma (Horner)
Soma Compound [CD]
(Horner)

Drug Family: Muscle Relaxant

Prescription Required: Yes (Controlled Drug, U.S. Schedule 3)

Available Dosage Forms and Strengths
Tablets — 350 mg.
Capsules — 250 mg.

How This Drug Works

Intended Therapeutic Effect(s):   Relief of discomfort resulting from spasm of voluntary muscles.

Location of Drug Action(s):   Not completely established. This drug is thought to act on those nerve pathways in the brain and spinal cord that are involved in the reflex activity of voluntary muscles.

Method of Drug Action(s):   Not completely established. It is thought that this drug may relieve muscle spasm and pain by blocking the transmission of nerve impulses over reflex pathways and/or by producing a sedative effect that decreases the perception of pain.

THIS DRUG SHOULD NOT BE TAKEN IF

—you have had an allergic reaction to any dosage form of it previously.
—you have a history of acute intermittent porphyria.
—it is prescribed for a child under 5 years of age.

INFORM YOUR PHYSICIAN BEFORE TAKING THIS DRUG IF

—you are allergic or sensitive to any chemically related drugs: meprobamate, tybamate (see Drug Profiles for brand names).
—you have cerebral palsy.
—you are taking sedatives, sleep-inducing drugs, tranquilizers, antidepressants, or anti-convulsants.

Time Required for Apparent Benefit

Approximately 30 to 60 minutes.

Possible Side-Effects *(natural, expected, and unavoidable drug actions)*

Drowsiness, lethargy, sense of weakness. (The elderly are susceptible to standard doses. It is advisable to use with caution if 60 years of age or older.)

Possible Adverse Effects *(unusual, unexpected, and infrequent reactions)*

IF ANY OF THE FOLLOWING DEVELOP, DISCONTINUE DRUG AND NOTIFY
YOUR PHYSICIAN AS SOON AS POSSIBLE

Mild Adverse Effects

Allergic Reactions: Skin rashes (various kinds), fever, burning of eyes.
Dizziness, unsteadiness in stance and gait, tremor, headache, fainting.
Heart palpitation, nausea, indigestion.

Serious Adverse Effects

Allergic Reactions: Anaphylactic reaction (see Glossary), high fever, asthmatic breathing.

Idiosyncratic Reaction (may occur with first dose):   Extreme weakness,
temporary paralysis of arms and legs, dizziness, temporary loss of vision,
slurred speech, confusion.

Advisability of Use During Pregnancy

Safety not established. Prudent use is best determined by the physician's
evaluation.

Advisability of Use While Nursing Infant

Drug is known to be present in milk. Ask physician for guidance.

Habit-Forming Potential

This drug can produce psychological and (possibly) physical dependence if
used in large doses for an extended period of time.

Effects of Overdosage

With Moderate Overdose: Dizziness, impaired stance, staggering gait,
slurred speech, marked drowsiness.

With Large Overdose: Stupor progressing to deep sleep and coma, depression of breathing and heart function.

Possible Effects of Extended Use

Psychological and (possibly) physical dependence.

Recommended Periodic Examinations While Taking This Drug

None.

While Taking This Drug, Observe the Following

Foods: No restrictions.

Beverages: No restrictions.

Alcohol: Use with extreme caution until combined effect is determined.
Alcohol combined with carisoprodol can cause severe impairment of mental and physical functions.

Tobacco Smoking: No interactions expected.

Other Drugs

Carisoprodal may *increase* the effects of

• sedatives, sleep-inducing drugs, tranquilizers, antidepressants, and narcotic drugs. Use such drugs with caution until combined effect has been
determined. Ask physician for guidance regarding dosage adjustment.

The following drugs may *increase* the effects of carisoprodol:
- tricyclic antidepressants (see Drug Family, Section Four) may increase the sedative action of carisoprodol.
- mono-amine oxidase (MAO) inhibitor drugs (see Drug Family, Section Four) may increase the muscle relaxant and sedative actions of carisoprodol.

The following drugs may *decrease* the effects of carisoprodol
- barbiturate drugs, especially phenobarbital, may hasten its destruction and elimination.
- some antihistamines, such as Benadryl and Fedrazil, may hasten its destruction and elimination.

Driving a Vehicle, Piloting a Plane, Operating Machinery: This drug may impair mental alertness, judgment, and physical coordination. Avoid hazardous activities.

Exposure to Sun: No restrictions.

Exposure to Heat: No restrictions.

Heavy Exercise or Exertion: No restrictions, but muscular strength and endurance may appear reduced.

Special Storage Instructions
Keep in a dry, tightly closed container.

CEPHALEXIN

Year Introduced: 1971

Brand Names

USA	Canada
Keflex (Lilly)	Ceporex (Glaxo)
	Keflex (Lilly)

Drug Family: Antibiotic (Anti-infective) [Cephalosporins]

Prescription Required: Yes

Available Dosage Forms and Strengths
Tablets — 500 mg.
Capsules — 250 mg., 500 mg.
Oral Suspension — 125 mg., 250 mg. per teaspoonful
Pediatric Drops — 100 mg. per ml.

How This Drug Works
Intended Therapeutic Effect(s): The elimination of infections responsive to the action of this drug.

Location of Drug Action(s): Any body tissue or fluid in which sufficient concentration of the drug can be achieved.

Method of Drug Action(s):   This drug destroys susceptible infecting bacteria by interfering with their ability to produce new protective cell walls as they multiply and grow.

THIS DRUG SHOULD NOT BE TAKEN IF
—you are allergic to any cephalosporin antibiotics (Ancef, Anspor, Ceporan, Ceporex, Kafocin, Keflex, Keflin, Kefzol, Loridine, Velosef).

INFORM YOUR PHYSICIAN BEFORE TAKING THIS DRUG IF
—you have a history of allergy to any form of penicillin (see Drug Family, Section Four).
—you have impaired kidney function.

Time Required for Apparent Benefit
Varies with nature of infection under treatment; usually from 2 to 5 days.

Possible Side-Effects *(natural, expected, and unavoidable drug actions)*
Superinfections (see Glossary).

Possible Adverse Effects *(unusual, unexpected, and infrequent reactions)*

IF ANY OF THE FOLLOWING DEVELOP, DISCONTINUE DRUG AND NOTIFY YOUR PHYSICIAN AS SOON AS POSSIBLE

Mild Adverse Effects
Allergic Reactions: Skin rash (various kinds).
Headache, drowsiness, dizziness, nausea, vomiting, diarrhea, indigestion, abdominal cramping, irritation of mouth or tongue.

Serious Adverse Effects
Allergic Reactions: Anaphylactic reaction (see Glossary), fever, sore throat.

Advisability of Use During Pregnancy
Safety not established. Prudent use is best determined by the physician's evaluation.

Advisability of Use While Nursing Infant
Drug may be present in milk and may sensitize infant to cephalosporins (and possibly to penicillin). Ask physician for guidance.

Habit-Forming Potential
None.

Effects of Overdosage
Nausea, vomiting, abdominal cramping, and/or diarrhea.

Possible Effects of Extended Use
Superinfections (see Glossary).

Recommended Periodic Examinations While Taking This Drug
Complete blood cell counts.
Liver and kidney function tests.

While Taking This Drug, Observe the Following
Foods: No restrictions of food selection. Drug is most effective when taken 1 hour before or 2 hours after eating, but may be taken at any time.

Beverages: No restrictions.

Alcohol: No interactions expected.

Tobacco Smoking: No interactions expected.

Other Drugs
Cephalexin may *increase* the effects of oral anticoagulants, and make it necessary to reduce their dosage.

The following drugs may *increase* the effects of cephalexin:
• probenecid (Benemid) may increase its blood level and prolong its action.

Driving a Vehicle, Piloting a Plane, Operating Machinery: No restrictions unless drug causes dizziness.

Exposure to Sun: No restrictions.

Discontinuation: Certain infections require that this drug be taken for 10 days to prevent the development of rheumatic fever. Ask your physician for guidance regarding the recommended duration of treatment.

Special Storage Instructions
Tablets and capsules should be kept in a tightly closed container. Oral suspension and drops should be refrigerated.

Do Not Take the Oral Suspension or Drops of This Drug If It Is Older Than
14 days—when kept at room temperature or refrigerated.

CEPHRADINE
Year Introduced: 1974

Brand Names

USA	Canada
Anspor (Smith Kline & French)	Velosef (Squibb)
Velosef (Squibb)	

Drug Family: Antibiotic (Anti-infective) [Cephalosporins]

Prescription Required: Yes

Available Dosage Forms and Strengths
Capsules — 250 mg., 500 mg.
Oral Suspension — 125 mg., 250 mg. per teaspoonful

How This Drug Works
Intended Therapeutic Effect(s):   The elimination of infections responsive to the action of this drug.

Location of Drug Action(s):   Any body tissue or fluid in which sufficient concentration of the drug can be achieved.

Method of Drug Action(s):   This drug destroys susceptible infecting bacteria by interfering with their ability to produce new protective cell walls as they multiply and grow.

THIS DRUG SHOULD NOT BE TAKEN IF

—you are allergic to any cephalosporin antibiotic (Ancef, Anspor, Ceporan, Ceporex, Kafocin, Keflex, Keflin, Kefzol, Loridine, Velosef).

INFORM YOUR PHYSICIAN BEFORE TAKING THIS DRUG IF

—you have a history of allergy to any form of penicillin (see Drug Family, Section Four).

—you have impaired kidney function.

Time Required for Apparent Benefit

Varies with nature of infection under treatment; usually from 2 to 5 days.

Possible Side-Effects *(natural, expected, and unavoidable drug actions)*

Superinfections (see Glossary).

Possible Adverse Effects *(unusual, unexpected, and infrequent reactions)*

IF ANY OF THE FOLLOWING DEVELOP, DISCONTINUE DRUG AND NOTIFY YOUR PHYSICIAN AS SOON AS POSSIBLE

Mild Adverse Effects

Allergic Reactions: Skin rash (various kinds).

Headache, drowsiness, dizziness, nausea, vomiting, diarrhea, indigestion, abdominal cramping, irritation of mouth or tongue.

Serious Adverse Effects

Allergic Reactions: Anaphylactic reaction (see Glossary), fever, sore throat.

Advisability of Use During Pregnancy

Safety not established. Prudent use is best determined by the physician's evaluation.

Advisability of Use While Nursing Infant

Drug may be present in milk and can sensitize infant to cephalosporins (and possibly to penicillin). Ask physician for guidance.

Habit-Forming Potential

None.

Effects of Overdosage

Nausea, vomiting, abdominal cramping, and/or diarrhea.

Possible Effects of Extended Use

Superinfections (see Glossary).

Recommended Periodic Examinations While Taking This Drug

Complete blood cell counts.

Liver and kidney function tests.

While Taking This Drug, Observe the Following

Foods: No restrictions of food selection. Drug is most effective when taken 1 hour before or 2 hours after eating, but may be taken at any time.

Beverages: No restrictions.

Alcohol: No interactions expected.

Tobacco Smoking: No interactions expected.

Other Drugs

Cephradine may *increase* the effects of

• oral anticoagulants, and make it necessary to reduce their dosage.

The following drugs may *increase* the effects of cephradine:

• probenecid (Benemid) may increase its blood level and prolong its action.

Driving a Vehicle, Piloting a Plane, Operating Machinery: No restrictions unless drug causes dizziness.

Exposure to Sun: No restrictions.

Discontinuation: Certain infections require that this drug be taken continuously for 10 days to prevent the development of rheumatic fever or nephritis. Ask your physician for guidance regarding the recommended duration of treatment.

Special Storage Instructions

Capsules should be kept in a tightly closed container. Oral suspension should be refrigerated.

Do Not Take the Oral Suspension of This Drug If It Is Older Than

14 days—when kept at room temperature or refrigerated.

CHLORAL HYDRATE

Year Introduced: 1860

Brand Names

USA	Canada
Aquachloral (Webcon)	Chloralex (Regal)
Cohidrate (Coastal)	Chloralixir (Dymond)
Dormal (Ingram)	Chloralvan (ICN)
Felsules	Nigracap (Nordic)
(Fellows-Testagar)	Noctec (Squibb)
H.S. Need (Hanlon)	Novochlorhydrate
Kessodrate (McKesson)	(Novopharm)
Noctec (Squibb)	
Oradrate (Coast)	
Rectules	
(Fellows-Testagar)	
Somnos (Merck Sharp &	
Dohme)	

Drug Family: Sleep Inducer (Hypnotic)

Prescription Required: Yes (Controlled Drug, U.S. Schedule 4)

Available Dosage Forms and Strengths
Capsules — 250 mg., 500 mg., 1 Gm.
Syrup — 500 mg. per teaspoonful
Elixir — 500 mg. per teaspoonful
Suppositories — 325 mg., 650 mg., 975 mg., 1.25 Gms.

How This Drug Works
Intended Therapeutic Effect(s)
• with low dosage, relief of mild to moderate anxiety or tension (sedative effect).
• with higher dosage taken at bedtime, relief of insomnia (hypnotic effect).
Location of Drug Action(s):   Not completely established. Thought to be the wake-sleep centers of the brain, possibly the reticular activating system.
Method of Drug Action(s):   Not established.

THIS DRUG SHOULD NOT BE TAKEN IF
—you have had an allergic reaction to any dosage form of it previously.
—you have a history of severe impairment of liver or kidney function.
—you have active inflammation of the stomach (gastritis).

INFORM YOUR PHYSICIAN BEFORE TAKING THIS DRUG IF
—you are taking sedatives, other sleep-inducing drugs, tranquilizers, pain relievers, antihistamines, or narcotic drugs of any kind.
—you plan to have surgery under general anesthesia in the near future.

Time Required for Apparent Benefit
Approximately 30 to 60 minutes.

Possible Side-Effects *(natural, expected, and unavoidable drug actions)*
Lightheadedness in upright position, unsteadiness in stance and gait, weakness.

Possible Adverse Effects *(unusual, unexpected, and infrequent reactions)*
IF ANY OF THE FOLLOWING DEVELOP, DISCONTINUE DRUG AND NOTIFY
YOUR PHYSICIAN AS SOON AS POSSIBLE

Mild Adverse Effects
Allergic Reactions: Skin rashes (various kinds), hives.
Indigestion, nausea, heartburn, vomiting.
Nightmares, "hangover" effects.

Serious Adverse Effects
Allergic Reactions: Severe skin reactions.
Idiosyncratic Reactions: Paradoxical excitement and delirium, sleepwalking.

Advisability of Use During Pregnancy
Apparently safe. Use in small doses and avoid continuous use.

Advisability of Use While Nursing Infant
This drug is known to be present in milk. Observe nursing infant for indications of sedation. Ask physician for guidance.

Habit-Forming Potential
This drug can cause psychological and/or physical dependence (see Glossary).
Avoid large doses and continuous use.

Effects of Overdosage
With Moderate Overdose: Marked drowsiness, confusion, incoordination, slurred speech, staggering gait, weakness, vomiting.
With Large Overdose: Stupor, deep sleep, flushing of the skin, weak pulse, slow and shallow breathing, dilated pupils.

Possible Effects of Extended Use
Psychological and/or physical dependence.
Kidney damage.

Recommended Periodic Examinations While Taking This Drug
Kidney function studies.

While Taking This Drug, Observe the Following
Foods: No restrictions.
Beverages: Capsules should be taken with a full glass of liquid (water, milk, or fruit juice) to reduce stomach irritation that might occur in some individuals. The syrup and elixir should be taken in one-half glass of water, milk, or fruit juice.
Alcohol: Avoid completely for 6 hours before taking this drug. Alcohol can increase greatly the sedative and depressant actions of this drug on brain function.
Tobacco Smoking: No interactions expected.

Other Drugs

Chloral hydrate may *increase* the effects of

• oral anticoagulants, and cause abnormal bleeding or hemorrhage. Ask physician for guidance regarding prothrombin time testing and adjustment (reduction) of anticoagulant dosage.

• other sedatives, sleep-inducing drugs, tranquilizers, antihistamines, pain relievers, and narcotic drugs. Dosage adjustments may be necessary.

Chloral hydrate may *decrease* the effects of

• cortisone and related drugs, by hastening their elimination from the body. Dosage adjustments may be necessary.

The following drugs may *increase* the effects of chloral hydrate:

• mono-amine oxidase (MAO) inhibitor drugs (see Drug Family, Section Four) may increase the sedative action of chloral hydrate and cause oversedation.

• some phenothiazine and antihistamine drugs may increase the sedative action of chloral hydrate. It is advisable to use this combination with caution.

Driving a Vehicle, Piloting a Plane, Operating Machinery: This drug can impair mental alertness, judgment, physical coordination, and reaction time. Avoid hazardous activities until all sensation of drowsiness has disappeared.

Exposure to Sun: No restrictions.

Discontinuation: If it has been necessary to use this drug for an extended period of time, do not discontinue abruptly. Ask physician for guidance regarding dosage reduction and withdrawal. Ask physician for guidance regarding dosage adjustment of certain other drugs taken concurrently with chloral hydrate, such as oral anticoagulants and cortisone.

Special Storage Instructions

Keep in a tightly closed container.

Keep suppositories refrigerated.

CHLORAMPHENICOL

Year Introduced: 1947

Brand Names

USA	Canada
Amphicol (McKesson)	Chloromycetin (P.D. &
Antibiopto (Softcon)	Co.)
Chloromycetin	Chloroptic (Allergan)
(Parke-Davis)	Fenicol (Alcon)
Chloroptic (Allergan)	Isopto Fenicol (Alcon)
Mychel (Rachelle)	Mycinol (Horner)
Ophthochlor	Novochlorocap
(Parke-Davis)	(Novopharm)
	Pentamycetin
	(Pentagone)

Drug Family: Antibiotic (Anti-infective)

Prescription Required: Yes

Available Dosage Forms and Strengths

Capsules — 50 mg., 100 mg., 250 mg.
Oral Suspension — 125 mg. per teaspoonful
Eye Solution — 0.5%
Eye Ointment — 1%
Ear Solution — 0.5%
Cream — 1%

How This Drug Works

Intended Therapeutic Effect(s):   The elimination of infections responsive to the action of this drug.

Location of Drug Action(s):   Any body tissue or fluid in which sufficient concentration of the drug can be achieved.

Method of Drug Action(s):   This drug prevents the growth and multiplication of susceptible bacteria by interfering with their formation of essential proteins.

THIS DRUG SHOULD NOT BE TAKEN IF

—you have had an allergic reaction to any dosage form of it previously.
—it is prescribed for a mild or trivial infection such as a cold, sore throat, or "flu"-like illness.
—it is prescribed for a premature or newborn infant (under 2 weeks of age).

INFORM YOUR PHYSICIAN BEFORE TAKING THIS DRUG IF

—you have a history of liver or kidney disease.
—you have a history of a blood or bone marrow disease.
—you are taking anticoagulants.

Time Required for Apparent Benefit

Varies with nature of infection under treatment; usually 2 to 5 days.

Possible Side-Effects *(natural, expected, and unavoidable drug actions)*
Superinfections (see Glossary).

Possible Adverse Effects *(unusual, unexpected, and infrequent reactions)*

**IF ANY OF THE FOLLOWING DEVELOP, DISCONTINUE DRUG AND NOTIFY
YOUR PHYSICIAN AS SOON AS POSSIBLE**

Mild Adverse Effects
  Allergic Reactions: Skin rash (various kinds), hives, swelling of face or
    extremities, fever.
  Nausea, vomiting, diarrhea, irritation of mouth or tongue, "black tongue."
  Headache, confusion.
  Peripheral neuritis (see Glossary), numbness, tingling, pain (often burning),
    weakness in hands and/or feet.
Serious Adverse Effects
  Allergic Reactions: Anaphylactic reaction (see Glossary), jaundice (rare).
  †Bone marrow depression (see Glossary)—weakness, fever, sore throat,
    unusual bleeding or bruising.

Advisability of Use During Pregnancy
Safety not established. Prudent use is best determined by the physician's
evaluation.

Advisability of Use While Nursing Infant
Drug can be present in milk and can have adverse effects on infant. Ask
physician for guidance.

Habit-Forming Potential
None.

Effects of Overdosage
Possible nausea, vomiting, and/or diarrhea.

Possible Effects of Extended Use
Impaired vision, bone marrow depression, superinfections.

Recommended Periodic Examinations While Taking This Drug
Complete blood cell counts, which should be performed before treatment is
  started and repeated every 2 days during administration of drug.
Periodic liver and kidney function tests.

While Taking This Drug, Observe the Following
Foods: No restrictions.
Beverages: No restrictions.
Alcohol: Avoid while taking chloramphenicol if:
  • you have a history of liver disease.
  • you do not know your sensitivity to this combination. In some people, the
    concurrent use of chloramphenicol and alcohol can produce a "disulfi-

---

†A rare but potentially dangerous reaction that can occur after both short-term and
long-term treatment with this drug.

ram-like" reaction (see Glossary). Use alcohol cautiously until combined effect is determined.

Tobacco Smoking: No interactions expected.

Other Drugs

Chloramphenicol may *increase* the effects of
- oral anti-diabetic (hypoglycemic) drugs; these are: chlorpropamide (Diabinese), acetohexamide (Dymelor), tolbutamide (Orinase), tolazamide (Tolinase).
- dicumarol.
- phenytoin (Dantoin, Dilantin, etc.).

Chloramphenicol may *decrease* the effects of
- cyclophosphamide (Cytoxan).
- penicillin drugs.

Driving a Vehicle, Piloting a Plane, Operating Machinery: No restrictions.
Exposure to Sun: No restrictions.

Special Storage Instructions
Keep in a tightly closed, light-resistant container.

CHLORDIAZEPOXIDE

Year Introduced: 1960

Brand Names

USA		Canada
Libritabs (Roche)	Chemdipoxide	Nack (Nordic)
Librium (Roche)	(Chemo)	Novopoxide
	Corax (ICN)	(Novopharm)
	C-Tran (M & M)	Protensin
	Diapax (Therapex)	(Elliott-Marion)
	Dymopoxide	Relaxil (Maney)
	(Dymond)	Solium (Horner)
	Gene-Poxide	Sterium (Sterilab)
	(Franca)	Trilium (Trianon)
	Librium (Roche)	Via-Quil (Denver)
	Medilium (Medic)	

Drug Family: Tranquilizer, Mild (Anti-anxiety) [Benzodiazepines]

Prescription Required: Yes (Controlled Drug, U.S. Schedule 4)

Available Dosage Forms and Strengths
Tablets — 5 mg., 10 mg., 25 mg.
Capsules — 5 mg., 10 mg., 25 mg.
Injection — 100 mg. per 5 ml.

How This Drug Works

Intended Therapeutic Effect(s):   Relief of mild to moderate anxiety and nervous tension, without significant sedation.

Location of Drug Action(s):   Thought to be the limbic system of the brain, one of the centers that influence emotional stability.

Method of Drug Action(s):   Not established. Present thinking is that this drug may reduce the activity of certain parts of the limbic system.

THIS DRUG SHOULD NOT BE TAKEN IF

—you have had an allergic reaction to any dosage form of it previously.
—you are subject to acute intermittent porphyria.
—you have myasthenia gravis.
—it is prescribed for a child under 6 years of age.

INFORM YOUR PHYSICIAN BEFORE TAKING THIS DRUG IF

—you are allergic to any drugs chemically related to chlordiazepoxide: clorazepate, diazepam, flurazepam, oxazepam (see Drug Profiles for brand names).
—you have diabetes.
—you have epilepsy.
—you are taking sedative, sleep-inducing, tranquilizer, or anti-convulsant drugs of any kind.
—you are taking anticoagulant drugs.
—you plan to have surgery under general or spinal anesthesia in the near future.

Time Required for Apparent Benefit

Approximately 2 to 4 hours. For severe symptoms of some duration, benefit may require regular medication for several days.

Possible Side-Effects *(natural, expected, and unavoidable drug actions)*

Drowsiness, lethargy, unsteadiness in stance and gait.

Increase in the level of blood sugar in some cases of diabetes.

In the elderly (over 60 years of age) and debilitated: lightheadedness, confusion, weakness, impaired bladder control, constipation. (The elderly are very susceptible to standard doses. Small doses are advisable until tolerance has been determined.)

Possible Adverse Effects *(unusual, unexpected, and infrequent reactions)*

IF ANY OF THE FOLLOWING DEVELOP, DISCONTINUE DRUG AND NOTIFY YOUR PHYSICIAN AS SOON AS POSSIBLE

Mild Adverse Effects

Allergic Reactions: Skin rashes (various kinds).

Dizziness, fainting, blurred vision, double vision, slurred speech, nausea, menstrual irregularity, vivid dreaming.

Serious Adverse Effects

Allergic Reactions: Jaundice (see Glossary), impaired resistance to infection manifested by fever and/or sore throat, unusual bleeding or bruising.

Parkinson-like disorders (see Glossary), depression.

Paradoxical Reactions: Acute excitement, hallucinations, rage.

Advisability of Use During Pregnancy
The findings of some recent studies suggest a possible association between the use of this drug during early pregnancy and the occurrence of birth defects, such as cleft lip. It is advisable to avoid this drug completely during the first 3 months of pregnancy.

Advisability of Use While Nursing Infant
With recommended dosage, drug is present in milk and can affect infant. Avoid use if possible. Ask physician for guidance.

Habit-Forming Potential
This drug can produce psychological and/or physical dependence (see Glossary) if used in large doses for an extended period of time.

Effects of Overdosage
With Moderate Overdose: Marked drowsiness, weakness, feeling of drunkenness, staggering gait, tremor.

With Large Overdose: Stupor progressing to deep sleep and coma.

Possible Effects of Extended Use
Psychological and/or physical dependence.
Impairment of blood cell production.
Impairment of liver function.

Recommended Periodic Examinations While Taking This Drug
Blood cell counts and liver function tests during long-term use.
Blood sugar measurements (in presence of diabetes).

While Taking This Drug, Observe the Following
Food: No restrictions.

Beverages: Large intake of coffee, tea, or cola drinks (because of their caffeine content) may reduce the calming action of this drug.

Alcohol: Use with extreme caution until the combined effect is determined. Alcohol may increase the sedative effects of chlordiazepoxide. Chlordiazepoxide may increase the intoxicating effects of alcohol.

Tobacco Smoking: Heavy smoking may reduce the calming action of chlordiazepoxide.

Other Drugs

Chlordiazepoxide may *increase* the effects of

- other sedatives, sleep-inducing drugs, tranquilizers, anti-convulsants, and narcotic drugs. Use these only under supervision of a physician. Careful dosage adjustment is necessary.
- oral anticoagulants of the coumarin family; ask physician for guidance regarding need for dosage adjustment to prevent bleeding.
- anti-hypertensives, producing excessive lowering of the blood pressure.

Chlordiazepoxide *taken concurrently* with

- anti-convulsants, may cause an increase in the frequency or severity of seizures; an increase in the dose of the anti-convulsant may be necessary.
- mono-amine oxidase (MAO) inhibitor drugs (see Drug Family, Section Four), may cause extreme sedation, convulsions, or paradoxical excitement or rage.

The following drugs may *increase* the effects of chlordiazepoxide

• tricyclic antidepressants (see Drug Family, Section Four) may increase the sedative effects of chlordiazepoxide.

Driving a Vehicle, Piloting a Plane, Operating Machinery: This drug can impair mental alertness, judgment, physical coordination, and reaction time. Avoid hazardous activities.

Exposure to Sun: Use caution until sensitivity is determined. Chlordiazepoxide may cause photosensitivity (see Glossary).

Exposure to Heat: Use caution until effect of excessive perspiration is determined. Because of reduced urine volume, chlordiazepoxide may accumulate in the body and produce effects of overdosage.

Heavy Exercise or Exertion: No restrictions in cool or temperate weather.

Discontinuation: If it has been necessary to use this drug for an extended period of time, do not discontinue it abruptly. Ask physician for guidance regarding dosage reduction and withdrawal. The dosage of other drugs taken concurrently with chlordiazepoxide may also require adjustment.

Special Storage Instructions
Keep in a dry, tightly closed, light-resistant container.

CHLOROTHIAZIDE

Year Introduced: 1958

Brand Names

USA	Canada
Diuril (Merck Sharp & Dohme)	Diuril (Frosst)
Aldoclor [CD] (Merck Sharp & Dohme)	Diupres [CD] (MSD)
Diupres [CD] (Merck Sharp & Dohme)	

Drug Family: Anti-hypertensive (Hypotensive); Diuretic [Thiazides]

Prescription Required: Yes

Available Dosage Forms and Strengths
Tablets — 250 mg., 500 mg.
Oral Suspension — 250 mg. per teaspoonful

How This Drug Works
Intended Therapeutic Effect(s)
• elimination of excessive fluid retention (edema).
• reduction of high blood pressure.

Location of Drug Action(s): Principal actions occur in
- the tubular systems of the kidney that determine the final composition of the urine
- the walls of the smaller arteries.

Method of Drug Action(s)

By increasing the elimination of salt and water from the body (through increased urine production), this drug reduces the volume of fluid in the blood and body tissues and lowers the sodium content throughout the body.

By relaxing the walls of the smaller arteries and allowing them to expand, this drug significantly increases the total capacity of the arterial system.

The combined effect of these two actions (reduced blood volume in expanded space) results in lowering of the blood pressure.

THIS DRUG SHOULD NOT BE TAKEN IF

—you have had an allergic reaction to any dosage form of it previously.

INFORM YOUR PHYSICIAN BEFORE TAKING THIS DRUG IF

—you are allergic to any form of "sulfa" drug.
—you are pregnant and your physician does not know it.
—you have a history of kidney disease or liver disease, or impaired kidney or liver function.
—you have diabetes (or a tendency to diabetes).
—you have a history of gout.
—you have a history of lupus erythematosus.
—you are taking any form of cortisone, digitalis, oral anti-diabetic drugs, or insulin.
—you plan to have surgery under general anesthesia in the near future.

Time Required for Apparent Benefit

Increased urine volume begins in 2 hours, reaches a maximum in 4 to 6 hours, and subsides in 8 to 12 hours. Continuous use on a regular schedule will be necessary for 2 to 3 weeks to determine this drug's effectiveness in lowering your blood pressure.

Possible Side-Effects *(natural, expected, and unavoidable drug actions)*

Lightheadedness on arising from sitting or lying position (see orthostatic hypotension in Glossary).

Increase in level of blood sugar, affecting control of diabetes.

Increase in level of blood uric acid, affecting control of gout.

Decrease in the level of blood potassium, resulting in muscle weakness and cramping.

CAUTION

The elderly (over 60 years of age) are frequently quite sensitive to the effects of standard doses. It is advisable to use this drug with caution until extent and duration of response have been determined.

Possible Adverse Effects *(unusual, unexpected, and infrequent reactions)*

IF ANY OF THE FOLLOWING DEVELOP, DISCONTINUE DRUG AND NOTIFY
YOUR PHYSICIAN AS SOON AS POSSIBLE

Mild Adverse Effects
Allergic Reactions: Skin rash (various kinds), hives, drug fever.
Reduced appetite, indigestion, nausea, vomiting, diarrhea.
Headache, dizziness, yellow vision, blurred vision.

Serious Adverse Effects
Allergic Reactions: Hepatitis with jaundice (see Glossary), anaphylactic
reaction (see Glossary), severe skin reactions.
Inflammation of the pancreas—severe abdominal pain.
Bone marrow depression (see Glossary)—fatigue, weakness, fever, sore
throat, unusual bleeding or bruising.

Advisability of Use During Pregnancy
This drug should not be used during pregnancy unless a very serious complication of pregnancy occurs for which this drug is significantly beneficial. This
type of diuretic can have adverse effects on the fetus.

Advisability of Use While Nursing Infant
This drug is known to be present in milk. Prudent use is best determined by
the physician's evaluation.

Habit-Forming Potential
None.

Effects of Overdosage
With Moderate Overdose: Dryness of mouth, thirst, lethargy, weakness,
muscle pain and cramping, nausea, vomiting.
With Large Overdose: Drowsiness progressing to stupor and coma, weak
and rapid pulse.

Possible Effects of Extended Use
Impaired balance of water, salt, and potassium in blood and body tissues.
Development of diabetes (in predisposed individuals).

Recommended Periodic Examinations While Taking This Drug
Complete blood cell counts.
Measurements of blood levels of sodium, potassium, chloride, sugar, and uric
acid.
Liver function tests.
Kidney function tests.

While Taking This Drug, Observe the Following
Foods: It is recommended that you include in your daily diet liberal servings of foods rich in potassium (unless directed otherwise by your physician). The following foods have a high potassium content:

All-bran cereals	Bananas, fresh
Almonds	Beans (navy and lima)
Apricots (dried)	Beef

Carrots (raw)	Lonalac
Chicken	Milk
Citrus fruits	Peaches
Coconut	Peanut butter
Coffee	Peas
Crackers (rye)	Pork
Dates and figs (dried)	Potato Chips
Fish, fresh	Prunes, dried
Lentils	Raisins
Liver, beef	Tomato Juice

- *Note:* Avoid licorice in large amounts while taking this drug. Follow your physician's instructions regarding the use of salt.

Beverages: No restrictions unless directed by your physician.

Alcohol: Use with caution until the combined effect has been determined. Alcohol can exaggerate the blood pressure-lowering effect of this drug and cause orthostatic hypotension.

Tobacco Smoking: No interactions expected with this drug. Follow your physician's advice regarding smoking.

Other Drugs

Chlorothiazide may *increase* the effects of

- other anti-hypertensive drugs. Careful adjustment of dosages is necessary to prevent excessive lowering of the blood pressure.
- drugs of the phenothiazine family, and cause excessive lowering of the blood pressure. (The thiazides and related drugs and the phenothiazines may both cause orthostatic hypotension).

Chlorothiazide may *decrease* the effects of

- oral anti-diabetic drugs and insulin, by raising the level of blood sugar. Careful dosage adjustment is necessary to maintain proper control of diabetes.
- allopurinol (Zyloprim), by raising the level of blood uric acid. Careful dosage adjustment is required to maintain proper control of gout.
- probenecid (Benemid), by raising the level of blood uric acid. Careful dosage adjustments are necessary to maintain control of gout.

Chlorothiazide *taken concurrently* with

- cortisone and cortisone-related drugs, may cause excessive loss of potassium from the body.
- digitalis and related drugs, requires very careful monitoring and dosage adjustments to prevent serious disturbances of heart rhythm.
- tricyclic antidepressants (Elavil, Sinequan, etc.), may cause excessive lowering of the blood pressure.

The following drugs may *increase* the effects of chlorothiazide:

- barbiturates may exaggerate its blood pressure-lowering action.
- mono-amine oxidase (MAO) inhibitor drugs (see Drug Family, Section Four) may increase urine volume by delaying this drug's elimination from the body.

• pain relievers (analgesics), both narcotic and non-narcotic, may exaggerate its blood pressure-lowering action.

The following drugs may *decrease* the effects of chlorothiazide:

• cholestyramine (Cuemid, Questran) may interfere with its absorption. Take cholestyramine 30 to 60 minutes before any oral diuretic.

Driving a Vehicle, Piloting a Plane, Operating Machinery: Use caution until the possibility of orthostatic hypotension (lightheadedness, dizziness, incoordination) has been determined.

Exposure to Sun: Use caution until sensitivity has been determined. This drug can cause photosensitivity (see Glossary).

Exposure to Heat: Avoid excessive perspiring which could cause additional loss of water and salt from the body.

Heavy Exercise or Exertion: Avoid exertion that produces lightheadedness, excessive fatigue, or muscle cramping.

Occurrence of Unrelated Illness: Illnesses which cause vomiting or diarrhea can produce a serious imbalance of important body chemistry. Discontinue this drug and ask your physician for guidance.

Discontinuation: It may be advisable to discontinue this drug approximately 5 to 7 days before major surgery. Ask your physician, surgeon, and/or anesthesiologist for guidance regarding dosage reduction or withdrawal.

Special Storage Instructions
Keep in a dry, tightly closed container.

CHLORPHENIRAMINE
Year Introduced: 1950

Brand Names

USA	Canada
Chlor-Trimeton (Schering)	Chlor-Tripolon (Schering)
Histaspan (USV Pharmaceutical)	Chlortrone (Barlowe Cote)
Polaramine* (Schering)	Histalon (ICN)
Teldrin (Smith Kline & French)	Histaspan (Arlington)
(Numerous other brand and combination brand names)	Novopheniram (Novopharm)

Drug Family: Antihistamines

Prescription Required: For tablets of 2 mg. and 4 mg. and for syrup—No
For all other dosage forms—Yes

*A brand of the closely related generic drug dexchlorpheniramine.

Available Dosage Forms and Strengths

Tablets — 2 mg., 4 mg.

Prolonged Action Tablets — 4 mg., 6 mg., 8 mg., 12 mg.

Prolonged Action Capsules — 8 mg., 12 mg.

Syrup — 2 mg. per teaspoonful

Injection — 10 mg. per ml., 100 mg. per ml.

How This Drug Works

Intended Therapeutic Effect(s):   Relief of symptoms associated with hayfever (allergic rhinitis) and with allergic reactions in the skin, such as itching,
swelling, hives, and rash.

Location of Drug Action(s):   Those hypersensitive tissues that release excessive histamine as part of an allergic reaction. The principal tissue sites are
the eyes, the nose, and the skin.

Method of Drug Action(s):   This drug reduces the intensity of the allergic
response by blocking the action of histamine after it has been released from
sensitized tissue cells.

THIS DRUG SHOULD NOT BE TAKEN IF

—you have had an allergic reaction to any dosage form of it previously.

INFORM YOUR PHYSICIAN BEFORE TAKING THIS DRUG IF

—you have had any unfavorable reaction to previous use of antihistamines.

—you have glaucoma (narrow-angle type).

—you have difficulty in emptying the urinary bladder.

—you plan to have surgery under general anesthesia in the near future.

Time Required for Apparent Benefit

Drug action usually begins in 15 to 30 minutes, reaches maximal effect in 1
to 2 hours, and subsides in 3 to 6 hours.

Possible Side-Effects *(natural, expected, and unavoidable drug actions)*

Drowsiness, sense of weakness, dryness of the nose, mouth, and throat.

Possible Adverse Effects *(unusual, unexpected, and infrequent reactions)*

**IF ANY OF THE FOLLOWING DEVELOP, DISCONTINUE DRUG AND NOTIFY
YOUR PHYSICIAN AS SOON AS POSSIBLE**

Mild Adverse Effects

Allergic Reactions: Skin rash (rare).

Headache, nervous agitation, dizziness, double vision, blurred vision, ringing in the ears, tremors.

Reduced appetite, heartburn, nausea, vomiting, diarrhea.

Reduced tolerance for contact lenses.

Serious Adverse Effects

Reduced production of white blood cells possibly resulting in fever and/or
sore throat.

Advisability of Use During Pregnancy

Safety not established. If necessary to use any antihistamine, limit use to small
doses and for short periods of time.

Advisability of Use While Nursing Infant
Drug is present in milk in small quantities. Ask physician for guidance.

Habit-Forming Potential
None.

Effects of Overdosage
With **Moderate Overdose:**   Excitement, incoordination, staggering gait, hallucinations, muscular tremors and spasms.

With **Large Overdose:**   Stupor progressing to coma, convulsions, dilated pupils, flushed face, fever, shallow respiration, weak and rapid pulse.

Possible Effects of Extended Use
Tardive dyskinesia (see Glossary).

Bone marrow depression (see Glossary).

(Note: Prolonged, continuous use of antihistamines should be avoided.)

Recommended Periodic Examinations While Taking This Drug
Complete blood cell counts.

While Taking This Drug, Observe the Following
Foods: No restrictions.

Beverages: Coffee and tea can help to offset the drowsiness produced by most antihistamines.

Alcohol: Use with extreme caution until combined effects have been determined. The combination of alcohol and antihistamines can produce rapid and marked sedation.

Tobacco Smoking: No interactions expected.

Other Drugs

Chlorpheniramine may *increase* the effects of

• all sedatives, sleep-inducing drugs, tranquilizers, analgesics, and narcotic drugs, and produce oversedation.

Chlorpheniramine may *decrease* the effects of

• oral anticoagulants, by hastening their elimination from the body. Consult physician regarding prothrombin time testing and dosage adjustment.

The following drugs may *increase* the effects of chlorpheniramine

• all sedatives, sleep-inducing drugs, tranquilizers, analgesics, and narcotic drugs may exaggerate its sedative action.

• mono-amine oxidase (MAO) inhibitor drugs (see Drug Family, Section Four) may prolong the action of antihistamines.

Driving a Vehicle, Piloting a Plane, Operating Machinery: This drug can impair mental alertness, judgment, coordination, and reaction time. Avoid hazardous activities until full sedative effects have been determined.

Exposure to Sun: No restrictions.

Special Storage Instructions
Keep tablets and capsules in a dry, tightly closed container.

Protect liquid drug preparations from light to prevent discoloration.

CHLORPROMAZINE

Year Introduced: 1951

Brand Names

USA
Chlor-PZ (USV
  Pharmaceutical)
Klorazine (Myers-Carter)
Promachlor (Geneva)
Promapar (Parke-Davis)
Sonazine (Tutag)
Thorazine (Smith Kline
  & French)

Canada
Chlor-Promanyl (Maney)
Chlorprom-Ez-Ets
  (Barlowe Cote)
Largactil (Poulenc)

Drug Family: Tranquilizer, Strong (Anti-psychotic)
Antinausea (Anti-emetic) [Phenothiazines]

Prescription Required: Yes

Available Dosage Forms and Strengths

Tablets — 10 mg., 25 mg., 50 mg., 100 mg., 200 mg.
Capsules — 30 mg., 75 mg., 150 mg., 200 mg., 300 mg.
Suppositories — 25 mg., 100 mg.
Syrup — 10 mg. per teaspoonful
Concentrated Solution — 30 mg. per ml., 100 mg. per ml.
Injection — 25 mg. per ml.

How This Drug Works

Intended Therapeutic Effect(s):   Restoration of emotional calm. Relief of severe anxiety, agitation, and psychotic behavior.

Location of Drug Action(s):   Those nerve pathways in the brain that utilize the tissue chemical dopamine for the transmission of nerve impulses.

Method of Drug Action(s):   Not completely established. Present theory is that by inhibiting the action of dopamine, this drug acts to correct an imbalance of nerve impulse transmissions that is thought to be responsible for certain mental disorders.

THIS DRUG SHOULD NOT BE TAKEN IF

—you are allergic to any of the drugs bearing the brand names listed above.
—you have a disorder of the blood or bone marrow.
—it is prescribed for a child under 6 months of age.

INFORM YOUR PHYSICIAN BEFORE TAKING THIS DRUG IF

—you are allergic or sensitive to any phenothiazine drug (see Drug Family, Section Four).
—you are taking sedatives, sleep-inducing drugs, tranquilizers, antidepressants, antihistamines, or narcotic drugs of any kind.
—you have glaucoma.
—you have epilepsy.

—you have a liver, heart, or lung disorder, especially asthma or emphysema.
—you have a history of peptic ulcer.
—you plan to have surgery under general or spinal anesthesia in the near future.

Time Required for Apparent Benefit
Approximately 1 to 2 hours. Maximal benefit may require regular use for several weeks.

Possible Side-Effects *(natural, expected, and unavoidable drug actions)*
Drowsiness (usually during the first 2 weeks), dryness of the mouth, nasal congestion, constipation, impaired urination.
Pink or purple coloration of the urine, of no significance.

Possible Adverse Effects *(unusual, unexpected, and infrequent reactions)*
IF ANY OF THE FOLLOWING DEVELOP, DISCONTINUE DRUG AND NOTIFY YOUR PHYSICIAN AS SOON AS POSSIBLE

Mild Adverse Effects
Allergic Reactions: Skin rashes (various kinds), hives, low-grade fever.
Lowering of body temperature, especially in the elderly (over 60 years of age).
Lightheadedness or faintness in upright position, dizziness, heart palpitation.
Increased appetite and weight gain.
Breast fullness, tenderness, and milk production.
Menstrual irregularity.
False positive pregnancy tests.

Serious Adverse Effects
Allergic Reactions: Hepatitis with jaundice (see Glossary)—usually occurs between second and fourth week, high fever, asthma, anaphylactic reaction (see Glossary).
Bone marrow depression (see Glossary)—fatigue, weakness, fever, sore throat, unusual bleeding or bruising.
Parkinson-like disorders (see Glossary).
Muscle spasms affecting the jaw, neck, back, hands, or feet.
Eye-rolling, muscle twitching, convulsions.
Prolonged drop in blood pressure with weakness, perspiration, and fainting.

Advisability of Use During Pregnancy
Safety not established. Prudent use is best determined by the physician's evaluation.

Advisability of Use While Nursing Infant
Drug is known to be present in milk. Ask physician for guidance.

Habit-Forming Potential
None.

Effects of Overdosage
With **Moderate Overdose:**   Marked drowsiness, weakness, tremor, impairment of stance and gait, agitation.
With **Large Overdose:**   Stupor, deep sleep, coma, convulsions.

Possible Effects of Extended Use
Tardive dyskinesia (see Glossary).
Pigmentation of skin, gray to violet in color, usually in exposed areas, more common in women.
Eye changes—cataracts and pigmentation of retina, with impairment of vision.

Recommended Periodic Examinations While Taking This Drug
Complete blood cell counts, especially between the fourth and tenth weeks of treatment.
Liver function tests.
Complete eye examinations, including eye structures and vision.
Careful inspection of the tongue for early evidence of fine, involuntary, wave-like movements that could indicate the beginning of tardive dyskinesia.
Periodic electrocardiograms.

While Taking This Drug, Observe the Following
Foods: No restrictions.
Beverages: No restrictions.
Alcohol: Avoid completely. Alcohol can increase the sedative action of chlorpromazine and accentuate its depressant effects on brain function and blood pressure. Chlorpromazine can increase the intoxicating effects of alcohol.
Tobacco Smoking: No interactions expected.
Other Drugs
Chlorpromazine may *increase* the effects of
• all drugs containing atropine or having an atropine-like action (see Drug Family, Section Four).
• all sedatives, sleep-inducing drugs, other tranquilizers, antidepressants, antihistamines, and narcotic drugs, and produce oversedation.
• methyldopa (Aldomet), and cause excessive lowering of the blood pressure.
• pargyline (Eutonyl), and cause excessive lowering of the blood pressure.
• phenytoin (Dantoin, Dilantin, etc.).
• reserpine (and related drugs), and cause excessive lowering of the blood pressure.

Chlorpromazine may *decrease* the effects of
• oral anticoagulants, by hastening their destruction and elimination. Dosage adjustments of the anticoagulant may be necessary.
• oral anti-diabetic drugs and insulin, and reduce their effectiveness in regulating blood sugar.

- chlorphentermine (Pre-Sate), and reduce its effectiveness in controlling appetite.
- guanethidine (Ismelin), and reduce its effectiveness in lowering blood pressure.
- levodopa (Dopar, Larodopa, Parda), and reduce its effectiveness in the treatment of Parkinson's disease (shaking palsy).
- phenmetrazine (Preludin), and reduce its effectiveness in controlling appetite.

Chlorpromazine *taken concurrently* with
- quinidine, may impair heart function. Avoid the concurrent use of these two drugs.
- orphenadrine (Norflex, Norgesic, Disipal), may cause severe lowering of the blood sugar and unconsciousness (see hypoglycemia in Glossary).

Driving a Vehicle, Piloting a Plane, Operating Machinery: This drug can impair mental alertness, judgment, and physical coordination. Avoid hazardous activities.

Exposure to Sun: Use caution until sensitivity has been determined. This drug can produce photosensitivity (see Glossary).

Exposure to Heat: Use caution and avoid excessive heat as much as possible. This drug may impair the regulation of body temperature and increase the risk of heat stroke.

Heavy Exercise or Exertion: Use caution. Ask physician for guidance.

Discontinuation: If it has been necessary to use this drug for an extended period of time, do not discontinue it suddenly. Ask physician for guidance regarding dosage reduction and withdrawal. Upon discontinuation of this drug, it may also be necessary to adjust the dosages of other drugs taken concurrently with it.

Special Storage Instructions
Keep in a tightly closed, light-resistant container.

CHLORPROPAMIDE

Year Introduced: 1958

Brand Names

USA	Canada
Diabinese (Pfizer)	Chloromide (ICN)
	Chloronase (Hoechst)
	Diabinese (Pfizer)
	Novopropamide
	(Novopharm)
	Stabinol (Horner)

Drug Family: Anti-diabetic, Oral (Hypoglycemic) [Sulfonylureas]

Prescription Required: Yes

Available Dosage Forms and Strengths
Tablets—100 mg., 250 mg.

How This Drug Works
Intended Therapeutic Effect(s):   The correction of insulin deficiency in adult (maturity-onset) diabetes of moderate severity.
Location of Drug Action(s):   The insulin-producing tissues of the pancreas.
Method of Drug Action(s):   It is well established that sulfonylurea drugs stimulate the secretion of insulin (by a pancreas capable of responding to stimulation). Therapeutic doses may increase the amount of available insulin.

THIS DRUG SHOULD NOT BE TAKEN IF
—you have had an allergic reaction to any dosage form of it previously.
—you have severe impairment of liver function or kidney function.

INFORM YOUR PHYSICIAN BEFORE TAKING THIS DRUG IF
—your diabetes has been difficult to control in the past ("brittle type").
—you have a history of peptic ulcer of the stomach or duodenum.
—you have a history of poryphyria.
—you do not know how to recognize or treat hypoglycemia (see Glossary).

Time Required for Apparent Benefit
A single dose may lower the blood sugar within 2 to 4 hours. Regular use for 1 to 2 weeks may be needed to determine this drug's effectiveness in controlling your diabetes.

Possible Side-Effects *(natural, expected, and unavoidable drug actions)*
Usually none. If drug dosage is excessive or food intake is inadequate, abnormally low blood sugar (hypoglycemia) will occur as a predictable drug effect.

CAUTION
The elderly (over 60 years of age) require smaller doses and are more likely to experience episodes of prolonged hypoglycemia when taking this drug.

Possible Adverse Effects *(unusual, unexpected, and infrequent reactions)*

IF ANY OF THE FOLLOWING DEVELOP, DISCONTINUE DRUG AND NOTIFY YOUR PHYSICIAN AS SOON AS POSSIBLE

Mild Adverse Effects

Allergic Reactions: Skin rashes (various kinds), hives, itching, drug fever. Headache, ringing in ears.

Indigestion, heartburn, nausea, diarrhea.

Serious Adverse Effects

Allergic Reactions: Hepatitis with jaundice (see Glossary).

Idiosyncratic Reactions: Hemolytic anemia in susceptible individuals (see Glossary).

Bone marrow depression (see Glossary)—fatigue, weakness, fever, sore throat, unusual bleeding or bruising.

Advisability of Use During Pregnancy

Safety not established. Prudent use is best determined by the physician's evaluation.

Advisability of Use While Nursing Infant

Drug is known to be present in milk. Ask physician for guidance.

Habit-Forming Potential

None

Effects of Overdosage

With Moderate Overdose: Symptoms of mild to moderate hypoglycemia: headache, lightheadedness, faintness, nervousness, confusion, tremor, sweating, heart palpitation, weakness, and hunger.

With Large Overdose: Hypoglycemic coma (see Glossary).

Possible Effects of Extended Use

Reduced function of the thyroid gland (hypothyroidism), resulting in lowered metabolism.

Reports of increased frequency and severity of heart and blood vessel diseases associated with long-term use of the members of this drug family are highly controversial and inconclusive. A direct cause-and-effect relationship (see Glossary) has not been established to date. Ask your physician for guidance regarding extended use.

Recommended Periodic Examinations While Taking This Drug

Complete blood cell counts.

Liver function tests.

Thyroid function tests.

Periodic evaluation of heart and circulatory system.

While Taking This Drug, Observe the Following

Foods: Follow the diabetic diet prescribed by your physician.

Beverages: As directed in the diabetic diet prescribed by your physician.

Alcohol: Use with extreme caution until the combined effect has been determined. This drug can cause a marked intolerance to alcohol resulting in a disulfiram-like reaction (see Glossary).

Tobacco Smoking: No restrictions unless imposed as part of your overall treatment program. Ask physician for guidance.

Other Drugs

Chlorpropamide may *increase* the effects of

- sedatives and sleep-inducing drugs, by slowing their elimination from the body.
- "sulfa" drugs, by slowing their elimination from the body.

Chlorpropamide *taken concurrently* with

- oral anticoagulants, may cause unpredictable changes in anticoagulant drug actions. Ask physician for guidance regarding prothrombin blood tests and dosage adjustment.
- propranolol (Inderal), may allow hypoglycemia to develop without adequate warning. Follow diet and dosage schedules very carefully.

The following drugs may *increase* the effects of chlorpropamide

- bishydroxycoumarin (Dicumarol, Dufalone)
- chloramphenicol (Chloromycetin, etc.)
- clofibrate (Atromid-S)
- mono-amine oxidase (MAO) inhibitors (see Drug Family, Section Four)
- oxyphenbutazone (Oxalid, Tandearil)
- phenformin (DBI)
- phenylbutazone (Azolid, Butazolidin, etc.)
- phenyramidol (Analexin)
- probenecid (Benemid)
- propranolol (Inderal)
- salicylates (aspirin, sodium salicylate)
- sulfaphenazole (Orisul, Sulfabid)
- sulfisoxazole (Gantrisin, Novosoxazole, etc.)

The following drugs may *decrease* the effects of chlorpropamide

- chlorpromazine (Thorazine, Largactil, etc.)
- cortisone and related drugs (see Drug Family, Section Four)
- estrogens (Premarin, Menotrol, Ogen, etc.)
- isoniazid (INH, Isozide, etc.)
- nicotinic acid (Niacin, etc.)
- oral contraceptives (see Drug Family, Section Four)
- pyrazinamide (Aldinamide)
- thiazide diuretics (see Drug Family, Section Four)
- thyroid preparations

Driving a Vehicle, Piloting a Plane, Operating Machinery: Regulate your dosage schedule, eating schedule, and physical activities very carefully to prevent hypoglycemia. Be able to recognize the early symptoms of hypoglycemia and avoid hazardous activities if you suspect that hypoglycemia is developing.

Exposure to Sun: Use caution until sensitivity has been determined. This drug can cause photosensitivity (see Glossary).

Exposure to Heat: No restrictions.

Exposure to Cold: No restrictions.

Heavy Exercise or Exertion: Use caution. Excessive exercise may result in hypoglycemia.

Occurrence of Unrelated Illness: Acute infections, illnesses causing vomiting or diarrhea, serious injuries, and the need for surgery can interfere with diabetic control and may require a change in medication. If any of these conditions occur, ask your physician for guidance regarding the continued use of this drug.

Discontinuation: If you find it necessary to discontinue this drug for any reason, notify your physician and ask for guidance regarding necessary changes in your treatment program for diabetic control.

Special Storage Instructions
Keep in a dry, tightly closed container.

CHLORTETRACYCLINE

Year Introduced: 1948

Brand Names

USA	Canada
Aureomycin (Lederle)	Aureomycin (Lederle)

Drug Family: Antibiotic (Anti-infective) [Tetracyclines]

Prescription Required: Yes

Available Dosage Forms and Strengths
Capsules — 250 mg.
Eye Ointment — 1%
Skin Ointment — 3%

How This Drug Works
Intended Therapeutic Effect(s):   The elimination of infections responsive to the action of this drug.

Location of Drug Action(s):   Any body tissue or fluid in which sufficient concentration of the drug can be achieved.

Method of Drug Action(s):   This drug prevents the growth and multiplication of susceptible bacteria by interfering with their formation of essential proteins.

THIS DRUG SHOULD NOT BE TAKEN IF
—you are allergic to any tetracycline drug (see Drug Family, Section Four).
—you are pregnant or breastfeeding.
—it is prescribed for a child under 9 years of age.

INFORM YOUR PHYSICIAN BEFORE TAKING THIS DRUG IF
—you have a history of liver or kidney disease.
—you have systemic lupus erythematosus.

—you are taking any penicillin drug.

—you are taking any anticoagulant drug.

—you plan to have surgery under general anesthesia in the near future.

Time Required for Apparent Benefit

Varies with nature of infection under treatment; usually 2 to 5 days.

Possible Side-Effects *(natural, expected, and unavoidable drug actions)*

Superinfections (see Glossary), often due to yeast organisms. These can occur in the mouth, intestinal tract, rectum, and/or vagina, resulting in rectal and vaginal itching.

Possible Adverse Effects *(unusual, unexpected, and infrequent reactions)*

IF ANY OF THE FOLLOWING DEVELOP, DISCONTINUE DRUG AND NOTIFY YOUR PHYSICIAN AS SOON AS POSSIBLE

Mild Adverse Effects

Allergic Reactions: Skin rash (various kinds), hives, itching of hands and feet, swelling of face or extremities.

Photosensitivity Reactions: Exaggerated sunburn or skin irritation occurs commonly with some tetracyclines (see Glossary).

Loss of appetite, nausea, vomiting, diarrhea.

Irritation of mouth or tongue, "black tongue," sore throat, abdominal pain or cramping.

Serious Adverse Effects

Allergic Reactions: Anaphylactic reaction (see Glossary), asthma, fever, painful swollen joints, unusual bleeding or bruising, jaundice (see Glossary).

Permanent discoloration and/or malformation of teeth when taken under 9 years of age, including unborn child and infant.

Advisability of Use During Pregnancy

Tetracyclines can have adverse effects on mother and fetus. Avoid use.

Advisability of Use While Nursing Infant

Tetracyclines can be present in milk and can have adverse effects on infant. Avoid use.

Habit-Forming Potential

None.

Effects of Overdosage

Possible nausea, vomiting, diarrhea.

Acute liver damage (rare).

Possible Effects of Extended Use

Impairment of bone marrow, liver, or kidney function (all rare).

Superinfections.

Recommended Periodic Examinations While Taking This Drug

Complete blood cell counts.

Liver and kidney function tests.

During extended use, sputum and stool examinations may detect early super-infections due to yeast organisms.

While Taking This Drug, Observe the Following

Foods: Dairy products can interfere with absorption. Tetracyclines should be taken 1 hour before or 2 hours after eating.

Beverages: Avoid milk for 1 hour before and after each dose of a tetracycline.

Alcohol: Avoid while taking a tetracycline if you have a history of liver disease.

Tobacco Smoking: No interactions expected.

Other Drugs

Tetracyclines may *increase* the effects of
• oral anticoagulants, and make it necessary to reduce their dosage.

Tetracyclines may *decrease* the effects of
• the penicillins, and impair their effectiveness in treating infections.

The following drugs may *decrease* the effects of tetracyclines
• antacids may reduce drug absorption.
• iron and mineral preparations may reduce drug absorption.

Driving a Vehicle, Piloting a Plane, Operating Machinery: No restrictions.

Exposure to Sun: Avoid as much as possible. Photosensitivity (see Glossary) is common with some tetracyclines.

Special Storage Instructions
Keep in a tightly closed, light-resistant container.

CHLORTHALIDONE

Year Introduced: 1960

Brand Names

USA
Hygroton (USV
    Pharmaceutical)
Regroton [CD] (USV
    Pharmaceutical)

Canada
Hygroton (Geigy)
Uridon (ICN)
Novothalidone
    (Novopharm)

Drug Family: Anti-hypertensive (Hypotensive); Diuretic

Prescription Required: Yes

Available Dosage Forms and Strengths
Tablets—50 mg., 100 mg.

How This Drug Works

Intended Therapeutic Effect(s)
- elimination of excessive fluid retention (edema).
- reduction of high blood pressure.

Location of Drug Action(s):   Principal actions occur in:
- the tubular systems of the kidney that determine the final composition of the urine.
- the walls of the smaller arteries.

Method of Drug Action(s)

By increasing the elimination of salt and water from the body (through increased urine production), this drug reduces the volume of fluid in the blood and body tissues and lowers the sodium content throughout the body.

By relaxing the walls of the smaller arteries and allowing them to expand, this drug significantly increases the total capacity of the arterial system. The combined effect of these two actions (reduced blood volume in expanded space) results in lowering of the blood pressure.

THIS DRUG SHOULD NOT BE TAKEN IF

—you have had an allergic reaction to any dosage form of it previously.

INFORM YOUR PHYSICIAN BEFORE TAKING THIS DRUG IF

—you are allergic to any form of "sulfa" drug.

—you are pregnant and your physician does not know it.

—you have a history of kidney disease or liver disease, or impaired kidney or liver function.

—you have diabetes (or a tendency to diabetes).

—you have a history of gout.

—you have a history of lupus erythematosus.

—you are taking any form of cortisone, digitalis, oral anti-diabetic drugs, or insulin.

—you plan to have surgery under general anesthesia in the near future.

Time Required for Apparent Benefit

Increased urine volume begins in 2 hours, reaches a maximum in 6 to 18 hours, and gradually subsides within 48 to 72 hours. Continuous use on a regular schedule will be necessary for 2 to 3 weeks to determine this drug's effectiveness in lowering your blood pressure.

Possible Side-Effects *(natural, expected, and unavoidable drug actions)*

Lightheadedness on arising from sitting or lying position (see orthostatic hypotension in Glossary).

Increase in the level of blood sugar, affecting control of diabetes.

Increase in the level of blood uric acid, affecting control of gout.

Decrease in the level of blood potassium, resulting in muscle weakness and cramping.

CAUTION
The elderly (over 60 years of age) are frequently quite sensitive to the effects of standard doses. It is advisable to use this drug with caution until extent and duration of response have been determined.

Possible Adverse Effects *(unusual, unexpected, and infrequent reactions)*

IF ANY OF THE FOLLOWING DEVELOP, DISCONTINUE DRUG AND NOTIFY YOUR PHYSICIAN AS SOON AS POSSIBLE

Mild Adverse Effects
Allergic Reactions: Skin rash (various kinds), hives, drug fever.
Reduced appetite, indigestion, nausea, vomiting, diarrhea.
Headache, dizziness, yellow vision, blurred vision.

Serious Adverse Effects
Allergic Reactions: Hepatitis with jaundice (see Glossary), anaphylactic reaction (see Glossary), severe skin reactions.
Inflammation of the pancreas—severe abdominal pain.
Bone marrow depression (see Glossary)—fatigue, weakness, fever, sore throat, unusual bleeding or bruising.

Advisability of Use During Pregnancy
This drug should not be used during pregnancy unless a very serious complication of pregnancy occurs for which this drug is significantly beneficial. This type of diuretic can have adverse effects on the fetus. Prudent use is best determined by the physician's evaluation.

Advisability of Use While Nursing Infant
This drug is known to be present in milk. Ask physician for guidance.

Habit-Forming Potential
None.

Effects of Overdosage
With Moderate Overdose: Dryness of mouth, thirst, lethargy, weakness, muscle pain and cramping, nausea, vomiting.
With Large Overdose: Drowsiness progressing to stupor and coma, weak and rapid pulse.

Possible Effects of Extended Use
Impaired balance of water, salt, and potassium in blood and body tissues.
Development of diabetes (in predisposed individuals).

Recommended Periodic Examinations While Taking This Drug
Complete blood cell counts.
Measurements of blood levels of sodium, potassium, chloride, sugar, and uric acid.
Liver function tests.
Kidney function tests.

While Taking This Drug, Observe the Following

Foods: It is recommended that you include in your daily diet liberal servings of foods rich in potassium (unless directed otherwise by your physician). The following foods have a high potassium content

All-bran cereals	Fish, fresh
Almonds	Lentils
Apricots (dried)	Liver, beef
Bananas, fresh	Lonalac
Beans (navy and lima)	Milk
Beef	Peaches
Carrots (raw)	Peanut butter
Chicken	Peas
Citrus fruits	Pork
Coconut	Potato Chips
Coffee	Prunes (dried)
Crackers (rye)	Raisins
Dates and figs (dried)	Tomato Juice

Note: Avoid licorice in large amounts while taking this drug. Follow your physician's instructions regarding the use of salt.

Beverages: No restrictions unless directed by your physician.

Alcohol: Use with caution until the combined effect has been determined. Alcohol can exaggerate the blood pressure-lowering effect of this drug and cause orthostatic hypotension

Tobacco Smoking: No interactions expected with this drug. Follow your physician's advise regarding smoking.

Other Drugs

Chlorthalidone may *increase* the effects of

- other anti-hypertensive drugs. Careful adjustment of dosages is necessary to prevent excessive lowering of the blood pressure.
- drugs of the phenothiazine family, and cause excessive lowering of the blood pressure. (The thiazides and related drugs and the phenothiazines may both cause orthostatic hypotension).

Chlorthalidone may *decrease* the effects of

- oral anti-diabetic drugs and insulin, by raising the level of blood sugar. Careful dosage adjustment is necessary to maintain proper control of diabetes.
- allopurinol (Zyloprim), by raising the level of blood uric acid. Careful dosage adjustment is required to maintain proper control of gout.
- probenecid (Benemid), by raising the level of blood uric acid. Careful dosage adjustments are necessary to maintain control of gout.

Chlorthalidone *taken concurrently* with

- cortisone and cortisone-related drugs, may cause excessive loss of potassium from the body.
- digitalis and related drugs, requires very careful monitoring and dosage adjustments to prevent serious disturbances of heart rhythm.

• tricyclic antidepressants (Elavil, Sinequan, etc.), may cause excessive lowering of the blood pressure.

The following drugs may *increase* the effects of chlorthalidone
• barbiturates may exaggerate its blood pressure-lowering action.
• mono-amine oxidase (MAO) inhibitor drugs (see Drug Family, Section Four) may increase urine volume by delaying this drug's elimination from the body.
• pain relievers (analgesics), both narcotic and non-narcotic, may exaggerate its blood pressure-lowering action.

The following drugs may *decrease* the effects of chlorthalidone
• cholestyramine (Cuemid, Questran) may interfere with its absorption. Take cholestyramine 30 to 60 minutes before any oral diuretic.

Driving a Vehicle, Piloting a Plane, Operating Machinery: Use caution until the possibility of orthostatic hypotension (lightheadedness, dizziness, incoordination) has been determined.

Exposure to Sun: Use caution until sensitivity has been determined. This drug can cause photosensitivity (see Glossary).

Exposure to Heat: Avoid excessive perspiring which could cause additional loss of water and salt from the body.

Heavy Exercise or Exertion: Avoid exertion that produces lightheadedness, excessive fatigue, or muscle cramping.

Occurrence of Unrelated Illness: Illnesses which cause vomiting or diarrhea can produce a serious imbalance of important body chemistry. Discontinue this drug and ask your physician for guidance.

Discontinuation: It may be advisable to discontinue this drug approximately 5 to 7 days before major surgery. Ask your physician, surgeon, and/or anesthesiologist for guidance regarding dosage reduction or withdrawal.

Special Storage Instructions
Keep in a dry, tightly closed container.

CHLORZOXAZONE
Year Introduced: 1958

Brand Names

USA	Canada
Paraflex (McNeil)	Parafon Forte [CD]
Parafon Forte [CD]	(McNeil)
(McNeil)	

Drug Family: Muscle Relaxant

Prescription Required: Yes

Available Dosage Forms and Strengths
Tablets—250 mg.

How This Drug Works
Intended Therapeutic Effect(s):   Relief of discomfort resulting from spasm of voluntary muscles.

Location of Drug Action(s):   Not completely established. This drug is thought to act on those nerve pathways in the brain and spinal cord that are involved in the reflex activity of voluntary muscles.

Method of Drug Action(s):   Not completely established. It is thought that this drug may relieve muscle spasm and pain by blocking the transmission of nerve impulses over reflex pathways and/or by producing a sedative effect that decreases the perception of pain.

THIS DRUG SHOULD NOT BE TAKEN IF
—you have had an allergic reaction to any dosage form of it previously.

INFORM YOUR PHYSICIAN BEFORE TAKING THIS DRUG IF
—you have experienced any unfavorable reactions to muscle relaxant drugs in the past.
—you have a history of liver disease or impaired liver function.

Time Required for Apparent Benefit
Drug action begins in 1 hour, reaches a maximal effect in 3 to 4 hours, and subsides in 5 to 6 hours.

Possible Side-Effects *(natural, expected, and unavoidable drug actions)*
Drowsiness, orange or red-purple discoloration of the urine (of no significance).

Possible Adverse Effects *(unusual, unexpected, and infrequent reactions)*

IF ANY OF THE FOLLOWING DEVELOP, DISCONTINUE DRUG AND NOTIFY YOUR PHYSICIAN AS SOON AS POSSIBLE

Mild Adverse Effects
  Allergic Reactions: Skin rash, hives, itching.
  Lightheadedness, dizziness, lethargy.
  Nausea, indigestion, heartburn.
Serious Adverse Effects
  Allergic Reactions: Spontaneous bruising of skin (not due to injury).
  Idiosyncratic Reactions: Overstimulation, disorientation, amnesia.
  Bleeding from the stomach or intestine—black or dark colored stools.
  Hepatitis with or without jaundice (see Glossary)—yellow eyes and skin, dark colored urine, light colored stools.

Advisability of Use During Pregnancy
Safety not established. Prudent use is best determined by the physician's evaluation.

Advisability of Use While Nursing Infant
This drug is known to be present in milk. Safety for infant not established. Ask physician for guidance.

Habit-Forming Potential
None.

Effects of Overdosage
With Moderate Overdose: Nausea, vomiting, diarrhea, drowsiness, dizziness, headache, sluggishness.
With Large Overdose: Marked weakness, sense of paralysis of arms and legs, rapid and irregular breathing.

Possible Effects of Extended Use
None reported.

Recommended Periodic Examinations While Taking This Drug
Liver function tests.

While Taking This Drug, Observe the Following
Foods: No restrictions.
Beverages: No restrictions.
Alcohol: Use with caution until the combined effect has been determined. This drug may add to the depressant action of alcohol on the brain.
Tobacco Smoking: No interactions expected.
Other Drugs
   The following drugs may *decrease* the effects of chlorzoxazone:
   • testosterone is reported to reduce its ability to relax muscles in spasm.
Driving a Vehicle, Piloting a Plane, Operating Machinery: This drug may cause drowsiness, lightheadedness, or dizziness in susceptible individuals. Avoid hazardous activities if these drug effects occur.
Exposure to Sun: No restrictions.

Special Storage Instructions
Keep in a dry, tightly closed container. Protect from light.

CLIDINIUM

Year Introduced: 1961

Brand Names

USA	Canada
Librax [CD] (Roche)	Librax [CD] (Roche)

Drug Family: Antispasmodic, Atropine-like Drug [Anticholinergics]

Prescription Required: Yes

Available Dosage Forms and Strengths
Capsules — 2.5 mg. (+ 5 mg. chlordiazepoxide)
(Note: In the United States and Canada this drug is available only in combination with chlordiazepoxide. To be fully informed on the use of Librax, read Drug Profiles of both components.)

How This Drug Works
Intended Therapeutic Effect(s):   Relief of discomfort resulting from excessive activity and spasm of the digestive tract (esophagus, stomach, intestine, and colon).

Location of Drug Action(s):   The terminal nerve fibers of the parasympathetic nervous system that control the activity of the gastrointestinal tract.

Method of Drug Action(s):   By blocking the action of the chemical (acetylcholine) that transmits impulses at parasympathetic nerve endings, this drug prevents stimulation of muscular contraction and glandular secretion within the organs involved. This results in reduced overall activity, including the prevention or relief of muscle spasms.

THIS DRUG SHOULD NOT BE TAKEN IF
—you have had an allergic reaction to any dosage form of it previously.
—your stomach cannot empty properly into the intestine (pyloric obstruction).
—you are unable to empty the urinary bladder completely.
—you have glaucoma (narrow-angle type).
—you have severe ulcerative colitis.

INFORM YOUR PHYSICIAN BEFORE TAKING THIS DRUG IF
—you have glaucoma (open-angle type).
—you have angina or coronary heart disease.
—you have chronic bronchitis.
—you have a hiatal hernia.
—you have enlargement of the prostate gland.
—you have myasthenia gravis.
—you have a history of peptic ulcer disease.
—you plan to have surgery under general anesthesia in the near future.

Time Required for Apparent Benefit
Drug action begins in 1 to 2 hours and persists for approximately 4 hours.

Possible Side-Effects *(natural, expected, and unavoidable drug actions)*
Blurring of vision (impairment of focus), dryness of the mouth and throat, constipation, hesitancy in urination. (Nature and degree of side effects depend upon individual susceptibility and drug dosage.)

CAUTION
The elderly (over 60 years of age) are often more sensitive to the actions of this drug. Small doses are advisable until tolerance has been determined.

Possible Adverse Effects *(unusual, unexpected, and infrequent reactions)*

IF ANY OF THE FOLLOWING DEVELOP, DISCONTINUE DRUG AND NOTIFY
YOUR PHYSICIAN AS SOON AS POSSIBLE

Mild Adverse Effects

Allergic Reactions: Skin rash, hives.

Dilation of pupils, causing sensitivity to light.

Flushing and dryness of the skin (reduced sweating).

Rapid heart action.

Lightheadedness, dizziness, unsteady gait.

Serious Adverse Effects

Idiosyncratic Reactions: Acute confusion, delirium, and behavioral abnormalities.

Development of acute glaucoma (in susceptible individuals).

Advisability of Use During Pregnancy

Safety not established. Avoid use completely. (See CHLORDIAZEPOXIDE Drug Profile.)

Advisability of Use While Nursing Infant

Drug is known to be present in milk. Ask physician for guidance.

Habit-Forming Potential

For clidinium, none (see CHLORDIAZEPOXIDE Drug Profile).

Effects of Overdosage

With Moderate Overdose: Marked dryness of the mouth, dilated pupils, blurring of near vision, rapid pulse, heart palpitation, headache, difficulty in urination.

With Large Overdose: Extremely dilated pupils, rapid pulse and breathing, hot skin, high fever, excitement, confusion, hallucinations, delirium, eventual loss of consciousness, convulsions, and coma.

Possible Effects of Extended Use

Chronic constipation, severe enough to result in fecal impaction. (Constipation should be treated promptly with effective laxatives.)

Recommended Periodic Examinations While Taking This Drug

Measurement of internal eye pressure to detect any significant increase that might indicate developing glaucoma.

While Taking This Drug, Observe the Following

Foods: No interaction with drug. Effectiveness is greater if drug is taken one-half to 1 hour before eating. Follow diet prescribed for condition under treatment.

Beverages: No interactions. As allowed by prescribed diet.

Alcohol: No interactions expected with this drug (see CHLORDIAZEPOXIDE Drug Profile).

Tobacco Smoking: No interactions expected with clidinium (see CHLORDIAZEPOXIDE Drug Profile).

Other Drugs

Clidinium may *increase* the effects of

- all other drugs having atropine-like actions (see Drug Family, Section Four).

Clidinium may *decrease* the effects of

- pilocarpine eye drops, and reduce their effectiveness in lowering internal eye pressure (in the treatment of glaucoma).

Clidinium *taken concurrently* with

- mono-amine oxidase (MAO) inhibitor drugs, may cause an exaggerated response to normal doses of atropine-like drugs. It is best to avoid atropine-like drugs for 2 weeks after the last dose of any MAO inhibitor drug (see Drug Family, Section Four).
- haloperidol (Haldol), may significantly increase internal eye pressure (dangerous in glaucoma).

The following drugs may *increase* the effects of clidinium:

- tricyclic antidepressants (see Drug Family, Section Four)
- those antihistamines that have an atropine-like action
- meperidine (Demerol, pethidine)
- methylphenidate (Ritalin)
- orphenadrine (Disipal, Norflex)
- those phenothiazines that have an atropine-like action (see Drug Family, Section Four)

The following drugs may *decrease* the effects of clidinium:

- Vitamin C reduces its effectiveness by hastening its elimination from the body. Avoid large doses of Vitamin C during treatment with this drug.

Driving a Vehicle, Piloting a Plane, Operating Machinery: This drug may produce blurred vision, drowsiness, or dizziness. Avoid hazardous activities if these drug effects occur.

Exposure to Sun: No restrictions.

Exposure to Heat: Use extreme caution. The use of this drug in hot environments may significantly increase the risk of heat stroke.

Heavy Exercise or Exertion: Use caution in warm or hot environments. This drug may impair normal perspiration (heat loss) and interfere with the regulation of body temperature.

Special Storage Instructions
Keep in a tightly closed container. Protect from light.

CLINDAMYCIN

Year Introduced: 1973

Brand Names

USA	Canada
Cleocin (Upjohn)	Dalacin C (Upjohn)

Drug Family: Antibiotic (Anti-infective)

Prescription Required: Yes

Available Dosage Forms and Strengths
Capsules — 75 mg., 150 mg.
Oral Solution — 75 mg. per teaspoonful

How This Drug Works
Intended Therapeutic Effect(s):   The elimination of infections responsive to the action of this drug.
Location of Drug Action(s):   Any body tissue or fluid in which sufficient concentration of the drug can be achieved.
Method of Drug Action(s):   This drug prevents the growth and multiplication of susceptible bacteria by interfering with their formation of essential proteins.

THIS DRUG SHOULD NOT BE TAKEN IF
—you are allergic to lincomycin or clindamycin.
—it is prescribed for a mild or trivial infection such as a cold, sore throat, or "flu"-like illness.
—you have a history of ulcerative colitis.
—it is prescribed for an infant under 1 month of age.

INFORM YOUR PHYSICIAN BEFORE TAKING THIS DRUG IF
—you have a history of allergy to any drug.
—you are allergic by nature (hayfever, asthma, hives, eczema).
—you have a history of previous yeast infections.
—you have liver or kidney disease or impaired liver or kidney function.
—you plan to have surgery under general anesthesia in the near future.

Time Required for Apparent Benefit
Varies with nature of infection under treatment; usually 2 to 5 days.

Possible Side-Effects *(natural, expected, and unavoidable drug actions)*
Superinfections (see Glossary).

Possible Adverse Effects *(unusual, unexpected, and infrequent reactions)*

IF ANY OF THE FOLLOWING DEVELOP, DISCONTINUE DRUG AND NOTIFY YOUR PHYSICIAN AS SOON AS POSSIBLE

Mild Adverse Effects
Allergic Reactions: Skin rash (various kinds), hives.
Nausea, vomiting, diarrhea, abdominal pain.

Serious Adverse Effects
Allergic Reactions: Painful, swollen joints, jaundice (see Glossary).
†*Severe colitis with persistent diarrhea;* stools may contain blood and/or mucus.

Advisability of Use During Pregnancy
Safety not established. Prudent use is best determined by the physician's evaluation.

Advisability of Use While Nursing Infant
Drug can be present in milk. Safety for infant not established. Ask physician for guidance.

Habit-Forming Potential
None.

Effects of Overdosage
Nausea, vomiting, cramping, diarrhea.

Possible Effects of Extended Use
†*Severe colitis with persistent diarrhea.*
Superinfections (see Glossary), expecially from yeast organisms.

Recommended Periodic Examinations While Taking This Drug
Complete blood cell counts.
Liver function tests.

While Taking This Drug, Observe the Following
Foods: No restrictions of food selection. Drug may be taken at any time with relationship to eating.
Beverages: No restrictions.
Alcohol: No interactions expected.
Tobacco Smoking: No interactions expected.
Other Drugs
   The following drugs may *decrease* the effects of clindamycin:
   • anti-diarrheal preparations
   • erythromycin
Driving a Vehicle, Piloting a Plane, Operating Machinery: No restrictions.
Exposure to Sun: Use caution until sensitivity is determined.
Discontinuation: When used to treat infections that predispose to rheumatic fever or kidney disease (nephritis), take continuously in full dosage for no less than 10 days. Ask physician for guidance regarding the recommended duration of therapy.

Special Storage Instructions
Capsules should be kept in a dry, tightly closed container.
Oral solution should be kept at room temperature; do *not* refrigerate.

Do Not Take the Oral Solution of This Drug If It Is Older Than
14 days.

†An infrequent but potentially dangerous reaction characteristic of this drug.

CLOFIBRATE

Year Introduced: 1967

Brand Names

USA	Canada
Atromid-S (Ayerst)	Atromid-S (Ayerst)

Drug Family: Cholesterol Reducer (Antihyperlipemic)

Prescription Required: Yes

Available Dosage Forms and Strengths
Capsules — 500 mg.

How This Drug Works
Intended Therapeutic Effect(s):   Reduction of high blood levels of cholesterol and/or triglycerides.
Location of Drug Action(s):   Not completely established. Thought to be those liver cells responsible for the production of cholesterol.
Method of Drug Action(s):   Not completely established. It is thought that this drug may reduce blood levels of cholesterol and triglycerides by inhibiting their production and hastening their removal from the blood.

THIS DRUG SHOULD NOT BE TAKEN IF
—you have had an allergic reaction to any dosage form of it previously.
—you have impaired function of the liver or kidneys.

INFORM YOUR PHYSICIAN BEFORE TAKING THIS DRUG IF
—you are taking any anticoagulant drug.
—you have a history of liver disease or jaundice.
—you have a history of peptic ulcer.
—you have diabetes.

Time Required for Apparent Benefit
Continuous use for 2 to 3 months may be needed to determine the extent of this drug's ability to lower blood levels of either cholesterol or triglycerides.

Possible Side-Effects *(natural, expected, and unavoidable drug actions)*
Gain in weight occurs frequently.

Possible Adverse Effects *(unusual, unexpected, and infrequent reactions)*
IF ANY OF THE FOLLOWING DEVELOP, DISCONTINUE DRUG AND NOTIFY YOUR PHYSICIAN AS SOON AS POSSIBLE
Mild Adverse Effects
Allergic Reactions: Skin rash, hives, itching, loss of scalp hair.
Nausea, vomiting, indigestion, diarrhea.
Headache, dizziness, fatigue, drowsiness.
"Flu"-like muscle and joint aching and cramping.
Impairment of sexual function.
Serious Adverse Effects
Allergic Reactions: Kidney tissue injury (rare).

Liver damage (without jaundice).
Abnormally low red blood cells (anemia) and white blood cells.

Advisability of Use During Pregnancy
Safety not established. Prudent use is best determined by the physician's evaluation.

Advisability of Use While Nursing Infant
Safety for infant not established. Ask physician for guidance.

Habit-Forming Potential
None.

Effects of Overdosage
With Moderate Overdose: Nausea, vomiting, abdominal distress, diarrhea.
With Large Overdose: Headache, muscular pain, weakness.

Possible Effects of Extended Use
None reported.

Recommended Periodic Examinations While Taking This Drug
Complete blood cell counts.
Liver function tests.

While Taking This Drug, Observe the Following
Foods: Follow the low animal fat and/or low carbohydrate diet prescribed by your physician.
Beverages: No restrictions.
Alcohol: No interactions expected; follow diet prescribed.
Tobacco Smoking: No interactions expected; follow physician's advice regarding smoking.
Other Drugs
Clofibrate may *increase* the effects of
• oral anticoagulants of the coumarin family (see Drug Family, Section Four). The usual dose of the anticoagulant must be reduced by one-third or one-half to prevent abnormal bleeding or hemorrhage. Consult physician regarding prothrombin time testing and dosage adjustment.
• oral anti-diabetics of the sulfonylurea family (see Drug Family, Section Four). Dosage adjustments may be necessary to prevent hypoglycemia (see Glossary) and to establish correct control of diabetes.
• insulin preparations, which may also require dosage adjustments to prevent hypoglycemia.

The following drugs may *increase* the effects of clofibrate
• thyroid preparations may enhance the lowering of blood cholesterol.

The following drugs may *decrease* the effects of clofibrate
• oral contraceptives may prevent the lowering of blood cholesterol or triglycerides.
• estrogens (Premarin, etc.) may prevent the lowering of cholesterol.

Driving a Vehicle, Piloting a Plane, Operating Machinery: Usually no restrictions, but be alert to the possible occurrence of drowsiness or dizziness. Avoid hazardous activities if these occur.

Exposure to Sun: No restrictions.

Discontinuation: This drug should be discontinued after 3 months if significant lowering of the blood cholesterol and/or triglycerides has not occurred. Withdrawal should be gradual, not sudden. Ask physician for guidance.

Special Storage Instructions
Keep in a dry, tightly closed container. Protect from light.

CLONIDINE

Year Introduced: 1966 (Europe)

Brand Names

USA	Canada
Catapres (Boehringer Ingelheim)	Catapres (Boehringer)
Combipres [CD] (Boehringer Ingelheim)	Combipres [CD] (Boehringer)

Drug Family: Anti-hypertensive (Hypotensive)

Prescription Required: Yes

Available Dosage Forms and Strengths
Tablets — 0.1 mg., 0.2 mg.

How This Drug Works
Intended Therapeutic Effect(s):   Reduction of high blood pressure.

Location of Drug Action(s):   The vasomotor center in the brain that influences the control of the sympathetic nervous system over blood vessels (principally arterioles) throughout the body.

Method of Drug Action(s):   By decreasing the activity of the vasomotor center, this drug reduces the ability of the sympathetic nervous system to maintain the degree of blood vessel constriction responsible for elevation of the blood pressure. This change results in relaxation of blood vessel walls and lowering of the blood pressure.

THIS DRUG SHOULD NOT BE TAKEN IF
—you have had an allergic reaction to any dosage form of it previously.
—it is prescribed for a child under 12 years of age.

INFORM YOUR PHYSICIAN BEFORE TAKING THIS DRUG IF
—you have a history of heart or circulatory disease (angina, heart attack, stroke).
—you plan to have surgery under general anesthesia in the near future.

Time Required for Apparent Benefit
Blood pressure is lowered within 1 to 4 hours. Drug action subsides in 6 to 8 hours.

Possible Side-Effects *(natural, expected, and unavoidable drug actions)*
Drowsiness, dryness of the nose and mouth, constipation, lightheadedness on arising from a sitting or lying position (see orthostatic hypotension in Glossary).

CAUTION
Do not discontinue this drug suddenly. Be sure to keep an adequate supply on hand. Sudden withdrawal can produce a severe and possibly fatal reaction. Include notation of the use of this drug on your card of personal identification (see Table 14 and Section Seven).

Possible Adverse Effects *(unusual, unexpected, and infrequent reactions)*
IF ANY OF THE FOLLOWING DEVELOP, NOTIFY YOUR PHYSICIAN AS SOON AS POSSIBLE

Mild Adverse Effects
Allergic Reactions: Skin rash, hives, localized swellings, itching.
Dizziness, depression, insomnia, nightmares.
Nausea, vomiting.
Dryness and burning of the eyes. Breast enlargement.
Serious Adverse Effects
None reported.

Advisability of Use During Pregnancy
Safety not established. Prudent use is best determined by physician's evaluation.

Advisability of Use While Nursing Infant
Presence of drug in milk is not known. Ask physician for guidance.

Habit-Forming Potential
None.

Effects of Overdosage
With Moderate Overdose: Marked drowsiness, weakness, slow and weak pulse.
With Large Overdose: Deep sleep, lowered body temperature.

Possible Effects of Extended Use
Weight gain due to salt and water retention.
Temporary sexual impotence.

Recommended Periodic Examinations While Taking This Drug
Monitoring of weight to detect possible water retention.
Eye examinations for changes in retina or impairment of vision.

While Taking This Drug, Observe the Following
Foods: Follow prescribed diet. Ask physician for guidance regarding use of salt.

Beverages: No restrictions.

Alcohol: Use with extreme caution until combined effect has been determined. This combination can cause marked drowsiness and exaggerated reduction of blood pressure.

Tobacco Smoking: No interactions expected with this drug. Follow your physician's advice regarding smoking.

Other Drugs

Clonidine may *increase* the effects of

- sedatives, sleep-inducing drugs, tranquilizers, antihistamines, pain relievers, and narcotic drugs, and cause oversedation.
- thiazide diuretics and other anti-hypertensive drugs, and cause exaggerated lowering of the blood pressure. Careful dosage adjustments are necessary.

The following drugs may *decrease* the effects of clonidine

- tricyclic antidepressants (Elavil, Tofranil, Sinequan, etc.) may interfere with its blood pressure-lowering action. Dosage adjustments may be necessary.

Driving a Vehicle, Piloting a Plane, Operating Machinery: This drug can cause drowsiness and orthostatic hypotension (see Glossary). Avoid hazardous activities until its effect on mental alertness, judgment, and coordination have been determined.

Exposure to Sun: No restrictions.

Exposure to Heat: No restrictions.

Exposure to Cold: Use caution until combined effect has been determined. This drug may cause painful blanching and numbness of the hands and feet on exposure to cold air or water.

Heavy Exercise or Exertion: Use caution. Ask physician for guidance.

Occurrence of Unrelated Illness: If an illness causes vomiting and prevents the intake of this drug on a regular basis, notify your physician as soon as possible.

Discontinuation: Do not discontinue this drug suddenly. A severe withdrawal reaction can occur within 12 to 48 hours. If drug is to be discontinued for any reason, ask your physician for guidance regarding dosage reduction and gradual withdrawal.

Special Storage Instructions

Keep in a dry, tightly closed container.

CLORAZEPATE

Year Introduced: 1972

Brand Names

USA	Canada
Tranxene (Abbott)	Tranxene (Abbott)

Drug Family: Tranquilizer, Mild (Anti-anxiety) [Benzodiazepines]

Prescription Required: Yes (Controlled Drug, U.S. Schedule 4)

Available Dosage Forms and Strengths
Capsules—3.75 mg., 7.5 mg., 15 mg.

How This Drug Works

Intended Therapeutic Effect(s): Relief of mild to moderate anxiety and nervous tension, without significant sedation.

Location of Drug Action(s): Thought to be the limbic system of the brain, one of the centers that influence emotional stability.

Method of Drug Action(s): Not established. Present thinking is that this drug may reduce the activity of certain parts of the limbic system.

THIS DRUG SHOULD NOT BE TAKEN IF

—you have had an allergic reaction to any dosage form of it previously.
—you have glaucoma (narrow-angle type).
—you have myasthenia gravis.
—it is prescribed for an infant under 6 months of age.

INFORM YOUR PHYSICIAN BEFORE TAKING THIS DRUG IF

—you are allergic to any drugs chemically related to clorazepate: chlordiazepoxide, diazepam, flurazepam, oxazepam (see Drug Profiles for brand names).
—you have epilepsy.
—you have glaucoma (open-angle type).
—you are taking sedative, sleep-inducing, tranquilizer, antidepressant, or anticonvulsant drugs of any kind.
—you plan to have surgery under general anesthesia in the near future.

Time Required For apparent Benefit

Approximately 1 to 2 hours. For severe symptoms of some duration, relief may require regular medication for several days.

Possible Side-Effects *(natural, expected, and unavoidable drug actions)*

Drowsiness, lethargy, unsteadiness in stance and gait.

In the elderly (over 60 years of age) and debilitated: confusion, weakness, loss of bladder control, constipation. (The elderly are very susceptible to standard doses.)

Possible Adverse Effects *(unusual, unexpected, and infrequent reactions)*

IF ANY OF THE FOLLOWING DEVELOP, DISCONTINUE DRUG AND NOTIFY
YOUR PHYSICIAN AS SOON AS POSSIBLE

Mild Adverse Effects
Allergic Reactions: Skin rashes (various kinds).
Dizziness, fainting, blurred vision, double vision, slurred speech, nausea,
    menstrual irregularity.
Serious Adverse Effects
Allergic Reactions: Jaundice (see Glossary), fever, sore throat.
Eye pain (possibly glaucoma), depression.
Paradoxical Reactions: Acute excitement, hallucinations, rage.

Advisability of Use During Pregnancy
The findings of some recent studies suggest a possible association between the
use of a drug closely related to clorazepate during early pregnancy and the
occurrence of birth defects, such as cleft lip. It is advisable to avoid this drug
completely during the first 3 months of pregnancy.

Advisability of Use While Nursing Infant
With recommended dosage, drug is present in milk. Avoid use if possible. Ask
physician for guidance.

Habit-Forming Potential
This drug can cause psychological and/or physical dependence (see Glossary)
if used in large doses for an extended period of time.

Effects of Overdosage
With Moderate Overdose: Marked drowsiness, weakness, drunkenness, im-
    pairment of stance and gait.
With Large Overdose: Stupor progressing to deep sleep and coma.

Possible Effects of Extended Use
Psychological and/or physical dependence.
Impairment of blood cell production.
Impairment of liver function.

Recommended Periodic Examinations While Taking This Drug
Blood cell counts and liver function tests during long-term use.

While Taking This Drug, Observe the Following
Foods: No restrictions.
Beverages: Large intake of coffee, tea, or cola drinks (because of their caf-
    feine content) may reduce the calming action of this drug.
Alcohol: Use with extreme caution until the combined effect is determined.
    Alcohol may increase the sedative effects of clorazepate. Clorazepate may
    increase the intoxicating effects of alcohol.
Tobacco Smoking: Heavy smoking may reduce the calming action of clo-
    razepate.

Other Drugs

Clorazepate may *increase* the effects of

- other sedatives, sleep-inducing drugs, tranquilizers, anti-convulsants, and narcotic drugs. Use these only under supervision of a physician. Careful dosage adjustments are necessary.
- oral anticoagulants of the coumarin family (see Drug Family, Section Four). Ask physician for guidance regarding need for dosage adjustments to prevent bleeding.
- anti-hypertensives, producing excessive lowering of the blood pressure.

Clorazepate *taken concurrently* with

- anti-convulsants, may cause an increase in the frequency or severity of seizures; an increase in the dose of the anti-convulsant may be necessary.
- mono-amine oxidase (MAO) inhibitor drugs (see Drug Family, Section Four), may cause extreme sedation, convulsions, or paradoxical excitement or rage.

The following drugs may *increase* the effects of clorazepate

- tricyclic antidepressants (see Drug Family, Section Four) may increase the sedative effects of clorazepate.

Driving a Vehicle, Piloting a Plane, Operating Machinery: This drug can impair mental alertness, judgment, physical coordination, and reaction time. Avoid hazardous activities.

Exposure to Sun: No restrictions.

Exposure to Heat: Use caution until effect of excessive perspiration is determined. Because of reduced urine volume, clorazepate may accumulate in the body and produce effects of overdosage.

Heavy Exercise or Exertion: No restrictions in cool or temperate weather.

Discontinuation: If it has been necessary to use this drug for an extended period of time, ask physician for guidance regarding dosage reduction and withdrawal. The dosage of other drugs taken concurrently with clorazepate may also require adjustment.

Special Storage Instructions

Keep in a dry, tightly closed, light-resistant container.

CLOXACILLIN

Year Introduced: 1962

Brand Names

USA	Canada
Tegopen (Bristol)	Orbenin (Ayerst)
	Tegopen (Will)

Drug Family: Antibiotic (Anti-infective) [Penicillins]

Prescription Required: Yes

Available Dosage Forms and Strengths
Capsules — 250 mg., 500 mg.
Oral Solution — 125 mg. per teaspoonful

How This Drug Works
Intended Therapeutic Effect(s):   The elimination of infections responsive to the action of this drug.

Location of Drug Action(s):   Any body tissue or fluid in which sufficient concentration of the drug can be achieved.

Method of Drug Action(s):   This drug destroys susceptible infecting bacteria by interfering with their ability to produce new protective cell walls as they multiply and grow.

THIS DRUG SHOULD NOT BE TAKEN IF
—you have had an allergic reaction to any dosage form of it previously.
—you are certain you are allergic to any form of penicillin.

INFORM YOUR PHYSICIAN BEFORE TAKING THIS DRUG IF
—you suspect you may be allergic to penicillin or you have a history of a previous "reaction" to penicillin.
—you are allergic to cephalosporin antibiotics (Ancef, Ceporan, Ceporex, Kafocin, Keflex, Keflin, Kefzol, Loridine).
—you are allergic by nature (hayfever, asthma, hives, eczema).

Time Required for Apparent Benefit
Varies with the nature of the infection under treatment; usually from 2 to 5 days.

Possible Side-Effects *(natural, expected, and unavoidable drug actions)*
Superinfections (see Glossary).

Possible Adverse Effects *(unusual, unexpected, and infrequent reactions)*

IF ANY OF THE FOLLOWING DEVELOP, DISCONTINUE DRUG AND NOTIFY YOUR PHYSICIAN AS SOON AS POSSIBLE

Mild Adverse Effects
Allergic Reactions: Skin rashes (various kinds).
Irritation of mouth or tongue, "black tongue," nausea, vomiting, diarrhea, gaseous indigestion.

Serious Adverse Effects
Allergic Reactions: †Anaphylactic reaction (see Glossary), severe skin reactions, high fever, swollen painful joints, sore throat, unusual bleeding or bruising.

Advisability of Use During Pregnancy
Safety not established. Prudent use is best determined by the physician's evaluation.

Advisability of Use While Nursing Infant
Drug may be present in milk and may sensitize infant to penicillin. Ask physician for guidance.

---

†A rare but potentially dangerous reaction characteristic of penicillins.

Habit-Forming Potential
None.

Effects of Overdosage
Possible nausea, vomiting, and/or diarrhea.

Possible Effects of Extended Use
Superinfections (see Glossary).

Recommended Periodic Examinations While Taking This Drug
Complete blood cell counts.
Liver and kidney function tests.

While Taking This Drug, Observe the Following
Foods: No restrictions of food selection. Drug is most effective when taken on empty stomach, 1 hour before or 2 hours after eating.
Beverages: No restrictions.
Alcohol: No interactions expected.
Tobacco Smoking: No interactions expected.
Other Drugs
The following drugs may *decrease* the effects of cloxacillin
• antacids can reduce absorption of cloxacillin.
• chloramphenicol (Chloromycetin)
• erythromycin (Erythrocin, E-Mycin, etc.)
• paromomycin (Humatin)
• tetracyclines (Achromycin, Declomycin, Minocin, etc.; see Drug Family, Section Four)
• troleandomycin (Cyclamycin, TAO)
Driving a Vehicle, Piloting a Plane, Operating Machinery: No restrictions.
Exposure to Sun: No restrictions.

Special Storage Instructions
Capsules: keep in tightly closed container at room temperature.
Oral Solution: keep refrigerated.

Do Not Take the Oral Solution of This Drug If It Is Older Than
3 days—when kept at room temperature.
14 days—when kept refrigerated.

CODEINE

Year Introduced: 1886

Brand Names

USA	Canada
No brand names for codeine as a single entity drug product. Many brand names for combination drug products containing codeine.	Paveral [a codeine syrup] (Desbergers) Many brand names for combination drug products containing codeine.

Drug Family: Analgesic, Mild (Narcotic)

Prescription Required: Yes (Controlled Drug, U.S. Schedule 2)

Available Dosage Forms and Strengths
Tablets — 15 mg., 30 mg., 60 mg.
Syrup — 10 mg. per ml.
Injection — 15 mg., 30 mg., 60 mg. per ml.

How This Drug Works
Intended Therapeutic Effect(s)
• relief of moderate pain.
• control of coughing.
Location of Drug Action(s)
• those areas of the brain and spinal cord involved in the perception of pain.
• those areas of the brain and spinal cord involved in the cough reflex.
Method of Drug Action(s):   Not completely established. It is thought that this drug affects tissue sites that react specifically with opium and its derivatives to relieve pain and cough.

THIS DRUG SHOULD NOT BE TAKEN IF
—you have had an allergic reaction to any dosage form of it previously.

INFORM YOUR PHYSICIAN BEFORE TAKING THIS DRUG IF
—you are taking sedatives, other analgesics, sleep-inducing drugs, tranquilizers, antidepressants, or narcotic drugs of any kind.
—you have impaired liver or kidney function.
—you have underactive thyroid function.
—you plan to have surgery under general anesthesia in the near future.

Time Required for Apparent Benefit
Usually 15 to 30 minutes when taken orally.

Possible Side-Effects *(natural, expected, and unavoidable drug actions)*
Drowsiness, lightheadedness, constipation.

Possible Adverse Effects *(unusual, unexpected, and infrequent reactions)*

**IF ANY OF THE FOLLOWING DEVELOP, DISCONTINUE DRUG AND NOTIFY
YOUR PHYSICIAN AS SOON AS POSSIBLE**

Mild Adverse Effects
   Allergic Reactions: Skin rashes, hives, itching.
   Nausea, vomiting.
   Dizziness, sensation of drunkenness. These may be more apparent in the
      elderly (over 60 years of age), for whom reduced dosage may be neces-
      sary.
Serious Adverse Effects
   None reported.

Advisability of Use During Pregnancy
Wide use for 90 years has resulted in no reports of serious adverse effects on
the course of pregnancy, the mother, or the fetus. However, use of codeine
during pregnancy should be limited to the smallest effective dose and for
short periods of time. Ask physician for guidance.

Advisability of Use While Nursing Infant
Drug is known to be present in milk and may have a depressant effect on
infant. Ask physician for guidance.

Habit-Forming Potential
This drug can produce psychological and physical dependence (see Glossary)
when used in large doses for an extended period of time.

Effects of Overdosage
   With Moderate Overdose: Marked drowsiness, nausea, vomiting, restless-
      ness, agitation.
   With Large Overdose: Stupor progressing to deep sleep, convulsions, cold
      and clammy skin, slow and shallow breathing.

Possible Effects of Extended Use
Psychological and physical dependence.

Recommended Periodic Examinations While Taking This Drug
None.

While Taking This Drug, Observe the Following
Foods: No restrictions.
Beverages: No restrictions.
Alcohol: Use with extreme caution until combined effects have been deter-
   mined. Codeine can intensify the intoxicating effects of alcohol, and alcohol
   can intensify the depressant effects of codeine on brain function, breathing,
   and circulation.
Tobacco Smoking: No interactions expected.
Other Drugs
   Codeine may *increase* the effects of
      all sedatives, analgesics, sleep-inducing drugs, tranquilizers, antidepres-
      sants, and other narcotic drugs.

Codeine *taken concurrently* with
• chlordiazepoxide (Librium), may cause extreme sedation and coma.

The following drugs may *increase* the effects of codeine:
• aspirin increases the analgesic action of codeine.
• chloramphenical (Chloromycetin) increases the analgesic action of codeine.
• phenothiazines increase the sedative action of codeine (see Drug Family,
Section Four).
• tricyclic antidepressants increase the sedative action of codeine (see Drug
Family, Section Four).
• mono-amine oxidase (MAO) inhibitor drugs increase the sedative action
of codeine (see Drug Family, Section Four).

Driving a Vehicle, Piloting a Plane, Operating Machinery: This drug can
impair mental alertness, judgment, reaction time, and physical coordination. Avoid hazardous activities.

Exposure to Sun: No restrictions.

Discontinuation: If it has been necessary to use codeine for an extended
period of time, ask physician for guidance regarding dosage reduction and
withdrawal.

Special Storage Instructions
Keep in a dry, tightly closed, light-resistant container.

COLISTIN

Year Introduced: 1962

Brand Names

USA	Canada
Coly-Mycin S	None
(Warner/Chilcott)	

Drug Family: Antibiotic (Anti-infective) [Polymyxins]

Prescription Required: Yes

Available Dosage Forms and Strengths
Oral Suspension—25 mg. per teaspoonful (5 ml.)

How This Drug Works
Intended Therapeutic Effect(s):   The elimination of infections responsive to
the action of this drug.

Location of Drug Action(s):   Any body tissue or fluid in which sufficient
concentration of the drug can be achieved.

Method of Drug Action(s):   This drug destroys susceptible bacteria by altering the membranes of their cell walls and allowing the cell contents to leak
through.

THIS DRUG SHOULD NOT BE TAKEN IF
—you have had an allergic reaction to any dosage form of it previously.

INFORM YOUR PHYSICIAN BEFORE GIVING THIS DRUG IF
—the patient has a history of serious kidney disease or impaired kidney function.

Time Required for Apparent Benefit
Varies with nature and severity of infection; usually 2 to 4 days.

Possible Side-Effects *(natural, expected, and unavoidable drug actions)*
Superinfections (see Glossary).

Possible Adverse Effects *(unusual, unexpected, and infrequent reactions)*

IF ANY OF THE FOLLOWING DEVELOP, DISCONTINUE DRUG AND NOTIFY YOUR PHYSICIAN AS SOON AS POSSIBLE

Mild Adverse Effects
None reported at recommended doses.
Stomach pain, cramps, diarrhea reported with high doses.

Serious Adverse Effects
None reported at recommended doses and in the presence of normal kidney function.

Habit-Forming Potential
None.

Effects of Overdosage
With Moderate Overdose: Possible nausea, vomiting, abdominal pain, diarrhea.
With Large Overdose: Possible kidney damage.

Possible Effects of Extended Use
Superinfections (see Glossary).

Recommended Periodic Examinations While Taking This Drug
Urine analysis and kidney function tests.

While Taking This Drug, Observe the Following
Foods: No restrictions of food selection related to drug action. Follow prescribed diet.
Beverages: No restrictions of beverage selection related to drug action.
Alcohol: Avoid in presence of diarrhea. No interaction with drug expected.
Other Drugs: No interactions reported.
Exposure to Sun: No restrictions.
Discontinuation: Ask physician for guidance when symptoms have cleared. Avoid prolonged and unnecessary use.

Special Storage Instructions
Keep in a tightly closed, light-resistant container at a temperature between 59° and 86°F. (15° and 30°C.).

Do Not Take the Oral Suspension of This Drug If It Is Older Than
14 days.

CROMOLYN/DISODIUM CROMOGLYCATE

Year Introduced: 1968

Brand Names

USA	Canada
Aarane (Syntex)	Intal (Fisons)
Intal (Fisons)	Rynacrom (Fisons)

Drug Family: Asthma Preventive

Prescription Required: Yes

Available Dosage Forms and Strengths
Powder, Inhalation (in cartridges)—20 mg.

How This Drug Works
Intended Therapeutic Effect(s):   Prevention of acute attacks of bronchial asthma. (Of no value in relieving asthma after the attack has begun.)

Location of Drug Action(s):   The mast cells within the tissues that line the bronchial tubes.

Method of Drug Action(s):   By blocking the release of histamine that normally occurs in allergic reactions, this drug acts to prevent the sequence of tissue changes that leads to constriction of the bronchial tubes and the development of asthma.

THIS DRUG SHOULD NOT BE TAKEN IF
—you have had an allergic reaction to any dosage form of it previously.

INFORM YOUR PHYSICIAN BEFORE TAKING THIS DRUG IF
—you have not been instructed fully in the proper use and care of the inhaler which is used to administer the drug.

Time Required for Apparent Benefit
Continuous use on a regular schedule for 2 to 4 weeks is usually necessary to determine this drug's effectiveness in preventing acute attacks of asthma.

Possible Side-Effects *(natural, expected, and unavoidable drug actions)*
Mild throat irritation, hoarseness, cough. (These can be minimized by a few swallows of water after each inhalation.)

CAUTION
1. Do not swallow the cartridges. The contents are intended for inhalation into the air passages of the lungs. (If the cartridge is swallowed inadvertently, the drug will cause no ill effects. Since it is not absorbed into the blood stream, it will have no beneficial effects.)
2. Obtain complete instruction in the proper use of the specially designed inhaler.
3. Remember that this drug acts solely as a preventive; its effectiveness is limited to the pretreatment phase of asthma—before the onset of acute bronchial constriction (asthmatic wheezing).
4. This drug does *not* interfere with the actions of those drugs used to relieve asthma after it has begun.

Possible Adverse Effects *(unusual, unexpected, and infrequent reactions)*

IF ANY OF THE FOLLOWING DEVELOP, DISCONTINUE DRUG AND NOTIFY YOUR PHYSICIAN AS SOON AS POSSIBLE

Mild Adverse Effects
Allergic Reactions: Skin rash, hives.
Cough.

Serious Adverse Effects
Allergic Reactions: Allergic pneumonitis (allergic reaction of lung tissue resembling pneumonia).
Spasm of bronchial tubes resulting in acute shortness of breath.

Avisability of Use During Pregnancy
Safety not established. Ask physician for guidance.

Advisability of Use While Nursing Infant
The presence of this drug in milk is not known. Ask physician for guidance.

Habit-Forming Potential
None.

Effects of Overdosage
With Moderate Overdose: No significant effects.
With Large Overdose: No significant effects.

Possible Effects of Extended Use
Allergic reaction of lung tissue resembling pneumonia (very rare).

Recommended Periodic Examinations While Taking This Drug
Examination of the lungs by sputum and X-ray if symptoms suggest an allergic reaction of lung tissue.

While Taking This Drug, Observe the Following
Foods: Follow diet prescribed by your physician. Avoid all foods to which you may be allergic.

Beverages: Avoid all beverages to which you may be allergic.

Alcohol: No interactions expected.

Tobacco Smoking: Follow physician's advice regarding smoking.

Other Drugs: Cromolyn may make it possible to reduce the dosage of cortisone-like drugs in the management of chronic asthma. Consult your physician regarding dosage adjustment.

Driving a Vehicle, Piloting a Plane, Operating Machinery: No restrictions or precautions.

Exposure to Sun: No restrictions.

Discontinuation: If the regular use of cromolyn has made it possible to reduce or discontinue maintenance doses of cortisone-like drugs, and you find it necessary to discontinue cromolyn for any reason, observe closely for a sudden return of acute asthma. It may be necessary to resume a cortisone-like drug and to institute other measures for satisfactory management.

Special Storage Instructions

Keep in a dry, tightly closed container. Store in a cool place, but not in the refrigerator. Do not handle the cartridges or the inhaler when hands are wet.

CYCLANDELATE

Year Introduced: 1952

Brand Names

USA	Canada
Cyclospasmol (Ives)	Cyclospasmol (Wyeth)

Drug Family: Vasodilator

Prescription Required: Yes

Available Dosage Forms and Strengths

Tablets — 100 mg.
Capsules — 200 mg.

How This Drug Works

Intended Therapeutic Effect(s):   Relief of symptoms associated with
  • impaired circulation of blood in the extremities.
  • impaired circulation of blood within the brain (in carefully selected cases).
Location of Drug Action(s):   The muscles in the walls of blood vessels. The principal therapeutic action is on the small arteries (arterioles).
Method of Drug Action(s):   By causing direct relaxation and expansion of blood vessel walls, this drug increases the volume of blood flowing through the vessels. The resulting increase in oxygen and nutrients relieves the symptoms attributable to deficient circulation. The mechanism responsible for the direct relaxation of muscle is not known.

THIS DRUG SHOULD NOT BE TAKEN IF

—you have had an allergic reaction to any dosage form of it previously.

INFORM YOUR PHYSICIAN BEFORE TAKING THIS DRUG IF

—you have glaucoma.
—you have had a heart attack or a stroke.
—you suffer from poor circulation to the brain or heart (angina).

Time Required for Apparent Benefit

Continuous use on a regular schedule for several weeks is needed to determine this drug's effectiveness. Beneficial results from short-term use are unlikely.

Possible Side-Effects *(natural, expected, and unavoidable drug actions)*

Flushing and warm sensation, tingling of face and extremities, sweating.

CAUTION

Individuals with extensive or severe impairment of circulation to the brain or heart may respond unfavorably to this drug. Observe closely until the true nature of the response has been determined. Discontinue drug if condition worsens.

Possible Adverse Effects *(unusual, unexpected, and infrequent reactions)*

IF ANY OF THE FOLLOWING DEVELOP, DISCONTINUE DRUG AND NOTIFY YOUR PHYSICIAN AS SOON AS POSSIBLE

Mild Adverse Effects
Stomach irritation, heartburn, nausea.
Headache, dizziness, weakness.
Heart palpitation (rapid heart action).

Serious Adverse Effects
None reported.

Advisability of Use During Pregnancy
Safety not established. Prudent use is best determined by physician's evaluation.

Advisability of Use While Nursing Infant
Safety not established. Ask physician for guidance.

Habit-Forming Potential
None.

Effects of Overdosage
Headache, dizziness, flushed and hot face, nausea and vomiting.

Possible Effects of Extended Use
None reported.

Recommended Periodic Examinations While Taking This Drug
Measurement of internal eye pressure (if glaucoma is present).

While Taking This Drug, Observe the Following
Foods: No restrictions of food selection. Drug may be taken with or immediately following meals to reduce stomach irritation or nausea.
Beverages: No restrictions.
Alcohol: No interactions expected.
Tobacco Smoking: Nicotine can reduce this drug's ability to dilate blood vessels and to improve circulation. Follow physician's advice regarding smoking.
Other Drugs: No significant drug interactions reported.
Driving a Vehicle, Piloting a Plane, Operating Machinery: No restrictions.
Exposure to Sun: No restrictions.
Exposure to Heat: Use caution. This drug may cause excessive sweating in hot environments.
Exposure to Cold: Avoid as much as possible. This drug may be less effective in cold environments or with the handling of cold objects.
Heavy Exercise or Exertion: No restrictions.

Special Storage Instructions
Keep in a dry, tightly closed container. Protect from light and excessive hea

CYCLIZINE

Year Introduced: 1953

Brand Names

USA	Canada
Marezine (Burroughs Wellcome)	Marzine (Calmic)
Migral [CD] (Burroughs Wellcome)	

Drug Family: Antihistamines; Antinausea (Anti-emetic)

Prescription Required: USA: Tablets — No
Other forms — Yes
Canada: Yes

Available Dosage Forms and Strengths
Tablets — 50 mg.
Suppositories — 50 mg., 100 mg.
Injection — 50 mg. per ml.

How This Drug Works
Intended Therapeutic Effect(s):   Prevention and management of the na
sea, vomiting, and dizziness associated with motion sickness.
Location of Drug Action(s):   The nerve pathways connecting the organ
equilibrium (the labyrinth) in the inner ear with the vomiting center in th
brain.
Method of Drug Action(s):   This drug reduces the sensitivity of the ner
endings in the labyrinth and blocks the transmission of excessive ner
impulses to the vomiting center.

THIS DRUG SHOULD NOT BE TAKEN IF
—you have had an allergic reaction to any dosage form of it previously.
—you are taking, or have taken during the past 2 weeks, any mono-amir
oxidase (MAO) inhibitor drug (see Drug Family, Section Four).

INFORM YOUR PHYSICIAN BEFORE TAKING THIS DRUG IF
—you have had an unfavorable reaction to any antihistamine in the past.

Time Required for Apparent Benefit
Drug action begins in 30 to 60 minutes and persists for 4 to 6 hours.

Possible Side-Effects *(natural, expected, and unavoidable drug actions)*
Drowsiness, dryness of nose, mouth, or throat.

Possible Adverse Effects *(unusual, unexpected, and infrequent reactions)*

IF ANY OF THE FOLLOWING DEVELOP, DISCONTINUE DRUG AND NOTIFY YOUR PHYSICIAN AS SOON AS POSSIBLE

Mild Adverse Effects
Allergic Reactions: Skin rash, hives.
Blurring of vision.

Serious Adverse Effects
Allergic Reactions: Anaphylactic reaction (see Glossary).

Advisability of Use During Pregnancy
Safety not established. Prudent use is best determined by the physician's evaluation.

Advisability of Use While Nursing Infant
Safety for infant not established. Ask physician for guidance.

Habit-Forming Potential
None.

Effects of Overdosage
With Moderate Overdose: Marked drowsiness, confusion, incoordination, unsteady gait, muscle tremors. In children: excitement, hallucinations, over-activity, convulsions.

With Large Overdose: Stupor progressing to coma, fever, flushed face, dilated pupils, weak pulse, shallow breathing.

Possible Effects of Extended Use
None reported.

Recommended Periodic Examinations While Taking This Drug
Complete blood cell counts.

While Taking This Drug, Observe the Following
Foods: No restrictions. Stomach irritation can be reduced if drug is taken after eating.

Beverages: Coffee and tea may help to reduce the drowsiness caused by most antihistamines.

Alcohol: Use with extreme caution until combined effect has been determined. The combination of alcohol and antihistamines can cause rapid and marked sedation.

Tobacco Smoking: No interactions expected.

Other Drugs
Cyclizine may *increase* the effects of
• sedatives, sleep-inducing drugs, tranquilizers, antidepressants, pain relievers, and narcotic drugs, and result in oversedation. Careful dosage adjustments are necessary.
• atropine and drugs with atropine-like action (see Drug Family, Section Four).

The following drugs may *increase* the effects of cyclizine:

- all sedatives, sleep-inducing drugs, tranquilizers, pain relievers, and narcotic drugs may exaggerate its sedative action and cause oversedation.
- mono-amine oxidase (MAO) inhibitor drugs (see Drug Family, Section Four) may delay its elimination from the body, thus exaggerating and prolonging its action.

The following drugs may *decrease* the effects of cyclizine

- amphetamines (Benzedrine, Dexedrine, Desoxyn, etc.) may reduce the drowsiness caused by most antihistamines.

Driving a Vehicle, Piloting a Plane, Operating Machinery: This drug may impair mental alertness, judgment, physical coordination, and reaction time. Avoid hazardous activities until degree of drowsiness has been determined.

Exposure to Sun: No restrictions.

Special Storage Instructions
Keep in a dry, tightly closed container.

CYPROHEPTADINE

Year Introduced: 1961

Brand Names

USA	Canada
Periactin (Merck Sharp & Dohme)	Periactin (MSD) Vimicon (Frosst)

Drug Family: Antihistamines; Anti-itching (Antipruritic)

Prescription Required: Yes

Available Dosage Forms and Strengths
Tablets — 4 mg.
Syrup — 2 mg. per teaspoonful

How This Drug Works
Intended Therapeutic Effect(s):   Relief of symptoms associated with hayfever (allergic rhinitis) and with allergic reactions in the skin, such as itching, swelling, hives, and rash.

Location of Drug Action(s):   Those hypersensitive tissues that release excessive histamine as part of an allergic reaction. The principal tissue sites are the eyes, the nose, and the skin.

Method of Drug Action(s):   This drug reduces the intensity of the allergic response by blocking the action of histamine after it has been released from sensitized tissue cells.

THIS DRUG SHOULD NOT BE TAKEN IF
—you have had an allergic reaction to any dosage form of it previously.
—you are subject to acute attacks of asthma.
—you have glaucoma (narrow-angle type).

—you have difficulty emptying the urinary bladder.
—you are taking, or have taken during the past 2 weeks, any mono-amine oxidase (MAO) inhibitor drugs (see Drug Family, Section Four).
—it has been prescribed for a newborn infant.

INFORM YOUR PHYSICIAN BEFORE TAKING THIS DRUG IF
—you have had an unfavorable reaction to any antihistamine drug in the past.
—you have a history of peptic ulcer disease.
—you plan to have surgery under general anesthesia in the near future.

Time Required for Apparent Benefit
Drug action begins in approximately 30 minutes, reaches a maximum in 1 hour, and subsides in 4 to 6 hours.

Possible Side-Effects *(natural, expected, and unavoidable drug actions)*
Drowsiness, sense of weakness, dryness of nose, mouth, and throat, constipation.

CAUTION
The elderly (over 60 years of age) may be more susceptible to the adverse effects of this drug. Small doses are advisable until tolerance is determined.

Possible Adverse Effects *(unusual, unexpected, and infrequent reactions)*
IF ANY OF THE FOLLOWING DEVELOP, DISCONTINUE DRUG AND NOTIFY YOUR PHYSICIAN AS SOON AS POSSIBLE

Mild Adverse Effects
Allergic Reactions: Skin rash, hives.
Headache, dizziness, inability to concentrate, nervousness, blurring of vision, double vision, difficulty in urination.
Nausea, vomiting, diarrhea.

Serious Adverse Effects
Idiosyncratic Reactions: Behavioral disturbances—confusion, delirium, excitement, hallucinations.

Advisability of Use During Pregnancy
No reports of adverse effects on mother or fetus. Limit use to small doses and for the shortest periods of time possible.

Advisability of Use While Nursing Infant
This drug may impair milk formation and make nursing difficult. In addition, the drug is known to be present in milk. Ask physician for guidance.

Habit-Forming Potential
None.

Effects of Overdosage
With Moderate Overdose: Marked drowsiness, confusion, incoordination, unsteady gait, muscle tremors. In children: excitement, hallucinations, overactivity, convulsions.
With Large Overdose: Stupor progressing to coma, fever, flushed face, dilated pupils, weak pulse, shallow breathing.

Possible Effects of Extended Use
None reported.

Recommended Periodic Examinations While Taking This Drug
Complete blood cell counts.

While Taking This Drug, Observe the Following
Foods: No restrictions. Stomach irritation can be reduced if drug is taken after eating.

Beverages: Coffee and tea may help to reduce the drowsiness caused by most antihistamines.

Alcohol: Use with extreme caution until combined effect has been determined. The combination of alcohol and antihistamines can cause rapid and marked sedation.

Tobacco Smoking: No interactions expected.

Other Drugs

Cyproheptadine may *increase* the effects of

- sedatives, sleep-inducing drugs, tranquilizers, antidepressants, pain relievers, and narcotic drugs, and result in oversedation. Careful dosage adjustments are necessary.
- atropine and drugs with atropine-like action (see Drug Family, Section Four).

The following drugs may *increase* the effects of cyproheptadine:

- all sedatives, sleep-inducing drugs, tranquilizers, pain relievers, and narcotic drugs may exaggerate its sedative action and cause oversedation.
- mono-amine oxidase (MAO) inhibitor drugs (see Drug Family, Section Four) may delay its elimination from the body, thus exaggerating and prolonging its action.

The following drugs may *decrease* the effects of cyproheptadine

- amphetamines (Benzedrine, Dexedrine, Desoxyn, etc.) may reduce the drowsiness caused by most antihistamines.

Driving a Vehicle, Piloting a Plane, Operating Machinery: This drug may impair mental alertness, judgment, physical coordination, and reaction time. Avoid hazardous activities until full sedative effect has been determined.

Exposure to Sun: No restrictions.

Special Storage Instructions
Keep in a dry, tightly closed container.

DEMECLOCYCLINE

Year Introduced: 1959

Brand Names

USA	Canada
Declomycin (Lederle)	Declomycin (Lederle)

Drug Family: Antibiotic (Anti-infective) [Tetracyclines]

Prescription Required: Yes

Available Dosage Forms and Strengths
Tablets — 75 mg., 150 mg., 300 mg.
Capsules — 150 mg.
Oral Suspension — 75 mg. per teaspoonful
Syrup — 75 mg. per teaspoonful
Pediatric Drops — 60 mg. per ml.

How This Drug Works
Intended Therapeutic Effect(s):   The elimination of infections responsive to the action of this drug.

Location of Drug Action(s):   Any body tissue or fluid in which sufficient concentration of the drug can be achieved.

Method of Drug Action(s):   This drug prevents the growth and multiplication of susceptible bacteria by interfering with their formation of essential proteins.

THIS DRUG SHOULD NOT BE TAKEN IF
—you are allergic to any tetracycline drug (see Drug Family, Section Four).
—you are pregnant or breast feeding.
—it is prescribed for a child under 9 years of age.

INFORM YOUR PHYSICIAN BEFORE TAKING THIS DRUG IF
—you have a history of liver or kidney disease.
—you have systemic lupus erythematosus.
—you are taking any penicillin drug.
—you are taking any anticoagulant drug.
—you plan to have surgery under general anesthesia in the near future.

Time Required for Apparent Benefit
Varies with nature of infection under treatment; usually 2 to 5 days.

Possible Side-Effects *(natural, expected, and unavoidable drug actions)*
Superinfections (see Glossary), often due to yeast organisms. These can occur in the mouth, intestinal tract, rectum, and/or vagina, resulting in rectal and vaginal itching.

Possible Adverse Effects *(unusual, unexpected, and infrequent reactions)*

IF ANY OF THE FOLLOWING DEVELOP, DISCONTINUE DRUG AND NOTIFY
YOUR PHYSICIAN AS SOON AS POSSIBLE

Mild Adverse Effects

Allergic Reactions: Skin rash (various kinds), hives, itching of hands and feet, swelling of face or extremities.

Photosensitivity Reactions: Exaggerated sunburn or skin irritation occurs commonly with some tetracyclines (see Glossary).

Loss of appetite, nausea, vomiting, diarrhea.

Irritation of mouth or tongue, "black tongue," sore throat, abdominal pain or cramping.

Serious Adverse Effects

Allergic Reactions: Anaphylactic reaction (see Glossary), asthma, fever, painful swollen joints, unusual bleeding or bruising, jaundice (see Glossary).

Permanent discoloration and/or malformation of teeth when taken under 9 years of age, including unborn child and infant.

Advisability of Use During Pregnancy
Tetracyclines can have adverse effects on mother and fetus. Avoid use.

Advisability of Use While Nursing Infant
Tetracyclines can be present in milk and can have adverse effects on infant. Avoid use or avoid nursing.

Habit-Forming Potential
None.

Effects of Overdosage
Possible nausea, vomiting, diarrhea.
Acute liver damage (rare).

Possible Effects of Extended Use
Impairment of bone marrow, liver, or kidney function (all rare).
Superinfections.

Recommended Periodic Examinations While Taking This Drug
Complete blood cell counts.
Liver and kidney function tests.
During extended use, sputum and stool examinations may detect early superinfections due to yeast organisms.

While Taking This Drug, Observe the Following
Foods: Dairy products can interfere with absorption. Tetracyclines should be taken 1 hour before or 2 hours after eating.

Beverages: Avoid milk for 1 hour before and after each dose of a tetracycline.

Alcohol: Avoid while taking a tetracycline if you have a history of liver disease.

Tobacco Smoking: No interactions expected.

Other Drugs

Tetracyclines may *increase* the effects of
• oral anticoagulants, and make it necessary to reduce their dosage.

Tetracyclines may *decrease* the effects of
• the penicillins, and impair their effectiveness in treating infections.

The following drugs may *decrease* the effects of tetracyclines
• antacids may reduce drug absorption.
• iron and mineral preparations may reduce drug absorption.

Driving a Vehicle, Piloting a Plane, Operating Machinery: No restrictions

Exposure to Sun: Avoid as much as possible. Photosensitivity (see Glossary) is common with some tetracyclines.

Special Storage Instructions
Keep in a tightly closed, light-resistant container.

DESIPRAMINE

Year Introduced: 1964

Brand Names

USA	Canada
Norpramin	Norpramin (Merrell)
(Merrell-National)	Pertofrane (Geigy)
Pertofrane (USV	
Pharmaceutical)	

Drug Family: Antidepressant, Tricyclic (Anti-psychotic)

Prescription Required: Yes

Available Dosage Forms and Strengths
Tablets — 25 mg., 50 mg.
Capsules — 25 mg., 50 mg.

How This Drug Works
Intended Therapeutic Effect(s):   Gradual improvement of mood and relief of emotional depression.

Location of Drug Action(s):   Those areas of the brain that determine mood and emotional stability.

Method of Drug Action(s):   Not established. Present thinking is that this drug slowly restores to normal levels certain constituents of brain tissue (such as norepinephrine) that transmit nerve impulses.

THIS DRUG SHOULD NOT BE TAKEN IF
—you have had an allergic reaction to any dosage form of it previously.
—you are taking or have taken within the past 14 days any mono-amine oxidase (MAO) inhibitor drug (see Drug Family, Section Four).

—you are recovering from a recent heart attack.
—you have glaucoma (narrow-angle type).
—it is prescribed for a child under 12 years of age.

INFORM YOUR PHYSICIAN BEFORE TAKING THIS DRUG IF
—you are allergic or sensitive to any other tricyclic antidepressant (see Drug Family, Section Four).
—you have a history of any of the following: diabetes, epilepsy, glaucoma, heart disease, prostate gland enlargement, or overactive thyroid function.
—you plan to have surgery under general anesthesia in the near future.

Time Required for Apparent Benefit
Some benefit may be apparent within the first 1 to 2 weeks. Adequate response may require continuous treatment for 4 to 6 weeks.

Possible Side-Effects *(natural, expected, and unavoidable drug actions)*
Drowsiness, blurring of vision, dryness of mouth, constipation, impaired urination.

CAUTION
The possibility of adverse effects from this drug is greater in the elderly (over 60 years of age). Small doses are advisable until tolerance has been determined.

Possible Adverse Effects *(unusual, unexpected, and infrequent reactions)*

IF ANY OF THE FOLLOWING DEVELOP, DISCONTINUE DRUG AND NOTIFY YOUR PHYSICIAN AS SOON AS POSSIBLE

Mild Adverse Effects
Allergic Reactions: Skin rash, hives, swelling of face or tongue, drug fever.
Nausea, indigestion, irritation of tongue or mouth, peculiar taste.
Headache, dizziness, weakness, fainting, unsteady gait, tremors.
Swelling of testicles, breast enlargement, milk formation.
Fluctuation of blood sugar levels.

Serious Adverse Effects
Allergic Reactions: Hepatitis with jaundice (see Glossary).
Confusion (especially in the elderly), hallucinations, agitation, restlessness, nightmares.
Heart palpitation and irregular rhythm.
Bone marrow depression (see Glossary)—fatigue, weakness, fever, sore throat, unusual bleeding or bruising.
Numbness, tingling, pain, loss of strength in arms and legs.
Parkinson-like disorders (see Glossary)—usually mild and infrequent; more likely to occur in the elderly.

Advisability of Use During Pregnancy
Safety not established. Prudent use is best determined by the physician's evaluation.

Advisability of Use While Nursing Infant
This drug may be present in milk in small quantities. Ask physician for guidance.

Habit-Forming Potential
Psychological or physical dependence is rare and unexpected.

Effects of Overdosage
With Moderate Overdose: Confusion, hallucinations, extreme drowsiness, drop in body temperature, heart palpitation, dilated pupils, tremors.
With Large Overdose: Stupor, deep sleep, coma, convulsions.

Possible Effects of Extended Use
None reported.

Recommended Periodic Examinations While Taking This Drug
Complete blood cell counts.
Liver function tests.
Serial blood pressure readings and electrocardiograms.

While Taking This Drug, Observe the Following
Foods: No restrictions.
Beverages: No restrictions.
Alcohol: Avoid completely. This drug can increase markedly the intoxicating effects of alcohol and accentuate its depressant action on brain function.
Tobacco Smoking: No interactions expected.
Other Drugs
Desipramine may *increase* the effects of
 • atropine and drugs with atropine-like actions (see Drug Family, Section Four).
 • sedatives, sleep-inducing drugs, tranquilizers, antihistamines, and narcotic drugs, and cause oversedation. Dosage adjustments may be necessary.
 • levodopa (Dopar, Larodopa, etc.), in its control of Parkinson's disease.

Desipramine may *decrease* the effects of
 • guanethidine, and reduce its effectiveness in lowering blood pressure.
 • other commonly used anti-hypertensive drugs. Ask physician for guidance regarding the need to monitor blood pressure readings and to adjust dosage of anti-hypertensive medications. (The action of Aldomet is not decreased by tricyclic antidepressants.)

Desipramine *taken concurrently* with
 • thyroid preparations, may cause impairment of heart rhythm and function. Ask physician for guidance regarding thyroid dosage adjustment.
 • ethchlorvynol (Placidyl), may cause delirium.
 • quinidine, may cause impairment of heart rhythm and function. Avoid the combined use of these two drugs.
 • mono-amine oxidase (MAO) inhibitor drugs (see Drug Family, Section Four), may cause high fever, delirium, and convulsions.

The following drugs may *increase* the effects of Desipramine
• thiazide diuretics (see Drug Family, Section Four) may slow its elimination from the body. Overdosage may occur.

Driving a Vehicle, Piloting a Plane, Operating Machinery: This drug may impair mental alertness, judgment, physical coordination, and reaction time. Avoid hazardous activities.

Exposure to Sun: Use caution until sensitivity to sun has been determined. This drug may cause photosensitivity (see Glossary).

Discontinuation: If it has been necessary to use this drug for an extended period of time, do not discontinue it abruptly. Ask physician for guidance regarding dosage reduction and withdrawal. It may be necessary to adjust the dosage of other drugs taken concurrently.

Special Storage Instructions
Keep in a dry, tightly closed container.

DEXAMETHASONE

Year Introduced: 1958

Brand Names

USA	Canada
Decadron (Merck Sharp & Dohme)	Decadron (MSD)
	Dexamethadrone
Deronil (Schering)	(Barlowe Cote)
Dexameth (USV Pharmaceutical)	Dexasone (ICN)
	Hexadrol (Organon)
Dezone (Tutag)	Maxidex (Alcon)
Gammacorten (CIBA)	Novadex (Nova)
Hexadrol (Organon)	

Drug Family: Cortisone-like Drug [(Adrenocortical Steroids (Glucocorticoids)]

Prescription Required: Yes

Available Dosage Forms and Strengths
Tablets — 0.25 mg., 0.5 mg., 0.75 mg., 1.5 mg.
Elixir — 0.5 mg. per teaspoonful
Aerosol Inhaler — 18 mg. in 12.6 gm.
Aerosol Skin Spray — 10 mg. in 90 gm.
Cream — 0.1%
Eye Ointment and Solution — 0.05%, 0.1%

How This Drug Works
Intended Therapeutic Effect(s):   The symptomatic relief of inflammation (swelling, redness, heat and pain) in any tissue, and from many causes. (Cortisone-like drugs do not correct the underlying disease process.)

Location of Drug Action(s): Significant biological effects occur in most tissues throughout the body. The principal actions of therapeutic doses occur at sites of inflammation and/or allergic reaction, regardless of the nature of the causative injury or illness.

Method of Drug Action(s): Not completely established. Present thinking is that cortisone-like drugs probably inhibit several mechanisms within the tissues that induce inflammation. Well-regulated dosage aids the body in restoring normal stability. However, prolonged use or excessive dosage can impair the body's defense mechanisms against infectious disease.

THIS DRUG SHOULD NOT BE TAKEN IF
—you have had an allergic reaction to any dosage form of it previously.
—you have an active peptic ulcer (stomach or duodenum).
—you have an active infection of the eye caused by the herpes simplex virus (ask your eye doctor for guidance).
—you have active tuberculosis.

INFORM YOUR PHYSICIAN BEFORE TAKING THIS DRUG IF
—you have had an unfavorable reaction to any cortisone-like drug in the past.
—you have a history of tuberculosis.
—you have diabetes or a tendency to diabetes.
—you have a history of peptic ulcer disease.
—you have glaucoma or a tendency to glaucoma.
—you have a deficiency of thyroid function (hypothyroidism).
—you have high blood pressure.
—you have myasthenia gravis.
—you have a history of thrombophlebitis.
—you plan to have surgery of any kind in the near future, especially if under general anesthesia.

Time Required for Apparent Benefit
Evidence of beneficial drug action is usually apparent in 24 to 48 hours. Dosage must be individualized to give reasonable improvement. This is usually accomplished in 4 to 10 days. It is unwise to demand complete relief of all symptoms. The effective dose varies with the nature of the disease and with the patient. During long-term use it is essential that the smallest effective dose be determined and maintained.

Possible Side-Effects *(natural, expected, and unavoidable drug actions)*
Increased appetite, weight gain.
Increased susceptibility to infections.
Retention of salt and water. This occurs less frequently than with other cortisone-like drugs.

CAUTION
1. It is advisable to carry a card of personal identification with a notation that you are taking this drug if your course of treatment is to exceed 1 week (see Table 14 and Section Seven).
2. Do not discontinue this drug abruptly.
3. While taking this drug, immunization procedures should be given with

caution. If vaccination against measles, smallpox, rabies, or yellow fever is required, discontinue this drug 72 hours before vaccination and do not resume for at least 14 days after vaccination.

Possible Adverse Effects *(unusual, unexpected, and infrequent reactions)*

IF ANY OF THE FOLLOWING DEVELOP, DISCONTINUE DRUG AND NOTIFY YOUR PHYSICIAN AS SOON AS POSSIBLE

Mild Adverse Effects
Allergic Reactions: Skin rash.
Headache, dizziness, insomnia.
Acid indigestion, abdominal distention.
Muscle cramping and weakness.
Irregular menstrual periods.
Acne, excessive growth of facial hair.

Serious Adverse Effects
Mental and emotional disturbances of serious magnitude.
Reactivation of latent tuberculosis.
Development of peptic ulcer.
Increased blood pressure.
Development of inflammation of the pancreas.
Thrombophlebitis (inflammation of a vein with the formation of blood clot) —pain or tenderness in thigh or leg, with or without swelling of the foot, ankle, or leg.
Pulmonary embolism (movement of blood clot to the lung)—sudden shortness of breath, pain in the chest, coughing, bloody sputum.

Advisability of Use During Pregnancy
Safety has not been established. If possible, avoid completely. If use of this drug is considered necessary, limit dosage and duration of use as much as possible. Following birth, the infant should be examined for possible defective function of the adrenal glands (deficiency of adrenal cortical hormones).

Advisability of Use While Nursing Infant
Drug is known to be present in milk. Ask physician for guidance.

Habit-Forming Potential
Use of this drug to suppress symptoms over an extended period of time may produce a state of functional dependence (see Glossary). In the treatment of conditions like rheumatoid arthritis and asthma, it is advisable to try alternate-day drug administration to keep the daily dose as small as possible and to attempt drug withdrawal after periods of reasonable improvement. Such procedures may reduce the degree of "steroid rebound"—the return of symptoms as the drug is withdrawn.

Effects of Overdosage
With Moderate Overdose: Fatigue, muscle weakness, stomach irritation, acid indigestion, excessive sweating.
With Large Overdose: Marked flushing of the face, increased blood pressure, retention of fluid with swelling of extremities, muscle cramping, marked emotional and behavioral disturbances.

Possible Effects of Extended Use

Development of increased blood sugar, possibly diabetes.

Increased fat deposits on the trunk of the body ("buffalo hump"), rounding of the face ("moon face"), and thinning of the arms and legs.

Thinning and fragility of the skin, easy bruising.

Loss of texture and strength of the bones, resulting in spontaneous fractures.

Development of increased internal eye pressure, possibly glaucoma.

Development of cataracts.

Retarded growth and development in children.

Recommended Periodic Examinations While Taking This Drug

Measurement of blood potassium levels.

Measurement of blood sugar levels 2 hours after eating.

Measurement of blood pressure at regular intervals.

Complete eye examination at regular intervals.

Chest X-ray if history of previous tuberculosis.

Determination of the rate of development of the growing child to detect retardation of normal growth.

While Taking This Drug, Observe the Following

Foods: No interactions. Ask physician regarding need to restrict salt intake or to eat potassium-rich foods. During long-term use of this drug it is advisable to have a high protein diet.

Beverages: No restrictions.

Alcohol: No interactions expected.

Tobacco Smoking: Nicotine increases the blood levels of naturally produced cortisone and related hormones. Heavy smoking may add to the expected actions of this drug and requires close observation for excessive effects.

Other Drugs

Dexamethasone may *increase* the effects of

- barbiturates and other sedatives and sleep-inducing drugs, causing oversedation.

Dexamethasone may *decrease* the effects of

- insulin and oral anti-diabetic drugs, by raising the level of blood sugar. Doses of anti-diabetic drugs may have to be raised.
- anticoagulants of the coumarin family. Monitor prothrombin times closely and adjust doses accordingly.
- choline-like drugs (Mestinon, pilocarpine, Prostigmin), by reducing their effectiveness in treating glaucoma and myasthenia gravis.

Dexamethasone *taken concurrently* with

- thiazide diuretics, may cause excessive loss of potassium. Monitor blood levels of potassium on physician's advice.
- atropine-like drugs, may cause increased internal eye pressure and initiate or aggravate glaucoma (see Drug Family, Section Four).
- digitalis preparations, requires close monitoring of body potassium stores to prevent digitalis toxicity.

• stimulant drugs (adrenalin, amphetamines, ephedrine, etc.), may increase internal eye pressure and initiate or aggravate glaucoma.

The following drugs may *increase* the effects of Dexamethasone:
• indomethacin (Indocin, Indocid)
• aspirin

The following drugs may *decrease* the effects of dexamethasone:
• barbiturates
• phenytoin (Dantoin, Dilantin, etc.)
• antihistamines (some)
• chloral hydrate (Noctec, Somnos)
• glutethimide (Doriden)
• phenylbutazone (Azolid, Butazolidin, etc.) may reduce its effectiveness following a brief, initial increase in effectiveness.
• Propranolol (Inderal)

Driving a Vehicle, Piloting a Plane, Operating Machinery: No restrictions or precautions.

Exposure to Sun: No restrictions.

Occurrence of Unrelated Illness

This drug may decrease natural resistance to infection. Notify your physician if you develop an infection of any kind.

This drug may reduce your body's ability to respond appropriately to the stress of acute illness, injury, or surgery. Keep your physician fully informed of any significant changes in your state of health.

Discontinuation

If you have been taking this drug for an extended period of time, do not discontinue it abruptly. Ask physician for guidance regarding gradual withdrawal.

For a period of 2 years after discontinuing this drug, it is essential in the event of illness, injury, or surgery that you inform attending medical personnel that you used this drug in the past. The period of inadequate response to stress following the use of cortisone-like drugs may last for 1 to 2 years.

Special Storage Instructions

Keep in a tightly closed container. Protect from light.

DEXTROAMPHETAMINE
(d-Amphetamine)

Year Introduced: 1944

Brand Names

USA	Canada
Dexedrine (Smith Kline & French)	Dexedrine (SK&F)
Bamadex [CD] (Lederle)	Dexamyl [CD] (SK&F)
Biphetamine [CD] (Pennwalt)	
Dexamyl [CD] (Smith Kline & French)	
Eskatrol [CD] (Smith Kline & French)	

Drug Family: Stimulant [Sympathomimetics] [Amphetamines]
Appetite Suppressant (Anorexian)

Prescription Required: Yes (Controlled Drug, U.S. Schedule 2)

Available Dosage Forms and Strengths
Tablets — 5 mg.
Prolonged Action Capsules — 5 mg., 10 mg., 15 mg.
Elixir — 5 mg. per teaspoonful (5 ml.)

How This Drug Works
Intended Therapeutic Effect(s)
- prevention or reduction in the frequency of episodes of sleep epilepsy (narcolepsy)—sudden attacks of sleep occurring at irregular intervals.
- reduction of restlessness, distractability, and impulsive behavior characteristic of the abnormally hyperactive child (as seen with minimal brain dysfunction).
- suppression of appetite in the management of weight reduction using low-calorie diets.

Location of Drug Action(s)
- the wake-sleep center within the brain.
- areas within the outer layer (cortex) of the brain that are responsible for higher mental functions and behavioral reactions.
- the appetite-regulating center within the hypothalamus of the brain.

Method of Drug Action(s)
By increasing the release of the nerve impulse transmitter norepinephrine, this drug produces wakefulness and accelerated mental activity.
The increased availability of norepinephrine may also improve alertness, concentration, and attention span. (The primary action that calms the overactive child is not known.)
By altering the chemical control of nerve impulse transmission within the appetite-regulating center, this drug can temporarily reduce or abolish hunger.

THIS DRUG SHOULD NOT BE TAKEN IF
—you have had an allergic reaction to any dosage form of it previously. A combination drug [CD] should not be taken if you are allergic to *any* of its ingredients.
—you have advanced hardening of the arteries.
—you have heart disease that requires treatment.
—you are being treated for high blood pressure.
—you have glaucoma.
—you have an overactive thyroid disorder (hyperthyroidism).
—you have severe anxiety or nervous tension.
—you are taking, or have taken within the past 14 days, any mono-amine oxidase (MAO) inhibitor drug (see Drug Family, Section Four).
—it is prescribed for a child under 3 years of age.

INFORM YOUR PHYSICIAN BEFORE TAKING THIS DRUG IF
—you have a history of high blood pressure, heart disease, or stroke.
—you have diabetes.
—you have experienced any form of drug dependence in the past (see Glossary).

Time Required for Apparent Benefit
Drug action begins in 30 to 60 minutes and persists for 4 to 6 hours. The effects of the prolonged action capsule may persist for 10 to 14 hours.

Possible Side-Effects *(natural, expected, and unavoidable drug actions)*
Nervousness, increased heart rate, insomnia.

CAUTION
1. To reduce the possibility of insomnia, do not take this drug within 6 hours of retiring.
2. It is advisable to determine the lowest effective dose for each individual and to maintain dosage at this level.
3. The appetite-suppressing action of this drug may disappear after several weeks of continuous use, regardless of the size of the dose. *Do not increase the dose* beyond that prescribed.

Possible Adverse Effects *(unusual, unexpected, and infrequent reactions)*

IF ANY OF THE FOLLOWING DEVELOP, DISCONTINUE DRUG AND NOTIFY YOUR PHYSICIAN AS SOON AS POSSIBLE

Mild Adverse Effects
    Allergic Reactions: Hives.
    Headache, dizziness, overstimulation, tremor, euphoria.
    Dryness of the mouth, unpleasant taste.
    Heart palpitation, rapid and/or irregular heart action.
Serious Adverse Effects
    Alteration of insulin requirements in the management of diabetes.
    Increased blood pressure.
    Changes in libido, sexual impotence.
    Behavioral disturbances, psychotic episodes.

Advisability of Use During Pregnancy
Avoid completely during the first 3 months. Safety not established for use at any time during pregnancy. Prudent use is best determined by the physician's evaluation.

Advisability of Use While Nursing Infant
This drug is known to be present in milk in very small amounts. Ask physician for guidance.

Habit-Forming Potential
This drug can cause severe psychological dependence (see Glossary; this is the most serious problem related to the use of amphetamines). Avoid large doses and prolonged use if possible. Observe closely for indications of developing dependence.

Effects of Overdosage
With Moderate Overdose: Nervous irritability, overactivity, insomnia, personality changes, tremor, rapid heart rate, headache.

With Large Overdose: Nausea, vomiting, diarrhea, dizziness, dilated pupils, blurred vision, confusion, high fever, gasping respirations, profuse sweating, hallucinations, convulsions, coma.

Possible Effects of Extended Use
With low dosage, excessive weight loss.

With moderate to high dosage (chronic intoxication), skin eruptions, insomnia, excitability, personality changes, severe mental disturbances resembling schizophrenia.

Severe psychological dependence.

Recommended Periodic Examinations While Taking This Drug
Observation for evidence of developing dependence.

Measurement of blood pressure to detect any tendency to abnormal elevation.

While Taking This Drug, Observe the Following
Foods: When used to suppress appetite, take this drug 30 to 60 minutes before eating. Follow weight reduction diet as prescribed. Avoid foods rich in tyramine (see Glossary). This drug in combination with tyramine may cause excessive rise in blood pressure.

Beverages: Avoid beverages prepared from meat or yeast extracts. Avoid sour cream.

Alcohol: Avoid beer (unpasteurized), Chianti, and vermouth wines.

Tobacco Smoking: No interactions expected.

Other Drugs

Dextroamphetamine may *increase* the effects of
• meperidine (pethidine, Demerol).

Dextroamphetamine may *decrease* the effects of
• bethanidine (Esbaloid).
• guanethidine (Ismelin).

- hydralazine (Apresoline).
- methyldopa (Aldomet).
- reserpine (Serpasil, Ser-Ap-Es, etc.).

Dextroamphetamine *taken concurrently* with

- mono-amine oxidase (MAO) inhibitor drugs, may cause acute, severe rise in blood pressure that could be dangerous (see Drug Family, Section Four).

The following drugs may *increase* the effects of dextroamphetamine:
- acetazolamide (Diamox)
- antacids containing sodium bicarbonate (see ANTACID Drug Profile)
- thiazide diuretics (see Drug Family, Section Four)
- tricyclic antidepressants (see Drug Family, Section Four)

The following drugs may *decrease* the effects of dextroamphetamine:
- amantadine (Symmetrel)
- methenamine (Mandelamine)
- phenothiazines (see Drug Family, Section Four)
- Vitamin C, in large doses

Driving a Vehicle, Piloting a Plane, Operating Machinery: This drug may impair the ability to engage safely in hazardous activities. Use caution until full effect has been determined.

Exposure to Sun: No restrictions.

Exposure to Heat: No restrictions.

Heavy Exercise or Exertion: Use caution if you have high blood pressure. Ask your physician for guidance.

Discontinuation: Abrupt withdrawal of this drug after prolonged use at moderate to high dosage may cause extreme fatigue and mental depression. Ask your physician for guidance regarding gradual reduction and discontinuation.

Special Storage Instructions
Keep tablets and capsules in a dry, tightly closed container.
Keep elixir in a tightly closed, light-resistant container.

DIAZEPAM

Year Introduced: 1963

Brand Names

USA	Canada
Valium (Roche)	Anxium-5 (Ethica)
	Canazepam (Maney)
	D-Tran (M & M)
	E-Pam (ICN)
	Erital (Eri)
	Meval (Medic)
	Neo-Calme (Neo)
	Novodipam (Novopharm)
	Paxel (Elliott-Marion)
	Serenack (Nordic)
	Valium (Roche)
	Vivol (Horner)

Drug Family: Tranquilizer, Mild (Anti-anxiety) [Benzodiazepines]

Prescription Required: Yes (Controlled Drug, U.S. Schedule 4)

Available Dosage Forms and Strengths
Tablets — 2 mg., 5 mg., 10 mg.
Injection — 5 mg. per ml.

How This Drug Works
Intended Therapeutic Effect(s):   Relief of mild to moderate anxiety and nervous tension, without significant sedation.
Location of Drug Action(s):   Thought to be the limbic system of the brain, one of the centers that influence emotional stability.
Method of Drug Action(s):   Not established. Present thinking is that this drug may reduce the activity of certain parts of the limbic system.

THIS DRUG SHOULD NOT BE TAKEN IF
—you are allergic to any of the drugs bearing the brand names listed above.
—you have glaucoma (narrow-angle type).
—you have myasthenia gravis.
—it is prescribed for an infant under 6 months of age.

INFORM YOUR PHYSICIAN BEFORE TAKING THIS DRUG IF
—you are allergic to any drugs chemically related to diazepam: chlordiazepoxide, clorazepate, flurazepam, oxazepam (see Drug Profiles for brand names).
—you have diabetes.
—you have glaucoma (open-angle type).
—you have epilepsy.
—you are taking sedative, sleep-inducing, tranquilizer, or anti-convulsant drugs of any kind.
—you plan to have surgery under general anesthesia in the near future.

Time Required for Apparent Benefit
Approximately 1 to 2 hours. For severe symptoms of some duration, benefit may require regular medication for several days.

Possible Side-Effects *(natural, expected, and unavoidable drug actions)*
Drowsiness, lethargy, unsteadiness in stance and gait.
Increase in the level of blood sugar in some cases of diabetes.
In the elderly (over 60 years of age) and debilitated: lightheadedness, confusion, weakness, impaired bladder control, constipation. (The elderly may be very susceptible to standard doses.)

Possible Adverse Effects *(unusual, unexpected, and infrequent reactions)*
IF ANY OF THE FOLLOWING DEVELOP, DISCONTINUE DRUG AND NOTIFY YOUR PHYSICIAN AS SOON AS POSSIBLE

Mild Adverse Effects
Allergic Reactions: Skin rashes (various kinds).
Dizziness, fainting, blurred vision, double vision, slurred speech, nausea, menstrual irregularity.

Serious Adverse Effects
Allergic Reactions: Jaundice (see Glossary), impaired resistance to infection manifested by fever and/or sore throat.
Eye pain, possibly glaucoma, emotional depression.
Paradoxical Reactions: Acute excitement, hallucinations, rage.

Advisability of Use During Pregnancy
The findings of some recent studies suggest a possible association between the use of this drug during early pregnancy and the occurrence of birth defects, such as cleft lip. It is advisable to avoid this drug completely during the first 3 months of pregnancy.

Advisability of Use While Nursing Infant
With recommended dosage, drug is present in milk and can affect infant. Ask physician for guidance.

Habit-Forming Potential
This drug can produce psychological and/or physical dependence (see Glossary) if used in large doses for an extended period of time.

Effects of Overdosage
With Moderate Overdose: Marked drowsiness, weakness, feeling of drunkenness, staggering gait, tremor.
With Large Overdose   Stupor progressing to deep sleep or coma.

Possible Effects of Extended Use
Psychological and/or physical dependence.
Reduction of white blood cells.
Impairment of liver function.

Recommended Periodic Examinations While Taking This Drug
Blood cell counts and liver function tests during long-term use.
Blood sugar measurements (in presence of diabetes).

While Taking This Drug, Observe the Following

Foods: No restrictions.

Beverages: Large intake of coffee, tea, or cola drinks (because of their caffeine content) may reduce the calming action of this drug.

Alcohol: Use with extreme caution until the combined effect is determined. Alcohol may increase the sedative effects of diazepam. Diazepam may increase the intoxicating effects of alcohol.

Tobacco Smoking: Heavy smoking may reduce the calming action of diazepam.

Other Drugs

Diazepam may *increase* the effects of

- other sedatives, sleep-inducing drugs, tranquilizers, antidepressants, and narcotic drugs. Use these only under supervision of a physician. Careful dosage adjustment is necessary.
- oral anticoagulants of the coumarin family; ask physician for guidance regarding need for dosage adjustment to prevent bleeding.
- anti-hypertensives, and produce excessive lowering of the blood pressure.

Diazepam *taken concurrently* with

- anti-convulsants, may cause an increase in the frequency or severity of seizures; an increase in the dose of the anti-convulsant may be necessary.
- mono-amine oxidase (MAO) inhibitor drugs (see Drug Family, Section Four), may cause extreme sedation, convulsions, or paradoxical excitement or rage.

The following drugs may *increase* the effects of diazepam

- tricyclic antidepressants (see Drug Family, Section Four) may increase the sedative effects of diazepam.

Driving a Vehicle, Piloting a Plane, Operating Machinery: This drug can impair mental alertness, judgment, physical coordination, and reaction time. Avoid hazardous activities.

Exposure to Sun: No restrictions.

Exposure to Heat: Use caution until effect of excessive perspiration is determined. Because of reduced urine volume, diazepam may accumulate in the body and produce effects of overdosage.

Heavy Exercise or Exertion: No restrictions in cool or temperate weather.

Discontinuation: If it has been necessary to use this drug for an extended period of time do not discontinue it abruptly. Ask physician for guidance regarding dosage reduction and withdrawal. The dosage of other drugs taken concurrently with diazepam may also require adjustment.

Special Storage Instructions

Keep in a dry, tightly closed, light-resistant container.

DICLOXACILLIN

Year Introduced: 1965

Brand Names

USA	Canada
Dynapen (Bristol-Myers)	Dynapen (Bristol)
Pathocil (Wyeth)	
Veracillin (Ayerst)	

Drug Family: Antibiotic (Anti-infective) [Penicillins]

Prescription Required: Yes

Available Dosage Forms and Strengths
Capsules — 125 mg., 250 mg.
Oral Suspension — 62.5 mg. per teaspoonful

How This Drug Works
Intended Therapeutic Effect(s):   The elimination of infections responsive to the action of this drug.
Location of Drug Action(s):   Any body tissue or fluid in which sufficient concentration of the drug can be achieved.
Method of Drug Action(s):   This drug destroys susceptible infecting bacteria by interfering with their ability to produce new protective cell walls as they multiply and grow.

THIS DRUG SHOULD NOT BE TAKEN IF
—you have had an allergic reaction to any dosage form of it previously.
—you are certain you are allergic to any form of penicillin.

INFORM YOUR PHYSICIAN BEFORE TAKING THIS DRUG IF
—you suspect you may be allergic to penicillin or you have a history of a previous "reaction" to penicillin.
—you are allergic to cephalosporin antibiotics (Ancef, Ceporan, Ceporex, Kafocin, Keflex, Keflin, Kefzol, Loridine).
—you are allergic by nature (hayfever, asthma, hives, eczema).

Time Required for Apparent Benefit
Varies with the nature of the infection under treatment; usually from 2 to 5 days.

Possible Side-Effects *(natural, expected, and unavoidable drug actions)*
Superinfections (see Glossary).

Possible Adverse Effects *(unusual, unexpected, and infrequent reactions)*

IF ANY OF THE FOLLOWING DEVELOP, DISCONTINUE DRUG AND NOTIFY YOUR PHYSICIAN AS SOON AS POSSIBLE

Mild Adverse Effects
Allergic Reactions: Skin rashes (various kinds).
Irritation of mouth or tongue, "black tongue," nausea, vomiting, diarrhea, gaseous indigestion.

Serious Adverse Effects
Allergic Reactions: †Anaphylactic reaction (see Glossary), severe skin reactions, high fever, swollen painful joints, sore throat, unusual bleeding or bruising.

Advisability of Use During Pregnancy
Safety not established. Prudent use is best determined by the physician's evaluation.

Advisability of Use While Nursing Infant
Drug may be present in milk and may sensitize infant to penicillin. Ask physician for guidance.

Habit-Forming Potential
None.

Effects of Overdosage
Possible nausea, vomiting, and/or diarrhea.

Possible Effects of Extended Use
Superinfections (see Glossary).

Recommended Periodic Examinations While Taking This Drug
Complete blood cell counts.
Liver and kidney function tests.

While Taking This Drug, Observe the Following
Foods: No restrictions of food selection. Drug is most effective when taken on an empty stomach, 1 hour before or 2 hours after eating.
Beverages: No restrictions.
Alcohol: No interactions expected.
Tobacco Smoking: No interactions expected.
Other Drugs
The following drugs may *decrease* the effects of dicloxacillin:
• antacids can reduce absorption of dicloxacillin.
• chloramphenicol (Chloromycetin)
• erythromycin (Erythrocin, E-Mycin, etc.)
• paromomycin (Humatin)
• tetracyclines (Achromycin, Declomycin, Minocin, etc.; see Drug Family, Section Four)
• troleandomycin (Cyclamycin, TAO)
Driving a Vehicle, Piloting a Plane, Operating Machinery: No restrictions.
Exposure to Sun: No restrictions.

Special Storage Instructions
Keep capsules in a tightly closed container at room temperature.
Keep oral suspension refrigerated.

---

†A rare but potentially dangerous reaction characteristic of penicillins.

Do Not Take the Oral Suspension of This Drug if It Is Older Than
3 days—when kept at room temperature.
14 days—when kept refrigerated.

DICUMAROL
(Formerly Bishydroxycoumarin)

Year Introduced: 1941

Brand Names

USA	Canada
Dicumarol (Abbott, Columbia, Lilly)	Dufalone (Frosst)

Drug Family: Anticoagulant [Coumarins]

Prescription Required: Yes

Available Dosage Forms and Strengths
Tablets — 25 mg., 50 mg., 100 mg.
Capsules — 25 mg., 50 mg., 100 mg.

How This Drug Works
Intended Therapeutic Effect(s):   A deliberate reduction in the ability of the blood to clot. This effect is often beneficial in the management of stroke, heart attack, abnormal clotting in arteries and veins (thrombosis), and the movement of a blood clot from vein to lung (pulmonary embolism).

Location of Drug Action(s):   Those tissues in the liver that use Vitamin K to produce prothrombin (and other factors) essential to the clotting of the blood.

Method of Drug Action(s):   The oral anticoagulants interfere with the production of four essential blood-clotting factors by blocking the action of Vitamin K. This leads to a deficiency of these clotting factors in circulating blood and inhibits blood-clotting mechanisms.

THIS DRUG SHOULD NOT BE TAKEN IF
—you have had an allergic reaction to any dosage form of it previously.
—you have a history of a bleeding disorder.
—you have an active peptic ulcer.
—you have ulcerative colitis.

INFORM YOUR PHYSICIAN BEFORE TAKING THIS DRUG IF
—you are now taking *any other drugs*—either drugs prescribed by another physician, or non-prescription drugs you purchased over-the-counter (see OTC Drugs in Glossary).
—you have high blood pressure.
—you have abnormally heavy or prolonged menstrual bleeding.
—you have diabetes.
—you are using an indwelling catheter.

—you have a history of serious liver or kidney disease, or impaired liver or kidney function.

—you plan to have a surgical or dental procedure in the near future.

Time Required for Apparent Benefit

Drug action begins in 24 to 36 hours, produces desired effects within 36 to 48 hours, and persists for 5 to 6 days. Continuous use on a regular schedule for up to 2 weeks (with daily prothrombin testing and dosage adjustment) is needed to determine the correct maintenance dose for each individual.

Possible Side-Effects *(natural, expected, and unavoidable drug actions)*

Minor episodes of bleeding may occur even when dosage is well within the recommended range. If in doubt regarding its significance, consult your physician regarding the need for prothrombin testing.

CAUTION

1. Always carry with you a card of personal identification that includes a statement indicating that *you are using an anticoagulant* (see Table 14 and Section Seven).
2. While you are taking an anticoagulant drug, always consult your physician *before* starting any new drug, changing the dosage schedule of any drug, or discontinuing any drug.

Possible Adverse Effects *(unusual, unexpected, and infrequent reactions)*

IF ANY OF THE FOLLOWING DEVELOP, DISCONTINUE DRUG AND NOTIFY YOUR PHYSICIAN AS SOON AS POSSIBLE

Mild Adverse Effects

Allergic Reactions: Skin rash, hives, loss of scalp hair, drug fever. Nausea, vomiting, diarrhea.

Serious Adverse Effects

Abnormal bruising, major bleeding, or hemorrhage. Notify physician of nose bleeds, bleeding gums, bloody sputum, blood-tinged urine, bloody or tarry stools. (The incidence of significant bleeding is 2 to 4%.)

Advisability of Use During Pregnancy

This drug can cause hemorrhage in the fetus. Avoid use completely if possible.

Advisability of Use While Nursing Infant

This drug is present in milk and may cause bleeding or hemorrhage in the nursing infant. Avoid drug or avoid nursing. Ask physician for guidance.

Habit-Forming Potential

None.

Effects of Overdosage

With Moderate Overdose: Episodes of minor bleeding: blood spots in white portion of eye, nose bleeds, gum bleeding, small bruises, prolonged bleeding from minor cuts received while shaving or from other small lacerations.

With Large Overdose: Episodes of major internal bleeding: vomiting of blood, grossly bloody urine or stools.

Possible Effects of Extended Use
None reported.

Recommended Periodic Examinations While Taking This Drug
Regular determination of prothrombin time is essential to safe dosage and proper control.
Occasional urine analysis for red blood cells.

While Taking This Drug, Observe the Following
Foods: A larger intake than usual of foods high in Vitamin K may reduce the effectiveness of this drug and make larger doses necessary. Foods rich in Vitamin K include: cabbage, cauliflower, fish, kale, liver, spinach.

Beverages: No restrictions

Alcohol: Use with caution until combined effect has been determined. Alcohol can either increase or decrease the effect of this drug. It is advisable to use alcohol sparingly while taking anticoagulants. (Note: Heavy users of alcohol with liver damage may be very sensitive to anticoagulants and require smaller than usual doses.)

Tobacco Smoking: No interactions expected with this drug. Follow physician's advice regarding smoking (based upon condition under treatment).

Other Drugs
See WARFARIN Drug Profile. Drug interactions for dicumarol are essentially the same as for warfarin.

Driving a Vehicle, Piloting a Plane, Operating Machinery: No restrictions. Avoid unnecessary hazardous activities that could cause injury and result in excessive bleeding.

Exposure to Sun: No restrictions.

Exposure to Heat: Prolonged hot weather may increase the prothrombin time and make it advisable to reduce anticoagulant dosage. Ask physician for guidance.

Occurrence of Unrelated Illness: Any acute illness that causes fever, vomiting, or diarrhea can alter your response to this drug. Notify your physician so corrective action can be taken.

Discontinuation: Do not discontinue this drug abruptly unless abnormal bleeding occurs. Ask physician for guidance regarding gradual reduction of dosage over a period of 3 to 4 weeks.

Special Storage Instructions
Keep in a dry, tightly closed container. Protect from light.

DICYCLOMINE

Year Introduced: 1952

Brand Names

USA	Canada
Bentyl (Merrell-National)	Bentylol (Merrell)
Dispas (North Amer.	Cyclobec (Pharbec)
Pharm.)	Menospasm (Deca)
Dyspas (Savage)	Viscerol (Medic)
Nospaz (Tutag)	
Triactin [CD] (Norwich)	

Drug Family: Antispasmodic, Atropine-like Drug

Prescription Required: Yes

Available Dosage Forms and Strengths
Tablets — 20 mg.
Capsules — 10 mg.
Syrup — 10 mg. per teaspoonful
Injection — 10 mg. per ml.

How This Drug Works

Intended Therapeutic Effect(s):   Relief of discomfort resulting from muscle spasm of the gastrointestinal tract (esophagus, stomach, intestine, and colon).

Location of Drug Action(s):   The muscles of the gastrointestinal tract.

Method of Drug Action(s):   Not completely established. It has been suggested that this drug may relax gastrointestinal muscle by means of a local anesthetic action that blocks reflex activity responsible for contraction and motility.

THIS DRUG SHOULD NOT BE TAKEN IF

—you have had an allergic reaction to any dosage form of it previously.
—you are unable to empty the urinary bladder completely.
—your stomach cannot empty properly into the intestine (pyloric obstruction).
—you have ulcerative colitis.
—you have myasthenia gravis.

INFORM YOUR PHYSICIAN BEFORE TAKING THIS DRUG IF

—you have glaucoma.
—you have a history of peptic ulcer disease.
—you have enlargement of the prostate gland.
—you have a history of liver or kidney disease.

Time Required for Apparent Benefit

Drug action begins in 1 to 2 hours and persists for approximately 4 hours.

Possible Side-Effects *(natural, expected, and unavoidable drug actions)*

Dryness of the mouth, blurred vision, constipation, rapid pulse.

Possible Adverse Effects *(unusual, unexpected, and infrequent reactions)*

IF ANY OF THE FOLLOWING DEVELOP, DISCONTINUE DRUG AND NOTIFY
YOUR PHYSICIAN AS SOON AS POSSIBLE

Mild Adverse Effects

Allergic Reactions: Skin rash, hives.

Reduced appetite, nausea, vomiting.

Headache, dizziness, drowsiness, weakness.

Difficult urination, reduced sexual function.

Serious Adverse Effects

Allergic Reactions: Anaphylactic reaction (see Glossary).

Idiosyncratic Reactions: Excitement, confusion, disturbed behavior.

Increased internal eye pressure (dangerous in glaucoma).

Advisability of Use During Pregnancy

Safety not established. Prudent use is best determined by the physician's
evaluation.

Advisability of Use While Nursing Infant

This drug may impair milk formation and make nursing difficult. Safety for
infant not established. Ask physician for guidance.

Habit-Forming Potential

None.

Effects of Overdosage

With Moderate Overdose: Headache, dizziness, nausea, dryness of the
mouth, difficulty in swallowing.

With Large Overdose: Dilated pupils, hot and dry skin, fever, excitement,
restlessness.

Possible Effects of Extended Use

None reported.

Recommended Periodic Examinations While Taking This Drug

Measurements of internal eye pressure (in presence of glaucoma or suspected
glaucoma).

While Taking This Drug, Observe the Following

Foods: No interactions. Drug is more effective if taken one-half to 1 hour
before eating. Follow prescribed diet.

Beverages: No interactions. As allowed by prescribed diet.

Alcohol: No interactions expected with this drug. Follow physician's advice
regarding use of alcohol (based upon its effect on the disease under treatment).

Tobacco Smoking: No interactions expected. Follow physician's advice regarding smoking.

Other Drugs

Dicyclomine may *increase* the effects of

• all other drugs having atropine-like actions (see Drug Family, Section
Four).

Dicyclomine may *decrease* the effects of
• pilocarpine eye drops, and reduce their effectiveness in lowering internal eye pressure (in the treatment of glaucoma).

The following drugs may *increase* the effects of dicyclomine:
• tricyclic antidepressants
• antihistamines
• meperidine (Demerol, pethidine)
• methylphenidate (Ritalin)
• orphenadrine (Disipal, Norflex)
• phenothiazines

Driving a Vehicle, Piloting a Plane, Operating Machinery: This drug may produce blurred vision, drowsiness, or dizziness. Avoid hazardous activities if these drug effects occur.

Exposure to Sun: No restrictions.

Exposure to Heat: Use extreme caution. The use of this drug in hot environments may increase the risk of heat stroke.

Heavy Exercise or Exertion: Use caution in hot or warm environments. This drug may impair normal perspiration and interfere with the regulation of body temperature.

Special Storage Instructions
Keep in a tightly closed container. Protect from light.

DIETHYLPROPION

Year Introduced: 1958

Brand Names

USA	Canada
Tenuate	Dietec (Pharbec)
(Merrell-National)	D.I.P. (Eri)
Tepanil (Riker)	Nobesine - 25 (Nadeau)
	Regibon (Medic)
	Tenuate (Merrell)

Drug Family: Appetite Suppressant (Anorexiant), Amphetamine-like Drug [Sympathomimetics]

Prescription Required: Yes (Controlled Drug, U.S. Schedule 4)

Available Dosage Forms and Strengths
Tablets — 25 mg.
Prolonged Action Tablets — 75 mg.

How This Drug Works
Intended Therapeutic Effect(s):   The suppression of appetite in the management of weight reduction using low-calorie diets.

Location of Drug Action(s):   Not completely established. The site of therapeutic action is thought to be the appetite-regulating center located in the hypothalamus of the brain.

Method of Drug Action(s):   Not established. This drug is thought to resemble the amphetamines in its action, diminishing hunger by altering the chemical control of nerve impulse transmission in the brain center which regulates appetite.

THIS DRUG SHOULD NOT BE TAKEN IF

—you have had an allergic reaction to any dosage form of it previously.

—you have glaucoma.

—you are taking, or have taken during the past 2 weeks, any mono-amine oxidase (MAO) inhibitor drug (see Drug Family, Section Four).

—it is prescribed for a child under 12 years of age.

INFORM YOUR PHYSICIAN BEFORE TAKING THIS DRUG IF

—you have had an unfavorable reaction to any amphetamine-like drug in the past.

—you have high blood pressure or any form of heart disease.

—you have an overactive thyroid gland (hyperthyroidism).

—you have a history of serious anxiety or nervous tension.

—you have epilepsy.

Time Required for Apparent Benefit

Drug action begins in approximately 1 hour and persists for 3 to 4 hours (the regular tablet) or for 10 to 14 hours (the prolonged action tablet).

Possible Side-Effects *(natural, expected, and unavoidable drug actions)*

Nervousness, insomnia.

CAUTION

The appetite-suppressing action of this drug may disappear after several weeks of continuous use, regardless of the size of the dose. *Do not increase the dose* beyond that prescribed.

Possible Adverse Effects *(unusual, unexpected, and infrequent reactions)*

IF ANY OF THE FOLLOWING DEVELOP, DISCONTINUE DRUG AND NOTIFY YOUR PHYSICIAN AS SOON AS POSSIBLE

Mild Adverse Effects

Allergic Reactions: Skin rashes, hives, bruising.

Headache, dizziness, restlessness, tremor.

Dryness of the mouth, nausea, vomiting, diarrhea.

Fast, forceful, and irregular heart action (heart palpitation).

Menstrual irregularities, impaired sexual function.

Serious Adverse Effects

Idiosyncratic Reactions: Overstimulation, anxiety, euphoria, erratic behavior.

Increased frequency of epileptic seizures.

Bone marrow depression (see Glossary).

Advisability of Use During Pregnancy
Safety not established. Prudent use is best determined by the physician's evaluation.

Advisability of Use While Nursing Infant
Presence of drug in milk is not known. Safety for infant not established. Ask physician for guidance.

Habit-Forming Potential
This drug is related to amphetamine and can cause severe psychological dependence (see Glossary). Avoid large doses and prolonged use.

Effects of Overdosage
With Moderate Overdose: Nervous irritability, overactivity, insomnia, personality change, tremor.
With Large Overdose: Initial excitement, dilated pupils, rapid pulse, confusion, disorientation, bizarre behavior, hallucinations, convulsions, coma.

Possible Effects of Extended Use
Severe psychological dependence.
Skin eruptions.

Recommended Periodic Examinations While Taking This Drug
Complete blood cell counts.

While Taking This Drug, Observe the Following
Foods: Avoid foods rich in tyramine (see Glossary). This drug in combination with tyramine may cause excessive rise in blood pressure.
Beverages: Avoid beverages prepared from meat or yeast extracts; avoid chocolate drinks.
Alcohol: Avoid beer, Chianti wines and vermouth.
Tobacco Smoking: No interactions expected.
Other Drugs
   Diethylpropion may *decrease* the effects of
   • the major anti-hypertensive drugs, impairing their ability to lower blood pressure. The drugs most affected are: guanethidine (Ismelin), hydralazine (Apresoline), methyldopa (Aldomet), and reserpine (Serpasil, etc.).

   Diethylpropion *taken concurrently* with
   • mono-amine oxidase (MAO) inhibitor drugs (see Drug Family, Section Four), may cause a dangerous rise in blood pressure. Withhold the use of diethylpropion for a minimum of 2 weeks after discontinuing any MAO inhibitor drug.

Driving a Vehicle, Piloting a Plane, Operating Machinery: This drug may impair the ability to safely engage in hazardous activities. Use caution until full effect has been determined.
Exposure to Sun: No restrictions.
Discontinuation: If this drug has been used for an extended period of time, do not discontinue it suddenly. Ask physician for guidance regarding gradual reduction and withdrawal.

Special Storage Instructions
Keep in a dry, tightly closed container.

DIGITALIS

Year Introduced: 1775

Brand Names

USA	Canada
Digifortis (Parke-Davis)	Chemdigtal (Chemo)
Digiglusin (Lilly)	Digitalis (Dymond)
Digitalis (Various	(Powell)
Manufacturers)	
Digitora (Upjohn)	
Pil-Digis (Lakeside)	

Drug Family: Digitalis Preparations (Cardiotonic)

Prescription Required: Yes

Available Dosage Forms and Strengths
Tablets — 30 mg. (0.5 gr.), 45 mg. (0.75 gr.), 65 mg. (1 gr.), 100 mg. (1.5 gr
Pills — 30 mg. (0.5 gr.), 45 mg. (0.75 gr.), 65 mg. (1 gr.)
Capsules — 65 mg. (1 gr.), 100 mg. (1.5 gr.)
Tincture — 73%, 100 mg. (1.5 gr.) per ml.

How This Drug Works
Intended Therapeutic Effect(s)
• improvement of the contraction force of the heart muscle, of benefit i
the treatment of congestive heart failure.
• correction of certain heart rhythm disorders.
Location of Drug Action(s)
• the heart muscle.
• the pacemaker and tissues that comprise the electrical conduction syster
of the heart.
Method of Drug Action(s)
By increasing the availability of calcium within the heart muscle, this dru
improves the efficiency of the conversion of chemical energy to mechan
cal energy, thus increasing the force of muscular contraction.
By slowing the activity of the pacemaker and delaying the transmission c
electrical impulses through the conduction system of the heart, this dru
assists in restoring normal heart rate and rhythm.

THIS DRUG SHOULD NOT BE TAKEN IF
—you have had an allergic reaction to any dosage form of it previously.

INFORM YOUR PHYSICIAN BEFORE TAKING THIS DRUG IF

—you have taken *any* digitalis preparation (including digitoxin and digoxin) within the past 2 weeks.

—you are now taking (or have recently taken) any diuretic (urine-producing) drugs.

—you have impaired liver or kidney function.

—you have a history of thyroid deficiency (hypothyroidism).

Time Required for Apparent Benefit

Drug action begins in 1 to 2 hours, reaches a maximum between 4 and 12 hours, and persists for 48 to 72 hours. (Some activity may persist for as long as 2 to 3 weeks.) Continuous use of this drug on a regular schedule (with careful, individualized dosage adjustment) is needed to achieve full benefit.

Possible Side-Effects *(natural, expected, and unavoidable drug actions)*

This drug may produce enlargement and/or sensitivity of the male breast tissue (rare). This is due to an estrogen-like (female hormone) action of certain digitalis preparations.

CAUTION

1. This drug has a narrow margin of safe use. Adhere strictly to prescribed dosage. Do not raise or lower the dose without first consulting your physician.
2. It is advisable to carry a card of personal identification that includes a notation that *you are taking this drug* (see Table 14 and Section Seven).
3. The elderly (over 60 years of age) are often more sensitive to the actions of this drug. Small doses are advisable until individual response has been determined.

Possible Adverse Effects *(unusual, unexpected, and infrequent reactions)*

IF ANY OF THE FOLLOWING DEVELOP, DISCONTINUE DRUG AND NOTIFY YOUR PHYSICIAN AS SOON AS POSSIBLE

Mild Adverse Effects

Allergic Reactions: Skin rash (various kinds), hives.

Drowsiness, lethargy, changes in vision ("halo" effect, yellow-green vision, blurring, "spots", double vision), confusion, headache.

Serious Adverse Effects

Confusion, disorientation (usually in the elderly).

Advisability of Use During Pregnancy

Adverse effects on the fetus have been reported. If use of drug is necessary, adhere to a carefully adjusted dosage schedule to reduce chance of overdosage.

Advisability of Use While Nursing Infant

Drug is probably present in milk. Safety for infant not established. Ask physician for guidance.

Habit-Forming Potential

None.

Effects of Overdosage
With Moderate Overdose: Loss of appetite, excessive saliva, nausea, vomiting, diarrhea. (These effects are usually the earliest indicators of an overdosage.)

With Large Overdose: Serious disturbance of heart rhythm and rate, intestinal bleeding, drowsiness, headache, confusion, delirium, hallucinations, convulsions.

Possible Effects of Extended Use
Impaired color vision: a red-green color perception defect that is reversible.

Recommended Periodic Examinations While Taking This Drug
Electrocardiograms.
Measurement of blood potassium level.

While Taking This Drug, Observe the Following
Foods: No interactions with drug. Follow prescribed diet.

Beverages: It is advisable to use caffeine-containing beverages (coffee, tea, cola) sparingly.

Alcohol: No interactions expected. Follow physician's advice.

Tobacco Smoking: Follow physician's advice regarding smoking. Nicotine can cause irritability of the heart muscle and may confuse interpretation of your response to this drug.

Other Drugs

Digitalis *taken concurrently* with

- ephedrine or epinephrine (adrenaline), may cause serious disturbance of heart rhythm.
- cortisone and related drugs, may lead to digitalis toxicity (due to excessive loss of potassium from the body).
- diuretics (other than spironolactone and triamterene), may cause serious digitalis toxicity (due to excessive loss of potassium).
- reserpine, may cause additional slowing of the heart and may increase the possibility of digitalis toxicity.
- thyroid preparations, requires that the combined effect be monitored very closely to prevent digitalis toxicity.

The following drugs may *increase* the effects of digitalis:

- phenytoin (Dantoin, Dilantin, etc.) may cause overdosage effects initially and reduced effects later.
- guanethidine may cause additional slowing of the heart.
- propranolol (Inderal) may cause additional slowing of the heart. Use this drug in small doses and very cautiously.
- quinidine must be used cautiously and in small doses.

The following drugs may *decrease* the effects of digitalis:

- antacids may interfere with drug absorption.
- laxatives may hasten drug's elimination and cause reduced absorption.
- phenobarbital may hasten drug's elimination and reduce effectiveness.
- phenylbutazone (Azolid, Butazolidin, etc.) may hasten drug's elimination and reduce effectiveness.

Driving a Vehicle, Piloting a Plane, Operating Machinery: No restrictions.
Exposure to Sun: No restrictions.
Occurrence of Unrelated Illness: Any illness that causes vomiting, diarrhea, dehydration, or liver impairment (such as jaundice) can seriously disturb the proper control of this drug's action. Notify physician immediately so corrective action can be taken.
Discontinuation: This drug must be continued indefinitely (possibly for life). Do not discontinue it without consultation with your physician.

Special Storage Instructions
Keep in a tightly closed container. Protect from light.

DIGITOXIN

Year Introduced: 1945

Brand Names

USA	Canada
Crystodigin (Lilly)	Purodigin (Wyeth)
Digitaline Nativelle (Savage)	
Purodigin (Wyeth)	

Drug Family: Digitalis Preparations (Cardiotonic)

Prescription Required: Yes

Available Dosage Forms and Strengths
Tablets — 0.05 mg., 0.1 mg., 0.15 mg., 0.2 mg.
Oral Solution — 1 mg. per ml.
Injection — 0.1 mg. per ml., 0.2 mg. per ml.

How This Drug Works
Intended Therapeutic Effect(s)
• improvement of the contraction force of the heart muscle, of benefit in the treatment of congestive heart failure.
• correction of certain heart rhythm disorders.
Location of Drug Action(s)
• the heart muscle.
• the pacemaker and tissues that comprise the electrical conduction system of the heart.
Method of Drug Action(s)
By increasing the availability of calcium within the heart muscle, this drug improves the efficiency of the conversion of chemical energy to mechanical energy, thus increasing the force of muscular contraction.
By slowing the activity of the pacemaker and delaying the transmission of electrical impulses through the conduction system of the heart, this drug assists in restoring normal heart rate and rhythm.

THIS DRUG SHOULD NOT BE TAKEN IF
—you have had an allergic reaction to any dosage form of it previously.

INFORM YOUR PHYSICIAN BEFORE TAKING THIS DRUG IF
—you have experienced any unfavorable reaction to a digitalis preparation in the past.
—you have taken any digitalis preparation within the past 2 weeks.
—you are now taking (or have recently taken) any diuretic (urine-producing) drugs.
—you have impaired liver or kidney function.
—you have a history of thyroid deficiency (hypothyroidism).

Time Required for Apparent Benefit
Drug action begins in 1 to 2 hours, reaches a maximum between 4 and 12 hours, and persists for 48 to 72 hours. (Some activity may persist for as long as 2 to 3 weeks.) Continuous use of this drug on a regular schedule (with careful, individualized dosage adjustment) is needed to achieve full benefit.

Possible Side-Effects *(natural, expected, and unavoidable drug actions)*
This drug may produce enlargement and/or sensitivity of the male breast tissue (rare). This is due to an estrogen-like (female hormone) action of certain digitalis preparations.

CAUTION
1. This drug has a narrow margin of safe use. Adhere strictly to prescribed dosage. Do not raise or lower the dose without first consulting your physician.
2. It is advisable to carry a card of personal identification that includes a notation that *you are taking this drug* (see Table 14 and Section Seven).
3. The elderly (over 60 years of age) are often more sensitive to the actions of this drug. Small doses are advisable until individual response has been determined.

Possible Adverse Effects *(unusual, unexpected, and infrequent reactions)*

IF ANY OF THE FOLLOWING DEVELOP, DISCONTINUE DRUG AND NOTIFY YOUR PHYSICIAN AS SOON AS POSSIBLE

Mild Adverse Effects
 Allergic Reactions: Skin rash (various kinds), hives.
 Drowsiness, lethargy, changes in vision ("halo" effect, yellow-green vision blurring, "spots", double vision), confusion, headache.

Serious Adverse Effects
 Allergic Reactions: Abnormal bruising due to allergic destruction of blood platelets (see Glossary).
 Confusion, disorientation (usually in the elderly).

Advisability of Use During Pregnancy
Adverse effects on the fetus have been reported. If use of drug is necessary adhere to a carefully adjusted dosage schedule to reduce chance of overdosage.

Advisability of Use While Nursing Infant
Drug is probably present in milk. Safety for infant not established. Ask physician for guidance.

Habit-Forming Potential
None.

Effects of Overdosage
With Moderate Overdose: Loss of appetite, excessive saliva, nausea, vomiting, diarrhea. (These effects are usually the earliest indicators of an overdosage.)

With Large Overdose: Serious disturbance of heart rhythm and rate, intestinal bleeding, drowsiness, headache, confusion, delirium, hallucinations, convulsions.

Possible Effects of Extended Use
None reported.

Recommended Periodic Examinations While Taking This Drug
Complete blood cell counts.
Electrocardiograms.
Measurement of blood potassium level.

While Taking This Drug, Observe the Following
Foods: No interactions with drug. Follow prescribed diet.

Beverages: It is advisable to use caffeine-containing beverages (coffee, tea, cola) sparingly.

Alcohol: No interactions expected. Follow physician's advice.

Tobacco Smoking: Follow physician's advice regarding smoking. Nicotine can cause irritability of the heart muscle and may confuse interpretation of your response to this drug.

Other Drugs

Digitoxin *taken concurrently* with

- ephedrine or epinephrine (adrenaline), may cause serious disturbance of heart rhythm.
- cortisone and related drugs, may lead to digitalis toxicity (due to excessive loss of potassium from the body).
- diuretics (other than spironolactone and triamterene), may cause serious digitalis toxicity (due to excessive loss of potassium).
- reserpine, may cause additional slowing of the heart and may increase the possibility of digitalis toxicity.
- thyroid preparations, require that the combined effect be monitored very closely to prevent digitalis toxicity.

The following drugs may *increase* the effects of digitoxin

- phenytoin (Dantoin, Dilantin, etc.) may cause overdosage effects initially and reduced effects later.
- guanethidine may cause additional slowing of the heart.
- propranolol (Inderal) may cause additional slowing of the heart. Use this drug in small doses and very cautiously.
- quinidine must be used cautiously and in small doses.

The following drugs may *decrease* the effects of digitoxin
- antacids may interfere with drug absorption.
- laxatives may hasten drug's elimination and cause reduced absorption.
- phenobarbital may hasten drug's elimination and reduce effectiveness.
- phenylbutazone (Azolid, Butazolidin, etc.) may hasten drug's elimination and reduce effectiveness.

Driving a Vehicle, Piloting a Plane, Operating Machinery: No restrictions.

Exposure to Sun: No restrictions.

Occurrence of Unrelated Illness: Any illness that causes vomiting, diarrhea, dehydration, or liver impairment (such as jaundice) can seriously disturb the proper control of this drug's action. Notify physician immediately so corrective action can be taken.

Discontinuation: This drug must be continued indefinitely (possibly for life). Do not discontinue it without consultation with your physician.

Special Storage Instructions
Keep in a tightly closed container. Protect from light.

DIGOXIN

Year Introduced: 1934

Brand Names

USA	Canada
Davoxin (Lakeside)	Chemgoxin (Chemo)
Lanoxin (Burroughs	Lanoxin (B.W. Ltd.)
Wellcome)	Novodigoxin
Thegitoxin (Standex)	(Novopharm)
	Rougoxin (Rougier)

Drug Family: Digitalis Preparations (Cardiotonic)

Prescription Required: Yes

Available Dosage Forms and Strengths
Tablets — 0.125 mg., 0.25 mg., 0.5 mg.
Pediatric Elixir — 0.05 mg. per ml.
Injection — 0.1 mg. per ml., 0.25 mg. per ml.

How This Drug Works
Intended Therapeutic Effect(s)
- improvement of the contraction force of the heart muscle, of benefit in the treatment of congestive heart failure.
- correction of certain heart rhythm disorders.

Location of Drug Action(s)
- the heart muscle.
- the pacemaker and tissues that comprise the electrical conduction system of the heart.

Method of Drug Action(s)
By increasing the availability of calcium within the heart muscle, this drug improves the efficiency of the conversion of chemical energy to mechanical energy, thus increasing the force of muscular contraction.

By slowing the activity of the pacemaker and delaying the transmission of electrical impulses through the conduction system of the heart, this drug assists in restoring normal heart rate and rhythm.

THIS DRUG SHOULD NOT BE TAKEN IF
—you have had an allergic reaction to any dosage form of it previously.

INFORM YOUR PHYSICIAN BEFORE TAKING THIS DRUG IF
—you have experienced any unfavorable reaction to a digitalis preparation in the past.

—you have taken any digitalis preparation within the past 2 weeks.

—you are now taking (or have recently taken) any diuretic (urine-producing) drugs.

—you have impaired liver or kidney function.

—you have a history of thyroid deficiency (hypothyroidism).

Time Required for Apparent Benefit
Drug action begins in 1 hour, reaches a maximum in 6 to 7 hours, and persists for approximately 3 days. Elimination from the body is usually complete in 6 days.

Possible Side-Effects *(natural, expected, and unavoidable drug actions)*
This drug may produce enlargement and/or sensitivity of the male breast tissue (rare). This is due to an estrogen-like (female hormone) action of some digitalis preparations.

CAUTION
1. This drug has a narrow margin of safe use. Adhere strictly to prescribed dosage. Do not raise or lower the dose without first consulting your physician.
2. It is advisable to carry a card of personal identification that includes a notation that you are taking this drug (see Table 14 and Section Seven).
3. The elderly (over 60 years of age) are often more sensitive to the actions of this drug. Small doses are advisable until individual response has been determined.

Possible Adverse Effects *(unusual, unexpected, and infrequent reactions)*

IF ANY OF THE FOLLOWING DEVELOP, DISCONTINUE DRUG AND NOTIFY YOUR PHYSICIAN AS SOON AS POSSIBLE

Mild Adverse Effects
Allergic Reactions: Skin rash (various kinds), hives.

Drowsiness, lethargy, changes in vision ("halo" effect, yellow-green vision, blurring, "spots", double vision), confusion, headache.

Serious Adverse Effects
Confusion, disorientation (usually in the elderly).

Advisability of Use During Pregnancy
Adverse effects on the fetus have been reported. If use of drug is necessary, adhere to a carefully adjusted dosage schedule to reduce changes of overdosage.

Advisability of Use While Nursing Infant
Drug is known to be present in milk. Safety for infant not established. Ask physician for guidance.

Habit-Forming Potential
None.

Effects of Overdosage
With Moderate Overdose: Loss of appetite, excessive saliva, nausea, vomiting, diarrhea. (These effects are usually the earliest indicators of an overdosage.)
With Large Overdose: Serious disturbance of heart rhythm and rate, intestinal bleeding, drowsiness, headache, confusion, delirium, hallucinations, convulsions.

Possible Effects of Extended Use
None reported.

Recommended Periodic Examinations While Taking This Drug
Electrocardiograms.
Measurement of blood potassium level.

While Taking This Drug, Observe the Following
Foods: No interactions with drug. Follow prescribed diet.
Beverages: It is advisable to use caffeine-containing beverages (coffee, tea, cola) sparingly.
Alcohol: No interactions expected. Follow physician's advice.
Tobacco Smoking: Follow physician's advice regarding smoking. Nicotine can cause irritability of the heart muscle and may confuse interpretation of your response to this drug.
Other Drugs
Digoxin *taken concurrently* with
• ephedrine or epinephrine (adrenaline), may cause serious disturbance of heart rhythm.
• cortisone and related drugs, may lead to digitalis toxicity (due to excessive loss of potassium from the body).
• diuretics (other than spironolactone and triamterene), may cause serious digitalis toxicity (due to excessive loss of potassium).
• reserpine, may cause additional slowing of the heart and may increase the possibility of digitalis toxicity.
• thyroid preparations, require that the combined effect be monitored very closely to prevent digitalis toxicity.

The following drugs may *increase* the effects of digoxin

- phenytoin (Dantoin, Dilantin, etc.) may cause overdosage effects initially and reduced effects later.
- guanethidine may cause additional slowing of the heart.
- propranolol (Inderal) may cause additional slowing of the heart. Use this drug in small doses and very cautiously.
- quinidine must be used cautiously and in small doses.

The following drugs may *decrease* the effects of digoxin

- antacids may interfere with drug absorption.
- laxatives may hasten drug's elimination and cause reduced absorption.
- phenobarbital may hasten drug's elimination and reduce effectiveness.
- phenylbutazone (Azolid, Butazolidin, etc.) may hasten drug's elimination and reduce effectiveness.

Driving a Vehicle, Piloting a Plane, Operating Machinery: No restrictions.
Exposure to Sun: No restrictions.

Occurrence of Unrelated Illness: Any illness that causes vomiting, diarrhea, dehydration, or liver impairment (such as jaundice) can seriously disturb the proper control of this drug's action. Notify physician immediately so corrective action can be taken.

Discontinuation: This drug must be continued indefinitely (possibly for life). Do not discontinue it without consultation with your physician.

Special Storage Instructions
Keep in a tightly closed container. Protect from light.

DIHYDROERGOTOXINE
Dihydrogenated Ergot Alkaloids:
Dihydroergocornine
Dihydroergocristine
Dihydroergokryptine

Year Introduced: 1949

Brand Names

USA	Canada
Deapril-ST (Mead Johnson)	Hydergine (Sandoz)
Hydergine (Sandoz)	

Drug Family: Ergot Preparations

Prescription Required: Yes

Available Dosage Forms and Strengths
Tablets, Sublingual — 0.5 mg., 1.0 mg.
Injection — 0.3 mg. per ml.

How This Drug Works

Intended Therapeutic Effect(s):   Alleviation of disturbing mental symptoms commonly experienced by the elderly, such as reduced alertness, poor memory, confusion, lack of motivation, and emotional depression.

Location of Drug Action(s):   Those areas of the brain that are responsible for intellect, personality, and behavior.

Method of Drug Action(s):   Not completely established. Present theory is that by stimulating brain cell metabolism, this drug increases the brain's ability to utilize oxygen and nutrients. The resulting improvement in brain function is thought to contribute to the benefit seen in responsive patients.

THIS DRUG SHOULD NOT BE TAKEN IF

—you have had an allergic reaction to any dosage form of it previously.
—your pulse rate is below 60 beats per minute.
—your systolic blood pressure is consistently below 100.

INFORM YOUR PHYSICIAN BEFORE TAKING THIS DRUG IF

—you have a history of low blood pressure.
—you are taking any drugs for high blood pressure.
—you are taking any digitalis preparation.
—you are taking propranolol (Inderal).

Time Required for Apparent Benefit

Relief of symptoms is usually gradual. Continuous use on a regular schedule for 3 to 4 weeks may be necessary to produce improvement.

Possible Side-Effects *(natural, expected and unavoidable drug actions)*

None expected.

CAUTION

Numerous studies have demonstrated that this drug can be beneficial in relieving many complaints of the elderly related to memory, intellectual performance, and social adjustment. However, it is important to remember that the causes of such symptoms are poorly understood, that they can occur whether or not drugs are being taken, and that behavioral changes in the elderly are often frequent and unpredictable. It is therefore advisable to monitor the response to this drug very closely, and to notify the physician if any significant adverse personality changes occur. In some instances, the development of nervousness, hostility, confusion, and depression may be related to the use of the drug.

Possible Adverse Effects *(unusual, unexpected and infrequent reactions)*

IF ANY OF THE FOLLOWING DEVELOP, DISCONTINUE DRUG AND NOTIFY YOUR PHYSICIAN AS SOON AS POSSIBLE

Mild Adverse Effects

Allergic Reactions: Skin rash (various kinds), drug fever (see Glossary). Headache, dizziness, flushing, blurred vision.
Nasal stuffiness, reduced appetite, nausea, vomiting, abdominal cramping.

Serious Adverse Effects
Marked drop in blood pressure, fainting.
Marked slowing of the heart rate (pulse count 40 to 50 beats per minute), accompanied by reduced activity, sluggishness, drowsiness, emotional withdrawal, and apathy.

Habit-Forming Potential
None

Effects of Overdosage
With Moderate Overdose: Headache, flushing of the face, nasal stuffiness.
With Large Overdose: Nausea, vomiting, extreme drop in blood pressure, weakness, collapse, coma.

Possible Effects of Extended Use
None reported.

Recommended Periodic Examinations While Taking This Drug
Pulse counts and blood pressure measurements on a regular basis.

While Taking This Drug, Observe the Following
Foods: No restrictions.
Beverages: No restrictions.
Alcohol: Use with caution until combined effects have been determined. Sensitive individuals may experience an excessive drop in blood pressure.
Tobacco Smoking: No interactions expected.
Other Drugs

Dihydroergotoxine may *increase* the effects of
• antihypertensive drugs, and cause excessive lowering of the blood pressure.

Dihydroergotoxine *taken concurrently* with
• digitalis preparations may cause excessive slowing of the heart rate.
• propranolol (Inderal) may cause excessive slowing of the heart rate and/or excessive lowering of the blood pressure.

Driving a Vehicle, Piloting a Plane, Operating Machinery: No restrictions, unless dizziness or blurring of vision should occur with use of the drug.
Exposure to Sun: No restrictions.
Exposure to Heat: No restrictions.
Exposure to Cold: Use caution. Avoid exposure that could lower body temperature and impair metabolism.
Heavy Exercise or Exertion: No restriction, if exertion is in keeping with physical condition.

Special Storage Instructions
Keep in a tightly closed container. Do not store at temperature above 86°F. (30°C.).

DIMENHYDRINATE

Year Introduced: 1949

Brand Names

USA	Canada
Dramamine (Searle)	Dramamine (Searle)
(Numerous other brand	Dramavol (Barlowe Cote)
names)	Dymenol (Dymond)
	Gravol (Horner)
	Nauseal (Eri)
	Nauseatol (Demers)
	Novodimenate
	(Novopharm)
	Travamine (ICN)

Drug Family: Antihistamines; Anti-motion sickness (Anti-emetic)

Prescription Required: For tablets and liquid—No
For suppositories and injection—Yes

Available Dosage Forms and Strengths
Tablets — 50 mg.
Liquid — 12.5 mg. per teaspoonful
Suppositories — 100 mg.
Injection — 50 mg. per ml.

How This Drug Works
Intended Therapeutic Effect(s):   Prevention and management of the nausea, vomiting, and dizziness associated with motion sickness.
Location of Drug Action(s):   The nerve pathways connecting the organ of equilibrium (the labyrinth) in the inner ear with the vomiting center in the brain.
Method of Drug Action(s):   This drug reduces the sensitivity of the nerve endings in the labyrinth and blocks the transmission of excessive nerve impulses to the vomiting center.

THIS DRUG SHOULD NOT BE TAKEN IF
—you have had an allergic reaction to any dosage form of it previously.
—you are taking, or have taken during the past 2 weeks, any mono-amine oxidase (MAO) inhibitor drugs (see Drug Family, Section Four).
—it has been prescribed for a newborn infant.

INFORM YOUR PHYSICIAN BEFORE TAKING THIS DRUG IF
—you have had an unfavorable reaction to any antihistamine drug in the past.

Time Required for Apparent Benefit
Drug action begins in 30 to 60 minutes and persists for approximately 4 hours.

Possible Side-Effects *(natural, expected, and unavoidable drug actions)*
Drowsiness, lassitude, dry mouth.

Possible Adverse Effects *(unusual, unexpected, and infrequent reactions)*

IF ANY OF THE FOLLOWING DEVELOP, DISCONTINUE DRUG AND NOTIFY YOUR PHYSICIAN AS SOON AS POSSIBLE

Mild Adverse Effects
Allergic Reactions: Skin rash.
Nausea.

Serious Adverse Effects
None reported.

Advisability of Use During Pregnancy

No reports of adverse effects on mother or fetus. Limit use to small doses and for the shortest periods of time possible.

Advisability of Use While Nursing Infant

Presence of drug in milk is not known. Ask physician for guidance.

Habit-Forming Potential

None.

Effects of Overdosage

With Moderate Overdose: Marked drowsiness, dizziness, delirium, vomiting.

With Large Overdose: Stupor progressing to coma, convulsions, slow and shallow breathing.

Possible Effects of Extended Use

None reported.

Recommended Periodic Examinations While Taking This Drug

None required.

While Taking This Drug, Observe the Following

Foods: No restrictions.

Beverages: No restrictions.

Alcohol: Use caution until combined effects have been determined. Alcohol in combination with some antihistamines can cause rapid and marked sedation.

Tobacco Smoking: No interactions expected.

Other Drugs: No significant drug interactions reported.

Driving a Vehicle, Piloting a Plane, Operating Machinery: This drug may produce drowsiness that could impair mental alertness, coordination, and reaction time. Avoid hazardous activities until sedative effect has been determined.

Exposure to Sun: No restrictions.

Special Storage Instructions

Keep in a dry, tightly closed container.

DIPHENHYDRAMINE

Year Introduced: 1945

Brand Names

USA	Canada
*Ambodryl (Parke-Davis)	*Ambodryl (P.D. & Co.)
Benadryl (Parke-Davis)	Benadryl (P.D. & Co.)
Ambenyl [CD] (Parke-Davis)	Benhydramil (Barlowe Cote)
Benylin [CD] (Parke-Davis)	Ambenyl [CD] (P.D. & Co.)
(Numerous other brand and combination brand names)	Benylin [CD] (P.D. & Co.)

Drug Family: Antihistamines; Sleep Inducer (Hypnotic)

Prescription Required: Yes (Ambenyl is a Controlled Drug, U.S. Schedule 5)

Available Dosage Forms and Strengths

Capsules — 25 mg., 50 mg.
Elixir — 12.5 mg. per teaspoonful
Injection — 10 mg. per ml., 50 mg. per ml.

How This Drug Works

Intended Therapeutic Effect(s):   Relief of symptoms associated with hayfever (allergic rhinitis) and with allergic reactions in the skin, such as itching, swelling, hives, and rash.

Location of Drug Action(s):   Those hypersensitive tissues that release excessive histamine as part of an allergic reaction. The principal tissue sites are the eyes, the nose, and the skin.

Method of Drug Action(s):   This drug reduces the intensity of the allergic response by blocking the action of histamine after it has been released from sensitized tissue cells.

THIS DRUG SHOULD NOT BE TAKEN IF

—you have had an allergic reaction to any dosage form of it previously.
—you are subject to acute attacks of asthma.
—you have glaucoma (narrow-angle type).
—you have difficulty emptying the urinary bladder.
—you are taking, or have taken during the past 2 weeks, any mono-amine oxidase (MAO) inhibitor drugs (see Drug Family, Section Four).
—it has been prescribed for a newborn infant.

INFORM YOUR PHYSICIAN BEFORE TAKING THIS DRUG IF

—you have had an unfavorable reaction to any antihistamine drug in the past.
—you have a history of peptic ulcer disease.
—you plan to have surgery under general anesthesia in the near future.

*Ambodryl is bromodiphenhydramine and has the same characteristics as diphenhydramine.

Time Required for Apparent Benefit
Drug action begins in approximately 30 minutes, reaches a maximum in 1 hour, and subsides in 4 to 6 hours.

Possible Side-Effects *(natural, expected, and unavoidable drug actions)*
Drowsiness, sense of weakness, dryness of nose, mouth, and throat, constipation.

CAUTION
The elderly (over 60 years of age) may be more susceptible to the adverse effects of this drug. Small doses are advisable until tolerance is determined.

Possible Adverse Effects *(unusual, unexpected, and infrequent reactions)*

IF ANY OF THE FOLLOWING DEVELOP, DISCONTINUE DRUG AND NOTIFY YOUR PHYSICIAN AS SOON AS POSSIBLE

Mild Adverse Effects
Allergic Reactions: Skin rash, hives.
Headache, dizziness, inability to concentrate, nervousness, blurring of vision, double vision, difficulty in urination.
Nausea, vomiting, diarrhea.
Reduced tolerance for contact lenses.

Serious Adverse Effects
Allergic Reactions: Anaphylactic reaction (see Glossary).
Blood platelet destruction (see Glossary)—unusual bleeding or bruising.
Idiosyncratic Reactions: Behavioral disturbances—confusion, excitement, insomnia.
Hemolytic anemia (see Glossary).

Advisability of Use During Pregnancy
No reports of adverse effects on mother or fetus. Limit use to small doses and for the shortest periods of time possible.

Advisability of Use While Nursing Infant
This drug may impair milk formation and make nursing difficult. In addition, the drug is known to be present in milk. Ask physician for guidance.

Habit-Forming Potential
None.

Effects of Overdosage
With Moderate Overdose: Marked drowsiness, confusion, incoordination, unsteady gait, muscle tremors. In children: excitement, hallucinations, overactivity, convulsions.
With Large Overdose: Stupor progressing to coma, fever, flushed face, dilated pupils, weak pulse, shallow breathing.

Possible Effects of Extended Use
Hemolytic anemia (see Glossary).

Recommended Periodic Examinations While Taking This Drug
Complete blood cell counts.

While Taking This Drug, Observe the Following

Foods: No restrictions. Stomach irritation can be reduced if drug is taken after eating.

Beverages: Coffee and tea may help to reduce the drowsiness caused by most antihistamines.

Alcohol: Use with extreme caution until combined effect has been determined. The combination of alcohol and antihistamines can cause rapid and marked sedation.

Tobacco Smoking: No interactions expected.

Other Drugs

Diphenhydramine may *increase* the effects of

- sedatives, sleep-inducing drugs, tranquilizers, antidepressants, pain relievers, and narcotic drugs, and result in oversedation. Careful dosage adjustments are necessary.
- atropine and drugs with atropine-like action (see Drug Family, Section Four).

Diphenhydramine may *decrease* the effects of

- oral anticoagulants, and reduce their protective action. Consult physician regarding prothrombin time testing and dosage adjustment.
- cortisone and related drugs (see Drug Family, Section Four).

Diphenhydramine *taken concurrently* with

- phenytoin (Dantoin, Dilantin, etc.), may change the pattern of epileptic seizures. Dosage adjustments may be necessary for proper control of epilepsy.

The following drugs may *increase* the effects of diphenhydramine

- all sedatives, sleep-inducing drugs, tranquilizers, pain relievers, and narcotic drugs may exaggerate its sedative action and cause oversedation.
- mono-amine oxidase (MAO) inhibitor drugs (see Drug Family, Section Four) may delay its elimination from the body, thus exaggerating and prolonging its action.

The following drugs may *decrease* the effects of diphenhydramine

- the amphetamines (Benzedrine, Dexedrine, Desoxyn, etc.) may reduce the drowsiness caused by most antihistamines.

Driving a Vehicle, Piloting a Plane, Operating Machinery: This drug may impair mental alertness, judgment, physical coordination, and reaction time. Avoid hazardous activities until full sedative effect has been determined.

Exposure to Sun: Use caution until sensitivity has been determined. This drug may cause photosensitivity (see Glossary).

Special Storage Instructions

Keep in a dry, tightly closed, light-resistant container.

DIPHENOXYLATE

Year Introduced: 1960

Brand Names

USA	Canada
Lomotil [CD] (Searle)	Lomotil [CD] (Searle)

Drug Family: Anti-diarrheal

Prescription Required: Yes (Controlled Drug, U.S. Schedule 5)

Available Dosage Forms and Strengths
Tablets — 2.5 mg. (+ 0.025 mg. atropine)
Liquid — 2.5 mg. (+ 0.025 mg. atropine) per teaspoonful

How This Drug Works
Intended Therapeutic Effect(s):   Relief of intestinal cramping and diarrhea.
Location of Drug Action(s):   The nerve fibers in the wall of the stomach, the small intestine, and the colon.
Method of Drug Action(s):   Not completely established. It is thought that this drug acts directly on the nerve supply of the gastrointestinal tract to reduce its motility and propulsive contractions, thus relieving cramping and diarrhea.

THIS DRUG SHOULD NOT BE TAKEN IF
—you are allergic to either component of this drug.
—you have active jaundice.
—it is prescribed for a child under 2 years of age.

INFORM YOUR PHYSICIAN BEFORE TAKING THIS DRUG IF
—you have a history of liver disease or impaired liver function.
—you have ulcerative colitis.

Time Required for Apparent Benefit
Repeated dosage may be necessary for 12 to 24 hours to control diarrhea. Duration of effect may approach 30 hours.

Possible Side-Effects *(natural, expected, and unavoidable drug actions)*
Drowsiness, constipation.

CAUTION
Do not exceed recommended doses. Observe children closely for indications of atropine overdose (see ATROPINE Drug Profile).

Possible Adverse Effects *(unusual, unexpected, and infrequent reactions)*
IF ANY OF THE FOLLOWING DEVELOP, DISCONTINUE DRUG AND NOTIFY YOUR PHYSICIAN AS SOON AS POSSIBLE
Mild Adverse Effects
Allergic Reactions: Skin rash, hives, localized swellings, itching.
Headache, dizziness, weakness, euphoria.
Reduced appetite, nausea, vomiting, bloating.

Serious Adverse Effects
None reported.

Advisability of Use During Pregnancy
Safety not established. Prudent use is best determined by the physician's evaluation.

Advisability of Use While Nursing Infant
Both components of this drug are present in milk and can affect the nursing infant. Ask physician for guidance regarding safe dosage.

Habit-Forming Potential
Because of its similarity to meperidine (pethidine), this drug may cause physical and/or psychological dependence (see Glossary) if used in large doses over an extended period of time.

Effects of Overdosage
With Moderate Overdose: Marked drowsiness, lethargy, depression, numbness in arms and legs.

With Large Overdose: Dryness of skin and mouth, flushing, fever, rapid pulse, slow and shallow breathing, stupor progressing to coma.

Possible Effects of Extended Use
Physical and/or psychological dependence (see Glossary) is a remote possibility.

Recommended Periodic Examinations While Taking This Drug
None required.

While Taking This Drug, Observe the Following
Foods: No restrictions. Follow prescribed diet.

Beverages: No restrictions. As allowed in prescribed diet.

Alcohol: Use with extreme caution until combined effect has been determined. This drug may increase the depressant action of alcohol on the brain.

Tobacco Smoking: No interactions expected.

Other Drugs

Diphenoxylate may *increase* the effects of

• sedatives, tranquilizers, and sleep-inducing drugs, and cause excessive sedation. Dosage adjustments may be necessary.

Diphenoxylate *taken concurrently* with

• mono-amine oxidase (MAO) inhibitor drugs (see Drug Family, Section Four), will require close observation of the blood pressure to detect any tendency to excessive rise.

Driving a Vehicle, Piloting a Plane, Operating Machinery: This drug may cause drowsiness. Avoid hazardous activities until full effect has been determined.

Exposure to Sun: No restrictions.

Special Storage Instructions
Keep in a dry, tightly closed container.

DISULFIRAM

Year Introduced: 1948

Brand Names

USA	Canada
Antabuse (Ayerst)	Antabuse (Ayerst)

Drug Family: Anti-alcoholism (Alcohol-drinking Deterrent)

Prescription Required: Yes

Available Dosage Forms and Strengths
Tablets — 250 mg., 500 mg.

How This Drug Works
Intended Therapeutic Effect(s):   To deter the drinking of alcohol (in the management of alcoholism).

Location of Drug Action(s):   Specific enzyme systems within the liver.

Method of Drug Action(s):   Following the ingestion of alcohol, this drug interrupts normal liver enzyme activity after the conversion of alcohol to acetaldehyde. This causes excessive accumulation of acetaldehyde, a highly toxic substance that produces the disulfiram (Antabuse) reaction (see Glossary).

THIS DRUG SHOULD NOT BE TAKEN IF
—you have experienced a severe allergic reaction to disulfiram in the past. (The reaction of disulfiram and alcohol is *not* an allergic reaction.)
—you have used alcohol in any amount or in any form within the past 12 hours.
—you are taking (or have taken recently) metronidazole (Flagyl).
—you have heart disease.

INFORM YOUR PHYSICIAN BEFORE TAKING THIS DRUG IF
—you have used disulfiram in the past.
—you do *not* intend to avoid alcohol completely while taking this drug.
—you have not been given a full explanation of the reaction you will experience if you drink alcohol while taking this drug.
—you have a history of diabetes, epilepsy, liver, or kidney disease
—you are currently taking oral anticoagulants, digitalis, isoniazid, phenytoin (Dantoin, Dilantin, etc.).
—you plan to have surgery under general anesthesia while taking this drug.

Time Required for Apparent Benefit
Full effectiveness usually requires 3 weeks.

Possible Side-Effects *(natural, expected, and unavoidable drug actions)*
None.

CAUTION
1. This drug should *never* be given to an individual who is in a state of alcoholic intoxication.
2. The patient should be fully informed regarding the purpose and actions of this drug *before* treatment is started.

Possible Adverse Effects *(unusual, unexpected, and infrequent reactions)*
IF ANY OF THE FOLLOWING DEVELOP, DISCONTINUE DRUG AND NOTIFY YOUR PHYSICIAN AS SOON AS POSSIBLE
Mild Adverse Effects
Allergic Reactions: Skin rashes (various kinds), hives.
Drowsiness, lethargy, headache, tremor, dizziness.
Metallic or garlic-like taste, indigestion. (These usually appear during the first 2 weeks and then gradually subside.)
Serious Adverse Effects
Peripheral neuritis (see Glossary)—numbness or tingling, pain, weakness in arms or legs.
Optic neuritis—impaired vision.

Advisability of Use During Pregnancy
Safety not established. Prudent use is best determined by physician's evaluation.

Advisability of Use While Nursing Infant
Safety not established. Ask physician for guidance.

Habit-Forming Potential
None.

Effects of Overdosage
With Moderate Overdose: Marked lethargy, impaired memory, behavioral disturbances.
With Large Overdose: Headache, stomach pain, nausea, vomiting, diarrhea, confusion, impaired stance and gait, muscle weakness, temporary paralysis.

Possible Effects of Extended Use
No significant effects reported.

Recommended Periodic Examinations While Taking This Drug
Complete blood cell counts.
Liver function tests.

While Taking This Drug, Observe the Following
Foods: Avoid all foods prepared with alcohol, including sauces, marinades, vinegars, desserts, etc. (Inquire when dining out regarding the use of alcohol in food preparation.)
Beverages: Avoid all punches, fruit drinks, etc., that may contain alcohol.
Alcohol: Avoid completely in all forms while taking this drug and for 14

days following the last dose. The combination of disulfiram and alcohol—even in small amounts—produces the "disulfiram (Antabuse) reaction." This begins within 5 to 10 minutes after ingesting alcohol and consists of intense flushing and warming of the face, a severe throbbing headache, shortness of breath, chest pains, nausea, repeated vomiting, sweating, and weakness. If the amount of alcohol ingested is large enough, the reaction may progress to blurred vision, vertigo, confusion, marked drop in blood pressure, and loss of consciousness. Severe reactions may lead to convulsions and death. The reaction may last from 30 minutes to several hours, depending upon the amount of alcohol in the body. As the symptoms subside, the individual is exhausted and usually sleeps for several hours.

Tobacco Smoking: No interactions expected.

Other Drugs

Disulfiram may *increase* the effects of

• oral anticoagulants, and cause abnormal bleeding; dosage adjustments may be necessary.
• barbiturates, and cause oversedation (see Drug Family, Section Four).
• phenytoin (Dantoin, Dilantin, etc.), and cause toxic effects on the brain; dosage adjustments may be necessary.

Disulfiram *taken concurrently* with

• isoniazid (INH, etc.), may cause unsteady gait and acute mental disturbance, making it necessary to discontinue treatment.
• metronidazole (Flagyl), may cause acute mental and behavioral disturbances, making it necessary to discontinue treatment.
• OTC cough syrups, tonics, etc., containing alcohol, may cause a disulfiram (Antabuse) reaction (see OTC in Glossary).

Driving a Vehicle, Piloting a Plane, Operating Machinery: No restrictions if drowsiness and dizziness do not occur.

Exposure to Sun: No restrictions.

Discontinuation: Treatment with disulfiram is only part of your total treatment program. Do *not* discontinue this drug without the knowledge and agreement of your physician.

Special Storage Instructions

Keep in a dry, tightly closed container.

DOXEPIN

Year Introduced: 1969

Brand Names

USA	Canada
Adapin (Pennwalt)	Sinequan (Pfizer)
Sinequan (Pfizer)	

Drug Family: Antidepressant, Tricyclic (Anti-psychotic)

Prescription Required: Yes

Available Dosage Forms and Strengths
Capsules — 10 mg., 25 mg., 50 mg., 100 mg.
Oral Concentrate — 10 mg. per ml.

How This Drug Works
Intended Therapeutic Effect(s):   Gradual improvement of mood and relief of emotional depression.
Location of Drug Action(s):   Those areas of the brain that determine mood and emotional stability.
Method of Drug Action(s):   Not established. Present thinking is that this drug slowly restores to normal levels certain constituents of brain tissue (such as norepinephrine) that transmit nerve impulses.

THIS DRUG SHOULD NOT BE TAKEN IF
—you have had an allergic reaction to any dosage form of it previously.
—you are taking or have taken within the past 14 days any mono-amine oxidase (MAO) inhibitor drug (see Drug Family, Section Four).
—you are recovering from a recent heart attack.
—you have glaucoma (narrow-angle type).
—it is prescribed for a child under 12 years of age.

INFORM YOUR PHYSICIAN BEFORE TAKING THIS DRUG IF
—you are allergic or sensitive to any other tricyclic antidepressant (see Drug Family, Section Four).
—you have a history of any of the following: diabetes, epilepsy, glaucoma, heart disease, prostate gland enlargement, or overactive thyroid function.
—you plan to have surgery under general anesthesia in the near future.

Time Required for Apparent Benefit
Some benefit may be apparent within the first 2 weeks. Maximal response may require continuous treatment for 3 to 4 weeks.

Possible Side-Effects *(natural, expected, and unavoidable drug actions)*
Drowsiness, blurring of vision, dryness of mouth, constipation, impaired urination.

CAUTION
The possibility of adverse effects from this drug is greater in the elderly (over 60 years of age). Small doses are advisable until tolerance has been determined.

Possible Adverse Effects *(unusual, unexpected, and infrequent reactions)*
IF ANY OF THE FOLLOWING DEVELOP, DISCONTINUE DRUG AND NOTIFY YOUR PHYSICIAN AS SOON AS POSSIBLE

Mild Adverse Effects
Allergic Reactions: Skin rash, hives, swelling of face or tongue, drug fever. Nausea, indigestion, irritation of tongue or mouth, peculiar taste.

Headache, dizziness, weakness, fainting, unsteady gait, tremors.

Swelling of testicles, breast enlargement, milk formation.

Fluctuation of blood sugar levels.

Serious Adverse Effects

Allergic Reactions: Hepatitis with jaundice (see Glossary).

Bone marrow depression (see Glossary)—fatigue, fever, sore throat, unusual bleeding or bruising.

Parkinson-like disorders (see Glossary).

Confusion, hallucinations, agitation, and restlessness (especially in the elderly).

Advisability of Use During Pregnancy

Safety not established. Prudent use is best determined by physician's evaluation.

Advisability of Use While Nursing Infant

Presence of drug in milk is not known. Safety has not been established. Ask physician for guidance.

Habit-Forming Potential

None

Effects of Overdosage

With Moderate Overdose: Confusion, hallucinations, extreme drowsiness, drop in body temperature, heart palpitation, dilated pupils, tremors.

With Large Overdose: Stupor, deep sleep, coma, convulsions.

Possible Effects of Extended Use

None reported.

Recommended Periodic Examinations While Taking This Drug

Complete blood cell counts.

Liver function tests.

Serial blood pressure readings and electrocardiograms.

While Taking This Drug, Observe the Following

Foods: No restrictions.

Beverages: No restrictions.

Alcohol: Avoid completely. This drug can increase markedly the intoxicating effects of alcohol and accentuate its depressant action on brain function.

Tobacco Smoking: No interactions expected.

Other Drugs

Doxepin may *increase* the effects of

- atropine and drugs with atropine-like actions (see Drug Family, Section Four).
- sedatives, sleep-inducing drugs, tranquilizers, antihistamines, and narcotic drugs, and cause oversedation. Dosage adjustments may be necessary.
- levodopa (Dopar, Larodopa, etc.), in its control of Parkinson's disease.

Doxepin *taken concurrently* with
- thyroid preparations, may cause impairment of heart rhythm and function. Ask physician for guidance regarding thyroid dosage adjustment.
- ethchlorvynol (Placidyl), may cause delirium.
- quinidine, may cause impairment of heart rhythm and function. Avoid the combined use of these two drugs.
- mono-amine oxidase (MAO) inhibitor drugs (see Drug Family, Section Four), may cause high fever, delirium, and convulsions.

The following drugs may *increase* the effects of doxepin:
- diuretics of the thiazide family (see Drug Family, Section Four), may slow its elimination from the body. Overdosage may occur.

Driving a Vehicle, Piloting a Plane, Operating Machinery: This drug may impair mental alertness, judgment, physical coordination, and reaction time. Avoid hazardous activities.

Exposure to Sun: Use caution until sensitivity to sun has been determined. This drug may cause photosensitivity (see Glossary).

Discontinuation: If it has been necessary to use this drug for an extended period of time, do not discontinue it abruptly. Ask physician for guidance regarding dosage reduction and withdrawal. It may be necessary to adjust the dosage of other drugs taken concurrently.

Special Storage Instructions
Keep in a dry, tightly closed container.

DOXYCYCLINE

Year Introduced: 1967

Brand Names

USA	Canada
Doxychel (Rachelle)	Vibramycin (Pfizer)
Doxy-II (USV Pharmaceutical)	
Vibramycin (Pfizer)	

Drug Family: Antibiotic (Anti-infective) [Tetracyclines]

Prescription Required: Yes

Available Dosage Forms and Strengths
Capsules — 50 mg., 100 mg.
Syrup — 50 mg. per teaspoonful
Oral Suspension — 25 mg. per teaspoonful

How This Drug Works
Intended Therapeutic Effect(s):   The elimination of infections responsive to the action of this drug.

Location of Drug Action(s):   Any body tissue or fluid in which sufficient concentration of the drug can be achieved.

Method of Drug Action(s):   This drug prevents the growth and multiplication of susceptible bacteria by interfering with their formation of essential proteins.

THIS DRUG SHOULD NOT BE TAKEN IF
—you are allergic to any tetracycline drug (see Drug Family, Section Four).
—you are pregnant or breast feeding.
—it is prescribed for a child under 9 years of age.

INFORM YOUR PHYSICIAN BEFORE TAKING THIS DRUG IF
—you have a history of liver or kidney disease.
—you have systemic lupus erythematosus.
—you are taking any penicillin drug.
—you are taking any anticoagulant drug.
—you plan to have surgery under general anesthesia in the near future.

Time Required for Apparent Benefit
Varies with nature of infection under treatment; usually 2 to 5 days.

Possible Side-Effects *(natural, expected, and unavoidable drug actions)*
Superinfections (see Glossary), often due to yeast organisms. These can occur in the mouth, intestinal tract, rectum, and/or vagina, resulting in rectal and vaginal itching.

Possible Adverse Effects *(unusual, unexpected, and infrequent reactions)*

IF ANY OF THE FOLLOWING DEVELOP, DISCONTINUE DRUG AND NOTIFY YOUR PHYSICIAN AS SOON AS POSSIBLE

Mild Adverse Effects
    Allergic Reactions: Skin rash (various kinds), hives, itching of hands and feet, swelling of face or extremities.
    Photosensitivity Reactions: Exaggerated sunburn or skin irritation occurs commonly with some tetracyclines (see Glossary).
    Loss of appetite, nausea, vomiting, diarrhea.
    Irritation of mouth or tongue, "black tongue," sore throat, abdominal pain or cramping.
Serious Adverse Effects
    Allergic Reactions: Anaphylactic reaction (see Glossary), asthma, fever, painful swollen joints, unusual bleeding or bruising, jaundice (see Glossary).
    Permanent discoloration and/or malformation of teeth when taken under 9 years of age, including unborn child and infant.

Advisability of Use During Pregnancy
Tetracyclines can have adverse effects on mother and fetus. Avoid use.

Advisability of Use While Nursing Infant
Tetracyclines can be present in milk and can have adverse effects on infant. Avoid use or avoid nursing.

Habit-Forming Potential
None.

Effects of Overdosage
Possible nausea, vomiting, diarrhea.
Acute liver damage (rare).

Possible Effects of Extended Use
Impairment of bone marrow, liver, or kidney function (all rare).
Superinfections.

Recommended Periodic Examinations While Taking This Drug
Complete blood cell counts.
Liver and kidney function tests.
During extended use, sputum and stool examinations may detect early super-infections due to yeast organisms.

While Taking This Drug, Observe the Following
Foods: Dairy products can interfere with absorption. Tetracyclines should be taken 1 hour before or 2 hours after eating.

Beverages: Avoid milk for 1 hour before and after each dose of a tetracycline.

Alcohol: Avoid while taking a tetracycline if you have a history of liver disease.

Tobacco Smoking: No interactions expected.

Other Drugs

Tetracyclines may *increase* the effects of
• oral anticoagulants, and make it necessary to reduce their dosage.

Tetracyclines may *decrease* the effects of
• the penicillins, and impair their effectiveness in treating infections.

The following drugs may *decrease* the effects of tetracyclines:
• antacids may reduce drug absorption.
• iron and mineral preparations may reduce drug absorption.

Driving a Vehicle, Piloting a Plane, Operating Machinery: No restrictions.

Exposure to Sun: Avoid as much as possible. Photosensitivity (see Glossary) is common with some tetracyclines.

Special Storage Instructions
Keep in a tightly closed, light-resistant container.

DOXYLAMINE

Year Introduced: 1949

Brand Names

USA	Canada
Decapryn (Merrell-National) Bendectin [CD] (Merrell-National) Nyquil [CD] (Vick) (Other combination brand names)	Bendectin [CD] (Merrell)

Drug Family: Antihistàmines

Prescription Required: For low-strength formulations—No
For high-strength formulations—Yes

Available Dosage Forms and Strengths
Tablets — 12.5 mg., 25 mg.
Syrup — 6.25 mg. per teaspoonful

How This Drug Works
Intended Therapeutic Effect(s):   Relief of symptoms associated with hayfever (allergic rhinitis) and with allergic reactions in the skin, such as itching, swelling, hives, and rash.
Location of Drug Action(s):   Those hypersensitive tissues that release excessive histamine as part of an allergic reaction. The principal tissue sites are the eyes, the nose, and the skin.
Method of Drug Action(s):   This drug reduces the intensity of the allergic response by blocking the action of histamine after it has been released from sensitized tissue cells.

THIS DRUG SHOULD NOT BE TAKEN IF
—you have had an allergic reaction to any dosage form of it previously.
—you are taking, or have taken during the past 2 weeks, any mono-amine oxidase (MAO) inhibitor drug (see Drug Family, Section Four).
—it has been prescribed for a newborn infant.

INFORM YOUR PHYSICIAN BEFORE TAKING THIS DRUG IF
—you have had an unfavorable reaction to any antihistamine drug in the past.
—you have glaucoma.
—you have a history of asthma, peptic ulcer disease, or impairment of urinary bladder function.
—you plan to have surgery under general anesthesia in the near future.

Time Required for Apparent Benefit
Drug action begins in approximately 30 minutes, reaches a maximum in 1 hour, and subsides in 4 to 6 hours.

Possible Side-Effects *(natural, expected, and unavoidable drug actions)*
Drowsiness, sense of weakness, dryness of nose, mouth, and throat, constipation.

CAUTION
The elderly (over 60 years of age) may be more susceptible to the adverse effects of this drug. Small doses are advisable until tolerance is determined.

Possible Adverse Effects *(unusual, unexpected, and infrequent reactions)*
IF ANY OF THE FOLLOWING DEVELOP, DISCONTINUE DRUG AND NOTIFY YOUR PHYSICIAN AS SOON AS POSSIBLE

Mild Adverse Effects
Allergic Reactions: Skin rash, hives.
Headache, dizziness, inability to concentrate, nervousness, blurring of vision, double vision, difficulty in urination.
Nausea, vomiting, diarrhea.

Serious Adverse Effects
Idiosyncratic Reactions: Emotional and behavioral disturbances—confusion, agitation, inappropriate actions.

Advisability of Use During Pregnancy
No reports of adverse effects on mother or fetus, but complete safety has not been established. Limit use to small doses and for short periods of time.

Advisability of Use While Nursing Infant
This drug may impair milk formation and make nursing difficult. It is known to be present in milk. Ask physician for guidance.

Habit-Forming Potential
None.

Effects of Overdosage
With Moderate Overdose: Marked drowsiness, confusion, incoordination, unsteady gait, muscle tremors. In children: excitement, hallucinations, overactivity, convulsions.
With Large Overdose: Stupor progressing to coma, fever, flushed face, dilated pupils, weak pulse, shallow breathing.

Possible Effects of Extended Use
None reported.

Recommended Periodic Examinations While Taking This Drug
Complete blood cell counts.

While Taking This Drug, Observe the Following
Foods: No restrictions. Stomach irritation can be reduced if drug is taken after eating.
Beverages: Coffee and tea may help to reduce the drowsiness caused by most antihistamines.
Alcohol: Use with extreme caution until combined effect has been determined. The combination of alcohol and antihistamines can cause rapid and marked sedation.

Tobacco Smoking: No interactions expected.

Other Drugs

Doxylamine may *increase* the effects of

• sedatives, sleep-inducing drugs, tranquilizers, antidepressants, pain relievers, and narcotic drugs, and result in oversedation. Careful dosage adjustments are necessary.

• atropine and drugs with atropine-like action (see Drug Family, Section Four).

The following drugs may *increase* the effects of doxylamine:

• all sedatives, sleep-inducing drugs, tranquilizers, pain relievers, and narcotic drugs may exaggerate its sedative action and cause oversedation.

• mono-amine oxidase (MAO) inhibitor drugs (see Drug Family, Section Four) may delay its elimination from the body, thus exaggerating and prolonging its action.

The following drugs may *decrease* the effects of doxylamine:

• the amphetamines (Benzedrine, Dexedrine, Desoxyn, etc.) may reduce the drowsiness caused by most antihistamines.

Driving a Vehicle, Piloting a Plane, Operating Machinery: This drug may impair mental alertness, judgment, physical coordination, and reaction time. Avoid hazardous activities until full sedative effect has been determined.

Exposure to Sun: No restrictions.

Special Storage Instructions

Keep in a dry, tightly closed, light-resistant container.

EPHEDRINE

Year Introduced: 1924 (crude form in use in China for 5000 years)

Brand Names

USA		Canada
Amesec [CD] (Lilly)	Quelidrine [CD]	Acet-Am [CD]
Bronkaid [CD]	(Abbott)	(Organon)
(Drew)	Quibron Plus [CD]	Amesec [CD] (Lilly)
Bronkotabs [CD]	(Mead Johnson)	Bronkaid [CD]
(Breon)	Tedral [CD]	(Winthrop)
Calcidrine [CD]	(Warner/Chilcott)	Quadrinal [CD]
(Abbott)	Verequad [CD]	(Pentagone)
Duovent [CD] (Riker)	(Knoll)	Tedral [CD]
Epragen [CD] (Lilly)	(Numerous other	(Warner/Chilcott)
Gluco-Fedrin [CD]	brand and	
(Parke-Davis)	combination brand	
I-Sedrin [CD] (Lilly)	names)	
Marax [CD] (Roerig)		
Mudrane [CD]		
(Poythress)		
Nyquil [CD] (Vick)		
Quadrinal [CD]		
(Knoll)		

Drug Family: Anti-asthmatic (Bronchodilator) [Sympathomimetics]

Prescription Required: For low-strength formulations—No
For high-strength formulations—Yes

Available Dosage Forms and Strengths
Tablets — 25 mg., 50 mg.
Capsules — 25 mg., 50 mg.
Syrup — 4 mg. per ml., 20 mg. per teaspoonful
(Marketed generically and in a variety of combination tablets, capsules, syrups, and solutions. Strength varies according to drug product. Examine product label.)

How This Drug Works
Intended Therapeutic Effect(s)
• prevention and symptomatic treatment of bronchial asthma.
• relief of congestion of respiratory passages.
Location of Drug Action(s):   This drug affects all tissues activated by the sympathetic nervous system. Its principal action sites of therapeutic importance are:
• the muscles in the walls of the bronchial tubes.
• the small blood vessels (arterioles) in the tissues lining the respiratory passages.

Method of Drug Action(s)

By blocking the release of certain chemicals from sensitized tissue cells which are undergoing an allergic reaction, this drug acts to prevent the constriction of bronchial tubes which occurs as a manifestation of allergy.

By directly producing relaxation of the bronchial muscles, this drug reverses the bronchial constriction responsible for asthma.

By contracting the walls and thus reducing the size of the arterioles, this drug decreases the volume of blood in the tissues. This results in shrinkage of tissue mass (decongestion).

THIS DRUG SHOULD NOT BE TAKEN IF

—you have had an allergic reaction to any dosage form of it previously. A combination drug [CD] should not be taken if you are allergic to *any* of its ingredients.

INFORM YOUR PHYSICIAN BEFORE TAKING THIS DRUG IF

—you have high blood pressure or heart disease.
—you have an overactive thyroid gland (hyperthyroidism) or diabetes.
—you have difficulty emptying the urinary bladder.
—you are taking, or have taken during the past 2 weeks, any mono-amine oxidase (MAO) inhibitor drug (see Drug Family, Section Four).
—you are taking any form of digitalis (digitoxin, digoxin, Lanoxin, etc.).
—you plan to have surgery under general anesthesia in the near future.

Time Required for Apparent Benefit

Drug action begins in 30 to 60 minutes and persists for 3 to 4 hours.

Possible Side-Effects *(natural, expected, and unavoidable drug actions)*

Nervousness, insomnia.

CAUTION

This drug may lose its effectiveness if taken too frequently on a continuous basis for 3 to 4 days. Interrupt regular use when possible to prevent or reduce the development of tolerance (see Glossary). Effectiveness is restored after several days of discontinuation.

Possible Adverse Effects *(unusual, unexpected, and infrequent reactions)*

IF ANY OF THE FOLLOWING DEVELOP, DISCONTINUE DRUG AND NOTIFY YOUR PHYSICIAN AS SOON AS POSSIBLE

Mild Adverse Effects

Allergic Reactions: None reported when taken orally.

Headache, dizziness, rapid and forceful heart action, chest discomfort, sweating.

Nausea, vomiting.

Difficult urination.

Serious Adverse Effects

None reported.

Advisability of Use During Pregnancy

No adverse effects on mother or fetus reported. However, sparing use and small doses are advisable. Ask physician for guidance.

Advisability of Use While Nursing Infant
Drug is known to be present in milk and to have adverse effects on the young infant. Avoid drug or discontinue nursing. Ask physician for guidance.

Habit-Forming Potential
None.

Effects of Overdosage
With Moderate Overdose: Marked nervousness, restlessness, headache, heart palpitation, sweating, nausea, vomiting.

With Large Overdose: Anxiety, confusion, delirium, muscular tremors, rapid and irregular pulse.

Possible Effects of Extended Use
None reported with normal dosage.

A toxic form of mental derangement (toxic psychosis) has resulted from long-term use of excessive doses.

Long-term use in men with prostate gland enlargement may cause increased difficulty in emptying the urinary bladder.

Recommended Periodic Examinations While Taking This Drug
None required.

While Taking This Drug, Observe the Following
Foods: No restrictions.

Beverages: Excessive coffee or tea may add to the nervousness or insomnia caused by this drug in sensitive individuals.

Alcohol: No interactions expected.

Tobacco Smoking: No interactions expected; no restrictions unless advised otherwise by your physician.

Other Drugs

Ephedrine may *increase* the effects of
- epinephrine (Adrenalin, Bronkaid Mist, Vaponefrin, etc.), and cause excessive stimulation of the heart and an increase in blood pressure. Use caution and avoid excessive dosage.

Ephedrine may *decrease* the effects of
- anti-hypertensive drugs, and reduce their effectiveness in lowering blood pressure. Ask physician if any dosage adjustment is necessary to maintain proper blood pressure control.

Ephedrine *taken concurrently* with
- digitalis preparations (digitoxin, digoxin, etc.), may cause serious disturbances of heart rhythm.
- ergot-related preparations (Cafergot, Ergotrate, Migral, Wigraine, etc.), may cause serious increase in blood pressure.
- guanethidine, may result in reduced effectiveness of both drugs.

The following drugs may *increase* the effects of ephedrine
- mono-amine oxidase (MAO) inhibitor drugs (see Drug Family, Section Four). The combined effects may cause a dangerous increase in blood pressure.

• tricyclic antidepressants (see Drug Family, Section Four). The combined effect may cause excessive stimulation of the heart and blood pressure.

Driving a Vehicle, Piloting a Plane, Operating Machinery: No restrictions unless dizziness occurs.

Exposure to Sun: No restrictions.

Special Storage Instructions
Keep in a tightly closed, light-resistant container. Avoid excessive heat.

ERGOTAMINE

Year Introduced: 1926

Brand Names

USA	Canada
Ergomar (Fisons)	Gynergen (Sandoz)
Gynergen (Sandoz)	Medihaler-Ergotamine
Medihaler-Ergotamine	(Riker)
(Riker)	Ergomar (Fisons)
Bellergal [CD] (Sandoz)	Bellergal [CD] (Sandoz)
Cafergot [CD] (Sandoz)	Cafergot [CD] (Sandoz)
Migral [CD] (Burroughs	Wigraine [CD] (Organon)
Wellcome)	
Wigraine [CD] (Organon)	
(Several other	
combination brand	
names)	

Drug Family: Migraine Analgesic (Vasoconstrictor)

Prescription Required: Yes

Available Dosage Forms and Strengths
Tablets — 1 mg.
Sublingual Tablets — 2 mg.
Aerosol Inhaler — 9 mg. per ml.
Suppositories — 2 mg. (in combination with caffeine)
Injection — 0.5 mg. per ml., 1 mg. per ml.

How This Drug Works
Intended Therapeutic Effect(s):   Prevention and early relief of blood vessel (vascular) headaches, such as migraine, variations of migraine, and histamine headaches.

Location of Drug Action(s):   The principal site of therapeutic action is the muscular tissue of blood vessel walls.

Method of Drug Action(s):   By directly constricting the walls of blood vessels in the head, this drug prevents or relieves the excessive expansion (dilation) responsible for the pain of migraine-like headaches.

THIS DRUG SHOULD NOT BE TAKEN IF
—you have had an allergic reaction to any dosage form of it previously.
—you are pregnant.
—you are experiencing a severe infection.
—you have any of the following conditions:
angina pectoris
Buerger's disease
coronary artery disease
hardening of the arteries (arteriosclerosis)
high blood pressure (severe hypertension)
kidney disease (or impaired kidney function)
liver disease (or impaired liver function)
Raynaud's phenomenon
thrombophlebitis
severe itching

INFORM YOUR PHYSICIAN BEFORE TAKING THIS DRUG IF
—you have had an allergic reaction to *any* derivative of ergot in the past.

Time Required for Apparent Benefit
If taken at the onset of headache, relief is usually felt in 30 to 60 minutes. I
use of the drug is delayed, larger doses and a longer period of time are needed
to obtain relief.

Possible Side-Effects *(natural, expected, and unavoidable drug actions)*
Usually infrequent and mild with recommended dosage. Susceptible in
dividuals may notice a sensation of cold hands and feet with mild numbnes
and tingling.

CAUTION
Do not exceed a total dose of 6 mg. in 24 hours or 12 mg. in 1 week. Limi
use of this drug to the following:
Tablets—no more than 6 in 24 hours or 12 in 1 week.
Sublingual Tablets—no more than 3 in 24 hours or 6 in 1 week.
Aerosol Inhaler—no more than 6 inhalations in 24 hours or 15 in 1 week
Suppositories—no more than 3 in 24 hours or 6 in 1 week.
Injection—no more than 12 ml. in 24 hours or 24 ml. in 1 week. (If DHE-4
is used, no more than 6 ml. in 24 hours or 12 ml. in 1 week.)

Possible Adverse Effects *(unusual, unexpected, and infrequent reactions)*

**IF ANY OF THE FOLLOWING DEVELOP, DISCONTINUE DRUG AND NOTIFY
YOUR PHYSICIAN AS SOON AS POSSIBLE**

Mild Adverse Effects
Allergic Reactions: Localized swellings, itching.
Nausea, vomiting, diarrhea.
Chest pain, numbness and tingling of fingers and toes, muscle pains in arm
or legs.
Headache, dizziness, confusion, drowsiness.

Serious Adverse Effects

Gangrene of the intestine—severe abdominal pain and swelling; emergency surgery required.

Gangrene of the extremities—coldness, numbness, pain, dark discoloration, eventual loss of fingers, toes, or feet.

Advisability of Use During Pregnancy

Avoid completely during entire pregnancy.

Advisability of Use While Nursing Infant

Drug is known to be present in milk. Avoid use or avoid nursing. Ask physician for guidance.

Habit-Forming Potential

None.

Effects of Overdosage

With Moderate Overdose: Manifestation of "ergotism"—coldness of skin, severe muscle pains, tingling and burning pain in hands and feet, loss of blood supply to extremities resulting in tissue death (gangrene).

With Large Overdose: Ergot poisoning—nausea, vomiting, diarrhea, cold skin, rapid and weak pulse, numbness and tingling of extremities, confusion, convulsions, coma.

Possible Effects of Extended Use

Risk of developing "ergotism"—chronic overdosage (see above).

Recommended Periodic Examinations While Taking This Drug

Evaluation of circulatory status (blood flow) to extremities.

While Taking This Drug, Observe the Following

Foods: Avoid all foods to which you are allergic. Some migraine headaches are due to food allergies. (No foods are known to interact with this drug.)

Beverages: No restrictions. Coffee may be beneficial in relieving migraine headache.

Alcohol: Best avoided while using this drug to treat a vascular (blood vessel) headache.

Tobacco Smoking: Nicotine may reduce further the restricted circulation (blood flow) produced by this drug. Follow physician's advice regarding smoking.

Other Drugs

Ergotamine may *increase* the effects of

• amphetamines, Adrenalin, ephedrine, and pseudoephedrine, and cause a dangerous rise in blood pressure.

The following drugs may *increase* the effects of ergotamine:

• TAO (troleandomycin) may delay its elimination from the body and thus produce overdose ("ergotism").

• caffeine can add to this drug's ability to constrict blood vessels in the head and so relieve the pain of migraine headache.

Driving a Vehicle, Piloting a Plane, Operating Machinery: Usually no restrictions. Avoid hazardous activities if drowsiness or dizziness occurs.
Exposure to Sun: No restrictions.
Exposure to Cold: Avoid as much as possible. Cold environments and handling of cold objects will reduce further the restricted circulation (blood flow) to the arms and legs which is part of this drug's normal action.

Special Storage Instructions
Keep all preparations in a cool place. Protect from light and heat. Store suppositories in a refrigerator.

ERYTHRITYL TETRANITRATE
Year Introduced: 1957

Brand Names

USA	Canada
Anginar (Pasadena Res. Lab.)	Cardilate (Calmic)
Cardilate (Burroughs Wellcome)	

Drug Family: Anti-anginal; Vasodilator [Nitrates]

Prescription Required: Yes

Available Dosage Forms and Strengths
Tablets — 5 mg., 10 mg., 15 mg.
Chewable Tablets — 10 mg.

How This Drug Works
Intended Therapeutic Effect(s):   Reduction in the frequency and severity of pain associated with angina pectoris (coronary insufficiency).
Location of Drug Action(s):   The muscular tissue in the walls of the blood vessels. The principal site of the therapeutic action is the system of coronary arteries in the heart.
Method of Drug Action(s):   This drug acts directly on the muscle cell to produce relaxation. This permits expansion of blood vessels and increases the supply of blood and oxygen to meet the needs of the working heart muscle.

THIS DRUG SHOULD NOT BE TAKEN IF
—you have had an allergic reaction to any dosage form of it previously.

INFORM YOUR PHYSICIAN BEFORE TAKING THIS DRUG IF
—you have glaucoma.
—you have had an unfavorable response to any vasodilator drug in the past.

Time Required for Apparent Benefit
The action of sublingual use (dissolved under the tongue) or chewed tablets begins in approximately 5 minutes, reaches a maximum in 30 to 45 minutes, and persists for 3 to 4 hours. The action of the swallowed tablet begins in approximately 30 minutes, reaches a maximum in 60 to 90 minutes, and persists for 3 to 4 hours.

Possible Side-Effects *(natural, expected, and unavoidable drug actions)*
Flushing, lightheadedness in upright position (see orthostatic hypotension in Glossary).

Possible Adverse Effects *(unusual, unexpected, and infrequent reactions)*
IF ANY OF THE FOLLOWING DEVELOP, DISCONTINUE DRUG AND NOTIFY YOUR PHYSICIAN AS SOON AS POSSIBLE
Mild Adverse Effects
    Allergic Reactions: Skin rash.
    Headache (may be persistent), dizziness, fainting.
    Nausea, vomiting.
Serious Adverse Effects
    Allergic Reactions: Severe dermatitis with peeling of skin.

Advisability of Use During Pregnancy
Safety not established. Prudent use is best determined by the physician's evaluation.

Advisability of Use While Nursing Infant
Presence of drug in milk is not known. Safety for infant not established. Ask physician for guidance.

Habit-Forming Potential
None.

Effects of Overdosage
With Moderate Overdose: Headache, dizziness, marked flushing of the skin.
With Large Overdose: Vomiting, weakness, sweating, fainting, shortness of breath, coma.

Possible Effects of Extended Use
Development of tolerance (see Glossary) which may reduce the drug's effectiveness at recommended doses.
Development of abnormal hemoglobin (red blood cell pigment).

Recommended Periodic Examinations While Taking This Drug
Measurement of internal eye pressure in those individuals with glaucoma or a tendency to glaucoma.
Red blood cell counts and hemoglobin measurements.

While Taking This Drug, Observe the Following
Foods: No restrictions. Drug is likely to be more effective if taken one-half to 1 hour before eating.
Beverages: No restrictions.

Alcohol: Use with extreme caution until combined effects have been determined. Alcohol may exaggerate the drop in blood pressure experienced by some sensitive individuals. This could be dangerous.

Tobacco Smoking: Nicotine may reduce the effectiveness of this drug. Follow physician's advice regarding smoking, based upon its effect on the condition under treatment and its possible interaction with this drug.

Other Drugs

Erythrityl may *increase* the effects of

- atropine-like drugs (see Drug Family, Section Four), and cause an increase in internal eye pressure.
- tricyclic antidepressants (see Drug Family, Section Four), and cause excessive lowering of the blood pressure.

Erythrityl may *decrease* the effects of

- all choline-like drugs, such as Mestinon, Mytelase, pilocarpine, Prostigmin, and Urecholine.

Erythrityl *taken concurrently* with

- anti-hypertensive drugs, may cause severe drop in blood pressure. Careful monitoring of drug response and appropriate dosage adjustments are necessary.

The following drugs may *increase* the effects of erythrityl:

- propranolol (Inderal) may cause additional lowering of the blood pressure. Dosage adjustments may be necessary.

Driving a Vehicle, Piloting a Plane, Operating Machinery: Usually no restrictions. Before engaging in hazardous activities, determine that this drug will not cause you to have orthostatic hypotension (see Glossary).

Exposure to Sun: No restrictions.

Exposure to Cold: Cold environment may reduce the effectiveness of this drug.

Heavy Exercise or Exertion: This drug may improve your ability to be more active without the resulting angina pain. Use caution and avoid excessive exertion that could cause heart injury in the absence of warning pain.

Special Storage Instructions

Keep in a dry, tightly closed container and in a cool place. Protect from heat and light.

ERYTHROMYCIN

Year Introduced: 1952 (Erythromycin, early forms)
1958 (Erythromycin estolate)

Brand Names

USA	Canada
Bristamycin (Bristol)	Chemthromycin (Chemo)
Dowmycin-E (Dow)	Emcinka (ICN)
E-Biotic (Saron)	E-Mycin (Upjohn)
E-Mycin (Upjohn)	Erymycin (Squibb)
Erypar (Parke-Davis)	Erythrocin (Abbott)
Erythrocin (Abbott)	Erythromid (Abbott)
Ethril (Squibb)	Erythromyctine (Barlowe
Ilosone (Dista)	Cote)
Ilotycin (Dista)	Ilosone (Lilly)
Kesso-Mycin (McKesson)	Ilotycin (Lilly)
Pediamycin (Ross)	Novorythro (Novopharm)
Pfizer-E (Pfizer)	Robimycin (Robins)
QIDmycin (Mallinckrodt)	
Robimycin (Robins)	
RP-Mycin	
(Reid-Provident)	
SK-Erythromycin (Smith	
Kline & French)	

Drug Family: Antibiotic (Anti-infective)

Prescription Required: Yes

Available Dosage Forms and Strengths

Tablets — 100 mg., 250 mg., 500 mg.
Chewable Tablets — 125 mg., 200 mg.
Capsules — 125 mg., 250 mg.
Oral Suspension — 125 mg., 250 mg. per teaspoonful
Pediatric Suspension — 200 mg. per teaspoonful
Pediatric Drops — 100 mg. per 2.5 ml., 100 mg. per 1 ml., 40 mg. per 1 ml.
Suppositories — 125 mg.
Skin Ointment — 1%
Eye Ointment — 0.5%

How This Drug Works

Intended Therapeutic Effect(s):   The elimination of infections responsive to the action of this drug.

Location of Drug Action(s):   Any body tissue or fluid in which sufficient concentration of the drug can be achieved.

Method of Drug Action(s):   This drug prevents the growth and multiplication of susceptible bacteria by interfering with their formation of essential proteins.

THIS DRUG SHOULD NOT BE TAKEN IF
—you have had an allergic reaction to any dosage form of it previously.
—you have a history of liver disease or impaired liver function and one of the
preparations of erythromycin *estolate* has been prescribed for you. These
are:
Chemthromycin
Emcinka (Capsules and Liquid)
Erythromyctine
Ilosone
Novorythro

INFORM YOUR PHYSICIAN BEFORE TAKING THIS DRUG IF
—you have taken any form of erythromycin estolate in the past (see list above).

Time Required for Apparent Benefit
Varies with nature of infection under treatment; usually 2 to 5 days.

Possible Side-Effects *(natural, expected, and unavoidable drug actions)*
Superinfections (see Glossary).

Possible Adverse Effects *(unusual, unexpected, and infrequent reactions)*
**IF ANY OF THE FOLLOWING DEVELOP, DISCONTINUE DRUG AND NOTIFY
YOUR PHYSICIAN AS SOON AS POSSIBLE**

Mild Adverse Effects
Allergic Reactions: Skin rash, hives.
Nausea, vomiting, diarrhea (all infrequent).
Serious Adverse Effects
Erythromycin estolate preparations (see above) can cause liver damage
with jaundice (see Glossary). These forms of erythromycin should not be
used for long-term treatment.

Advisability of Use During Pregnancy
Safety not established. Prudent use is best determined by the physician's
evaluation.

Advisability of Use While Nursing Infant
Drug may be present in milk. Safety for infant not established. Ask physician
for guidance

Habit-Forming Potential
None.

Effects of Overdosage
Possible nausea, vomiting, abdominal discomfort, diarrhea.

Possible Effects of Extended Use
Superinfections.

Recommended Periodic Examinations While Taking This Drug
Liver function tests if estolate form of erythromycin is used (see above).

While Taking This Drug, Observe the Following
Foods: No restrictions of food selection. Most effective if taken 1 hour before or 2 hours after eating. Estolate forms may be taken with meals.

Beverages: No restrictions.

Alcohol: Avoid if
- you have a history of liver disease.
- you are using an estolate form of erythromycin.

Tobacco Smoking: No interactions expected.

Other Drugs

Erythromycin may *decrease* the effects of
- clindamycin.
- lincomycin.
- the penicillins.

Driving a Vehicle, Piloting a Plane, Operating Machinery: No restrictions.

Exposure to Sun: No restrictions.

Discontinuation: When used to treat infections that predispose to rheumatic fever or kidney disease, take continuously in full dosage for no less than 10 days. Ask physician for guidance regarding recommended duration of therapy.

Special Storage Instructions
Keep in a dry, tightly closed, light-resistant container, at temperatures not exceeding usual room temperature. Keep liquid forms refrigerated.

Do Not Take a Liquid Form of This Drug If It Is Older Than
14 days.

ESTROGEN
(Estrogenic Substances)
Conjugated Estrogens, Esterified Estrogens
(Estrone and Equilin)

Year Introduced: 1942

Brand Names

USA	Canada
Amnestrogen (Squibb)	Climestrone (Frosst)
Conestrone (Wyeth)	Conjugated Estrogens
Evex (Syntex)	(Sands)
Femogen (Fellows)	Menotrol (Squibb)
Genisis (Organon)	Oestrilin (Desbergers)
Menest (Beecham)	Premarin (Ayerst)
Menotabs (Fleming)	Formatrix [CD] (Ayerst)
Premarin (Ayerst)	Menrium [CD] (Roche)
SK-Estrogens (Smith	
Kline & French)	
Theogen (Sig: Pharm.)	
Formatrix [CD] (Ayerst)	
Menrium [CD] (Roche)	
Milprem [CD] (Wallace)	
PMB-200 [CD] (Ayerst)	
PMB-400 [CD] (Ayerst)	

Drug Family: Female Sex Hormones (Estrogens)

Prescription Required: Yes

Available Dosage Forms and Strengths
Tablets — 0.3 mg., 0.625 mg., 1.25 mg., 2.5 mg.
Injection — 2 mg. per ml.
Vaginal Cream — 0.625 mg. per gram

How This Drug Works
Intended Therapeutic Effect(s)
• regulation of the menstrual cycle.
• prevention of pregnancy.
• relief of symptoms due to the menopause.

Location of Drug Action(s): Principal actions occur in
• the female reproductive tract (the Fallopian tubes, uterus, and vagina).
• the breast tissues.
• a major control center in the brain known as the hypothalamus.
• the pituitary gland.

Method of Drug Action(s)
By cyclic increase and decrease in tissue stimulation, estrogens prepare the

uterus for pregnancy and (in the absence of conception) induce menstruation.

When estrogens are taken in sufficient dosage and on a regular basis, their blood and tissue levels increase to resemble those that occur during pregnancy. This prevents the pituitary gland from secreting the hormones that induce ovulation.

Estrogen preparations, taken to restore normal tissue levels, reduce the frequency and intensity of menopausal symptoms.

THIS DRUG SHOULD NOT BE TAKEN IF
—you are allergic to any of the drugs bearing the brand names listed above.
—you have seriously impaired liver function.
—you have a history of thrombophlebitis, embolism, stroke, or heart attack.
—you have abnormal and unexplained vaginal bleeding.

INFORM YOUR PHYSICIAN BEFORE TAKING THIS DRUG IF
—you have a history of cancer of the breast or reproductive organs.
—you have cystic disease of the breast (cystic mastitis).
—you have fibroid tumors of the uterus.
—you have a history of endometriosis.
—you have migraine headaches or epilepsy.
—you have a history of porphyria.
—you have diabetes.
—you have high blood pressure.

Time Required for Apparent Benefit
Continuous use on a regular schedule for 10 to 20 days may be needed to determine the degree of effectiveness in relieving symptoms.

Possible Side-Effects *(natural, expected, and unavoidable drug actions)*
Retention of fluid, gain in weight, "breakthrough" bleeding (spotting in middle of menstrual cycle), change in menstrual flow, resumption of menstrual flow (bleeding from the uterus) after a period of natural cessation (postmenopausal bleeding). There may be an increased susceptibility to yeast infection of the genital tissues.

CAUTION
To avoid prolonged stimulation of breast tissues and uterine tissues, estrogens should be taken in cycles of 3 weeks on and 1 week off medication.

Possible Adverse Effects *(unusual, unexpected, and infrequent reactions)*

IF ANY OF THE FOLLOWING DEVELOP, DISCONTINUE DRUG AND NOTIFY YOUR PHYSICIAN AS SOON AS POSSIBLE

Mild Adverse Effects
Allergic Reactions: Skin rash.
Nausea, vomiting, indigestion, bloating.
Accentuation of migraine headaches.
Breast enlargement, congestion, and tenderness.

Serious Adverse Effects
Idiosyncratic Reactions: Development of cutaneous porphyria—fragility and scarring of the skin.

Thrombophlebitis (inflammation of a vein with the formation of blood clot) —pain or tenderness in thigh or leg, with or without swelling of the foot, ankle, or leg.

Pulmonary embolism (movement of blood clot to the lung)—sudden shortness of breath, pain in the chest, coughing, bloody sputum.

Stroke (blood clot in the brain)—headaches, blackouts, sudden weakness or paralysis of any part of the body, severe dizziness, double vision, slurred speech, inability to speak.

Retinal thrombosis (blood clot in eye vessels)—sudden impairment or loss of vision.

Heart attack (blood clot in coronary artery)—sudden pain in chest, neck, jaw, or arm, accompanied by weakness, sweating, or nausea.

Rise in blood pressure in susceptible individuals.

Jaundice (see Glossary).

Emotional depression in susceptible individuals.

Advisability of Use During Pregnancy

The use of any estrogen during pregnancy should be avoided. Evidence exists to suggest a cause-and-effect relationship (see Glossary) in the development of very serious adverse effects in the children of mothers who were given estrogenic drugs during pregnancy.

Advisability of Use While Nursing Infant

These drugs are known to be present in milk and may affect the nursing infant. They also may impair the formation of milk. Ask physician for guidance.

Habit-Forming Potential

None.

Effects of Overdosage

With Moderate Overdose: Nausea, vomiting, fluid retention, breast enlargement and discomfort, abnormal vaginal bleeding.

With Large Overdose: No serious or dangerous effects reported.

Possible Effects of Extended Use

Increased growth of fibroid tumors of the uterus.

Recent reports suggest a possible association between the use of these drugs and the development of cancer in the lining of the uterus. Further studies are needed to establish a definite cause-and-effect relationship. Prudence dictates that women with uterus intact should use estrogens only when symptoms justify it.

Recommended Periodic Examinations While Taking This Drug

Regular examinations of the breasts and reproductive organs (pelvic examination of the uterus and ovaries, including "Pap" smear).

While Taking This Drug, Observe the Following

Foods: No restrictions. Ask physician for guidance regarding salt intake if you experience fluid retention.

Beverages: No restrictions.

Alcohol: No interactions expected.

Tobacco Smoking: There are reports suggesting that heavy smoking in association with the use of estrogens may increase the risk of abnormal blood clots leading to stroke (cerebral thrombosis) or heart attack (coronary thrombosis). A cause-and-effect relationship (see Glossary) has not been established. Follow physician's advice regarding smoking.

Other Drugs

Estrogens may *decrease* the effects of

• clofibrate (Atromid-S), and prevent the lowering of blood cholesterol or triglycerides.

Estrogens *taken concurrently* with

• anti-diabetic drugs, may cause unpredictable fluctuations in blood sugar levels. Estrogens can cause an increase in blood sugar; they can also increase the effects of oral anti-diabetics (Diabinese, Dymelor, Orinase, Tolinase). Monitor blood sugar closely and adjust dosages for best diabetic control.

The following drugs may *decrease* the effects of estrogens:

• meprobamate (Equanil, Miltown)
• phenobarbital

Driving a Vehicle, Piloting a Plane, Operating Machinery: No restrictions or precautions.

Exposure to Sun: Use caution until full effect is known. These drugs may cause photosensitivity (see Glossary).

Discontinuation: It is advisable to discontinue these drugs for one week out of four, that is, 3 weeks on and 1 week off medication. In addition, it is recommended that after 3 to 6 cycles all estrogens be discontinued for a period of individual evaluation. Treatment with estrogens should be resumed only if symptoms require it.

Special Storage Instructions

Keep in a dry, tightly closed container.

ETHCHLORVYNOL

Year Introduced: 1956

Brand Names

USA	Canada
Placidyl (Abbott)	Placidyl (Abbott)

Drug Family: Sleep Inducer (Hypnotic)

Prescription Required: Yes (Controlled Drug, U.S. Schedule 4)

Available Dosage Forms and Strengths

Capsules — 100 mg., 200 mg., 500 mg., 750 mg.

How This Drug Works
Intended Therapeutic Effect(s):   Relief of insomnia (hypnotic effect).
Location of Drug Action(s):   Not completely established. Thought to be the wake-sleep centers of the brain, possibly the reticular activating system.
Method of Drug Action(s):   Not established.

THIS DRUG SHOULD NOT BE TAKEN IF
—you have had an allergic reaction to any dosage form of it previously.
—you have a history of porphyria.
—it is prescribed for a child under 12 years of age.

INFORM YOUR PHYSICIAN BEFORE TAKING THIS DRUG IF
—you are taking other sedatives, sleep-inducing drugs, tranquilizers, antihistamines, pain relievers, or narcotic drugs of any kind.
—you have a history of liver or kidney disease.

Time Required for Apparent Benefit
Usually from 30 to 60 minutes.

Possible Side-Effects *(natural, expected, and unavoidable drug actions)*
Lightheadedness in upright position, unsteadiness.

CAUTION
The elderly (over 60 years of age) may not tolerate average adult doses. Use caution until intensity and duration of drug action has been determined.

Possible Adverse Effects *(unusual, unexpected, and infrequent reactions)*

IF ANY OF THE FOLLOWING DEVELOP, DISCONTINUE DRUG AND NOTIFY YOUR PHYSICIAN AS SOON AS POSSIBLE
Mild Adverse Effects
    Allergic Reactions: Hives.
    Dizziness, staggering gait, blurred vision.
    Indigestion, nausea, vomiting.
Serious Adverse Effects
    Allergic Reactions: Hepatitis with jaundice (see Glossary).
    Idiosyncratic Reactions: Prolonged sleep, extreme muscular weakness, fainting, excitement.
    Reduced number of blood platelets (see Glossary), resulting in unusual bleeding or bruising.

Advisability of Use During Pregnancy
Safety not established for use during the first 6 months of pregnancy. Use sparingly during the last 3 months. Avoid large doses and continuous use.

Advisability of Use While Nursing Infant
Presence of this drug in milk is not known. If used while nursing, observe infant for unusual drowsiness. Ask physician for guidance regarding size and timing of dosage.

Habit-Forming Potential
This drug can cause both psychological and physical dependence (see Glossary). Avoid continuous use.

Effects of Overdosage
With **Moderate Overdose:**   Excitement, delirium, incoordination, extreme drowsiness.
With **Large Overdose:**   Deep and prolonged coma.

Possible Effects of Extended Use
Impairment of vision.
Psychological and/or physical dependence.

Recommended Periodic Examinations While Taking This Drug
Complete blood cell counts.
Liver function tests.
Vision tests.

While Taking This Drug, Observe the Following
Foods: No restrictions.
Beverages: No restrictions.
Alcohol: Avoid completely. Alcohol can increase greatly the sedative and depressant actions of this drug on brain function.
Tobacco Smoking: No interactions expected.
Other Drugs
Ethchlorvynol may *increase* the effects of
- all sedatives, sleep-inducing drugs, tranquilizers, antihistamines, pain relievers, and narcotic drugs. Ask physician for guidance regarding dosage adjustments.

Ethchlorvynol may *decrease* the effects of
- oral anticoagulants, and reduce their protective action. Ask physician for guidance regarding tests of prothrombin time and dosage adjustment of the anticoagulant.

Ethchlorvynol *taken concurrently* with
- amitriptyline (Elavil, etc.), may cause delirium and excessive sedation. Use caution while taking ethchlorvynol with any tricyclic antidepressant (see Drug Family, Section Four).

The following drugs may *increase* the effects of ethchlorvynol
- mono-amine oxidase (MAO) inhibitor drugs may cause oversedation (see Drug Family, Section Four). Careful dosage adjustment is necessary.

Driving a Vehicle, Piloting a Plane, Operating Machinery: The "hangover" effects of this drug can impair mental alertness, judgment, physical coordination, and reaction time. Avoid hazardous activities until "hangover" effects have disappeared.

Exposure to Sun: No restrictions.
Discontinuation: If it has been necessary to use this drug for an extended period of time, do not discontinue it abruptly. Ask your physician for guid-

ance regarding dosage reduction and withdrawal. Also, it may be necessary to adjust the dosage of other drugs taken concurrently with it.

Special Storage Instructions
Keep in a dry, tightly closed container.

ETHINAMATE

Year Introduced: 1955

Brand Names

USA	Canada
Valmid (Dista)	Valmid (Lilly)

Drug Family: Sleep Inducer (Hypnotic)

Prescription Required: Yes (Controlled Drug, U.S. Schedule 4)

Available Dosage Forms and Strengths
Capsules — 500 mg.

How This Drug Works
Intended Therapeutic Effect(s):   Relief of insomnia (hypnotic effect).
Location of Drug Action(s):   Not completely established. Thought to be the wake-sleep centers of the brain, possibly the reticular activating system.
Method of Drug Action(s):   Not established.

THIS DRUG SHOULD NOT BE TAKEN IF
—you have had an allergic reaction to any dosage form of it previously.
—it is prescribed for a child under 12 years of age.

INFORM YOUR PHYSICIAN BEFORE TAKING THIS DRUG IF
—you are taking sedatives, other sleep-inducing drugs, tranquilizers, pain relievers, or narcotic drugs of any kind.
—you plan to have surgery under general anesthesia in the near future.

Time Required for Apparent Benefit
Approximately 30 minutes.

Possible Side-Effects *(natural, expected, and unavoidable drug actions)*
Lightheadedness in upright position, unsteadiness in stance and gait.

CAUTION
The elderly (over 60 years of age) may not tolerate large doses. Small doses are advisable until tolerance and duration of action have been determined.

Possible Adverse Effects *(unusual, unexpected, and infrequent reactions)*

IF ANY OF THE FOLLOWING DEVELOP, DISCONTINUE DRUG AND NOTIFY YOUR PHYSICIAN AS SOON AS POSSIBLE

Mild Adverse Effects
Allergic Reactions: Skin rashes.
Indigestion, nausea, vomiting.

Serious Adverse Effects
Idiosyncratic Reactions: Drug fever, paradoxical excitement. Reduction of blood platelets (see Glossary), resulting in unusual bleeding or bruising.

Advisability of Use During Pregnancy
Safety not established. Prudent use is best determined by the physician's evaluation.

Advisability of Use While Nursing Infant
Drug is known to be present in milk. Ask physician for guidance.

Habit-Forming Potential
This drug can cause both psychological and physical dependence (see Glossary). Avoid large doses and continuous use.

Effects of Overdosage
With Moderate Overdose: Extreme drowsiness, confusion, incoordination, slurred speech, staggering gait.
With Large Overdose: Stupor, deep sleep, coma, shallow breathing.

Possible Effects of Extended Use
Psychological and/or physical dependence.

Recommended Periodic Examinations While Taking This Drug
Complete blood cell counts.

While Taking This Drug, Observe the Following
Foods: No restrictions.
Beverages: No restrictions.
Alcohol: Avoid completely for 6 hours before taking this drug for sleep. Alcohol can increase greatly the sedative and depressant actions of this drug on brain function.
Tobacco Smoking: No interactions expected.
Other Drugs
Ethinamate may *increase* the effects of
• sedatives, other sleep-inducing drugs, tranquilizers, antihistamines, pain relievers, and narcotic drugs. Ask physician for guidance regarding dosage adjustments.

Driving a Vehicle, Piloting a Plane, Operating Machinery: This drug can impair mental alertness, judgment, physical coordination, and reaction time. Avoid hazardous activities until all sensation of drowsiness (or "hangover") has disappeared.
Exposure to Sun: No restrictions.

Discontinuation: If it has been necessary to use this drug for an extended period of time, do not discontinue it abruptly. Ask physician for guidance regarding dosage reduction and withdrawal.

Special Storage Instructions
Keep in a dry, tightly closed container.

FLUPHENAZINE

Year Introduced: 1959

Brand Names

USA	Canada
Permitil (Schering)	Moditen (Squibb)
Prolixin (Squibb)	

Drug Family: Tranquilizer, Strong (Anti-psychotic) [Phenothiazines]

Prescription Required: Yes

Available Dosage Forms and Strengths
Tablets — 0.25 mg., 1 mg., 2.5 mg., 5 mg., 10 mg.
Prolonged Action Tablets — 1 mg.
Concentrate — 5 mg. per ml.
Elixir — 0.5 mg. per ml., 2.5 mg. per teaspoonful
Injection — 2.5 mg. per ml., 25 mg. per ml.

How This Drug Works
Intended Therapeutic Effect(s):   Restoration of emotional calm. Relief of severe anxiety, agitation, and psychotic behavior.

Location of Drug Action(s):   Those nerve pathways in the brain that utilize the tissue chemical dopamine for the transmission of nerve impulses.

Method of Drug Action(s):   Not completely established. Present theory is that by inhibiting the action of dopamine, this drug acts to correct an imbalance of nerve impulse transmissions that is thought to be responsible for certain mental disorders.

THIS DRUG SHOULD NOT BE TAKEN IF
—you have had an allergic reaction to any dosage form of it previously.
—you have a history of brain damage.
—you have a history of impaired liver or kidney function.
—you have a blood or bone marrow disorder.
—it is prescribed for a child under 12 years of age.

INFORM YOUR PHYSICIAN BEFORE TAKING THIS DRUG IF
—you are allergic or sensitive to any phenothiazine drug (see Drug Family, Section Four).
—you are taking any sedatives, sleep-inducing drugs, other tranquilizers, antihistamines, antidepressants, or narcotic drugs of any kind.

—you have epilepsy.
—you have a history of asthma or emphysema.
—you have a history of peptic ulcer.
—you plan to have surgery under general or spinal anesthesia in the near future.

Time Required for Apparent Benefit
Some benefit may be apparent in first week.
Maximal benefit may require continuous use for several weeks.

Possible Side-Effects *(natural, expected, and unavoidable drug actions)*
Drowsiness (usually during the first few weeks), blurred vision.
Nasal stuffiness, dry mouth, constipation, impaired urination.

Possible Adverse Effects *(unusual, unexpected, and infrequent reactions)*
IF ANY OF THE FOLLOWING DEVELOP, DISCONTINUE DRUG AND NOTIFY YOUR PHYSICIAN AS SOON AS POSSIBLE

Mild Adverse Effects
Allergic Reactions: Skin rashes (various kinds), hives, itching.
Headache, dizziness, weakness.
Excitement, restlessness, unusual dreaming.
Menstrual irregularity, breast enlargement and tenderness, milk formation.

Serious Adverse Effects
Allergic Reactions: Severe skin reaction, "silent pneumonia", anaphylactic reaction (see Glossary).
Idiosyncratic Reactions: High fever (see idiosyncrasy in Glossary).
Parkinson-like disorders (see Glossary).
Spasm of the muscles of the face, neck, back, and extremities, causing rolling of the eyes, grimacing, clamping of the jaw, protrusion of the tongue, difficulty in swallowing, arching of the back, spasms of the hands and feet.
Hepatitis with jaundice (see Glossary).
Bone marrow depression (see Glossary)—fatigue, weakness, fever, sore throat, unusual bleeding or bruising.

Advisability of Use During Pregnancy
Safety not established. Prudent use is best determined by the physician's evaluation.

Advisability of Use While Nursing Infant
Safety not established. Ask physician for guidance.

Habit-Forming Potential
None

Effects of Overdosage
With Moderate Overdose: Extreme drowsiness, slow breathing, weakness.
With Large Overdose: Deep sleep, coma, perspiration, weak and rapid pulse, shallow breathing.

Possible Effects of Extended Use
Tardive dyskinesia (see Glossary).
Deposits in the cornea and lens of the eye.
Impaired liver function.

Recommended Periodic Examinations While Taking This Drug
Complete blood cell counts, especially during the first 3 months.
Liver and kidney function tests.
Complete eye examination including vision and eye structures.
Careful inspection of tongue for the early development of fine, wave-like, rippling surface movements (involuntary) that could indicate the beginning of tardive dyskinesia.
Periodic electrocardiograms and chest X-rays.

While Taking This Drug, Observe the Following
Foods: No restrictions.

Beverages: No restrictions.

Alcohol: Use extreme caution until combined effect has been determined. Alcohol can increase the sedative action of fluphenazine and accentuate its depressant effects on brain function and blood pressure. Fluphenazine can increase the intoxicating action of alcohol.

Tobacco Smoking: No interactions expected.

Other Drugs

Fluphenazine may *increase* the effects of

• all sedatives, sleep-inducing drugs, other tranquilizers, antidepressants, antihistamines, and narcotic drugs, and cause oversedation. Ask physician for guidance regarding dosage adjustment.

• atropine and drugs with atropine-like action (see Drug Family, Section Four).

Fluphenazine may *decrease* the effects of

• levodopa (Dopar, Larodopa, Parda, etc.), and reduce its effectiveness in the treatment of Parkinson's disease (shaking palsy).

• appetite suppressant drugs (Pre-Sate, Preludin, Benzedrine, Dexedrine, etc.).

Fluphenazine *taken concurrently* with

• anti-convulsants, may cause a change in the pattern of epileptic seizures. Ask physician for guidance regarding adjustment of anti-convulsant drug dosage.

• quinidine, may impair heart function. Avoid the combined use of these two drugs.

The following drugs may *increase* the effects of fluphenazine

• tricyclic antidepressants (see Drug Family, Section Four)

Driving a Vehicle, Piloting a Plane, Operating Machinery: This drug may impair mental alertness, judgment, physical coordination, or reaction time. Avoid hazardous activities.

Exposure to Sun: Use caution. Drugs closely related to this drug are known to produce photosensitivity (see Glossary).

Exposure to Heat: Use caution until combined effect has been determined. This drug may impair the regulation of body temperature and increase the risk of heat stroke.

Heavy Exercise or Exertion: No restrictions in mild to moderate temperatures.

Discontinuation: If it has been necessary to use this drug for an extended period of time, do not discontinue it suddenly. Ask physician for guidance regarding dosage reduction and withdrawal. It may also be necessary to adjust the dosage of other drugs taken concurrently with it.

Special Storage Instructions
Keep liquid dosage forms in tightly closed, amber glass containers.

Do Not Use the Injectable Form of This Drug If
—its color is darker than light amber.

FLURAZEPAM
Year Introduced: 1970

Brand Names

USA	Canada
Dalmane (Roche)	Dalmane (Roche)

Drug Family: Sleep Inducer (Hypnotic) [Benzodiazepines]

Prescription Required: Yes (Controlled Drug, U.S. Schedule 4)

Available Dosage Forms and Strengths
Capsules — 15 mg., 30 mg.

How This Drug Works

Intended Therapeutic Effect(s):   Prevention of insomnia. Restoration of normal sleep pattern.

Location of Drug Action(s):   Exact site not known. Possibly the hypothalamus and limbic system of the brain.

Method of Drug Action(s):   Not established. Principal action induces sleep that closely resembles natural sleep.

THIS DRUG SHOULD NOT BE TAKEN IF
—you are allergic to flurazepam.
—it is prescribed for a child under 15 years of age.

INFORM YOUR PHYSICIAN BEFORE TAKING THIS DRUG IF
—you are allergic to any drugs chemically related to flurazepam: chlordiazepoxide, clorazepate, diazepam, oxazepam (see Drug Profiles for brand names).
—you have epilepsy.
—you have a history of acute intermittent porphyria.
—you are taking sedative, other sleep-inducing, tranquilizer, antidepressant, or anti-convulsant drugs of any kind.
—you plan to have surgery under general anesthesia in the near future.

Time Required for Apparent Benefit
Approximately 30 to 60 minutes.

Possible Side-Effects *(natural, expected, and unavoidable drug actions)*
"Hangover" effects on arising—drowsiness, lethargy, unsteadiness in stance and gait.
In the elderly (over 60 years of age) and debilitated: confusion, weakness, incoordination, falling. The elderly may be very susceptible to standard doses. Use with caution until tolerance has been determined.

Possible Adverse Effects *(unusual, unexpected, and infrequent reactions)*
IF ANY OF THE FOLLOWING DEVELOP, DISCONTINUE DRUG AND NOTIFY YOUR PHYSICIAN AS SOON AS POSSIBLE
Mild Adverse Effects
    Allergic Reactions: Skin rashes (various kinds), burning eyes.
    Dizziness, lightheadedness, staggering, blurred vision, slurred speech, headache, nausea, indigestion.
Serious Adverse Effects
    Allergic Reactions: Jaundice (yellow skin coloration; see Glossary).
    Paradoxical Reactions: Restlessness, talkativeness, acute excitement, hallucinations.

Advisability of Use During Pregnancy
The findings of some recent studies suggest a possible association between the use of a drug closely related to flurazepam during early pregnancy and the occurrence of birth defects, such as cleft lip. It is advisable to avoid this drug completely during the first 3 months of pregnancy.

Advisability of Use While Nursing Infant
With recommended dosage, drug is probably present in milk. Ask physician for guidance.

Habit-Forming Potential
This drug is closely related to drugs that can cause psychological and/or physical dependence if used in large doses for an extended period of time. Avoid continuous use.

Effects of Overdosage
With Moderate Overdose: Marked drowsiness, weakness, drunkenness, impairment of stance and gait.
With Large Overdose: Stupor, deep sleep, coma.

Possible Effects of Extended Use
Psychological and/or physical dependence.
Impairment of liver function.

Recommended Periodic Examinations While Taking This Drug
Blood cell counts, liver and kidney function tests during long-term use.

While Taking This Drug, Observe the Following
Foods: No restrictions.
Beverages: Because of their caffeine content, large intakes of coffee, tea, or cola drinks within 4 hours of medication may reduce the sleep-inducing effect of flurazepam.
Alcohol: Avoid completely. Alcohol can increase the sedative action of flurazepam and depress vital brain functions.
Tobacco Smoking: Heavy smoking may reduce the duration of sedative action of flurazepam.

Other Drugs
Flurazepam *taken concurrently* with
• anti-convulsants, may cause a change in the pattern of seizures; observe closely to determine if an adjustment of the anti-convulsant dose is necessary.

The following drugs may *increase* the effects of flurazepam
• all sedatives, drugs for sleep, tranquilizers, antidepressants, anti-convulsants, and narcotic drugs may increase the sedative action of flurazepam and produce oversedation. Ask physician for guidance regarding dosage adjustment.

Driving a Vehicle, Piloting a Plane, Operating Machinery: The "hangover" effects of this drug can impair mental alertness, judgment, and physical coordination. Avoid hazardous activities until all such drug effects have disappeared.
Exposure to Sun: No restrictions.
Discontinuation: If it has been necessary to use this drug in large doses or for an extended period of time, ask physician for guidance regarding dosage reduction and withdrawal.

Special Storage Instructions
Keep in a dry, tightly closed, light-resistant container. Avoid excessive heat.

FURAZOLIDONE

Year Introduced: 1959

Brand Names

USA	Canada
Furoxone (Eaton)	Furoxone (Eaton)

Drug Family: Antimicrobial (Anti-infective) [Nitrofurans] [Mono-amine Oxidase Inhibitors]

Prescription Required: Yes

Available Dosage Forms and Strengths
Tablets — 100 mg.
Oral Suspension — 50 mg. per tablespoonful

How This Drug Works
Intended Therapeutic Effect(s):   The elimination of infections responsive to the action of this drug.
Location of Drug Action(s):   Any body tissue or fluid in which sufficient concentration of the drug can be achieved.
Method of Drug Action(s):   Not completely established. It is thought that this drug prevents growth and multiplication of susceptible bacteria by interfering with the function of essential enzyme systems.

THIS DRUG SHOULD NOT BE TAKEN IF
—you have had an allergic reaction to any dosage form of it previously.
—you cannot abstain from drinking alcohol.
—it is prescribed for an infant under 1 month of age.

INFORM YOUR PHYSICIAN BEFORE TAKING THIS DRUG IF
—you are taking any mono-amine oxidase inhibitor drug (see Drug Family, Section Four).
—you are taking any stimulant drugs.
—you are taking any tranquilizer, sedative, or antidepressant drug.

Time Required for Apparent Benefit
Usually 2 to 5 days.

Possible Side-Effects *(natural, expected, and unavoidable drug actions)*
A brown discoloration of the urine may occur. This is a normal consequence of drug excretion and does not represent any form of drug toxicity.

Possible Adverse Effects *(unusual, unexpected, and infrequent reactions)*
IF ANY OF THE FOLLOWING DEVELOP, DISCONTINUE DRUG AND NOTIFY YOUR PHYSICIAN AS SOON AS POSSIBLE
Mild Adverse Effects
Allergic Reactions: Skin rash, hives, fever, joint pains, drop in blood pressure.
Headache, lethargy, dizziness, nausea, vomiting.
Serious Adverse Effects
Idiosyncratic Reactions: Hemolytic anemia (see Glossary).
Hypoglycemia (see Glossary).
Sudden, severe rise in blood pressure (see tyramine in Glossary).

Advisability of Use During Pregnancy
Safety not established. Prudent use is best determined by the physician's evaluation.

Advisability of Use While Nursing Infant
Safety not established for infant. Ask physician for guidance.

Habit-Forming Potential
None.

Effects of Overdosage
Nausea, vomiting.
Possible development of sudden, severe high blood pressure.

Possible Effects of Extended Use
Development of sudden, severe high blood pressure.

Recommended Periodic Examinations While Taking This Drug
Complete blood cell counts.
Measurement of blood pressure at regular intervals.

While Taking This Drug, Observe the Following
Foods: Avoid all foods containing tyramine (see tyramine family of foods and beverages in Glossary).

Beverages: Avoid all beverages containing tyramine (see Glossary).

Alcohol: Avoid completely during drug administration and for 4 days following discontinuation to prevent a disulfiram-like reaction (see Glossary).

Tobacco Smoking: No interactions expected.

Other Drugs

Furazolidone may *increase* the effects of

• other mono-amine oxidase (MAO) inhibitor drugs (see Drug Family, Section Four).

• amphetamine-like drugs (see Drug Family, Section Four).

• phenylephrine, ephedrine (decongestants frequently used in cold remedies and nasal sprays).

Furazolidone *taken concurrently* with

• tricyclic antidepressants (see Drug Family, Section Four), may cause severe mental and behavioral disturbances.

Driving a Vehicle, Piloting a Plane, Operating Machinery: No restrictions unless dizziness occurs.

Exposure to Sun: No restrictions.

Discontinuation: Do not take this drug for more than 5 days unless advised to do so by your physician.

Special Storage Instructions
Keep in a tightly covered, light-resistant container.

FUROSEMIDE

Year Introduced: 1966

Brand Names

USA	Canada
Lasix (Hoechst-Roussel)	Furoside (ICN)
	Lasix (Hoechst)

Drug Family: Anti-hypertensive (Hypotensive); Diuretic

Prescription Required: Yes

Available Dosage Forms and Strengths
Tablets — 20 mg., 40 mg.

How This Drug Works
Intended Therapeutic Effect(s)
• elimination of excessive fluid retention (edema).
• reduction of high blood pressure.
Location of Drug Action(s): The tubular systems of the kidney that determine the final composition of the urine.
Method of Drug Action(s): By increasing the elimination of salt and water from the body (through increased urine production), this drug reduces the volume of fluid in the blood and body tissues and lowers the sodium content throughout the body. These changes may produce a lowering of blood pressure.

THIS DRUG SHOULD NOT BE TAKEN IF
—you have had an allergic reaction to any dosage form of it previously.

INFORM YOUR PHYSICIAN BEFORE TAKING THIS DRUG IF
—you are allergic to any form of "sulfa" drug.
—you are pregnant and your physician does not know it.
—you have a history of liver or kidney disease, or impaired liver or kidney function.
—you have diabetes (or a tendency to diabetes).
—you have a history of gout.
—you have impaired hearing.
—you are taking any form of cortisone, digitalis, oral anti-diabetic drugs, or insulin.
—you plan to have surgery under general anesthesia in the near future.

Time Required for Apparent Benefit
Increased urine volume begins in 1 hour, reaches a maximum in the second hour, and gradually subsides in 6 to 8 hours. Continuous use on a regular schedule for 1 to 2 weeks may be necessary to determine this drug's effectiveness in lowering your blood pressure.

Possible Side-Effects *(natural, expected, and unavoidable drug actions)*
Lightheadedness on arising from sitting or lying position (see orthostatic hypotension in Glossary).
Increase in level of blood sugar, affecting control of diabetes.

Increase in level of blood uric acid, affecting control of gout.
Decrease in the level of blood potassium, resulting in muscle weakness and
cramping.

CAUTION

The elderly (over 60 years of age) are frequently quite sensitive to the effects
of small doses. It is advisable to use this drug with caution until extent and
duration of response have been determined.

Possible Adverse Effects *(unusual, unexpected, and infrequent reactions)*

**IF ANY OF THE FOLLOWING DEVELOP, DISCONTINUE DRUG AND NOTIFY
YOUR PHYSICIAN AS SOON AS POSSIBLE**

Mild Adverse Effects

Allergic Reactions: Skin rash (various kinds), hives, itching.
Nausea, vomiting, diarrhea.
Dizziness, blurred vision.

Serious Adverse Effects

Allergic Reactions: Severe skin reactions.
Bone marrow depression (see Glossary)—fatigue, weakness, infection manifested by fever or sore throat, unusual bleeding or bruising.

Advisability of Use During Pregnancy

This drug should not be used during pregnancy unless a very serious complication of pregnancy occurs for which this drug is significantly beneficial. This
type of diuretic can have adverse effects on the fetus.

Advisability of Use While Nursing Infant

Reports indicate that this drug probably does appear in milk. Avoid use if
possible. Ask physician for guidance.

Habit-Forming Potential

None.

Effects of Overdosage

With Moderate Overdose: Weakness, lethargy, dizziness, confusion, nausea,
vomiting, leg muscle cramps, thirst.
With Large Overdose: Drowsiness progressing to stupor or deep sleep,
weak and rapid pulse.

Possible Effects of Extended Use

Impaired balance of water, salt, and potassium in blood and body tissues.
Development of diabetes (in predisposed individuals).

Recommended Periodic Examinations While Taking This Drug

Complete blood cell counts.
Measurements of blood levels of sodium, potassium, chloride, sugar and uric
acid.
Liver function tests.
Kidney function tests.

While Taking This Drug, Observe the Following

Foods: It is recommended that you include in your daily diet liberal servings of foods rich in potassium (unless directed otherwise by your physician). The following foods have a high potassium content:

All-bran cereals	Fish, fresh
Almonds	Lentils
Apricots (dried)	Liver, beef
Bananas, fresh	Lonalac
Beans (navy and lima)	Milk
Beef	Peaches
Carrots (raw)	Peanut butter
Chicken	Peas
Citrus fruits	Pork
Coconut	Potato chips
Coffee	Prunes (dried)
Crackers (rye)	Raisins
Dates and figs (dried)	Tomato juice

Note: Avoid licorice in large amounts while taking this drug.
Follow your physician's instructions regarding the use of salt.

Beverages: No restrictions unless directed by your physician.

Alcohol: Use with caution until the combined effect has been determined. Alcohol can exaggerate the blood pressure-lowering effect of this drug and cause orthostatic hypotension (see Glossary).

Tobacco Smoking: No interactions expected with this drug. Follow your physician's advice regarding smoking.

Other Drugs

Furosemide may *increase* the effects of

- other anti-hypertensive drugs. Careful adjustment of dosages is necessary to prevent excessive lowering of the blood pressure.
- drugs of the phenothiazine family, and cause excessive lowering of the blood pressure. (The thiazides and related drugs and the phenothiazines may both cause orthostatic hypotension.)

Furosemide may *decrease* the effects of

- oral anti-diabetic drugs and insulin, by raising the level of blood sugar. Careful dosage adjustment is necessary to maintain proper control of diabetes.
- allopurinol (Zyloprim), by raising the level of blood uric acid. Careful dosage adjustment is required to maintain proper control of gout.
- probenecid (Benemid), by raising the level of blood uric acid. Careful dosage adjustments are necessary to maintain control of gout.

Furosemide *taken concurrently* with

- salicylates (aspirin, etc.), may cause aspirin poisoning by interfering with its elimination from the body and causing elevation of blood and tissue levels.
- cortisone and cortisone-related drugs, may cause excessive loss of potassium from the body.

• digitalis and related drugs, requires very careful monitoring and dosage adjustments to prevent serious disturbances of heart rhythm.

• tricyclic antidepressants (Elavil, Sinequan, etc.), may cause excessive lowering of the blood pressure.

• oral anticoagulants, requires careful monitoring of the prothrombin time and appropriate adjustment of anticoagulant dosage to prevent abnormal blood clotting.

The following drugs may *increase* the effects of furosemide

• sedatives (especially barbiturates) and narcotic drugs may exaggerate its blood pressure-lowering action.

• mono-amine oxidase (MAO) inhibitor drugs (see Drug Family, Section Four) may greatly exaggerate its blood pressure-lowering action and drop the pressure to dangerous levels.

Driving a Vehicle, Piloting a Plane, Operating Machinery: Use caution until the possibility of orthostatic hypotension has been determined.

Exposure to Sun: No restrictions.

Exposure to Heat: Avoid excessive perspiring which could cause additional loss of water and salt from the body.

Heavy Exercise or Exertion: Avoid exertion that produces lightheadedness, excessive fatigue, or muscle cramping.

Occurrence of Unrelated Illness: Illnesses which cause vomiting or diarrhea can produce a serious imbalance of important body chemistry. Discontinue this drug and ask your physician for guidance.

Discontinuation: It may be advisable to discontinue this drug approximately 5 to 7 days before major surgery. Ask your physician, surgeon, and/or anesthesiologist for guidance regarding dosage reduction or withdrawal.

Special Storage Instructions
Keep in a dry, tightly closed, light-resistant container.

GLUTETHIMIDE
Year Introduced: 1954

Brand Names

USA	Canada
Doriden (USV Pharmaceutical)	Doriden (CIBA)
Dorimide (Cenci)	

Drug Family: Sleep Inducer (Hypnotic)

Prescription Required: Yes (Controlled Drug, U.S. Schedule 3)

Available Dosage Forms and Strengths
Tablets — 125 mg., 250 mg., 500 mg.
Capsules — 500 mg.

How This Drug Works
Intended Therapeutic Effect(s):   Relief of insomnia (hypnotic effect).
Location of Drug Action(s):   Not completely established. Thought to be the wake-sleep centers of the brain, possibly the reticular activating system.
Method of Drug Action(s):   Not established.

THIS DRUG SHOULD NOT BE TAKEN IF
—you have had an allergic reaction to any dosage form of it previously.
—it is prescribed for a child under 12 years of age.

INFORM YOUR PHYSICIAN BEFORE TAKING THIS DRUG IF
—you are taking sedatives, other sleep-inducing drugs, tranquilizers, pain relievers, antihistamines, or narcotic drugs of any kind.
—you have a history of porphyria.
—you plan to have surgery under general anesthesia in the near future.

Time Required for Apparent Benefit
Approximately 30 minutes.

Possible Side-Effects *(natural, expected, and unavoidable drug actions)*
Lightheadedness, unsteadiness in stance and gait.

CAUTION
The elderly (over 60 years of age) may not tolerate standard doses well. Small doses are advisable until tolerance and duration of action have been determined.

Possible Adverse Effects *(unusual, unexpected, and infrequent reactions)*

IF ANY OF THE FOLLOWING DEVELOP, DISCONTINUE DRUG AND NOTIFY YOUR PHYSICIAN AS SOON AS POSSIBLE

Mild Adverse Effects
Allergic Reactions: Skin rash (various kinds), hives.
"Hangover" effects, blurred vision.
Nausea.

Serious Adverse Effects
Allergic Reactions: Severe skin reactions.
Idiosyncratic Reactions: Paradoxical excitement and confusion.
Bone marrow depression (see Glossary)—fatigue, weakness, fever, sore throat, unusual bleeding or bruising.

Advisability of Use During Pregnancy
Safety not established. Prudent use is best determined by the physician's evaluation.

Advisability of Use While Nursing Infant
Drug is known to be present in milk. Ask physician for guidance.

Habit-Forming Potential
This drug can cause both psychological and physical dependence (see Glossary). Avoid large doses and continuous use.

Effects of Overdosage
With **Moderate Overdose:**   Extreme drowsiness, confusion, incoordination, slurred speech, staggering gait.
With **Large Overdose:**   Stupor, deep sleep, coma, shallow breathing.

Possible Effects of Extended Use
Psychological and/or physical dependence.

Recommended Periodic Examinations While Taking This Drug
Complete blood cell counts.   .

While Taking This Drug, Observe the Following
Foods: No restrictions.
Beverages: No restrictions.
Alcohol: Avoid completely for 6 hours before taking this drug for sleep. Alcohol can increase greatly the sedative and depressant actions of this drug on brain function.
Tobacco Smoking: No interactions expected.
Other Drugs
Glutethimide may *increase* the effects of
• sedatives, other sleep-inducing drugs, tranquilizers, antihistamines, pain relievers, and narcotic drugs. Ask physician for guidance regarding dosage adjustments.
• tricyclic antidepressants (Elavil, Tofranil, etc.). This can have adverse effects on glaucoma.

Glutethimide may *decrease* the effects of
• oral anticoagulants of the coumarin drug family, and reduce their protective action. Ask physician for guidance regarding prothrombin time testing and adjustment of anticoagulant dosage.
• cortisone and related drugs, by hastening their elimination from the body.
• griseofulvin (Fulvicin, Grifulvin, etc.), and reduce its antifungal action.

Glutethimide *taken concurrently* with
• phenytoin (Dantoin, Dilantin, etc.), may cause a significant change in the pattern of epileptic seizures by reducing the protective action of phenytoin. Dosage adjustment may be necessary for proper control of seizure disorders.

Driving a Vehicle, Piloting a Plane, Operating Machinery: This drug can impair mental alertness, judgment, physical coordination, and reaction time. Avoid hazardous activities until all sensation of drowsiness (or "hangover") has disappeared.
Exposure to Sun: No restrictions.
Discontinuation: If it has been necessary to use this drug for an extended period of time, do not discontinue it abruptly. Ask physician for guidance regarding dosage reduction and withdrawal. Ask physician for guidance

regarding dosage adjustment of other drugs taken concurrently with it, such as the coumarin anticoagulants and the anti-convulsants.

Special Storage Instructions
Keep in a dry, tightly closed container.

GLYBURIDE/GLIBENCLAMIDE

Year Introduced: 1973

Brand Names

USA	Canada
None	Diabeta (Hoechst)
	Euglucon (Roussel)

Drug Family: Anti-diabetic, Oral (Hypoglycemic) [Sulfonylureas]

Prescription Required: Yes

Available Dosage Forms and Strengths
Tablets — 5 mg.

How This Drug Works
Intended Therapeutic Effect(s): The correction of insulin deficiency in adult (maturity-onset) diabetes of moderate severity.

Location of Drug Action(s):   The insulin-producing tissues of the pancreas.

Method of Drug Action(s):   It is well established that sulfonylurea drugs stimulate the secretion of insulin (by a pancreas capable of responding to stimulation). Therapeutic doses may increase the amount of available insulin.

THIS DRUG SHOULD NOT BE TAKEN IF
—you have had an allergic reaction to any dosage form of it previously.
—you have a history of severe liver or kidney disease with impaired function of either one.

INFORM YOUR PHYSICIAN BEFORE TAKING THIS DRUG IF
—your diabetes has been difficult to control in the past ("brittle type").
—you have a history of peptic ulcer of the stomach or duodenum.
—you do not know how to recognize and treat hypoglycemia (see Glossary).

Time Required for Apparent Benefit
A single dose may lower the blood sugar within 2 to 4 hours. Regular use for 1 to 2 weeks may be needed to determine this drug's effectiveness in controlling your diabetes.

Possible Side-Effects *(natural, expected, and unavoidable drug actions)*
Usually none. If drug dosage is excessive or food intake is inadequate, abnormally low blood sugar (hypoglycemia) will occur as a predictable drug effect (see hypoglycemia in Glossary).

CAUTION
The elderly (over 60 years of age) require smaller doses and are more likely to experience episodes of prolonged hypoglycemia when taking this drug.

Possible Adverse Effects *(unusual, unexpected, and infrequent reactions)*

IF ANY OF THE FOLLOWING DEVELOP, DISCONTINUE DRUG AND NOTIFY YOUR PHYSICIAN AS SOON AS POSSIBLE

Mild Adverse Effects
Allergic Reactions: Skin rashes (various kinds).
Headache, blurred vision.
Nausea, indigestion, diarrhea.

Serious Adverse Effects
Bone marrow depression (see Glossary)—fever, sore throat, unusual bleeding or bruising.

Advisability of Use During Pregnancy
Safety not established. Prudent use is best determined by the physician's evaluation.

Advisability of Use While Nursing Infant
Drug is known to be present in milk. Ask physician for guidance.

Habit-Forming Potential
None.

Effects of Overdosage
With Moderate Overdose: Symptoms of mild to moderate hypoglycemia: Headache, lightheadedness, faintness, nervousness, confusion, tremor, sweating, heart palpitation, weakness, and hunger.
With Large Overdose: Hypoglycemic coma (see Glossary).

Possible Effects of Extended Use
Reduced function of the thyroid gland (hypothyroidism), resulting in lowered metabolism.
Reports of increased frequency and severity of heart and blood vessel diseases associated with long-term use of the members of this drug family are highly controversial and inconclusive. A direct cause-and-effect relationship (see Glossary) has not been established to date. Ask your physician for guidance regarding extended use.

Recommended Periodic Examinations While Taking This Drug
Complete blood cell counts.
Liver function tests.
Periodic evaluations of heart and circulatory system.

While Taking This Drug, Observe the Following
Foods: Follow the diabetic diet prescribed by your physician.
Beverages: As directed in the diabetic diet prescribed by your physician.
Alcohol: Use with extreme caution until the combined effect has been determined. This drug can cause a marked intolerance to alcohol resulting in a disulfiram-like reaction (see Glossary).

Tobacco Smoking: No restrictions unless imposed as part of your overall treatment program. Ask physician for guidance.

Other Drugs

Glyburide may *increase* the effects of

- sedatives and sleep-inducing drugs, by slowing their elimination from the body.
- "sulfa" drugs, by slowing their elimination from the body.

Glyburide *taken concurrently* with

- oral anticoagulants, may cause unpredictable changes in anticoagulant drug actions. Ask physician for guidance regarding prothrombin blood tests and dosage adjustment.
- propranolol (Inderal), may allow hypoglycemia to develop without adequate warning. Follow diet and dosage schedules very carefully.

The following drugs may *increase* the effects of glyburide

- bishydroxycoumarin (Dicumarol, Dufalone)
- chloramphenicol (Chloromycetin, etc.)
- clofibrate (Atromid-S)
- mono-amine oxidase (MAO) inhibitors (see Drug Family, Section Four)
- oxyphenbutazone (Oxalid, Tandearil)
- phenformin (DBI)
- phenylbutazone (Azolid, Butazolidin, etc.)
- phenyramidol (Analexin)
- probenecid (Benemid)
- propranolol (Inderal)
- salicylates (aspirin, sodium salicylate)
- sulfaphenazole (Orisul, Sulfabid)
- sulfisoxazole (Gantrisin, Novosoxazole, etc.)

The following drugs may *decrease* the effects of glyburide

- chlorpromazine (Thorazine, Largactil, etc.)
- cortisone and related drugs (see Drug Family, Section Four)
- estrogens (Premarin, Menotrol, Ogen, etc.)
- isoniazid (INH, Isozide, etc.)
- nicotinic acid (Niacin, etc.)
- oral contraceptives (see Drug Profile)
- pyrazinamide (Aldinamide)
- thiazide diuretics (see Drug Family, Section Four)
- thyroid preparations

Driving a Vehicle, Piloting a Plane, Operating Machinery: Regulate your dosage schedule, eating schedule, and physical activities very carefully to prevent hypoglycemia. Be able to recognize the early symptoms of hypoglycemia and avoid hazardous activities if you suspect that hypoglycemia is developing.

Exposure to Sun: Use caution until sensitivity has been determined. This drug can cause photosensitivity (see Glossary).

Heavy Exercise or Exertion: Use caution. Excessive exercise may result in hypoglycemia.

Occurrence of Unrelated Illness: Acute infections, illnesses causing vomiting or diarrhea, serious injuries, and the need for surgery can interfere with diabetic control and may require a change in medication. If any of these conditions occur, ask your physician for guidance regarding the continued use of this drug.

Discontinuation: If you find it necessary to discontinue this drug for any reason, notify your physician and ask for guidance regarding necessary changes in your treatment program for diabetic control.

Special Storage Instructions
Keep in a dry, tightly closed container.

GRISEOFULVIN

Year Introduced: 1959

Brand Names

USA	Canada
Fulvicin P/G (Schering)	Fulvicin-U/F (Schering)
Fulvicin-U/F (Schering)	Grisactin (Ayerst)
Grifulvin V (McNeil)	Grisovin-FP (Glaxo)
Grisactin (Ayerst)	
Grisowen (Owen)	

Drug Family: Antibiotic; Antifungal (Antimycotic)

Prescription Required: Yes

Available Dosage Forms and Strengths
Tablets — 125 mg., 250 mg., 500 mg.
Capsules — 125 mg., 250 mg.
Oral Suspension — 250 mg. per teaspoonful

How This Drug Works
Intended Therapeutic Effect(s):   The elimination of fungus infections responsive to the action of this drug.

Location of Drug Action(s):   Those areas of the skin, the hair, and the nails infected by certain strains of fungus, and in which an adequate concentration of the drug can be achieved.

Method of Drug Action(s):   This drug prevents the growth and multiplication of susceptible strains of fungus, probably by interfering with their essential metabolic activities.

THIS DRUG SHOULD NOT BE TAKEN IF
—you have had an allergic reaction to any dosage form of it previously.
—you have serious impairment of liver function.
—you have a history of acute intermittent porphyria.

—you have a mild or trivial fungus infection that will respond to local treatment.

INFORM YOUR PHYSICIAN BEFORE TAKING THIS DRUG IF
—you are allergic to any penicillin drug.
—you have lupus erythematosus.

Time Required for Apparent Benefit
From 2 to 10 days for skin infections; from 2 to 4 weeks for nail infections. Complete cure, however, may require continuous use for many weeks or months, depending upon nature and extent of infection.

Possible Side-Effects *(natural, expected, and unavoidable drug actions)*
Mild lowering of the blood pressure.
Superinfections (see Glossary).

Possible Adverse Effects *(unusual, unexpected, and infrequent reactions)*
IF ANY OF THE FOLLOWING DEVELOP, DISCONTINUE DRUG AND NOTIFY YOUR PHYSICIAN AS SOON AS POSSIBLE

Mild Adverse Effects
   Allergic Reactions: Skin rashes (various kinds), hives, photosensitivity (see Glossary).
   Headache, a feeling of head fullness, lethargy, dizziness, numbness or pain in the extremities, blurred vision, insomnia.
   Nausea, vomiting, diarrhea, irritation of mouth or tongue, "black tongue".

Serious Adverse Effects
   Allergic Reactions: Anaphylactic reaction (see Glossary), fever, swelling of face and extremities, painful swollen joints, aching muscles, enlarged and tender lymph glands, jaundice (rare).
   In children: occasional enlargement of breasts, darkening of nipples and genitals.

Advisability of Use During Pregnancy
Safety not established. Prudent use is best determined by the physician's evaluation.

Advisability of Use While Nursing Infant
Safety not established. Ask physician for guidance.

Habit-Forming Potential
None.

Effects of Overdosage
Possible nausea, vomiting, diarrhea.

Possible Effects of Extended Use
Superinfections, especially from yeast organisms.
Numbness and/or tingling of hands or feet (see peripheral neuritis in Glossary).

Recommended Periodic Examinations While Taking This Drug
Complete blood cell counts weekly during first 2 months of treatment; longer
if findings warrant it.
During extended use, liver and kidney function tests.

While Taking This Drug, Observe the Following
Foods: No restrictions of food selection. Absorption is improved if taken
with high fat foods.
Beverages: No restrictions.
Alcohol: Use cautiously until combined effect is determined. A disulfiram-
like reaction (see Glossary) can occur. In addition, for some individuals
griseofulvin can increase the intoxicating effects of alcohol.
Tobacco Smoking: No interactions expected.
Other Drugs
Griseofulvin may *decrease* the effects of
• oral anticoagulants. Ask physician for guidance regarding prothrombin
time testing and dosage adjustment.

The following drugs may *decrease* the effects of griseofulvin
• phenobarbital (and possibly other barbiturates) may reduce its absorption.
(Dose of griseofulvin may have to be raised.)
Driving a Vehicle, Piloting a Plane, Operating Machinery: No restrictions
unless dizziness or impaired vision occur.
Exposure to Sun: Use caution until sensitivity is determined. Photosen-
sitivity can occur (see Glossary).
Discontinuation: Relatively long-term treatment is required to obtain cure.
Do not discontinue drug until advised by physician.

Special Storage Instructions
Keep in a dry, tightly closed container. Store at room temperature of 59° to
86° F (15° to 30° C.).

GUANETHIDINE

Year Introduced: 1960

Brand Names

USA	Canada
Ismelin (CIBA)	Ismelin (CIBA)
Esimil [CD] (CIBA)	Ismelin-Esidrix [CD] (CIBA)

Drug Family: Anti-hypertensive (Hypotensive)

Prescription Required: Yes

Available Dosage Forms and Strengths
Tablets — 10 mg., 25 mg.

How This Drug Works
Intended Therapeutic Effect(s):   Reduction of high blood pressure.

Location of Drug Action(s):   The storage sites of the nerve impulse transmitter norepinephrine in the terminal fibers of the sympathetic nervous system that activate the muscles in blood vessel walls.

Method of Drug Action(s):   By displacing norepinephrine from its storage sites, this drug reduces the ability of the sympathetic nervous system to maintain the degree of blood vessel constriction responsible for elevation of the blood pressure. This depletion of norepinephrine results in relaxation of blood vessel walls and lowering of the blood pressure.

THIS DRUG SHOULD NOT BE TAKEN IF
—you have had an allergic reaction to any dosage form of it previously.

—you are taking or have taken within the past 2 weeks any mono-amine oxidase (MAO) inhibitor drug (see Drug Family, Section Four).

—you have a mild and uncomplicated case of high blood pressure.

INFORM YOUR PHYSICIAN BEFORE TAKING THIS DRUG IF
—you have a history of stroke, heart disease, asthma, or kidney disease.

—you have a history of peptic ulcer or chronic acid indigestion.

—you plan to have surgery under general anesthesia in the near future.

Time Required for Apparent Benefit
Continuous use on a regular schedule for several weeks may be necessary to determine this drug's effectiveness in lowering blood pressure and to establish correct dosage.

Possible Side-Effects *(natural, expected, and unavoidable drug actions)*
Lightheadedness, dizziness, weakness, feeling of impending faint in upright position (see orthostatic hypotension in Glossary). Blurred vision, nasal congestion (stuffiness), dry mouth, water retention.

CAUTION
Orthostatic hypotension can occur frequently and unexpectedly while using this drug. Avoid sudden arising from a lying or sitting position; avoid prolonged standing and excessive physical exertion. At the onset of lightheadedness, dizziness, or weakness, promptly sit down or lie down to prevent fainting. Ask your physician for guidance in adjusting dosage schedules and activities to prevent orthostatic hypotension.

Possible Adverse Effects *(unusual, unexpected, and infrequent reactions)*
IF ANY OF THE FOLLOWING DEVELOP, DISCONTINUE DRUG AND NOTIFY YOUR PHYSICIAN AS SOON AS POSSIBLE
Mild Adverse Effects

Allergic Reactions: Skin rash, soreness of salivary glands, loss of scalp hair.

Drowsiness, lethargy, weakness (most apparent during early days of treatment).

Acid indigestion, nausea, vomiting, diarrhea.

Mild muscular aches and pains.

Disturbance of urination. Impaired ejaculation.

Serious Adverse Effects
Bone marrow depression (see Glossary)—fatigue, weakness, fever, sore throat, unusual bleeding or bruising.
Activation of stomach or duodenal (peptic) ulcer.

Advisability of Use During Pregnancy
Safety not established. Prudent use is best determined by the physician's evaluation.

Advisability of Use While Nursing Infant
The presence of this drug in milk is unknown. Ask physician for guidance.

Habit-Forming Potential
None.

Effects of Overdosage
With Moderate Overdose: Marked drop in blood pressure, extreme weakness in upright position leading to falling and fainting, severe diarrhea.
With Large Overdose: Drop in blood pressure to shock levels, loss of consciousness, slow and weak pulse, cold and sweaty skin.

Possible Effects of Extended Use
Due to this drug's accumulative action, careful dosage adjustment will be necessary to prevent wide fluctuations in blood pressure and unexpected episodes of sudden drop in blood pressure accompanied by fainting.

Recommended Periodic Examinations While Taking This Drug
Complete blood cell counts.

While Taking This Drug, Observe the Following
Foods: No restrictions with regard to drug interactions. Avoid highly seasoned and irritating foods if you are subject to acid indigestion or peptic ulcer.
Beverages: Use carbonated beverages sparingly.
Alcohol: Use sparingly and with extreme caution until combined effect has been determined. Alcohol can increase the blood pressure-lowering action of this drug and cause the development of orthostatic hypotension.
Tobacco Smoking: Nicotine can cause an elevation of blood pressure in sensitive individuals. Follow your physician's advice regarding smoking.
Other Drugs
Guanethidine may *increase* the effects of
• other anti-hypertensives, and cause excessive lowering of the blood pressure. Careful dosage adjustments are necessary.
• insulin, and cause hypoglycemia (see Glossary).

Guanethidine *taken concurrently* with
• digitalis drugs, may cause marked reduction of heart rate. Careful monitoring and dosage adjustments are necessary.

The following drugs may *increase* the effects of guanethidine
- thiazide diuretics
- reserpine and related drugs

The following drugs may *decrease* the effects of guanethidine
- amphetamines (Benzedrine, Dexedrine, Methedrine, etc.) can reduce its blood pressure-lowering action.
- tricyclic antidepressants (Elavil, Tofranil, etc.) may completely reverse the anti-hypertensive action of guanethidine and render it ineffective. (Sinequan appears to be an exception to this interaction.)
- antihistamines may reduce its anti-hypertensive action.
- oral contraceptives significantly reduce the ability of guanethidine to lower the blood pressure.

Driving a Vehicle, Piloting a Plane, Operating Machinery: Be alert to the possibility of orthostatic hypotension developing while engaged in hazardous activities. This drug can also cause drowsiness and impair mental alertness, coordination, and reaction time.

Exposure to Sun: No restrictions.

Exposure to Heat: Hot weather and overheated environments favor the development of orthostatic hypotension. Avoid as much as possible.

Exposure to Cold: No restrictions.

Heavy Exercise or Exertion: Use caution until tolerance for physical activity and exercise are determined. Excessive exertion can induce orthostatic hypotension.

Discontinuation: Upon stopping this drug, the dosage schedules of other drugs taken concurrently with it will require readjustment. Ask physician for guidance.

Special Storage Instructions
Keep in a dry, tightly closed container.

HALOPERIDOL

Year Introduced: 1967

Brand Names

USA	Canada
Haldol (McNeil)	Haldol (McNeil)

Drug Family: Tranquilizer, Strong (Anti-psychotic) [Butyrophenones]

Prescription Required: Yes

Available Dosage Forms and Strengths
Tablets — 0.5 mg., 1 mg., 2 mg., 5 mg., 10 mg.
Concentrate — 2 mg. per ml.
Injection — 5 mg. per ml.

How This Drug Works

Intended Therapeutic Effect(s):   Restoration of emotional calm. Relief of severe anxiety, agitation, and psychotic behavior.

Location of Drug Action(s):   Those nerve pathways in the mesolimbic area of the brain that utilize the tissue chemical dopamine for the transmission of nerve impulses.

Method of Drug Action(s):   Not completely established. Present theory is that by inhibiting the action of dopamine, this drug acts to correct an imbalance of nerve impulse transmissions that is thought to be responsible for certain mental disorders.

THIS DRUG SHOULD NOT BE TAKEN IF

—you have had an allergic reaction to any dosage form of it previously.
—you are experiencing mental depression at the present time.
—you have any form of Parkinson's disease.
—it is prescribed for a child under 3 years of age.

INFORM YOUR PHYSICIAN BEFORE TAKING THIS DRUG IF

—you are allergic by nature, or have a history of allergic reactions to drugs.
—you have a history of mental depression.
—you have a history of liver or kidney disease, or impaired liver or kidney function.
—you have diabetes.
—you have epilepsy.
—you have glaucoma.
—you have any form of heart disease, especially angina (coronary insufficiency).
—you have high blood pressure.
—you drink alcoholic beverages daily.
—you are taking oral anticoagulant drugs.
—you are taking sedatives, sleep-inducing drugs, tranquilizers, antidepressants, antihistamines, or narcotic drugs of any kind.
—you plan to have surgery under general or spinal anesthesia in the near future.

Time Required for Apparent Benefit

Significant benefit may occur within 3 weeks. However, maximal benefit may require continuous use on a regular basis for several months.

Possible Side-Effects *(natural, expected, and unavoidable drug actions)*

Drowsiness, lethargy, blurred vision, dryness of the mouth, impaired urination, constipation, transient drop in blood pressure.

CAUTION

1.   The elderly (over 60 years of age) and the debilitated are more sensitive to standard doses. Small doses are advisable until the full effects have been determined.
2.   Dosage must be carefully individualized. The maintenance dose should be the lowest effective dose.

Possible Adverse Effects *(unusual, unexpected, and infrequent reactions)*

IF ANY OF THE FOLLOWING DEVELOP, DISCONTINUE DRUG AND NOTIFY YOUR PHYSICIAN AS SOON AS POSSIBLE

Mild Adverse Effects

Allergic Reactions: Skin rashes (various kinds), loss of hair.

Insomnia, restlessness, anxiety, agitation.

Headache, dizziness, weakness.

Lightheadedness or faintness in upright position, heart palpitation, rapid heart rate.

Reduced appetite, nausea, vomiting, diarrhea.

Breast fullness, tenderness, and milk production.

Serious Adverse Effects

Allergic Reactions: Jaundice (rarely; see Glossary).

Parkinson-like disorders (see Glossary).

Muscle spasms affecting the jaw, neck, back, hands, or feet.

Eye-rolling, muscle twitching, convulsions.

Depression, confusion, hallucinations.

Sexual impotence.

Reduced number of red blood cells (anemia).

Fluctuations in number of white blood cells.

Fluctuations in blood sugar levels.

Advisability of Use During Pregnancy

Safety not established. Definitely avoid use during the first 3 months. Prudent use during the last 6 months is best determined by the physician's evaluation.

Advisability of Use While Nursing Infant

The presence of this drug in milk is not known. Ask your physician for guidance.

Habit-Forming Potential

None.

Effects of Overdosage

With **Moderate Overdose:**   Marked drowsiness, weakness, muscle rigidity, tremors, confusion, dryness of mouth, blurred or double vision.

With **Large Overdose:**   Deep sleep progressing to coma, weak and rapid pulse, shallow and slow breathing, very low blood pressure, convulsions.

Possible Effects of Extended Use

Tardive dyskinesia (see Glossary).

Recommended Periodic Examinations While Taking This Drug

Complete blood cell counts.

Liver function tests.

Careful inspection of the tongue for early evidence of fine, involuntary, wave-like movements that could indicate the beginning of tardive dyskinesia.

While Taking This Drug, Observe the Following
Foods: No restrictions.

Beverages: No restrictions. The liquid concentrate form of this drug may be taken in water, in fruit or vegetable juices, or in milk.

Alcohol: Avoid completely. Alcohol can increase this drug's sedative action and accentuate its depressant effects on brain function. Haloperidol can increase the intoxicating effects of alcohol.

Tobacco Smoking: No interactions expected.

Other Drugs

Haloperidol may *increase* the effects of
- atropine-like drugs, and cause an increase in internal eye pressure in the presence of glaucoma.
- sedatives, sleep-inducing drugs, other tranquilizers, antihistamines, and narcotic drugs, and cause excessive sedation.

Haloperidol may *decrease* the effects of
- oral anticoagulants, and require adjustment of their dosage.
- bethanidine.
- guanethidine.
- levodopa.

Haloperidol *taken concurrently* with
- anti-convulsant drugs, may cause a change in the pattern of seizures. Dosage adjustment of the anti-convulsant may be necessary.
- anti-hypertensive drugs (some), may cause excessive lowering of the blood pressure.
- methyldopa, may cause serious mental and behavioral abnormalities.

The following drugs may *increase* the effects of haloperidol
- barbiturates may cause excessive sedation.
- other tranquilizers may cause excessive sedation.
- tricyclic antidepressants may cause excessive sedation.

Driving a Vehicle, Piloting a Plane, Operating Machinery: This drug can impair mental alertness, judgment, and physical coordination. Avoid all hazardous activities if you experience such drug effects.

Exposure to Sun: Use caution until full effect is known. This drug can cause photosensitivity.

Special Storage Instructions
Keep all forms of this drug in airtight containers. Protect from light.

HYDRALAZINE

Year Introduced: 1952

Brand Names

USA	Canada
Apresoline (CIBA)	Apresoline (CIBA)
Dralzine (Lemmon)	Ser-Ap-Es [CD] (CIBA)
Lopress (Tutag)	Serpasil-Apresoline [CD]
Apresazide [CD] (CIBA)	(CIBA)
Apresoline-Esidrix [CD]	
(CIBA)	
Dralserp [CD] (Lemmon)	
Ser-Ap-Es [CD] (CIBA)	
Serpasil-Apresoline [CD]	
(CIBA)	

Drug Family: Anti-hypertensive (Hypotensive)

Prescription Required: Yes

Available Dosage Forms and Strengths
Tablets — 10 mg., 25 mg., 50 mg., 100 mg.

How This Drug Works
Intended Therapeutic Effect(s):   Reduction of high blood pressure.

Location of Drug Action(s):   The muscles in the walls of blood vessels. The principal therapeutic action occurs in the small arteries (arterioles).

Method of Drug Action(s):   By causing direct relaxation and expansion of blood vessel walls, this drug lowers the pressure of the blood within. The mechanism of this direct action is not known.

THIS DRUG SHOULD NOT BE TAKEN IF
—you have had an allergic reaction to any dosage form of it previously.
—you have a history of coronary artery disease (angina, coronary insufficiency, heart attack).
—you have a history of rheumatic heart disease (consult your physician regarding specific contraindications).

INFORM YOUR PHYSICIAN BEFORE TAKING THIS DRUG IF
—you experience pain in the chest, neck, or arms on physical exertion (possible angina).
—you have a history of lupus erythematosus.
—you have had a stroke at any time.
—you have a history of kidney disease or impaired kidney function.
—you plan to have surgery under general anesthesia in the near future.

Time Required for Apparent Benefit
Continuous use on a regular schedule for several weeks may be necessary to determine this drug's effectiveness in lowering your blood pressure.

Possible Side-Effects *(natural, expected, and unavoidable drug actions)*
Lightheadedness on arising from a sitting or lying position (see orthostatic hypotension in Glossary).
Nasal congestion, constipation, difficult urination.

CAUTION
Toxic reactions are more likely to occur with large doses. Adhere strictly to prescribed dosage schedules. Keep appointments for periodic follow-up examinations.

Possible Adverse Effects *(unusual, unexpected, and infrequent reactions)*
IF ANY OF THE FOLLOWING DEVELOP, DISCONTINUE DRUG AND NOTIFY YOUR PHYSICIAN AS SOON AS POSSIBLE

Mild Adverse Effects
Allergic Reactions: Skin rash (various kinds), hives, itching, drug fever.
Headache, dizziness, heart palpitation, flushing.
Reduced appetite, nausea, vomiting, diarrhea.
Tremors, muscle cramps.

Serious Adverse Effects
Allergic Reactions: Hepatitis with or without jaundice (see Glossary).
Excessive stimulation of the heart resulting in chest pain on exertion (angina) in individuals with existing coronary artery disease.
Peripheral neuritis (see Glossary)—weakness, numbness, and tingling of the arms or legs.
Bone marrow depression (see Glossary)—weakness, fatigue, fever, sore throat, unusual bleeding or bruising.
Behavioral changes—nervousness, confusion, emotional depression.

Advisability of Use During Pregnancy
Safety not established. Prudent use is best determined by the physician's evaluation.

Advisability of Use While Nursing Infant
This drug is known to be present in milk. Ask physician for guidance.

Habit-Forming Potential
None.

Effects of Overdosage
With Moderate Overdose: Marked lightheadedness or dizziness in upright position (orthostatic hypotension), headache, rapid heart action, generalized flushing of skin.
With Large Overdose: Collapse of circulation—extreme weakness, loss of consciousness, cold and sweaty skin, weak and rapid pulse.

Possible Effects of Extended Use
Long-term use may cause an arthritic-like illness (lupus erythematosus) in susceptible individuals (see lupus erythematosus in Glossary).

Recommended Periodic Examinations While Taking This Drug
Complete blood cell counts.
Liver function tests.
Exercise electrocardiograms.

While Taking This Drug, Observe the Following
Foods: No restrictions. Ask physician regarding the advisability of supplementing your diet with Vitamin B–6 (pyridoxine) to prevent peripheral neuritis (see Glossary).

Beverages: No restrictions.

Alcohol: Use with extreme caution until combined effect has been determined. Alcohol can exaggerate the blood pressure-lowering action of this drug and cause excessive reduction.

Tobacco Smoking: The nicotine in tobacco can contribute significantly to this drug's ability to intensify coronary insufficiency (angina) in susceptible individuals. Follow your physician's advice regarding the use of tobacco.

Other Drugs

Hydralazine may *increase* the effects of
- other anti-hypertensive drugs, and cause excessive lowering of the blood pressure. Careful dosage adjustments are necessary.

The following drugs may *increase* the effects of hydralazine
- tricyclic antidepressants (Elavil, Tofranil, Sinequan, etc.) may increase the possibility of orthostatic hypotension.
- oral diuretics (Aldactone, Dyrenium, Edecrin, Lasix, and the thiazide drug family) can significantly enhance its blood pressure-lowering action. Dosage adjustments may be necessary.
- mono-amine oxidase (MAO) inhibitor drugs may increase its blood pressure-lowering action.

The following drugs may *decrease* the effects of hydralazine
- amphetamines (Benzedrine, Dexedrine, Synatan, etc.) can impair its blood pressure-lowering action.

Driving a Vehicle, Piloting a Plane, Operating Machinery: Avoid hazardous activities until the possibility of orthostatic hypotension has been determined.

Exposure to Sun: No restrictions.

Exposure to Heat: No restrictions.

Exposure to Cold: Use caution until combined effect has been determined. Cold may increase this drug's ability to cause coronary insufficiency (angina) in susceptible individuals.

Heavy Exercise or Exertion: Use caution until combined effect has been determined. Excessive exertion can increase this drug's ability to cause coronary insufficiency (angina) in susceptible individuals.

Special Storage Instructions
Keep in a dry, tightly closed container.

HYDROCHLOROTHIAZIDE

Year Introduced: 1959

Brand Names

USA	Canada
Esidrix (CIBA)	Chemhydrazide (Chemo)
HydroDiuril (Merck	Diuchlor H (Medic)
Sharp & Dohme)	Esidrix (CIBA)
Hydrozide-50 (Mayrand)	Hydrazide (Powell)
Hyperetic (Elder)	Hydrid (Nordic)
Oretic (Abbott)	Hydro-Aquil (M & M)
Thiuretic (Parke-Davis)	Hydrodiuretex (Barlow
Zide (Tutag)	Cote)
Aldactazide [CD] (Searle)	HydroDiuril (MSD)
Apresazide [CD] (CIBA)	Hydrosaluret (Saunders)
(Numerous combination	Hydrozide
brand names)	(Elliott-Marion)
	Neo-Codema (Neo)
	Novohydrazide
	(Novopharm)
	Urozide (ICN)

Drug Family: Anti-hypertensive (Hypotensive); Diuretic [Thiazides]

Prescription Required: Yes

Available Dosage Forms and Strengths
Tablets — 25 mg., 50 mg., 100mg.

How This Drug Works
Intended Therapeutic Effect(s)
- elimination of excessive fluid retention (edema).
- reduction of high blood pressure.

Location of Drug Action(s):   Principal actions occur in
- the tubular systems of the kidney that determine the final composition of the urine.
- the walls of the smaller arteries.

Method of Drug Action(s)
By increasing the elimination of salt and water from the body (through increased urine production), this drug reduces the volume of fluid in the blood and body tissues and lowers the sodium content throughout the body.

By relaxing the walls of the smaller arteries and allowing them to expand, this drug significantly increases the total capacity of the arterial system.

The combined effect of these two actions (reduced blood volume in expanded space) results in lowering of the blood pressure.

THIS DRUG SHOULD NOT BE TAKEN IF
—you are allergic to any of the drugs bearing the brand names listed above.

INFORM YOUR PHYSICIAN BEFORE TAKING THIS DRUG IF
—you are allergic to any form of "sulfa" drug.
—you are pregnant and your physician does not know it.
—you have a history of kidney disease or liver disease, or impaired kidney or liver function.
—you have diabetes (or a tendency to diabetes).
—you have a history of gout.
—you have a history of lupus erythematosus.
—you are taking any form of cortisone, digitalis, oral anti-diabetic drug, or insulin.
—you plan to have surgery under general anesthesia in the near future.

Time Required for Apparent Benefit
Increased urine volume begins in 2 hours, reaches a maximum in 4 to 6 hours, and subsides in 8 to 12 hours. Continuous use on a regular schedule will be necessary for 2 to 3 weeks to determine this drug's effectiveness in lowering your blood pressure.

Possible Side-Effects *(natural, expected, and unavoidable drug actions)*
Lightheadedness on arising from sitting or lying position (see orthostatic hypotension in Glossary).
Increase in level of blood sugar, affecting control of diabetes.
Increase in level of blood uric acid, affecting control of gout.
Decrease in level of blood potassium, resulting in muscle weakness and cramping.

CAUTION
The elderly (over 60 years of age) are frequently quite sensitive to the effects of standard doses. Use this drug with caution until extent and duration of response have been determined.

Possible Adverse Effects *(unusual, unexpected, and infrequent reactions)*
IF ANY OF THE FOLLOWING DEVELOP, DISCONTINUE DRUG AND NOTIFY YOUR PHYSICIAN AS SOON AS POSSIBLE

Mild Adverse Effects
  Allergic Reactions: Skin rash (various kinds), hives, drug fever. Reduced appetite, indigestion, nausea, vomiting, diarrhea. Headache, dizziness, yellow vision, blurred vision.

Serious Adverse Effects
  Allergic Reactions: Hepatitis with jaundice (see Glossary). Anaphylactic reaction (see Glossary). Severe skin reactions.
  Inflammation of the pancreas—severe abdominal pain.
  Bone marrow depression (see Glossary)—fatigue, weakness, fever, sore throat, unusual bleeding or bruising.

Advisability of Use During Pregnancy
This drug should not be used during pregnancy unless a very serious complication of pregnancy occurs for which this drug is significantly beneficial. This type of diuretic can have adverse effects on the fetus.

Advisability of Use While Nursing Infant
This drug is known to be present in milk. Ask physician for guidance.

Habit-Forming Potential
None.

Effects of Overdosage
With Moderate Overdose: Dryness of mouth, thirst, lethargy, weakness, muscle pain and cramping, nausea, vomiting.

With Large Overdose: Drowsiness progressing to stupor and coma, weak and rapid pulse.

Possible Effects of Extended Use
Impaired balance of water, salt, and potassium in blood and body tissues. Development of diabetes (in predisposed individuals).

Recommended Periodic Examinations While Taking This Drug
Complete blood cell counts.
Measurements of blood levels of sodium, potassium, chloride, sugar, and uric acid.
Liver function tests.
Kidney function tests.

While Taking This Drug, Observe the Following
Foods It is recommended that you include in your daily diet liberal servings of foods rich in potassium (unless directed otherwise by your physician). The following foods have a high potassium content:

All-bran cereals	Fish, fresh
Almonds	Lentils
Apricots (dried)	Liver, beef
Bananas, fresh	Lonalac
Beans (navy and lima)	Milk
Beef	Peaches
Carrots (raw)	Peanut butter
Chicken	Peas
Citrus fruits	Pork
Coconut	Potato Chips
Coffee	Prunes (dried)
Crackers (rye)	Raisins
Dates and figs (dried)	Tomato juice

Note: Avoid licorice in large amounts while taking this drug. Follow your physician's instructions regarding the use of salt.

Beverages: No restrictions unless directed by your physician.

Alcohol: Use with caution until the combined effect has been determined. Alcohol can exaggerate the blood pressure-lowering effect of this drug and cause orthostatic hypotension.

Tobacco Smoking: No interactions expected. Follow your physician's advice regarding smoking.

Other Drugs

Hydrochlorothiazide may *increase* the effects of
- other anti-hypertensive drugs. Careful adjustment of dosages is necessary to prevent excessive lowering of the blood pressure.
- drugs of the phenothiazine family, and cause excessive lowering of the blood pressure. (Thiazides and related drugs and the phenothiazines both may cause orthostatic hypotension).

Hydrochlorothiazide may *decrease* the effects of
- oral anti-diabetic drugs and insulin, by raising the level of blood sugar. Careful adjustment of dosages is necessary to maintain proper control of diabetes.
- allopurinol (Zyloprim), by raising the level of blood uric acid. Careful adjustment of dosages is required to maintain proper control of gout.
- probenecid (Benemid), by raising the level of blood uric acid. Careful dosage adjustment is necessary to maintain control of gout.

Hydrochlorothiazide *taken concurrently* with
- cortisone and cortisone-related drugs, may cause excessive loss of potassium from the body.
- digitalis and related drugs, requires very careful monitoring and dosage adjustments to prevent serious disturbances of heart rhythm.
- tricyclic antidepressants (Elavil, Sinequan, etc.), may cause excessive lowering of the blood pressure.

The following drugs may *increase* the effects of hydrochlorothiazide
- barbiturates may exaggerate its blood pressure-lowering action.
- mono-amine oxidase (MAO) inhibitor drugs may increase urine volume by delaying this drug's elimination from the body.
- pain relievers (analgesics), both narcotic and non-narcotic, may exaggerate its blood pressure-lowering action.

The following drugs may *decrease* the effects of hydrochlorothiazide
- cholestyramine (Cuemid, Questran) may interfere with its absorption. Take cholestyramine 30 to 60 minutes before any oral diuretic.

Driving a Vehicle, Piloting a Plane, Operating Machinery: Use caution until the possibility of orthostatic hypotension has been determined.

Exposure to Sun: Use caution until sensitivity has been determined. This drug can cause photosensitivity (see Glossary).

Exposure to Heat: Avoid excessive perspiring that could cause additional loss of water and salt from the body.

Heavy Exercise or Exertion: Avoid exertion that produces lightheadedness, excessive fatigue, or muscle cramping.

Occurrence of Unrelated Illness: Illnesses which cause vomiting or diarrhea can produce a serious imbalance of important body chemistry. Discontinue this drug and ask your physician for guidance.

Discontinuation: It may be advisable to discontinue this drug approximately 5 to 7 days before major surgery. Ask your physician, surgeon, and/or anesthesiologist for guidance regarding dosage reduction or withdrawal.

Special Storage Instructions
Keep in a dry, tightly closed container.

HYDROCORTISONE (CORTISOL)

Year Introduced: 1954

Brand Names

USA	Canada
Cortef (Upjohn)	Cortef (Upjohn)
Cortenema (Rowell)	Cortenema (ICN)
Cortril (Pfizer)	Cortril (Pfizer)
Hydrocortone (Merck Sharp & Dohme)	Hydrocortone (MSD)
(Numerous other brand and combination brand names)	(Numerous other brand and combination brand names)

Drug Family: Cortisone-like Drug [Adrenocortical Steroids (Glucocorticoids)]

Prescription Required: Yes

Available Dosage Forms and Strengths
Tablets — 5 mg., 10 mg., 20 mg.
Oral Suspension — 10 mg. per teaspoonful
Suppositories — 15 mg., 25 mg.
Enema Suspension — 100 mg. per 60 ml.
Ointments and Creams — 0.125%, 0.25%, 0.5%, 1%, 2%, 2.5%
Lotions — 0.5%, 1%, 2.5%
Eye Ointments and Suspensions — 0.5%, 1.5%, 2%, 2.5%

How This Drug Works
Intended Therapeutic Effect(s):   The symptomatic relief of inflammation (swelling, redness, heat and pain) in any tissue, and from many causes. (Cortisone-like drugs do not correct the underlying disease process).

Location of Drug Action(s):   Significant biological effects occur in most tissues throughout the body. The principal actions of therapeutic doses occur at sites of inflammation and/or allergic reaction, regardless of the nature of the causative injury or illness.

Method of Drug Action(s):   Not completely established. Present thinking is that cortisone-like drugs probably inhibit several mechanisms within the tissues that induce inflammation. Well-regulated dosage aids the body in restoring normal stability. However, prolonged use or excessive dosage can impair the body's defense mechanisms against infectious disease.

THIS DRUG SHOULD NOT BE TAKEN IF
—you have had an allergic reaction to any dosage form of it previously.
—you have an active peptic ulcer (stomach or duodenum).
—you have an active infection of the eye caused by the herpes simplex virus (ask your eye doctor for guidance).
—you have active tuberculosis.

INFORM YOUR PHYSICIAN BEFORE TAKING THIS DRUG IF
—you have had an unfavorable reaction to any cortisone-like drug in the past.
—you have a history of tuberculosis.
—you have diabetes or a tendency to diabetes.
—you have a history of peptic ulcer disease.
—you have glaucoma or a tendency to glaucoma.
—you have a deficiency of thyroid function (hypothyroidism).
—you have high blood pressure.
—you have myasthenia gravis.
—you have a history of thrombophlebitis.
—you plan to have surgery of any kind in the near future, especially if under general anesthesia.

Time Required for Apparent Benefit
Evidence of beneficial drug action is usually apparent in 24 to 48 hours. Dosage must be individualized to give reasonable improvement; this is usually accomplished in 4 to 10 days. It is unwise to demand complete relief of all symptoms. The effective dose varies with the nature of the disease and with the patient. During long-term use it is essential that the smallest effective dose be determined and maintained.

Possible Side-Effects *(natural, expected, and unavoidable drug actions)*
Retention of salt and water, gain in weight, increased sweating, increased appetite, increased susceptibility to infection.

CAUTION
1. It is advisable to carry a card of personal identification with a notation that you are taking this drug if your course of treatment is to exceed 1 week (see Table 14 and Section Seven).
2. Do not discontinue this drug abruptly.
3. While taking this drug, immunization procedures should be given with caution. If vaccination against measles, smallpox, rabies, or yellow fever is required, discontinue this drug 72 hours before vaccination and do not resume for at least 14 days after vaccination.

Possible Adverse Effects *(unusual, unexpected, and infrequent reactions)*
IF ANY OF THE FOLLOWING DEVELOP, DISCONTINUE DRUG AND NOTIFY YOUR PHYSICIAN AS SOON AS POSSIBLE

Mild Adverse Effects
Allergic Reactions: Skin rash.
Headache, dizziness, insomnia.
Acid indigestion, abdominal distention.
Muscle cramping and weakness.

Irregular menstrual periods.

Acne, excessive growth of facial hair.

Serious Adverse Effects

Mental and emotional disturbances of serious magnitude.

Reactivation of latent tuberculosis.

Development of peptic ulcer.

Increased blood pressure.

Development of inflammation of the pancreas.

Thrombophlebitis (inflammation of a vein with the formation of blood clot) —pain or tenderness in thigh or leg, with or without swelling of the foot, ankle, or leg.

Pulmonary embolism (movement of blood clot to the lung)—sudden shortness of breath, pain in the chest, coughing, bloody sputum.

Advisability of Use During Pregnancy

Safety has not been established. If possible, avoid completely. If use of·this drug is considered necessary, limit dosage and duration of use as much as possible. Following birth, the infant should be examined for possible defective function of the adrenal glands (deficiency of adrenal cortical hormones).

Advisability of Use While Nursing Infant

Drug is known to be present in milk. Ask physician for guidance.

Habit-Forming Potential

Use of this drug to suppress symptoms over an extended period of time may produce a state of functional dependence (see Glossary). In the treatment of conditions like rheumatoid arthritis and asthma, it is advisable to try alternate-day drug administration to keep the daily dose as small as possible and to attempt drug withdrawal after periods of reasonable improvement. Such procedures may reduce the degree of "steroid rebound"—the return of symptoms as the drug is withdrawn.

Effects of Overdosage

With Moderate Overdose: Excessive fluid retention, swelling of extremities, flushing of the face, nervousness, stomach irritation, weakness.

With Large Overdose: Severe headache, convulsions, heart failure in susceptible individuals, emotional and behavioral disturbances.

Possible Effects of Extended Use

Development of increased blood sugar, possibly diabetes.

Increased fat deposits on the trunk of the body ("buffalo hump"), rounding of the face ("moon face"), and thinning of the arms and legs.

Thinning and fragility of the skin, easy bruising.

Loss of texture and strength of the bones, resulting in spontaneous fractures.

Development of increased internal eye pressure, possibly glaucoma.

Development of cataracts.

Retarded growth and development in children.

Recommended Periodic Examinations While Taking This Drug
Measurement of blood potassium levels.
Measurement of blood sugar levels 2 hours after eating.
Measurement of blood pressure at regular intervals.
Complete eye examination at regular intervals.
Chest X-ray if history of previous tuberculosis.
Determination of the rate of development of the growing child to detect retardation of normal growth.

While Taking This Drug, Observe the Following
Foods: No interactions. Ask physician regarding need to restrict salt intake or to eat potassium-rich foods. During long-term use of this drug it is advisable to have a high protein diet.

Beverages: No restrictions.

Alcohol: No interactions expected.

Tobacco Smoking: Nicotine increases the blood levels of naturally produced cortisone and related hormones. Heavy smoking may add to the expected actions of this drug and requires close observation for excessive effects.

Other Drugs

Hydrocortisone may *increase* the effects of
- barbiturates and other sedatives and sleep-inducing drugs, causing oversedation.

Hydrocortisone may *decrease* the effects of
- insulin and oral anti-diabetic drugs, by raising the level of blood sugar. Doses of anti-diabetic drugs may have to be raised.
- anticoagulants of the coumarin family. Monitor prothrombin times closely and adjust dosage accordingly.
- choline-like drugs (Mestinon, pilocarpine, Prostigmin), by reducing their effectiveness in treating glaucoma and myasthenia gravis.

Hydrocortisone *taken concurrently* with
- thiazide diuretics, may cause excessive loss of potassium. Monitor blood levels of potassium on physician's advice.
- atropine-like drugs, may cause increased internal eye pressure and initiate or aggravate glaucoma (see Drug Family, Section Four).
- digitalis preparations, requires close monitoring of body potassium stores to prevent digitalis toxicity.
- stimulant drugs (adrenalin, amphetamines, ephedrine, etc.), may increase internal eye pressure and initiate or aggravate glaucoma.

The following drugs may *increase* the effects of hydrocortisone
- indomethacin (Indocid, Indocin)
- aspirin

The following drugs may *decrease* the effects of hydrocortisone
- barbiturates
- phenytoin (Dantoin, Dilantin, etc.)
- antihistamines (some)

- chloral hydrate (Noctec, Somnos)
- glutethimide (Doriden)
- phenylbutazone (Azolid, Butazolidin, etc.) may reduce its effectiveness following a brief, initial increase in effectiveness.
- propranolol (Inderal)

Driving a Vehicle, Piloting a Plane, Operating Machinery: No restrictions or precautions.

Exposure to Sun: No restrictions.

Occurrence of Unrelated Illness

This drug may decrease natural resistance to infection. Notify your physician if you develop an infection of any kind.

This drug may reduce your body's ability to respond appropriately to the stress of acute illness, injury, or surgery. Keep your physician fully informed of any significant changes in your state of health.

Discontinuation

If you have been taking this drug for an extended period of time, do not discontinue it abruptly. Ask physician for guidance regarding gradual withdrawal.

For a period of 2 years after discontinuing this drug, it is essential in the event of illness, injury, or surgery that you inform attending medical personnel that you used this drug in the past. The period of inadequate response to stress following the use of cortisone-like drugs may last for 1 to 2 years.

Special Storage Instructions

Keep in a tightly closed container. Protect from light.

HYDROFLUMETHIAZIDE

Year Introduced: 1959

Brand Names

USA	Canada
Diucardin (Ayerst)	Diucardin (Ayerst)
Saluron (Bristol)	Salutensin (CD) (Bristol)
Salutensin [CD] (Bristol)	

Drug Family: Anti-hypertensive (Hypotensive); Diuretic [Thiazides]

Prescription Required: Yes

Available Dosage Forms and Strengths

Tablets — 50 mg.

How This Drug Works

Intended Therapeutic Effect(s)
- elimination of excessive fluid retention (edema).
- reduction of high blood pressure.

Location of Drug Action(s):   Principal actions occur in:
• the tubular systems of the kidney that determine the final composition of the urine.
• the walls of the smaller arteries.

Method of Drug Action(s)

By increasing the elimination of salt and water from the body (through increased urine production), this drug reduces the volume of fluid in the blood and body tissues and lowers the sodium content throughout the body.

By relaxing the walls of the smaller arteries and allowing them to expand, this drug significantly increases the total capacity of the arterial system.

The combined effect of these two actions (reduced blood volume in expanded space) results in lowering of the blood pressure.

THIS DRUG SHOULD NOT BE TAKEN IF

—you have had an allergic reaction to any dosage form of it previously.

INFORM YOUR PHYSICIAN BEFORE TAKING THIS DRUG IF

—you are allergic to any form of "sulfa" drug.
—you are pregnant and your physician does not know it.
—you have a history of kidney disease or liver disease, or impaired kidney or liver function.
—you have diabetes (or a tendency to diabetes).
—you have a history of gout.
—you have a history of lupus erythematosus.
—you are taking any form of cortisone, digitalis, oral anti-diabetic drugs, or insulin.
—you plan to have surgery under general anesthesia in the near future.

Time Required for Apparent Benefit

Increased urine volume begins in 2 hours, reaches a maximum in 4 to 6 hours, and subsides in 8 to 12 hours. Continuous use on a regular schedule will be necessary for 2 to 3 weeks to determine this drug's effectiveness in lowering your blood pressure.

Possible Side-Effects *(natural, expected, and unavoidable drug actions)*

Lightheadedness on arising from sitting or lying position (see orthostatic hypotension in Glossary).

Increase in level of blood sugar, affecting control of diabetes.

Increase in level of blood uric acid, affecting control of gout.

Decrease in the level of blood potassium, resulting in muscle weakness and cramping.

CAUTION

The elderly (over 60 years of age) are frequently quite sensitive to the effects of standard doses. It is advisable to use this drug with caution until extent and duration of response have been determined.

Possible Adverse Effects *(unusual, unexpected, and infrequent reactions)*

IF ANY OF THE FOLLOWING DEVELOP, DISCONTINUE DRUG AND NOTIFY YOUR PHYSICIAN AS SOON AS POSSIBLE

Mild Adverse Effects

Allergic Reactions: Skin rash (various kinds), hives, drug fever.
Reduced appetite, indigestion, nausea, vomiting, diarrhea.
Headache, dizziness, yellow vision, blurred vision.

Serious Adverse Effects

Allergic Reactions: Hepatitis with jaundice (see Glossary).
Anaphylactic reaction (see Glossary).
Severe skin reactions.
Inflammation of the pancreas—severe abdominal pain.
Bone marrow depression (see Glossary)—fatigue, weakness, fever, sore throat, unusual bleeding or bruising.

Advisability of Use During Pregnancy

This drug should not be used during pregnancy unless a very serious complication of pregnancy occurs for which this drug is significantly beneficial. This type of diuretic can have adverse effects on the fetus.

Advisability of Use While Nursing Infant

This drug is known to be present in milk. Ask physician for guidance.

Habit-Forming Potential

None.

Effects of Overdosage

With Moderate Overdose: Dryness of mouth, thirst, lethargy, weakness, muscle pain and cramping, nausea, vomiting.

With Large Overdose: Drowsiness progressing to stupor and coma, weak and rapid pulse.

Possible Effects of Extended Use

Impaired balance of water, salt, and potassium in blood and body tissues.
Development of diabetes (in predisposed individuals).

Recommended Periodic Examinations While Taking This Drug

Complete blood cell counts.
Measurements of blood levels of sodium, potassium, chloride, sugar, and uric acid.
Liver function tests.
Kidney function tests.

While Taking This Drug, Observe the Following

Foods: It is recommended that you include in your daily diet liberal servings of foods rich in potassium (unless directed otherwise by your physician). The following foods have a high potassium content:

All-bran cereals	Bananas, fresh
Almonds	Beans (navy and lima)
Apricots (dried)	Beef

Carrots (raw)	Lonalac
Chicken	Milk
Citrus fruits	Peaches
Coconut	Peanut butter
Coffee	Peas
Crackers (rye)	Pork
Dates and figs (dried)	Potato Chips
Fish, fresh	Prunes (dried)
Lentils	Raisins
Liver, beef	Tomato Juice

Note: Avoid licorice in large amounts while taking this drug. Follow your physician's instructions regarding the use of salt.

Beverages: No restrictions unless directed by your physician.

Alcohol: Use with caution until the combined effect has been determined. Alcohol can exaggerate the blood pressure-lowering effect of this drug and cause orthostatic hypotension.

Tobacco Smoking: No interactions expected with this drug. Follow your physician's advice regarding smoking.

Other Drugs

Hydroflumethiazide may *increase* the effects of

• other anti-hypertensive drugs. Careful adjustment of dosages is necessary to prevent excessive lowering of the blood pressure.

• drugs of the phenothiazine family, and cause excessive lowering of the blood pressure. (The thiazides and related drugs and the phenothiazines may both cause orthostatic hypotension.)

Hydroflumethiazide may *decrease* the effects of

• oral anti-diabetic drugs and insulin, by raising the level of blood sugar. Careful dosage adjustment is necessary to maintain proper control of diabetes.

• allopurinol (Zyloprim), by raising the level of blood uric acid. Careful dosage adjustment is required to maintain proper control of gout.

• probenecid (Benemid), by raising the level of blood uric acid. Careful dosage adjustments are necessary to maintain control of gout.

Hydroflumethiazide *taken concurrently* with

• cortisone and cortisone-related drugs, may cause excessive loss of potassium from the body.

• digitalis and related drugs, requires very careful monitoring and dosage adjustments to prevent serious disturbances of heart rhythm.

• tricyclic antidepressants (Elavil, Sinequan, etc.), may cause excessive lowering of the blood pressure.

The following drugs may *increase* the effects of hydroflumethiazide:

• barbiturates may exaggerate its blood pressure-lowering action.

• mono-amine oxidase (MAO) inhibitor drugs (see Drug Family, Section Four) may increase urine volume by delaying this drug's elimination from the body.

• pain relievers (analgesics), both narcotic and non-narcotic, may exaggerate its blood pressure-lowering action.

The following drugs may *decrease* the effects of hydroflumethiazide

• cholestyramine (Cuemid, Questran) may interfere with its absorption. Take cholestyramine 30 to 60 minutes before any oral diuretic.

Driving a Vehicle, Piloting a Plane, Operating Machinery: Use caution until the possibility of orthostatic hypotension has been determined.

Exposure to Sun: Use caution until sensitivity has been determined. This drug can cause photosensitivity (see Glossary).

Exposure to Heat: Avoid excessive perspiring which could cause additional loss of water and salt from the body.

Heavy Exercise or Exertion: Avoid exertion that produces lightheadedness, excessive fatigue, or muscle cramping.

Occurrence of Unrelated Illness: Illnesses which cause vomiting or diarrhea can produce a serious imbalance of important body chemistry. Discontinue this drug and ask your physician for guidance.

Discontinuation: It may be advisable to discontinue this drug approximately 5 to 7 days before major surgery. Ask your physician, surgeon, and/or anesthesiologist for guidance regarding dosage reduction or withdrawal.

Special Storage Instructions
Keep in a dry, tightly closed container.

HYDROXYZINE

Year Introduced: 1956

Brand Names

USA	Canada
Atarax (Roerig)	Atarax (Pfizer)
Vistaril (Pfizer)	
Ataraxoid [CD] (Pfizer)	
Cartrax [CD] (Roerig)	
Enarax [CD] (Roerig)	
Marax [CD] (Roerig)	
Vistrax [CD] (Pfizer)	

Drug Family: Tranquilizer, Mild (Anti-anxiety); Antihistamines

Prescription Required: Yes

Available Dosage Forms and Strengths
Tablets — 10 mg., 25 mg., 50 mg., 100 mg.
Capsules — 25 mg., 50 mg., 100 mg.
Syrup — 10 mg. per teaspoonful
Suspension — 25 mg. per teaspoonful
Injection — 50 mg. per ml.

How This Drug Works
Intended Therapeutic Effect(s):   Restoration of emotional calm, relief of anxiety, tension, apprehension, and agitation.

Location of Drug Action(s):   Not established. Thought to be certain key areas of the brain that influence emotional stability.

Method of Drug Action(s):   Not established. Present thinking is that this drug may reduce excessive activity in these areas of the brain. The nature of this depressant action is unknown.

THIS DRUG SHOULD NOT BE TAKEN IF
—you have had an allergic reaction to any dosage form of it previously.

INFORM YOUR PHYSICIAN BEFORE TAKING THIS DRUG IF
—you have epilepsy.
—you are taking any sedative, sleep-inducing drugs, other tranquilizers, pain relievers, or narcotic drugs of any kind.
—you plan to have surgery under general anesthesia in the near future.

Time Required for Apparent Benefit
Drug action begins in 15 to 30 minutes and persists for approximately 4 hours.

Possible Side-Effects *(natural, expected, and unavoidable drug actions)*
Drowsiness.

Possible Adverse Effects *(unusual, unexpected, and infrequent reactions)*
IF ANY OF THE FOLLOWING DEVELOP, DISCONTINUE DRUG AND NOTIFY YOUR PHYSICIAN AS SOON AS POSSIBLE
Mild Adverse Effects
Allergic Reactions: Itching.
Dryness of the mouth, headache.
Serious Adverse Effects
None reported.

Advisability of Use During Pregnancy
Safety not established. Prudent use is best determined by the physician's evaluation.

Advisability of Use While Nursing Infant
Drug is known to be present in milk. Ask physician for guidance.

Habit-Forming Potential
None.

Effects of Overdosage
With Moderate Overdose: Marked drowsiness, unsteady stance and gait.

With Large Overdose: Agitation, purposeless movements, tremor, convulsions.

Possible Effects of Extended Use
Reduced effectiveness due to the development of tolerance (see Glossary).

Recommended Periodic Examinations While Taking This Drug
None required.

While Taking This Drug, Observe the Following
Foods: No restrictions.

Beverages: Large intake of coffee or tea may reduce this drug's calming action.

Alcohol: Use with extreme caution until combined effect has been determined. Alcohol can increase the sedative action of hydroxyzine. Hydroxyzine can increase the intoxicating effect of alcohol.

Tobacco Smoking: No interactions expected.

Other Drugs

Hydroxyzine may *increase* the effects of

• sedatives, sleep-inducing drugs, other tranquilizers, and narcotic drugs. Dosage adjustments may be necessary to prevent oversedation.
• oral anticoagulants of the coumarin family, and cause abnormal bleeding or hemorrhage. Consult physician regarding prothrombin time testing and dosage adjustment (see Drug Family, Section Four).

Hydroxyzine may *decrease* the effects of

• phenytoin (Dantoin, Dilantin, etc.), by hastening its elimination from the body. It may be necessary to adjust the dose of phenytoin at any time hydroxyzine is started or stopped.

The following drugs may *increase* the effects of hydroxyzine

• all sedatives, sleep-inducing drugs, tranquilizers, antihistamines, pain relievers, and narcotic drugs. Dosage adjustments are necessary to prevent oversedation.

Driving a Vehicle, Piloting a Plane, Operating Machinery: This drug may impair mental alertness, judgment, coordination, or reaction time. Avoid hazardous activities.

Exposure to Sun: No restrictions.

Special Storage Instructions
Keep in a tightly closed container. Protect the liquid forms from light.

IBUPROFEN

Year Introduced: 1967

Brand Names

USA	Canada
Motrin (Upjohn)	Motrin (Upjohn)

Drug Family: Analgesic, Mild; Anti-inflammatory; Fever Reducer (Antipyretic)

Prescription Required: Yes

Available Dosage Forms and Strengths

Tablets — 300 mg., 400 mg.

How This Drug Works

Intended Therapeutic Effect(s):   Relief of joint pain, stiffness, inflammation, and swelling associated with arthritis.

Location of Drug Action(s):   Not completely established. It is thought that this drug acts in the brain (at the level of the hypothalamus) and in the inflamed tissues of arthritic joints.

Method of Drug Action(s):   Not completely known. It is thought that this drug reduces the tissue concentration of prostaglandins, chemicals involved in the production of inflammation and pain.

THIS DRUG SHOULD NOT BE TAKEN IF

—you have had an allergic reaction to any dosage form of it previously.

—you are allergic to aspirin (hives, nasal polyps, and/or asthma caused by aspirin).

—it has been prescribed for a child under 14 years of age.

INFORM YOUR PHYSICIAN BEFORE TAKING THIS DRUG IF

—you have a history of peptic ulcer disease.

—you have a history of gout.

Time Required for Apparent Benefit

Drug action begins within 1 hour and persists for 3 to 5 hours. Significant improvement may require continuous use on a regular schedule for 1 to 2 weeks.

Possible Side-Effects *(natural, expected, and unavoidable drug actions)*

None reported.

CAUTION

The dosage schedule must be determined individually. It is advisable to limit dosage to the smallest amount that produces reasonable improvement. Do not exceed 2400 mg. (6 to 8 tablets) daily.

Possible Adverse Effects *(unusual, unexpected, and infrequent reactions)*

IF ANY OF THE FOLLOWING DEVELOP, DISCONTINUE DRUG AND NOTIFY YOUR PHYSICIAN AS SOON AS POSSIBLE

Mild Adverse Effects
  Allergic Reactions: Skin rash (various kinds), hives, itching.
  Nausea, vomiting, stomach irritation, heartburn, cramping, excessive gas, diarrhea.
  Dizziness, lightheadedness, headache, ringing in the ears.
Serious Adverse Effects
  Blurring of vision, appearance of "colored lights."
  Development of peptic ulcer.
  Abnormally low white blood cell counts.
  Mild anemia due to "silent" blood loss from the stomach (less than that caused by aspirin).

Advisability of Use During Pregnancy
Safety not established. Prudent use is best determined by the physician's evaluation.

Advisability of Use While Nursing Infant
Reports indicate that this drug is not present in milk. Nursing should be safe for the infant. Ask physician for guidance regarding dosage.

Habit-Forming Potential
None apparent to date.

Effects of Overdosage
  With Moderate Overdose: Possible indigestion, nausea, vomiting, stomach irritation.
  With Large Overdose: No serious or threatening effects reported to date.

Possible Effects of Extended Use
None known.

Recommended Periodic Examinations While Taking This Drug
Complete blood cell counts.
Complete eye examinations if any change in vision occurs.

While Taking This Drug, Observe the Following
  Foods: This drug should be taken with milk or food if stomach irritation occurs.
  Beverages: No restrictions.
  Alcohol: Use with caution. The irritant action of alcohol on the stomach lining, added to the irritant action of ibuprofen in sensitive individuals, can increase the risk of stomach bleeding or ulceration.
  Tobacco Smoking: No interactions expected.
  Other Drugs
  No significant interactions reported to date.

Ibuprofen *taken concurrently* with
- oral anticoagulants, requires careful monitoring of combined effects until more experience establishes a predictable pattern. (No significant interaction reported to date.)

Driving a Vehicle, Piloting a Plane, Operating Machinery: No restrictions or precautions.

Exposure to Sun: No restrictions.

Special Storage Instructions
Keep in a dry, tightly closed container.

IMIPRAMINE

Year Introduced: 1959

Brand Names

USA	Canada
Presamine (USV Pharmaceutical)	Chemipramine (Chemo)
Tofranil (Geigy)	Impranil (Barlowe Cote)
	Impril (ICN)
	Novopramine (Novopharm)
	Tofranil (Geigy)

Drug Family: Antidepressant, Tricyclic (Anti-psychotic)

Prescription Required: Yes.

Available Dosage Forms and Strengths
Tablets — 10 mg., 25 mg., 50 mg.
Injection — 25 mg. per 2 ml.

How This Drug Works
Intended Therapeutic Effect(s):   Gradual improvement of mood and relie of emotional depression.

Location of Drug Action(s):   Those areas of the brain that determine moo and emotional stability.

Method of Drug Action(s):   Not established. Present thinking is that thi. drug slowly restores to normal levels certain constituents of brain tissu (such as norepinephrine) that transmit nerve impulses.

THIS DRUG SHOULD NOT BE TAKEN IF
—you have had an allergic reaction to any dosage form of it previously.
—you are taking or have taken within the past 14 days any mono-amine oxidas (MAO) inhibitor drug (see Drug Family, Section Four).
—you are recovering from a recent heart attack.
—you have glaucoma (narrow-angle type).
—it is prescribed for a child under 6 years of age.

INFORM YOUR PHYSICIAN BEFORE TAKING THIS DRUG IF
—you are allergic or sensitive to any other tricyclic antidepressant (see Drug Family, Section Four).
—you have a history of any of the following: diabetes, epilepsy, glaucoma, heart disease, prostate gland enlargement, or overactive thyroid function.
—you plan to have surgery under general anesthesia in the near future.

Time Required for Apparent Benefit
Some benefit may be apparent within 1 to 2 weeks. Adequate response may require continuous treatment for 4 to 6 weeks.

Possible Side-Effects *(natural, expected, and unavoidable drug actions)*
Drowsiness, blurring of vision, dryness of mouth, constipation, impaired urination.

CAUTION
The possibility of adverse effects from this drug is greater in the elderly (over 60 years of age). Small doses are advisable until tolerance has been determined.

Possible Adverse Effects *(unusual, unexpected, and infrequent reactions)*

IF ANY OF THE FOLLOWING DEVELOP, DISCONTINUE DRUG AND NOTIFY YOUR PHYSICIAN AS SOON AS POSSIBLE

Mild Adverse Effects
    Allergic Reactions: Skin rash, hives, swelling of face or tongue, drug fever.
    Nausea, indigestion, irritation of tongue or mouth, peculiar taste.
    Headache, dizziness, weakness, fainting, unsteady gait, tremors.
    Swelling of testicles, breast enlargement, milk formation.
    Fluctuation of blood sugar levels.

Serious Adverse Effects
    Allergic Reactions: Hepatitis with jaundice (see Glossary).
    Confusion (especially in the elderly), hallucinations, agitation, restlessness, nightmares.
    Heart palpitation and irregular rhythm.
    Bone marrow depression (see Glossary)—fatigue, weakness, fever, sore throat, unusual bleeding or bruising.
    Numbness, tingling, pain, loss of strength in arms and legs.
    Parkinson-like disorders (see Glossary)—usually mild and infrequent; more likely to occur in the elderly.

Advisability of Use During Pregnancy
Safety not established. Prudent use is best determined by the physician's evaluation.

Advisability of Use While Nursing Infant
This drug may be present in milk in small quantities. Ask physician for guidance.

Habit-Forming Potential
Psychological or physical dependence is rare and unexpected.

Effects of Overdosage

With Moderate Overdose: Confusion, hallucinations, extreme drowsines
drop in body temperature, heart palpitation, dilated pupils, tremors.
With Large Overdose: Stupor, deep sleep, coma, convulsions.

Possible Effects of Extended Use
None reported.

Recommended Periodic Examinations While Taking This Drug
Complete blood cell counts.
Liver function tests.
Serial blood pressure readings and electrocardiograms.

While Taking This Drug, Observe the Following
Foods: No restrictions.
Beverages: No restrictions.
Alcohol: Avoid completely. This drug can increase markedly the intoxica
ing effects of alcohol and accentuate its depressant action on brain functio
Tobacco Smoking: No interactions expected.
Other Drugs

Imipramine may *increase* the effects of

• atropine and drugs with atropine-like actions (see Drug Family, Sectio
Four).

• sedatives, sleep-inducing drugs, tranquilizers, antihistamines, and na
cotic drugs, and cause oversedation. Dosage adjustments may be nece
sary.

• levodopa (Dopar, Larodopa), in its control of Parkinson's disease.

Imipramine may *decrease* the effects of

• guanethidine, and reduce its effectiveness in lowering blood pressure.

• other commonly used anti-hypertensive drugs. Ask physician for gui
ance regarding the need to monitor blood pressure readings and to adju
dosage of anti-hypertensive medications. (The action of Aldomet is n
decreased by tricyclic antidepressants.)

Imipramine *taken concurrently* with

• thyroid preparations, may cause impairment of heart rhythm and fun
tion. Ask physician for guidance regarding thyroid dosage adjustment

• ethchlorvynol (Placidyl), may cause delirium.

• quinidine, may cause impairment of heart rhythm and function. Avoi
the combined use of these two drugs.

• mono-amine oxidase (MAO) inhibitor drugs (see Drug Family, Sectio
Four), may cause high fever, delirium, and convulsions.

The following drugs may *increase* the effects of imipramine

• thiazide diuretics, (see Drug Family, Section Four) may slow its elimin
tion from the body. Overdosage may occur.

Driving a Vehicle, Piloting a Plane, Operating Machinery: This drug ma
impair mental alertness, judgment, physical coordination, and reactic
time. Avoid hazardous activities.

Exposure to Sun: Use caution until sensitivity to sun has been determined. This drug may cause photosensitivity (see Glossary).

Discontinuation: If it has been necessary to use this drug for an extended period of time, do not discontinue it abruptly. Ask physician for guidance regarding dosage reduction and withdrawal. It may be necessary to adjust the dosage of other drugs taken concurrently.

Special Storage Instructions

Keep in a dry, tightly closed container.

INDOMETHACIN

Year Introduced: 1963

Brand Names

USA	Canada
Indocin (Merck Sharp & Dohme)	Indocid (MSD) Infrocin (Frosst)

Drug Family: Analgesic, Mild; Anti-inflammatory; Fever Reducer (Antipyretic)

Prescription Required: Yes

Available Dosage Forms and Strengths

Capsules — 25 mg., 50 mg.
Suppositories — 100 mg.

How This Drug Works

Intended Therapeutic Effect(s):   Relief of joint pain, stiffness, inflammation, and swelling associated with arthritis.

Location of Drug Action(s):   Not completely established. It is thought that this drug acts in the brain (at the level of the hypothalamus) and in the inflamed tissues of arthritic joints.

Method of Drug Action(s):   Not completely known. It is thought that this drug reduces the tissue concentration of prostaglandins, chemicals involved in the production of inflammation and pain.

THIS DRUG SHOULD NOT BE TAKEN IF

—you are allergic to aspirin or to any of the drugs bearing the brand names listed above.

—you have active gastritis (stomach inflammation), peptic ulcer, enteritis, ileitis, or ulcerative colitis.

—you are pregnant or nursing.

—you have had recent rectal bleeding and the suppository form of this drug has been prescribed for you.

—it is prescribed for a child under 15 years of age.

INFORM YOUR PHYSICIAN BEFORE TAKING THIS DRUG IF
—you have a history of stomach or intestinal disease, especially peptic ulcer or ulcerative colitis.
—you have a history of epilepsy, Parkinson's disease (shaking palsy), or mental illness.
—you have a history of kidney disease or impaired kidney function.

Time Required for Apparent Benefit
Some improvement may occur in 4 to 24 hours. Maximal benefit occurs within 3 weeks.

Possible Side-Effects *(natural, expected, and unavoidable drug actions)*
Because of indomethacin's ability to reduce fever and inflammation, it can hide or mask the symptoms and indications of infection. If you suspect an infection of any kind may be present, discontinue this drug for 48 hours and observe. Notify physician of your action.

CAUTION
The possibility of adverse effects from this drug is greater in the elderly (over 60 years of age).

Possible Adverse Effects *(unusual, unexpected, and infrequent reactions)*
IF ANY OF THE FOLLOWING DEVELOP, DISCONTINUE DRUG AND NOTIFY YOUR PHYSICIAN AS SOON AS POSSIBLE

Mild Adverse Effects
Allergic Reactions: Skin rashes (various kinds), hives, itching, swelling of face and/or extremities.
Headache, ringing in ears, drowsiness, lightheadedness, dizziness, feelings of detachment.
Loss of appetite, nausea, vomiting, diarrhea.
Temporary loss of hair.

Serious Adverse Effects
Allergic Reactions: Asthma, shortness of breath, unusual bleeding or bruising, irritation of mouth.
Blurring of vision, confusion, depression (may be severe).
Severe indigestion, abdominal pain, heartburn, need for antacids (possible developing peptic ulcer).
Gastro-intestinal bleeding; observe stools for evidence of blood (dark red to black discoloration).
Hepatitis and/or jaundice (see Glossary).
Bone marrow depression (see Glossary).
Numbness and/or tingling, pain, weakness in hands and/or feet.

Advisability of Use During Pregnancy
Safety not established. Avoid use.

Advisability of Use While Nursing Infant
Drug is known to be present in milk. Safety for infant not established. Ask physician for guidance.

Habit-Forming Potential
None.

Effects of Overdosage
With Moderate Overdose: Stomach irritation, nausea, vomiting, diarrhea, confusion, agitation.

With Large Overdose: Disorientation, incoherence, convulsions, coma, possible hemorrhage from stomach or intestine.

Possible Effects of Extended Use
Eye damage (deposits in the cornea, changes in the retina).

Recommended Periodic Examinations While Taking This Drug
Careful and complete examinations of vision and eye structures.
Complete blood cell counts.
Liver function tests.
Urine analysis.

While Taking This Drug, Observe the Following
Foods: No restrictions of food selection. Drug should be taken with or following food to minimize stomach irritation.

Beverages: No restrictions of beverage selection. Drug may be taken with milk to minimize stomach irritation.

Alcohol: No interactions expected.

Tobacco Smoking: No interactions expected.

Other Drugs

Indomethacin may *increase* the effects of
- oral anticoagulants of the coumarin type (see Drug Family, Section Four). Consult physician regarding dosage adjustments to prevent bleeding.
- cortisone and related drugs (see Drug Family, Section Four). Consult physician regarding dosage adjustments to prevent stomach ulceration and other effects of cortisone overdosage.

Indomethacin *taken concurrently* with
- phenylbutazone (Azolid, Butazolidin, etc.), increases the risk of stomach ulceration.
- thyroid medications, increases the risk of adverse effects on the heart and circulation.

The following drugs may *increase* the effects of indomethacin
- probenecid (Benemid) may delay the elimination of indomethacin in the urine.

The following drugs may *decrease* the effects of indomethacin
- aspirin may interfere with the absorption of indomethacin from the intestine.

Driving a Vehicle, Piloting a Plane, Operating Machinery: Use caution until the occurrence of drowsiness, lightheadedness, and/or dizziness is determined.

Exposure to Sun: No restrictions.

Discontinuation: Dosage adjustment may be necessary for any of the following drugs if taken concurrently with indomethacin: coumarin anticoagulants, cortisone and related drugs, thyroid medications.

Special Storage Instructions
Keep in a dry, tightly closed container.

INSULIN

Year Introduced: 1922

Brand Names

USA	Canada
Iletin Preparations (Lilly)	Insulin Preparations
Insulin Preparations	(Connaught)
(Squibb)	Lente Insulin
Globin Zinc Insulin	Neutral Insulin
Lente Insulin	NPH Insulin
NPH Insulin	Protamine Zinc Insulin
Protamine Zinc Insulin	Semilente Insulin
Regular Insulin	Sulphated Insulin
Semilente Insulin	Ultralente Insulin
Ultralente Insulin	

Drug Family: Anti-diabetic, Injectable (Hypoglycemic)

Prescription Required: No

Available Dosage Forms and Strengths
Injection — 40 units per ml., 80 units per ml., 100 units per ml., 500 units per ml.

How This Drug Works
Intended Therapeutic Effect(s)   Restoration of the body's ability to use sugar normally (control of diabetes).

Location of Drug Action(s):   Principal actions occur in the tissues of voluntary muscles, the heart muscle, and the liver.

Method of Drug Action(s):   By direct action on certain cell membranes, insulin facilitates the transport of sugar through the cell wall to the interior of the cell, where it is utilized.

THIS DRUG SHOULD NOT BE TAKEN IF
—the need for it and its correct dosage schedule have not been established by a properly qualified physician.

INFORM YOUR PHYSICIAN BEFORE TAKING THIS DRUG IF
—you have a history of allergic reaction to any form of insulin on previous use.
—you do not know how to recognize and treat abnormally low blood sugar (see hypoglycemia in Glossary).

—you are taking any mono-amine oxidase (MAO) inhibitor drug (see Drug Family, Section Four).

Time Required for Apparent Benefit:

Insulin Preparation	Action Onset	Peak	Duration
Regular and Neutral	½–1 hour	2–3 hrs.	5–7 hrs.
Semilente	½–1 hr.	5–8 hrs.	12–16 hrs.
Globin Zinc	1–2 hrs.	6–12 hrs.	18–24 hrs.
NPH	1–3 hrs.	10–18 hrs.	18–28 hrs.
Lente	1–3 hrs.	10–18 hrs.	18–28 hrs.
Protamine Zinc	3–7 hrs.	15–22 hrs.	24–36 hrs.
Ultralente	5–8 hrs.	16–24 hrs.	28–36 hrs.

Possible Side-Effects *(natural, expected, and unavoidable drug actions)*

In the management of stable diabetes, no side-effects occur when insulin dose, diet, and physical activity are correctly balanced and maintained. In the management of unstable ("brittle") diabetes, unexpected drops in blood sugar levels can occur, resulting in periods of hypoglycemia (see Glossary).

CAUTION

1. It is most important that you carry with you a card of personal identification with a notation that you have diabetes and are taking insulin (see Table 14 and Section Seven).
2. Be sure that you know how to recognize the onset of hypoglycemia and how to treat it. Always carry with you a readily available form of sugar such as hard candy or sugar cubes. Report episodes of hypoglycemia to your physician.
3. Improvement in vision may occur during the first several weeks of insulin treatment. It is advisable to defer examination for glasses for 6 weeks after starting insulin.

Possible Adverse Effects *(unusual, unexpected, and infrequent reactions)*

IF ANY OF THE FOLLOWING DEVELOP, DISCONTINUE DRUG AND NOTIFY YOUR PHYSICIAN AS SOON AS POSSIBLE

Mild Adverse Effects

Allergic Reactions: Local redness, swelling, and itching at point of injection. Occasional hives.

Thinning of subcutaneous tissue (beneath the skin) at points of injection.

Serious Adverse Effects

Allergic Reactions: Anaphylactic reaction (see Glossary).

Episodes of severe hypoglycemia (see Glossary).

Advisability of Use During Pregnancy

Diabetes may be more difficult to manage during pregnancy. To preserve the health of the mother and the welfare of the fetus, every effort must be made to establish the optimal dose of insulin and to prevent hypoglycemia.

Advisability of Use While Nursing Infant
Insulin treatment of the mother has no adverse effect on the nursing infant.

Habit-Forming Potential
None.

Effects of Overdosage
With Moderate Overdose: Fatigue, weakness, headache, nervousness, irritability, sweating, tremors, hunger, rapid pulse.

With Large Overdose: Confusion, delirium, abnormal behavior resembling drunkenness, unconsciousness, convulsions.

Possible Effects of Extended Use
None reported.

Recommended Periodic Examinations While Taking This Drug
Monitoring of urine sugar content as a guide to adjustment of diet and insulin dose.

Measurement of blood sugar levels at intervals recommended by physician.

While Taking This Drug, Observe the Following
Foods: Follow your prescribed diabetic diet conscientiously. Do not omit snack foods in midafternoon or at bedtime if they are prescribed to prevent hypoglycemia.

Beverages: According to prescribed diabetic diet.

Alcohol: Use with caution until combined effect has been determined. Remember that alcohol has caloric value and that it tends to lower blood sugar. Used excessively, alcohol may induce severe hypoglycemia, resulting in brain damage.

Tobacco Smoking: No interactions expected. Follow physician's advice regarding smoking.

Other Drugs

Insulin may *increase* the effects of
- oral anti-diabetic drugs.

Insulin *taken concurrently* with
- propranolol (Inderal), requires extreme care and attention to dosage of both drugs. Propranolol can mask the usual symptoms that indicate the development of hypoglycemia.

The following drugs may *increase* the effects of insulin
- oral anticoagulants
- isoniazid (INH) in small doses
- mono-amine oxidase (MAO) inhibitor drugs (see Drug Family, Section Four)
- oxyphenbutazone (Oxalid, Tandearil)
- phenylbutazone (Azolid, Butazolidin, etc.)
- salicylates (aspirin, sodium salicylate) in large doses
- "sulfa" drugs (see Drug Family, Section Four)
- sulfinpyrazone (Anturane)

The following drugs may *decrease* the effects of insulin
• chlorthalidone (Hygroton)
• cortisone-like drugs (see Drug Family, Section Four)
• furosemide (Lasix)
• oral contraceptives (see Drug Family, Section Four)
• phenytoin (Dantoin, Dilantin, etc.)
• thiazide diuretics (see Drug Family, Section Four)
• thyroid preparations

Driving a Vehicle, Piloting a Plane, Operating Machinery: No restrictions. Be prepared to stop and take corrective action if indications of impending hypoglycemia develop.

Exposure to Sun: No restrictions.

Heavy Exercise or Exertion: Use caution. Periods of unusual and unplanned heavy physical activity will hasten the burning of blood sugar and predispose to hypoglycemia.

Occurrence of Unrelated Illness: Report all illnesses that prevent regular eating. Meals omitted as a result of nausea, vomiting, or injury can lead to hypoglycemia. Consult physician for guidance regarding food intake and insulin dose.

Discontinuation: Do not discontinue this drug without consulting your physician. Diabetes that is insulin dependent requires continuous treatment on a regular basis. Omission of insulin will result in life threatening coma.

Special Storage Instructions
Keep in refrigerator. Protect from freezing. Protect from strong light and high temperatures when not refrigerated.

Do Not Take This Drug If It Is Older Than
The expiration date on the vial. (Always use fresh, "within date" insulin.)

ISONIAZID

Year Introduced: 1956

Brand Names

USA	Canada
Hyzyd (Mallinckrodt)	Isotamine (ICN)
INH (CIBA)	Rimifon (Roche)
Laniazid (Lannett)	
Niconyl (Parke-Davis)	
Nydrazid (Squibb)	
Teebaconin (Consol. Midland)	
Triniad (Kasar)	
Uniad (Kasar)	

Drug Family: Antimicrobial, Anti-tuberculosis (Anti-infective)

Prescription Required: Yes

Available Dosage Forms and Strengths
Tablets — 50 mg., 100 mg., 300 mg.
Syrup — 10 mg. per ml. (50 mg. per teaspoonful)

How This Drug Works
Intended Therapeutic Effect(s):   The prevention or treatment of active tuberculosis.

Location of Drug Action(s):   Any body tissue or fluid in which adequate concentration of the drug can be achieved.

Method of Drug Action(s):   Not completely established. It is thought that the drug destroys susceptible tuberculosis organisms by interfering with several of their essential metabolic activities.

THIS DRUG SHOULD NOT BE TAKEN IF
—you have had an allergic reaction to any dosage form of it previously.
—you have active liver disease.
—you are within the first 6 months of pregnancy.

INFORM YOUR PHYSICIAN BEFORE TAKING THIS DRUG IF
—you have serious impairment of liver or kidney function.
—you have epilepsy.
—you have diabetes.
—you have systemic lupus erythematosus.
—you plan to have surgery under general anesthesia in the near future.

Time Required for Apparent Benefit
From 3 to 6 months.

Possible Side-Effects *(natural, expected, and unavoidable drug actions)*
None.

Possible Adverse Effects *(unusual, unexpected, and infrequent reactions)*

IF ANY OF THE FOLLOWING DEVELOP, DISCONTINUE DRUG AND NOTIFY YOUR PHYSICIAN AS SOON AS POSSIBLE

Mild Adverse Effects
Allergic Reactions: Skin rashes (various kinds), fever, swollen glands, painful muscles and joints.
Nausea, indigestion, vomiting.
Numbness, tingling, pain (often burning), and weakness first noted in hands and feet (see peripheral neuritis in Glossary).

Serious Adverse Effects
Allergic Reactions: Hepatitis, with or without jaundice (see Glossary). Inform physician promptly if you develop any of the early indications of possible hepatitis—loss of appetite, nausea, fatigue, fever, itching, dark-colored urine, light-colored stools, yellow discoloration of eyes or skin.
Acute mental and behavioral disturbance, convulsions, impaired vision.
Increase in epileptic seizures.

Bone marrow depression (see Glossary)—fatigue, weakness, fever, sore throat, unusual bleeding or bruising.
Elevated blood sugar.
Breast enlargement or discomfort.

Advisability of Use During Pregnancy
Safety not established for use during the first 6 months of pregnancy. Prudent use during the last 3 months is best determined by the physician's evaluation.

Advisability of Use While Nursing Infant
Drug may be present in milk. Safety for infant not established. Ask physician for guidance.

Habit-Forming Potential
None.

Effects of Overdosage
With Moderate Overdose: Nausea, vomiting, dizziness, blurred vision, visual hallucinations, slurred speech.
With Large Overdose: Difficult breathing, stupor, coma, convulsions.

Possible Effects of Extended Use
Nerve damage in arms or legs if a deficiency of Vitamin B-6 (pyridoxine) develops.

Recommended Periodic Examinations While Taking This Drug
Consult physician regarding advisability of determining whether you are a "slow" or a "rapid" inactivator of isoniazid. This has a bearing on the likelihood of your developing adverse effects.
Liver function tests monthly.
Complete blood cell counts.
Careful examination of eye structures and visual acuity.

While Taking This Drug, Observe the Following
Foods: No restrictions.
Beverages: No restrictions.
Alcohol: Best avoided; alcohol can reduce effectiveness of isoniazid.
Tobacco Smoking: No interactions expected with isoniazid. Ask physician for guidance regarding smoking.
Other Drugs
Pyridoxine (Vitamin B-6) should be taken concurrently with isoniazid to prevent nerve damage in the extremities.

Isoniazid may *increase* the effects of
- phenytoin (Dantoin, Dilantin, etc.) to an excessive degree; dosage reduction of phenytoin may be necessary to prevent toxicity.
- disulfiram (Antabuse), causing incoordination and abnormal behavior.
- oral anticoagulants; reduced dosage may be necessary.
- oral anti-diabetic drugs; dosage may require adjustment up or down. Monitor blood and urine sugar closely.
- anti-hypertensive drugs; reduced dosage may be necessary if blood pressure falls too low.

- atropine-like drugs; caution required in presence of glaucoma.
- sedatives and narcotic drugs; caution required to avoid oversedation.
- stimulant drugs; caution required to avoid overstimulation of nervous system.

Driving a Vehicle, Piloting a Plane, Operating Machinery: No restrictions unless dizziness occurs.

Exposure to Sun: No restrictions.

Discontinuation: Long-term therapy required. Do not discontinue drug without physician's advice.

Special Storage Instructions
Keep in a tightly closed, light-resistant container.

ISOPROPAMIDE

Year Introduced: 1957

Brand Names

USA	Canada
Darbid (Smith Kline & French)	Darbid (SK&F)
Combid [CD] (Smith Kline & French)	Combid [CD] (SK&F)
Ornade [CD] (Smith Kline & French)	Ornade [CD] (SK&F)

Drug Family: Antispasmodic, Atropine-like Drugs [Anticholinergics]

Prescription Required: Yes

Available Dosage Forms and Strengths
Tablets — 5 mg.

How This Drug Works

Intended Therapeutic Effect(s):   Relief of discomfort resulting from excessive activity and spasm of the digestive tract (esophagus, stomach, intestine, and colon).

Location of Drug Action(s):   The terminal nerve fibers of the parasympathetic nervous system that control the activity of the gastrointestinal tract.

Method of Drug Action(s):   By blocking the action of the chemical (acetylcholine) that transmits impulses at parasympathetic nerve endings, this drug prevents stimulation of muscular contraction and glandular secretion within the organ involved. This results in reduced overall activity, including the prevention of relief of muscle spasm.

THIS DRUG SHOULD NOT BE TAKEN IF
—you have had an allergic reaction to any dosage form of it previously.

—your stomach cannot empty properly into the intestine (pyloric obstruction).
—you are unable to empty the urinary bladder completely.
—you have glaucoma (narrow-angle type).
—you have severe ulcerative colitis.

INFORM YOUR PHYSICIAN BEFORE TAKING THIS DRUG IF
—you have glaucoma (open-angle type).
—you have angina or coronary heart disease.
—you have chronic bronchitis.
—you have a hiatal hernia.
—you have enlargement of the prostate gland.
—you have myasthenia gravis.
—you have a history of peptic ulcer disease.
—you plan to have surgery under general anesthesia in the near future.

Time Required for Apparent Benefit
Drug action begins in 1 to 2 hours and persists for 10 to 12 hours.

Possible Side-Effects *(natural, expected, and unavoidable drug actions)*
Blurring of vision (impairment of focus), dryness of the mouth and throat, constipation, hesitancy in urination. (Nature and degree of side effects depend upon individual susceptibility and drug dosage.)

CAUTION
The elderly (over 60 years of age) may be more susceptible to all of the actions of this drug. Small doses are advisable until response has been determined.

Possible Adverse Effects *(unusual, unexpected, and infrequent reactions)*
IF ANY OF THE FOLLOWING DEVELOP, DISCONTINUE DRUG AND NOTIFY YOUR PHYSICIAN AS SOON AS POSSIBLE
Mild Adverse Effects
  Allergic Reactions: Skin rash, hives.
  Dilation of pupils, causing sensitivity to light.
  Flushing and dryness of the skin (reduced sweating).
  Rapid heart action.
  Lightheadedness, dizziness, unsteady gait.
Serious Adverse Effects
  Idiosyncratic Reactions: Acute confusion, delirium, and erratic behavior.
  Development of acute glaucoma (in susceptible individuals).

Advisability of Use During Pregnancy:
Safety not established. Prudent use is best determined by the physician's evaluation.

Advisability of Use While Nursing Infant
Presence of drug in milk is not known. Safety for infant not established. Ask physician for guidance.

Habit-Forming Potential
None.

Effects of Overdosage

With Moderate Overdose: Marked dryness of the mouth, dilated pupils, blurring of near vision, rapid pulse, heart palpitation, headache, difficulty in urination.

With Large Overdose: Extremely dilated pupils, rapid pulse and breathing, hot skin, high fever, excitement, confusion, hallucinations, delirium, eventual loss of consciousness, convulsions and coma.

Possible Effects of Extended Use

Chronic constipation, severe enough to result in fecal impaction. (Constipation should be treated promptly with effective laxatives.)

Recommended Periodic Examinations While Taking This Drug

Measurement of internal eye pressure to detect any significant increase that could indicate developing glaucoma.

While Taking This Drug, Observe the Following

Foods: No interaction with drug. Effectiveness is greater if drug is taken one-half to 1 hour before eating. Follow diet prescribed for condition under treatment.

Beverages: No interactions. As allowed by prescribed diet.

Alcohol: No interactions expected with this drug. Follow physician's advice regarding use of alcohol (based upon its effect on the condition under treatment).

Tobacco Smoking: No interactions expected. Follow physician's advice regarding smoking.

Other Drugs

Isopropamide may *increase* the effects of

- all other drugs having atropine-like actions (see Drug Family, Section Four).

Isopropamide may *decrease* the effects of

- pilocarpine eye drops, and reduce their effectiveness in lowering internal eye pressure in the treatment of glaucoma.

Isopropamide *taken concurrently* with

- mono-amine oxidase (MAO) inhibitor drugs (see Drug Family, Section Four), may cause an exaggerated response to normal doses of atropine-like drugs. It is best to avoid atropine-like drugs for 2 weeks after the last dose of any MAO inhibitor drug.
- haloperidol (Haldol), may significantly increase internal eye pressure (dangerous in glaucoma).

The following drugs may *increase* the effects of isopropamide

- tricyclic antidepressants
- those antihistamines that have an atropine-like action
- meperidine (Demerol, pethidine)
- methylphenidate (Ritalin)
- orphenadrine (Disipal, Norflex)

• those phenothiazines that have an atropine-like action (see Drug Family, Section Four).

Driving a Vehicle, Piloting a Plane, Operating Machinery: This drug may produce blurred vision, drowsiness, or dizziness. Avoid hazardous activities if these drug effects occur.

Exposure to Sun: No restrictions.

Exposure to Heat: Use extreme caution. The use of this drug in hot environments may significantly increase the risk of heat stroke.

Heavy Exercise or Exertion: Use caution in warm or hot environments. This drug may impair normal perspiration (heat loss) and interfere with the regulation of body temperature.

Special Storage Instructions
Keep in a tightly closed container. Protect from light.

ISOPROTERENOL/ISOPRENALINE
Year Introduced: 1948

Brand Names

USA	Canada
Isuprel (Winthrop)	Isuprel (Winthrop)
Medihaler-Iso (Riker)	Medihaler-Iso (Riker)
Norisodrine (Abbott)	Norisodrine (Abbott)
Brondilate [CD] (Walker)	Duo-Medihaler [CD]
Duohaler [CD] (Riker)	(Riker)
Duo-Medihaler [CD]	Isuprel-Neo [CD]
(Riker)	(Winthrop)
Iso-Asminyl [CD] (Cole)	
Isuprel Compound [CD]	
(Winthrop)	

Drug Family: Anti-asthmatic (Bronchodilator) [Sympathomimetics]

Prescription Required: Yes

Available Dosage Forms and Strengths
Sublingual Tablets — 10 mg., 15 mg.
Aerosol, Inhalation — 2 mg. per ml., 2.8 mg. per ml., 4 mg. per ml., 5.6 mg. per ml., 11.2 mg. per ml.
Powder, Inhalation — 10%, 25%
Syrup — 18 mg. per ounce (30 ml.)

How This Drug Works
Intended Therapeutic Effect(s):   Relief of difficult breathing associated with acute attacks of bronchial asthma and with other disorders characterized by spasm of the bronchial tubes, such as bronchitis and emphysema.

Location of Drug Action(s):   Those nerve terminals of the sympathetic nervous system that activate the muscles in the walls of bronchial tubes to produce dilation.

Method of Drug Action(s):   By stimulating certain sympathetic nerve terminals, this drug acts to dilate those bronchial tubes that are in sustained constriction, thereby increasing the size of the airway and improving the ability to breathe.

THIS DRUG SHOULD NOT BE TAKEN IF

—you have had an allergic reaction to any dosage form of it previously. A combination drug [CD] should not be taken if you are allergic to *any* of its ingredients.

—you have a serious heart rhythm disorder.

—you are taking, or have taken during the past 2 weeks, any mono-amine oxidase (MAO) inhibitor drug (see Drug Family, Section Four).

INFORM YOUR PHYSICIAN BEFORE TAKING THIS DRUG IF

—you are overly sensitive to drugs that stimulate the sympathetic nervous system.

—you are currently using epinephrine (Adrenalin) to relieve asthmatic breathing.

—you have high blood pressure.

—you have diabetes.

—you have a history of heart disease, especially angina (coronary insufficiency).

—you have a history of overactivity of the thyroid gland (hyperthyroidism).

—you are taking any form of digitalis.

Time Required for Apparent Benefit

Action begins within 2 to 4 minutes and persists for 30 to 60 minutes when this drug is inhaled or dissolved under the tongue.

Possible Side-Effects *(natural, expected, and unavoidable drug action)*

Nervousness, heart palpitation.

The saliva or sputum may appear pink or red after inhalation of this drug. This is a normal response, and is not indicative of bleeding or an adverse effect of any kind.

CAUTION

1. Do not chew or swallow the sublingual tablets. Allow them to dissolve under the tongue, and avoid swallowing until the tablet has been absorbed completely.

2. Avoid excessive use. Inhalation repeated too frequently can induce a resistance to this drug's bronchodilating action and render it ineffective. Limit use to the fewest number of inhalations necessary to produce relief.

3. The total daily dose of the sublingual tablets should not exceed 60 mg. for adults or 30 mg. for children.

4. Do not use this drug concurrently with epinephrine (Adrenalin). These two drugs may be used alternately if an interval of 4 hours is allowed between doses.

Possible Adverse Effects *(unusual, unexpected, and infrequent reactions)*

IF ANY OF THE FOLLOWING DEVELOP, DISCONTINUE DRUG AND NOTIFY YOUR PHYSICIAN AS SOON AS POSSIBLE

Mild Adverse Effects
  Headache, flushing, dizziness, tremor.
  Nausea, vomiting.
Serious Adverse Effects
  Intensification of angina in the presence of coronary artery insufficiency.
  Slight elevation of blood sugar levels.

Advisability of Use During Pregnancy
No reports of adverse effects on the fetus or on the course of pregnancy. Ask physician for guidance.

Advisability of Use While Nursing Infant
This drug does not appear in milk. Ask physician for guidance.

Habit-Forming Potential
None.

Effects of Overdosage
  With Moderate Overdose: Excessive nervousness, heart palpitation, rapid heart rate, sweating.
  With Large Overdose: Headache, tremor, vomiting, chest pain, marked drop in blood pressure, circulatory failure, irregular heart rhythm.

Possible Effects of Extended Use
Swelling of the salivary (parotid) glands.
Ulceration of the mouth, with prolonged use of the sublingual tablets.

Recommended Periodic Examinations While Taking This Drug
Dental examinations to detect any destructive effects on teeth during extended use of sublingual tablets.

While Taking This Drug, Observe the Following
Foods: No restrictions.
Beverages: No restrictions.
Alcohol: No interactions expected.
Tobacco Smoking: No interactions expected. Follow physician's advice regarding smoking as it affects the condition under treatment.
Other Drugs
  Isoproterenol may *increase* the effects of
  • ephedrine, and cause excessive stimulation of the heart and an increase in blood pressure.
  • tricyclic antidepressants (see Drug Family, Section Four).

  Isoproterenol *taken concurrently* with
  • epinephrine (Adrenalin), may cause serious disturbances of heart rhythm. Allow an interval of at least 4 hours between the use of these two drugs.

  The following drugs may *increase* the effects of isoproterenol
  • tricyclic antidepressants (see Drug Family, Section Four)

The following drugs may *decrease* the effects of isoproterenol
• propranolol (Inderal)

Driving a Vehicle, Piloting a Plane, Operating Machinery: No restrictions. Use caution if excessive nervousness or dizziness occurs.

Exposure to Sun: No restrictions.

Discontinuation: If this drug fails to provide relief after adequate trial, discontinue it and consult your physician regarding alternate drug therapy. Do not increase the dosage or the frequency of use. To do so could be dangerous.

Special Storage Instructions
Keep all forms of this drug in an airtight, nonmetallic container. Protect from light.

Do Not Take Any Form of This Drug If
It has become discolored. Do not use the aerosol solution if cloudy.

ISOSORBIDE DINITRATE

Year Introduced: 1959

Brand Names

USA	Canada
Angidil (Saron)	Coronex (Elliott-Marion)
Isordil (Ives)	Isordil (Wyeth)
Laserdil (Laser)	
Neo-Corovas-80	
(Amfre-Grant)	
Sorbitrate (Stuart)	
Sorquad (Tutag)	

Drug Family: Anti-anginal (Vasodilator) [Nitrates]

Prescription Required: Yes

Available Dosage Forms and Strengths
Tablets — 5 mg., 10 mg., 20 mg.
Sublingual Tablets — 2.5 mg., 5 mg.
Prolonged Action Tablets — 40 mg.
Prolonged Action Capsules — 40 mg.

How This Drug Works
Intended Therapeutic Effect(s):   Reduction in the frequency and severity of pain associated with angina pectoris (coronary insufficiency).

Location of Drug Action(s):   The muscular tissue in the walls of the blood vessels. The principal site of the therapeutic action is the system of coronary arteries in the heart.

Method of Drug Action(s):   This drug acts directly on the muscle cells to produce relaxation. This permits expansion of blood vessels and increases the supply of blood and oxygen to meet the needs of the working heart muscle.

THIS DRUG SHOULD NOT BE TAKEN IF
—you have had an allergic reaction to any dosage form of it previously.

INFORM YOUR PHYSICIAN BEFORE TAKING THIS DRUG IF
—you have glaucoma.
—you have had an unfavorable response to any vasodilator drug in the past.

Time Required for Apparent Benefit
The action of the sublingual tablet (dissolved under the tongue) begins in 2 to 5 minutes and persists for 1 to 2 hours. The action of the oral tablet (swallowed) begins in 30 to 60 minutes and persists for 4 to 6 hours.

Possible Side-Effects *(natural, expected, and unavoidable drug actions)*
Flushing, lightheadedness in upright position (see orthostatic hypotension in Glossary).

Possible Adverse Effects *(unusual, unexpected, and infrequent reactions)*

IF ANY OF THE FOLLOWING DEVELOP, DISCONTINUE DRUG AND NOTIFY YOUR PHYSICIAN AS SOON AS POSSIBLE

Mild Adverse Effects
  Allergic Reactions: Skin rash.
  Headache (may be persistent), dizziness, fainting.
  Nausea, vomiting.
Serious Adverse Effects
  Allergic Reactions: Severe dermatitis with peeling of skin.

Advisability of Use During Pregnancy
Safety not established. Prudent use is best determined by the physician's evaluation.

Advisability of Use While Nursing Infant
Presence of drug in milk is not known. Safety for infant not established. Ask physician for guidance.

Habit-Forming Potential
None.

Effects of Overdosage
  With Moderate Overdose: Headache, dizziness, marked flushing of the skin.
  With Large Overdose: Vomiting, weakness, sweating, fainting, shortness of breath, coma.

Possible Effects of Extended Use
  Development of tolerance (see Glossary), which may reduce the drug's effectiveness at recommended doses.
  Development of abnormal hemoglobin (red blood cell pigment).

Recommended Periodic Examinations While Taking This Drug

Measurement of internal eye pressure in those individuals with glaucoma or a tendency to glaucoma.

Red blood cell counts and hemoglobin measurements.

While Taking This Drug, Observe the Following

Foods: No restrictions. This drug is likely to be more effective if taken one-half to 1 hour before eating.

Beverages: No restrictions.

Alcohol: Use with extreme caution until combined effects have been determined. Alcohol may exaggerate the drop in blood pressure experienced by some sensitive individuals. This can be dangerous.

Tobacco Smoking: Nicotine may reduce the effectiveness of this drug. Follow physician's advice regarding smoking, based upon its effect on the condition under treatment and its possible interaction with this drug.

Other Drugs

Isosorbide may *increase* the effects of

- atropine-like drugs (see Drug Family, Section Four), and cause an increase in internal eye pressure.
- tricyclic antidepressants (see Drug Family, Section Four), and cause excessive lowering of the blood pressure.

Isosorbide may *decrease* the effects of

- all choline-like drugs, such as Mestinon, Mytelase, pilocarpine, Prostigmin, and Urecholine.

Isosorbide *taken concurrently* with

- anti-hypertensive drugs, may cause severe drop in blood pressure. Careful monitoring of drug response and appropriate dosage adjustments are necessary.

The following drugs may *increase* the effects of isosorbide

- propranolol (Inderal) may cause additional lowering of the blood pressure. Dosage adjustments may be necessary.

Driving a Vehicle, Piloting a Plane, Operating Machinery: Usually no restrictions. Before engaging in hazardous activities, determine that this drug will not cause you to have orthostatic hypotension (see Glossary).

Exposure to Sun: No restrictions.

Exposure to Cold: Cold environments may reduce the effectiveness of this drug.

Heavy Exercise or Exertion: This drug may improve your ability to be more active without resulting angina pain. Use caution and avoid excessive exertion that could cause heart injury in the absence of warning pain.

Special Storage Instructions

Keep in a dry, tightly closed container and in a cool place. Protect from heat and light.

ISOXSUPRINE

Year Introduced: 1955

Brand Names

USA	Canada
Vasodilan (Mead Johnson)	Vasodilan (Mead Johnson)

Drug Family: Vasodilator

Prescription Required: Yes

Available Dosage Forms and Strengths
Tablets — 10 mg., 20 mg.

How This Drug Works
Intended Therapeutic Effect(s):   Relief of symptoms associated with
• impaired circulation of blood in the extremities.
• impaired circulation of blood within the brain (in carefully selected cases).
Location of Drug Action(s):   Those sympathetic nerve terminals in the muscles of blood vessel walls that are responsible for vessel dilation.
Method of Drug Action(s):   By stimulating the action of those nerve terminals responsible for blood vessel dilation, this drug produces expansion of vessel walls. The resulting dilation increases the volume of blood flowing through the vessels. The increase in oxygen and nutrients relieves the symptoms attributable to deficient circulation.

THIS DRUG SHOULD NOT BE TAKEN IF
—you have had an allergic reaction to any dosage form of it previously.

INFORM YOUR PHYSICIAN BEFORE TAKING THIS DRUG IF
—you have high blood pressure.

Time Required for Apparent Benefit
Drug action begins in approximately 1 hour and persists for 3 hours.

Possible Side-Effects *(natural, expected, and unavoidable drug actions)*
Lightheadedness and lethargy (lowered blood pressure).

CAUTION
Individuals with extensive or severe impairment of circulation to the brain or heart may respond unfavorably to this drug. Observe closely until the true nature of the response has been determined. Discontinue drug if condition worsens.

Possible Adverse Effects *(unusual, unexpected, and infrequent reactions)*
IF ANY OF THE FOLLOWING DEVELOP, DISCONTINUE DRUG AND NOTIFY YOUR PHYSICIAN AS SOON AS POSSIBLE
Mild Adverse Effects
Allergic Reactions: Severe skin rash.
Weakness, dizziness, rapid heart action, headache.
Nausea, vomiting.

Serious Adverse Effects
None reported.

Advisability of Use During Pregnancy
Safety not established. Prudent use is best established by the physician's evaluation.

Advisability of Use While Nursing Infant
Safety not established. Ask physician for guidance.

Habit-Forming Potential
None.

Effects of Overdosage
Sudden drop in blood pressure, dizziness, heart palpitation, sense of weakness.

Possible Effects of Extended Use
None reported.

Recommended Periodic Examinations While Taking This Drug
Measurement of blood pressure in lying, sitting, and standing positions.

While Taking This Drug, Observe the Following
Foods: No restrictions of food selection. Drug may be taken with or immediately following meals to reduce stomach irritation or nausea.

Beverages: No restrictions.

Alcohol: No interactions expected.

Tobacco Smoking: Nicotine can reduce this drug's ability to dilate blood vessels and to improve circulation. Follow physician's advice regarding smoking.

Other Drugs: No significant drug interactions reported.

Driving a Vehicle, Piloting a Plane, Operating Machinery: Be alert to possible drop in blood pressure with resulting dizziness and weakness. Be prepared to stop and lie down.

Exposure to Sun: No restrictions.

Exposure to Cold: Avoid as much as possible. This drug may be less effective in cold environments or with the handling of cold objects.

Special Storage Instructions
Keep in a dry, tightly closed container.

LEVODOPA

Year Introduced: 1967

Brand Names

USA	Canada
Bendopa (ICN)	Dopar (Eaton)
Dopar (Eaton)	Larodopa (Roche)
Larodopa (Roche)	Levopa (ICN)
Levopa (ICN)	Sinemet [CD] (MSD)
Parda (Parke-Davis)	
Sinemet [CD] (Merck	
Sharp & Dohme)	

Drug Family: Anti-parkinsonism

Prescription Required: Yes

Available Dosage Forms and Strengths
     Tablets — 100 mg., 250 mg., 500 mg.
     Capsules — 100 mg., 250 mg., 500 mg.

How This Drug Works
     Intended Therapeutic Effect(s):   Reduction of the rigidity, tremor, sluggish movement, and gait disturbances characteristic of Parkinson's disease.
     Location of Drug Action(s):   A regulating center in the brain (the corpus striatum) that governs the coordination and efficiency of bodily movements.
     Method of Drug Action(s):   Not completely established. Present thinking is that levodopa enters the brain tissue and is converted to dopamine. After sufficient dosage, this corrects the deficiency of dopamine (thought to be the cause of Parkinsonism) and restores a more normal balance of the chemicals responsible for the transmission of nerve impulses.

THIS DRUG SHOULD NOT BE TAKEN IF
—you are allergic to any of the drugs bearing the brand names listed above.
—you are taking, or have taken during the past 2 weeks, any mono-amine oxidase (MAO) inhibitor drug (see Drug Family, Section Four).
—you have glaucoma (narrow-angle type).

INFORM YOUR PHYSICIAN BEFORE TAKING THIS DRUG IF
—you have diabetes.
—you have epilepsy.
—you have a history of high blood pressure or heart or lung disease.
—you have a history of liver or kidney disease.
—you have a history of peptic ulcer disease.
—you have a history of malignant melanoma.
—you plan to have surgery under general anesthesia in the near future.

Time Required for Apparent Benefit
Improvement usually occurs in 2 to 3 weeks. Regular use for 6 weeks or longer is needed to determine this drug's maximal effectiveness. Careful dosage adjustment according to individual response is necessary.

Possible Side-Effects *(natural, expected, and unavoidable drug actions)*
Fatigue, lethargy, lightheadedness in upright position (see orthostatic hypotension in Glossary).

Pink to red coloration of urine (which turns black after exposure to air), of no significance.

CAUTION
1. To reduce the high frequency of serious adverse effects, it is advisable to begin treatment with small doses, and to increase dosage gradually until the desired response is achieved.
2. As improvement occurs, avoid excessive and hurried activity (which often causes falls and injury).

Possible Adverse Effects *(unusual, unexpected, and infrequent reactions)*
IF ANY OF THE FOLLOWING DEVELOP, DISCONTINUE DRUG AND NOTIFY YOUR PHYSICIAN AS SOON AS POSSIBLE

Mild Adverse Effects
Allergic Reactions: Skin rash, itching.
Reduced appetite, nausea, vomiting.
Headache, dizziness, faintness, unsteadiness, blurred vision.
Heart palpitation.
Difficulty in emptying the urinary bladder.
Unusual, unpleasant taste sensation.
Offensive body odor.

Serious Adverse Effects
Emotional depression, confusion, abnormal thinking and behavior.
Abnormal, purposeless movements of the head, face, arms, or legs.
Development of peptic ulcer, stomach or intestinal bleeding.
Hemolytic anemia (see Glossary).
Abnormally low white blood cell count, resulting in lowered resistance to infection—fever, sore throat.

Advisability of Use During Pregnancy
Safety not established. Prudent use is best determined by the physician's evaluation.

Advisability of Use While Nursing Infant
This drug may be present in milk. Ask physician for guidance.

Habit-Forming Potential
None.

Effects of Overdosage
With Moderate Overdose: Muscle twitching, spastic closure of the eyelids, nausea, vomiting, diarrhea.

With Large Overdose: Irregular and rapid pulse, weakness, fainting, confusion, agitation, hallucinations.

Possible Effects of Extended Use
Development of involuntary, abnormal, purposeless movements of the head, face, mouth, tongue, arms, or legs. These developments are reversible and gradually disappear when the drug is discontinued.

Recommended Periodic Examinations While Taking This Drug
Complete blood cell counts.
Liver and kidney function tests.
Regular measurement of internal eye pressure (in presence of open-angle glaucoma).
Regular measurement of blood pressure in lying, sitting, and standing positions to detect any tendency to orthostatic hypotension.

While Taking This Drug, Observe the Following
Foods: No restrictions of food selection. Drug is best taken with meals to reduce stomach irritation or nausea.
Beverages: No restrictions.
Alcohol: No interactions expected.
Tobacco Smoking: No interactions expected.
Other drugs

Levodopa may *increase* the effects of
- anti-hypertensive drugs such as methyldopa (Aldomet), reserpine preparations, and pargyline, and cause excessive lowering of the blood pressure. Dosage adjustments may be necessary.

Levodopa *taken concurrently* with
- mono-amine oxidase (MAO) inhibitor drugs (see Drug Family, Section Four) may cause a dangerous rise in blood pressure and body temperature. Do not use these drugs concurrently.

The following drugs may *increase* the effects of levodopa
- other anti-Parkinsonism drugs (Artane, Cogentin, Kemadrin, etc.) may improve its effectiveness in treating Parkinsonism. Individual dosage adjustment is essential to determine the combined effect.

The following drugs may *decrease* the effects of levodopa
- haloperidol (Haldol)
- methyldopa (Aldomet)
- papaverine (Cerespan, Pavabid, Vasospan, etc.)
- phenothiazines (see Drug Family, Section Four)
- pyridoxine (Vitamin B-6) can reduce or even abolish the beneficial action of levodopa. Be sure that any vitamin preparation you are taking does not contain pyridoxine.
- reserpine (and related drugs)

Driving a Vehicle, Piloting a Plane, Operating Machinery: Be alert to the possible occurrence of orthostatic hypotension while engaged in hazardous activities. Be prepared to stop and lie down to prevent fainting.

Exposure to Sun: No restrictions.

Heavy Exercise or Exertion: Use caution as ability to be more active improves. Rapid, excessive, or unrestrained activity often causes falls and serious injury.

Special Storage Instructions

Keep in a dry, tightly closed container. Protect from light.

LINCOMYCIN

Year Introduced: 1966

Brand Names

USA	Canada
Lincocin (Upjohn)	Lincocin (Upjohn)

Drug Family: Antibiotic (Anti-infective)

Prescription Required: Yes

Available Dosage Forms and Strengths

Capsules — 250 mg., 500 mg.

Syrup — 250 mg. per teaspoonful

How This Drug Works

Intended Therapeutic Effect(s):   The elimination of infections responsive to the action of this drug.

Location of Drug Action(s):   Any body tissue or fluid in which sufficient concentration of the drug can be achieved.

Method of Drug Action(s):   This drug prevents the growth and multiplication of susceptible bacteria by interfering with their formation of essential proteins.

THIS DRUG SHOULD NOT BE TAKEN IF

—you are allergic to lincomycin or clindamycin.

—it is prescribed for a mild or trivial infection such as a cold, sore throat, or "flu"-like illness.

—you have a history of ulcerative colitis.

—it is prescribed for an infant under 1 month of age.

INFORM YOUR PHYSICIAN BEFORE TAKING THIS DRUG IF

—you have a history of allergy to *any* drugs.

—you are allergic by nature (hayfever, asthma, hives, eczema).

—you have a history of previous yeast infections.

—you have liver or kidney disease, or impaired liver or kidney function.

—you plan to have surgery under general anesthesia in the near future.

Time Required for Apparent Benefit

Varies with nature of infection under treatment; usually 2 to 5 days.

Possible Side-Effects *(natural, expected, and unavoidable drug actions)*
Superinfections (see Glossary).

Possible Adverse Effects *(unusual, unexpected, and infrequent reactions)*

IF ANY OF THE FOLLOWING DEVELOP, DISCONTINUE DRUG AND NOTIFY YOUR PHYSICIAN AS SOON AS POSSIBLE

Mild Adverse Effects

Allergic Reactions: Skin rash (various kinds), hives, swelling of face or extremities, irritation of mouth or tongue.

Nausea, vomiting, cramping, diarrhea.

Dizziness, ringing in the ears.

Serious Adverse Effects

Allergic Reactions: Anaphylactic reaction (see Glossary), fever, painful swollen joints, severe skin reactions.

Possible bone marrow depression (see Glossary)—weakness, fever, sore throat, unusual bleeding or bruising.

†Severe colitis with persistent diarrhea; stools may contain blood and/or mucus.

Advisability of Use During Pregnancy
Safety not established. Prudent use is best determined by the physician's evaluaton.

Advisability of Use While Nursing Infant
Drug may be present in milk. Safety for infant not established. Ask physician for guidance.

Habit-Forming Potential
None.

Effects of Overdosage
Nausea, vomiting, cramping, diarrhea.

Possible Effects of Extended Use
†Severe colitis with persistent diarrhea.
Superinfections (see Glossary), especially from yeast organisms.

Recommended Periodic Examinations While Taking This Drug
Complete blood cell counts.
Liver function tests.

While Taking This Drug, Observe the Following

Foods: Avoid all forms of cyclamate artificial sweeteners and foods containing cyclamates. For best absorption, take nothing but water for 1 to 2 hours before and after each dose.

Beverages: Avoid all beverages containing cyclamate artificial sweeteners.

Alcohol: No interactions expected.

Tobacco Smoking: No interactions expected.

†An infrequent but potentially dangerous reaction characteristic of this drug.

Other Drugs
The following drugs may *decrease* the effects of lincomycin:
- anti-diarrheal preparations
- erythromycin

Driving a Vehicle, Piloting a Plane, Operating Machinery: No restrictions unless dizziness occurs.

Exposure to Sun: Use caution until sensitivity is determined. Photosensitivity has been reported (see Glossary).

Discontinuation: When used to treat infections that predispose to rheumatic fever or nephritis (kidney disease), take continuously in full dosage for no less than 10 days. Ask physician for guidance regarding the recommended duration of therapy.

Special Storage Instructions
Keep in a tightly closed container.

LIOTHYRONINE
(T–3)

Year Introduced: 1956

Brand Names

USA
Cytomel (Smith Kline & French)
Liomel (Western Research)
Euthyroid [CD] (Warner/Chilcott)
Thyrolar [CD] (Armour)

Canada
Cytomel (SK&F)
Tertroxin (Glaxo)
Thyrolar [CD] (Harris)

Drug Family: Thyroid Hormones

Prescription Required: Yes

Available Dosage Forms and Strengths
Tablets — 0.005 mg., 0.025 mg., 0.05 mg.

How This Drug Works
Intended Therapeutic Effect(s):   Correction of thyroid hormone deficiency (hypothyroidism) by replacement therapy.

Location of Drug Action(s):   Affects the biochemical activity of all tissues throughout the body.

Method of Drug Action(s):   By altering the processes of cellular chemistry that store energy in an inactive (reserve) form, this drug makes more energy available for biochemical activity and increases the rate of cellular metabolism.

THIS DRUG SHOULD NOT BE TAKEN IF
—you have had an allergic reaction to any dosage form of it previously.

—you are recovering from a recent heart attack (ask physician for guidance).
—you are using it to lose weight and you do not have a thyroid deficiency (your thyroid function is normal).

INFORM YOUR PHYSICIAN BEFORE TAKING THIS DRUG IF
—you have any form of heart disease.
—you have high blood pressure.
—you have diabetes.
—you have Addison's disease or a history of adrenal gland deficiency.
—you are using Adrenalin, ephedrine, or isoproterenol to treat asthma.
—you are taking any anticoagulant drugs.

Time Required for Apparent Benefit
Drug action begins within the first 12 hours, reaches a maximum in 2 to 3 days, and gradually subsides within 5 days. Full effectiveness requires continuous use on a regular schedule for several weeks.

Possible Side-Effects *(natural, expected, and unavoidable drug actions)*
None if dosage is adjusted correctly.

CAUTION
1. Thyroid hormones are used to correct conditions due to thyroid deficiency and to treat thyroid gland enlargement (goiter) and thyroid cancer. They should not be used to treat obesity if diagnostic studies indicate that there is no thyroid deficiency contributing to the obesity.
2. The need for and response to thyroid hormone treatment varies greatly from person to person. Careful supervision of individual response is necessary to determine correct dosage. Do not change your dosage schedule without consulting your physician.
3. The elderly (over 60 years of age) are usually more sensitive to thyroid hormone action. Small doses are advisable until nature of response has been determined.

Possible Adverse Effects *(unusual, unexpected, and infrequent reactions)*
IF ANY OF THE FOLLOWING DEVELOP, DISCONTINUE DRUG AND NOTIFY YOUR PHYSICIAN AS SOON AS POSSIBLE.
Mild Adverse Effects
  Allergic Reactions: Skin rash, hives.
  Headache may occur in sensitive individuals even with proper dosage adjustment.
  Change in menstrual pattern may occur during dosage adjustment.
Serious Adverse Effects
  Increased frequency or intensity of angina in the presence of coronary artery disease.

Advisability of Use During Pregnancy
Thyroid hormones do not reach the fetus (cross the placenta) in significant amounts. This drug is safe to use in pregnancy but *only* if given to correct a true thyroid deficiency and the dosage is properly adjusted.

Advisability of Use While Nursing Infant
Thyroid hormones are present in milk. Nursing is safe when the mother's dose of thyroid hormones is correctly adjusted to maintain normal thyroid activity.

Habit-Forming Potential
None.

Effects of Overdosage
With Moderate Overdose: Sense of increased body heat, heart palpitation, nervousness, increased sweating, hand tremors, insomnia.

With Large Overdose: Rapid and irregular pulse, fever, headache, marked nervousness and irritability, diarrhea, weight loss, muscle spasm and cramping.

Possible Effects of Extended Use
None with correct dosage adjustment.

Recommended Periodic Examinations While Taking This Drug
Physician's assessment of response to treatment, with evaluation of subjective and objective changes due to thyroid hormone activity.

Measurement of thyroid hormone levels in the blood.

While Taking This Drug, Observe the Following
Foods: To improve absorption this drug should be taken on arising and before eating. Avoid heavy use of soybean preparations because of their ability to interfere with thyroid function.

Beverages: No restrictions.

Alcohol: No interactions expected.

Tobacco Smoking: No interactions expected.

Other Drugs

Liothyronine may *increase* the effects of

- stimulants such as adrenalin, ephedrine, the amphetamines (Dexedrine), methylphenidate (Ritalin), etc., and cause excessive stimulation. Dosage adjustment may be necessary.
- oral anticoagulants of the coumarin family (see Drug Family, Section Four), and cause bleeding or hemorrhage. Reduction in dosage of the anticoagulant is usually necessary.
- tricyclic antidepressants (see Drug Family, Section Four).
- digitalis preparations (see Drug Family, Section Four). Careful dosage adjustment is necessary to prevent digitalis toxicity.

Liothyronine may *decrease* the effects of

- barbiturates, making larger doses necessary for effective sedation.

Liothyronine *taken concurrently* with

- all anti-diabetic drugs (insulin and oral anti-diabetic medications), may require an increase in the dosage of the anti-diabetic agent to obtain proper control of blood sugar levels. After the correct doses of both drugs have been determined, a reduction in the dose of thyroid will require a simultaneous reduction in the dose of the anti-diabetic drug to prevent hypoglycemia.

• cortisone-like drugs, requires careful dosage adjustment to prevent the development of cortisone deficiency.

The following drugs may *increase* the effects of liothyronine
• aspirin (in large doses and with continuous use)
• phenytoin (Dantoin, Dilantin, etc.)

The following drugs may *decrease* the effects of liothyronine
• cholestyramine (Cuemid, Questran) may reduce its absorption. Intake of the two drugs should be 5 hours apart.

Driving a Vehicle, Piloting a Plane, Operating Machinery: No restrictions or precautions.

Exposure to Sun: No restrictions.

Exposure to Heat: This drug may decrease individual tolerance to warm environments, increasing the discomfort due to heat. Avoid excessive sweating.

Exposure to Cold: This drug may increase individual tolerance to cold, decreasing the discomfort due to cold.

Heavy Exercise or Exertion: Use caution in the presence of angina and known coronary artery disease. This drug may increase the frequency of angina during physical activity.

Discontinuation: This drug must be taken continuously on a regular schedule to correct thyroid deficiency. Do not discontinue it without consulting your physician.

Special Storage Instructions
Keep in a dry, tightly closed container at room temperature. Protect from light.

LITHIUM

Year Introduced: 1949

Brand Names

USA	Canada
Eskalith (Smith Kline & French)	Carbolith (ICN)
Lithane (Roerig)	Lithane (Pfizer)
Lithonate (Rowell)	
Lithotabs (Rowell)	

Drug Family: Tranquilizer, Strong (Anti-manic)

Prescription Required: Yes

Available Dosage Forms and Strengths
Tablets — 300 mg.
Capsules — 300 mg.

How This Drug Works

Intended Therapeutic Effect(s): Normalization of mood and behavior in chronic manic-depressive mental illness.

Location of Drug Action(s): Those areas of the brain that determine mood and emotional stability.

Method of Drug Action(s): Not established. Present thinking is that lithium may act to correct chemical imbalances in certain nerve impulse transmitters that influence emotional status and behavior.

THIS DRUG SHOULD NOT BE TAKEN IF

—you are allergic to any of the drugs bearing the brand names listed above.
—you have serious heart or kidney disease.
—it is prescribed for a child under 12 years of age.

INFORM YOUR PHYSICIAN BEFORE TAKING THIS DRUG IF

—you are taking any type of diuretic (urine producing) drug (see Drug Family, Section Four).
—you have diabetes.
—you have epilepsy.

Time Required for Apparent Benefit

Improvement in the manic phase may occur in 1 to 3 weeks. Improvement in the depressive phase may require continuous use for several months.

Possible Side-Effects *(natural, expected, and unavoidable drug actions)*

Increased urine volume and thirst, drowsiness or lethargy (in sensitive individuals).

CAUTION

This drug has a very narrow margin of safe use. The level of drug required to be effective is quite close to the level that can cause adverse effects. Careful dosage adjustments based on periodic measurements of blood levels are mandatory. Follow instructions exactly regarding blood examinations and drug dosage. The elderly (over 60 years of age) often show a reduced tolerance for this drug.

Possible Adverse Effects *(unusual, unexpected, and infrequent reactions)*

IF ANY OF THE FOLLOWING DEVELOP, DISCONTINUE DRUG AND NOTIFY YOUR PHYSICIAN AS SOON AS POSSIBLE

Mild Adverse Effects

Allergic Reactions: Generalized itching, skin rash.

Headache, dizziness, †drowsiness, †sluggishness, hand tremors, †muscle twitching, blurred vision.

Irregular pulse, heart palpitation.

Loss of appetite, nausea, †vomiting, †diarrhea, metallic taste.

Serious Adverse Effects

Severe, involuntary, spasmodic movements of arms or legs, impaired balance, staggering gait.

Blackout spells, epileptic-like seizures.

Loss of bladder or rectal control.

†May be an early sign of lithium toxicity, indicating need for dosage adjustment.

Advisability of Use During Pregnancy
Safety not established. This drug may produce adverse effects on the fetus. Prudent use is best determined by the physician's evaluation.

Advisability of Use While Nursing Infant
Lithium is known to be present in milk and in the blood of the nursing infant. It is advisable to avoid drug or to refrain from nursing. Ask physician for guidance.

Habit-Forming Potential
None.

Effects of Overdosage
With Moderate Overdose: Drowsiness, muscular weakness, lack of coordination, nausea, vomiting, diarrhea, tremors, muscular spasms.

With Large Overdose: Blurred vision, ringing in the ears, dizziness, staggering gait, increased urine volume, slurred speech, confusion, stupor progressing to coma, convulsions.

Possible Effects of Extended Use
The development of thyroid gland enlargement (goiter), with or without reduced thyroid function (hypothyroidism).

Recommended Periodic Examinations While Taking This Drug
Regular determinations of blood lithium levels are absolutely essential to the safe and effective use of this drug.
Periodic evaluation of thyroid gland size and functional status.

While Taking This Drug, Observe the Following
Foods: Maintain a normal diet. Do *not* restrict your use of salt.

Beverages: Drink at least 2 and one-half to 3 quarts of liquids every 24 hours.

Alcohol: Use with caution until combined effect has been determined. Avoid alcohol completely if symptoms of lithium toxicity appear (see Effects of Overdosage, above).

Tobacco Smoking: No interactions expected.

Other Drugs

Lithium *taken concurrently* with

- diuretics (urine promoting drugs), may cause severe lithium toxicity due to excessive loss of sodium and water and to excessive retention of lithium in the body.

The following drugs may *decrease* the effects of lithium:

- chlorpromazine (Thorazine, Largactil) may reduce lithium's effectiveness by hastening its excretion from the body. Dosage adjustments may be necessary.

Driving a Vehicle, Piloting a Plane, Operating Machinery: This drug can impair mental alertness, judgment, physical coordination, and reaction time. Avoid all hazardous activities if these drug effects occur.

Exposure to Sun: No restrictions.

Exposure to Heat   Excessive sweating may cause lithium toxicity. Avoid hot environments as much as possible.

Heavy Exercise or Exertion: Use good judgment. In hot environments avoid exercise that could induce excessive sweating.

Occurrence of Unrelated Illness: Any illness that causes fever, heavy perspiration, nausea, or vomiting can greatly increase the risk of lithium toxicity. Notify your physician of all such illnesses and ask for guidance.

Special Storage Instructions
Keep in a dry, tightly closed container.

MECLIZINE

Year Introduced: 1954

Brand Names

USA	Canada
Antivert (Roerig)	Bonamine (Pfizer)
Bonine (Pfizer)	Mecazine (Barlowe Cote)
Vertrol (Saron)	Antivert [CD] (Pfizer)
	Bonadoxin [CD] (Pfizer)

Drug Family: Antihistamines; Antinausea (Anti-emetic)

Prescription Required: Yes
For Bonine—No

Available Dosage Forms and Strengths
Tablets — 12.5 mg., 25 mg.
Chewable Tablets — 25 mg.

How This Drug Works
Intended Therapeutic Effect(s):   Prevention and management of the nausea, vomiting, and dizziness associated with motion sickness.

Location of Drug Action(s):   The nerve pathways connecting the organ of equilibrium (the labyrinth) in the inner ear with the vomiting center in the brain.

Method of Drug Action(s):   This drug reduces the sensitivity of the nerve endings in the labyrinth and blocks the transmission of excessive nerve impulses to the vomiting center.

THIS DRUG SHOULD NOT BE TAKEN IF
—you have had an allergic reaction to any dosage form of it previously.
—you are taking, or have taken during the past 2 weeks, any mono-amine oxidase (MAO) inhibitor drug (see Drug Family, Section Four).
—you are, or think you may be, pregnant.

INFORM YOUR PHYSICIAN BEFORE TAKING THIS DRUG IF
—you have had an unfavorable reaction to any antihistamine in the past.

Time Required for Apparent Benefit
Drug action begins in approximately 1 hour and persists for 12 to 24 hours.

Possible Side-Effects *(natural, expected, and unavoidable drug actions)*
Drowsiness, dryness of nose, mouth, or throat.

Possible Adverse Effects *(unusual, unexpected, and infrequent reactions)*

IF ANY OF THE FOLLOWING DEVELOP, DISCONTINUE DRUG AND NOTIFY
YOUR PHYSICIAN AS SOON AS POSSIBLE

Mild Adverse Effects
  Blurring of vision.
Serious Adverse Effects
  None reported.

Advisability of Use During Pregnancy
Safety not established. Avoid use completely.

Advisability of Use While Nursing Infant
Safety for infant not established. Ask physician for guidance.

Habit-Forming Potential
  None.

Effects of Overdosage
With Moderate Overdose: Marked drowsiness, confusion, incoordination, unsteady gait, muscle tremors. In children: excitement, hallucinations, over-activity, convulsions.
With Large Overdose: Stupor progressing to coma, fever, flushed face, dilated pupils, weak pulse, shallow breathing.

Possible Effects of Extended Use
  None reported.

Recommended Periodic Examinations While Taking This Drug
  None required.

While Taking This Drug, Observe the Following
Foods: No restrictions. Stomach irritation can be reduced if drug is taken after eating.
Beverages: Coffee and tea may help to reduce the drowsiness caused by most antihistamines.
Alcohol: Use with extreme caution until combined effect has been determined. The combination of alcohol and antihistamines can cause rapid and marked sedation.
Tobacco Smoking: No interactions expected.
Other Drugs
  Meclizine may *increase* the effects of
- sedatives, sleep-inducing drugs, tranquilizers, antidepressants, pain relievers, and narcotic drugs, and result in oversedation. Careful dosage adjustments are necessary.
- atropine and drugs with atropine-like action (see Drug Family, Section Four).

The following drugs may *increase* the effects of meclizine:
- all sedatives, sleep-inducing drugs, tranquilizers, pain relievers, and narcotic drugs may exaggerate its sedative action and cause oversedation.
- mono-amine oxidase (MAO) inhibitor drugs (see Drug Family, Section Four) may delay its elimination from the body, thus exaggerating and prolonging its action.

The following drugs may *decrease* the effects of meclizine:
- amphetamines (Benzedrine, Dexedrine, Desoxyn, etc.) may reduce the drowsiness caused by most antihistamines.

Driving a Vehicle, Piloting a Plane, Operating Machinery: This drug may impair mental alertness, judgment, physical coordination, and reaction time. Avoid hazardous activities until degree of drowsiness has been determined.

Exposure to Sun: No restrictions.

Special Storage Instructions
Keep in a dry, tightly closed container.

MEDROXYPROGESTERONE
Year Introduced: 1959

Brand Names

USA	Canada
Amen (Carnrick)	Provera (Upjohn)
Provera (Upjohn)	

Drug Family: Female Sex Hormones (Progestins)

Prescription Required: Yes

Available Dosage Forms and Strengths
Tablets — 2.5 mg., 10 mg.

How This Drug Works
Intended Therapeutic Effect(s):   Correction of menstrual disorders due to hormone imbalance. Progesterone and related drugs (progestins) are also used to prevent pregnancy.

Location of Drug Action(s)
- the hypothalamus and the pituitary gland in the brain.
- the lining of the uterus.
- the mucus-producing glands in the neck (cervix) of the uterus.

Method of Drug Action(s)
By inducing and maintaining a lining in the uterus that resembles pregnancy, this drug can prevent uterine bleeding.

By suppressing the release of the pituitary gland hormone that induces ovulation, this drug can prevent ovulation (contraceptive effect).

By stimulating the secretion of mucus (by the uterine cervix) that resists the passage of sperm, this drug increases its contraceptive effect.

THIS DRUG SHOULD NOT BE TAKEN IF
—you have had an allergic reaction to any dosage form of it previously.
—you have seriously impaired liver function.
—you have a history of cancer of the breast or genital organs.
—you have a history of thrombophlebitis, embolism, or stroke.
—you have abnormal and unexplained vaginal bleeding.

INFORM YOUR PHYSICIAN BEFORE TAKING THIS DRUG IF
—you have migraine headaches.
—you have epilepsy.
—you have diabetes (or a tendency to diabetes).

Time Required for Apparent Benefit
Improvement in control of abnormal menstrual bleeding may occur in 24 to 48 hours. Long-range benefit requires regular use on a cyclic schedule adjusted to individual needs.

Possible Side-Effects *(natural, expected, and unavoidable drug actions)*
Retention of fluid, gain in weight, changes in menstrual timing and flow, spotting between periods.

Possible Adverse Effects *(unusual, unexpected, and infrequent reactions)*
IF ANY OF THE FOLLOWING DEVELOP, DISCONTINUE DRUG AND NOTIFY YOUR PHYSICIAN AS SOON AS POSSIBLE

Mild Adverse Effects
Allergic Reactions: Skin rashes, hives, itching.
Breast tenderness and secretion.
Excessive hair growth.

Serious Adverse Effects
Hepatitis with jaundice (see Glossary)—yellow eyes and skin, dark-colored urine, light-colored stools.
Thrombophlebitis (inflammation of a vein with the formation of blood clot) —pain or tenderness in thigh or leg, with or without swelling of the foot, ankle, or leg.
Pulmonary embolism (movement of blood clot to the lung)—sudden shortness of breath, pain in the chest, coughing, bloody sputum.
Stroke (blood clot in the brain)—headaches, blackouts, sudden weakness or paralysis of any part of the body, severe dizziness, double vision, slurred speech, inability to speak.
Retinal thrombosis (blood clot in blood vessels of the eye)—sudden impairment or loss of vision.

Advisability of Use During Pregnancy
The use of progestins during pregnancy should be avoided. Evidence exists to suggest a cause-and-effect relationship (see Glossary) between the use of these drugs and the occurrence of serious birth defects in the child.

Advisability of Use While Nursing Infant
These drugs are known to be present in milk. Safety for the nursing infant has not been established. Ask physician for guidance.

Habit-Forming Potential
None.

Effects of Overdosage
With Moderate Overdose: Nausea, vomiting, fluid retention, breast enlargement and discomfort, abnormal vaginal bleeding.
With Large Overdose: No serious or dangerous effects reported.

Possible Effects of Extended Use
None reported.

Recommended Periodic Examinations While Taking This Drug
Regular examinations of the breasts and reproductive organs (pelvic examination of the uterus and ovaries, including "Pap" smear).

While Taking This Drug, Observe the Following
Foods: No restrictions. If you experience fluid retention, ask physician for guidance regarding salt intake.
Beverages: No restrictions.
Alcohol: No interactions expected.
Tobacco Smoking: It is advisable to smoke lightly or not at all. Follow physician's advice.
Other Drugs
Medroxyprogesterone may *increase* the effects of
- phenothiazines.

The following drugs may *decrease* the effects of medroxyprogesterone
- antihistamines
- phenobarbital
- phenylbutazone (Azolid, Butazolidin, etc.)

Driving a Vehicle, Piloting a Plane, Operating Machinery: No restrictions or precautions.
Exposure to Sun: No restrictions.

Special Storage Instructions
Keep in a dry, tightly closed container. Protect from light.

MEPERIDINE/PETHIDINE

Year Introduced: 1939

Brand Names

USA	Canada
Demerol (Winthrop)	Demerol (Winthrop)
	Demer-Idine (Demers)

Drug Family: Analgesic, Strong (Synthetic Narcotic)

Prescription Required: Yes (Controlled Drug, U.S. Schedule 2)

Available Dosage Forms and Strengths
Tablets — 50 mg., 100 mg.
Syrup — 50 mg. per teaspoonful
Injection — 25 mg., 50 mg., 75 mg., 100 mg. per ml.

How This Drug Works
Intended Therapeutic Effect(s): Relief of moderate to severe pain.
Location of Drug Action(s): Those areas of the brain and spinal cord involved in the perception of pain.
Method of Drug Action(s): Not completely established. It has been suggested that the resulting increase of chemicals that transmit nerve impulses somehow contributes to the analgesic effect of this drug.

THIS DRUG SHOULD NOT BE TAKEN IF
—you have had an allergic reaction to any dosage form of it previously.
—you are taking now, or have taken within the past 14 days, any mono-amine oxidase (MAO) inhibitor drug (see Drug Family, Section Four).

INFORM YOUR PHYSICIAN BEFORE TAKING THIS DRUG IF
—you are taking sedatives, sleep-inducing drugs, tranquilizers, antidepressants, or narcotic drugs of any kind.
—you plan to have surgery under general anesthesia in the near future.
—you are subject to attacks of asthma.
—you have epilepsy.
—you have impaired liver or kidney function.
—you are being treated for glaucoma.

Time Required for Apparent Benefit
Usually from 15 minutes to 1 hour when taken orally.

Possible Side-Effects *(natural, expected, and unavoidable drug actions)*
Drowsiness, lightheadedness, weakness, euphoria, dryness of the mouth, constipation.

Possible Adverse Effects *(unusual, unexpected, and infrequent reactions)*
IF ANY OF THE FOLLOWING DEVELOP, DISCONTINUE DRUG AND NOTIFY YOUR PHYSICIAN AS SOON AS POSSIBLE
Mild Adverse Effects
Allergic Reactions: Skin rash, hives, itching.
Headache, dizziness, visual disturbances, agitation.
Nausea, vomiting.
Flushing of face, sweating, heart palpitation, faintness.
Serious Adverse Effects
Drop in blood pressure, causing severe weakness and fainting.
Disorientation, hallucinations, unstable gait, tremor, muscle twitching.
Interference with urination.

Advisability of Use During Pregnancy
Safety not established. Prudent use is best determined by the physician's evaluation.

Advisability of Use While Nursing Infant
Drug is known to be present in milk. Ask physician for guidance.

Habit-Forming Potential
This drug can produce psychological and physical dependence (see Glossary).

Effects of Overdosage
With Moderate Overdose: Marked drowsiness, confusion, tremors, convulsions, extreme weakness.
With Large Overdose: Stupor progressing to coma, cold and clammy skin, slow and shallow breathing.

Possible Effects of Extended Use
Psychological and physical dependence.

Recommended Periodic Examinations While Taking This Drug
None.

While Taking This Drug, Observe the Following
Foods: No restrictions.
Beverages: No restrictions.
Alcohol: Use with extreme caution until combined effects have been determined. Alcohol can greatly increase the sedative effect of meperidine as well as its depressant action on breathing, heart function, and circulation.
Tobacco Smoking: No interactions expected.
Other Drugs
  Meperidine/pethidine may *increase* the effects of
  • all other sedatives, sleep-inducing drugs, tranquilizers, antidepressants, and narcotic drugs. Appropriate dosage adjustments are mandatory. Ask physician for guidance.

  Meperidine/pethidine may *decrease* the effects of
  • eye drops prescribed for the treatment of glaucoma. Ask physician for guidance regarding dosage adjustment.

  Meperidine/pethidine *taken concurrently* with
  • mono-amine oxidase (MAO) inhibitor drugs (see Drug Family, Section Four), can cause the equivalent of acute narcotic overdose—unconsciousness, severe depression of breathing, heart action, and circulation. A variation of this reaction can be excitability, convulsions, high fever, and rapid heart action.
  • anti-hypertensive (anti-high blood pressure) drugs, may cause excessive lowering of the blood pressure and result in severe dizziness and fainting (see Drug Family, Section Four).

  The following drugs may *increase* the effects of meperidine/pethidine
  • mild and strong tranquilizers, especially the phenothiazines (see respective Drug Families, Section Four)
  • antidepressants may enhance the unfavorable effect of meperidine on glaucoma.

• nitrates and nitrites used to treat angina and coronary heart disease can enhance the blood pressure-lowering effect of meperidine (see Drug Family, Section Four).

Driving a Vehicle, Piloting a Plane, Operating Machinery: This drug can impair mental alertness, judgment, reaction time, and physical coordination. Avoid hazardous activities.

Exposure to Sun: No restrictions.

Discontinuation: If used for an extended period of time, ask physician for guidance regarding dosage reduction and withdrawal.

Special Storage Instructions
Keep in a dry, tightly closed container.

MEPROBAMATE

Year Introduced: 1955

Brand Names

USA		Canada
Amosene (Ferndale)	Miltown (Wallace)	Equanil (Wyeth)
Arcoban (Arcum)	Pax 400 (Kenyon)	Lan-Dol (Bio-Chem.)
Bamate (Century)	Promate (Kay)	Meditran (Medic)
Bamo 400 (Misemer)	QIDbamate	Meprospan-400
Coprobate (Coastal)	(Mallinckrodt)	(Horner)
Equanil (Wyeth)	Robamate (Robinson)	Miltown (Horner)
Kalmm (Scrip)	Saronil (Saron)	Neo-Tran (Neo)
Kesso-Bamate	SK-Bamate (Smith	Novomepro
(McKesson)	Kline & French)	(Novopharm)
Maso-Bamate (Mason)	Tranmep	Probal (Nadeau)
Meprocon (CMC)	(Reid-Provident)	Quietal (Deca)
Meprospan (Wallace)		Trelmar
Meprotab (Wallace)		(Elliott-Marion)
Meribam (Merit)		Wescomep (Saunders)

Drug Family: Tranquilizer, Mild (Anti-anxiety)

Prescription Required: Yes (Controlled Drug, U.S. Schedule 4)

Available Dosage Forms and Strengths
Tablets — 200 mg., 400 mg., 600 mg.
Sustained Release Capsules — 200 mg., 400 mg.
Liquid Suspension — 200 mg. per teaspoonful

How This Drug Works
Intended Therapeutic Effect(s)
• relief of mild to moderate anxiety and tension (sedative effect).
• relief of insomnia due to anxiety and tension (hypnotic effect).

Location of Drug Action(s):   Not completely established. It is thought that this drug acts on multiple sites in the brain, including the thalamus and limbic systems.

Method of Drug Action(s):   Not known.

THIS DRUG SHOULD NOT BE TAKEN IF

—you have had an allergic reaction to any dosage form of it previously.

—you are allergic or sensitive to any chemically related drugs: carbromal, carisoprodol, tybamate (see Drug Profiles for brand names).

—you have a history of intermittent porphyria.

—it is prescribed for a child under 6 years of age.

INFORM YOUR PHYSICIAN BEFORE TAKING THIS DRUG IF

—you have epilepsy.

—you have impaired liver or kidney function.

—you are taking sedatives, sleep-inducing drugs, tranquilizers, antidepressants, or anti-convulsants.

Time Required for Apparent Benefit

Approximately 1 to 2 hours. For severe symptoms of some duration, benefit may require regular medication for several days.

Possible Side-Effects *(natural, expected, and unavoidable drug actions)*

Drowsiness, lethargy, unsteadiness in stance and gait.

In the elderly (over 60 years of age) and debilitated: Lightheadedness, confusion, weakness. The elderly are very susceptible to standard doses.

Possible Adverse Effects *(unusual, unexpected, and infrequent reactions)*

IF ANY OF THE FOLLOWING DEVELOP, DISCONTINUE DRUG AND NOTIFY YOUR PHYSICIAN AS SOON AS POSSIBLE

Mild Adverse Effects

Allergic Reactions: Skin rashes (various kinds), swelling of hands or feet, swelling of glands, low-grade fever.

Dizziness, slurred speech, headache, blurred vision, nausea, diarrhea, heart palpitation, fainting.

Serious Adverse Effects

Allergic Reactions: Anaphylactic reaction (see Glossary), high fever, asthmatic breathing, reduced urine formation, unusual bruising or bleeding.

Paradoxical Reactions: Excitement, overactivity.

Bone marrow depression (see Glossary)—fatigue, weakness, impaired resistance to infection, fever, sore throat, unusual bleeding.

Sudden drop in blood pressure, which may be hazardous in those with heart disease and impaired circulation.

Advisability of Use During Pregnancy

The findings of some recent studies suggest a possible association between the use of this drug during early pregnancy and the occurrence of birth defects, such as cleft lip. It is advisable to avoid this drug completely during the first 3 months of pregnancy.

Advisability of Use While Nursing Infant
Drug is known to be present in milk. Avoid use if possible. Ask physician for guidance.

Habit-Forming Potential
This drug can produce psychological and/or physical dependence (see Glossary) if used in large doses for an extended period of time.

Effects of Overdosage
With Moderate Overdose: Dizziness, slurred speech, impaired stance, staggering gait.

With Large Overdose: Stupor progressing to deep sleep and coma; depression of breathing and heart function.

Possible Effects of Extended Use
Psychological and/or physical dependence.
Impairment of blood cell production.

Recommended Periodic Examinations While Taking This Drug
Complete blood cell counts during long-term use.

While Taking This Drug, Observe the Following
Foods: No restrictions.

Beverages: Large intake of coffee, tea, or cola drinks (because of their caffeine content) may reduce the calming action of this drug.

Alcohol: Use with extreme caution until combined effect is determined. Alcohol can increase the sedative effects of meprobamate. The combination can cause serious depression of vital brain functions.

Tobacco Smoking: No interactions expected.

Other Drugs

Meprobamate may *increase* the effects of
- other sedatives, sleep-inducing drugs, tranquilizers, antidepressants, and narcotic drugs, resulting in oversedation.

Meprobamate may *decrease* the effects of
- oral anticoagulants, making it necessary to increase their dosage to maintain their intended action.
- estrogens used in the treatment of menopause, by hastening their destruction and elimination.
- oral contraceptives, by hastening their destruction and elimination.

Meprobamate *taken concurrently* with
- anti-convulsants, may cause a change in the pattern of seizures, making it necessary to adjust the dosage of the anti-convulsant. Observe closely to determine combined effect of the two drugs.

The following drugs may *increase* the effects of meprobamate
- mono-amine oxidase (MAO) inhibitor drugs (see Drug Family, Section Four) can increase the sedative and brain-depressant effects of meprobamate. Ask physician for guidance regarding dosage adjustment.

Driving a Vehicle, Piloting a Plane, Operating Machinery: This drug can impair mental alertness, judgment, physical coordination, and reaction time. Avoid hazardous activities.

Exposure to Sun: No restrictions.

Discontinuation: If it has been necessary to use this drug for an extended period of time, ask physician for guidance regarding reduction of dose and withdrawal. The dosage of other drugs taken concurrently with meprobamate may also require adjustment.

Special Storage Instructions

Keep in a dry, tightly closed container.

MESORIDAZINE

Year Introduced: 1970

Brand Names

USA	Canada
Serentil (Sandoz)	Serentil (Sandoz)

Drug Family: Tranquilizer, Strong (Anti-psychotic) [Phenothiazines]

Prescription Required: Yes

Available Dosage Forms and Strengths

Tablets — 10 mg., 25 mg., 50 mg., 100 mg.
Concentrate — 25 mg. per ml.
Injection — 25 mg. per ml.

How This Drug Works

Intended Therapeutic Effect(s):   Restoration of emotional calm. Relief of severe anxiety, agitation, and psychotic behavior.

Location of Drug Action(s):   Those nerve pathways in the brain that utilize the tissue chemical dopamine for the transmission of nerve impulses.

Method of Drug Action(s):   Not completely established. Present theory is that by inhibiting the action of dopamine, this drug acts to correct an imbalance of nerve impulse transmissions that is thought to be responsible for certain mental disorders.

THIS DRUG SHOULD NOT BE TAKEN IF

—you have had an allergic reaction to any dosage form of it previously.

—it is prescribed for a child under 12 years of age.

INFORM YOUR PHYSICIAN BEFORE TAKING THIS DRUG IF

—you are allergic or sensitive to any phenothiazine drug (see Drug Family, Section Four).

—you are taking any sedatives, sleep-inducing drugs, other tranquilizers, antidepressants, antihistamines, or narcotic drugs of any kind.

—you have epilepsy.

—you have a history of heart disease.

—you plan to have surgery under general or spinal anesthesia in the near future.

Time Required for Apparent Benefit
Some benefit usually apparent in first week. Maximal benefit may require regular dosage for several weeks.

Possible Side-Effects *(natural, expected, and unavoidable drug actions)*
Drowsiness, lethargy, blurred vision, nasal stuffiness, dryness of the mouth, constipation, impaired urination.

Possible Adverse Effects *(unusual, unexpected, and infrequent reactions)*

IF ANY OF THE FOLLOWING DEVELOP, DISCONTINUE DRUG AND NOTIFY YOUR PHYSICIAN AS SOON AS POSSIBLE

Mild Adverse Effects
Allergic Reactions: Skin rash (various kinds), hives, swelling of the salivary glands, fever.
Headache, lightheadedness, and faintness in upright position (see orthostatic hypotension in Glossary).
Confusion, agitation, restlessness.
Breast congestion, milk formation, menstrual irregularity.
Nausea, vomiting, loss of appetite.

Serious Adverse Effects
Allergic Reactions: Hepatitis with jaundice (see Glossary), very rare with this drug.
Bone marrow depression (see Glossary), usually mild.
Convulsions.
Parkinson-like disorders (see Glossary), less frequent than with other phenothiazines.

Advisability of Use During Pregnancy
Safety not established. Prudent use is best determined by the physician's evaluation.

Advisability of Use While Nursing Infant
Safety not established. Ask physician for guidance.

Habit-Forming Potential
None.

Effects of Overdosage
With Moderate Overdose: Marked drowsiness, confusion, disorientation, blurred vision, nasal congestion, marked dryness of mouth, weakness.
With Large Overdose: Deep sleep, coma, convulsions, drop in body temperature, shallow breathing.

Possible Effects of Extended Use
Tardive dyskinesia (see Glossary).
Discoloration (pigmentation) of the skin and/or surface structures of the eye.
Opacities in the cornea or lens of the eye, resembling cataracts.

Recommended Periodic Examinations While Taking This Drug

Complete eye examinations for changes in vision and pigment deposits in the retina.

Complete blood cell counts and liver function tests.

Periodic electrocardiograms.

Periodic examinations of the tongue for the appearance of fine, involuntary, wave-like movements that could indicate the development of tardive dyskinesia.

While Taking This Drug, Observe the Following

Foods: No restrictions.

Beverages: No restrictions.

Alcohol: Use extreme caution until combined effects have been determined. Alcohol can increase the sedative action of mesoridazine and accentuate its depressant effects on brain function. Mesoridazine may increase the intoxicating effects of alcohol.

Tobacco Smoking: No interactions expected.

Other Drugs

Mesoridazine may *increase* the effects of

- all sedatives, sleep-inducing drugs, other tranquilizers, antidepressants, antihistamines, and narcotic drugs, and produce oversedation. Ask physician for guidance regarding dosage adjustments.
- all drugs containing atropine or having atropine-like actions (see Drug Family, Section Four).

Mesoridazine may *decrease* the effects of

- levodopa (Dopar, Larodopa, etc.), and reduce its effectiveness in the treatment of Parkinson's disease (shaking palsy).
- appetite suppressant drugs (Pre-Sate, Preludin, Benzedrine, Dexedrine, etc.).

Mesoridazine *taken concurrently* with

- quinidine may impair heart function. Avoid the use of these two drugs at the same time.

The following drugs may *increase* the effects of mesoridazine

- tricyclic antidepressants (see Drug Family, Section Four)

Driving a Vehicle, Piloting a Plane, Operating Machinery: This drug can impair mental alertness, judgment, and physical coordination. Avoid hazardous activities.

Exposure to Sun: Use caution until sensitivity has been determined. This drug may produce photosensitivity (see Glossary).

Exposure to Heat: Use caution and avoid excessive heat. This drug may impair the regulation of body temperature and increase the risk of heat stroke.

Heavy Exercise or Exertion: Use caution and follow your physician's instructions if you have any form of heart disease.

Discontinuation: If it has been necessary to use this drug for an extended period of time, do not discontinue it suddenly. Ask physician for guidance regarding dosage reduction and withdrawal. Upon discontinuation of this drug, it may also be necessary to adjust the dosages of other drugs taken concurrently with it.

Special Storage Instructions
Store liquid concentrate in a tightly closed, amber glass container, at temperatures below 86° F. (30°C.).

METFORMIN

Year Introduced: 1972

Brand Names

USA	Canada
None	Glucophage (Nordic)

Drug Family: Anti-diabetic, Oral (Hypoglycemic) [Biguanides]

Prescription Required: Yes

Available Dosage Forms and Strengths
Tablets — 500 mg.

How This Drug Works
Intended Therapeutic Effect(s):   Lowering of blood sugar levels in the management of stable adult (maturity-onset) diabetes of moderate severity.

Location of Drug Action(s):   · In those tissues responsive to the action of insulin.

Method of Drug Action(s):   Not completely established. It is thought that this drug may promote an increase in the utilization of sugar by improving the efficiency of insulin activity.

THIS DRUG SHOULD NOT BE TAKEN IF
—you have had an allergic reaction to any dosage form of it previously.
—you have a history of kidney disease with impaired kidney function.
—you have a history of alcoholism or excessive drinking of alcoholic beverages.

INFORM YOUR PHYSICIAN BEFORE TAKING THIS DRUG IF
—your diabetes has been difficult to control in the past ("brittle type").
—you have a history of liver disease.
—you do not know how to recognize and treat hypoglycemia (see Glossary).

Time Required for Apparent Benefit
A single dose lowers the blood sugar within 2 to 6 hours. Regular use for 1 to 2 weeks may be needed to determine this drug's effectiveness in controlling your diabetes.

Possible Side-Effects *(natural, expected, and unavoidable drug actions)*
None. However, excessive dosage and/or inadequate food intake may result in episodes of hypoglycemia. This is most likely to occur if metformin is used concurrently with insulin or another oral anti-diabetic drug.

CAUTION
Because of the increased frequency of heart and blood vessel disease in the elderly, this drug should be used with caution by those over 60 years of age.

Possible Adverse Effects *(unusual, unexpected, and infrequent reactions)*

IF ANY OF THE FOLLOWING DEVELOP, DISCONTINUE DRUG AND NOTIFY YOUR PHYSICIAN AS SOON AS POSSIBLE

Mild Adverse Effects
Allergic Reactions: Hives (rare).
Loss of appetite, nausea, vomiting, unpleasant metallic taste, diarrhea. Weakness, fatigue.

Serious Adverse Effects
† Lactic acidosis, manifested by nausea, vomiting, drowsiness, abdominal pain, and heavy, exaggerated breathing. This requires immediate treatment.

Advisability of Use During Pregnancy
Safety not established. Prudent use is best determined by the physician's evaluation.

Advisability of Use While Nursing Infant
Presence of drug in milk has not been determined. Safety for infants has not been established. Ask physician for guidance.

Habit-Forming Potential
None.

Effects of Overdosage
With Moderate Overdose: Marked nausea, vomiting, diarrhea, mild to moderate hypoglycemia.
With Large Overdose: Severe lactic acidosis, drop in blood pressure and body temperature, heart failure (more common in the elderly).

Possible Effects of Extended Use
Interference with the absorption of Vitamin B–12, resulting in anemia.
Reports of increased frequency and severity of heart and blood vessel diseases following long-term use of oral anti-diabetic drugs are controversial and inconclusive. A direct cause-and-effect relationship (see Glossary) has not been established to date. Ask physician for guidance regarding long-term use.

Recommended Periodic Examinations While Taking This Drug
Frequent urine examinations for sugar and acetone.
Complete blood cell counts.
Liver function and kidney function tests.
Periodic evaluation of heart and circulatory system.

While Taking This Drug, Observe the Following
Foods: Follow diabetic diet prescribed by your physician. Take this drug with meals to reduce the possibility of nausea and stomach irritation.
Beverages: As indicated in the diabetic diet prescribed by your physician.
Alcohol: Use with extreme caution and in small quantities until combined

---

†A rare adverse effect important to recognize.

effects have been determined. Alcohol can interact with this drug to produce nausea, vomiting, severe drop in blood pressure, and marked acidosis.
Tobacco Smoking: No interactions expected. No restrictions other than those imposed by your physician as part of your total treatment program.
Other Drugs
Metformin may *increase* the effects of
• all oral anti-diabetic drugs (the sulfonylureas), increasing the possibility of hypoglycemia. Adhere strictly to properly adjusted dosage schedules.
• insulin (all types), increasing the possibility of hypoglycemia.
• clofibrate (Atromid-S).

Driving a Vehicle, Piloting a Plane, Operating Machinery: Maintain properly adjusted dosage schedule, eating schedule, and physical activities to prevent hypoglycemia. Know how to recognize and treat hypoglycemia.
Exposure to Sun: No restrictions.
Heavy Exercise or Exertion: Avoid excessive exercise that could cause hypoglycemia.
Occurrence of Unrelated Illness: Consult your physician if acute infection, vomiting, diarrhea, serious injury, or need for surgery arises. Your dosage of this drug will require adjustment.
Discontinuation: If you find it necessary to discontinue this drug abruptly, notify your physician as soon as possible. Ask for guidance regarding control of your diabetes.

Special Storage Instructions
Keep in a dry, tightly closed container.

METHACYCLINE
Year Introduced: 1969

Brand Names

USA	Canada
Rondomycin (Wallace)	Rondomycin (Elliott-Marion)

Drug Family: Antibiotic (Anti-infective) [Tetracylines]

Prescription Required: Yes

Available Dosage Forms and Strengths
Capsules — 150 mg., 300 mg.
Syrup — 75 mg. per teaspoonful

How This Drug Works
Intended Therapeutic Effect(s):   The elimination of infections responsive to the action of this drug.

Location of Drug Action(s):   Any body tissue or fluid in which sufficient concentration of the drug can be achieved.

Method of Drug Action(s):   This drug prevents the growth and multiplication of susceptible bacteria by interfering with their formation of essential proteins.

THIS DRUG SHOULD NOT BE TAKEN IF

—you are allergic to any tetracycline drug (see Drug Family, Section Four).

—you are pregnant or breast feeding.

—it is prescribed for a child under 9 years of age.

INFORM YOUR PHYSICIAN BEFORE TAKING THIS DRUG IF

—you have a history of liver or kidney disease.

—you have systemic lupus erythematosus.

—you are taking any penicillin drug.

—you are taking any anticoagulant drug.

—you plan to have surgery under general anesthesia in the near future.

Time Required for Apparent Benefit

Varies with nature of infection under treatment; usually 2 to 5 days.

Possible Side-Effects *(natural, expected, and unavoidable drug actions)*

Superinfections (see Glossary), often due to yeast organisms. These can occur in the mouth, intestinal tract, rectum, and/or vagina, resulting in rectal and vaginal itching.

Possible Adverse Effects *(unusual, unexpected, and infrequent reactions)*

IF ANY OF THE FOLLOWING DEVELOP, DISCONTINUE DRUG AND NOTIFY YOUR PHYSICIAN AS SOON AS POSSIBLE

Mild Adverse Effects

Allergic Reactions: Skin rash (various kinds), hives, itching of hands and feet, swelling of face or extremities.

Photosensitivity Reactions: Exaggerated sunburn or skin irritation occurs commonly with some tetracyclines (see Glossary).

Loss of appetite, nausea, vomiting, diarrhea.

Irritation of mouth or tongue, "black tongue," sore throat, abdominal pain or cramping.

Serious Adverse Effects

Allergic Reactions: Anaphylactic reaction (see Glossary), asthma, fever, painful swollen joints, unusual bleeding or bruising, jaundice (see Glossary).

Permanent discoloration and/or malformation of teeth when taken under 9 years of age, including unborn child and infant.

Advisability of Use During Pregnancy

Tetracyclines can have adverse effects on mother and fetus. Avoid use.

Advisability of Use While Nursing Infant

Tetracyclines can be present in milk and can have adverse effects on infant. Avoid use.

Habit-Forming Potential

None.

Effects of Overdosage
Possible nausea, vomiting, diarrhea.
Acute liver damage (rare).

Possible Effects of Extended Use
Impairment of bone marrow, liver, or kidney function (all rare).
Superinfections.

Recommended Periodic Examinations While Taking This Drug
Complete blood cell counts.
Liver and kidney function tests.
During extended use, sputum and stool examinations may detect early super-infections due to yeast organisms.

While Taking This Drug, Observe the Following
Foods: Dairy products can interfere with absorption. Tetracyclines should be taken 1 hour before or 2 hours after eating.

Beverages: Avoid milk for 1 hour before and after each dose of a tetracycline.

Alcohol: Avoid while taking a tetracycline if you have a history of liver disease.

Tobacco Smoking: No interactions expected.

Other Drugs

Tetracyclines may *increase* the effects of
• oral anticoagulants, and make it necessary to reduce their dosage.

Tetracyclines may *decrease* the effects of
• the penicillins, and impair their effectiveness in treating infections.

The following drugs may *decrease* the effects of tetracyclines
• antacids may reduce drug absorption.
• iron and mineral preparations may reduce drug absorption.

Driving a Vehicle, Piloting a Plane, Operating Machinery: No restrictions.

Exposure to Sun: Avoid as much as possible. Photosensitivity (see Glossary) is common with some tetracyclines.

Special Storage Instructions
Keep in a tightly closed, light-resistant container.

METHADONE
Year Introduced: 1948

Brand Names

USA	Canada
Dolophine (Lilly)	None

Drug Family: Analgesic, Strong (Synthetic Narcotic)

Prescription Required: Yes (Controlled Drug, U.S. Schedule 2)

Available Dosage Forms and Strengths
Tablets — 5 mg., 10mg.
Syrup — 10 mg. per 30 ml. (1 ounce)
Injection — 10 mg. per ml.

How This Drug Works
Intended Therapeutic Effect(s):   Relief of moderate to severe pain.
Location of Drug Action(s):   Those areas of the brain and spinal cord involved in the perception of pain.
Method of Drug Action(s):   Not completely established. It has been suggested that the resulting increase of chemicals that transmit nerve impulses somehow contributes to the analgesic effect of this drug.

THIS DRUG SHOULD NOT BE TAKEN IF
—you have had an allergic reaction to any dosage form of it previously.

INFORM YOUR PHYSICIAN BEFORE TAKING THIS DRUG IF
—you are taking now, or have taken within the past 14 days, any mono-amine oxidase (MAO) inhibitor drug (see Drug Family, Section Four).
—you are taking sedatives, sleep-inducing drugs, tranquilizers, antidepressants, or other narcotic drugs of any kind.
—you plan to have surgery under general anesthesia in the near future.
—you are subject to attacks of asthma.
—you have impaired liver or kidney function.

Time Required for Apparent Benefit
Usually 30 minutes to 1 hour when taken orally.

Possible Side-Effects *(natural, expected, and unavoidable drug actions)*
Drowsiness, lightheadedness, weakness, euphoria, dryness of the mouth, constipation.

Possible Adverse Effects *(unusual, unexpected, and infrequent reactions)*
IF ANY OF THE FOLLOWING DEVELOP, DISCONTINUE DRUG AND NOTIFY YOUR PHYSICIAN AS SOON AS POSSIBLE
Mild Adverse Effects
Allergic Reactions: Skin rash, hives, itching.
Headache, dizziness, visual disturbances, agitation.
Nausea, vomiting.
Flushing of face, sweating, heart palpitation, faintness.
Serious Adverse Effects
Drop in blood pressure, causing severe weakness and fainting.
Disorientation, hallucinations, unstable gait, tremor, muscle twitching.
Interference with urination.

Advisability of Use During Pregnancy
Safety not established. Prudent use is best determined by the physician's evaluation.

Advisability of Use While Nursing Infant
Drug is known to be present in milk. Avoid use if possible. Ask physician for guidance.

Habit-Forming Potential
This drug can produce psychological and physical dependence (see Glossary).

Effects of Overdosage
With Moderate Overdose: Marked drowsiness, confusion, tremors, convulsions, extreme weakness.
With Large Overdose: Stupor progressing to coma, cold and clammy skin, slow and shallow breathing.

Possible Effects of Extended Use
Psychological and physical dependence.

Recommended Periodic Examinations While Taking This Drug
None required.

While Taking This Drug, Observe the Following
Foods: No restrictions.
Beverages: No restrictions.
Alcohol: Use with extreme caution until combined effects have been determined. Alcohol can greatly increase the sedative effect of methadone as well as its depressant effect on breathing, heart function, and circulation.
Tobacco Smoking: No interactions expected.
Other Drugs
Methadone may *increase* the effects of
• all other sedatives, sleep-inducing drugs, tranquilizers, antidepressants, and narcotic drugs. Appropriate dosage adjustments are mandatory. Ask physician for guidance.

Methadone *taken concurrently* with
• pentazocine, may result in withdrawal symptoms if the methadone is being used as maintenance treatment for narcotic addiction.
• anti-hypertensive (anti-high blood pressure) drugs may cause excessive lowering of blood pressure and result in severe dizziness and fainting (see Drug Family, Section Four).

The following drugs may *increase* the effects of methadone
• isoniazid (INH, etc.)
• mild and strong tranquilizers, especially the phenothiazines (see respective Drug Families, Section Four)

The following drugs may *decrease* the effects of methadone
• cyproheptadine (Periactin) may interfere with its analgesic action.
• methysergide (Sansert) may interfere with its analgesic action.

Driving a Vehicle, Piloting a Plane, Operating Machinery: This drug can impair mental alertness, judgment, reaction time, and physicial coordination. Avoid hazardous activities.
Exposure to Sun: No restrictions.
Discontinuation: If used for an extended period of time, do not discontinue abruptly. Ask physician for guidance regarding dosage reduction and withdrawal.

Special Storage Instructions
Keep in a dry, tightly closed container.

METHAQUALONE

Year Introduced: 1965

Brand Names

USA	Canada
Parest (Parke-Davis)	Hyptor (Bio-Chem.)
Quaalude (Rorer)	Mequelon (Frosst)
Sopor (Arnar-Stone)	Methadorm (Eri)
Somnafac (Cooper)	Quaalude (Rorer)
	Sedalone (Pharbec)
	Triador (Trianon)
	Tualone (ICN)
	Mandrax [CD] (Roussel)

Drug Family: Sleep Inducer (Hypnotic)

Prescription Required: Yes (Controlled Drug, U.S. Schedule 2)

Available Dosage Forms and Strengths
Tablets — 150 mg., 300 mg.

How This Drug Works
Intended Therapeutic Effect(s)
  • with low dosage, relief of mild to moderate anxiety or tension (sedative effect).
  • with higher dosage taken at bedtime, relief of insomnia (hypnotic effect).
Location of Drug Action(s):   Not completely established. Thought to be the wake-sleep centers of the brain, possibly the reticular activating system.
Method of Drug Action(s):   Not established.

THIS DRUG SHOULD NOT BE TAKEN IF
—you have had an allergic reaction to any dosage form of it previously.
—you are pregnant or planning pregnancy.
—it is prescribed for a child under 12 years of age.

INFORM YOUR PHYSICIAN BEFORE TAKING THIS DRUG IF
—you are taking sedatives, other sleep-inducing drugs, tranquilizers, antihistamines, pain relievers, or narcotic drugs of any kind.
—you have a history of liver disease or impaired liver function.
—you plan to have surgery under general anesthesia in the near future.

Time Required for Apparent Benefit
Approximately 20 to 30 minutes.

Possible Side-Effects *(natural, expected, and unavoidable drug actions)*
Lightheadedness in the upright position, weakness, unsteadiness in stance and gait.

CAUTION
The elderly (over 60 years of age) may not tolerate standard doses. Small doses are advisable until tolerance and duration of action have been determined.

Possible Adverse Effects *(unusual, unexpected, and infrequent reactions)*

IF ANY OF THE FOLLOWING DEVELOP, DISCONTINUE DRUG AND NOTIFY YOUR PHYSICIAN AS SOON AS POSSIBLE

Mild Adverse Effects

Allergic Reactions: Skin rashes, hives.

Headache, "hangover" effects, dizziness, numbness and tingling in the arms and legs.

Indigestion, nausea, vomiting, diarrhea.

Serious Adverse Effects

Bone marrow depression (see Glossary)—fatigue, weakness, fever, sore throat, unusual bleeding or bruising.

Advisability of Use During Pregnancy

Safety not established. Avoid use.

Advisability of Use While Nursing Infant

Presence of drug in milk is not known. Ask physician for guidance.

Habit-Forming Potential

This drug can cause both psychological and physical dependence (see Glossary). Avoid large doses and continuous use.

Effects of Overdosage

With Moderate Overdose: Marked drowsiness, confusion, delirium, incoordination, vomiting.

With Large Overdose: Stupor progressing to coma, convulsions, swelling due to fluid retention, abnormal bleeding.

Possible Effects of Extended Use

Psychological and/or physical dependence.

Note: This drug should not be taken continuously for more than 3 months.

Recommended Periodic Examinations While Taking This Drug

Complete blood cell counts.

While Taking This Drug, Observe the Following

Foods: No restrictions.

Beverages: No restrictions.

Alcohol: Avoid completely for 6 hours before taking this drug for sleep. Alcohol can increase greatly the sedative and depressant actions of this drug on brain function.

Tobacco Smoking: No interactions expected.

Other Drugs

Methaqualone may *increase* the effects of

• sedatives, other sleep-inducing drugs, tranquilizers, antihistamines, pain relievers, and narcotic drugs. Ask physician for guidance regarding dosage adjustments.

• oral anticoagulants, and cause bleeding if it is taken in large doses.

Driving a Vehicle, Piloting a Plane, Operating Machinery: This drug can impair mental alertness, judgment, physical coordination, and reaction time. Avoid hazardous activities until all sensation of drowsiness (or "hang-over") has disappeared.

Exposure to Sun: No restrictions.

Discontinuation: If it has been necessary to use this drug for an extended period of time, do not discontinue it abruptly. Ask physician for guidance regarding dosage reduction and withdrawal. Also, it may be necessary to adjust the dosage of other drugs taken concurrently with it, such as coumarin anticoagulants and anti-convulsants.

Special Storage Instructions
Keep in a dry, tightly closed container.

METHSCOPOLAMINE

Year Introduced: 1953

Brand Names

USA

Pamine (Upjohn)
Scoline (Westerfield)
Pamine PB [CD]
(Upjohn)
Synt-PB [CD] (Scrip)
(Numerous other
combination brand
names)

Canada

Pamine (Upjohn)
Pamiphen [CD] (Upjohn)

Drug Family: Antispasmodic, Atropine-like Drug [Anticholinergics]

Prescription Required: Yes

Available Dosage Forms and Strengths
Tablets — 2.5 mg.
Injection — 1 mg. per ml.

How This Drug Works
Intended Therapeutic Effect(s): Relief of discomfort associated with
• excessive activity and spasm of the digestive tract (esophagus, stomach, intestine, and colon) and the gall bladder.
• irritation and spasm of the lower urinary tract (bladder and urethra).
• painful menstruation (cramping of the uterus).
Location of Drug Action(s): The terminal nerve fibers of the parasympathetic nervous system that control the activity of the gastrointestinal tract and the genitourinary tract.

Method of Drug Action(s):   By blocking the action of the chemical (acetyl-choline) that transmits impulses at parasympathetic nerve endings, this drug prevents stimulation of muscular contraction and glandular secretion within the organs involved. This results in reduced overall activity, including the prevention or relief of muscle spasm.

THIS DRUG SHOULD NOT BE TAKEN IF
—you have had an allergic reaction to any dosage form of it previously.
—your stomach cannot empty properly into the intestine (pyloric obstruction).
—you are unable to empty the urinary bladder completely.
—you have glaucoma (narrow-angle type).
—you have severe ulcerative colitis.

INFORM YOUR PHYSICIAN BEFORE TAKING THIS DRUG IF
—you have glaucoma (open-angle type).
—you have angina or coronary heart disease.
—you have chronic bronchitis.
—you have a hiatal hernia.
—you have enlargement of the prostate gland.
—you have myasthenia gravis.
—you have a history of peptic ulcer disease.
—you plan to have surgery under general anesthesia in the near future.

Time Required for Apparent Benefit
Drug action begins in 1 to 2 hours and persists for approximately 8 hours.

Possible Side-Effects *(natural, expected, and unavoidable drug actions)*
Blurring of vision (impairment of focus), dryness of the mouth and throat, constipation, hesitancy in urination. (Nature and degree of side effects depend upon individual susceptibility and drug dosage.)

CAUTION
The elderly (over 60 years of age) may be more susceptible to all of the actions of this drug. Small doses are advisable until response has been determined.

Possible Adverse Effects *(unusual, unexpected, and infrequent reactions)*

IF ANY OF THE FOLLOWING DEVELOP, DISCONTINUE DRUG AND NOTIFY YOUR PHYSICIAN AS SOON AS POSSIBLE

Mild Adverse Effects
 Allergic Reactions: Skin rash, hives.
 Dilation of pupils, causing sensitivity to light.
 Flushing and dryness of the skin (reduced sweating).
 Rapid heart action.
 Lightheadedness, dizziness, unsteady gait.
Serious Adverse Effects
 Idiosyncratic Reactions: Acute confusion, delirium, and erratic behavior.
 Development of acute glaucoma (in susceptible individuals).

Advisability of Use During Pregnancy
Safety not established. Prudent use is best determined by the physician's evaluation.

Advisability of Use While Nursing Infant
This drug may impair the formation of milk and make nursing difficult. Sufficient quantities of drug may be present in the milk to affect the infant. Avoid drug or avoid nursing, as directed by your physician.

Habit-Forming Potential
None.

Effects of Overdosage
With Moderate Overdose: Marked dryness of the mouth, dilated pupils, blurring of near vision, rapid pulse, heart palpitation, headache, difficulty in urination.

With Large Overdose: Extremely dilated pupils, rapid pulse and breathing, hot skin, high fever, excitement, confusion, hallucinations, delirium, eventual loss of consciousness, convulsions, and coma.

Possible Effects of Extended Use
Chronic constipation, severe enough to result in fecal impaction. (Constipation should be treated promptly with effective laxatives.)

Recommended Periodic Examinations While Taking This Drug
Measurement of internal eye pressure to detect any significant increase that could indicate developing glaucoma.

While Taking This Drug, Observe the Following
Foods: No interaction with drug. Effectiveness is greater if drug is taken one-half to 1 hour before eating. Follow diet prescribed for condition under treatment.

Beverages: No interactions. As allowed by prescribed diet.

Alcohol: No interactions expected with this drug. Follow physician's advice regarding use of alcohol (based upon its effect on the condition under treatment).

Tobacco Smoking: No interactions expected. Follow physician's advice regarding smoking.

Other Drugs

Methscopolamine may *increase* the effects of
- all other drugs having atropine-like actions (see Drug Family, Section Four).

Methscopolamine may *decrease* the effects of
- pilocarpine eye drops, and reduce their effectiveness in lowering internal eye pressure in the treatment of glaucoma.

Methscopolamine *taken concurrently* with
- mono-amine oxidase (MAO) inhibitor drugs, may cause an exaggerated response to normal doses of atropine-like drugs. It is best to avoid atropine-like drugs for 2 weeks after the last dose of any MAO inhibitor drug (see Drug Family, Section Four).
- haloperidol (Haldol), may significantly increase internal eye pressure (dangerous in glaucoma).

The following drugs may *increase* the effects of methscopolamine
• tricyclic antidepressants
• those antihistamines that have an atropine-like action
• meperidine (Demerol, pethidine)
• methylphenidate (Ritalin)
• orphenadrine (Disipal, Norflex)
• those phenothiazines that have an atropine-like action
(see Drug Family, Section Four, for specific brand names)

The following drugs may *decrease* the effects of methscopolamine
• Vitamin C reduces its effectiveness by hastening its elimination from the body. Avoid large doses of Vitamin C during treatment with this drug.

Driving a Vehicle, Piloting a Plane, Operating Machinery: This drug may produce drowsiness or blurred vision. Avoid hazardous activities if these drug effects occur.

Exposure to Sun: No restrictions.

Exposure to Heat: Use extreme caution. The use of this drug in hot environments may significantly increase the risk of heat stroke.

Heavy Exercise or Exertion: Use caution in warm or hot environments. This drug may impair normal perspiration (heat loss) and interfere with the regulation of body temperature.

Special Storage Instructions
Keep in a tightly closed container. Protect from light.

METHYCLOTHIAZIDE
Year Introduced: 1960

Brand Names

USA	Canada
Enduron (Abbott)	Duretic (Abbott)
Diutensen [CD] (Mallinckrodt)	
Diutensen-R [CD] (Mallinckrodt)	
Enduronyl [CD] (Abbott)	

Drug Family: Anti-hypertensive (Hypotensive); Diuretic [Thiazides]

Prescription Required: Yes

Available Dosage Forms and Strengths
Tablets — 2.5 mg., 5 mg.

How This Drug Works

Intended Therapeutic Effect(s)
- elimination of excessive fluid retention (edema).
- reduction of high blood pressure.

Location of Drug Action(s):   Principal actions occur in
- the tubular systems of the kidney that determine the final composition of the urine.
- the walls of the smaller arteries.

Method of Drug Action(s)

By increasing the elimination of salt and water from the body (through increased urine production), this drug reduces the volume of fluid in the blood and body tissues and lowers the sodium content throughout the body.

By relaxing the walls of the smaller arteries and allowing them to expand, this drug significantly increases the total capacity of the arterial system. The combined effect of these two actions (reduced blood volume in expanded space) results in lowering of the blood pressure.

THIS DRUG SHOULD NOT BE TAKEN IF

—you have had an allergic reaction to any dosage form of it previously. A combination drug [CD] should not be taken if you are allergic to *any* of its ingredients.

INFORM YOUR PHYSICIAN BEFORE TAKING THIS DRUG IF

—you are allergic to any form of "sulfa" drug.
—you are pregnant and your physician does not know it.
—you have a history of kidney disease or liver disease, or impaired kidney or liver function.
—you have diabetes (or a tendency to diabetes).
—you have a history of gout.
—you have a history of lupus erythematosus.
—you are taking any form of cortisone, digitalis, oral anti-diabetic drugs, or insulin.
—you plan to have surgery under general anesthesia in the near future.

Time Required for Apparent Benefit

Increased urine volume begins in 2 hours, reaches a maximum in 6 hours, and subsides in 24 hours. Continuous use on a regular schedule will be necessary for 2 to 3 weeks to determine this drug's effectiveness in lowering your blood pressure.

Possible Side-Effects *(natural, expected, and unavoidable drug actions)*

Lightheadedness on arising from sitting or lying position (see orthostatic hypotension in Glossary).

Increase in level of blood sugar, affecting control of diabetes.

Increase in level of blood uric acid, affecting control of gout.

Decrease in level of blood potassium, resulting in muscle weakness and cramping.

CAUTION
The elderly (over 60 years of age) are frequently quite sensitive to the effects of standard doses. Use this drug with caution until extent and duration of response have been determined.

Possible Adverse Effects *(unusual, unexpected, and infrequent reactions)*
IF ANY OF THE FOLLOWING DEVELOP, DISCONTINUE DRUG AND NOTIFY YOUR PHYSICIAN AS SOON AS POSSIBLE

Mild Adverse Effects
Allergic Reactions: Skin rash (various kinds), hives, drug fever.
Reduced appetite, indigestion, nausea, vomiting, diarrhea.
Headache, dizziness, yellow vision, blurred vision.

Serious Adverse Effects
Allergic Reactions: Hepatitis with jaundice (see Glossary). Anaphylactic reaction (see Glossary). Severe skin reactions.
Inflammation of the pancreas—severe abdominal pain.
Bone marrow depression (see Glossary)—fatigue, weakness, fever, sore throat, unusual bleeding or bruising.

Advisability of Use During Pregnancy
This drug should not be used during pregnancy unless a very serious complication of pregnancy occurs for which this drug is significantly beneficial. This type of diuretic can have adverse effects on the fetus.

Advisability of Use While Nursing Infant
This drug is known to be present in milk. Ask physician for guidance.

Habit-Forming Potential
None.

Effects of Overdosage
With Moderate Overdose: Dryness of mouth, thirst, lethargy, weakness, dizziness, muscle pain and cramping, nausea, vomiting.
With Large Overdose: Drowsiness progressing to stupor and coma, weak and rapid pulse.

Possible Effects of Extended Use
Impaired balance of water, salt, and potassium in blood and body tissues.
Development of diabetes (in predisposed individuals).

Recommended Periodic Examinations While Taking This Drug
Complete blood cell counts.
Measurement of blood levels of sodium, potassium, chloride, sugar, and uric acid.
Liver function tests.
Kidney function tests.

While Taking This Drug, Observe the Following

Foods: It is recommended that you include in your daily diet liberal servings of foods rich in potassium (unless directed otherwise by your physician). The following foods have a high potassium content:

All-bran cereals	Fish, fresh
Almonds	Lentils
Apricots (dried)	Liver, beef
Bananas, fresh	Lonalac
Beans (navy and lima)	Milk
Beef	Peaches
Carrots (raw)	Peanut butter
Chicken	Peas
Citrus fruits	Pork
Coconut	Potato chips
Coffee	Prunes (dried)
Crackers (rye)	Raisins
Dates and figs (dried)	Tomato juice

Note: Avoid licorice in large amounts while taking this drug. Follow your physician's instructions regarding the use of salt.

Beverages: No restrictions unless directed by your physician.

Alcohol: Use with caution until the combined effect has been determined. Alcohol can exaggerate the blood pressure-lowering effect of this drug and cause orthostatic hypotension.

Tobacco Smoking: No interactions expected. Follow your physician's advice regarding smoking.

Other Drugs

Methyclothiazide may *increase* the effects of

- other anti-hypertensive drugs. Careful adjustment of dosages is necessary to prevent excessive lowering of the blood pressure.
- drugs of the phenothiazine drug family, and cause excessive lowering of the blood pressure. (The thiazide and related drugs and the phenothiazines both may cause orthostatic hypotension).

Methyclothiazide may *decrease* the effects of

- the oral anti-diabetic drugs and insulin, by raising the level of blood sugar. Careful adjustment of dosages is necessary to maintain proper control of diabetes.
- allopurinol (Zyloprim), by raising the level of blood uric acid. Careful adjustment of dosages is required to maintain proper control of gout.
- probenecid (Benemid), by raising the level of blood uric acid. Careful dosage adjustment is necessary to maintain control of gout.

Methyclothiazide *taken concurrently* with

- cortisone and cortisone-related drugs, may cause excessive loss of potassium from the body.
- digitalis and related drugs, requires very careful monitoring and dosage adjustments to prevent serious disturbances of heart rhythm.
- tricyclic antidepressants (Elavil, Sinequan, etc.), may cause excessive lowering of the blood pressure.

The following drugs may *increase* the effects of methyclothiazide
• the barbiturates may exaggerate its blood pressure-lowering action.
• the mono-amine oxidase (MAO) inhibitor drugs may increase urine volume by delaying this drug's elimination from the body.
• the pain relievers (analgesics), both narcotic and non-narcotic, may exaggerate its blood pressure-lowering action.

The following drugs may *decrease* the effects of methyclothiazide
• cholestyramine (Cuemid, Questran) may interfere with its absorption. Take cholestyramine 30 to 60 minutes before any oral diuretic.

Driving a Vehicle, Piloting a Plane, Operating Machinery: Use caution until the possibility of orthostatic hypotension has been determined.

Exposure to Sun: Use caution until sensitivity has been determined. This drug may cause photosensitivity (see Glossary).

Exposure to Heat: Avoid excessive perspiring which could cause additional loss of water and salt from the body.

Heavy Exercise or Exertion: Avoid exertion that produces lightheadedness, excessive fatigue, or muscle cramping.

Occurrence of Unrelated Illness: Illnesses which cause vomiting or diarrhea can produce a serious imbalance of important body chemistry. Discontinue this drug and ask your physician for guidance.

Discontinuation: It may be advisable to discontinue this drug approximately 5 to 7 days before major surgery. Ask your physician, surgeon, and/or anesthesiologist for guidance regarding dosage reduction or withdrawal.

Special Storage Instructions
Keep in a dry, tightly closed container.

METHYLDOPA

Year Introduced: 1963

Brand Names

USA	Canada
Aldomet (Merck Sharp & Dohme)	Aldomet (MSD)
	Dopamet (ICN)
Aldoclor [CD] (Merck Sharp & Dohme)	Novomedopa (Novopharm)
Aldoril [CD] (Merck Sharp & Dohme)	Aldoril [CD] (MSD)

Drug Family: Anti-hypertensive (Hypotensive)

Prescription Required: Yes

Available Dosage Forms and Strengths
Tablets — 125 mg., 250 mg., 500 mg.

How This Drug Works
Intended Therapeutic Effect(s):   Reduction of high blood pressure.

Location of Drug Action(s):   The vasomotor center in the brain that influences the control of the sympathetic nervous system over blood vessels (principally arterioles) throughout the body.

Method of Drug Action(s):   By decreasing the activity of the vasomotor center, this drug reduces the ability of the sympathetic nervous system to maintain the degree of blood vessel constriction responsible for elevation of the blood pressure. This change results in relaxation of blood vessel walls and lowering of the blood pressure.

THIS DRUG SHOULD NOT BE TAKEN IF

—you have had an allergic reaction to any dosage form of it previously.

—you have active liver disease.

—you have a mild and uncomplicated case of hypertension.

INFORM YOUR PHYSICIAN BEFORE TAKING THIS DRUG IF

—you have a history of liver disease or impaired liver function.

—you are taking any tricyclic antidepressant (Elavil, Tofranil, Sinequan, etc.; (see Drug Family, Section Four).

—you are taking any mono-amine oxidase (MAO) inhibitor drug (Eutonyl, Marplan, Nardil, Niamid, etc.; see Drug Family, Section Four).

—you plan to have surgery under general anesthesia in the near future.

Time Required for Apparent Benefit

Continuous use with periodic dosage adjustment for 2 to 4 weeks may be necessary to determine this drug's effectiveness in controlling high blood pressure.

Possible Side-Effects *(natural, expected, and unavoidable drug actions)*

Drowsiness, lethargy, weakness, which may occur during first few weeks and then subside.

Lightheadedness in upright position (see orthostatic hypotension in Glossary).

Nasal stuffiness, dryness of the mouth.

CAUTION

The elderly (over 60 years of age) may not tolerate large doses. Small doses are advisable to determine tolerance and avoid fainting.

Possible Adverse Effects *(unusual, unexpected, and infrequent reactions)*

IF ANY OF THE FOLLOWING DEVELOP, DISCONTINUE DRUG AND NOTIFY YOUR PHYSICIAN AS SOON AS POSSIBLE

Mild Adverse Effects

Allergic Reactions: Skin rash, joint and muscle discomfort.

Headache, dizziness.

Nausea, vomiting, irritation of tongue, diarrhea.

Water retention and weight gain.

Breast enlargement, milk production, impaired sex drive and performance.

Serious Adverse Effects

Allergic Reactions: Hepatitis with jaundice (see Glossary).

Idiosyncratic Reactions: Episodes of high fever (not due to infection).

Bone marrow depression (see Glossary)—fatigue, weakness, fever, sore throat, unusual bleeding or bruising.

Inflammation of the pancreas—abdominal pain, fever, nausea, vomiting.

Parkinson-like disorders (see Glossary).

Behavioral changes—confusion, depression, nightmares.

Advisability of Use During Pregnancy
Safety not established. Prudent use is best determined by the physician's evaluation.

Advisability of Use While Nursing Infant
This drug's presence in milk is not known. Ask physician for guidance.

Habit-Forming Potential
None.

Effects of Overdosage
With Moderate Overdose: Marked drowsiness, weakness, sense of exhaustion, orthostatic hypotension.

With Large Overdose: Stupor, confusion, slow and weak pulse.

Possible Effects of Extended Use
Development of hemolytic anemia (see Glossary).

Retention of salt and water with gain in weight.

Recommended Periodic Examinations While Taking This Drug
Complete blood cell counts.

Coombs' test of red blood cells.

Liver function tests.

While Taking This Drug, Observe the Following
Foods: Ask physician for guidance regarding intake of salt.

Beverages: Drink enough water to satisfy thirst and prevent constipation.

Alcohol: Use with extreme caution until combined effect has been determined. Alcohol can exaggerate this drug's sedative effect and can add to its ability to lower the blood pressure. Excessive drop in blood pressure may result from this combination.

Tobacco Smoking: Follow your physician's advice regarding the use of tobacco. Nicotine can raise the blood pressure in sensitive individuals.

Other Drugs

Methyldopa may *increase* the effects of

- oral anticoagulants, and cause bleeding or hemorrhage. Careful dosage adjustments are necessary.
- other anti-hypertensive drugs. Careful dosage adjustments are necessary to prevent excessive drop in blood pressure.

Methyldopa may *decrease* the effects of

- levodopa (L-Dopa, Larodopa, Dopar, etc.), and reduce its effectiveness in treating Parkinson's disease.

Methyldopa *taken concurrently* with
- tricyclic antidepressants (Elavil, Tofranil, Sinequan, etc.) may cause dangerous elevation of the blood pressure. Avoid combined use.
- mono-amine oxidase (MAO) inhibitor drugs (Eutonyl, Marplan, Nardil, Niamid, etc.) may cause dangerous elevation of the blood pressure. Avoid combined use.

The following drugs may *increase* the effects of methyldopa
- thiazide diuretics usually enhance its blood pressure-lowering action.

The following drugs may *decrease* the effects of methyldopa
- amphetamines (Benzedrine, Dexedrine, Desoxyn, etc.) can reduce its effectiveness in lowering blood pressure.

Driving a Vehicle, Piloting a Plane, Operating Machinery: Avoid hazardous activities until the early manifestations of drowsiness and lethargy have subsided. Be alert to the occurrence of orthostatic hypotension.

Exposure to Sun: No restrictions.

Heavy Exercise or Exertion: Use caution. Excessive physical activity may increase the possibility of orthostatic hypotension.

Discontinuation: Consult physician for guidance regarding the need to readjust the dosage schedule of other drugs taken concurrently with methyldopa, such as anticoagulants and other anti-hypertensives.

Special Storage Instructions
Keep in a dry, tightly closed container.

METHYLPHENIDATE
Year Introduced: 1956

Brand Names

USA	Canada
Ritalin (CIBA)	Methidate (ICN)
	Ritalin (CIBA)

Drug Family: Stimulant, Amphetamine-like Drug [Sympathomimetics]

Prescription Required: Yes (Controlled Drug, U.S. Schedule 2)

Available Dosage Forms and Strengths
Tablets — 5 mg., 10 mg., 20 mg.

How This Drug Works
Intended Therapeutic Effect(s)
- Improvement of mood, confidence, initiative, and performance in states of fatigue and depression.
- reduction of restlessness, distractability, and impulsive behavior characteristic of the abnormally hyperactive child (as seen with minimal brain damage).

Location of Drug Action(s):   Areas within the outer layer (cortex) of the brain that are responsible for higher mental functions and behavioral reactions.

Method of Drug Action(s):   Not established. Present thinking is that this drug may increase the release of the nerve impulse transmitter, norepinephrine. The resulting stimulation of brain tissue improves alertness and concentration, and increases learning ability and attention span. (The primary action that calms the overactive child is not known.)

THIS DRUG SHOULD NOT BE TAKEN IF

—you are allergic to either of the drugs bearing the brand names listed above.

—you have glaucoma.

—you are experiencing a period of severe anxiety, nervous tension, or emotional depression.

—it has been prescribed for a child under 6 years of age.

INFORM YOUR PHYSICIAN BEFORE TAKING THIS DRUG IF

—you have epilepsy.

—you have high blood pressure.

—you are taking any mono-amine oxidase (MAO) inhibitor drug (see Drug Family, Section Four).

Time Required for Apparent Benefit

It is advisable to start with low dosage and increase gradually. Continuous use, with dosage adjustments, may be needed for a full month to determine this drug's effectiveness.

Possible Side-Effects *(natural, expected, and unavoidable drug actions)*

Nervousness, insomnia.

CAUTION

Careful dosage adjustments on an individual basis are essential. In a paradoxical reaction, aggravation of symptoms may occur (see Glossary).

Possible Adverse Effects *(unusual, unexpected, and infrequent reactions)*

IF ANY OF THE FOLLOWING DEVELOP, DISCONTINUE DRUG AND NOTIFY YOUR PHYSICIAN AS SOON AS POSSIBLE

Mild Adverse Effects

Allergic Reactions: Skin rash, hives, drug fever, joint pains.

Reduced appetite, nausea, abdominal discomfort.

Headache, dizziness, drowsiness.

Rapid and forceful heart palpitation.

Serious Adverse Effects

Allergic Reactions: Severe skin reactions, extensive bruising due to destruction of blood platelets (see Glossary).

Idiosyncratic Reactions: Abnormal patterns of behavior.

Abnormally low red blood cells and white blood cells.

Advisability of Use During Pregnancy
Safety not established. Prudent use is best determined by the physician's evaluation.

Advisability of Use While Nursing Infant
The presence of this drug in milk is not known. Safety for infant not established. Ask physician for guidance.

Habit-Forming Potential
This drug can produce tolerance and psychological dependence, a potentially dangerous characteristic of amphetamine-like drugs (see Glossary). Avoid excessive dosage and long-term use if possible.

Effects of Overdosage
With Moderate Overdose: Vomiting, agitation, tremors, muscle twitching, headache, sweating, dryness of the mouth.

With Large Overdose: High fever, rapid and irregular pulse, confusion, hallucinations, convulsions, coma.

Possible Effects of Extended Use
Suppression of growth (in weight and/or height) has been reported in children. Monitor growth carefully during long-term use of this drug.

Recommended Periodic Examinations While Taking This Drug
Measurement of blood pressure on a regular basis to detect any tendency to abnormal elevation.
Complete blood cell counts.

While Taking This Drug, Observe the Following
Foods: Avoid foods rich in tyramine (see Glossary). This drug in combination with tyramine may cause excessive rise in blood pressure.

Beverages: Avoid beverages prepared from meat or yeast extracts; avoid chocolate drinks.

Alcohol: Avoid beer, Chianti wines and vermouth.

Tobacco Smoking: No interactions expected.

Other Drugs

Methylphenidate may *increase* the effects of
- oral anticoagulants of the coumarin family.
- anti-convulsants such as phenobarbital, phenytoin, and primidone.
- phenylbutazone (Azolid, Butazolidin, etc.).
- tricyclic antidepressants.
- atropine-like drugs.

(Consult appropriate Drug Family, Section Four, to see if you are taking any drugs that may require reduction in dosage.)

Methylphenidate may *decrease* the effects of
- guanethidine (Ismelin), and reduce its ability to lower blood pressure.

Methylphenidate *taken concurrently* with
- anti-convulsants, may cause a significant change in the pattern of epilep-

tic seizures. Dosage adjustments may be necessary for proper control.
• mono-amine oxidase (MAO) inhibitor drugs (see Drug Family, Section Four), may cause a dangerous rise in blood pressure. The simultaneous use of these two drugs should be avoided.

Driving a Vehicle, Piloting a Plane, Operating Machinery: Usually no restrictions. Use caution if drowsiness or dizziness occurs.

Exposure to Sun: No restrictions.

Discontinuation: If it has been necessary to use this drug for an extended period of time, do not discontinue it abruptly. Careful supervision is necessary during withdrawal to prevent severe depression and erratic behavior.

Special Storage Instructions
Keep in a dry, tightly closed container.

METHYLPREDNISOLONE
Year Introduced: 1957

Brand Names

USA	Canada
Medrol (Upjohn)	Medrol (Upjohn)

Drug Family: Cortisone-like Drug [Adrenocortical Steroids (Glucocorticoids)]

Prescription Required: Yes

Available Dosage Forms and Strengths
Tablets — 2 mg., 4 mg., 16 mg.
Capsules — 2 mg., 4 mg.
Enema Suspension — 40 mg.
Ointment — 0.25%, 1%

How This Drug Works
Intended Therapeutic Effect(s):   The symptomatic relief of inflammation (swelling, redness, heat and pain) in any tissue, and from many causes. (Cortisone-like drugs do not correct the underlying disease process).

Location of Drug Action(s):   Significant biological effects occur in most tissues throughout the body. The principal actions of therapeutic doses occur at sites of inflammation and/or allergic reaction, regardless of the nature of the causative injury or illness.

Method of Drug Action(s):   Not completely established. Present thinking is that cortisone-like drugs probably inhibit several mechanisms within the tissues that induce inflammation. Well-regulated dosage aids the body in restoring normal stability. However, prolonged use or excessive dosage can impair the body's defense mechanisms against infectious disease.

THIS DRUG SHOULD NOT BE TAKEN IF
—you have had an allergic reaction to any dosage form of it previously.
—you have an active peptic ulcer (stomach or duodenum).

INFORM YOUR PHYSICIAN BEFORE TAKING THIS DRUG IF
—you have had an unfavorable reaction to any cortisone-like drug in the past.
—you have a history of tuberculosis.
—you have diabetes or a tendency to diabetes.
—you have a history of peptic ulcer disease.
—you have glaucoma or a tendency to glaucoma.
—you have a deficiency of thyroid function (hypothyroidism).
—you have high blood pressure.
—you have myasthenia gravis.
—you have a history of thrombophlebitis.
—you plan to have surgery of any kind in the near future, especially if under general anesthesia.

Time Required for Apparent Benefit
Evidence of beneficial drug action is usually apparent in 24 to 48 hours. Dosage must be individualized to give reasonable improvement; this is usually accomplished in 4 to 10 days. It is unwise to demand complete relief of all symptoms. The effective dose varies with the nature of the disease and with the patient. During long-term use it is essential that the smallest effective dose be determined and maintained.

Possible Side-Effects *(natural, expected, and unavoidable drug actions)*
The retention of salt and water (common with some cortisone-like drugs) is less likely to occur with this drug. Increased susceptibility to infection may occur.

CAUTION
1. It is advisable to carry a card of personal identification with a notation that you are taking this drug if your course of treatment is to exceed 1 week (see Table 14 and Section Seven).
2. Do not discontinue this drug abruptly.
3. While taking this drug, immunization procedures should be given with caution. If vaccination against measles, smallpox, rabies, or yellow fever is required, discontinue this drug 72 hours before vaccination and do not resume for at least 14 days after vaccination.

Possible Adverse Effects *(unusual, unexpected, and infrequent reactions)*

IF ANY OF THE FOLLOWING DEVELOP, DISCONTINUE DRUG AND NOTIFY YOUR PHYSICIAN AS SOON AS POSSIBLE

Mild Adverse Effects
　Allergic Reactions: Skin rash.
　Headache, dizziness, insomnia.
　Acid indigestion, abdominal distention.
　Muscle cramping and weakness.
　Irregular menstrual periods.
　Acne, excessive growth of facial hair.

Serious Adverse Effects
Mental and emotional disturbances of serious magnitude.
Reactivation of latent tuberculosis.
Development of peptic ulcer.
Increased blood pressure.
Development of inflammation of the pancreas.
Thrombophlebitis (inflammation of a vein with the formation of blood clot) —pain or tenderness in thigh or leg, with or without swelling of the foot, ankle, or leg.
Pulmonary embolism (movement of blood clot to the lung)—sudden shortness of breath, pain in the chest, coughing, bloody sputum.

Advisability of Use During Pregnancy
Safety has not been established. If possible, avoid completely. If use of this drug is considered necessary, limit dosage and duration of use as much as possible. Following birth, the infant should be examined for possible defective function of the adrenal glands (deficiency of adrenal cortical hormones).

Advisability of Use While Nursing Infant
Drug is known to be present in milk. Ask physician for guidance.

Habit-Forming Potential
Use of this drug to suppress symptoms over an extended period of time may produce a state of functional dependence (see Glossary). In the treatment of conditions like rheumatoid arthritis and asthma, it is advisable to try alternate-day drug administration to keep the daily dose as small as possible and to attempt drug withdrawal after periods of reasonable improvement. Such procedures may reduce the degree of "steroid rebound"—the return of symptoms as the drug is withdrawn.

Effects of Overdosage
With Moderate Overdose: Excessive fluid retention, swelling of extremities, flushing of the face, nervousness, stomach irritation, weakness.
With Large Overdose: Severe headache, convulsions, heart failure in susceptible individuals, emotional and behavioral disturbances.

Possible Effects of Extended Use
Development of increased blood sugar, possibly diabetes.
Increased fat deposits on the trunk of the body ("buffalo hump"), rounding of the face ("moon face"), and thinning of the arms and legs.
Thinning and fragility of the skin, easy bruising.
Loss of texture and strength of the bones, resulting in spontaneous fractures.
Development of increased internal eye pressure, possibly glaucoma.
Development of cataracts.
Retarded growth and development in children.

Recommended Periodic Examinations While Taking This Drug
Measurement of blood potassium levels.
Measurement of blood sugar levels 2 hours after eating.
Measurement of blood pressure at regular intervals.

Complete eye examination at regular intervals.

Chest X-ray if history of previous tuberculosis.

Determination of the rate of development of the growing child to detect retardation of normal growth.

While Taking This Drug, Observe the Following

Foods: No interactions. Ask physician regarding need to restrict salt intake or to eat potassium-rich foods. During long-term use of this drug it is advisable to have a high protein diet.

Beverages: No restrictions.

Alcohol: No interactions expected.

Tobacco Smoking: Nicotine increases the blood levels of naturally produced cortisone and related hormones. Heavy smoking may add to the expected actions of this drug and requires close observation for excessive effects.

Other Drugs

Methylprednisolone may *increase* the effects of

- barbiturates and other sedatives and sleep-inducing drugs, causing over-sedation.

Methylprednisolone may *decrease* the effects of

- insulin and oral anti-diabetic drugs, by raising the level of blood sugar. Doses of anti-diabetic drugs may have to be raised.
- anticoagulants of the coumarin family. Monitor prothrombin times closely and adjust dosage accordingly.
- choline-like drugs (Mestinon, pilocarpine, Prostigmin), and reduce their effectiveness in treating glaucoma and myasthenia gravis.

Methylprednisolone *taken concurrently* with

- thiazide diuretics, may cause excessive loss of potassium. Monitor blood levels of potassium on physician's advice.
- atropine-like drugs, may cause increased internal eye pressure and initiate or aggravate glaucoma (see Drug Family, Section Four).
- digitalis preparations, requires close monitoring of body potassium stores to prevent digitalis toxicity.
- stimulant drugs (Adrenalin, amphetamines, ephedrine, etc.), may increase internal eye pressure and initiate or aggravate glaucoma.

The following drugs may *decrease* the effects of methylprednisolone

- indomethacin (Indocin, Indocid)
- aspirin

The following drugs may *increase* the effects of methylprednisolone

- barbiturates
- phenytoin (Dantoin, Dilantin, etc.)
- antihistamines (some)
- chloral hydrate (Noctec, Somnos)
- glutethimide (Doriden)
- phenylbutazone (Azolid, Butazolidin, etc.) may reduce its effectiveness following a brief, initial increase in effectiveness.
- propranolol (Inderal)

Driving a Vehicle, Piloting a Plane, Operating Machinery: No restrictions or precautions.

Exposure to Sun: No restrictions.

Occurrence of Unrelated Illness

This drug may decrease natural resistance to infection. Notify your physician if you develop an infection of any kind.

This drug may reduce your body's ability to respond appropriately to the stress of acute illness, injury, or surgery. Keep your physician fully informed of any significant changes in your state of health.

Discontinuation

If you have been taking this drug for an extended period of time, do not discontinue it abruptly. Ask physician for guidance regarding gradual withdrawal.

For a period of 2 years after discontinuing this drug, it is essential in the event of illness, injury, or surgery that you inform attending medical personnel that you used this drug in the past. The period of inadequate response to stress following the use of cortisone-like drugs may last for 1 to 2 years.

Special Storage Instructions

Keep in a tightly closed container. Protect from light.

METHYPRYLON

Year Introduced: 1955

Brand Names

USA	Canada
Noludar (Roche)	Noludar (Roche)

Drug Family: Sleep Inducer (Hypnotic)

Prescription Required: Yes (Controlled Drug, U.S. Schedule 3)

Available Dosage Forms and Strengths

Tablets — 50 mg., 200 mg.
Capsules — 300 mg.

How This Drug Works

Intended Therapeutic Effect(s):   Relief of insomnia (hypnotic effect).

Location of Drug Action(s):   Not completely established. Thought to be the wake-sleep centers of the brain, possibly the reticular activating system.

Method of Drug Action(s):   Not established.

THIS DRUG SHOULD NOT BE TAKEN IF

—you have had an allergic reaction to any dosage form of it previously.
—it is prescribed for a child under 3 months of age.

INFORM YOUR PHYSICIAN BEFORE TAKING THIS DRUG IF

—you are taking sedatives, other sleep-inducing drugs, tranquilizers, antihistamines, pain relievers, or narcotic drugs of any kind.

—you have a history of liver disease or impaired liver function.

—you plan to have surgery under general anesthesia in the near future.

Time Required for Apparent Benefit

Approximately 45 to 60 minutes.

Possible Side-Effects *(natural, expected, and unavoidable drug actions)*

Lightheadedness in the upright position, weakness, unsteadiness in stance and gait.

CAUTION

The elderly (over 60 years of age) may not tolerate large doses. Small doses are advisable until tolerance and duration of action have been determined.

Possible Adverse Effects *(unusual, unexpected, and infrequent reactions)*

IF ANY OF THE FOLLOWING DEVELOP, DISCONTINUE DRUG AND NOTIFY YOUR PHYSICIAN AS SOON AS POSSIBLE

Mild Adverse Effects

Allergic Reactions: Skin rashes, hives.

Headache, "hangover" effects, dizziness, numbness and tingling in the arms and legs.

Indigestion, nausea, vomiting, diarrhea.

Serious Adverse Effects

Bone marrow depression (see Glossary)—fatigue, weakness, fever, sore throat, unusual bleeding or bruising.

Advisability of Use During Pregnancy

Safety not established. Prudent use is best determined by the physician's evaluation.

Advisability of Use While Nursing Infant

Presence of drug in milk is not known. Ask physician for guidance.

Habit-Forming Potential

This drug can cause both psychological and physical dependence (see Glossary). Avoid large doses and continuous use.

Effects of Overdosage

With Moderate Overdose: Marked drowsiness, confusion, delirium, incoordination, weakness.

With Large Overdose: Stupor progressing to deep sleep and coma, slow and shallow breathing.

Possible Effects of Extended Use

Psychological and/or physical dependence.

Recommended Periodic Examinations While Taking This Drug
Complete blood cell counts.

While Taking This Drug, Observe the Following
Foods: No restrictions.
Beverages: No restrictions.
Alcohol: Avoid completely for 6 hours before taking this drug for sleep. Alcohol can increase greatly the sedative and depressant actions of this drug on brain function.
Tobacco Smoking: No interactions expected.
Other Drugs
Methyprylon may *increase* the effects of
• sedatives, other sleep-inducing drugs, tranquilizers, antihistamines, pain relievers, and narcotic drugs. Ask physician for guidance regarding dosage adjustments.

Driving a Vehicle, Piloting a Plane, Operating Machinery: This drug can impair mental alertness, judgment, physical coordination, and reaction time. Avoid hazardous activities until all sensation of drowsiness (or "hangover") has disappeared.
Exposure to Sun: No restrictions.
Discontinuation: If it has been necessary to use this drug for an extended period of time, do not discontinue it abruptly. Ask physician for guidance regarding dosage reduction and withdrawal. It may be necessary to adjust the dosage of other drugs taken concurrently with methyprylon, such as coumarin anticoagulants and anti-convulsants.

Special Storage Instructions
Keep in a tightly closed, light-resistant container.

METHYSERGIDE
Year Introduced: 1961

Brand Names

USA	Canada
Sansert (Sandoz)	Sansert (Sandoz)

Drug Family: Migraine Preventive (Antiserotonin)

Prescription Required: Yes

Available Dosage Forms and Strengths
Tablets — 2 mg.

How This Drug Works
Intended Therapeutic Effect(s):   Prevention of blood vessel (vascular) headaches of the migraine type, or reduction of their frequency or severity.

Location of Drug Action(s):   Those blood vessels in the head that undergo excessive constriction in response to stimulation by the tissue chemical serotonin.

Method of Drug Action(s):   Not fully established. It is thought that by blocking the action of serotonin, this drug prevents the blood vessel constriction that initiates the migraine syndrome.

THIS DRUG SHOULD NOT BE TAKEN IF
—you have had an allergic reaction to any dosage form of it previously
—you are pregnant.
—you are experiencing a severe infection.
—you have any of the following conditions:
  angina pectoris
  Buerger's disease
  chronic lung disease
  connective tissue (collagen) disease
  coronary artery disease
  hardening of the arteries (arteriosclerosis)
  heart valve disease
  high blood pressure (severe hypertension)
  kidney disease (or impaired kidney function)
  liver disease (or impaired liver function)
  phlebitis of any kind
  Raynaud's disease or phenomenon

INFORM YOUR PHYSICIAN BEFORE TAKING THIS DRUG IF
—you have had an allergic reaction to *any other forms of ergot.*
—you have a history of peptic ulcer disease.

Time Required for Apparent Benefit
This drug is used solely to *prevent* migraine headaches. If it has not proved to be effective after a trial of 3 weeks, it should be discontinued.

Possible Side-Effects *(natural, expected, and unavoidable drug actions)*
Weight gain, fluid retention (in some individuals).

CAUTION
Continuous use without interruption must not exceed 6 months. There should be a drug-free period of 1 month between each 6-month course of treatment.

Possible Adverse Effects *(unusual, unexpected, and infrequent reactions)*
IF ANY OF THE FOLLOWING DEVELOP, DISCONTINUE DRUG AND NOTIFY YOUR PHYSICIAN AS SOON AS POSSIBLE

Mild Adverse Effects
  Allergic Reactions: Skin rashes, flushing of the face, transient loss of scalp hair.
  Heartburn, nausea, vomiting, diarrhea.
  Drowsiness, dizziness, unsteadiness.
  Transient muscle and joint pains.

Serious Adverse Effects
Idiosyncratic Reactions: Nightmares, hallucinations, acute mental disturbances.
The development of cold, numb and painful hands and feet, leg cramps on walking, pain in the chest, abdomen, or back, fatigue or fever, urinary disturbance.
Abnormally low white blood cell counts.
Hemolytic anemia (see Glossary).

Advisability of Use During Pregnancy
Avoid completely during entire pregnancy.

Advisability of Use While Nursing Infant
Drug is probably present in milk. Avoid use or avoid nursing. Ask physician for guidance.

Habit-Forming Potential
None.

Effects of Overdosage
With Moderate Overdose: Nausea, vomiting, abdominal pain, diarrhea, incoordination.

Possible Effects of Extended Use
Formation of scar tissue inside chest cavity or abdominal cavity, on heart valves, in lung tissue, and surrounding major blood vessels and internal organs. (This tissue reaction is referred to as fibrosis.) The possibility of this potentially dangerous reaction requires close and continuous medical supervision while taking this drug.

Recommended Periodic Examinations While Taking This Drug
Careful examination at regular intervals for scar tissue formation or circulatory complications.
Complete blood cell counts.
Kidney function tests.
Serial sedimentation rates (of red blood cells).

While Taking This Drug, Observe the Following
Foods: No restrictions other than foods to which you are allergic. (Some migraine headaches are due to food allergy.) Drug should be taken with meals.
Beverages: No restrictions.
Alcohol: No interactions expected with this drug. Observe closely to determine if alcoholic beverages can initiate a migraine-like headache.
Tobacco Smoking: Because of the constrictive action of nicotine on blood vessels (reducing blood flow), heavy smoking should be avoided. Follow physician's advice regarding smoking.
Other Drugs
Methysergide may *decrease* the effects of
• narcotic analgesics (morphine, codeine, oxycodone, meperidine, methadone, etc.), reducing their ability to relieve pain.

Driving a Vehicle, Piloting a Plane, Operating Machinery: Usually no restrictions. Avoid hazardous activities if drowsiness or dizziness occurs.
Exposure to Sun: No restrictions.
Exposure to Cold: Use caution until combined effect has been determined. Cold environment may increase the occurrence of reduced circulation (blood flow) to the extremities.
Discontinuation: If this drug has been used for an extended period of time, do not discontinue it abruptly. Gradual withdrawal can prevent the occurrence of "rebound" headaches. Ask physician for instructions.

Special Storage Instructions
Keep in a dry, tightly closed container. Protect from light and heat. Store in a cool place.

METRONIDAZOLE

Year Introduced: 1960

Brand Names

USA	Canada
Flagyl (Searle)	Flagyl (Poulenc)
	Neo-Tric (Neo)
	Novonidazol
	(Novopharm)
	Trikacide (ICN)
	Trikamon (Elliott-Marion)

Drug Family: Antimicrobial, Antiprotozoal (Anti-infective)

Prescription Required: Yes

Available Dosage Forms and Strengths
Tablets — 250 mg.
Vaginal Inserts — 500 mg.

How This Drug Works
Intended Therapeutic Effect(s):   The elimination of protozoal infections responsive to the action of this drug.
Location of Drug Action(s):   Those body tissues and fluids infected by certain protozoal microorganisms, and in which adequate concentration of the drug can be achieved.
Method of Drug Action(s):   Not established.

THIS DRUG SHOULD NOT BE TAKEN IF
—you have had an allergic reaction to any dosage form of it previously.
—you have or have had a disease of the bone marrow or blood cells (a blood dyscrasia).

INFORM YOUR PHYSICIAN BEFORE TAKING THIS DRUG IF
—you have an active disorder of the nervous system (brain or spinal cord).
—you use alcoholic beverages frequently or heavily.

Time Required for Apparent Benefit
Drug action begins in 1 hour, reaches a maximum in 2 to 3 hours, and persists for 12 hours. Continuous treatment for up to 10 days may be needed to cure infection.

Possible Side-Effects *(natural, expected, and unavoidable drug actions)*
A sharp, metallic, unpleasant taste.
Dark discoloration of the urine (of no significance).
Superinfection (see Glossary) by yeast organisms in the mouth or vagina.

Possible Adverse Effects *(unusual, unexpected,and infrequent reactions)*
IF ANY OF THE FOLLOWING DEVELOP, DISCONTINUE DRUG AND NOTIFY YOUR PHYSICIAN AS SOON AS POSSIBLE
Mild Adverse Effects
Allergic Reactions: Skin rash, hives, flushing, itching.
Reduced appetite, nausea, vomiting, abdominal pain, cramping, diarrhea, altered taste, irritation of mouth or tongue.
Headache, dizziness, unsteadiness, incoordination.
Sense of numbness or abnormal sensation in the extremities.
Serious Adverse Effects
Idiosyncratic Reactions: Behavioral disturbances, irritability, confusion, depression, insomnia.
Abnormally low white blood cell count.

Advisability of Use During Pregnancy
Safety not established. Avoid use completely.

Advisability of Use While Nursing Infant
Drug is known to be present in milk. Avoid use or discontinue nursing. Ask physician for guidance.

Habit-Forming Potential
None.

Effects of Overdosage
With Moderate Overdose: Weakness, stomach irritation, nausea, vomiting.
With Large Overdose: Disorientation, confusion.

Possible Effects of Extended Use
None reported.

Recommended Periodic Examinations While Taking This Drug
Complete blood cell counts.

While Taking This Drug, Observe the Following
Foods: No restrictions. Drug may be taken after eating to reduce stomach irritation or nausea.
Beverages: No restrictions.

Alcohol: Avoid completely. This drug combined with alcohol may produce a disulfiram-like reaction (see Glossary).

Tobacco Smoking: No interactions expected.

Other Drugs

Metronidazole *taken concurrently* with

• disulfiram (Antabuse), may cause severe emotional and behavioral disturbances.

The following drugs may *decrease* the effects of metronidazole

• oxytetracycline (Terramycin, etc.) may reduce its effectiveness in treating trichomonas infection.

Driving a Vehicle, Piloting a Plane, Operating Machinery: Use caution until tolerance has been determined. Avoid hazardous activities if dizziness or incoordination occurs.

Exposure to Sun: No restrictions.

Special Storage Instructions

Keep in a dry, tightly closed container. Protect from light.

MINOCYCLINE

Year Introduced: 1970

Brand Names

USA	Canada
Minocin (Lederle)	Minocin (Lederle)
Vectrin (Parke-Davis)	Ultramycin (P.D. & Co.)

Drug Family: Antibiotic (Anti-infective) [Tetracyclines]

Prescription Required: Yes

Available Dosage Forms and Strengths

Capsules — 50 mg., 100 mg.

Syrup — 50 mg. per teaspoonful

How This Drug Works

Intended Therapeutic Effect(s):   The elimination of infections responsive to the action of this drug.

Location of Drug Action(s):   Any body tissue or fluid in which sufficient concentration of the drug can be achieved.

Method of Drug Action(s):   This drug prevents the growth and multiplication of susceptible bacteria by interfering with their formation of essential proteins.

THIS DRUG SHOULD NOT BE TAKEN IF

—you are allergic to *any* tetracycline drug (see Drug Family, Section Four).

—you are pregnant or breast feeding.

—it is prescribed for a child under 9 years of age.

INFORM YOUR PHYSICIAN BEFORE TAKING THIS DRUG IF
—you have a history of liver or kidney disease.
—you have systemic lupus erythematosus.
—you are taking any penicillin drug.
—you are taking any anticoagulant drug.
—you plan to have surgery under general anesthesia in the near future.

Time Required for Apparent Benefit
Varies with nature of infection under treatment; usually 2 to 5 days.

Possible Side-Effects *(natural, expected, and unavoidable drug actions)*
Superinfections (see Glossary).

Possible Adverse Effects *(unusual, unexpected, and infrequent reactions)*

IF ANY OF THE FOLLOWING DEVELOP, DISCONTINUE DRUG AND NOTIFY YOUR PHYSICIAN AS SOON AS POSSIBLE

Mild Adverse Effects
Allergic Reactions: Skin rash (various kinds), hives, itching of hands and feet, swelling of face or extremities.
Photosensitivity Reactions: Exaggerated sunburn occurs with the use of some tetracyclines, but this has not been reported with minocycline (see Glossary).
Loss of appetite, nausea, vomiting, diarrhea.
Sensation of lightheadedness or dizziness (this is relatively common and usually occurs during first 3 days).

Serious Adverse Effects
Allergic Reactions: Anaphylactic reaction (see Glossary), asthma, fever, unusual bleeding or bruising.
Stomach irritation, superinfections, rectal or vaginal itching.
Permanent discoloration and/or malformation of teeth when taken under 9 years of age, including unborn child or infant.

Advisability of Use During Pregnancy
Tetracyclines can have adverse effects on mother and fetus. Avoid use.

Advisability of Use While Nursing Infant
Tetracyclines can be present in milk and can have adverse effects on infant. Avoid use.

Habit-Forming Potential
None.

Effects of Overdosage
Possible nausea, vomiting, diarrhea, dizziness.
Acute liver damage (rare).

Possible Effects of Extended Use
Impairment of bone marrow, liver, or kidney function (all rare).
Superinfections.

Recommended Periodic Examinations While Taking This Drug
Complete blood cell counts.
Liver and kidney function tests.
During extended use, sputum and stool examinations may detect early super-infections due to yeast organisms.

While Taking This Drug, Observe the Following
Foods: No restrictions of food selection. Drug may be taken at any time with relationship to eating.
Beverages: No restrictions.
Alcohol: Avoid while taking minocycline if you have a history of liver disease.
Tobacco Smoking: No interactions expected.
Other Drugs

Minocycline may *increase* the effects of
- oral anticoagulants, and make it necessary to reduce their dosage.

Minocycline may *decrease* the effects of
- the penicillins, and impair their effectiveness in treating infections.

The following drugs may *decrease* the effects of minocycline
- antacids may reduce drug absorption.
- iron and mineral preparations may reduce drug absorption.

Driving a Vehicle, Piloting a Plane, Operating Machinery: Avoid all hazardous activities if lightheaded or dizzy.
Exposure to Sun: Photosensitivity (see Glossary) is common with some tetracyclines. Use caution until sensitivity is determined.

Special Storage Instructions
Keep in a tightly closed, light-resistant container. Avoid temperatures above 90°F. (32°C.). Syrup need not be refrigerated.

NAFCILLIN

Year Introduced: 1961

Brand Names

USA	Canada
Unipen (Wyeth)	Unipen (Wyeth)

Drug Family: Antibiotic (Anti-infective) [Penicillins]

Prescription Required: Yes

Available Dosage Forms and Strengths
Tablets — 500 mg.
Capsules — 250 mg.
Oral Solution — 250 mg. per teaspoonful

How This Drug Works

Intended Therapeutic Effect(s):   The elimination of infections responsive to the action of this drug.

Location of Drug Action(s):   Any body tissue or fluid in which sufficient concentration of the drug can be achieved.

Method of Drug Action(s):   This drug destroys susceptible infecting bacteria by interfering with their ability to produce new protective cell walls as they multiply and grow.

THIS DRUG SHOULD NOT BE TAKEN IF

—you have had an allergic reaction to any dosage form of it previously.
—you are certain you are allergic to any form of penicillin.

INFORM YOUR PHYSICIAN BEFORE TAKING THIS DRUG IF

—you suspect you may be allergic to penicillin, or you have a history of a previous "reaction" to penicillin.
—you are allergic to cephalosporin antibiotics (Ancef, Ceporan, Ceporex, Kafocin, Keflex, Keflin, Kefzol, Loridine).
—you are allergic by nature (hayfever, asthma, hives, eczema).

Time Required for Apparent Benefit

Varies with the nature of the infection under treatment; usually from 2 to 5 days.

Possible Side-Effects *(natural, expected, and unavoidable drug actions)*

Superinfections (see Glossary).

Possible Adverse Effects *(unusual, unexpected, and infrequent reactions)*

IF ANY OF THE FOLLOWING DEVELOP, DISCONTINUE DRUG AND NOTIFY YOUR PHYSICIAN AS SOON AS POSSIBLE

Mild Adverse Effects
Allergic Reactions: Skin rashes (various kinds).
Irritation of mouth or tongue, "black tongue," nausea, vomiting, diarrhea, gaseous indigestion.

Serious Adverse Effects
Allergic Reactions: †Anaphylactic reaction (see Glossary), severe skin reactions, high fever, swollen painful joints, sore throat, unusual bleeding or bruising.

Advisability of Use During Pregnancy

Safety not established. Prudent use is best determined by the physician's evaluation.

Advisability of Use While Nursing Infant

Drug may be present in milk and can sensitize infant to penicillin. Ask physician for guidance.

Habit-Forming Potential

None.

---

†A rare but potentially dangerous reaction characteristic of penicillins.

Effects of Overdosage
Possible nausea, vomiting, and/or diarrhea.

Possible Effects of Extended Use
Superinfections.

Recommended Periodic Examinations While Taking This Drug
Complete blood cell counts.
Liver and kidney function tests.

While Taking This Drug, Observe the Following
Foods: No restrictions of food selection. Drug is most effective when taken on an empty stomach, 1 hour before or 2 hours after eating.
Beverages: No restrictions.
Alcohol: No interactions expected.
Tobacco Smoking: No interactions expected.
Other Drugs
   The following drugs may *decrease* the effects of nafcillin
   • antacids can reduce absorption of nafcillin.
   • chloramphenicol (Chloromycetin, etc.)
   • erythromycin (Erythrocin, E-Mycin, etc.)
   • paromomycin (Humatin)
   • tetracyclines (Achromycin, Declomycin, Minocin, etc.; see Drug Family, Section Four)
   • troleandomycin (Cyclamycin, TAO)
Driving a Vehicle, Piloting a Plane, Operating Machinery: No restrictions.
Exposure to Sun: No restrictions.

Special Storage Instructions
Keep tablets and capsules in a tightly closed container at room temperature.
Refrigerate oral solution.

Do Not Take the Oral Solution of This Drug If It Is Older Than
1 week—when kept refrigerated.

NALIDIXIC ACID
Year Introduced: 1963

Brand Names

USA	Canada
NegGram (Winthrop)	NegGram (Winthrop)

Drug Family: Antimicrobial (Anti-infective)

Prescription Required: Yes

Available Dosage Forms and Strengths
Tablets — 250 mg., 500 mg.
Suspension — 250 mg. per teaspoonful (5 ml.)

How This Drug Works
Intended Therapeutic Effect(s):   The elimination of infections in the urinary tract that are responsive to the action of this drug.
Location of Drug Action(s):   Primarily within the organs of the urinary tract —the kidneys, ureters, bladder, and urethra.
Method of Drug Action(s):   This drug destroys susceptible bacteria by inhibiting the formation of essential nuclear protein (DNA).

THIS DRUG SHOULD NOT BE TAKEN IF
—you have had an allergic reaction to any dosage form of it previously.
—you have any type of convulsive disorder (seizures, epilepsy).
—it is prescribed for an infant under 3 months of age.

INFORM YOUR PHYSICIAN BEFORE TAKING THIS DRUG IF
—you have a history of liver disease, or impaired liver function.
—you have a history of kidney disease, or impaired kidney function.
—you have impaired circulation within the brain.
—you have any form of parkinsonism.

Time Required for Apparent Benefit
From 1 to 2 weeks. Periodic urine examinations are required to evaluate response.

Possible Side-Effects *(natural, expected, and unavoidable drug actions)*
None reported.

CAUTION
1. Infants, young children, and the elderly (over 60 years of age) are more susceptible to behavioral disturbances and convulsions while taking this drug.
2. Some bacteria can develop resistance to this drug rapidly and render it ineffective. Adhere to dosage schedules closely, and take the full amount prescribed.
3. This drug can cause *false* positive results when any of these reagents are used to test the urine for sugar: Benedict's solution, Fehling's solution, Clinitest tablets. A false positive test result does *not* occur with the use of Clinistix or Tes-Tape.

Possible Adverse Effects *(unusual, unexpected, and infrequent reactions)*

IF ANY OF THE FOLLOWING DEVELOP, DISCONTINUE DRUG AND NOTIFY YOUR PHYSICIAN AS SOON AS POSSIBLE

Mild Adverse Effects
Allergic Reactions: Itching, skin rash, hives, localized swellings, joint pain and swelling.
Headache, dizziness, drowsiness, weakness.
Visual disturbances such as overbrightness of lights, changes in color per-

ception, difficulty in focusing, double vision.
Nausea, vomiting, abdominal discomfort, diarrhea.
Numbness and/or tingling.

Serious Adverse Effects
Allergic Reactions: Anaphylactic reaction (see Glossary).
Drug fever (see Glossary).
Idiosyncratic Reactions: Hemolytic anemia (see Glossary).
Behavioral disturbances (toxic psychosis).
Convulsions, usually brief.
Hepatitis with jaundice (see Glossary).
Abnormally low white blood cells and/or blood platelets (see Glossary).

Advisability of Use During Pregnancy
Avoid completely during the first 3 months. Use only if necessary and with extreme caution during the last 6 months. Prudent use is best determined by physician's evaluation.

Advisability of Use While Nursing Infant
No significant amounts of this drug have been found in the milk of mothers with normal kidney function. It can be present in the milk of mothers with reduced kidney function, and it can affect the nursing infant. Ask physician for guidance.

Habit-Forming Potential
None.

Effects of Overdosage
With Moderate Overdose: Nausea, vomiting, lethargy.
With Large Overdose: Behavioral disturbance (toxic psychosis), convulsions, shift of acid-alkaline balance of body chemistry resulting in acidosis with stupor and deep, exaggerated breathing.

Possible Effects of Extended Use
None reported.

Recommended Periodic Examinations While Taking This Drug
Complete blood cell counts.
Liver function tests.
Kidney function tests.

While Taking This Drug, Observe the Following
Foods: No restrictions. Absorption is best when drug is taken 1 hour before eating. However, it may be taken with food if necessary to prevent stomach distress.
Beverages: No restrictions. May be taken with milk.
Alcohol: Use caution until combined effect has been determined. This drug in combination with alcohol may impair alertness, judgment, and physical coordination.
Tobacco Smoking: No interactions expected.

Other Drugs

Nalidixic acid may *increase* the effects of

• dicumarol.

• warfarin (Coumadin, etc.).

The following drugs may *increase* the effects of nalidixic acid

• Vitamin C (in large doses)

The following drugs may *decrease* the effects of nalidixic acid

• antacids may reduce its absorption.

• nitrofurantoin (Furadantin, Macrodantin, etc.)

Driving a Vehicle, Piloting a Plane, Operating Machinery: Use caution until full effects of drug have been determined. Drowsiness, dizziness, or visual disturbance can impair ability to engage safely in hazardous activities.

Exposure to Sun: Use caution until sensitivity has been determined. This drug can cause severe and prolonged photosensitivity (see Glossary).

Special Storage Instructions

Keep in a tightly closed container. Protect from light.

NAPROXEN

Year Introduced: 1975

Brand Names

USA	Canada
Naprosyn (Syntex)	Naprosyn (Syntex)

Drug Family: Analgesic, Mild; Anti-inflammatory; Fever Reducer (Antipyretic)

Prescription Required: Yes

Available Dosage Forms and Strengths

Tablets — 125 mg., 250 mg.

How This Drug Works

Intended Therapeutic Effect(s): Relief of joint pain, stiffness, inflammation, and swelling associated with arthritis.

Location of Drug Action(s): Not completely established. It is thought that this drug acts in the brain (at the level of the hypothalamus) and in the inflamed tissues of arthritic joints.

Method of Drug Action(s): Not completely known. It is thought that this drug reduces the tissue concentration of prostaglandins, chemicals involved in the production of inflammation and pain.

THIS DRUG SHOULD NOT BE TAKEN IF

—you have had an allergic reaction to any dosage form of it previously.

—you are allergic to aspirin (hives, nasal polyps, or asthma caused by aspirin).

—you have an active peptic ulcer, active gastritis, duodenitis, ileitis, or ulcerative colitis.
—it is prescribed for a child under 16 years of age.

INFORM YOUR PHYSICIAN BEFORE TAKING THIS DRUG IF
—you have a history of peptic ulcer or recurrent gastritis, duodenitis, ileitis, or colitis.
—you have diverticulosis.
—you have a history of heart disease.
—you have a tendency to retain water and develop edema.
—you have a history of kidney disease or reduced kidney function.

Time Required for Apparent Benefit
Drug action begins in 1 to 2 hours, reaches a maximum in 2 to 4 hours, and gradually subsides within 24 to 26 hours. Significant improvement may require continuous use on a regular schedule for 1 to 2 weeks.

Possible Side-Effects *(natural, expected, and unavoidable drug actions)*
Prolongation of bleeding time.

CAUTION
1. The elderly (over 60 years of age) are more susceptible to stomach bleeding with the use of this drug.
2. This drug's anti-inflammatory and antipyretic effects can make it more difficult to recognize the presence of infection. If you develop any symptoms that suggest an active infection, inform your physician promptly.

Possible Adverse Effects *(unusual, unexpected, and infrequent reactions)*
IF ANY OF THE FOLLOWING DEVELOP, DISCONTINUE DRUG AND NOTIFY YOUR PHYSICIAN AS SOON AS POSSIBLE

Mild Adverse Effects
Allergic Reactions: Itching, rash, hives, localized swellings, spontaneous bruising.
Headache, lightheadedness, dizziness, ringing in the ears, drowsiness, fatigue, inability to concentrate.
Nausea, vomiting, heartburn, indigestion, abdominal pain, diarrhea, irritation of mouth.
Mild fluid retention (edema) in face or legs.

Serious Adverse Effects
Stomach or intestinal bleeding, mild to severe, with or without the development of ulcer. (Observe for dark-colored stools.)
Hepatitis with jaundice (see Glossary).
Visual disturbances due to corneal changes, lens opacities, retinal changes.
Hearing impairment.
Reduction of white blood cells and/or blood platelets (see Glossary).
Diverticulitis.

Advisability of Use During Pregnancy
Safety not established. Prudent use is best determined by the physician's evaluation.

Advisability of Use While Nursing Infant
This drug is known to be present in milk in very small amounts. Ask physician for guidance.

Habit-Forming Potential
None.

Effects of Overdosage
With Moderate Overdose: Nausea, vomiting, heartburn.
With Large Overdose: Drowsiness. No other serious or threatening effects reported to date.

Possible Effects of Extended Use
Eye changes such as opacities in the cornea or lens, deterioration of the retina (macular area).

Recommended Periodic Examinations While Taking This Drug
Complete blood cell counts to detect development of:
Anemia, due to silent bleeding from the stomach.
Reduction of white blood cells.
Reduction of blood platelets.
Liver function tests.
Complete eye examinations if any change in vision occurs.
Hearing examinations if ringing in the ears or hearing impairment develops.

While Taking This Drug, Observe the Following
Foods: No restrictions. This drug should be taken with food if stomach irritation occurs.
Beverages: No restrictions. May be taken with milk.
Alcohol: Use with caution. The irritant action of alcohol on the stomach lining added to the irritant action of naproxen in sensitive individuals can increase the risk of stomach bleeding or ulceration.
Tobacco Smoking: No interactions expected.
Other Drugs
Naproxen may *increase* the effects of
• anticoagulants of the coumarin family (see Drug Family, Section Four).
• anti-diabetic drugs of the sulfonylurea family (see Drug Family, Section Four).
• phenytoin (Dantoin, Dilantin, etc.).
• sulfonamides (see Drug Family, Section Four).

The following drug may *decrease* the effects of naproxen
• aspirin may hasten its elimination from the body.
Driving a Vehicle, Piloting a Plane, Operating Machinery: Use caution until full effect has been determined. This drug can cause drowsiness and dizziness and can impair the ability to engage safely in hazardous activities.
Exposure to Sun: No restrictions.

Special Storage Instructions
Keep in a dry, tightly closed container.

NICOTINIC ACID/NIACIN

Year Introduced: 1937

Brand Names

USA	Canada
Niacin (Various Manufacturers)	Niacin (Various Manufacturers)
Nicalex (Merrell-National)	Novoniacin (Novopharm)
Nicobid (Armour)	Nico-Metrazol [CD]
Nicolar (Armour)	(Pentagone)
Nico-Span (Key)	
Nicotinex Elixir (Fleming)	
(Numerous other brand and combination brand names)	

Drug Family: Vasodilator; Cholesterol Reducer (Antihyperlipemic)

Prescription Required: For tablets and elixir—No
For prolonged action capsules—Yes

Available Dosage Forms and Strengths
Tablets — 25 mg., 50 mg., 100 mg., 500 mg.
Prolonged Action Capsules — 125 mg., 250 mg., 400 mg.
Elixir — 500 mg. per tablespoonful

How This Drug Works
Intended Therapeutic Effect(s)
- prevention and treatment of pellagra, a disease resulting from deficiency of nicotinic acid and characterized by dermatitis, diarrhea, and mental disturbances.
- increased circulation of blood to the head, thought to be of benefit in the treatment of vertigo, ringing in the ears, and premenstrual headache.
- reduction of the blood levels of cholesterol and triglycerides (using doses of 3 grams daily).

Location of Drug Action(s)
- tissues throughout the body that require nicotinic acid as a component of essential enzyme systems.
- blood vessels in the skin of the "blush area" (the face and neck).
- fatty tissues throughout the body; possibly the liver.

Method of Drug Action(s)

By correcting a deficiency of nicotinic acid in the tissues, this drug in adequate dosage can prevent or relieve the manifestations of pellagra. Dilation of blood vessels is thought to be limited to the skin, an action of questionable therapeutic value. Increased blood flow within the brain has not been demonstrated.

It is thought that this drug (in large dosage) reduces the initial production of cholesterol and prevents the conversion of fatty tissue to cholesterol and triglycerides.

THIS DRUG SHOULD NOT BE TAKEN IF

—you have had an allergic reaction to any dosage form of it previously. A combination drug [CD] should not be taken if you are allergic to *any* of its ingredients.

—you have impaired liver function.

—you have an active peptic ulcer (stomach or duodenum).

INFORM YOUR PHYSICIAN BEFORE TAKING THIS DRUG IF

—you have a history of peptic ulcer, liver disease, jaundice, or gall bladder disease.

—you have diabetes.

—you have gout.

Time Required for Apparent Benefit

Drug action begins in approximately 15 to 20 minutes and persists for 1 hour.

Possible Side-Effects *(natural, expected, and unavoidable drug actions)*

Flushing, itching, or tingling sensations, and feeling of warmth. Sensitive individuals may experience orthostatic hypotension (see Glossary).

CAUTION

Small doses (as used for vasodilation) are usually well tolerated and free of serious adverse effects. Large doses used for prolonged periods of time may be more hazardous.

Possible Adverse Effects *(unusual, unexpected, and infrequent reactions)*

IF ANY OF THE FOLLOWING DEVELOP, DISCONTINUE DRUG AND NOTIFY YOUR PHYSICIAN AS SOON AS POSSIBLE

Mild Adverse Effects

Allergic Reactions: Skin rash, itching, hives.
Headache, dimness of vision.
Nausea, indigestion, vomiting, diarrhea.
Dryness of skin, grayish-black pigmentation of skin folds.

Serious Adverse Effects

Activation of peptic ulcer.
Hepatitis with jaundice (see Glossary)—yellow eyes and skin, dark-colored urine, light-colored stools.
Worsening of diabetes and gout.

Advisability of Use During Pregnancy
Safety not established for the use of this drug in large doses. Prudent use is best determined by the physician's evaluation.

Advisability of Use While Nursing Infant
Presence of drug in milk is not known. Safety for infant not established. Ask physician for guidance.

Habit-Forming Potential
None.

Effects of Overdosage
With Moderate Overdose: Severe generalized flushing, nausea, vomiting, abdominal cramping, diarrhea.
With Large Overdose: Weakness, lightheadedness, fainting, sweating.

Possible Effects of Extended Use
Disturbance of liver function.

Recommended Periodic Examinations While Taking This Drug
Liver function tests.
Measurement of blood sugar (glucose) levels.
Measurement of blood uric acid levels.

While Taking This Drug, Observe the Following
Foods: No interactions. Advisable to take drug with or following food to reduce stomach irritation.
Beverages: No restrictions.
Alcohol: Use caution until combined effects have been determined. Alcohol used with large doses of this drug may cause excessive lowering of the blood pressure.
Tobacco Smoking: The nicotine in tobacco can cause blood vessel constriction, the opposite of the dilation produced by nicotinic acid. Smoking may reduce the effectiveness of this drug.
Other Drugs
Nicotinic acid may *increase* the effects of
- some anti-hypertensive drugs, and cause excessive lowering of the blood pressure. Dosage adjustments may be necessary for guanethidine (Ismelin, Esimil), mecamylamine (Inversine), methyldopa (Aldomet), pargyline (Eutonyl), and propranolol (Inderal).

Nicotinic acid may *decrease* the effects of
- anti-diabetic drugs, by raising the level of blood sugar. Doses of insulin or oral anti-diabetic drugs may have to be raised or the diet may have to be modified.

Driving a Vehicle, Piloting a Plane, Operating Machinery: Usually no restrictions. Determine first that this drug does not cause orthostatic hypotension.
Exposure to Sun: No restrictions.

Special Storage Instructions
Keep in a dry, tightly closed container.

NITROFURANTOIN

Year Introduced: 1953

Brand Names

USA

Furachel (Rachelle)
Furadantin (Eaton)
Furalan (Lannett)
Furaloid (Edwards)
Furantoin (North Amer.
  Pharm.)
Macrodantin (Eaton)
Nitrex (Star)
Nitrodan (Century)
Parfuran (Parke-Davis)
Sarodant (Saron)
Trantoin (McKesson)
Urotoin (Scruggs)

Canada

Furadantin (Eaton)
Furanex (Elliott-Marion)
Furanite (Saunders)
Furatine (ICN)
Macrodantin (Eaton)
Nephronex (Cortunon)
Nifuran (Maney)
Novofuran (Novopharm)

Drug Family: Antimicrobial (Anti-infective) [Nitrofurans]

Prescription Required: Yes

Available Dosage Forms and Strengths
Tablets — 50 mg., 100 mg.
Capsules — 25 mg., 50 mg., 100 mg.
Oral Suspension — 25 mg. per teaspoonful

How This Drug Works

Intended Therapeutic Effect(s):   The elimination of infections responsive to the action of this drug.

Location of Drug Action(s):   Any body tissue or fluid in which sufficient concentration of the drug can be achieved.

Method of Drug Action(s):   Not completely established. It is thought that this drug prevents growth and multiplication of susceptible bacteria by interfering with the function of essential enzyme systems.

THIS DRUG SHOULD NOT BE TAKEN IF

—you have had an allergic reaction to any dosage form of it previously.
—you have serious impairment of kidney function.
—you are in the last month of pregnancy.
—you cannot abstain from drinking alcohol.
—it is prescribed for an infant under 1 month of age.

INFORM YOUR PHYSICIAN BEFORE TAKING THIS DRUG IF
—you are allergic to any nitrofuran drug.
—you have a history of kidney disease.

Time Required for Apparent Benefit
From 1 to 2 weeks. Periodic urine examinations required to evaluate response.

Possible Side-Effects *(natural, expected, and unavoidable drug actions)*
Brown discoloration of the urine, of no significance.

Possible Adverse Effects *(unusual, unexpected, and infrequent reactions)*
IF ANY OF THE FOLLOWING DEVELOP, DISCONTINUE DRUG AND NOTIFY
YOUR PHYSICIAN AS SOON AS POSSIBLE

Mild Adverse Effects
Allergic Reactions: Skin rashes (various kinds), hives, itching, swelling of
face or extremities, fever, chills.
Nausea, vomiting, diarrhea, abdominal cramps.
Headache, dizziness, drowsiness, muscle aching, temporary loss of hair,
impaired color vision, burning and tearing of eyes.

Serious Adverse Effects
Allergic Reactions: Anaphylactic reaction (see Glossary), severe allergic
reaction in lungs (giving the appearance of pneumonia), asthma, jaun-
dice, drop in blood pressure, joint pain.
Idiosyncratic Reaction: Hemolytic anemia (see Glossary).
Peripheral neuritis (see Glossary).
Liver damage with jaundice (see Glossary).
Superinfections (see Glossary).

Advisability of Use During Pregnancy
Safety not established. Prudent use is best determined by the physician's
evaluation.

Advisability of Use While Nursing Infant
Drug can be present in milk. Safety for infant not established. Ask physician
for guidance.

Habit-Forming Potential
None.

Effects of Overdosage
Nausea, vomiting, abdominal pain, diarrhea.

Possible Effects of Extended Use
Varying degrees of allergic reaction within the lungs, from mild to severe.
(Physician should be informed of chest pain, shortness of breath, or cough.)
Superinfections (see Glossary) within the urinary system.

Recommended Periodic Examinations While Taking This Drug
Complete blood cell counts.
Liver function tests.
X-ray examination of lungs (during extended use of drug).

While Taking This Drug, Observe the Following
Foods: No restrictions of food selection. Drug should be taken with meals, or with food or milk if taken at bedtime.

Beverages: No restrictions.

Alcohol: Use with extreme caution until combined effects have been determined. This drug, in combination with alcohol, may cause a disulfiram-like reaction in sensitive individuals (see Glossary).

Tobacco Smoking: No interactions expected.

Other Drugs

The following drugs may *increase* the effects of nitrofurantoin
• probenecid (Benemid) may delay its elimination from the body.

The following drugs may *decrease* the effects of nitrofurantoin
• phenobarbital may reduce its absorption and hasten its elimination from the body.
• nalidixic acid (NegGram) may reduce its antimicrobial action and impair its effectiveness in treatment.

Driving a Vehicle, Piloting a Plane, Operating Machinery: No restrictions unless dizziness occurs.

Exposure to Sun: No restrictions.

Special Storage Instructions
Keep in a tightly closed, light-resistant container.

NITROGLYCERIN
Year Introduced: 1890

Brand Names

USA	Canada
Nitrobid (Marion)	Nitrol (K-U)
Nitroglyn (Key	Nitrong (U.S. Ethicals)
Pharmaceuticals)	Nitrostabilin (A & H)
Nitro-Span (USV	Nitrostat (P.D. & Co.)
Pharmaceutical)	
Nitrostat (Parke-Davis)	
(Numerous other brand	
names)	

Drug Family: Anti-anginal (Vasodilator) [Nitrates]

Prescription Required: Yes

Available Dosage Forms and Strengths
Sublingual Tablets — 0.15 mg., 0.3 mg., 0.4 mg., 0.6 mg.
Prolonged Action Tablets — 1.3 mg., 2.6 mg., 6.5 mg.
Prolonged Action Capsules — 2.5 mg., 6.5 mg.

How This Drug Works
Intended Therapeutic Effect(s):   Reduction in the frequency and severity of pain associated with angina pectoris (coronary insufficiency).
Location of Drug Action(s):   The muscular tissue in the walls of the blood vessels. The principal site of therapeutic action is the system of coronary arteries in the heart.
Method of Drug Action(s):   This drug acts directly on the muscle cell to produce relaxation. This permits expansion of blood vessels and increases the supply of blood and oxygen to meet the needs of the working heart muscle.

THIS DRUG SHOULD NOT BE TAKEN IF
—you have had an allergic reaction to any dosage form of it previously.

INFORM YOUR PHYSICIAN BEFORE TAKING THIS DRUG IF
—you have glaucoma.
—you have had an unfavorable response to any vasodilator drug in the past.

Time Required for Apparent Benefit
The action of the sublingual tablet (dissolved under the tongue) begins in 1 to 3 minutes and persists for approximately 20 minutes. The action of the prolonged action preparations begins in approximately 30 minutes and persists for 8 to 12 hours.

Possible Side-Effects *(natural, expected, and unavoidable drug actions)*
Flushing of the face, throbbing in the head, increased heart rate (faster pulse), lightheadedness in upright position (see orthostatic hypotension in Glossary)

Possible Adverse Effects *(unusual, unexpected, and infrequent reactions)*

IF ANY OF THE FOLLOWING DEVELOP, DISCONTINUE DRUG AND NOTIFY YOUR PHYSICIAN AS SOON AS POSSIBLE

Mild Adverse Effects
Allergic Reactions: Skin rash.
Headache (may be persistent), dizziness, fainting.
Nausea, vomiting.
Serious Adverse Effects
Allergic Reactions: Severe dermatitis with peeling of skin.

Advisability of Use During Pregnancy
Safety not established. Prudent use is best determined by the physician's evaluation.

Advisability of Use While Nursing Infant
Presence of drug in milk is not known. Safety for infant not established. Ask physician for guidance.

Habit-Forming Potential
None.

Effects of Overdosage
With Moderate Overdose: Headache, dizziness, marked flushing of the skin.

With Large Overdose: Vomiting, weakness, sweating, fainting, shortness of breath, coma.

Possible Effects of Extended Use
The development of tolerance (see Glossary), which may reduce the drug's effectiveness at recommended doses.

The development of abnormal hemoglobin (red blood cell pigment).

Recommended Periodic Examinations While Taking This Drug
Measurement of internal eye pressure in those individuals with glaucoma or a tendency to glaucoma.

Red blood cell counts and hemoglobin measurements.

While Taking This Drug, Observe the Following
Foods: No restrictions.

Beverages: No restrictions.

Alcohol: Use extreme caution until combined effects have been determined. Avoid alcohol completely in the presence of any side effects or adverse effects from nitroglycerin. Never use alcohol in the presence of a nitroglycerin headache.

Tobacco Smoking: Nicotine may reduce the effectiveness of this drug. Follow physician's advice regarding smoking, based upon its effect on the condition under treatment and its possible interaction with this drug.

Other Drugs

Nitroglycerin may *increase* the effects of

• atropine-like drugs (see Drug Family, Section Four), and cause an increase in internal eye pressure.

• tricyclic antidepressants (see Drug Family, Section Four), and cause excessive lowering of the blood pressure.

Nitroglycerin may *decrease* the effects of

• all choline-like drugs, such as Mestinon, Mytelase, pilocarpine, Prostigmin, and Urecholine.

Nitroglycerin *taken concurrently* with

• anti-hypertensive drugs, may cause severe drop in blood pressure. Careful monitoring of drug response and appropriate dosage adjustments are necessary.

The following drugs may *increase* the effects of nitroglycerin

• propranolol (Inderal) may cause additional lowering of the blood pressure. Dosage adjustments may be necessary.

Driving a Vehicle, Piloting a Plane, Operating Machinery: Usually no restrictions. Before engaging in hazardous activities, determine that this drug will not cause you to have orthostatic hypotension.

Exposure to Sun: No restrictions.

Exposure to Cold: Cold environment may reduce the effectiveness of this drug.

Heavy Exercise or Exertion: This drug may improve your ability to be more active without resulting anginal pain. Use caution and avoid excessive exertion that could cause heart injury if warning pain is delayed.

Special Storage Instructions
To prevent loss of strength
- keep tablets in the original glass container.
- do not transfer tablets to a plastic or metallic container (such as a pill box).
- do not place absorbent cotton, paper (such as the prescription label), or other material inside the container.
- do not store other drugs in the same container.
- close the container tightly immediately after each use.
- store at room temperature (59° to 86° F, 15° to 30° C).

Do Not Use the Sublingual Tablet of This Drug If Older Than
60 days from the date of opening the original container. With repeated exposure to air, nitroglycerin gradually loses its strength and becomes ineffective.

NORTRIPTYLINE

Year Introduced: 1964

Brand Names

USA	Canada
Aventyl (Lilly)	Aventyl (Lilly)

Drug Family: Antidepressant, Tricyclic (Anti-psychotic)

Prescription Required: Yes

Available Dosage Forms and Strengths
Capsules — 10 mg., 25 mg.
Oral Liquid — 10 mg. per teaspoonful

How This Drug Works
Intended Therapeutic Effect(s):   Gradual improvement of mood and relief of emotional depression.

Location of Drug Action(s):   Those areas of the brain that determine mood and emotional stability.

Method of Drug Action(s):   Not established. Present thinking is that this drug slowly restores to normal levels certain constitutents of brain tissue (such as norepinephrine) that transmit nerve impulses.

THIS DRUG SHOULD NOT BE TAKEN IF
—you have had an allergic reaction to any dosage form of it previously.

—you are taking or have taken within the past 14 days any mono-amine oxidase (MAO) inhibitor drug (see Drug Family, Section Four).
—you are recovering from a recent heart attack.
—you have glaucoma (narrow-angle type).
—it is prescribed for a child under 12 years of age.

INFORM YOUR PHYSICIAN BEFORE TAKING THIS DRUG IF
—you are allergic or sensitive to any other tricyclic antidepressant (see Drug Family, Section Four).
—you have a history of any of the following: diabetes, epilepsy, glaucoma, heart disease, prostate gland enlargement, or overactive thyroid function.
—you plan to have surgery under general anesthesia in the near future.

Time Required for Apparent Benefit
Some benefit may be apparent within the first 1 to 2 weeks. Adequate response may require continuous treatment for 4 to 6 weeks.

Possible Side-Effects *(natural, expected, and unavoidable drug actions)*
Drowsiness, blurring of vision, dryness of mouth, constipation, impaired urination.

CAUTION
The possibility of adverse effects from this drug is greater in the elderly (over 60 years of age). Small doses are advisable until tolerance has been determined.

Possible Adverse Effects *(unusual, unexpected, and infrequent reactions)*
IF ANY OF THE FOLLOWING DEVELOP, DISCONTINUE DRUG AND NOTIFY YOUR PHYSICIAN AS SOON AS POSSIBLE
Mild Adverse Effects
Allergic Reactions: Skin rash, hives, swelling of face or tongue, drug fever.
Nausea, indigestion, irritation of tongue or mouth, peculiar taste.
Headache, dizziness, weakness, fainting, unsteady gait, tremors.
Swelling of testicles, breast enlargement, milk formation.
Fluctuation of blood sugar levels.
Serious Adverse Effects
Allergic Reactions: Hepatitis with jaundice (see Glossary).
Confusion (especially in the elderly), hallucinations, agitation, restlessness, nightmares.
Heart palpitation and irregular rhythm.
Bone marrow depression (see Glossary)—fatigue, weakness, fever, sore throat, unusual bleeding or bruising.
Peripheral neuritis (see Glossary)—numbness, tingling, pain, loss of strength in arms and legs.
Parkinson-like disorders (see Glossary)—usually mild and infrequent; more likely to occur in the elderly (over 60 years of age).

Advisability of Use During Pregnancy
Safety not established. Prudent use is best determined by the physician's evaluation.

Advisability of Use While Nursing Infant
This drug may be present in milk in small quantities. Ask physician for guidance.

Habit-Forming Potential
Psychological or physical dependence is rare and unexpected.

Effects of Overdosage
With Moderate Overdose: Confusion, hallucinations, extreme drowsiness, drop in body temperature, heart palpitation, dilated pupils, tremors.
With Large Overdose: Stupor, deep sleep, coma, convulsions.

Possible Effects of Extended Use
None reported.

Recommended Periodic Examinations While Taking This Drug
Complete blood cell counts.
Liver function tests.
Serial blood pressure readings and electrocardiograms.

While Taking This Drug, Observe the Following
Foods: No restrictions.
Beverages: No restrictions.
Alcohol: Avoid completely. This drug can increase markedly the intoxicating effects of alcohol and accentuate its depressant action on brain function.
Tobacco Smoking: No interactions expected.
Other Drugs

Nortriptyline may *increase* the effects of
- atropine and drugs with atropine-like actions (see Drug Family, Section Four).
- sedatives, sleep-inducing drugs, tranquilizers, antihistamines, and narcotic drugs, and cause oversedation. Dosage adjustments may be necessary.
- levodopa (Dopar, Larodopa, etc.), in its control of Parkinson's disease.

Nortriptyline may *decrease* the effects of
- guanethidine, and reduce its effectiveness in lowering blood pressure.
- other commonly used anti-hypertensive drugs. Ask physician for guidance regarding the need to monitor blood pressure readings and to adjust dosage of antihypertensive medications. (The action of Aldomet is not decreased by tricyclic antidepressants.)

Nortriptyline *taken concurrently* with
- thyroid preparations, may cause impairment of heart rhythm and function. Ask physician for guidance regarding thyroid dosage adjustment.
- ethchlorvynol (Placidyl), may cause delirium.
- quinidine, may cause impairment of heart rhythm and function. Avoid the combined use of these two drugs.
- mono-amine oxidase (MAO) inhibitor drugs (see Drug Family, Section Four), may cause high fever, delirium, and convulsions.

The following drugs may *increase* the effects of nortriptyline
• thiazide diuretics (see Drug Family, Section Four) may slow its elimination from the body. Overdosage may occur.

Driving a Vehicle, Piloting a Plane, Operating Machinery: This drug may impair mental alertness, judgment, physical coordination, and reaction time. Avoid hazardous activities.

Exposure to Sun: Use caution until sensitivity to sun has been determined. This drug may cause photosensitivity (see Glossary).

Discontinuation: If it has been necessary to use this drug for an extended period of time, do not discontinue it abruptly. Ask physician for guidance regarding dosage reduction and withdrawal. It may be necessary to adjust the dosage of other drugs taken concurrently.

Special Storage Instructions
Keep in a dry, tightly closed container.

NYSTATIN

Year Introduced: 1954

Brand Names

USA	Canada
Mycostatin (Squibb)	Mycostatin (Squibb)
Nilstat (Lederle)	Nadostine (Nadeau)
O-V Statin (Squibb)	Nilstat (Lederle)
Declostatin [CD] (Lederle)	
Mycolog [CD] (Squibb)	
(Others)	

Drug Family: Antibiotic, Antifungal (Antimycotic)

Prescription Required: Yes

Available Dosage Forms and Strengths
Tablets — 500,000 units
Vaginal Tablets — 100,000 units
Suspension — 100,000 units per ml.
Ointment and Cream — 100,000 units per gram

How This Drug Works
Intended Therapeutic Effect(s): The elimination of fungus infections responsive to the action of this drug.

Location of Drug Action(s): Those body tissues and fluids infected by certain strains of fungus, and in which an adequate concentration of the drug can be achieved.

Method of Drug Action(s):   This drug prevents the growth and multiplication of susceptible strains of fungus by attacking the walls of the infecting organism and causing the leakage of essential internal components.

THIS DRUG SHOULD NOT BE TAKEN IF
—you have had an allergic reaction to any dosage form of it previously.

Time Required for Apparent Benefit
Drug action begins immediately on contact with the infecting yeast organisms. Complete cure may require continuous use on a regular schedule for 1 to 3 weeks depending upon the location and extent of the infection.

Possible Side-Effects *(natural, expected, and unavoidable drug actions)*
None reported.

CAUTION
To accomplish complete cure of infection, it is advisable to continue treatment several days after all symptoms (indications of infection) have disappeared.

Possible Adverse Effects *(unusual, unexpected, and infrequent reactions)*
IF ANY OF THE FOLLOWING DEVELOP, DISCONTINUE DRUG AND NOTIFY YOUR PHYSICIAN AS SOON AS POSSIBLE
Mild Adverse Effects
   Allergic Reactions: Irritation and itching of tissues on local application.
Serious Adverse Effects
   None reported.

Advisability of Use During Pregnancy
This drug is not absorbed into the bloodstream. It is considered safe to use during pregnancy.

Advisability of Use While Nursing Infant
This drug does not appear in the milk. It is considered safe to use while nursing infant.

Habit-Forming Potential
   None.

Effects of Overdosage
   With Moderate Overdose: Nausea, vomiting, diarrhea.
   With Large Overdose: No significant or threatening effects.

Possible Effects of Extended Use
   None known.

Recommended Periodic Examinations While Taking This Drug
   Laboratory examination at end of treatment course to determine degree of response.

While Taking This Drug, Observe the Following
   Foods: No restrictions.
   Beverages: No restrictions.

Alcohol: No interactions expected.
Tobacco Smoking: No interactions expected.
Other Drugs: No interactions reported.
Driving a Vehicle, Piloting a Plane, Operating Machinery: No restrictions or precautions.
Exposure to Sun: No restrictions.

Special Storage Instructions
Keep tablets in a dry, tightly closed container, at room temperature. Keep liquid preparations in a cool place. Protect from light and high temperatures. Use within one week after preparation.

ORAL CONTRACEPTIVES
"The Pill"

Year Introduced: 1960

Brand Names

USA	Canada
Combination Type*	Combination Type*
Demulen (Searle)	Anoryol (Desbergers)
Enovid-E (Searle)	Demulen (Searle)
Enovid 5 mg. (Searle)	Enovid (Searle)
Enovid 10 mg. (Searle)	Enovid-E (Searle)
Loestrin 1/20	Loestrin 1.5/30 (P.D.
(Parke-Davis)	& Co.)
Loestrin 1.5/30	Logest 1/50 (Lederle)
(Parke-Davis)	Logest 1.5/30 (Lederle)
Lo/Ovral (Wyeth)	Lyndiol-22 (Organon)
Norinyl 1+50 (Syntex)	Min-Ovral (Wyeth)
Norinyl 1+80 (Syntex)	Norinyl-1 (Syntex)
Norinyl 2 mg. (Syntex)	Norinyl 1+80 (Syntex)
Norlestrin 1/50	Norinyl-2 (Syntex)
(Parke-Davis)	Norlestrin 1.0 mg.
Norlestrin 2.5/50	(P.D. & Co.)
(Parke-Davis)	Norlestrin 2.5 mg.
Norlestrin Fe 1/50	(P.D. & Co.)
(Parke-Davis)	Novinol (Desbergers)
Norlestrin Fe 2.5/50	Ortho-Novum 0.5 mg.
(Parke-Davis)	(Ortho)
Ortho-Novum 1/50	Ortho-Novum 1/50
(Ortho)	(Ortho)

*Contains estrogen and progestin.

(continued)

Ortho-Novum 1/80	Ortho-Novum 1/80
(Ortho)	(Ortho)
Ortho-Novum 2 mg.	Ortho-Novum 2 mg.
(Ortho)	(Ortho)
Ortho-Novum 10 mg.	Ortho-Novum 5 mg.
(Ortho)	(Ortho)
Ovral (Wyeth)	Ovral (Wyeth)
Ovulen (Searle)	Ovulen 0.5 mg. (Searle)
Zorane (Lederle)	Ovulen 1 mg. (Searle)
"Mini-Pill" Type**	"Mini-Pill" Type**
Micronor 0.35 mg.	Micronor (Ortho)
(Ortho)	Noriday (Syntex)
Nor-Q.D. (Syntex)	Ovrette (Wyeth)
Ovrette (Wyeth)	

Drug Family: Oral Contraceptives (Estrogen + Progestin)

Prescription Required: Yes

Available Dosage Forms and Strengths

Tablets — Numerous combinations of varying strengths (examine package label of drug prescribed)

How This Drug Works

Intended Therapeutic Effect(s):   The prevention of pregnancy by suppression of ovulation.

Location of Drug Action(s):   Principal actions occur in
- a major control center in the brain known as the hypothalamus.
- the pituitary gland.

Method of Drug Action(s):   When the combination of an estrogen and a progestin are taken in sufficient dosage and on a regular basis, their blood and tissue levels increase to resemble those that occur during pregnancy. This results in suppression of the two pituitary gland hormones that normally produce ovulation (the formation and release of an egg by the ovary).

THIS DRUG SHOULD NOT BE TAKEN IF

—you are allergic to either of the drugs contained in the brand prescribed (see package label).

—you have now, or have had in the past, any form of phlebitis, embolism, stroke, angina, or heart attack (coronary thrombosis).

—you have active liver disease or impaired liver function.

—you have a history of cancer of the breast or reproductive organs.

—you have abnormal and unexplained vaginal bleeding.

**Contains progestin only.

INFORM YOUR PHYSICIAN BEFORE TAKING THIS DRUG IF

—you have had an unfavorable reaction of any kind to any oral contraceptive in the past.
—you have cystic disease of the breasts (cystic mastitis).
—you have fibroid tumors of the uterus.
—you have a history of migraine headaches.
—you have epilepsy.
—you have a history of asthma or heart disease.
—you have diabetes or a tendency to diabetes.
—you have high blood pressure.
—you have a history of endometriosis.
—you plan to have surgery within 1 month.
—you smoke 15 or more cigarettes daily.

Time Required for Apparent Benefit

When the dosage schedule is followed exactly (one pill every scheduled day at the same time), the effectiveness of these drugs approaches 100%. Missed doses are the main reason for treatment failure and the occurrence of pregnancy. However, during the first 10 days of the first month of treatment, another method of birth control is advisable since early ovulation (and possible pregnancy) may occur before these drugs have become fully effective.

Possible Side-Effects *(natural, expected, and unavoidable drug actions)*

Retention of fluid, gain in weight, "breakthrough" bleeding (spotting in middle of menstrual cycle), change in menstrual flow, absence of menstrual flow (during regular use and after permanent withdrawal). There may be an increased tendency to acquire a yeast infection of the genital tissues.

CAUTION

1. The incidence of serious adverse effects due to the use of these drugs is very low.* However, you should report any unusual development to your physician promptly for evaluation.
2. Recent studies suggest that women over 40 years of age who use oral contraceptives are at significantly greater risk of having a heart attack than nonusers.*
3. Certain commonly used drugs may reduce the effectiveness of oral contraceptives (some of these are listed in the section Other Drugs, below).

Possible Adverse Effects *(unusual, unexpected, and infrequent reactions)*

IF ANY OF THE FOLLOWING DEVELOP, DISCONTINUE DRUG AND NOTIFY YOUR PHYSICIAN AS SOON AS POSSIBLE

Mild Adverse Effects

Allergic Reactions: Skin rashes, itching, hives.
Headache, nervous tension, and irritability.

*See tables at the end of this Profile.

Accentuation of migraine headaches.

Nausea, vomiting, bloating.

Breast enlargement, tenderness, and secretion.

Tannish pigmentation of the face.

Reduced tolerance to contact lenses.

Impaired color vision: blue tinge to objects, blue halo around lights.

Serious Adverse Effects

Idiosyncratic Reactions: Muscle and joint pains.

Thrombophlebitis (inflammation of a vein with the formation of blood clot) —pain or tenderness in thigh or leg, with or without swelling of the foot, ankle, or leg.

Pulmonary embolism (movement of blood clot to the lung)—sudden shortness of breath and/or pain in the chest, coughing, bloody sputum.

Stroke (blood clot in the brain)—headaches, blackouts, sudden weakness or paralysis of any part of the body, severe dizziness, drooping of eyelid, double vision, slurred speech, inability to speak.

Rise in blood pressure—increasing headaches.

Coronary thrombosis (heart attack)—sudden pain in heart area, weakness.

Retinal thrombosis (blood clot in eye vessels)—sudden impairment or loss of vision.

Hepatitis with jaundice (see Glossary)—yellow eyes and skin, dark-colored urine, light-colored stools.

Emotional depression (may be severe).

Formation of benign liver tumors—discomfort in the right upper abdomen, acute pain in the abdomen due to internal bleeding (from liver tumor).

Gall bladder disease—indigestion and discomfort in the right upper abdomen after eating fatty foods. (Recent studies suggest an increased risk of gall bladder disease in oral contraceptive users.)

Advisability of Use During Pregnancy

There is a possibility that this drug could be taken during the early weeks of an unrecognized pregnancy. Safety for the fetus has not been established. Usage during pregnancy should be avoided. If you have 2 consecutive cycles without menstruation (following the 7-day withdrawal of the drug), notify your physician so an examination for pregnancy can be made.

Advisability of Use While Nursing Infant

The components of this drug are known to be present in milk. Safety for the infant has not been established. Ask physician for guidance. It is generally felt that this drug should not be taken while nursing.

Habit-Forming Potential

None.

Effects of Overdosage

With Moderate Overdose: Headache, nausea, vomiting, fluid retention, abnormal vaginal bleeding, breast enlargement and discomfort.

With Large Overdose: Drowsiness (in some individuals). No serious or dangerous effects reported.

Possible Effects of Extended Use

Increased growth of fibroid tumors of the uterus.

Gradual rise in blood pressure.

Delayed resumption of normal menstruation after discontinuation of drug, with associated difficulty in establishing pregnancy (impaired fertility).

Recommended Periodic Examinations While Taking This Drug

Regular examinations of the breasts and reproductive organs (pelvic examination of uterus and ovaries, including "Pap" smear).

Liver function tests.

While Taking This Drug, Observe the Following

Foods: No restrictions. Ask physician for guidance regarding salt intake if you experience fluid retention. Ask physician regarding the need for supplemental folic acid (Vitamin Bc).

Beverages: No restrictions.

Alcohol: No interactions expected.

Tobacco Smoking: Recent studies strongly suggest that heavy smoking (15 or more cigarettes daily) in association with the use of oral contraceptives significantly increases the risk of heart attack (coronary thrombosis). Heavy smoking should be considered a relative contraindication to the use of oral contraceptives.

Other Drugs

Oral contraceptives may *increase* the effects of

• meperidine (Demerol, pethidine).

• promazine (Sparine).

Oral contraceptives may *decrease* the effects of

• anticoagulants of the coumarin family. Dosage adjustment may be necessary to protect against clotting.

• anti-diabetic drugs (oral tablets and insulin). Dosage adjustment may be necessary to control diabetes.

• clofibrate (Atromid-S), and prevent the lowering of blood cholesterol or triglycerides.

• guanethidine (Ismelin), and reduce its ability to lower the blood pressure.

The following drugs may *decrease* the effects of oral contraceptives

• antihistamines (some)

• meprobamate (Equanil, Miltown, etc.)

• mineral oil

• phenobarbital (possibly other barbiturates)

• phenylbutazone (Azolid, Butazolidin, etc.)

• phenytoin (Dantoin, Dilantin, etc.)

• rifampin (Rifadin, Rifomycin, Rimactane)

Driving a Vehicle, Piloting a Plane, Operating Machinery: No restrictions or precautions.

Exposure to Sun: Use caution until full effect is known. These drugs may cause photosensitivity (see Glossary).

Occurrence of Unrelated Illness: Notify your physician of any illness that causes vomiting or diarrhea; these can interfere with absorption of the drug and reduce its effectiveness.

Discontinuation

If spotting or "breakthrough" bleeding occurs, do not discontinue the drug. If bleeding does not subside, notify your physician.

Remember: failure to take the drug for even 1 day of the dosage schedule may allow pregnancy to occur; use another contraceptive method for the remaining part of the cycle.

It is considered advisable to avoid pregnancy for 6 months after discontinuing these drugs. (This recommendation is based upon the finding of significantly increased chromosome abnormalities in aborted fetuses from women who became pregnant within 6 months of discontinuing oral contraceptives.)

Consult your physician regarding the advisability of continuing or discontinuing this drug prior to any surgery.

Special Storage Instructions

Keep in a dry, tightly closed container. Use of the original container will reduce dosage error.

Comparison of deaths associated with pregnancy and childbirth and with use of oral contraceptives

Age group	Deaths from pregnancy and childbirth*	Deaths from use of oral contraceptives**
15 – 19	10.8	1.3
20 – 24	8.5	1.3
25 – 29	12.1	1.3
30 – 34	25.1	4.8
35 – 39	41.0	6.9
40 – 44	69.1	24.5

*Ratio per 100,000 live births.
**Rate per 100,000 users per year.

Comparison of annual nonfatal heart attacks per 100,000 users and nonusers of oral contraceptives

Age group	OC users	OC nonusers
30 – 39	5.6	2.1
40 – 44	56.9	9.9

Comparison of annual fatal heart attacks per 100,000 users and nonusers of oral contraceptives

Age group	OC users	OC nonusers
30 – 39	5.4	1.9
40 – 44	32.0	12.0

ORPHENADRINE

Year Introduced: 1957

Brand Names

USA	Canada
Disipal (Riker)	Disipal (Riker)
Norflex (Riker)	Norflex (Riker)
Norgesic [CD] (Riker)	Norgesic [CD] (Riker)

Drug Family: Muscle Relaxant; Antihistamines, Anti-parkinsonism, Atropine-like Drug [Anticholinergics]

Prescription Required: Yes

How This Drug Works
  Intended Therapeutic Effect(s)
  • relief of discomfort associated with acutely painful muscle strain.
  • relief of the rigidity, tremor, sluggish movement, and impaired gait associated with Parkinson's disease.

Location of Drug Action(s)
- the site of drug action within the brain responsible for the relief of pain due to muscle spasm is unknown.
- the site of drug action beneficial in the management of Parkinson's disease is the regulating center in the brain (the basal ganglia) that governs the coordination and efficiency of bodily movements.

Method of Drug Action(s)
The action responsible for the relief of pain associated with muscle strain is not fully established. It may be related to sedative and analgesic effects. This drug does not directly relax muscle in spasm due to strain.

The improvement in Parkinson's disease results from the restoration of a more normal balance of the chemical activities responsible for the transmission of nerve impulses within the basal ganglia.

THIS DRUG SHOULD NOT BE TAKEN IF
—you have had an allergic reaction to any dosage form of it previously.

INFORM YOUR PHYSICIAN BEFORE TAKING THIS DRUG IF
—you have glaucoma.
—you have myasthenia gravis.
—you have difficulty emptying the urinary bladder.
—you have a history of heart disease or disturbance of heart rhythm.
—you have a history of peptic ulcer disease.

Time Required for Apparent Benefit
Drug action usually begins in 1 to 2 hours and persists for 8 to 12 hours.

Possible Side-Effects *(natural, expected, and unavoidable drug actions)*
Dryness of the mouth, blurred vision, constipation, slowed urination, drowsiness.

CAUTION
The elderly (over 60 years of age) may experience confusion with the use of this drug. Small doses are advisable until sensitivity and tolerance have been determined.

Possible Adverse Effects *(unusual, unexpected, and infrequent reactions)*

IF ANY OF THE FOLLOWING DEVELOP, DISCONTINUE DRUG AND NOTIFY YOUR PHYSICIAN AS SOON AS POSSIBLE

Mild Adverse Effects
Allergic Reactions: Skin rash, hives, itching.
Headache, lightheadedness, dizziness, weakness, fainting.
Nausea, vomiting.
Palpitation, rapid heart action.

Serious Adverse Effects
Idiosyncratic Reactions: Agitation, hallucinations, tremor.

Advisability of Use During Pregnancy
Safety not established. Prudent use is best determined by the physician's evaluation.

Advisability of Use While Nursing Infant
Presence of drug in milk is not known. Safety for infant not established. Ask physician for guidance.

Habit-Forming Potential
None.

Effects of Overdosage
With Moderate Overdose: Marked dryness of mouth and throat, drowsiness, muscle tremors, fainting.
With Large Overdose: Confusion, convulsions, coma, widely dilated pupils, rapid pulse.

Possible Effects of Extended Use
Increased internal eye pressure, possibly glaucoma.
Safety for continuous long-term use has not been established.

Recommended Periodic Examinations While Taking This Drug
Measurement of internal eye pressure (glaucoma detection) on a regular basis.
Complete blood cell counts.

While Taking This Drug, Observe the Following
Foods: No restrictions. May be taken with or after food to prevent stomach irritation.
Beverages: No restrictions.
Alcohol: Use with caution until combined effect has been determined. Alcohol may increase the drowsiness produced by this drug in sensitive individuals.
Tobacco Smoking: No interactions expected.
Other Drugs
Orphenadrine may *increase* the effects of
• other atropine-like drugs, and intensify their side effects. Dosage adjustments may be necessary.
• levodopa (Dopar, Larodopa, etc.), and improve its effectiveness in the treatment of parkinsonism.

Orphenadrine may *decrease* the effects of
• griseofulvin (Fulvicin, Grifulvin, etc.), and reduce its effectiveness in treating fungus infections.
• phenylbutazone (Azolid, Butazolidin, etc.), and reduce its effectiveness in relieving inflammation and pain.

Orphenadrine *taken concurrently* with

• propoxyphene (Darvon), may cause confusion, nervousness, and tremors in sensitive individuals (probably very rare).

• chlorpromazine (Thorazine), may cause hypoglycemia (see Glossary) in sensitive individuals.

Driving a Vehicle, Piloting a Plane, Operating Machinery: This drug may impair mental alertness, physical control, coordination, and reaction time. Determine tolerance before undertaking hazardous activities.

Exposure to Sun: No restrictions.

Special Storage Instructions
Keep in a dry, tightly closed container. Protect from light.

OXACILLIN

Year Introduced: 1961

Brand Names

USA	Canada
Bactocill (Beecham)	Prostaphlin (Bristol)
Prostaphlin (Bristol)	

Drug Family: Antibiotic (Anti-infective) [Penicillins]

Prescription Required: Yes

Available Dosage Forms and Strengths
Capsules — 250 mg., 500 mg.
Oral Suspension — 250 mg. per teaspoonful

How This Drug Works
Intended Therapeutic Effect(s):   The elimination of infections responsive to the action of this drug.

Location of Drug Action(s):   Any body tissue or fluid in which sufficient concentration of the drug can be achieved.

Method of Drug Action(s):   This drug destroys susceptible infecting bacteria by interfering with their ability to produce new protective cell walls as they multiply and grow.

THIS DRUG SHOULD NOT BE TAKEN IF
—you have had an allergic reaction to any dosage form of it previously.

—you are certain you are allergic to any form of penicillin.

INFORM YOUR PHYSICIAN BEFORE TAKING THIS DRUG IF

—you suspect you may be allergic to penicillin, or you have a history of a previous "reaction" to penicillin.

—you are allergic to cephalopsporin antibiotics (Ancef, Ceporan, Ceporex, Kafocin, Keflex, Keflin, Kefzol, Loridine).

—you are allergic by nature (hayfever, asthma, hives, eczema).

Time Required for Apparent Benefit

Varies with the nature of the infection under treatment; usually from 2 to 5 days.

Possible Side-Effects *(natural, expected, and unavoidable drug actions)*

Superinfections (see Glossary).

Possible Adverse Effects *(unusual, unexpected, and infrequent reactions)*

IF ANY OF THE FOLLOWING DEVELOP, DISCONTINUE DRUG AND NOTIFY YOUR PHYSICIAN AS SOON AS POSSIBLE

Mild Adverse Effects

Allergic Reactions: Skin rashes (various kinds).

Irritation of mouth or tongue, "black tongue," nausea, vomiting, diarrhea, gaseous indigestion.

Serious Adverse Effects

Allergic Reactions: †Anaphylactic reaction (see Glossary), severe skin reactions, high fever, swollen painful joints, sore throat, unusual bleeding or bruising.

Advisability of Use During Pregnancy

Safety not established. Prudent use is best determined by the physician's evaluation.

Advisability of Use While Nursing Infant

Drug may be present in milk and may sensitize infant to penicillin. Ask physician for guidance.

Habit-Forming Potential

None.

Effects of Overdosage

Possible nausea, vomiting, and/or diarrhea.

Possible Effects of Extended Use

Superinfections.

Recommended Periodic Examinations While Taking This Drug

Complete blood cell counts.

Liver and kidney function tests.

---

†A rare but potentially dangerous reaction characteristic of penicillins.

While Taking This Drug, Observe the Following

Foods: No restrictions of food selection. Drug is most effective when taken on an empty stomach, 1 hour before or 2 hours after eating.

Beverages: No restrictions.

Alcohol: No interactions expected.

Tobacco Smoking: No interactions expected.

Other Drugs

The following drugs may *decrease* the effects of oxacillin

- antacids can reduce absorption of oxacillin.
- chloramphenicol (Chloromycetin)
- erythromycin (Erythrocin, E-Mycin, etc.)
- paromomycin (Humatin)
- tetracyclines (Achromycin, Declomycin, Minocin, etc.; see Drug Family, Section Four)
- troleandomycin (Cyclamycin, TAO)

Driving a Vehicle, Piloting a Plane, Operating Machinery: No restrictions.

Exposure to Sun: No restrictions.

Special Storage Instructions

Keep capsules in a tightly closed container, at room temperature. Keep oral suspension refrigerated.

Do Not Take the Oral Suspension of This Drug If It Is Older Than

3 days — when kept at room temperature.

14 days — when kept refrigerated.

OXAZEPAM

Year Introduced: 1965

Brand Names

USA	Canada
Serax (Wyeth)	Serax (Wyeth)

Drug Family: Tranquilizer, Mild (Anti-anxiety) [Benzodiazepines]

Prescription Required: Yes (Controlled Drug, U.S. Schedule 4)

Available Dosage Forms and Strengths

Tablets — 15 mg.

Capsules — 10 mg., 15 mg., 30 mg.

How This Drug Works

Intended Therapeutic Effect(s):   Relief of mild to moderate anxiety and nervous tension, without significant sedation.

Location of Drug Action(s):   Thought to be the limbic system of the brain, one of the centers that influence emotional stability.

Method of Drug Action(s):   Not established. Present thinking is that this drug may reduce the activity of certain parts of the limbic system.

THIS DRUG SHOULD NOT BE TAKEN IF
—you have had an allergic reaction to any dosage form of it previously.
—it is prescribed for a child under 6 years of age.

INFORM YOUR PHYSICIAN BEFORE TAKING THIS DRUG IF
—you are allergic to any drugs chemically related to oxazepam: chlordiazepoxide, clorazepate, diazepam, flurazepam (see Drug Profiles for brand names).
—you have epilepsy.
—you are taking sedative, sleep-inducing, tranquilizer, antidepressant, or anticonvulsant drugs of any kind.
—you plan to have surgery under general anesthesia in the near future.

Time Required for Apparent Benefit
Approximately 1 to 2 hours. For severe symptoms of some duration, relief may require regular medication for several days.

Possible Side-Effects *(natural, expected, and unavoidable drug actions)*
Drowsiness, lethargy, unsteadiness in stance and gait.
In the elderly (over 60 years of age) and debilitated: Confusion, weakness, constipation. The elderly are very susceptible to standard doses.

Possible Adverse Effects *(unusual, unexpected, and infrequent reactions)*

IF ANY OF THE FOLLOWING DEVELOP, DISCONTINUE DRUG AND NOTIFY YOUR PHYSICIAN AS SOON AS POSSIBLE

Mild Adverse Effects
   Allergic Reactions: Skin rashes (various kinds), swelling of face.
   Dizziness, fainting, blurred vision, double vision, slurred speech, headache, nausea.
Serious Adverse Effects
   Allergic Reactions: Jaundice (yellow skin coloration; see Glossary), impaired resistance to infection manifested by fever and/or sore throat.
   Prolonged drop in blood pressure; may be hazardous in the elderly.
   Paradoxical Reactions: Acute excitement, overactivity.

Advisability of Use During Pregnancy
The findings of some recent studies suggest a possible association between the use of a drug closely related to oxazepam during early pregnancy and the occurrence of birth defects, such as cleft lip. It is advisable to avoid this drug completely during the first 3 months of pregnancy.

Advisability of Use While Nursing Infant
With recommended dosage, drug is probably present in milk. Avoid use if possible. Ask physician for guidance.

Habit-Forming Potential
This drug can cause psychological and/or physical dependence (see Glossary) if used in large doses for an extended period of time.

Effects of Overdosage
With Moderate Overdose: Marked drowsiness, weakness, drunkenness, impairment of stance and gait.
With Large Overdose: Stupor progressing to deep sleep or coma.

Possible Effects of Extended Use
Psychological and/or physical dependence.
Impairment of blood cell production.
Impairment of liver function.

Recommended Periodic Examinations While Taking This Drug
Blood cell counts and liver function tests during long-term use.

While Taking This Drug, Observe the Following
Foods: No restrictions.
Beverages: Large intake of coffee, tea, or cola drinks (because of their caffeine content) may reduce the calming action of this drug.
Alcohol: Use with extreme caution until the combined effect is determined. Alcohol may increase the sedative effects of oxazepam. Oxazepam may increase the intoxicating effects of alcohol.
Tobacco Smoking: Heavy smoking may reduce the calming action of oxazepam.
Other Drugs
Oxazepam may *increase* the effects of
• other sedatives, sleep-inducing drugs, tranquilizers, anti-convulsants, and narcotic drugs. Use these only under supervision of a physician. Careful dosage adjustment is necessary.
• oral anticoagulants of the coumarin drug family; ask physician for guidance regarding need for dosage adjustment to prevent bleeding.
• anti-hypertensives, producing excessive lowering of the blood pressure.

Oxazepam *taken concurrently* with
• anti-convulsants, may cause an increase in the frequence or severity of seizures; an increase in the dose of the anti-convulsant may be necessary.
• monoamine oxidase (MAO) inhibitor drugs (see Drug Family, Section Four) may cause extreme sedation, convulsions, or paradoxical excitement or rage.

The following drugs may *increase* the effects of oxazepam
• tricyclic anti-depressants (see Drug Family, Section Four) may increase the sedative effects of oxazepam.
Driving a Vehicle, Piloting a Plane, Operating Machinery: This drug can impair mental alertness, judgment, physical coordination, and reaction time. Avoid hazardous activities.
Exposure to Sun: No restrictions.
Exposure to Heat: Use caution until effect of excessive perspiration is determined. Because of reduced urine volume, oxazepam may accumulate in the body and produce effects of overdosage.
Heavy Exercise or Exertion: No restrictions in cool or temperate weather.

Discontinuation: If it has been necessary to use this drug for an extended period of time do not discontinue it abruptly. Ask physician for guidance regarding dosage reduction and withdrawal. The dosage of other drugs taken concurrently with oxazepam may also require adjustment.

Special Storage Instructions
Keep in a dry, tightly closed, light-resistant container.

OXYCODONE

Year Introduced: 1950

Brand Names

USA	Canada
*Percobarb [CD] (Endo)	Percodan [CD] (Endo)
Percocet-5 [CD] (Endo)	
Percodan [CD] (Endo)	

Drug Family: Analgesic, Mild (Narcotic)

Prescription Required: Yes (Controlled Drug, U.S. Schedule 2)

Available Dosage Forms and Strengths
Tablets — 2.44 mg., 4.88 mg. (in combination with other drugs)

How This Drug Works
Intended Therapeutic Effect(s)
• relief of moderate pain.
• control of coughing.
Location of Drug Action(s)
• those areas of the brain and spinal cord involved in the perception of pain.
• those areas of the brain and spinal cord involved in the cough reflex.
Method of Drug Action(s):   Not completely established. It is thought that this drug affects tissue sites that react specifically with opium and its derivatives to relieve pain and cough.

THIS DRUG SHOULD NOT BE TAKEN IF
—you have had an allergic reaction to any dosage form of it previously.
—it is prescribed for a child under 6 years of age.

INFORM YOUR PHYSICIAN BEFORE TAKING THIS DRUG IF
—you have had an unfavorable reaction to any narcotic drug in the past.
—you are taking any sedatives, sleep-inducing drugs, tranquilizers, other pain-relieving drugs, or antihistamines.
—you have difficulty emptying the urinary bladder.

Time Required for Apparent Benefit
Drug action begins within the first hour and persists for 4 to 5 hours.

*Percobarb contains hexobarbital, a sedative of the barbiturate drug family.

Possible Side-Effects *(natural, expected, and unavoidable drug actions)*
Drowsiness, unsteadiness in stance and gait, constipation.

CAUTION
The elderly (over 60 years of age) may have a reduced tolerance for this drug. Small doses are advisable until full effect has been determined.

Possible Adverse Effects *(unusual, unexpected, and infrequent reactions)*
IF ANY OF THE FOLLOWING DEVELOP, DISCONTINUE DRUG AND NOTIFY YOUR PHYSICIAN AS SOON AS POSSIBLE
Mild Adverse Effects
Allergic Reactions: Itching.
Lightheadedness, dizziness, euphoria.
Nausea, vomiting.
Serious Adverse Effects
None reported.

Advisability of Use During Pregnancy
Safety not established. Prudent use is best determined by the physician's evaluation.

Advisability of Use While Nursing Infant
Safety not established. Avoid use or avoid nursing. Ask physician for guidance.

Habit-Forming Potential
This drug can produce both psychological and physical dependence (see Glossary). Avoid use over an extended period of time.

Effects of Overdosage
With Moderate Overdose: Marked drowsiness, staggering gait, incoordination.
With Large Overdose: Stupor progressing to coma, slow and shallow breathing, cold and clammy skin, weak and slow pulse.

Possible Effects of Extended Use
Psychological and physical dependence.

Recommended Periodic Examinations While Taking This Drug
None required.

While Taking This Drug, Observe The Following
Foods: No restrictions.
Beverages: No restrictions.
Alcohol: Use with extreme caution. Alcohol can increase this drug's sedative and depressant action on brain function. This drug can increase the intoxicating action of alcohol.
Tobacco Smoking: No interactions expected.
Other Drugs
Oxycodone may *increase* the effects of
• sedatives, sleep-inducing drugs, tranquilizers, pain-relieving drugs, nar-

cotic drugs, and antihistamines. Dosage adjustments are necessary to prevent excessive sedation.

Oxycodone *taken concurrently* with
• phenytoin (Dantoin, Dilantin, etc.), may cause excessive depression of brain function. Ask physician for guidance regarding dosage adjustment for proper control of seizures.

The following drugs may *increase* the effects of oxycodone
• all drugs with a sedative action: calming drugs, sleep-inducing drugs, tranquilizers, pain relievers, other narcotic drugs, antihistamines. Dosage adjustments are usually necessary to prevent excessive sedation.

The following drugs may *decrease* the effects of oxycodone
• cyproheptadine (Periactin) may reduce its ability to relieve pain.
• methysergide (Sansert) may reduce its ability to relieve pain.

Driving a Vehicle, Piloting a Plane, Operating Machinery: This drug can impair mental alertness, judgment, physical coordination, and reaction time. Avoid hazardous activities.

Exposure to Sun: No restrictions.

Discontinuation: If it has been necessary to use this drug for an extended period of time, ask physician for guidance regarding gradual reduction and withdrawal.

Special Storage Instructions
Keep in a dry, tightly closed container. Protect from light.

OXYMETAZOLINE

Year Introduced: 1964

Brand Names

USA	Canada
Afrin (Schering)	Nafrine (Schering)

Drug Family: Decongestant [Sympathomimetics]

Prescription Required: No

Available Dosage Forms and Strengths
Nasal Solution — 0.025%, 0.05%
Nasal Spray — 0.025%, 0.05%

How This Drug Works
Intended Therapeutic Effect(s): Relief of congestion of the nose, sinuses, and throat associated with allergic disorders and infections.
Location of Drug Action(s): The small blood vessels (arterioles) in the tissues lining the nasal passages, the sinuses, and the throat.

Method of Drug Action(s):   By contracting the walls and thus reducing the size of the arterioles, this drug decreases the volume of blood in the tissues, resulting in shrinkage of tissue mass (decongestion). This expands the nasal airway and enlarges the openings into the sinuses and eustachian tubes.

THIS DRUG SHOULD NOT BE TAKEN IF
—you have had an allergic reaction to any dosage form of it previously.
—it is prescribed for a child under 6 years of age.

INFORM YOUR PHYSICIAN BEFORE TAKING THIS DRUG IF
—you have high blood pressure or heart disease.
—you have diabetes or an overactive thyroid gland (hyperthyroidism).
—you are taking, or have taken within the past 2 weeks, any mono-amine oxidase (MAO) inhibitor drug (see Drug Family, Section Four).

Time Required for Apparent Benefit
Drug action is usually felt within 5 to 30 minutes after application to nasal membranes and may persist for periods of 4 to 12 hours.

Possible Side-Effects *(natural, expected, and unavoidable drug actions)*
Dryness of nose, nervousness, insomnia.

CAUTION
Too frequent application of nose drops and sprays containing this drug may cause a secondary "rebound" congestion resulting in a form of dependence (see dependence, functional, in Glossary).

Possible Adverse Effects *(unusual, unexpected, and infrequent reactions)*

IF ANY OF THE FOLLOWING DEVELOP, DISCONTINUE DRUG AND NOTIFY YOUR PHYSICIAN AS SOON AS POSSIBLE
Mild Adverse Effects
   Allergic Reactions: None reported.
   Burning and stinging of nose, headache, lightheadedness, heart palpitation, tremor.
Serious Adverse Effects
   None reported.

Advisability of Use During Pregnancy
Safety not established. Prudent use is best determined by the physician's evaluation.

Advisability of Use While Nursing Infant
Safety not established. Ask physician for guidance regarding time and frequency of use with relationship to nursing.

Habit-Forming Potential
Frequent or excessive use may cause functional dependence.

Effects of Overdosage
With Moderate Overdose: Headache, restlessness, sweating, heart palpitation.
With Large Overdose: Anxiety, agitation, rapid and irregular pulse.

Possible Effects of Extended Use
Secondary "rebound" congestion and chemical irritation of nasal membranes.

Recommended Periodic Examinations While Taking This Drug
None required.

While Taking This Drug, Observe the Following
Foods: No restrictions.
Beverages: Heavy use of coffee or tea may add to the nervousness or insomnia experienced by sensitive individuals.
Alcohol: No interactions expected.
Tobacco Smoking: No interactions expected. No restrictions (unless directed otherwise by the physician).
Other Drugs
Oxymetazoline *used concurrently* with
• mono-amine oxidase (MAO) inhibitor drugs, may cause dangerous elevation of the blood pressure.
Driving a Vehicle, Piloting a Plane, Operating Machinery: No restrictions.
Exposure to Sun: No restrictions.

Special Storage Instructions
Keep in a tightly closed container.

OXYPHENBUTAZONE
Year Introduced: 1961

Brand Names

USA	Canada
Oxalid (USV Pharmaceutical)	Tandearil (Geigy)
Tandearil (Geigy)	

Drug Family: Analgesic, Mild; Anti-inflammatory; Fever Reducer (Antipyretic) [Pyrazolines]

Prescription Required: Yes

Available Dosage Forms and Strengths
Tablets — 100 mg.

How This Drug Works
Intended Therapeutic Effect(s): Symptomatic relief of inflammation, swelling, pain, and tenderness associated with arthritis, tendinitis, bursitis, and superficial phlebitis. (This drug does not correct the underlying disease process.)

Location of Drug Action(s):   Areas of inflammation in:
- the soft tissue structures of joints (tendons, ligaments, bursas, etc.).
- the superficial veins.

Method of Drug Action(s):   Not completely established. Present thinking is that this drug acts somewhat like aspirin, by suppressing the formation of prostaglandins (chemicals involved in the production of inflammation).

THIS DRUG SHOULD NOT BE TAKEN IF

—you are allergic to any of the drugs bearing the brand names listed above or to the related drug phenylbutazone (see PHENYLBUTAZONE Drug Profile for brand names).

—you have had a severe reaction to any drug in the past. (Ask physician for guidance.)

—you have a history of blood or bone marrow disease.

—you have a history of stomach or intestinal ulceration, or recurrent indigestion of a serious nature.

—you have a history of disease or impaired function of the thyroid, heart, liver, or kidneys.

—you have high blood pressure.

—it is prescribed for a mild or trivial condition.

—it is prescribed for a child under 15 years of age.

—it is prescribed for anyone in a state of senility.

INFORM YOUR PHYSICIAN BEFORE TAKING THIS DRUG IF

—you are taking any other drugs at this time, either prescription or over-the-counter drugs.

—you are on long-term anticoagulant drugs.

—you have glaucoma.

Time Required for Apparent Benefit
Usually 2 to 7 days.

Possible Side-Effects *(natural, expected, and unavoidable drug actions)*
Retention of salt and water in the body with decreased formation of urine.

CAUTION
The elderly (over 60 years of age) are more likely to experience adverse effects from this drug. Small doses initially and careful observation are advisable.

Possible Adverse Effects *(unusual, unexpected, and infrequent reactions)*

IF ANY OF THE FOLLOWING DEVELOP, DISCONTINUE DRUG AND NOTIFY YOUR PHYSICIAN AS SOON AS POSSIBLE

Mild Adverse Effects
    Allergic Reactions: Skin rashes (various kinds), hives, itching, fever.
    Indigestion, stomach pain, nausea, vomiting, diarrhea.
    Progressive gain in weight and rise in blood pressure due to water retention; these are indications to discontinue this drug.

Serious Adverse Effects
    Allergic Reactions: Severe skin reactions, high fever, swollen and painful

joints, salivary gland enlargement, anaphylactic reaction (see Glossary). Bone marrow depression (see Glossary)—fatigue, weakness, fever, sore throat, mouth irritation, unusual bleeding or bruising.
Hepatitis with or without jaundice (see Glossary).
Kidney damage with impaired function.
Stomach and intestinal ulceration and/or bleeding, with dark red to black discoloration of stools.
Blood pressure elevation, heart damage.
Eye damage: injury to optic nerve and retina with impaired vision.
Ear damage: hearing loss.
Lethargy, confusion, nervousness.

Advisability of Use During Pregnancy
Safety not established. Avoid use if possible.

Advisability of Use While Nursing Infant
Drug known to be present in milk. Safety for infant not established. Avoid use if possible. Ask physician for guidance.

Habit-Forming Potential
None.

Effects of Overdosage
With **Moderate Overdose:**   Headache, insomnia, dizziness, mental and behavioral disturbance.
With **Large Overdose:**   Hallucinations, convulsions, coma.

Possible Effects of Extended Use
Bone marrow depression (see Glossary).
Development of thyroid gland enlargement (goiter) with or without impaired function.

Recommended Periodic Examinations While Taking This Drug
Complete blood cell counts and urine analysis should be made *before* drug is taken and *during* course of treatment at intervals of 1 to 2 weeks.

While Taking This Drug, Observe the Following
Foods: Avoid heavily salted foods. Drug should be taken with or following food to minimize stomach irritation.
Beverages: No restrictions of beverage selection. May be taken with milk to minimize stomach irritation.
Alcohol: Best avoided because of its irritant effect on stomach with increased risk of ulceration.
Tobacco Smoking: No interactions expected.
Other Drugs
Oxyphenbutazone may *increase* the effects of
• oral anti-diabetics (see sulfonylurea Drug Family, Section Four); consult physician regarding dosage adjustment to prevent hypoglycemia.
• insulin preparations; consult physician regarding dosage adjustment to prevent "insulin reaction" (hypoglycemia).

- sulfonamide ("sulfa") drugs (see Drug Family, Section Four).
- oral anticoagulants of the coumarin type (see Drug Family, Section Four); consult physician regarding need for dosage adjustment to prevent bleeding.
- the penicillins (see Drug Family, Section Four).

Oxyphenbutazone may *decrease* the effects of
- antihistamines (see Drug Family, Section Four).
- barbiturates (see Drug Family, Section Four).
- digitoxin; consult physician regarding need for dosage adjustment.
- oral contraceptives, by hastening their destruction.
- griseofulvin, by hastening its destruction.
- zoxazolamine (Flexin), by hastening its destruction.

Oxyphenbutazone *taken concurrently* with
- phenytoin (Dantoin, Dilantin, etc.), may cause excessive levels of phenytoin resulting in toxic effects on the brain; dosage reduction may be necessary.
- indomethacin, may increase the risk of stomach ulceration.

The following drugs may *decrease* the effects of oxyphenbutazone
- tricyclic antidepressants (Elavil, Tofranil, etc.) may interfere with its absorption.
- aspirin and related drugs (see salicylate Drug Family, Section Four)
- barbiturates (see Drug Family, Section Four).

Driving a Vehicle, Piloting a Plane, Operating Machinery: Use caution until occurrence of lethargy, confusion, impairment of vision or hearing is determined.

Exposure to Sun: Use caution until sensitivity is determined. Oxyphenbutazone can cause photosensitivity (see Glossary).

Discontinuation: This drug should be discontinued after 7 days if a favorable response has not occurred. If drug has been used for a longer period of time, ask physician for guidance regarding discontinuation or dosage adjustment of the following drugs if taken concurrently with oxyphenbutazone:

> oral anticoagulant drugs of the coumarin type
> oral anti-diabetic medications
> insulin preparations
> barbiturates
> digitoxin
> phenytoin

Special Storage Instructions
Keep in a dry, tightly closed container.

OXYTETRACYCLINE

Year Introduced: 1950

Brand Names

USA	Canada
Dalimycin (Dalin)	Terramycin (Pfizer)
Oxlopar (Parke-Davis)	
Oxy-Kesso-Tetra	
(McKesson)	
Oxy-Tetrachel (Rachelle)	
Terramycin (Pfizer)	
Uri-tet (American	
Urologicals)	
Terrastatin [CD] (Pfizer)	
Urobiotic [CD] (Pfizer)	

Drug Family: Antibiotic (Anti-infective) [Tetracyclines]

Prescription Required: Yes

Available Dosage Forms and Strengths

Tablets — 250 mg.
Capsules — 125 mg., 250 mg.
Syrups — 125 mg. per teaspoonful
Pediatric Drops — 100 mg. per ml.
Vaginal Tablets — 100 mg.
Skin Ointment — 3%
Eye Ointment — 0.5%

How This Drug Works

Intended Therapeutic Effect(s):   The elimination of infections responsive to the action of this drug.

Location of Drug Action(s):   Any body tissue or fluid in which sufficient concentration of the drug can be achieved.

Method of Drug Action(s):   This drug prevents the growth and multiplication of susceptible bacteria by interfering with their formation of essential proteins.

THIS DRUG SHOULD NOT BE TAKEN IF

—you are allergic to any tetracycline drug (see Drug Family, Section Four).
—you are pregnant or breast feeding.
—it is prescribed for a child under 9 years of age.

INFORM YOUR PHYSICIAN BEFORE TAKING THIS DRUG IF

—you have a history of liver or kidney disease.
—you have systemic lupus erythematosus.
—you are taking any penicillin drug.
—you are taking any anticoagulant drug.
—you plan to have surgery under general anesthesia in the near future.

Time Required for Apparent Benefit
Varies with nature of infection under treatment; usually 2 to 5 days.

Possible Side-Effects *(natural, expected, and unavoidable drug actions)*
Superinfections (see Glossary), often due to yeast organisms. These can occur in the mouth, intestinal tract, rectum, and/or vagina, resulting in rectal and vaginal itching.

Possible Adverse Effects *(unusual, unexpected, and infrequent reactions)*
IF ANY OF THE FOLLOWING DEVELOP, DISCONTINUE DRUG AND NOTIFY YOUR PHYSICIAN AS SOON AS POSSIBLE

Mild Adverse Effects
Allergic Reactions: Skin rash (various kinds), hives, itching of hands and feet, swelling of face or extremities.
Photosensitivity Reactions: Exaggerated sunburn or skin irritation occurs commonly with some tetracyclines (see Glossary).
Loss of appetite, nausea, vomiting, diarrhea.
Irritation of mouth or tongue, "black tongue," sore throat, abdominal pain or cramping.

Serious Adverse Effects
Allergic Reactions: Anaphylactic reaction (see Glossary), asthma, fever, painful swollen joints, unusual bleeding or bruising, jaundice (see Glossary).
Permanent discoloration and/or malformation of teeth when taken under 9 years of age, including unborn child and infant.

Advisability of Use During Pregnancy
Tetracyclines can have adverse effects on mother and fetus. Avoid use.

Advisability of Use While Nursing Infant
Tetracyclines can be present in milk and can have adverse effects on infant. Avoid use.

Habit-Forming Potential
None.

Effects of Overdosage
Possible nausea, vomiting, diarrhea.
Acute liver damage (rare).

Possible Effects of Extended Use
Impairment of bone marrow, liver, or kidney function (all rare).
Superinfections.

Recommended Periodic Examinations While Taking This Drug
Complete blood cell counts.
Liver and kidney function tests.
During extended use, sputum and stool examinations can detect early superinfections.

While Taking This Drug, Observe the Following

Foods: Dairy products interfere with absorption. Tetracycline should be taken 1 hour before or 2 hours after eating.

Beverages: Avoid milk for 1 hour before and after each dose of a tetracycline.

Alcohol: Avoid while taking a tetracycline if you have a history of liver disease.

Tobacco Smoking: No interactions expected.

Other Drugs

Tetracyclines may *increase* the effects of
• oral anticoagulants, and make it necessary to reduce their dosage.

Tetracyclines may *decrease* the effects of
• the penicillins, and impair their effectiveness in treating infections.

The following drugs may *decrease* the effects of tetracyclines
• antacids may reduce drug absorption.
• iron and mineral preparations may reduce drug absorption.

Driving a Vehicle, Piloting a Plane, Operating Machinery: No restrictions.

Exposure to Sun: Avoid as much as possible. Photosensitivity (see Glossary) is common with some tetracyclines.

Special Storage Instructions

Keep in a tightly closed, light-resistant container.

PAPAVERINE

Year Introduced: 1937

Brand Names

USA	Canada
Cerespan (USV Pharmaceutical)	Papaverine (Frosst)
Pavabid (Marion)	
Vasospan (Ulmer)	
Copavin [CD] (Lilly)	
(Numerous other brand names and combinations)	

Drug Family: Vasodilator

Prescription Required: Yes

Available Dosage Forms and Strengths

Tablets — 30 mg., 60 mg., 100 mg., 200 mg.
Prolonged Action Capsules — 150 mg.

How This Drug Works

Intended Therapeutic Effect(s):   Relief of symptoms associated with
• impaired circulation of blood in the extremities.
• impaired circulation of blood within the brain (in carefully selected cases).
Location of Drug Action(s):   The muscles in the walls of blood vessels. The
principal therapeutic action is on the small arteries (arterioles).
Method of Drug Action(s):   By causing direct relaxation and expansion of
blood vessel walls, this drug increases the volume of blood flowing through
the vessels. The resulting increase in oxygen and nutrients relieves the
symptoms attributable to deficient circulation. The mechanism responsible
for the direct relaxation of muscle is not known.

THIS DRUG SHOULD NOT BE TAKEN IF

—you have had an allergic reaction to any dosage form of it previously.

INFORM YOUR PHYSICIAN BEFORE TAKING THIS DRUG IF

—you have glaucoma.
—you have had a heart attack or a stroke.
—you suffer from poor circulation to the brain or heart (angina).

Time Required for Apparent Benefit

Drug action begins in 30 to 60 minutes and persists for 4 to 6 hours.

Possible Side-Effects *(natural, expected, and unavoidable drug actions)*

Lightheadedness and lethargy (lowered blood pressure), flushing of the face,
sweating, mild constipation.

CAUTION

Individuals with extensive or severe impairment of circulation to the brain
or heart may respond unfavorably or not at all to this drug. Observe closely
to determine if drug effects are beneficial. Discontinue drug if the condition
worsens.

Possible Adverse Effects *(unusual, unexpected, and infrequent reactions)*

IF ANY OF THE FOLLOWING DEVELOP, DISCONTINUE DRUG AND NOTIFY YOUR PHYSICIAN AS SOON AS POSSIBLE

Mild Adverse Effects
    Allergic Reactions: Itching, skin rash.
    Stomach irritation, indigestion, nausea, dryness of mouth and throat.
    Drowsiness, dizziness, headache.
Serious Adverse Effects
    Allergic Reactions: Hepatitis with jaundice (see Glossary).

Advisability of Use During Pregnancy

No reports of adverse effects on mother or fetus. However, use should be
limited to the smallest effective dose and for the shortest periods possible.

Advisability of Use While Nursing Infant

Drug is known to be present in milk. Safety for infant not established. Ask
physician for guidance.

Habit-Forming Potential
None.

Effects of Overdosage
With Moderate Overdose: Nausea, vomiting, marked drowsiness, severe constipation.

With Large Overdose: Weakness, faintness in upright position, flushed and warm face, excessive sweating, stupor, irregular pulse.

Possible Effects of Extended Use
None reported.

Recommended Periodic Examinations While Taking This Drug
Liver function tests.

Measurement of internal eye pressure (if glaucoma is present).

While Taking This Drug, Observe the Following
Foods: No restrictions of food selection. Drug may be taken with or immediately following meals to reduce stomach irritation or nausea.

Beverages: No restrictions.

Alcohol: No interactions expected.

Tobacco Smoking: Nicotine can reduce this drug's ability to dilate blood vessels and improve circulation. Follow physician's advice regarding smoking.

Other Drugs

The following drugs may *increase* the effects of papaverine

• sedatives, sleep-inducing drugs, tranquilizers, pain relievers, and narcotic drugs. Observe for excessive sedation.

Driving a Vehicle, Piloting a Plane, Operating Machinery: Determine if drug causes drowsiness or dizziness before undertaking hazardous activities.

Exposure to Sun: No restrictions.

Exposure to Heat: Use caution. This drug may cause excessive sweating in hot environments.

Exposure to Cold: Avoid as much as possible. This drug may be less effective in cold environments or with the handling of cold objects.

Heavy Exercise or Exertion: No restrictions.

Special Storage Instructions
Keep in a dry, tightly closed container. Protect from light and excessive heat.

PARA-AMINOSALICYLIC ACID (PAS)

Year Introduced: 1946

Brand Names

USA	Canada
Pamisyl (Parke-Davis)	Nemasol (ICN)
Parasal (Panray)	
P.A.S. (Lilly)	
P.A.S. Acid (Kasar)	
Pasna (Barnes-Hind)	
Rezipas (Squibb)	

Drug Family: Antimicrobial, Anti-tuberculosis (Anti-infective)

Prescription Required: Yes

Available Dosage Forms and Strengths
Tablets — 0.5 Gm., 1 Gm., 2 Gm.
Capsules — 0.5 Gm.
Resin Powder — 8 Gm. packets

How This Drug Works
Intended Therapeutic Effect(s):   To increase the effectiveness of other drugs used in the treatment of active tuberculosis.
Location of Drug Action(s):   Those body tissues and fluids in which adequate concentration of the drug can be achieved.
Method of Drug Action(s):   This drug prevents the growth and multiplication of susceptible tuberculosis organisms and renders them more vulnerable to the destructive action of more potent drugs.

THIS DRUG SHOULD NOT BE TAKEN IF
—you are allergic to any of the drugs bearing the brand names listed above or to any form of aminosalicylic acid.

INFORM YOUR PHYSICIAN BEFORE TAKING THIS DRUG IF
—you have a history of liver or kidney disease.
—you have a history of peptic ulcer (stomach or duodenum).
—you are taking anticoagulant drugs.
—you have epilepsy.

Time Required for Apparent Benefit
From 3 to 6 months.

Possible Side-Effects *(natural, expected, and unavoidable drug actions)*
Interference with the absorption of Vitamin B–12. (This may result in the development of anemia.)

Possible Adverse Effects *(unusual, unexpected, and infrequent reactions)*

IF ANY OF THE FOLLOWING DEVELOP, DISCONTINUE DRUG AND NOTIFY
YOUR PHYSICIAN AS SOON AS POSSIBLE

Mild Adverse Effects
Allergic Reactions: Skin rashes (various kinds), fever, swollen glands.
Loss of appetite, nausea, vomiting, diarrhea, stomach pain and burning (all
common).
Headaches, pains in the arms and/or legs.

Serious Adverse Effects
Allergic Reactions: Hepatitis, with or without jaundice (see Glossary).
Bone marrow depression (see Glossary)—fatigue, weakness, fever, sore
throat, unusual bleeding or bruising.
Mental and behavioral disturbances.
Peptic ulceration of stomach.

Advisability of Use During Pregnancy
Safety not established. Prudent use is best determined by the physician's
evaluation.

Advisability of Use While Nursing Infant
Safety for infant not established. Avoid use if possible. Ask physician for
guidance.

Habit-Forming Potential
None.

Effects of Overdosage
Severe nausea, vomiting, abdominal pain, diarrhea.

Possible Effects of Extended Use
Impaired thyroid function with enlargement of thyroid gland (goiter).

Recommended Periodic Examinations While Taking This Drug
Complete blood cell counts.
Serial determination of blood potassium levels.
Liver, kidney, and thyroid function tests.

While Taking This Drug, Observe the Following
Foods: No restrictions of food selection. Take PAS with meals to reduce
stomach irritation.
Beverages: No restrictions.
Alcohol: Avoid completely if you have a history of liver disease.
Tobacco Smoking: No interactions expected with PAS. Ask physician for
guidance regarding smoking.

Other Drugs
PAS may *increase* the effects of
• oral anticoagulants, and cause bleeding. Monitor prothrombin time and
adjust dosage of anticoagulant as necessary.
• phenytoin (Dantoin, Dilantin, etc.), to an excessive degree. Dosage reduction of phenytoin may be necessary to prevent toxicity.
• barbiturates, and cause oversedation.

PAS may *decrease* the effects of
- rifampin, by reducing its absorption. Separate doses of each drug by 8 to 12 hours.
- "sulfa" drugs (see Drug Family, Section Four).

PAS *taken concurrently* with
- aspirin, may cause excessive irritation of the stomch, increasing the possibility of stomach ulceration or bleeding.

Driving a Vehicle, Piloting a Plane, Operating Machinery: No restrictions.
Exposure to Sun: No restrictions.
Discontinuation: Long-term treatment is required for cure. If you cannot tolerate PAS because of severe stomach irritation, consult your physician so your treatment program can be modified.

Special Storage Instructions
Keep in a tightly closed, light-resistant container. PAS solutions must be refrigerated and kept in a dark place.

Do Not Take the Liquid Form of This Drug If It Is Older Than
24 hours.

PAREGORIC
(Camphorated Tincture of Opium)

Year Introduced: 1885

Brand Names

USA	Canada
Brown Mixture [CD] (Lilly)	Diban [CD] (Robins)
CM with Paregoric [CD] (Beecham)	Donnagel-PG [CD] (Robins)
Donnagel-PG [CD] (Robins)	Parepectolin [CD] (Rorer)
Kaoparin [CD] (McKesson)	Pomalin [CD] (Winthrop)
Parepectolin [CD] (Rorer) (Others)	

Drug Family: Anti-diarrheal (Narcotic)

Prescription Required: Yes (Controlled Drug, U.S. Schedule 5)

Available Dosage Forms and Strengths
Oral Liquid Mixtures — Opium content 15 to 24 mg. per ounce

How This Drug Works
Intended Therapeutic Effect(s)
- relief of mild to moderate pain.
- relief of intestinal cramping and diarrhea.

Location of Drug Action(s)
- those areas of the brain and spinal cord involved in the perception of pain.
- the membranes lining the intestine and the nerve fibers in the wall of the intestine.

Method of Drug Action(s):   Not completely established. It is thought that this drug affects tissue sites that react specifically with opium and its derivatives to relieve pain. Morphine, the active ingredient in paregoric, acts in two ways to relieve cramping and diarrhea: It acts as a local anesthetic on surface membranes and it blocks the release of acetylcholine, the chemical that transmits stimulating nerve impulses to the muscular walls of the intestine.

THIS DRUG SHOULD NOT BE TAKEN IF
—you are allergic to any opium derivative (morphine, codeine, papaverine).

INFORM YOUR PHYSICIAN BEFORE TAKING THIS DRUG IF
—you are taking any other sedative, sleep-inducing, tranquilizing, or narcotic drugs at this time.
—you have impaired liver or kidney function.

Time Required for Apparent Benefit
Control of cramping and diarrhea may require several doses over a period of 2 to 6 hours.

Possible Side-Effects *(natural, expected, and unavoidable drug actions)*
Mild drowsiness, lightheadedness, sweating, constipation.

Possible Adverse Effects *(unusual, unexpected, and infrequent reactions)*

IF ANY OF THE FOLLOWING DEVELOP, DISCONTINUE DRUG AND NOTIFY YOUR PHYSICIAN AS SOON AS POSSIBLE

Mild Adverse Effects
Allergic Reactions: Skin rash, hives, itching.
Nausea, vomiting (in sensitive individuals).
Dizziness, unsteadiness (more common in the elderly, over 60 years of age).

Serious Adverse Effects
None reported.

Advisability of Use During Pregnancy
Wide use for over 90 years has resulted in no reports of serious adverse effects on the course of pregnancy, either to the mother or to the fetus. However, use of opium (or any of its derivatives) should be limited to the smallest effective dose and for short periods of time.

Advisability of Use While Nursing Infant
The active drug (morphine) is known to be present in milk and may have a depressant effect on the infant. Ask physician for guidance.

Habit-Forming Potential
This drug may produce both psychological and physical dependence (see Glossary) if used in large doses for an extended period of time.

Effects of Overdosage
With Moderate Overdose: Increased drowsiness, nausea, vomiting, constipation.
With Large Overdose: Stupor progressing to deep sleep, slow breathing, slow pulse, flushed and warm skin, small (constricted) pupils.

Possible Effects of Extended Use
Psychological and physical dependence.

Recommended Periodic Examinations While Taking This Drug
None required.

While Taking This Drug, Observe the Following
Foods: Follow diet prescribed to combat diarrhea.
Beverages: No interactions.
Alcohol: Best avoided until diarrhea is controlled. Use with caution if taken concurrently with this drug. Opium (morphine) can intensify the intoxicating effects of alcohol. Alcohol can intensify the depressant action of opium on brain function.
Tobacco Smoking: No interactions expected.
Other Drugs
Paregoric may *increase* the effects of
• all sedatives, analgesics, sleep-inducing drugs, tranquilizers, and narcotic drugs, causing excessive sedation.

The following drugs may *increase* the effects of paregoric
• phenothiazines may enhance its sedative effect.
• tricyclic antidepressants may enhance its sedative effect.

Driving a Vehicle, Piloting a Plane, Operating Machinery: Usually no restrictions. However, if used in large doses this drug may impair mental alertness, judgment, reaction time, or coordination. If so, avoid hazardous activities.
Exposure to Sun: No restrictions.

Special Storage Instructions
Keep in a tightly closed, light-resistant container. Avoid exposure to direct sunlight and to excessive heat.

PENICILLIN G

Year Introduced: 1941

Brand Names

USA
Arcocillin (Arcum)
Biotic-T-500 (Scrip)
Cryspen 400 (Knight)
Deltapen (Trimen)
G-Recillin-T
(Reid-Provident)
Hyasorb (Key
Pharmaceuticals)
K-Cillin (Mayrand)
Kesso-Pen (McKesson)
K-Pen (Kay)
Lanacillin (Lannett)
Palocillin-S (Palmedico)
Palocillin-5 (Palmedico)
Pentids (Squibb)
Pfizerpen G (Pfizer)
QIDpen G (Mallinckrodt)
Sugracillin (Upjohn)

Canada
Abbocillin (Abbott)
Crystapen (Glaxo)
Dymocillin (Dymond)
Falapen (Frosst)
Hylenta (Ayerst)
Ka-Pen (Pfizer)
Megacillin (Frosst)
Novopen G (Novopharm)
P-50 (Horner)
Pencitabs (M & M)
Penioral 500 (Wyeth)
Pentids (Squibb)
P.G.A. (A & H)
Therapen K (Therapex)
Wescopen (Saunders)

Drug Family: Antibiotic (Anti-infective) [Penicillins]

Prescription Required: Yes

Available Dosage Forms and Strengths

Tablets — 50,000 units, 100,000 units, 200,000 units, 250,000 units, 400,000 units, 500,000 units, 800,000 units, 1,000,000 units
Capsules — 400,000 units
Solutions — 100,000 units, 125,000 units, 200,000 units, 250,000 units, 400,000 units, 500,000 units per teaspoonful
Syrups — 200,000 units, 250,000 units, 400,000 units, 500,000 units per teaspoonful
Suspension — 150,000 units, 300,000 units per teaspoonful
Ointment — 1,000 units per gram (use not recommended)

How This Drug Works

Intended Therapeutic Effects(s):   The elimination of infections responsive to the action of this drug.

Location of Drug Action(s):   Any body tissue or fluid in which sufficient concentration of the drug can be achieved.

Method of Drug Action(s):   This drug destroys susceptible infecting bacteria by interfering with their ability to produce new protective cell walls as they multiply and grow.

THIS DRUG SHOULD NOT BE TAKEN IF
—you have had an allergic reaction to any dosage form of it previously.
—you are certain you are allergic to any form of penicillin.

INFORM YOUR PHYSICIAN BEFORE TAKING THIS DRUG IF
—you suspect you may be allergic to penicillin or you have a history of a previous "reaction" to penicillin
—you are allergic to cephalosporin antibiotics (Ancef, Ceporan, Ceporex, Kafocin, Keflex, Keflin, Kefzol, Loridine).
—you are allergic by nature (hayfever, asthma, hives, eczema).

Time Required for Apparent Benefit
Varies with the nature of the infection under treatment; usually from 2 to 5 days.

Possible Side-Effects *(natural, expected, and unavoidable drug actions)*
Superinfections (see Glossary).

Possible Adverse Effects *(unusual, unexpected, and infrequent reactions)*

IF ANY OF THE FOLLOWING DEVELOP, DISCONTINUE DRUG AND NOTIFY YOUR PHYSICIAN AS SOON AS POSSIBLE

Mild Adverse Effects
  Allergic Reactions: Skin rashes (various kinds).
  Irritations of mouth or tongue, "black tongue," nausea, vomiting, diarrhea, dizziness (rare).
Serious Adverse Effects
  Allergic Reactions: †Anaphylactic reaction (see Glossary), severe skin reactions, high fever, swollen painful joints, sore throat, unusual bleeding or bruising.

Advisability of Use During Pregnancy
Apparently safe. No evidence of adverse effect on mother or fetus.

Advisability of Use While Nursing Infant
Drug may be present in milk and may sensitize infant to penicillin. Ask physician for guidance.

Habit-Forming Potential
None.

Effects of Overdosage
Possible nausea, vomiting, and/or diarrhea.

Possible Effects of Extended Use
Superinfections.

Recommended Periodic Examinations While Taking This Drug
Complete blood cell counts. Liver and kidney function tests.

†A rare but potentially dangerous reaction characteristic of penicillins.

While Taking This Drug, Observe the Following

Foods: No restrictions of food selection. To insure effectiveness, take at least 1 hour before or 2 hours after eating.

Beverages: No restrictions.

Alcohol: No interactions expected.

Tobacco Smoking: No interactions expected.

Other Drugs

The following drugs may *decrease* the effectiveness of penicillin G
- antacids may reduce absorption of penicillin G.
- chloramphenicol (Chloromycetin)
- erythromycin (Erythrocin, E-Mycin, etc.)
- paromomycin (Humatin)
- tetracyclines (Achromycin, Declomycin, Minocin, etc.; see Drug Family, Section Four)
- troleandomycin (Cyclamycin, TAO)

Driving a Vehicle, Piloting a Plane, Operating Machinery: No restrictions.

Exposure to Sun: No restrictions.

Discontinuation: Certain infections require that this drug be taken for 10 days to prevent the development of rheumatic fever. Ask your physician for guidance regarding the recommended duration of treatment.

Special Storage Instructions

Keep tablets and capsules in a tightly closed, light-resistant container, preferably below 85°F. (30°C). Keep solutions, syrups, and suspensions refrigerated.

Do Not Take a Liquid Form of This Drug If It Is Older Than

7 days—when kept at room temperature.
14 days—when kept refrigerated.

PENICILLIN V

Year Introduced: 1953

Brand Names

USA

Betapen VK (Bristol)
Compocillin V & VK
  (Ross)
Dowpen VK (Dow)
Kesso-Pen V & VK
  (McKesson)
Ledercillin VK (Lederle)
Penapar VK
  (Parke-Davis)
Pen-Vee K (Wyeth)
Pfizerpen VK (Pfizer)
QIDpen VK
  (Mallinckrodt)
Repen VK
  (Reid-Provident)
Robicillin-VK (Robins)
Ro-Cillin-VK (Rowell)
SK-Penicillin VK (Smith
  Kline & French)
Uticillin VK (Upjohn)
V-Cillin (Lilly)
V-Cillin K (Lilly)
Veetids (Squibb)

Canada

Hi-Pen (Abbott)
Ledercillin VK (Lederle)
Nadopen-V (Nadeau)
Novopen-V-500
  (Novopharm)
Penebec-V (Pharbec)
Pen-Vee (Wyeth)
"PVF" K (Frosst)
Sigmavin (Sigma)
Therapen V (Therapex)
V-Cillin K (Lilly)
VC-K 500 (Lilly)
Win-V-K (ICN)

Drug Family: Antibiotic (Anti-infective) [Penicillins]

Prescription Required: Yes

Available Dosage Forms and Strengths

Tablets — 125 mg., 250 mg., 300 mg., 500 mg.
Chewable Tablets — 125 mg., 250 mg.
Capsules — 125 mg., 250 mg.
Oral Solutions — 125 mg., 250 mg. per teaspoonful
Oral Suspensions — 90 mg., 180 mg. per teaspoonful
Pediatric Oral Suspensions — 125 mg., 250 mg. per teaspoonful
Pediatric Drops — 90 mg. per 1 ml., 125 mg. per 0.6 ml., 125
mg. per 2.5 ml.

How This Drug Works

Intended Therapeutic Effect(s):   The elimination of infections responsive to the action of this drug.

Location of Drug Action(s):   Any body tissue or fluid in which sufficient concentration of the drug can be achieved.

Method of Drug Action(s):   This drug destroys susceptible infecting bacteria by interfering with their ability to produce new protective cell walls as they multiply and grow.

THIS DRUG SHOULD NOT BE TAKEN IF
—you have had an allergic reaction to any dosage form of it previously
—you are certain you are allergic to any form of penicillin.

INFORM YOUR PHYSICIAN BEFORE TAKING THIS DRUG IF
—you suspect you may be allergic to penicillin or you have a history of a previous "reaction" to penicillin.
—you are allergic to cephalosporin antibiotics (Ancef, Ceporan, Ceporex, Kafocin, Keflex, Keflin, Kefzol, Loridine).
—you are allergic by nature (hayfever, asthma, hives, eczema).

Time Required for Apparent Benefit
Varies with the nature of the infection under treatment; usually from 2 to 5 days.

Possible Side-Effects *(natural, expected, and unavoidable drug actions)*
Superinfections (see Glossary).

Possible Adverse Effects *(unusual, unexpected, and infrequent reactions)*

IF ANY OF THE FOLLOWING DEVELOP, DISCONTINUE DRUG AND NOTIFY YOUR PHYSICIAN AS SOON AS POSSIBLE
Mild Adverse Effects
  Allergic Reactions: Skin rashes (various kinds).
  Irritations of mouth or tongue, "black tongue," nausea, vomiting, diarrhea.
Serious Adverse Effects
  Allergic Reactions: †Anaphylactic reaction (see Glossary), severe skin reactions, high fever, swollen painful joints, sore throat, unusual bleeding or bruising.

Advisability of Use During Pregnancy
Apparently safe. No evidence of adverse effect on mother or fetus.

Advisability of Use While Nursing Infant
Drug may be present in milk and may sensitize infant to penicillin. Ask physician for guidance.

Habit-Forming Potential
None.

Effects of Overdosage
Possible nausea, vomiting, and/or diarrhea.

Possible Effects of Extended Use
Superinfections.

---

†A rare but potentially dangerous reaction characteristic of penicillins.

Recommended Periodic Examinations While Taking This Drug
Complete blood cell counts.
Liver and kidney function tests.

While Taking This Drug, Observe the Following
Foods: No restrictions of food selection. May be taken at any time (before, during, or after eating, or between meals).
Beverages: No restrictions.
Alcohol: No interactions expected.
Tobacco Smoking: No interactions expected.
Other Drugs
The following drugs may *decrease* the effectiveness of penicillin V
• chloramphenicol (Chloromycetin)
• erythromycin (Erythrocin, E-Mycin, etc.)
• paromomycin (Humatin)
• tetracyclines (Achromycin, Declomycin, Minocin, etc.; see Drug Family, Section Four)
• troleandomycin (Cyclamycin, TAO)
Driving a Vehicle, Piloting a Plane, Operating Machinery: No restrictions.
Exposure to Sun: No restrictions.
Discontinuation: Certain infections require that this drug be taken for 10 days to prevent the development of rheumatic fever. Ask your physician for guidance regarding the recommended duration of treatment.

Special Storage Instructions
Keep tablets and capsules in a tightly closed, light-resistant container, preferably below 85°F. (30°C). Keep liquid preparations refrigerated.

Do Not Take a Liquid Form of This Drug If It Is Older Than
7 days—when kept at room temperature.
14 days—when kept refrigerated.

PENTAERYTHRITOL TETRANITRATE

Year Introduced: 1951

Brand Names

USA

Perispan (USV
Pharmaceutical)
Peritrate
(Warner/Chilcott)
P.E.T.N. (Ulmer)
SK-Petn. (Smith Kline &
French)
Cartrax [CD] (Roerig)
Equanitrate [CD]
(Wyeth)
Miltrate [CD] (Wallace)
(Numerous other brand
and combination brand
names)

Canada

Dilanca (Anca)
Neo-Corodil (Ethica)
Niritol (ICN)
Peritrate
(Warner/Chilcott)
Perynitrate (Barlowe
Cote)
P-T (Dymond)
Tetranite Bitab (Nordic)

Drug Family: Anti-anginal (Vasodilator) [Nitrates]

Prescription Required: Yes

Available Dosage Forms and Strengths

Tablets — 10 mg., 20 mg.
Prolonged Action Tablets — 60 mg., 80 mg.

How This Drug Works

Intended Therapeutic Effect(s):   Reduction in the frequency and severity of pain associated with angina pectoris (coronary insufficiency).

Location of Drug Action(s):   The muscular tissue in the walls of the blood vessels. The principal site of the therapeutic action is the system of coronary arteries in the heart.

Method of Drug Action(s):   This drug acts directly on the muscle cell to produce relaxation. This permits expansion of blood vessels and increases the supply of blood and oxygen to meet the needs of the working heart muscle.

THIS DRUG SHOULD NOT BE TAKEN IF

—you have had an allergic reaction to any dosage form of it previously. A combination drug [CD] should not be taken if you are allergic to *any* of its ingredients.

INFORM YOUR PHYSICIAN BEFORE TAKING THIS DRUG IF

—you have glaucoma.
—you have had an unfavorable response to any vasodilator drug in the past.

Time Required for Apparent Benefit

Drug action begins in 30 to 60 minutes and persists for 4 to 5 hours.

Possible Side-Effects *(natural, expected, and unavoidable drug actions)*
Flushing, lightheadedness in upright position (see orthostatic hypotension in Glossary).

Possible Adverse Effects *(unusual, unexpected, and infrequent reactions)*
IF ANY OF THE FOLLOWING DEVELOP, DISCONTINUE DRUG AND NOTIFY YOUR PHYSICIAN AS SOON AS POSSIBLE

Mild Adverse Effects
Allergic Reactions: Skin rash.
Headache (may be persistent), dizziness, fainting.
Nausea, vomiting.
Serious Adverse Effects
Allergic Reactions: Severe dermatitis with peeling of skin.

Advisability of Use During Pregnancy
Safety not established. Prudent use is best determined by the physician's evaluation.

Advisability of Use While Nursing Infant
Presence of drug in milk is not known. Safety for infant not established. Avoid use if possible. Ask physician for guidance.

Habit-Forming Potential
None.

Effects of Overdosage
With Moderate Overdose: Headache, dizziness, marked flushing of the skin.
With Large Overdose: Vomiting, weakness, sweating, fainting, shortness of breath, coma.

Possible Effects of Extended Use
Development of tolerance (see Glossary), which may reduce the drug's effectiveness at recommended doses.
Development of abnormal hemoglobin (red blood cell pigment).

Recommended Periodic Examinations While Taking This Drug
Measurement of internal eye pressure in those individuals with glaucoma or a tendency to glaucoma.
Red blood cell counts and hemoglobin measurements.

While Taking This Drug, Observe the Following
Foods: No restrictions. This drug is likely to be more effective if taken one-half to 1 hour before eating.
Beverages: No restrictions.
Alcohol: Use with extreme caution until combined effects have been determined. Alcohol may exaggerate the drop in blood pressure experienced by some sensitive individuals. This could be dangerous.
Tobacco Smoking: Nicotine may reduce the effectiveness of this drug. Follow physician's advice regarding smoking, based upon its effect on the condition under treatment and its possible interaction with this drug.

Other Drugs

Pentaerythritol may *increase* the effects of

- atropine-like drugs (see Drug Family, Section Four), and cause an increase in internal eye pressure.
- tricyclic antidepressants (see Drug Family, Section Four), and cause excessive lowering of the blood pressure.

Pentaerythritol may *decrease* the effects of

- all choline-like drugs, such as Mestinon, Mytelase, pilocarpine, Prostigmin, and Urecholine.

Pentaerythritol *taken concurrently* with

- anti-hypertensive drugs, may cause severe drop in blood pressure. Careful monitoring of drug response and appropriate dosage adjustments are necessary.

The following drugs may *increase* the effects of pentaerythritol

- propranolol (Inderal) may cause additional lowering of the blood pressure. Dosage adjustments may be necessary.

Driving a Vehicle, Piloting a Plane, Operating Machinery: Usually no restrictions. Before engaging in hazardous activities, determine that this drug will not cause orthostatic hypotension.

Exposure to Sun: No restrictions.

Exposure to Cold: Cold environment may reduce the effectiveness of this drug.

Heavy Exercise or Exertion: This drug may improve your ability to be more active without resulting angina pain. Use caution and avoid excessive exertion that could cause heart injury if warning pain is delayed.

Special Storage Instructions

Keep in a dry, tightly closed container and in a cool place. Protect from heat and light.

PENTAZOCINE

Year Introduced: 1967

Brand Names

USA	Canada
Talwin (Winthrop)	Talwin (Winthrop)

Drug Family: Analgesic, Mild (Non-narcotic)

Prescription Required: Yes (Controlled Drug, Canada Schedule G)

Available Dosage Forms and Strengths

Tablets — 50 mg.

How This Drug Works

Intended Therapeutic Effect(s):   Relief of mild to moderate pain.

Location of Drug Action(s):   Those areas of the brain and spinal cord involved in the perception of pain.

Method of Drug Action(s):   Not completely established. It has been suggested that the resulting increase in chemicals that transmit nerve impulses somehow contributes to the analgesic effect of this drug.

THIS DRUG SHOULD NOT BE TAKEN IF

—you have had an allergic reaction to any dosage form of it previously.

—it is prescribed for a child under 12 years of age.

INFORM YOUR PHYSICIAN BEFORE TAKING THIS DRUG IF

—you are taking sedatives, sleep-inducing drugs, tranquilizers, antidepressants, or narcotic drugs of any kind.

—you have a history of impaired liver or kidney function.

—you have epilepsy.

—you plan to have surgery under general anesthesia in the near future.

Time Required for Apparent Benefit

Usually 15 minutes to 1 hour when taken orally.

Possible Side-Effects *(natural, expected, and unavoidable drug actions)*

Drowsiness, lightheadedness, weakness, constipation.

Possible Adverse Effects *(unusual, unexpected, and infrequent reactions)*

IF ANY OF THE FOLLOWING DEVELOP, DISCONTINUE DRUG AND NOTIFY YOUR PHYSICIAN AS SOON AS POSSIBLE

Mild Adverse Effects

Allergic Reactions: Skin rash, hives, swelling of face.

Nausea, vomiting, indigestion, diarrhea.

Headache, dizziness, blurring of vision, flushing and sweating.

Serious Adverse Effects

Marked drop in blood pressure, which may produce fainting.

Mental and behavioral disturbances, hallucinations, tremor.

Bone marrow depression (see Glossary) of a mild and reversible nature (rare).

Interference with urination.

Advisability of Use During Pregnancy

Safety not established. Prudent use is best determined by physician's evaluation.

Advisability of Use While Nursing Infant

Safety not established. Avoid use if possible. Ask physician for guidance.

Habit-Forming Potential

This drug can produce psychological and physical dependence (see Glossary) if used in large doses for an extended period of time.

Effects of Overdosage
With Moderate Overdose: Anxiety, disturbed thoughts, hallucinations, nightmares, progressive drowsiness.

With Large Overdose: Stupor, depressed respiration.

Possible Effects of Extended Use
Psychological and physical dependence.

Recommended Periodic Examinations While Taking This Drug
Complete blood cell counts, if used for an extended period of time.

While Taking This Drug, Observe the Following
Foods: No restrictions.

Beverages: No restrictions.

Alcohol: Use with caution until combined effect is determined. Pentazocine may increase the intoxicating effects of alcohol.

Tobacco Smoking: Heavy smoking may reduce the effectiveness of pentazocine. Consult physician regarding need for dosage adjustment.

Other Drugs

Pentazocine may *increase* the effects of

• all sedatives, sleep-inducing drugs, tranquilizers, antidepressants. Ask physician for guidance regarding need for dosage adjustment.

Pentazocine may *decrease* the effects of

• narcotic drugs (to a slight degree).

Driving a Vehicle, Piloting a Plane, Operating Machinery: This drug can impair mental alertness, judgment, reaction time, and physical coordination. Use caution until the occurrence of drowsiness, dizziness, and weakness is determined. Avoid hazardous activities.

Exposure to Sun: No restrictions.

Discontinuation: If this drug has been taken for an extended period of time, do not discontinue it abruptly. Ask physician for guidance.

Special Storage Instructions
Keep in a dry, tightly closed container.

PENTOBARBITAL

Year Introduced: 1930

Brand Names

USA	Canada
Nembutal (Abbott)	Butylone (Hartz)
Night-Caps (Bowman)	Hypnol (Stickley)
Penital (Kay)	Hypnotal (M & M)
Penta (Dunhall)	Ibatal (I & B)
Carbrital [CD]	Nembutal (Abbott)
(Parke-Davis)	Nova-Rectal (Nova)
(Numerous combination	Pental (Saunders)
brand names)	Pentanca (Anca)
	Pentogen (Maney)
	Carbrital [CD] (P.D. & Co.)

Drug Family: Sedative, Mild; Sleep Inducer (Hypnotic) [Barbiturates]

Prescription Required: Yes (Controlled Drug, U.S. Schedule 2)

Available Dosage Forms and Strengths
Tablets — 100 mg.
Capsules — 30 mg., 50 mg., 100 mg.
Elixir — 20 mg. per teaspoonful
Suppositories — 30 mg., 60 mg., 120 mg., 200 mg.

How This Drug Works
Intended Therapeutic Effect(s)
• with low dosage, relief of mild to moderate anxiety or tension (sedative effect).
• with higher dosage taken at bedtime, sedation sufficient to induce sleep (hypnotic effect).
Location of Drug Action(s):   The connecting points (synapses) in the nerve pathways that transmit impulses between the wake-sleep centers of the brain.
Method of Drug Action(s):   Not completely established. Present thinking is that this drug selectively blocks the transmission of nerve impulses by reducing the amount of available norepinephrine, one of the chemicals responsible for impulse transmission.

THIS DRUG SHOULD NOT BE TAKEN IF
—you have had an allergic reaction to any dosage form of it previously.
—you have a history of porphyria.

INFORM YOUR PHYSICIAN BEFORE TAKING THIS DRUG IF
—you are allergic or sensitive to any barbiturate drug.
—you are taking any sedative, sleep-inducing drugs, tranquilizers, antihistamines, pain relievers, or narcotic drugs of any kind.
—you have epilepsy.

—you have a history of liver or kidney disease.
—you plan to have surgery under general anesthesia in the near future.

Time Required for Apparent Benefit
Approximately 30 minutes.

Possible Side-Effects *(natural, expected, and unavoidable drug actions)*
Drowsiness, lethargy, a sense of mental and physical sluggishness.

CAUTION
The elderly (over 60 years of age) and the debilitated may experience agitation, excitement, confusion, and delirium with standard doses. Small doses are advisable until tolerance has been determined.

Possible Adverse Effects *(unusual, unexpected, and infrequent reactions)*

IF ANY OF THE FOLLOWING DEVELOP, DISCONTINUE DRUG AND NOTIFY YOUR PHYSICIAN AS SOON AS POSSIBLE

Mild Adverse Effects
Allergic Reactions: Skin rash (various kinds), hives, localized swellings of eyelids, face, or lips, drug fever.
"Hangover" effect, dizziness, unsteadiness.
Nausea, vomiting, diarrhea.
Joint and muscle pains, most often in the neck, shoulders, and arms.

Serious Adverse Effects
Allergic Reactions: Hepatitis with jaundice (see Glossary). Severe skin reactions.
Idiosyncratic Reactions: Paradoxical excitement and delirium (rather than sedation).
Anemia, manifested by weakness and fatigue.
Reduction of blood platelets (see Glossary), resulting in unusual bleeding or bruising.

Advisability of Use During Pregnancy
Safety not established. Prudent use is best determined by the physician's evaluation.

Advisability of Use While Nursing Infant
Drug is known to be present in milk. Avoid use if possible. Ask physician for guidance.

Habit-Forming Potential
This drug can cause both psychological and physical dependence (see Glossary).

Effects of Overdosage
With Moderate Overdose: Behavior similar to alcoholic intoxication: confusion, slurred speech, physical incoordination, staggering gait, drowsiness.
With Large Overdose: Deepening sleep, coma, slow and shallow breathing, weak and rapid pulse, cold and sweaty skin.

Possible Effects of Extended Use
Psychological and/or physical dependence.

Anemia.

If dose is excessive, a form of chronic drug intoxication can occur—headache, impaired vision, slurred speech, and depression.

Recommended Periodic Examinations While Taking This Drug
Complete blood cell counts.

Liver function tests.

While Taking This Drug, Observe the Following
Foods: No restrictions.

Beverages: No restrictions.

Alcohol: Avoid completely. Alcohol can increase greatly the sedative and depressant actions of this drug on brain function.

Tobacco Smoking: No interactions expected.

Other Drugs

Pentobarbital may *increase* the effects of

• other sedatives, sleep-inducing drugs, tranquilizers, antihistamines, pain relievers, and narcotic drugs, and cause oversedation. Ask your physician for guidance regarding dosage adjustment.

Pentobarbital may *decrease* the effects of

• oral anticoagulants of the coumarin family (see Drug Family, Section Four). Ask physician for guidance regarding prothrombin time testing and adjustment of the anticoagulant dosage.

• aspirin, and reduce its pain-relieving action.

• cortisone and related drugs, by hastening their elimination from the body.

• oral contraceptives, by hastening their elimination from the body.

• griseofulvin (Fulvicin, Grisactin, etc.), and reduce its effectiveness in treating fungus infections.

• phenylbutazone (Azolid, Butazolidin, etc.), and reduce its effectiveness in treating inflammation and pain.

Pentobarbital *taken concurrently* with

• anti-convulsants, may cause a change in the pattern of epileptic seizures. Careful dosage adjustments are necessary to achieve a balance of actions that will give the best protection from seizures.

The following drugs may *increase* the effects of pentobarbital

• both mild and strong tranquilizers may increase the sedative and sleep-inducing actions of barbiturate drugs and cause oversedation.

• isoniazid (INH, Isozide, etc.) may prolong the action of barbiturate drugs.

• antihistamines may increase the sedative effects of barbiturate drugs.

• oral anti-diabetic drugs of the sulfonylurea type may prolong the sedative effects of barbiturate drugs.

• mono-amine oxidase (MAO) inhibitor drugs (see Drug Family, Section Four) may prolong the sedative effects of barbiturate drugs.

Driving a Vehicle, Piloting a Plane, Operating Machinery: This drug can produce drowsiness and impair mental alertness, judgment, physical coordination, and reaction time. Avoid hazardous activities.

Exposure to Sun: Use caution until sensitivity has been determined. Some barbiturates can cause photosensitivity (see Glossary).

Exposure to Cold: The elderly may experience excessive lowering of body temperature while taking this drug. Keep dosage to a minimum during winter and dress warmly.

Discontinuation: If it has been necessary to use this drug for an extended period of time, do not discontinue it abruptly. Ask physician for guidance regarding dosage adjustment and withdrawal. It may also be necessary to adjust the dose of other drugs taken concurrently with it.

Special Storage Instructions
Keep tablets and capsules in a dry, tightly closed container. Keep elixir in a tightly closed, amber glass container.

PERPHENAZINE
Year Introduced: 1963

Brand Names

USA	Canada
Trilafon (Schering)	Phenazine (ICN)
Etrafon [CD] (Schering)	Trilafon (Schering)
Triavil [CD] (Merck	Etrafon [CD] (Schering)
Sharp & Dohme)	Triavil [CD] (MSD)

Drug Family: Tranquilizer, Strong (Anti-psychotic) [Phenothiazines]

Prescription Required: Yes

Available Dosage Forms and Strengths
Tablets — 2 mg., 4 mg., 8 mg., 16 mg.
Prolonged Action Tablets — 8 mg.
Syrup — 2 mg. per teaspoonful
Concentrate — 16 mg. per teaspoonful
Injection — 5 mg. per ml.

How This Drug Works
Intended Therapeutic Effect(s):   Restoration of emotional calm. Relief of severe anxiety, agitation, and psychotic behavior.

Location of Drug Action(s):   Those nerve pathways in the brain that utilize the tissue chemical dopamine for the transmission of nerve impulses.

Method of Drug Action(s):   Not completely established. Present theory is that by inhibiting the action of dopamine, this drug acts to correct an imbalance of nerve impulse transmissions that is thought to be responsible for certain mental disorders.

THIS DRUG SHOULD NOT BE TAKEN IF
—you have had an allergic reaction to any dosage form of it previously.
—you have a blood or bone marrow disorder.
—you have impaired liver function.
—it is prescribed for a child under 12 years of age.

INFORM YOUR PHYSICIAN BEFORE TAKING THIS DRUG IF
—you are allergic or sensitive to any phenothiazine drug (see Drug Family, Section Four).
—you are taking sedatives, sleep-inducing drugs, other tranquilizers, antidepressants, antihistamines, or narcotic drugs of any kind.
—you have epilepsy.
—you plan to have surgery under general or spinal anesthesia in the near future.

Time Required for Apparent Benefit
Some benefit may be apparent during first week. Maximal benefit may require continuous use for several weeks.

Possible Side-Effects *(natural, expected, and unavoidable drug actions)*
Drowsiness (usually mild), blurring of vision, nasal congestion, dryness of mouth, constipation, impaired urination.

Possible Adverse Effects *(unusual, unexpected, and infrequent reactions)*

IF ANY OF THE FOLLOWING DEVELOP, DISCONTINUE DRUG AND NOTIFY YOUR PHYSICIAN AS SOON AS POSSIBLE

Mild Adverse Effects
Allergic Reactions: Skin rashes (various kinds), hives, itching, local or generalized swelling.
Headaches, mild insomnia.

Serious Adverse Effects
Allergic Reactions: Anaphylactic reaction (see Glossary), severe skin reactions, asthma.
Idiosyncratic Reactions: High fever.
Parkinson-like disorders (see Glossary).
Hepatitis with jaundice (see Glossary).
Bone marrow depression (see Glossary)—usually mild and very rare.
Muscle spasms involving the face and neck—rolling eyes, grimacing, clamping jaws, difficult speech and swallowing, twisting and bending of the neck, rounding and protrusion of the tongue.
Generalized convulsions.

Advisability of Use During Pregnancy
Safety not established. Prudent use is best determined by the physician's evaluation.

Advisability of Use While Nursing Infant
Safety not established. Avoid use if possible. Ask physician for guidance.

Habit-Forming Potential
None.

Effects of Overdosage
With Moderate Overdose: Marked drowsiness, weakness, slurred speech, staggering gait, muscle spasms of face, neck, arms, and legs, convulsions.
With Large Overdose: Stupor progressing to deep sleep and coma.

Possible Effects of Extended Use
Tardive dyskinesia (see Glossary).

Recommended Periodic Examinations While Taking This Drug
Complete blood cell counts, especially during first 3 months.
Liver function tests.
Periodic electrocardiograms.
Periodic examinations of tongue for development of fine, wave-like, rippling movements (involuntary) that could indicate the beginning of tardive dyskinesia.

While Taking This Drug, Observe the Following
Foods: No restrictions.
Beverages: No restrictions.
Alcohol: Use extreme caution until combined effects have been determined. Alcohol may increase the sedative action of perhenazine and accentuate its depressant effects on brain function. Perphenazine may increase the intoxicating action of alcohol.
Tobacco Smoking: No interactions expected.
Other Drugs
Perphenazine may *increase* the effects of
- all sedatives, sleep-inducing drugs, other tranquilizers, antidepressants, antihistamines, and narcotic drugs, and cause oversedation. Ask physician for guidance regarding dosage adjustment.
- mono-amine oxidase (MAO) inhibitor drugs (see Drug Family, Section Four), and cause excessive lowering of the blood pressure.
- reserpine (and related drugs), and cause excessive lowering of the blood pressure.
- atropine and atropine-like drugs (see Drug Family, Section Four).

Perphenazine may *decrease* the effects of
- appetite suppressant drugs (Pre-Sate, Preludin, Dexedrine, etc.).
- levodopa (Dopar, Larodopa, Parda, etc.), and reduce its effectiveness in the treatment of Parkinson's disease (shaking palsy).

Perphenazine *taken concurrently* with
- anti-convulsants, may cause a change in the pattern of epileptic seizures. Ask physician for guidance regarding dosage adjustment of the anti-convulsant.
- anti-hypertensive drugs (see Drug Family, Section Four), may cause excessive lowering of the blood pressure. Use this combination very cautiously and ask physician for guidance regarding dosage adjustment.

•quinidine, may impair heart function. Avoid this combination of drugs.

The following drugs may *increase* the effects of perphenazine
• tricyclic antidepressants (see Drug Family, Section Four)
• all sedatives, sleep-inducing drugs, and other tranquilizers, both mild and strong

Driving a Vehicle, Piloting a Plane, Operating Machinery: This drug may impair mental alertness, judgment, physical coordination, and reaction time. Avoid hazardous activities.

Exposure to Sun: Use caution until sensitivity has been determined. This drug may cause photosensitivity (see Glossary).

Exposure to Heat: Use caution until combined effect has been determined. This drug may impair regulation of body temperature and produce increased risk of heat stroke.

Heavy Exercise or Exertion: No restriction in moderate temperatures.

Discontinuation: If it has been necessary to use this drug for an extended period of time, do not discontinue it suddenly. Ask physician for guidance regarding dosage reduction and withdrawal. It may also be necessary to adjust the dosage of other drugs taken concurrently with it.

Special Storage Instructions
Keep liquid concentrate in a tightly closed, amber glass container. Protect all liquid forms from light.

PHENACETIN
(Acetophenetidin)

Year Introduced: 1886

Brand Names

USA		Canada
A.P.C. Tablets [CD] (Various Manufacturers)	Norgesic [CD] (Riker) P.A.C. Compound [CD] (Upjohn)	None
Bromo-Seltzer [CD] (Warner-Lambert)	Percodan [CD] (Endo)	
Empirin Compound [CD] (Burroughs Wellcome)	Sinubid [CD] (Warner/Chilcott) (Others)	
Fiorinal [CD] (Sandoz)		

Drug Family: Analgesic, Mild; Fever Reducer (Antipyretic)

Prescription Required: In combination with aspirin and caffeine—No
In combination with barbiturates, codeine, etc.—Yes

Available Dosage Forms and Strengths
Tablets—300 mg.
Also numerous combination drugs containing 130 to 194 mg. of phenacetin.

How This Drug Works
Intended Therapeutic Effect(s)
- relief of mild to moderate pain.
- reduction of high fever.

Location of Drug Action(s):   Principal actions occur in
- areas of injury, muscle spasm, or inflammation in many body tissues.
- the heat-regulating center, located in the hypothalamus of the brain.

Method of Drug Action(s):   Not fully established. It is thought that this drug relieves both pain and fever by reducing the tissue concentration of prostaglandins, chemicals involved in the production of pain, fever, and inflammation.

THIS DRUG SHOULD NOT BE TAKEN IF
—you have had an allergic reaction to any dosage form of it previously.

INFORM YOUR PHYSICIAN BEFORE TAKING THIS DRUG IF
—you have a history of serious kidney disease or impaired kidney function.

Time Required for Apparent Benefit
Drug action begins in 15 to 30 minutes, reaches a maximum in approximately 60 minutes, and persists for 2 to 3 hours.

Possible Side-Effects *(natural, expected, and unavoidable drug actions)*
Mild drowsiness (in sensitive individuals).
Flushing and sweating (in the presence of fever).

CAUTION
This drug may damage the kidneys when used in large amounts or for a long period of time. Check product label and do not exceed 2 grams (7 to 8 tablets) in 24 hours. Do not take regularly on a daily basis for more than 10 days without consulting your physician.

Possible Adverse Effects *(unusual, unexpected, and infrequent reactions)*
IF ANY OF THE FOLLOWING DEVELOP, DISCONTINUE DRUG AND NOTIFY YOUR PHYSICIAN AS SOON AS POSSIBLE
Mild Adverse Effects
Allergic Reactions: Skin rash, hives.
Impaired thinking and concentration.

Serious Adverse Effects
Allergic Reactions: Abnormal bruising and bleeding due to destruction of blood platelets (see Glossary).
Idiosyncratic Reactions: Possible hemolytic anemia (see Glossary).
Development of abnormal hemoglobin (methemoglobin).
Bone marrow depression (see Glossary)—fatigue, weakness, fever, sore throat, abnormal bleeding or bruising.

Advisability of Use During Pregnancy
Avoid completely if possible. This drug may cause the formation of abnormal hemoglobin in the fetus or newborn infant.

Advisability of Use While Nursing Infant
This drug is known to be present in milk. Safety for the nursing infant is not established. Ask physician for guidance.

Habit-Forming Potential
With prolonged use this drug may cause a mild form of psychological dependence (see Glossary).

Effects of Overdosage
With Moderate Overdose: Nausea, vomiting, drowsiness, dizziness, tremors, yellow vision.
With Large Overdose: Profuse sweating, bloody urine, convulsions, coma.

Possible Effects of Extended Use
Serious damage to kidney tissues.
Development of abnormal hemoglobin.

Recommended Periodic Examinations While Taking This Drug
Kidney function tests, including urine analysis.
Complete blood cell counts and examination for abnormal hemoglobin (methemoglobin).

While Taking This Drug, Observe the Following
Foods: No restrictions.
Beverages: No restrictions. Total liquid intake should be no less than 5 to 6 pints every 24 hours.
Alcohol: No interactions expected.
Tobacco Smoking: No interactions expected.
Other Drugs
The following drugs may *decrease* the effects of phenacetin
• phenobarbital may hasten its elimination from the body.
Driving a Vehicle, Piloting a Plane, Operating Machinery: No restrictions when used in recommended doses.
Exposure to Sun: No restrictions.

Special Storage Instructions
Keep in a dry, tightly closed container.

PHENAZOPYRIDINE

Year Introduced: 1927

Brand Names

USA	Canada
Pyridium	Phenazo (ICN)
(Warner/Chilcott)	Pyridium
Azo Gantanol [CD]	(Warner/Chilcott)
(Roche)	Azo Gantrisin [CD]
Azo Gantrisin [CD]	(Roche)
(Roche)	Azo-Mandelamine [CD]
Azo-Mandelamine [CD]	(Warner/Chilcott)
(Warner/Chilcott)	Azotrex [CD] (Bristol)
Azotrex [CD] (Bristol)	
Thiosulfil-A [CD] (Ayerst)	
Urobiotic [CD] (Pfizer)	
(Numerous other brand	
and combination	
brand names)	

Drug Family: Urinary Analgesic

Prescription Required: Yes

Available Dosage Forms and Strengths
Tablets—100 mg., 200 mg.

How This Drug Works

Intended Therapeutic Effect(s):   Relief of pain and discomfort associated with acute irritation of the lower urinary tract, as in cystitis, urethritis, and prostatitis.

Location of Drug Action(s):   The sensory nerve endings in the lining of the lower urinary tract (bladder and urethra).

Method of Drug Action(s):   By its local anesthetic effect on the tissues lining the lower urinary tract, this drug provides symptomatic relief of pain, burning, pressure, and sense of urgency to void.

THIS DRUG SHOULD NOT BE TAKEN IF

—you have had an allergic reaction to any dosage form of it previously.
—you have active hepatitis.

INFORM YOUR PHYSICIAN BEFORE TAKING THIS DRUG IF

—you have a history of serious liver or kidney disease.

Time Required for Apparent Benefit

Drug action usually begins in 1 to 2 hours and persists for 3 to 5 hours.

Possible Side-Effects *(natural, expected, and unavoidable drug actions)*

Reddish-orange discoloration of the urine, of no significance.

Possible Adverse Effects *(unusual, unexpected, and infrequent reactions)*

IF ANY OF THE FOLLOWING DEVELOP, DISCONTINUE DRUG AND NOTIFY YOUR PHYSICIAN AS SOON AS POSSIBLE

Mild Adverse Effects
Allergic Reactions: Skin rash.
Headache, dizziness.
Indigestion, abdominal cramping.

Serious Adverse Effects
Allergic Reactions: Hepatitis with or without jaundice (see Glossary).
Idiosyncratic Reactions: Hemolytic anemia (see Glossary) in sensitive individuals (may occur in the presence of impaired kidney function).

Advisability of Use During Pregnancy
Safety not established. It is advisable to limit use to small doses for short periods of time.

Advisability of Use While Nursing Infant
Presence of drug in milk is not known. Ask physician for guidance.

Habit-Forming Potential
None.

Effects of Overdosage
With Moderate Overdose: Nausea, indigestion, abdominal distress, vomiting.
With Large Overdose: Hemolytic anemia (in sensitive individuals), skin discoloration, altered hemoglobin resulting in shortness of breath and weakness.

Possible Effects of Extended Use
Orange-yellow discoloration of the skin.
Hemolytic anemia.

Recommended Periodic Examinations While Taking This Drug
If used on a long-term basis, red blood cell counts and liver function tests.

While Taking This Drug, Observe the Following
Foods: No restrictions.
Beverages: No restrictions.
Alcohol: No interactions expected.
Tobacco Smoking: No interactions expected.
Other Drugs: No significant interaction with other drugs has been reported.
Driving a Vehicle, Piloting a Plane, Operating Machinery: No restrictions.
Exposure to Sun: No restrictions.

Special Storage Instructions
Keep in a dry, tightly closed container.

PHENFORMIN*

Year Introduced: 1956

Brand Names

USA	Canada
DBI (Geigy)	DBI (Arlington)
DBI-TD (Geigy)	DBI-TD (Arlington)
Meltrol (USV Pharmaceutical)	

Drug Family: Anti-diabetic, Oral (Hypoglycemic) [Biguanides]

Prescription Required: Yes

Available Dosage Forms and Strengths

Tablets — 25 mg.
Prolonged Action Capsules — 50 mg., 100 mg.

How This Drug Works

Intended Therapeutic Effect(s):   Lowering of blood sugar levels in the management of stable adult (maturity-onset) diabetes of moderate severity.

Location of Drug Action(s):   In those tissues responsive to the action of insulin.

Method of Drug Action(s):   Not completely established. It is thought that this drug may promote an increase in the utilization of sugar by improving the efficiency of insulin activity.

THIS DRUG SHOULD NOT BE TAKEN IF

—you have had an allergic reaction to any dosage form of it previously.
—you have a history of kidney disease with impaired kidney function.
—you have a history of alcoholism or excessive drinking of alcoholic beverages.

INFORM YOUR PHYSICIAN BEFORE TAKING THIS DRUG IF

—your diabetes has been difficult to control in the past ("brittle type").
—you have a history of liver disease or heart disease.
—you do not know how to recognize and treat hypoglycemia (see Glossary).

Time Required for Apparent Benefit

A single dose lowers the blood sugar within 2 to 6 hours. Regular use for 1 to 2 weeks may be needed to determine this drug's effectiveness in controlling your diabetes.

Possible Side-Effects *(natural, expected, and unavoidable drug actions)*

None. However, excessive dosage and/or inadequate food intake may result in episodes of hypoglycemia. This is most likely to occur if phenformin is used concurrently with insulin or another oral anti-diabetic drug.

CAUTION

1. Because of the increased frequency of heart and blood vessel disease in the elderly, this drug should be used with caution by those over 60 years of age.
2. The daily dose should not exceed 100 mg.

*This drug is being removed from the market in the U.S. and Canada. It will not be available for general use after October 25, 1977.

Possible Adverse Effects *(unusual, unexpected, and infrequent reactions)*

IF ANY OF THE FOLLOWING DEVELOP, DISCONTINUE DRUG AND NOTIFY YOUR PHYSICIAN AS SOON AS POSSIBLE

Mild Adverse Effects
Allergic Reactions: Hives (rare).
Loss of appetite, nausea, vomiting, unpleasant metallic taste, diarrhea. Weakness, fatigue.

Serious Adverse Effects
†Lactic acidosis—nausea, vomiting, drowsiness, abdominal pain, and heavy, exaggerated breathing. This requires immediate treatment.

Advisability of Use During Pregnancy
Safety not established. Prudent use is best determined by the physician's evaluation.

Advisability of Use While Nursing Infant
Presence of drug in milk has not been determined. Safety for infant has not been established. Ask physician for guidance.

Habit-Forming Potential
None.

Effects of Overdose
With Moderate Overdose: Marked nausea, vomiting, diarrhea, mild to moderate hypoglycemia.
With Large Overdose: Severe lactic acidosis, drop in blood pressure and body temperature, heart failure (more common in the elderly).

Possible Effects of Extended Use
Reports of increased frequency and severity of heart and blood vessel diseases following long-term use of phenformin are controversial and inconclusive. A direct cause-and-effect relationship (see Glossary) has not been established to date. Ask physician for guidance regarding long-term use.

Recommended Periodic Examinations While Taking This Drug
Frequent urine examinations for sugar and acetone.
Complete blood cell counts.
Liver function and kidney function tests.
Periodic evaluation of heart and circulatory system.

While Taking This Drug, Observe the Following
Foods: Follow diabetic diet prescribed by your physician. Take this drug with meals to reduce the possibility of nausea and stomach irritation.
Beverages: As indicated in the diabetic diet prescribed by your physician.
Alcohol: Use with extreme caution and in small quantities until combined effects have been determined. Alcohol can interact with this drug to produce nausea, vomiting, severe drop in blood pressure, and marked acidosis.
Tobacco Smoking: No interactions expected. No restrictions other than those imposed by your physician as part of your total treatment program.

†A rare adverse effect important to recognize.

Other Drugs
Phenformin may *increase* the effects of
• all oral anti-diabetic drugs (sulfonylureas), increasing the possibility of hypoglycemia. Adhere strictly to properly adjusted dosage schedules.
• insulin (all types), increasing the possibility of hypoglycemia.
• clofibrate (Atromid-S).

Driving a Vehicle, Piloting a Plane, Operating Machinery: Maintain properly adjusted dosage schedule, eating schedule, and physical activities to prevent hypoglycemia. Know how to recognize and treat hypoglycemia.

Exposure to Sun: No restrictions.

Heavy Exercise or Exertion: Avoid excessive exercise that could cause hypoglycemia.

Occurrence of Unrelated Illness: Consult your physician if acute infection, vomiting, diarrhea, serious injury, or need for surgery arises. Your dosage of this drug will require adjustment.

Discontinuation: If you find it necessary to discontinue this drug abruptly, notify your physician as soon as possible. Ask for guidance regarding control of your diabetes.

Special Storage Instructions
Keep in a dry, tightly closed container.

PHENIRAMINE

Year Introduced: 1951

Brand Names

USA	Canada
Inhiston (Plough)	Triaminic [CD] (Anca)
Robitussin-AC [CD]	Triaminicin [CD] (Anca)
(Robins)	Triaminicol [CD] (Anca)
Triaminic [CD] (Dorsey)	
Triaminicin [CD] (Dorsey)	
Triaminicol [CD] (Dorsey)	
Tussagesic [CD] (Dorsey)	
Tussaminic [CD] (Dorsey)	
Ursinus [CD] (Dorsey)	
(Numerous other brand and combination brand names)	

Drug Family: Antihistamines

Prescription Required: For low-strength formulations—No
For high-strength formulations—Yes

Available Dosage Forms and Strengths
Tablets — 40 mg.
Tablets — 12.5 mg., 25 mg. (in combination with other drugs)
Syrup — 6.25 mg. per teaspoonful (in combination with other drugs)
Pediatric Drops — 10 mg. per ml. (in combination with other drugs)

How This Drug Works
Intended Therapeutic Effect(s):   Relief of symptoms associated with hayfever (allergic rhinitis) and with allergic reactions in the skin, such as itching, swelling, hives, and rash.

Location of Drug Action(s):   Those hypersensitive tissues that release excessive histamine as part of an allergic reaction. The principal tissue sites are the eyes, the nose, and the skin.

Method of Drug Action(s):   This drug reduces the intensity of the allergic response by blocking the action of histamine after it has been released from sensitized tissue cells.

THIS DRUG SHOULD NOT BE TAKEN IF
—you have had an allergic reaction to any dosage form of it previously.
—you are taking, or have taken during the past 2 weeks, any mono-amine oxidase (MAO) inhibitor drug (see Drug Family, Section Four).
—it has been prescribed for a newborn infant.

INFORM YOUR PHYSICIAN BEFORE TAKING THIS DRUG IF
—you have had an unfavorable reaction to any antihistamine drug in the past.
—you have glaucoma.
—you have a history of asthma, peptic ulcer disease, or impairment of urinary bladder function.
—you plan to have surgery under general anesthesia in the near future.

Time Required for Apparent Benefit
Drug action begins in approximately 30 minutes, reaches a maximum in 1 hour, and subsides in 4 to 6 hours.

Possible Side-Effects *(natural, expected, and unavoidable drug actions)*
Drowsiness, sense of weakness, dryness of nose, mouth, and throat, constipation.

CAUTION
The elderly (over 60 years of age) may be more susceptible to the adverse effects of this drug. Small doses are advisable until tolerance is determined.

Possible Adverse Effects *(unusual, unexpected, and infrequent reactions)*

IF ANY OF THE FOLLOWING DEVELOP, DISCONTINUE DRUG AND NOTIFY YOUR PHYSICIAN AS SOON AS POSSIBLE

Mild Adverse Effects
Allergic Reactions: Skin rash, hives.

Headache, dizziness, inability to concentrate, nervousness, blurring of vision, double vision, difficulty in urination.

Nausea, vomiting, diarrhea.

Serious Adverse Effects

Idiosyncratic Reactions: Emotional and behavioral disturbances: Confusion, agitation, inappropriate actions.

dvisability of Use During Pregnancy

No reports of adverse effects on mother or fetus, but complete safety has not been established. Limit use to small doses and for short periods of time.

dvisability of Use While Nursing Infant

This drug may impair milk formation and make nursing difficult. It is known to be present in milk. Avoid use or stop nursing. Ask physician for guidance.

abit-Forming Potential

None.

ffects of Overdosage

With Moderate Overdose: Marked drowsiness, confusion, incoordination, unsteady gait, muscle tremors. In children: excitement, hallucinations, overactivity, convulsions.

With Large Overdose: Stupor progressing to coma, fever, flushed face, dilated pupils, weak pulse, shallow breathing.

ossible Effects of Extended Use

None reported.

ecommended Periodic Examinations While Taking This Drug

Complete blood cell counts.

hile Taking This Drug, Observe the Following

Foods: No restrictions. Stomach irritation can be reduced if drug is taken after eating.

Beverages: Coffee and tea may help to reduce the drowsiness caused by most antihistamines.

Alcohol: Use with extreme caution until combined effect has been determined. The combination of alcohol and antihistamines can cause rapid and marked sedation.

Tobacco Smoking: No interactions expected.

Other Drugs

Pheniramine may *increase* the effects of

- sedatives, sleep-inducing drugs, tranquilizers, antidepressants, pain relievers, and narcotic drugs, and result in oversedation. Careful dosage adjustments are necessary.
- atropine and drugs with atropine-like action (see Drug Family, Section Four).

The following drugs may *increase* the effects of pheniramine

- all sedatives, sleep-inducing drugs, tranquilizers, pain relievers, and narcotic drugs may exaggerate its sedative action and cause oversedation.

- mono-amine oxidase (MAO) inhibitor drugs (see Drug Family, Section Four) may delay its elimination from the body, thus exaggerating and prolonging its action.

The following drugs may *decrease* the effects of pheniramine

- amphetamines (Benzedrine, Dexedrine, Desoxyn, etc.) may reduce the drowsiness caused by most antihistamines.

Driving a Vehicle, Piloting a Plane, Operating Machinery: This drug may impair mental alertness, judgment, physical coordination, and reaction time. Avoid hazardous activities until full sedative effect has been determined.

Exposure to Sun: No restrictions.

Special Storage Instructions
Keep in a dry, tightly closed, light-resistant container.

PHENOBARBITAL/PHENOBARBITONE

Year Introduced: 1912

Brand Names

USA	Canada
Barbipil (North Amer. Pharm.)	Epilol (I&B)
Barbita (North Amer. Pharm.)	Epsylone (Powell)
Bar-15, -25, -100 (Scrip)	Eskabarb (SK&F)
Eskabarb (Smith Kline & French)	Fenosed (Nordic)
Floramine (Lemmon)	Gardenal (Poulenc)
Henomint (Bowman)	Hypnolone (Hartz)
Hypnette (Fleming)	Luminal (Winthrop)
Luminal (Winthrop)	Mediphen (Medic)
Oprine (Pennwalt)	Nova-Pheno (Nova)
Solu-barb (Fellows-Testagar)	PEBA (Powell)
Stental (Robins)	Phen Bar (Saunders)
(Numerous other combination brand names)	Sedabar (Saunders)

Drug Family: Sedative, Mild; Sleep Inducer (Hypnotic) [Barbiturates]

Prescription Required: Yes (Controlled Drug, U.S. Schedule 4)

Available Dosage Forms and Strengths

Tablets — 16 mg., 32 mg., 50 mg., 64 mg., 100 mg.
Prolonged Action Capsules — 65 mg., 100 mg.
Elixir — 20 mg. per teaspoonful

How This Drug Works

Intended Therapeutic Effect(s)
- with low dosage, relief of mild to moderate anxiety or tension (sedative effect).
- with higher dosage taken at bedtime, sedation sufficient to induce sleep (hypnotic effect).
- with continuous dosage on a regular schedule, prevention of epileptic seizures (anti-convulsant effect).

Location of Drug Action(s):   The connecting points (synapses) in the nerve pathways that transmit impulses between the wake-sleep centers of the brain.

Method of Drug Action(s):   Not completely established. Present thinking is that this drug selectively blocks the transmission of nerve impulses by reducing the amount of available norepinephrine, one of the chemicals responsible for impulse transmission.

THIS DRUG SHOULD NOT BE TAKEN IF

—you have had an allergic reaction to any dosage form of it previously.
—you have a history of porphyria.

INFORM YOUR PHYSICIAN BEFORE TAKING THIS DRUG IF

—you are allergic or sensitive to any barbiturate drug.
—you are taking any sedative, sleep-inducing drugs, tranquilizers, antihistamines, pain relievers, or narcotic drugs of any kind.
—you have epilepsy.
—you have a history of liver or kidney disease.
—you plan to have surgery under general anesthesia in the near future.

Time Required for Apparent Benefit

Approximately 1 hour.

Possible Side-Effects (natural, expected, and unavoidable drug actions)

Drowsiness, lethargy, a sense of mental and physical sluggishness.

CAUTION

The elderly (over 60 years of age) and the debilitated may experience agitation, excitement, confusion, and delirium with standard doses. Small doses are advisable until tolerance has been determined.

Possible Adverse Effects (unusual, unexpected, and infrequent reactions)

IF ANY OF THE FOLLOWING DEVELOP, DISCONTINUE DRUG AND NOTIFY YOUR PHYSICIAN AS SOON AS POSSIBLE

Mild Adverse Effects
    Allergic Reactions: Skin rash (various kinds), hives, localized swellings of eyelids, face, or lips, drug fever. (See Glossary).
    "Hangover" effect, dizziness, unsteadiness.
    Nausea, vomiting, diarrhea.
    Joint and muscle pains, most often in the neck, shoulders, and arms.

Serious Adverse Effects
Allergic Reactions: Hepatitis with jaundice (see Glossary). Severe skin reactions.

Idiosyncratic Reactions: Paradoxical excitement and delirium (rather than sedation).

Anemia, manifested by weakness and fatigue.

Reduction of blood platelets (see Glossary), resulting in unusual bleeding or bruising.

Advisability of Use During Pregnancy
Safety not established. Prudent use is best determined by the physician's evaluation.

Advisability of Use While Nursing Infant
Drug is known to be present in milk. Avoid use if possible. Ask physician for guidance.

Habit-Forming Potential
This drug can cause both psychological and physical dependence (see Glossary).

Effects of Overdosage
With Moderate Overdose: Behavior similar to alcoholic intoxication: confusion, slurred speech, physical incoordination, staggering gait, drowsiness.

With Large Overdose: Deepening sleep, coma, slow and shallow breathing, weak and rapid pulse, cold and sweaty skin.

Possible Effects of Extended Use
Psychological and/or physical dependence.

Anemia.

If dose is excessive, a form of chronic drug intoxication can occur: headache, impaired vision, slurred speech, and depression.

Recommended Periodic Examinations While Taking This Drug
Complete blood cell counts.

Liver function tests.

While Taking This Drug, Observe the Following
Foods: No restrictions.

Beverages: No restrictions.

Alcohol: Avoid completely. Alcohol can increase greatly the sedative and depressant actions of this drug on brain function.

Tobacco Smoking: No interactions expected.

Other Drugs

Phenobarbital may *increase* the effects of

- other sedatives, sleep-inducing drugs, tranquilizers, antihistamines, pain relievers, and narcotic drugs, and cause oversedation. Ask your physician for guidance regarding dosage adjustments.

Phenobarbital may *decrease* the effects of

- oral anticoagulants of the coumarin family. Ask physician for guidance regarding prothrombin time testing and adjustment of the anticoagulant dosage.
- aspirin, and reduce its pain relieving action.
- cortisone and related drugs, by hastening their elimination from the body.
- oral contraceptives, by hastening their elimination from the body.
- griseofulvin (Fulvicin, Grisactin, etc.), and reduce its effectiveness in treating fungus infections.
- phenylbutazone (Azolid, Butazolidin, etc.), and reduce its effectiveness in treating inflammation and pain.

Phenobarbital *taken concurrently* with

- anti-convulsants, may cause a change in the pattern of epileptic seizures. Careful dosage adjustments are necessary to achieve a balance of actions that will give the best protection from seizures.

The following drugs may *increase* the effects of phenobarbital

- both mild and strong tranquilizers may increase the sedative and sleep-inducing actions of barbiturate drugs and cause oversedation.
- isoniazid (INH, Isozide, etc.) may prolong the action of barbiturate drugs.
- antihistamines may increase the sedative effects of barbiturate drugs.
- oral anti-diabetic drugs of the sulfonylurea type may prolong the sedative effect of barbiturate drugs.
- mono-amine oxidase (MAO) inhibitor drugs may prolong the sedative effects of barbiturate drugs.

Driving a Vehicle, Piloting a Plane, Operating Machinery: This drug can produce drowsiness and can impair mental alertness, judgment, physical coordination, and reaction time. Avoid hazardous activities.

Exposure to Sun: Use caution until sensitivity has been determined. Some barbiturates can cause photosensitivity (see Glossary).

Exposure to Cold: The elderly may experience excessive lowering of body temperature while taking this drug. Keep dosage to a minimum during winter and dress warmly.

Discontinuation: If it has been necessary to use this drug for an extended period of time, do not discontinue it abruptly. Ask physician for guidance regarding dosage adjustment and withdrawal. It may also be necessary to adjust the doses of other drugs taken concurrently with it.

Special Storage Instructions

Keep tablets and capsules in a dry, tightly closed container. Keep elixir in a tightly closed, amber glass bottle.

PHENOXYBENZAMINE

Year Introduced: 1953

Brand Names

USA	Canada
Dibenzyline (Smith Kline & French)	None

Drug Family: Vasodilator (Alpha-Adrenergic Blocker) [Sympatholytics]

Prescription Required: Yes

Available Dosage Forms and Strengths
Capsules—10 mg.

How This Drug Works
Intended Therapeutic Effect(s)
- relief of impaired circulation associated with Raynaud's phenomenon, acrocyanosis, and the aftereffects of frostbite.
- control of the high blood pressure and sweating associated with adrenalin-producing tumors (pheochromocytoma).

Location of Drug Action(s):   Those sympathetic nerve terminals in the muscles of blood vessel walls that are responsible for vessel constriction.

Method of Drug Action(s):   By blocking the action of those nerve terminals responsible for maintaining vessel constriction, this drug permits the blood vessel walls to relax and expand. The resulting dilation increases the volume of blood flowing through the vessels and lowers the blood pressure.

THIS DRUG SHOULD NOT BE TAKEN IF
—you have had an allergic reaction to any dosage form of it previously.
—you have a condition that would make it dangerous for you to have a sudden drop in blood pressure (such as angina or impaired circulation to the brain).

INFORM YOUR PHYSICIAN BEFORE TAKING THIS DRUG IF
—you have a history of stroke or heart disease.
—you are taking any medicine for high blood pressure.
—you have diabetes.

Time Required for Apparent Benefit
Drug action may be felt during the first 24 hours. However, regular use for at least 2 weeks is necessary to determine proper dosage adjustment. Maximal benefit may require several additional weeks.

Possible Side-Effects *(natural, expected, and unavoidable drug actions)*
Lightheadedness in upright position (see orthostatic hypotension in Glossary), nasal stuffiness, rapid heart action, skin warmth and flushing. (These tend to decrease with continued use of the drug.)

CAUTION
Adhere strictly to prescribed doses. To prevent overdosage, the same dosage should be continued for at least 4 days before any increase. Increase dosage only on advice of physician.

Possible Adverse Effects *(unusual, unexpected, and infrequent reactions)*

IF ANY OF THE FOLLOWING DEVELOP, DISCONTINUE DRUG AND NOTIFY YOUR PHYSICIAN AS SOON AS POSSIBLE

Mild Adverse Effects
Drowsiness, lethargy, dryness of the mouth.
Indigestion, nausea, vomiting (with large doses).
Impaired ejaculation.
Serious Adverse Effects
None reported.

Advisability of Use During Pregnancy
No reports of adverse effects on mother or fetus. If used, keep dose as small as possible.

Advisability of Use While Nursing Infant
Presence of drug in milk is not known. Avoid use or avoid nursing. Ask physician for guidance.

Habit-Forming Potential
None

Effects of Overdosage
With Moderate Overdose: Extreme weakness, dizziness, fainting, vomiting, rapid heart beat.
With Large Overdose: Constricted pupils, stupor, collapse of circulation causing cold and sweaty skin, weak and rapid pulse.

Possible Effects of Extended Use
None reported.

Recommended Periodic Examinations While Taking This Drug
None required.

While Taking This Drug, Observe the Following
Foods: No specific restrictions. However, a large meal may increase the possibility of orthostatic hypotension.
Beverages: No restrictions.
Alcohol: Use caution until combined effect has been determined. Alcohol can add to the drop in blood pressure produced by this drug.
Tobacco Smoking: Avoid completely. Nicotine can reduce this drug's effectiveness in dilating blood vessels and improving circulation.
Other Drugs
Phenoxybenzamine may *increase* the effects of
• anti-hypertensive drugs, and cause excessive lowering of the blood pressure. Careful dosage adjustments are necessary.

Phenoxybenzamine *taken concurrently* with
• Adrenalin (and similar drugs used for asthma), may cause a dangerous drop in blood pressure. Avoid the concurrent use of these two drugs if possible.

• insulin and oral anti-diabetic drugs, may make it difficult to recognize the onset of hypoglycemia (see Glossary). Use extra caution to reduce the possibility of hypoglycemia.

The following drugs may *increase* the effects of phenoxybenzamine

• most anti-hypertensive drugs may exaggerate its blood pressure-lowering action and cause excessive drop in pressure. Careful dosage adjustment is necessary.

Driving a Vehicle, Piloting a Plane, Operating Machinery: This drug can cause orthostatic hypotension. Be alert to this possibility while engaged in hazardous activities. Be prepared to stop and lie down to prevent fainting.

Exposure to Sun: No restrictions.

Exposure to Heat: No restrictions.

Exposure to Cold: Keep to a minimum. Cold reduces the ability of this drug to dilate blood vessels and improve circulation.

Heavy Exercise or Exertion: Use extreme caution until combined effect has been determined. Excessive physical activity can increase the drop in blood pressure produced by this drug.

Discontinuation: The action of this drug is quite prolonged. Drug effects may continue for up to a week after the last dose. Use caution until all effects have disappeared.

Special Storage Instructions
Keep in a dry, tightly closed container.

PHENTERMINE

Year Introduced: 1952

Brand Names

USA	Canada
Fastin (Beecham)	Ionamin (Pennwalt)
Ionamin(Pennwalt)	
Tora (Tutag)	
Wilpo (Dorsey)	

Drug Family: Appetite Suppressant (Anorexiant), Amphetamine-like Drug [Sympathomimetics]

Prescription Required: Yes (Controlled Drug, U.S. Schedule 4)

Available Dosage Forms and Strengths
Tablets — 8 mg.
Capsules — 15 mg.
Prolonged Action Capsules — 15 mg., 30 mg.

How This Drug Works
Intended Therapeutic Effect(s)   The suppression of appetite in the management of weight reduction using low-calorie diets.

Location of Drug Action(s):   Not completely established. The site of therapeutic action is thought to be the appetite-regulating center located in the hypothalamus of the brain.

Method of Drug Action(s):   Not established. This drug is thought to resemble the amphetamines in its action, diminishing hunger by altering the chemical control of nerve impulse transmission in the brain center which regulates appetite.

THIS DRUG SHOULD NOT BE TAKEN IF
—you have had an allergic reaction to any dosage form of it previously.

—you have glaucoma.

—you are taking, or have taken during the past 2 weeks, any mono-amine oxidase (MAO) inhibitor drug (see Drug Family, Section Four).

—it is prescribed for a child under 12 years of age.

INFORM YOUR PHYSICIAN BEFORE TAKING THIS DRUG IF
—you have had an unfavorable reaction to any amphetamine-like drug in the past

—you have high blood pressure or any form of heart disease.

—you have an overactive thyroid gland (hyperthyroidism).

—you have a history of serious anxiety or nervous tension.

Time Required for Apparent Benefit
Drug action begins in approximately 1 hour and persists for 10 to 14 hours (if the prolonged action capsule is used).

Possible Side-Effects *(natural, expected, and unavoidable drug actions)*
Nervousness, insomnia.

CAUTION
The appetite-suppressing action of this drug may disappear after several weeks of continuous use, regardless of the size of the dose. *Do not increase the dose* beyond that prescribed.

Possible Adverse Effects *(unusual, unexpected, and infrequent reactions)*
IF ANY OF THE FOLLOWING DEVELOP, DISCONTINUE DRUG AND NOTIFY YOUR PHYSICIAN AS SOON AS POSSIBLE
Mild Adverse Effects
Allergic Reactions: Skin rash, hives.
Dryness of the mouth, nausea, diarrhea.
Headache, dizziness, restlessness, tremor.
Fast and forceful heart action (heart palpitation).
Serious Adverse Effects
None reported.

Advisability of Use During Pregnancy
Safety not established. Prudent use is best determined by the physician's evaluation.

Advisability of Use While Nursing Infant
Drug is present in milk. Safety for infant not established. Ask physician for guidance.

Habit-Forming Potential
This drug is related to amphetamine and can cause severe psychological dependence (see Glossary). Avoid large doses and prolonged use.

Effects of Overdosage
With Moderate Overdose: Nervous irritability, overactivity, insomnia, personality change, tremor.

With Large Overdose: Initial excitement, dilated pupils, rapid pulse, confusion, disorientation, bizarre behavior, hallucinations, convulsions, and coma.

Possible Effects of Extended Use
Severe psychological dependence.
Skin eruptions.

Recommended Periodic Examinations While Taking This Drug
None required.

While Taking This Drug, Observe the Following
Foods: Avoid foods rich in tyramine (see Glossary). This drug in combination with tyramine may cause excessive rise in blood pressure.

Beverages: Avoid beverages prepared from meat or yeast extracts. Avoid chocolate drinks.

Alcohol: Avoid beer, Chianti wines, and vermouth.

Tobacco Smoking: No interactions expected.

Other Drugs

Phentermine may *decrease* the effects of

- the major anti-hypertensive drugs, impairing their ability to lower blood pressure. The drugs most affected are guanethidine (Ismelin), hydralazine (Apresoline), methldopa (Aldomet), reserpine (Serpasil, etc.).

Phentermine *taken concurrently* with

- mono-amine oxidase (MAO) inhibitor drugs (see Drug Family, Section Four), may cause a dangerous rise in blood pressure. Withhold the use of phentermine for a minimum of 2 weeks after discontinuing any MAO inhibitor drug.

Driving a Vehicle, Piloting a Plane, Operating Machinery: This drug may impair the ability to safely engage in hazardous activities. Use caution until full effect has been determined.

Exposure to Sun: No restrictions.

Discontinuation: If this drug has been used for an extended period of time, do not discontinue it suddenly. Ask physician for guidance regarding gradual reduction and withdrawal.

Special Storage Instructions
Keep in a dry, tightly closed container.

PHENYLBUTAZONE

Year Introduced: 1949

Brand Names

USA		Canada
Azolid (USV	Algoverine (Rougier)	Nadozone (Nadeau)
Pharmaceutical)	Anevral (Deca)	Neo-Zoline (Neo)
Butazolidin (Geigy)	Butadyne (Bio-Chem.)	Novophenyl
Azolid-A [CD] (USV	Butagesic (Maney)	(Novopharm)
Pharmaceutical)	Butazolidin (Geigy)	Phenbutazone (ICN)
Butazolidin alka [CD]	Chembutazone	Phenylbetazone
(Geigy)	(Chemo)	(Barlowe Cote)
Sterazolidin [CD]	Eributazone (Eri)	Phenylone (Medic)
(Geigy)	Intrabutazone	Tazone (Nordic)
	(Organon)	Wescozone (Saunders)
	Malgesic (M & M)	

Drug Family: Analgesic, Mild; Anti-inflammatory; Fever Reducer (Antipyretic) [Pyrazolines]

Prescription Required: Yes

Available Dosage Forms and Strengths
Tablets — 100 mg.
Capsules — 100 mg. (in combination with antacids)

How This Drug Works
Intended Therapeutic Effect(s):   Symptomatic relief of inflammation, swelling, pain, and tenderness associated with arthritis, tendinitis, bursitis, and superficial phlebitis. (This drug does not correct the underlying disease process.)

Location of Drug Action(s):   Areas of inflammation in:
• the soft tissue structures of joints (tendons, ligaments, bursas, etc.).
• the superficial veins.

Method of Drug Action(s):   Not completely established. Present thinking is that this drug acts somewhat like aspirin, by suppressing the formation of prostaglandins (chemicals involved in the production of inflammation).

THIS DRUG SHOULD NOT BE TAKEN IF
—you are allergic to any of the drugs bearing the brand names listed above or to oxyphenbutazone (Oxalid, Tandearil).
—you have had a severe reaction to any drug in the past. (Ask physician for guidance.)
—you have a history of blood or bone marrow disease.

—you have a history of stomach or intestinal ulceration, or recurrent indigestion of a serious nature.

—you have a history of disease or impaired function of the thyroid, heart, liver, or kidneys.

—you have high blood pressure.

—it is prescribed for a mild or trivial condition.

—it is prescribed for a child under 15 years of age.

—it is prescribed for anyone in a state of senility.

INFORM YOUR PHYSICIAN BEFORE TAKING THIS DRUG IF

—you are taking any other drugs at this time, either prescription drugs or over-the-counter drugs.

—you are on long-term anticoagulant drugs.

—you have glaucoma.

Time Required for Apparent Benefit
Usually 2 to 7 days.

Possible Side-Effects *(natural, expected, and unavoidable drug actions)*
Retention of salt and water in the body with decreased formation of urine.

CAUTION
The elderly (over 60 years of age) are more likely to experience adverse effects from this drug. It is advisable to use small doses initially and to monitor all drug effects carefully.

Possible Adverse Effects *(unusual, unexpected, and infrequent reactions)*

IF ANY OF THE FOLLOWING DEVELOP, DISCONTINUE DRUG AND NOTIFY YOUR PHYSICIAN AS SOON AS POSSIBLE

Mild Adverse Effects
Allergic Reactions: Skin rashes (various kinds), hives, itching, fever.
Indigestion, stomach pain, nausea, vomiting, diarrhea.
Progressive gain in weight and rise in blood pressure due to water retention; these are indications to discontinue this drug.

Serious Adverse Effects
Allergic Reactions: Severe skin reactions, high fever, swollen and painful joints, salivary gland enlargement, anaphylactic reaction (see Glossary).
Bone marrow depression (see Glossary)—fatigue, weakness, fever, sore throat, mouth irritation, unusual bleeding or bruising.
Hepatitis with or without jaundice (see Glossary).
Kidney damage with impaired function.
Stomach and intestinal ulceration and/or bleeding, with dark red to black discoloration of stools.
Blood pressure elevation, heart damage.
Eye damage: injury to optic nerve and retina, with impaired vision.
Ear damage: hearing loss.
Lethargy, confusion, nervousness.

Advisability of Use During Pregnancy
Safety not established. Avoid use if possible.

Advisability of Use While Nursing Infant
Drug is known to be present in milk. Safety for infant not established. Ask physician for guidance.

Habit-Forming Potential
None.

Effects of Overdosage
With Moderate Overdose: Headache, insomnia, dizziness, mental and behavioral disturbance.
With Large Overdose: Hallucinations, convulsions, coma.

Possible Effects of Extended Use
Bone marrow depression (see Glossary).
Development of thyroid gland enlargement (goiter), with or without impaired function.

Recommended Periodic Examinations While Taking This Drug
Complete blood cell counts and urine analysis should be made before drug is taken and during course of treatment at intervals of 1 to 2 weeks. Evaluation of thyroid gland size and functional status.

While Taking This Drug, Observe the Following
Foods: Avoid heavily salted foods. Drug should be taken with or following food to minimize stomach irritation.
Beverages: No restrictions of beverage selection. May be taken with milk to minimize stomach irritation.
Alcohol: Best avoided because of its irritant effect on stomach, with increased risk of ulceration and bleeding.
Tobacco Smoking: No interactions expected.
Other Drugs
Phenylbutazone may *increase* the effects of
  • oral anticoagulants of the coumarin type (see Drug Family, Section Four); consult physician regarding need for dosage adjustment to prevent bleeding.
  • oral anti-diabetic medications (see sulfonylurea Drug Family, Section Four). Consult physician regarding dosage adjustment to prevent hypoglycemia.
  • insulin preparations; consult physician regarding dosage adjustment to prevent "insulin reaction" (hypoglycemia).
  • the penicillins (see Drug Family, Section Four).
  • sulfonamide ("sulfa") drugs (see Drug Family, Section Four).

Phenylbutazone may *decrease* the effects of
  • antihistamines (see Drug Family, Section Four).
  • barbiturates (see Drug Family, Section Four).
  • digitoxin; consult physician regarding need for dosage adjustment.
  • griseofulvin, by hastening its destruction.
  • oral contraceptives, by hastening their destruction.
  • zoxazolamine (Flexin), by hastening its destruction.

Phenylbutazone *taken concurrently* with
• indomethacin, may increase the risk of stomach ulceration.
• phenytoin (Dantoin, Dilantin, etc.), may cause excessive levels of phenytoin, resulting in toxic effects on the brain. Dosage reduction may be necessary.

The following drugs may *decrease* the effects of phenylbutazone
• aspirin and related drugs (see salicylate Drug Family, Section Four)
• barbiturates (see Drug Family, Section Four)
• tricyclic antidepressants (Elavil, Tofranil, etc.)

Driving a Vehicle, Piloting a Plane, Operating Machinery: Use caution until occurrence of lethargy, confusion, and impairment of vision or hearing is determined.

Exposure to Sun: Use caution until sensitivity is determined. Phenylbutazone can cause photosensitivity (see Glossary).

Discontinuation: This drug should be discontinued after 7 days if a favorable response has not occurred. If drug has been used for a longer period of time, consult physician regarding dosage adjustment for any of the following drugs taken concurrently with phenylbutazone: oral anticoagulant drugs, oral anti-diabetic medications, insulin preparations, barbiturates, digitoxin, phenytoin.

Special Storage Instructions
Keep in a dry, tightly closed container.

PHENYLEPHRINE

Year Introduced: 1949

Brand Names

USA		Canada
Alcon-Efrim	Chlor-Trimeton	Degest (Barnes-Hind)
(Webcon)	Expectorant [CD]	Isopto Frin (Alcon)
Anti-B Nasal Spray	(Schering)	Neo-Synephrine
(DePree)	Clistin-D [CD]	(Winthrop)
Isophrin (Riker)	(McNeil)	Prefrin (Allergan)
Neo-Synephrine	Co-Tylenol [CD]	
(Winthrop)	(McNeil)	
Op-Isophrin (Riker)	4-Way Tablets, Nasal	
Sinarest Nasal Spray	Spray [CD]	
(Pharmacraft)	(Bristol-Myers)	
Synasal Spray (Texas	Sinex [CD] (Vick)	
Pharm.)	(Numerous other	
	combination brand	
	names)	

Drug Family: Decongestant [Sympathomimetics]

Prescription Required: No

Available Dosage Forms and Strengths
Tablets — 5 mg. (in combination with other drugs)
Elixir — 5 mg. per teaspoonful
Nasal Solution — 0.125%, 0.25%, 0.5%, 1%
Nasal Spray — 0.25%, 0.5%
Nasal Jelly — 0.5%
(Examine drug label of combination products.)

How This Drug Works
Intended Therapeutic Effect(s):   Relief of congestion of the nose, sinuses, and throat associated with allergic disorders and infections.
Location of Drug Action(s):   The small blood vessels (arterioles) in the tissues lining the nasal passages, the sinuses, and the throat.
Method of Drug Action(s):   By contracting the walls and thus reducing the size of the arterioles, this drug decreases the volume of blood in the tissues, resulting in shrinkage of tissue mass (decongestion). This expands the nasal airway and enlarges the openings into the sinuses and eustachian tubes.

THIS DRUG SHOULD NOT BE TAKEN IF
—you have had an allergic reaction to any dosage form of it previously.

INFORM YOUR PHYSICIAN BEFORE TAKING THIS DRUG IF
—you have high blood pressure or heart disease.
—you have diabetes or an overactive thyroid gland (hyperthyroidism).
—you are taking, or have taken within the past 2 weeks, any mono-amine oxidase (MAO) inhibitor drug (see Drug Family, Section Four).

Time Required for Apparent Benefit
Drug action is usually felt within 5 to 30 minutes after application to nasal membranes and may persist for 4 hours.

Possible Side-Effects *(natural, expected, and unavoidable drug actions)*
Dryness of the nose and throat.

CAUTION
Too frequent application of nose drops and sprays containing this drug may cause a secondary "rebound" congestion resulting in functional dependence (see Glossary).

Possible Adverse Effects *(unusual, unexpected, and infrequent reactions)*
IF ANY OF THE FOLLOWING DEVELOP, DISCONTINUE DRUG AND NOTIFY YOUR PHYSICIAN AS SOON AS POSSIBLE

Mild Adverse Effects
  Allergic Reactions: None reported.
  Burning and stinging of nose, headache, lightheadness, heart palpitation, tremor.
Serious Adverse Effects
  None reported.

Advisability of Use During Pregnancy
Safety not established. Ask physician for guidance.

Advisability of Use While Nursing Infant
Safety not established. Ask physician for guidance regarding time and frequency of use with relationship to nursing.

Habit-Forming Potential
Frequent or excessive use may cause functional dependence.

Effects of Overdosage
With Moderate Overdose: Headache, heart palpitation, vomiting.
With Large Overdose: Elevation of blood pressure, slow and forceful pulse.

Possible Effects of Extended Use
Secondary "rebound" congestion and chemical irritation of nasal membranes.

Recommended Periodic Examinations While Taking This Drug
None required.

While Taking This Drug, Observe the Following
Foods: No restrictions. Oral dosage forms should be taken after eating to reduce stomach irritation.
Beverages: No restrictions.
Alcohol: No interactions expected.
Tobacco Smoking: No interactions expected. No restrictions (unless directed otherwise by physician).

Other Drugs
Phenylephrine *taken concurrently* with
• mono-amine oxidase (MAO) inhibitor drugs (see Drug Family, Section Four), may cause dangerous elevation of the blood pressure.
Driving a Vehicle, Piloting a Plane, Operating Machinery: No restrictions.
Exposure to Sun: No restrictions.

Special Storage Instructions
Keep in a tightly closed container. Protect from light.

PHENYLPROPANOLAMINE
Year Introduced: 1948

Brand Names

USA		Canada
Propadrine (Merck Sharp & Dohme)	Sinutab [CD] (Warner/Chilcott)	Naldecol [CD] (Bristol)
Allerest [CD] (Pharmacraft)	Triaminic [CD] (Dorsey)	Ornade [CD] (SK&F) Ornex [CD] (SK&F)
Contac [CD] (Menley & James)	Triaminicin [CD] (Dorsey)	Sinutab [CD] (Warner/Chilcott)
4-Way Nasal Spray [CD] (Bristol-Myers)	Triaminicol [CD] (Dorsey)	Triaminic [CD] (Anca)
Naldecon [CD] (Bristol)	Tussagesic [CD] (Dorsey)	Triaminicin [CD] (Anca)
Ornacol [CD] (Smith Kline & French)	Tussaminic [CD] (Dorsey)	Tuss-Ornade [CD] (SK&F)
Ornade [CD] (Smith Kline & French)	Tuss-Ornade [CD] (Smith Kline & French)	
Ornex [CD] (Smith Kline & French)	(Numerous other combination brand names)	
Sinubid [CD] (Warner/Chilcott)		

Drug Family: Decongestant [Sympathomimetics]

Prescription Required: For low-strength formulations—No
For high-strength formulations—Yes

Available Dosage Forms and Strengths
Capsules — 25 mg., 50 mg.
Elixir — 20 mg. per teaspoonful
(Also marketed in a variety of tablets, capsules, syrups, solutions, and sprays in combination with other drugs. Strength varies according to drug product; examine drug label.)

How This Drug Works

Intended Therapeutic Effect(s):   Relief of congestion of the nose, sinuses, and throat associated with allergic disorders and infections.

Location of Drug Action(s):   The small blood vessels (arterioles) in the tissues lining the nasal passages, the sinuses, and the throat.

Method of Drug Action(s):   By contracting the walls and thus reducing the size of the arterioles, this drug decreases the volume of blood in the tissues, resulting in shrinkage of tissue mass (decongestion). This expands the nasal airway and enlarges the openings into the sinuses and eustachian tubes.

THIS DRUG SHOULD NOT BE TAKEN IF

—you have had an allergic reaction to any dosage form of it previously.

INFORM YOUR PHYSICIAN BEFORE TAKING THIS DRUG IF

—you have high blood pressure or heart disease.
—you have an overactive thyroid gland (hyperthyroidism) or diabetes.
—you have difficulty emptying the urinary bladder.
—you are taking, or have taken during the past 2 weeks, any mono-amine oxidase (MAO) inhibitor drug (see Drug Family, Section Four).
—you are taking any form of digitalis (Digitoxin, Digoxin, etc.).
—you plan to have surgery under general anesthesia in the near future.

Time Required for Apparent Benefit

Drug action begins in 30 to 60 minutes and persists for 3 to 4 hours.

Possible Side-Effects *(natural, expected, and unavoidable drug actions)*

Nervousness, insomnia.

CAUTION

Do not exceed recommended dose. Large doses can cause dangerous increase in blood pressure. Too frequent application of nose drops and sprays containing this drug may cause a secondary "rebound" congestion resulting in functional dependence (see Glossary).

Possible Adverse Effects *(unusual, unexpected, and infrequent reactions)*

IF ANY OF THE FOLLOWING DEVELOP, DISCONTINUE DRUG AND NOTIFY YOUR PHYSICIAN AS SOON AS POSSIBLE

Mild Adverse Effects
Allergic Reactions: None reported when drug is taken orally.
Headache, dizziness, rapid and forceful heart action.
Nausea, vomiting.

Serious Adverse Effects
Idiosyncratic Reactions: Acute temporary mental derangement (psychotic episodes).

Advisability of Use During Pregnancy

No adverse effects on mother or fetus reported. However, it is advisable to use sparingly and in small doses. Ask physician for guidance.

Advisability of Use While Nursing Infant

Drug is known to be present in milk and to have adverse effects on the infant. Avoid drug or stop nursing. Ask physician for guidance.

Habit-Forming Potential
Frequent or excessive use of nasal solutions containing this drug may lead to functional dependence.

Effects of Overdosage
With Moderate Overdose: Marked nervousness, restlessness, headache, heart palpitation, sweating, nausea, vomiting.

With Large Overdose: Anxiety, confusion, delirium, muscular tremors, rapid and irregular pulse.

Possible Effects of Extended Use
Secondary "rebound" congestion of nasal membranes.

Recommended Periodic Examinations While Taking This Drug
None required.

While Taking This Drug, Observe the Following
Foods: No restrictions.

Beverages: Excessive coffee or tea may add to the nervousness or insomnia caused by this drug in sensitive individuals.

Alcohol: No interactions expected.

Tobacco Smoking: No interactions expected. No restrictions (unless advised otherwise by your physician).

Other Drugs

Phenylpropanolamine may *increase* the effects of

• epinephrine (Adrenalin, Bronkaid Mist, Vaponefrin, etc.), and cause excessive stimulation of the heart and an increase in blood pressure. Use caution and avoid excessive dosage.

Phenylpropanolamine may *decrease* the effects of

• the anti-hypertensive drugs, and reduce their effectiveness in lowering blood pressure. Ask physician if any dosage adjustment is necessary to maintain proper blood pressure control.

Phenylpropanolamine *taken concurrently* with

• digitalis preparations (Digitoxin, Digoxin, etc.), may cause serious disturbances of heart rhythm.

• ergot-related preparations (Cafergot, Ergotrate, Migral, Wigraine, etc.), may cause serious increase in blood pressure.

• guanethidine, may result in reduced effectiveness of both drugs.

The following drugs may *increase* the effects of phenylpropanolamine

• mono-amine oxidase (MAO) inhibitor drugs (see Drug Family, Section Four). The combined effects may cause a dangerous increase in blood pressure.

• tricyclic antidepressants (see Drug Family, Section Four). The combined effects may cause excessive stimulation of the heart and blood pressure.he heart and blood pressure.

Driving a Vehicle, Piloting a Plane, Operating Machinery: No restrictions unless dizziness occurs.

Exposure to Sun: No restrictions.

Special Storage Instructions
Keep in a tightly closed, light-resistant container. Avoid excessive heat.

PHENYTOIN
(formerly Diphenylhydantoin)

Year Introduced: 1938

Brand Names

USA
Didan-TDC-250
(Canfield)
Dihycon (Consol.
Midland)
Dilantin (Parke-Davis)
Di-Phen (North Amer.
Pharm.)
Diphenyl (Drug
Industries)
Diphenylan (Lannett)
Ekko (Fleming)
Kessodanten (McKesson)
SDPH (Rachelle)

Canada
Dantoin (Sterilab)
Dilantin (P.D. & Co.)
Diphentyn (ICN)
Divulsan (Dymond)
Novodiphenyl
(Novopharm)

Drug Family: Anti-convulsant [Hydantoins]

Prescription Required: Yes

Available Dosage Forms and Strengths
Tablets — 50 mg.
Capsules — 30 mg., 100 mg.
Suspension — 30 mg., 125 mg. per teaspoonful
Suppositories — 200 mg.
Injection — 50 mg. per ml.

How This Drug Works
Intended Therapeutic Effect(s):   Prevention of epileptic seizures (anti-convulsant effect).

Location of Drug Action(s): Those areas of the brain that initiate and sustain episodes of excessive electrical discharges responsible for epileptic seizures.

Method of Drug Action(s): Not completely established. It is thought that by promoting the loss of sodium from nerve fibers, this drug lowers and stabilizes their excitability and inhibits the repetitious spread of electrical impulses along nerve pathways. This action may prevent seizures altogether, or it may reduce their frequency and severity.

THIS DRUG SHOULD NOT BE TAKEN IF
—you are allergic to any of the drugs bearing the brand names listed above or you have had an allergic reaction or an unfavorable response to any hydantoin drug.

INFORM YOUR PHYSICIAN BEFORE TAKING THIS DRUG IF
—you have a history of liver disease or impaired liver function.
—you plan to have surgery under general anesthesia in the near future.

Time Required for Apparent Benefit
Dosage must be individualized. Continuous use on a regular schedule for 7 to 10 days is needed to achieve satisfactory response.

Possible Side-Effects *(natural, expected, and unavoidable drug actions)*
Sluggishness or drowsiness (in sensitive individuals).
Pink to red to brown coloration of the urine.

CAUTION
1. When used for the treatment of epilepsy, this drug must not be stopped abruptly.
2. The wide variation of this drug's action from person to person requires careful individualization of dosage schedules.
3. The elderly (over 60 years of age) may show evidence of overdosage or toxicity earlier than younger individuals.
4. Total daily dosage should not exceed 600 mg. for adults (proportionately less for children).
5. Regularity of drug use is essential for the successful management of seizure disorders.
6. Shake the suspension form of this drug to mix it thoroughly before measuring the dose. Use a standard measuring device to assure that the dose is based upon a 5 ml. teaspoon.
7. Side-effects and mild adverse effects are usually most apparent during the first several days of treatment, and often subside with continued use.
8. It may be necessary to take Vitamin Bc (folic acid) to prevent anemia while taking this drug. Consult your physician.
9. It is advisable to carry a card of personal identification with a notation that you are taking this drug. (See Table 14 and Section Seven.)

Possible Adverse Effects *(unusual, unexpected, and infrequent reactions)*

IF ANY OF THE FOLLOWING DEVELOP, DISCONTINUE DRUG AND NOTIFY YOUR PHYSICIAN AS SOON AS POSSIBLE

Mild Adverse Effects

Allergic Reactions: Skin rash, drug fever. (See Glossary).

Headache, dizziness, staggering, slurred speech, confusion, muscle twitching.

Nausea, vomiting, constipation.

Joint aches and pains.

Excessive growth of hair (more common in young girls).

Serious Adverse Effects

Allergic Reactions: Severe skin reactions—peeling, bruising, blistering. Enlargement of lymph glands.

Idiosyncratic Reactions: Hemolytic anemia (see Glossary).

Bone marrow depression (see Glossary)—weakness, fever, sore throat, abnormal bruising or bleeding.

Swelling and tenderness of the gums (more common in children).

Hepatitis with jaundice (see Glossary)—yellow eyes and skin, dark-colored urine, light-colored stools.

Advisability of Use During Pregnancy

Over 90 percent of epileptic mothers treated with anti-convulsant drugs during pregnancy give birth to normal children. However, recent reports suggest a possible association between the use of this drug during the first 3 months of pregnancy and the development of birth defects in the fetus. Discuss with your physician the advantages and possible disadvantages of using this drug during pregnancy. It is advisable to use the smallest maintenance dose that will prevent seizures.

The newborn infants of mothers who take this drug during pregnancy may develop abnormal bleeding or serious hemorrhage due to a deficiency of certain clotting factors in the blood. Consult your physician regarding the advisability of taking Vitamin K during the last month of pregnancy.

Advisability of Use While Nursing Infant

This drug is known to be present in milk. Ask physician for guidance with regard to nursing.

Habit-Forming Potential

None.

Effects of Overdosage

With Moderate Overdose: Jerky eye movements, staggering gait, imbalance, slurred speech, drowsiness.

With Large Overdose: Deep sleep progressing to coma, drop in blood pressure, slow and shallow breathing.

Possible Effects of Extended Use

Development of lymph gland enlargement and toxic change.

Development of peripheral neuritis (see Glossary).

Recommended Periodic Examinations While Taking This Drug
Complete blood cell counts.
Liver function tests.
Evaluation of lymph glands.

While Taking This Drug, Observe the Following
Foods: No interactions. The drug may be taken with or following food to reduce the possibility of nausea. Consult physician regarding the need for additional Vitamin D.

Beverages: No restrictions.

Alcohol: Use with extreme caution until combined effects have been determined. Alcohol (in large quantities or with continuous use) may reduce this drug's effectiveness in preventing seizures.

Tobacco Smoking: No interactions expected.

Other Drugs

Phenytoin may *increase* the effects of

- anticoagulants of the coumarin family (see Drug Family, Section Four), and cause abnormal bleeding or hemorrhage.
- anti-hypertensive drugs, and cause excessive lowering of the blood pressure.
- sedatives and sleep-inducing drugs, and cause oversedation.
- griseofulvin (Fulvicin, Grifulvin, etc.).
- methotrexate.
- propranolol (Inderal).
- quinidine.

Phenytoin may *decrease* the effects of

- cortisone and related drugs (see Drug Family, Section Four).
- oral contraceptives

Phenytoin *taken concurrently* with

- barbiturates, may cause an initial change in the pattern of seizures. Dosage adjustments may be necessary.
- tricyclic antidepressants, may require adjustment of the phenytoin dosage to control seizures produced by the antidepressants (when they are used in high doses).
- digitalis preparations, may cause unpredictable toxic effects by either drug. Careful observation and dosage adjustments are essential.

The following drugs may *increase* the effects of phenytoin

- anticoagulants of the coumarin family (see Drug Family, Section Four)
- disulfiram (Antabuse)
- isoniazid (INH, Niconyl, Isozide, Rimifon)
- phenylbutazone (Azolid, Butazolidin, etc.)
- para-aminosalicylic acid (PAS)
- aspirin (in large doses)
- mild tranquilizers (Librium, Valium, Serax, Dalmane)
- chloramphenicol (Chloromycetin)
- estrogens (Premarin, etc.)

- methylphenidate (Ritalin)
- phenothiazines (Compazine, Thorazine)
- certain "sulfa" drugs (Gantrisin, Orisul)

Reduced doses of phenytoin may be necessary to prevent phenytoin toxicity.

The following drugs may *decrease* the effects of phenytoin

- alcohol
- antihistamines (some)
- glutethimide (Doriden)

Driving a Vehicle, Piloting a Plane, Operating Machinery: Use caution until the full effects of this drug have been determined. Rarely, it can cause drowsiness, and impair mental alertness, vision, and physical coordination. Avoid hazardous activities if such symptoms occur. It is essential that you adhere to a schedule of drug dosage that will prevent seizures.

Exposure to Sun: Use caution until full effect has been determined. This drug may cause photosensitivity (see Glossary).

Occurrence of Unrelated Illness: Notify your physician of any illness or injury that causes you to make any alterations in your regular dosage schedule.

Discontinuation: Do not discontinue this drug abruptly if you are taking it for epilepsy or seizure disorders. Sudden withdrawal of any anti-convulsant drug can cause severe and repeated seizures.

Special Storage Instructions

Keep in a dry, tightly closed container.

PILOCARPINE

Year Introduced: 1875

Brand Names

USA	Canada
Almocarpine (Ayerst)	Isopto-Carpine (Alcon)
Isopto-Carpine (Alcon)	Miocarpine (Cooper)
Mi-Pilo (Barnes-Hind)	Nova-Carpine (Nova)
Ocusert Pilo-20 and 40 (Alza)	Ocusert Pilo-20 and 40 (Alza)
Pilocar (Smith, Miller & Patch)	Pentacarpine (Pentagone)
Pilocel (Softcon)	P.V. Carpine (Allergan)
Pilomiotin (Smith, Miller & Patch)	
(Also several combination brand names)	

Drug Family: Anti-glaucoma (Miotic) [Parasympathomimetics]

Prescription Required: Yes

Available Dosage Forms and Strengths

Eye Drop Solution — 0.25%, 0.5%, 1%, 1.5%, 2%, 3%, 4%, 5%, 6%, 8%, 10%

Ocuserts — 20 mcg., 40 mcg.

How This Drug Works

Intended Therapeutic Effect(s):   Reduction of elevated internal eye pressure, of benefit in the management of glaucoma.

Location of Drug Action(s):   The parasympathetic nerve terminals in the muscles of the eye that constrict the pupil.

Method of Drug Action(s):   By directly stimulating constriction of the pupil, this drug enlarges the canal in the anterior chamber of the eye and promotes the drainage of excess fluid (aqueous humor), thus lowering the internal eye pressure.

THIS DRUG SHOULD NOT BE TAKEN IF

—you have had an allergic reaction to any dosage form of it previously.
—you are subject to attacks of bronchial asthma.

INFORM YOUR PHYSICIAN BEFORE TAKING THIS DRUG IF

—you have a history of bronchial asthma.

Time Required for Apparent Benefit

Drug action begins in 15 to 30 minutes, reaches a maximal effect in 60 to 75 minutes, and gradually subsides in 4 to 8 hours. Continuous use on a regular schedule is necessary to control internal eye pressure (as in the treatment of glaucoma).

Possible Side-Effects *(natural, expected, and unavoidable drug actions)*
Temporary impairment of vision, usually lasting 2 to 3 hours after installation of drops.

Possible Adverse Effects *(unusual, unexpected, and infrequent reactions)*
IF ANY OF THE FOLLOWING DEVELOP, DISCONTINUE DRUG AND NOTIFY YOUR PHYSICIAN AS SOON AS POSSIBLE
Mild Adverse Effects
Allergic Reactions: Itching of the eyes, itching and/or swelling of the eyelids.
Headache, heart palpitation, trembling.
Serious Adverse Effects
Provocation of acute asthma in susceptible individuals.

Advisability of Use During Pregnancy
Use with caution. Safety has not been established. Limit use to the smallest effective dose.

Advisability of Use While Nursing Infant
Drug may be present in milk in small quantities. Ask physician for guidance.

Habit-Forming Potential
None.

Effects of Overdosage
With Moderate Overdose: Flushing of the face, increased flow of saliva, and sweating may result from absorption with excessive use of pilocarpine eye drops.
With Large Overdose: If solution is swallowed: nausea, vomiting, diarrhea, profuse sweating, rapid pulse, difficult breathing, loss of consciousness.

Possible Effects of Extended Use
Continuous use may lead to the development of tolerance and the loss of effectiveness in reducing internal eye pressure. Ask physician how this may be avoided.

Recommended Periodic Examinations While Taking This Drug
Measurements of internal eye pressure on a regular basis.
Examination of the eyes for the development of cataracts.

While Taking This Drug, Observe the Following
Foods: No restrictions.
Beverages: No restrictions.
Alcohol: Use caution until combined effect has been determined. This drug may prolong the action of alcohol on the brain.
Tobacco Smoking: No interactions expected.
Other Drugs
The following drugs may *decrease* the effects of pilocarpine
• atropine and atropine-like drugs (see Drug Family, Section Four)
• amphetamine and related drugs (see Drug Family, Section Four)
• cortisone and related drugs (see Drug Family, Section Four)

• members of the phenothiazine family (see Drug Family, Section Four). Consult physician regarding the need for dosage adjustments.

Driving a Vehicle, Piloting a Plane, Operating Machinery: Use caution until full effect on vision (ability to focus properly) has been determined.

Exposure to Sun: No restrictions.

Discontinuation: Periodic discontinuation of this drug and temporary substitution of another drug may be necessary to preserve its effectiveness in treating glaucoma.

Special Storage Instructions
Keep in a tightly closed, light-resistant bottle.

Do Not Use This Drug If It Is Older Than
the expiration date stated on the label.

POTASSIUM

Year Introduced: 1939

Brand Names

USA	Canada
Kaochlor (Warren-Teed)	Kaochlor (Warren-Teed)
Kaon (Warren-Teed)	Kaon (Warren-Teed)
Kay Ciel (Cooper)	Kay Ciel (Cooper)
K-Lor (Abbott)	KCl-Rougier (Rougier)
Klorvess (Dorsey)	K-Lyte (Mead Johnson)
K-Lyte (Mead Johnson)	Potassium-Rougier
Pfiklor (Pfizer)	(Rougier)
Potassium Triplex (Lilly)	Potassium-Sandoz
Slow-K (CIBA)	(Sandoz)
	Slow-K (CIBA)

Drug Family: Potassium Preparations

Prescription Required: In USA—Yes
In Canada—No

Available Dosage Forms and Strengths:
Tablets — 5 mEq.*
Slow-Release Tablets — 6.67 mEq., 8 mEq.
Effervescent Tablets — 20 mEq., 25 mEq.
Powder — 15 mEq., 20 mEq., 25 mEq. per packet
Elixir — 20 mEq. per tablespoonful (15 ml.)
Oral Liquid — 15 mEq. per teaspoonful (5 ml.)
— 10 mEq. per tablespoonful (15 ml.)
— 20 mEq. per tablespoonful (15 ml.)
— 40 mEq. per tablespoonful (15 ml.)

*Milliequivalent—the number of grams of potassium contained in one milliliter of a normal solution.

How This Drug Works

Intended Therapeutic Effect(s):   The prevention or treatment of potassium deficiency.

Location of Drug Action(s):   Within the cells of most body tissues.

Method of Drug Action(s):   By maintaining or replenishing the normal potassium content of cells, this drug preserves or restores such normal cellular functions as the transmission of nerve impulses, the contraction of muscle fibers, the regulation of kidney function, and the secretion of stomach juices.

THIS DRUG SHOULD NOT BE TAKEN IF

—you have had an allergic reaction to any of the drugs bearing the brand names listed above or to any potassium preparation previously.

—you have severe impairment of kidney function.

—you are taking any drug that contains either spironolactone or triamterene.

INFORM YOUR PHYSICIAN BEFORE TAKING THIS DRUG IF

—you are taking any cortisone-like drug (see Drug Family, Section Four).

—you are taking any digitalis preparation.

—you are taking any diuretic drug (see Drug Family, Section Four).

—you have Addison's disease (adrenal gland deficiency).

—you have diabetes.

—you have any form of heart disease.

—you have a history of kidney disease or impaired kidney function.

—you have a history of intestinal obstruction.

—you have a history of familial periodic paralysis.

Time Required for Apparent Benefit

When used to correct potassium deficiency, these preparations are usually beneficial within 12 to 24 hours.

Possible Side-Effects *(natural, expected, and unavoidable drug actions)*

A mild laxative effect for some individuals.

CAUTION

1. Dosage must be individualized. Periodic evaluation of overall condition and blood potassium levels is essential to safe and effective management. Excessively high blood levels of potassium can occur without warning. Do not exceed the prescribed dose.
2. Inform your physician promptly if you are taking a tablet form of this drug and you become aware of any difficulty in swallowing.
3. If you have chronic constipation, it is advisable that you avoid potassium in tablet form.
4. Some salt substitutes contain a large amount of potassium. If you are using a salt substitute, consult your physician regarding its continued use or any necessary adjustment in the dosage of your potassium preparation.

Possible Adverse Effects *(unusual, unexpected, and infrequent reactions)*

IF ANY OF THE FOLLOWING DEVELOP, DISCONTINUE DRUG AND NOTIFY YOUR PHYSICIAN AS SOON AS POSSIBLE

Mild Adverse Effects

Nausea, vomiting, abdominal discomfort, diarrhea. (These usually occur if potassium is taken undiluted or on an empty stomach.)

Serious Adverse Effects

Potassium accumulation, resulting in abnormally high blood levels (see Effects of Overdosage, below). Immediate treatment is mandatory.

Potassium in enteric-coated tablets can cause ulceration, perforation, narrowing, and obstruction of the small intestine. Report promptly the development of abdominal pain, vomiting, or evidence of intestinal bleeding.

Potassium in slow-release (wax matrix) tablets can cause ulceration of the stomach. Report the development of persistent indigestion or stomach discomfort.

Advisability of Use During Pregnancy

Potassium preparations can be used safely during pregnancy. Adhere strictly to prescribed dosage. Inform your physician promptly if symptoms suggestive of overdosage develop.

Advisability of Use While Nursing Infant

The presence of these drugs in milk is not known. Ask your physician for guidance.

Habit-Forming Potential

None.

Effects of Overdosage

With Moderate Overdose: Lethargy, weakness and heaviness of legs, numbness and tingling in the extremities, confusion.

With Large Overdose: Paralysis of the extremities, irregular heart rhythm, drop in blood pressure, convulsions, coma, heart arrest.

Possible Effects of Extended Use

Reduced absorption of Vitamin B-12, resulting in anemia (in some individuals).

Recommended Periodic Examinations While Taking This Drug

Measurement of blood potassium levels.

Electrocardiograms, to monitor changes that reflect the potassium content of blood and body tissues.

Measurement of red blood cell counts and hemoglobin levels to detect development of anemia during extended use of drug.

While Taking This Drug, Observe the Following

Foods: Consult your physician regarding the advisability of eating potassium-rich foods. Potassium preparations should be taken with or following food to reduce the possibility of stomach irritation.

Beverages: The effervescent tablets, powder, elixir, and oral liquid preparations of potassium should be well diluted in cold water or juice and taken after meals. If you are on a low-sodium diet, consult your physician regarding the selection of beverage to use for dissolving potassium powder or diluting potassium liquids. Beverages with a high sodium content include Clamato juice, Gatorade, tomato juice, and V-8 juice.

Alcohol: No interactions expected. However, alcoholic beverages can intensify any stomach irritation due to potassium preparations.

Tobacco Smoking: No interactions expected.

Other Drugs

Potassium *taken concurrently* with

- spironolactone or triameterene, may cause an excessive rise in the blood potassium level. This can be extremely dangerous; avoid the concurrent use of these diuretics and any form of potassium.
- digitalis preparations, requires very careful minitoring of the dosage and effects of both drugs.

The following drugs may *decrease* the effects of potassium

- thiazide diuretics (see Drug Family, Section Four) may promote the loss of potassium from the body (hence the need for potassium preparations to maintain normal blood and tissue levels).

Driving a Vehicle, Piloting a Plane, Operating Machinery: No restrictions in the absence of symptoms indicative of overdosage.

Exposure to Sun: No restrictions.

Occurrence of Unrelated Illness: Inform your physician of any illness that causes vomiting or diarrhea.

Discontinuation: Do not discontinue any potassium preparation suddenly if you are taking digitalis. Ask your physician for guidance if you find it necessary to reduce or discontinue potassium medication for any reason.

Special Storage Instructions

Keep all tablets in a dry, tightly closed container.

Keep elixir and oral liquid in tightly closed, light-resistant containers.

PREDNISOLONE

ear Introduced: 1955

rand Names

USA	Canada
Delta-Cortef (Upjohn)	Delta-Cortef (Upjohn)
Fernisolone (Ferndale)	Inflamase (Cooper)
Hydeltra (Merck Sharp & Dohme)	Isopto Prednisolone (Alcon)
Prednis (USV Pharmaceutical)	Nova-Pred (Nova)
Sterane (Pfizer)	
(Others)	

rug Family: Cortisone-like Drug [Adrenocortical Steroids (Glucocorticoids)]

rescription Required: Yes

vailable Dosage Forms and Strengths
Tablets—1 mg., 2.5 mg., 5 mg.

ow This Drug Works

Intended Therapeutic Effect(s):   The symptomatic relief of inflammation (swelling, redness, heat and pain) in any tissue, and from many causes. (Cortisone-like drugs do not correct the underlying disease process.)

Location of Drug Action(s):   Significant biological effects occur in most tissues throughout the body. The principal actions of therapeutic doses occur at sites of inflammation and/or allergic reaction, regardless of the nature of the causative injury or illness.

Method of Drug Action(s):   Not completely established. Present thinking is that cortisone-like drugs probably inhibit several mechanisms within the tissues that induce inflammation. Well-regulated dosage aids the body in restoring normal stability. However, prolonged use or excessive dosage can impair the body's defense mechanisms against infectious disease.

HIS DRUG SHOULD NOT BE TAKEN IF
-you have had an allergic reaction to any dosage form of it previously.
-you have an active peptic ulcer (stomach or duodenum).
-you have an active infection of the eye caused by the herpes simplex virus (ask your eye doctor for guidance).
-you have active tuberculosis.

IFORM YOUR PHYSICIAN BEFORE TAKING THIS DRUG IF
-you have had an unfavorable reaction to any cortisone-like drug in the past.
-you have a history of tuberculosis.
-you have diabetes or a tendency to diabetes.
-you have a history of peptic ulcer disease.
-you have glaucoma or a tendency to glaucoma.
-you have a deficiency of thyroid function (hypothyroidism).

—you have high blood pressure.
—you have myasthenia gravis.
—you have a history of thrombophlebitis.
—you plan to have surgery of any kind in the near future, especially if under general anesthesia.

Time Required for Apparent Benefit
Evidence of beneficial drug action is usually apparent in 24 to 48 hours. Dosage must be individualized to give reasonable improvement. This is usually accomplished in 4 to 10 days. It is unwise to demand complete relief of all symptoms. The effective dose varies with the nature of the disease and with the patient. During long-term use it is essential that the smallest effective dose be determined and maintained.

Possible Side-Effects *(natural, expected, and unavoidable drug actions)*
Retention of salt and water, gain in weight, increased sweating, increased appetite, increased susceptibility to infection.

CAUTION
1. It is advisable to carry a card of personal identification with a notation that you are taking this drug if your course of treatment is to exceed 1 week (see Table 14 and Section Seven).
2. Do not discontinue this drug abruptly.
3. While taking this drug, immunization procedures should be given with caution. If vaccination against measles, smallpox, rabies, or yellow fever is required, discontinue this drug 72 hours before vaccination and do not resume for at least 14 days after vaccination.

Possible Adverse Effects *(unusual, unexpected, and infrequent reactions)*
IF ANY OF THE FOLLOWING DEVELOP, DISCONTINUE DRUG AND NOTIFY YOUR PHYSICIAN AS SOON AS POSSIBLE

Mild Adverse Effects
Allergic Reactions: Skin rash.
Headache, dizziness, insomnia.
Acid indigestion, abdominal distention.
Muscle cramping and weakness.
Irregular menstrual periods.
Acne, excessive growth of facial hair.

Serious Adverse Effects
Mental and emotional disturbances of serious magnitude.
Reactivation of latent tuberculosis.
Development of peptic ulcer.
Increased blood pressure.
Development of inflammation of the pancreas.
Thrombophlebitis (inflammation of a vein with the formation of blood clot
    —pain or tenderness in thigh or leg, with or without swelling of the foot
ankle, or leg.
Pulmonary embolism (movement of blood clot to the lung)—sudden short
ness of breath, pain in the chest, coughing, bloody sputum.

Advisability of Use During Pregnancy
Safety has not been established. If possible, avoid completely. If use of this drug is considered necessary, limit dosage and duration of use as much as possible. Following birth, the infant should be examined for possible defective function of the adrenal glands (deficiency of adrenal cortical hormones).

Advisability of Use While Nursing Infant
Drug is known to be present in milk. Ask physician for guidance.

Habit-Forming Potential
Use of this drug to suppress symptoms over an extended period of time may produce a state of functional dependence (see Glossary). In the treatment of conditions like rheumatoid arthritis and asthma, it is advisable to try alternate-day drug administration to keep the daily dose as small as possible and to attempt drug withdrawal after periods of reasonable improvement. Such procedures may reduce the degree of "steroid rebound"—the return of symptoms as the drug is withdrawn.

Effects of Overdosage
With Moderate Overdose: Excessive fluid retention, swelling of extremities, flushing of the face, nervousness, stomach irritation, weakness.
With Large Overdose: Severe headache, convulsions, heart failure in susceptible individuals, emotional and behavioral disturbances.

Possible Effects of Extended Use
Development of increased blood sugar, possibly diabetes.
Increased fat deposits on the trunk of the body ("buffalo hump"), rounding of the face ("moon face"), and thinning of the arms and legs.
Thinning and fragility of the skin, easy bruising.
Loss of texture and strength of the bones, resulting in spontaneous fractures.
Development of increased internal eye pressure, possibly glaucoma.
Development of cataracts.
Retarded growth and development in children.

Recommended Periodic Examinations While Taking This Drug
Measurement of blood potassium levels.
Measurement of blood sugar levels 2 hours after eating.
Measurement of blood pressure at regular intervals.
Eye examination at regular intervals.
Chest X-ray if history of previous tuberculosis.
Determination of the rate of development of the growing child to detect retardation of normal growth.

While Taking This Drug, Observe the Following
Foods: No interactions. Ask physician regarding need to restrict salt intake or to eat potassium-rich foods. During long-term use of this drug it is advisable to have a high protein diet.
Beverages: No restrictions.
Alcohol: No interactions expected.
Tobacco Smoking: Nicotine increases the blood levels of naturally pro-

duced cortisone and related hormones. Heavy smoking may add to the expected actions of this drug and requires close observation for excessive effects.

Other Drugs

Prednisolone may *increase* the effects of

- barbiturates and other sedatives and sleep-inducing drugs, causing over-sedation.

Prednisolone may *decrease* the effects of

- insulin and oral anti-diabetic drugs, by raising the level of blood sugar. Doses of anti-diabetic drugs may have to be raised.
- anticoagulants of the coumarin family. Monitor prothrombin times closely and adjust dosage accordingly.
- choline-like drugs (Mestinon, pilocarpine, Prostigmin), and reduce their effectiveness in treating glaucoma and myasthenia gravis.

Prednisolone *taken concurrently* with

- thiazide diuretics, may cause excessive loss of potassium. Monitor blood levels of potassium on physician's advice.
- atropine-like drugs, may cause increased internal eye pressure and initiate or aggravate glaucoma (see Drug Family, Section Four).
- digitalis preparations, requires close monitoring of body potassium stores to prevent digitalis toxicity.
- stimulant drugs (Adrenalin, amphetamines, ephedrine, etc.), may increase internal eye pressure and initiate or aggravate glaucoma.

The following drugs may *increase* the effects of prednisolone

- indomethacin (Indocin, Indocid)
- aspirin

The following drugs may *decrease* the effects of prednisolone

- barbiturates
- phenytoin (Dantoin, Dilantin, etc.)
- antihistamines (some)
- chloral hydrate (Noctec, Somnos)
- glutethimide (Doriden)
- phenylbutazone (Azolid, Butazolidin, etc.) may reduce its effectiveness following a brief, initial increase in effectiveness.
- propranolol (Inderal)

Driving a Vehicle, Piloting a Plane, Operating Machinery: No restrictions or precautions.

Exposure to Sun: No restrictions.

Occurrence of Unrelated Illness

This drug may decrease natural resistance to infection. Notify your physician if you develop an infection of any kind.

This drug may reduce your body's ability to respond appropriately to the stress of acute illness, injury, or surgery. Keep your physician fully informed of any significant changes in your state of health.

Discontinuation

If you have been taking this drug for an extended period of time, do not discontinue it abruptly. Ask physician for guidance regarding gradual withdrawal.

For a period of 2 years after discontinuing this drug, it is essential in the event of illness, injury, or surgery that you inform attending medical personnel that you used this drug in the past. The period of inadequate response to stress following the use of cortisone-like drugs may last for 1 to 2 years.

Special Storage Instructions

Keep in a tightly closed container. Protect from light.

PREDNISONE

Year Introduced: 1955

Brand Names

USA
Deltasone (Upjohn)
Delta (Merck Sharp & Dohme)
Meticorten (Schering)
Paracort (Parke-Davis)
Servisone (Lederle)
Sterazolidin [CD] (Geigy)

Canada
Colisone (Frosst)
Deltasone (Upjohn)
Paracort (P.D. & Co.)
Wescopred (Saunders)

Drug Family: Cortisone-like Drug [Adrenocortical Steroids (Glucocorticoids)]

Prescription Required: Yes

Available Dosage Forms and Strengths

Tablets—1 mg., 2.5 mg., 5 mg., 10 mg., 20 mg., 50 mg.

How This Drug Works

Intended Therapeutic Effect(s):   The symptomatic relief of inflammation (swelling, redness, heat and pain) in any tissue, and from many causes. (Cortisone-like drugs do not correct the underlying disease process.)

Location of Drug Action(s):   Significant biological effects occur in most tissues throughout the body. The principal actions of therapeutic doses occur at sites of inflammation and/or allergic reaction, regardless of the nature of the causative injury or illness

Method of Drug Action(s):   Not completely established. Present thinking is that cortisone-like drugs probably inhibit several mechanisms within the tissues that induce inflammation. Well-regulated dosage aids the body in restoring normal stability. However, prolonged use or excessive dosage can impair the body's defense mechanisms against infectious disease.

THIS DRUG SHOULD NOT BE TAKEN IF
—you are allergic to any of the drugs bearing the brand names listed above.
—you have an active peptic ulcer (stomach or duodenum).
—you have an active infection of the eye caused by the herpes simplex virus (ask your eye doctor for guidance).
—you have active tuberculosis.

INFORM YOUR PHYSICIAN BEFORE TAKING THIS DRUG IF
—you have had an unfavorable reaction to any cortisone-like drug in the past.
—you have a history of tuberculosis.
—you have diabetes or a tendency to diabetes.
—you have a history of peptic ulcer disease.
—you have glaucoma or a tendency to glaucoma.
—you have a deficiency of thyroid function (hypothyroidism).
—you have high blood pressure.
—you have myasthenia gravis.
—you have a history of thrombophlebitis.
—you plan to have surgery of any kind in the near future, especially if under general anesthesia.

Time Required for Apparent Benefit
Evidence of beneficial action is usually apparent in 24 to 48 hours. Dosage must be individualized to give reasonable improvement; this is usually accomplished in 4 to 10 days. It is unwise to demand complete relief of all symptoms. The effective dose varies with the nature of the disease and with the patient. During long-term use it is essential that the smallest effective dose be determined and maintained.

Possible Side-Effects *(natural, expected, and unavoidable drug actions)*
Retention of salt and water, gain in weight, increased sweating, increased appetite, increased susceptibility to infection.

CAUTION
1. It is advisable to carry a card of personal identification with a notation that you are taking this drug if your course of treatment is to exceed 1 week (see Table 14 and Section Seven).
2. Do not discontinue this drug abruptly.
3. While taking this drug, all immunization procedures should be used with caution. If vaccination against measles, smallpox, rabies, or yellow fever is required, discontinue this drug 72 hours before vaccination and do not resume it for at least 14 days after vaccination.

Possible Adverse Effects *(unusual, unexpected, and infrequent reactions)*
IF ANY OF THE FOLLOWING DEVELOP, DISCONTINUE DRUG AND NOTIFY YOUR PHYSICIAN AS SOON AS POSSIBLE

Mild Adverse Effects
Allergic Reactions: Skin rash.
Headache, dizziness, insomnia.
Acid indigestion, abdominal distention.
Muscle cramping and weakness.

Irregular menstrual periods.

Acne, excessive growth of facial hair.

Serious Adverse Effects

Mental and emotional disturbances of serious magnitude.

Reactivation of latent tuberculosis.

Development of peptic ulcer.

Increased blood pressure.

Development of inflammation of the pancreas.

Thrombophlebitis (inflammation of a vein with the formation of blood clot) —pain or tenderness in thigh or leg, with or without swelling of the foot, ankle, or leg.

Pulmonary embolism (movement of blood clot to the lung)—sudden shortness of breath, pain in the chest, coughing, bloody sputum.

Advisability of Use During Pregnancy

Safety has not been established. If possible, avoid completely. If use of this drug is considered necessary, limit dosage and duration of use as much as possible. Following birth, the infant should be examined for possible defective function of the adrenal glands (deficiency of adrenal cortical hormones).

Advisability of Use While Nursing Infant

Drug is known to be present in milk. Ask physician for guidance.

Habit-Forming Potential

Use of this drug to suppress symptoms over an extended period of time may produce a state of functional dependence (see Glossary). In the treatment of conditions like rheumatoid arthritis and asthma, it is advisable to try alternate-day drug administration to keep the daily dose as small as possible and to attempt drug withdrawal after periods of reasonable improvement. Such procedures may reduce the degree of "steroid rebound"—the return of symptoms as the drug is withdrawn.

Effects of Overdosage

With Moderate Overdose: Excessive fluid retention, swelling of extremities, flushing of the face, nervousness, stomach irritation, weakness.

With Large Overdose: Severe headache, convulsions, heart failure in susceptible individuals, emotional and behavioral disturbances.

Possible Effects of Extended Use

Development of increased blood sugar, possibly diabetes.

Increased fat deposits on the trunk of the body ("buffalo hump"), rounding of the face ("moon face"), and thinning of the arms and legs.

Thinning and fragility of the skin, easy bruising.

Loss of strength and texture of the bones, resulting in spontaneous fractures.

Development of increased internal eye pressure, possibly glaucoma.

Development of cataracts.

Retarded growth and development in children.

Recommended Periodic Examinations While Taking This Drug

Measurement of blood potassium levels.

Measurement of blood sugar levels 2 hours after eating.

Measurement of blood pressure at regular intervals.

Chest X-ray if history of previous tuberculosis.

Determination of the rate of development of the growing child to detect retardation of normal growth.

While Taking This Drug, Observe the Following

Foods: No interactions. Ask physician regarding need to restrict salt intake or to eat potassium-rich foods. During long-term use of this drug it is advisable to have a high protein diet.

Beverages: No restrictions.

Alcohol: No interactions expected.

Tobacco Smoking: Nicotine increases the blood levels of naturally produced cortisone and related hormones. Heavy smoking may add to the expected actions of this drug and requires close observation for excessive effects.

Other Drugs

Prednisone may *increase* the effects of

• barbiturates and other sedatives and sleep-inducing drugs, and cause oversedation.

Prednisone may *decrease* the effects of

• anticoagulants of the coumarin family. Monitor prothrombin times closely and adjust dosage accordingly.

• choline-like drugs (Mestinon, pilocarpine, Prostigmin), and reduce their effectiveness in treating glaucoma and myasthenia gravis.

• insulin and oral anti-diabetic drugs, by raising the level of blood sugar. Doses of anti-diabetic drugs may have to be raised.

Prednisone *taken concurrently* with

• atropine-like drugs, may cause increased internal eye pressure and initiate or aggravate glaucoma (see Drug Family, Section Four).

• digitalis preparations, requires close monitoring of body potassium stores to prevent digitalis toxicity.

• stimulant drugs (Adrenalin, amphetamines, ephedrine, etc.), may increase internal eye pressure and initiate or aggravate glaucoma.

• thiazide diuretics, may cause excessive loss of potassium. Monitor blood levels of potassium on physician's advice.

The following drugs may *increase* the effects of prednisone

• aspirin

• indomethacin (Indocin, Indocid)

The following drugs may *decrease* the effects of prednisone

• antihistamines (some)

• barbiturates

• chloral hydrate (Noctec, Somnos)

• glutethimide (Doriden)

• phenylbutazone (Azolid, Butazolidin, etc.) may reduce its effectiveness following a brief, initial increase in effectiveness.

• phenytoin (Dantoin, Dilantin, etc.)

• propranolol (Inderal)

Driving a Vehicle, Piloting a Plane, Operating Machinery: No restrictions or precautions.

Exposure to Sun: No restrictions.

Occurrence of Unrelated Illness

This drug may decrease natural resistance to infection. Notify your physician if you develop an infection of any kind.

This drug may reduce your body's ability to respond appropriately to the stress of acute illness, injury, or surgery. Keep your physician fully informed of any significant changes in your state of health.

Discontinuation

If you have been taking this drug for an extended period of time, do not discontinue it abruptly. Ask physician for guidance regarding gradual withdrawal.

For a period of 2 years after discontinuing this drug, it is essential in the event of illness, injury, or surgery that you inform attending medical personnel that you used this drug in the past. The period of inadequate response to stress following the use of cortisone-like drugs may last 1 to 2 years.

Special Storage Instructions

Keep in a tightly closed container. Protect from light.

PRIMIDONE

Year Introduced: 1954

Brand Names

USA	Canada
Mysoline (Ayerst)	Mysoline (Ayerst)

Drug Family: Anti-convulsant

Prescription Required: Yes

Available Dosage Forms and Strengths

Tablets — 50 mg., 250 mg.

Suspension — 250 mg. per teaspoonful (5 ml.)

How This Drug Works

Intended Therapeutic Effect(s):   Prevention of epileptic seizures (anti-convulsant effect).

Location of Drug Action(s):   Those areas of the brain that initiate and sustain episodes of excessive electrical discharges responsible for epileptic seizures.

Method of Drug Action(s):　Not completely established. This drug reduces and stabilizes the excitability of nerve fibers and inhibits the repetitious spread of electrical impulses along nerve pathways. This action may prevent seizures altogether, or it may reduce their frequency and severity. (Part of this drug's action is attributable to phenobarbital, one of its conversion products in the body.)

THIS DRUG SHOULD NOT BE TAKEN IF

—you have had an allergic reaction to any dosage form of it previously.
—you are allergic to phenobarbital.
—you have a history of porphyria.

INFORM YOUR PHYSICIAN BEFORE TAKING THIS DRUG IF

—you have had an allergic reaction to any barbiturate drug (see Drug Family, Section Four).
—you have a history of liver or kidney disease.
—you have a history of systemic lupus erythematosus.
—you plan to have surgery under general anesthesia in the near future.

Time Required for Apparent Benefit

Dosage must be individualized. Continuous use on a regular schedule for 2 to 3 weeks is needed to evaluate response. Dosage adjustments may be necessary from time to time.

Possible Side-Effects *(natural, expected, and unavoidable drug actions)*

Drowsiness, lethargy, a sense of mental and physical sluggishness.

CAUTION

1. This drug must not be stopped abruptly.
2. The wide variation of this drug's action from person to person requires careful individualization of dosage schedules.
3. The elderly (over 60 years of age) may show evidence of overdosage or toxicity earlier than younger individuals.
4. Total daily dosage should not exceed 2000 mg.
5. Regularity of drug use is essential for the successful management of seizure disorders.
6. Shake the suspension form of this drug to mix it thoroughly before measuring the dose. Use a standard measuring device to assure that the dose is based upon a 5 ml. teaspoon.
7. Side-effects and mild adverse effects are usually most apparent during the first several days of treatment and often subside with continued use.
8. It may be necessary to take Vitamin Bc (folic acid) to prevent anemia while taking this drug. Consult your physician.
9. It is advisable that you carry a card of personal identification with a notation that you are taking this drug (see Table 14 and Section Seven).

Possible Adverse Effects *(unusual, unexpected, and infrequent reactions)*

IF ANY OF THE FOLLOWING DEVELOP, DISCONTINUE DRUG AND NOTIFY YOUR PHYSICIAN AS SOON AS POSSIBLE

Mild Adverse Effects
Allergic Reactions: Skin rash.
Dizziness, vertigo, unsteadiness, impaired coordination.
Reduced appetite, nausea, vomiting.
Nervous irritability, emotional disturbances.

Serious Adverse Effects
Allergic Reactions: Enlargement of lymph glands.
Severe skin reactions.
Idiosyncratic Reactions: Anemia due to deficiency of Vitamin Bc (folic acid).
Visual disturbances, double vision.
Sexual impotence.
Personality changes, abnormal behavior.
Symptoms suggesting systemic lupus erythematosus (see Glossary).
Bone marrow depression (see Glossary)—fatigue, weakness, fever, sore throat, abnormal bruising or bleeding.

Advisability of Use During Pregnancy
Over 90% of epileptic mothers treated with anti-convulsant drugs during pregnancy give birth to normal children. However, recent reports suggest a possible association between the use of this drug during the first 3 months of pregnancy and the development of birth defects in the fetus. Discuss with your physician the advantages and possible disadvantages of using this drug during pregnancy. It is advisable to use the smallest maintenance dose that will prevent seizures.

The newborn infants of mothers who take this drug during pregnancy may develop abnormal bleeding or serious hemorrhage due to a deficiency of certain clotting factors in the blood. Consult your physician regarding the advisability of taking Vitamin K during the last month of pregnancy.

Advisability of Use While Nursing Infant
This drug is known to be present in milk in substantial amounts. Observe the nursing infant for drowsiness. Ask physician for guidance.

Habit-Forming Potential
None.

Effects of Overdosage
With Moderate Overdose: Drowsiness, jerky eye movements, blurred vision, staggering gait, incoordination, slurred speech.
With Large Overdose: Deep sleep progressing to coma, slow and shallow breathing, weak and rapid pulse.

Possible Effects of Extended Use
Lymph gland enlargement.
Thyroid gland enlargement.

Anemia.

Reduced blood levels of calcium and phosphorus, leading to rickets in children and loss of bone texture (osteomalacia) in adults.

Recommended Periodic Examinations While Taking This Drug

Complete blood cell counts.

Evaluation of lymph glands.

Measurements of blood levels of calcium and phosphorus.

While Taking This Drug, Observe the Following

Foods: No restrictions. This drug may be taken with or following food to reduce the possibility of nausea. Consult your physician regarding the need for additional Vitamin D.

Beverages: No restrictions.

Alcohol: Use with extreme caution until combined effects have been determined. Alcohol can increase the sedative action of this drug and (in large quantities or with continuous use) may reduce its effectiveness in preventing seizures.

Tobacco Smoking: No interactions expected.

Other Drugs: This drug is closely related to the barbiturates and yields phenobarbital as a conversion product in the body. See PHENOBARBITAL Drug Profile for possible interactions with other drugs.

Driving a Vehicle, Piloting a Plane, Operating Machinery: Use caution until the full effects of this drug have been determined. It can cause drowsiness and impair mental alertness, vision, and physical coordination. Avoid hazardous activities if such symptoms occur.

Exposure to Sun: No restrictions.

Occurrence of Unrelated Illness: Notify your physician of any illness or injury that prevents the use of this drug according to your regular dosage schedule.

Discontinuation: Do not discontinue this drug abruptly. Sudden withdrawal of any anti-convulsant drug can cause severe and repeated seizures.

Special Storage Instructions

Keep in a tightly closed container. Protect the liquid suspension from light.

PROBENECID

Year Introduced: 1951

Brand Names

USA
Benacen (Cenci)
Benemid (Merck Sharp &
Dohme)
Probalan (Lannett)
Colbenemid [CD] (Merck
Sharp & Dohme)

Canada
Benemid (MSD)
Benuryl (ICN)

Drug Family: Anti-gout [Uricosurics]

Prescription Required: Yes

Available Dosage Forms and Strengths
Tablets — 500 mg.

How This Drug Works
Intended Therapeutic Effect(s)
- prevention of acute episodes of gout through maintenance of normal uric acid blood levels.
- maintenance of high blood levels of penicillin.

Location of Drug Action(s)
- the tubular systems of the kidney that regulate the uric acid content of the urine.
- the tubular systems of the kidney that regulate the elimination of penicillin.

Method of Drug Action(s)
By acting on the tubular systems of the kidney to increase the amount of uric acid excreted in the urine, this drug reduces the level of uric acid in the blood and body tissues.

By acting on the tubular systems of the kidney to decrease the amount of penicillin excreted in the urine, this drug prolongs the presence of penicillin in the blood.

THIS DRUG SHOULD NOT BE TAKEN IF
—you have had an allergic reaction to any dosage form of it previously.
—you are experiencing an attack of acute gout at the present time.
—it is prescribed for a child under 2 years of age.

INFORM YOUR PHYSICIAN BEFORE TAKING THIS DRUG IF
—you have a history of kidney stones or kidney disease.
—you have a history of peptic ulcer disease.
—you have a disease of the bone marrow or blood cells.
—you are taking any drug product that contains aspirin or aspirin-like drugs

Time Required for Apparent Benefit
Drug action begins in 2 hours, reaches a peak in 4 hours, and subsides in 12 to 24 hours. Continuous use on a regular schedule for several months is needed to prevent acute attacks of gout.

Possible Side-Effects *(natural, expected, and unavoidable drug actions)*
Development of kidney stones (composed of uric acid). Ask physician for guidance regarding their prevention.

CAUTION
Acute attacks of gout may occur after this drug is started on a regular dosage schedule. If symptoms suggestive of gout develop, consult your physician for guidance.

Possible Adverse Effects *(unusual, unexpected, and infrequent reactions)*

IF ANY OF THE FOLLOWING DEVELOP, DISCONTINUE DRUG AND NOTIFY YOUR PHYSICIAN AS SOON AS POSSIBLE

Mild Adverse Effects
Allergic Reactions: Skin rashes, itching, drug fever (see Glossary).
Headache, dizziness, flushing.
Reduced appetite, nausea, vomiting, sore gums.

Serious Adverse Effects
Allergic Reactions: Anaphylactic reaction (see Glossary).
Idiosyncratic Reactions: Hemolytic anemia (see Glossary).
Bone marrow depression (see Glossary)—fatigue, weakness, fever, sore throat, unusual bleeding or bruising.
Liver damage.
Kidney damage.

Advisability of Use During Pregnancy
Safety not established. Prudent use is best determined by the physician's evaluation.

Advisability of Use While Nursing Infant
Presence of drug in milk is not known. Avoid use if possible.

Habit-Forming Potential
None.

Effects of Overdosage
With Moderate Overdose: Stomach irritation, nausea, vomiting.
With Large Overdose: Severe nervous agitation, delirium, convulsions, coma, difficulty in breathing.

Possible Effects of Extended Use
Development of kidney damage in sensitive individuals.

Recommended Periodic Examinations While Taking This Drug
Complete blood cell counts.
Liver and kidney function tests.

While Taking This Drug, Observe the Following

Foods: Follow physician's advice regarding the need for a low purine diet. Drug may be taken after eating to reduce stomach irritation or nausea.

Beverages: A large intake of coffee, tea, or cola beverages may reduce the effectiveness of treatment. It is advisable to drink no less than 5 to 6 pints of liquids every 24 hours.

Alcohol: No interactions expected with this drug, but alcohol may impair successful management of gout.

Tobacco Smoking: No interactions expected.

Other Drugs

Probenecid may *increase* the effects of

- acetohexamide (Dymelor), and cause hypoglycemia. Dosage adjustments may be necessary for smooth control of diabetes.
- allopurinol (Zyloprim), and add to its elimination of uric acid.
- oral anticoagulants (see Drug Family, Section Four), and increase the risk of abnormal bleeding or hemorrhage.
- indomethacin (Indocin, Indocid), and enhance its potential for causing adverse effects. Reduced dosage may be necessary.
- nitrofurantoin (Furadantin).
- sulfinpyrazone (Anturane).

Probenecid may *decrease* the effects of

- ethacrynic acid (Edecrin), and reduce its diuretic action.

Probenecid *taken concurrently* with

- penicillin preparations (see Drug Family, Section Four), may cause a threefold to fivefold increase in penicillin blood levels, greatly increasing the effectiveness of each penicillin dose.
- para-aminosalicylic acid (PAS), may slow its elimination and increase its blood levels by 50%.
- sulfonamide ("sulfa") drugs (see Drug Family, Section Four), may slow their elimination and cause excessive accumulation during long-term use.

The following drugs may *decrease* the effects of probenecid

- aspirin and aspirin-like drugs may reduce its effectiveness in eliminating uric acid from the body.
- ethacrynic acid (Edecrin) may reduce its effectiveness in eliminating uric acid from the body.
- thiazide diuretics (see Drug Family, Section Four) may impair its effectiveness by raising the levels of uric acid in the blood.

Driving a Vehicle, Piloting a Plane, Operating Machinery: No restrictions.

Exposure to Sun: No restrictions.

Discontinuation: Do not discontinue this drug without consulting your physician. At the time of discontinuation, consult the Other Drugs section (above) to see if you are taking any drugs which may require dosage adjustments.

Special Storage Instructions

Keep in a dry, tightly closed container.

PROCAINAMIDE

Year Introduced: 1950

Brand Names

USA	Canada
Pronestyl (Squibb)	Pronestyl (Squibb)
Sub-Quin (Scrip)	

Drug Family: Heart Rhythm Regulator (Anti-arrhythmic)

Prescription Required: Yes

Available Dosage Forms and Strengths
Tablets — 250 mg., 375 mg., 500 mg.
Capsules — 250 mg., 375 mg., 500 mg.
Injection — 100 mg. per ml., 500 mg. per ml.

How This Drug Works
Intended Therapeutic Effect(s):   Correction of certain heart rhythm disorders.
Location of Drug Action(s):   The heart muscle and the tissues that comprise the electrical conduction system of the heart.
Method of Drug Action(s):   By slowing the activity of the pacemaker and delaying the transmission of electrical impulses through the conduction system and muscle of the heart, this drug assists in restoring normal heart rate and rhythm.

THIS DRUG SHOULD NOT BE TAKEN IF
—you have had an allergic reaction to any dosage form of it previously.
—you have myasthenia gravis.

INFORM YOUR PHYSICIAN BEFORE TAKING THIS DRUG IF
—you are allergic to procaine (Novocain) or to other local anesthetics of the "–caine" drug family, such as those commonly used for measuring the internal eye pressure (glaucoma testing) and for dental procedures.
—you have a history of kidney disease or impaired kidney function.
—you have a history of liver disease or impaired liver function.
—you have a history of lupus erythematosus.
—you are taking any form of digitalis.
—you plan to have surgery under general anesthesia in the near future.

Time Required for Apparent Benefit
Drug action begins within 30 to 60 minutes when taken by mouth and within a few minutes when given by intramuscular or intravenous injection.

Possible Side-Effects *(natural, expected, and unavoidable drug actions)*
Drop in blood pressure, mild and infrequent with oral administration but more common and pronounced with intramuscular or intravenous administration.

CAUTION
1. The appearance of symptoms suggestive of arthritis should be reported immediately; they could indicate the development of a lupus erythematosus-like disorder.
2. Dosage schedules must be carefully individualized.

Possible Adverse Effects *(unusual, unexpected, and infrequent reactions)*

IF ANY OF THE FOLLOWING DEVELOP, DISCONTINUE DRUG AND NOTIFY YOUR PHYSICIAN AS SOON AS POSSIBLE

Mild Adverse Effects
Allergic Reactions: Itching, skin rash, hives, drug fever (see Glossary).
Nausea, vomiting, abdominal pain, bitter taste, diarrhea.
Weakness, lightheadedness.

Serious Adverse Effects
Idiosyncratic Reactions: Hemolytic anemia (see Glossary).
Mental depression, hallucinations, abnormal behavior.
Reduced white blood cell counts—fever, sore throat, respiratory tract infections.
Reduced blood platelet counts (see Glossary)—abnormal bleeding or bruising.

Advisability of Use During Pregnancy
Safety not established. Prudent use is best determined by the physician's evaluation.

Advisability of Use While Nursing Infant
The presence of this drug in milk is not known. Ask physician for guidance.

Habit-Forming Potential
None.

Effects of Overdosage
With Moderate Overdose: Loss of appetite, nausea, drop in blood pressure, lightheadedness, weakness, intensification of abnormal heart rhythm.
With Large Overdose: Stupor, failure of circulation, heart arrest.

Possible Effects of Extended Use
†Lupus erythematosus-like disorder (see Glossary; this is a frequent and serious reaction with prolonged use of this drug)—joint pain and swelling (may be several joints), muscle ache, chest pain associated with breathing (pleurisy), fever, skin rash.

Recommended Periodic Examinations While Taking This Drug
Complete blood cell counts.
Blood examinations for the development of lupus erythematosis (LE) cells and anti-nuclear antibodies.
Electrocardiograms to monitor the full effect of the drug on the mechanisms that influence heart rate and rhythm.

While Taking This Drug, Observe the Following

Foods: No restrictions or precautions.

Beverages: Avoid excessive coffee, tea, and cola beverages because of their caffeine content. Avoid iced drinks.

Alcohol: No interactions expected.

Tobacco Smoking: No interactions expected. It is advisable to discontinue all smoking in the presence of serious heart rhythm disorders. Ask physician for guidance.

Other Drugs

Procainamide may *increase* the effects of

• anti-hypertensive drugs, and cause excessive lowering of the blood pressure (see Drug Family, Section Four).

• atropine-like drugs (see Drug Family, Section Four).

Procainamide may *decrease* the effects of

• ambenonium (Mytelase).

• neostigmine (Prostigmin).

• pryridostigmine (Mestinon).

The beneficial effect of these three drugs in the treatment of myasthenia gravis may be reduced.

Procainamide *taken concurrently* with

• propranolol in the presence of recent heart damage (acute myocardial infarction), may increase the depressant action of propranolol on the heart muscle.

• kanamycin, neomycin, or streptomycin, may cause severe muscle weakness and impairment of breathing.

The following drugs may *increase* the effects of procainamide

• acetazolamide (Diamox)

• sodium bicarbonate (see ANTACIDS Drug Profile)

Driving a Vehicle, Piloting a Plane, Operating Machinery: No restrictions. Use caution if this drug causes lightheadedness.

Exposure to Sun: No restrictions.

Discontinuation: This drug should be discontinued if symptoms of lupus erythematosus develop.

Special Storage Instructions

Keep tablets and capsules in tightly closed containers and at room temperature.

Keep injectable form (vials) at room temperature. Protect from light, freezing, and excessive heat.

Do Not Use the Injectable Solution of This Drug if

It is darker than a pale yellow.

PROCHLORPERAZINE

Year Introduced: 1956

Brand Names

USA	**Canada**
Compazine (Smith Kline & French)	Stemetil (Poulenc)

Drug Family: Tranquilizer, Strong (Anti-psychotic) [Phenothiazines] Anti-nausea (Anti-emetic)

Prescription Required: Yes

Available Dosage Forms and Strengths

Tablets — 5 mg., 10 mg., 25 mg.
Capsules — 10 mg., 15 mg., 30 mg., 75 mg.
Syrup — 5 mg. per teaspoonful
Suppositories — 2.5 mg., 5 mg., 25 mg.
Concentrate — 10 mg. per ml.
Injection — 5 mg. per ml.

How This Drug Works

Intended Therapeutic Effect(s)

• relief of severe nausea and vomiting.
• restoration of emotional calm; relief of severe anxiety, agitation, and/or psychotic behavior.

Location of Drug Action(s)

• the nerve pathways in the brain that stimulate the vomiting center.
• the nerve pathways in the limbic system of the brain that influence emotion and behavior.

Method of Drug Action(s)

By blocking the action of one of the chemicals (acetylcholine) responsible for the transmission of nerve impulses, this drug prevents excessive stimulation of the vomiting center.

By blocking the action of another chemical (dopamine) responsible for the transmission of nerve impulses within certain brain structures, this drug restores a more normal balance of factors controlling emotional state and behavior.

THIS DRUG SHOULD NOT BE TAKEN IF

—you have had an allergic reaction to any dosage form of it previously.
—you have a blood or bone marrow disorder.
—it is prescribed for a child under 2 years of age or weighing under 20 pounds.

INFORM YOUR PHYSICIAN BEFORE TAKING THIS DRUG IF

—you are allergic or sensitive to any phenothiazine drug (see Drug Family, Section Four).
—you are taking sedatives, sleep-inducing drugs, tranquilizers, antidepressants, antihistamines, or narcotic drugs of any kind.
—you have glaucoma.

—you have epilepsy.
—you have a liver, heart, or lung disorder, especially asthma or emphysema.
—you have a history of peptic ulcer.
—you plan to have surgery under general or spinal anesthesia in the near future.

Time Required for Apparent Benefit

Approximately 1 to 2 hours. In treating nervous and mental disorders, maximal benefit may require regular use for several weeks.

Possible Side-Effects *(natural, expected, and unavoidable drug actions)*

Drowsiness, blurring of vision, dryness of the mouth, nasal congestion, constipation, impaired urination.

CAUTION

Children with acute illness ("flu"-like infections, measles, chickenpox, etc.) are very susceptible to adverse effects involving muscular spasms of the face, neck, back, or extremities when this drug is used to control nausea and vomiting. Observe closely and notify physician if such reactions occur.

Possible Adverse Effects *(unusual, unexpected, and infrequent reactions)*

IF ANY OF THE FOLLOWING DEVELOP, DISCONTINUE DRUG AND NOTIFY YOUR PHYSICIAN AS SOON AS POSSIBLE

Mild Adverse Effects
 Allergic Reactions: Skin rashes (various kinds), hives, low-grade fever.
 Dizziness, lightheadedness in upright position and feeling of impending faint (see orthostatic hypotension in Glossary).
 Menstrual irregularity.

Serious Adverse Effects
 Allergic Reactions: Hepatitis with jaundice (see Glossary), usually within the first 4 weeks.
 Bone marrow depression (see Glossary).
 Parkinson-like disorders (see Glossary).
 Spasms of the muscles of the face, neck, back, and extremities, causing rolling of the eyes, grimacing, clamping of the jaw, protrusion of the tongue, difficulty in swallowing, arching of the back, cramping of the hands and feet.

Advisability of Use During Pregnancy

Safety not established. Prudent use is best determined by the physician's evaluation.

Advisability of Use While Nursing Infant

Drug is known to be present in milk. Avoid use if possible. Ask physician for guidance.

Habit-Forming Potential

None.

Effects of Overdosage
With Moderate Overdose: Marked drowsiness, weakness, tremor, restlessness, agitation.
With Large Overdose: Stupor, deep sleep, coma, convulsions.

Possible Effects of Extended Use
Tardive dyskinesia (see Glossary).

Recommended Periodic Examinations While Taking This Drug
Complete blood cell counts, especially during first 3 months of treatment.
Liver function tests.
Careful inspection of the tongue for early evidence of fine, involuntary, wave-like movements that could indicate the beginning of tardive dyskinesia.

While Taking This Drug, Observe the Following
Foods: No restrictions.
Beverages: No restrictions.
Alcohol: Use with extreme caution until combined effect has been determined. Alcohol can increase the sedative action of prochlorperazine and accentuate its depressant effects on brain function. Prochlorperazine may increase the intoxicating effects of alcohol.
Tobacco Smoking: No interactions expected.
Other Drugs
Prochlorperazine may *increase* the effects of
• all sedatives, sleep-inducing drugs, other tranquilizers, antihistamines, and narcotic drugs, and produce oversedation. Ask physician for guidance regarding dosage adjustment.
• all drugs containing atropine or having an atropine-like action (see Drug Family, Section Four).
• phenytoin (Dantoin, Dilantin, etc.).

Prochlorperazine may *decrease* the effects of
• levodopa (Dopar, Larodopa, etc.), and reduce its effectiveness in the treatment of Parkinson's disease (shaking palsy).
• appetite suppressant drugs (Pre-Sate, Preludin, Benzedrine, Dexedrine, etc.).

Prochlorperazine *taken concurrently* with
• quinidine, may impair heart function. Avoid the combined use of these two drugs.

The following drugs may *increase* the effects of prochlorperazine
• tricyclic antidepressants (see Drug Family, Section Four).
Driving a Vehicle, Piloting a Plane, Operating Machinery: This drug can impair mental alertness, judgment, and physical coordination. Avoid hazardous activities.
Exposure to Sun: Use caution until sensitization has been determined. This drug can produce photosensitivity (see Glossary).

Exposure to Heat: Use caution and avoid excessive heat. This drug may impair the regulation of body temperature and increase the risk of heat stroke.

Heavy Exercise or Exertion: No restrictions.

Discontinuation: If it has been necessary to use this drug for an extended period of time, do not discontinue it suddenly. Ask physician for guidance regarding dosage reduction and withdrawal. Upon discontinuation of this drug, it may also be necessary to adjust the dosages of other drugs taken concurrently with it.

Special Storage Instructions
Keep in a tightly closed, light-resistant container.

PROCYCLIDINE

Year Introduced: 1948

Brand Names

USA	Canada
Kemadrin (Burroughs Wellcome)	Kemadrin (B.W. Ltd.)
	Procyclid (ICN)

Drug Family: Anti-parkinsonism, Atropine-like Drug [Anticholinergics]

Prescription Required: Yes

Available Dosage Forms and Strengths
Tablets — 2 mg., 5 mg.

How This Drug Works
Intended Therapeutic Effect(s): Relief of the rigidity, tremor, sluggish movement, and impaired gait associated with Parkinson's disease.

Location of Drug Action(s): The principal site of the desired therapeutic action is the regulating center in the brain (the basal ganglia) which governs the coordination and efficiency of bodily movements.

Method of Drug Action(s): The improvement in Parkinson's disease results from the restoration of a more normal balance of the chemical activities responsible for the transmission of nerve impulses within the basal ganglia.

THIS DRUG SHOULD NOT BE TAKEN IF
—you have had an allergic reaction to any dosage form of it previously.
—it is prescribed for a child under 3 years of age.

INFORM YOUR PHYSICIAN BEFORE TAKING THIS DRUG IF
—you have experienced an unfavorable response to atropine or atropine-like drugs in the past.
—you have glaucoma.
—you have high blood pressure or heart disease.

—you have a history of liver or kidney disease.
—you have difficulty emptying the urinary bladder.

Time Required for Apparent Benefit
Drug action begins in 1 to 2 hours and persists for approximately 24 hours. Daily dosage may be cumulative in some individuals. Regular use for 2 to 4 weeks may be needed to determine optimal dosage schedule.

Possible Side-Effects *(natural, expected, and unavoidable drug actions)*
Nervousness, blurring of vision, dryness of the mouth, constipation. (These often subside as drug use continues.)

CAUTION
The elderly (over 60 years of age) are often more sensitive to the actions of this drug. Small doses are advisable until tolerance has been determined.

Possible Adverse Effects *(unusual, unexpected, and infrequent reactions)*
IF ANY OF THE FOLLOWING DEVELOP, DISCONTINUE DRUG AND NOTIFY YOUR PHYSICIAN AS SOON AS POSSIBLE

Mild Adverse Effects
  Allergic Reactions: Skin rashes.
  Drowsiness, dizziness, headache.
  Nausea, vomiting.
  Urinary hesitancy, difficulty emptying bladder.
Serious Adverse Effects
  Idiosyncratic Reactions: Confusion, delusions, hallucinations, agitation, erratic behavior.

Advisability of Use During Pregnancy
Safety not established. Prudent use is best determined by the physician's evaluation.

Advisability of Use While Nursing Infant
Presence of drug in milk is not known. Safety for infant not established. Ask physician for guidance.

Habit-Forming Potential
None.

Effects of Overdosage
  With Moderate Overdose   Drowsiness, stupor, weakness, impaired vision, rapid pulse.
  With Large Overdose: Excitement, confusion, agitation, hallucinations, dry and hot skin, generalized skin rash, markedly dilated pupils.

Possible Effects of Extended Use
Increased internal eye pressure, possibly glaucoma.

Recommended Periodic Examinations While Taking This Drug
Measurement of internal eye pressure (glaucoma detection) at regular intervals.

While Taking This Drug, Observe the Following

Foods: No restrictions. Drug may be taken after food if it causes indigestion

Beverages: No restrictions.

Alcohol: No interactions expected.

Tobacco Smoking: No interactions expected.

Other Drugs

Procyclidine may *increase* the effects of

- levodopa (Dopar, Larodopa, etc.), and improve its effectiveness in the treatment of parkinsonism.
- mild and strong tranquilizers, and cause excessive sedation.

Procyclidine *taken concurrently* with

- cortisone (and related drugs) on an extended basis, may cause an increase in internal eye pressure, possibly glaucoma.
- primidone (Mysoline), may cause excessive sedation.
- phenothiazine drugs, may cause (in sensitive individuals) severe behavioral disturbances (toxic psychosis).

The following drugs may *increase* the effects of procyclidine

- antihistamines may add to the dryness of mouth and throat.
- tricyclic antidepressants may add to the effects on the eye and further increase internal eye pressure, dangerous in glaucoma.
- mono-amine oxidase (MAO) inhibitor drugs (see Drug Family, Section Four) may intensify all effects of this drug.
- meperidine (Demerol)
- methylphenidate (Ritalin)
- orphenadrine (Disipal, Norflex)
- quinidine

Driving a Vehicle, Piloting a Plane, Operating Machinery: Drowsiness and dizziness may occur in sensitive individuals. Avoid hazardous activities until full effects and tolerance have been determined.

Exposure to Sun: No restrictions.

Exposure to Heat: Use caution. This drug may reduce sweating, cause an increase in body temperature, and increase the risk of heat stroke.

Heavy Exercise or Exertion: Avoid in hot environments.

Discontinuation: Do not discontinue this drug suddenly. Ask physician for guidance in reducing dose gradually.

Special Storage Instructions

Keep in a dry, tightly closed container. Protect from light.

PROMAZINE

Year Introduced: 1957

Brand Names

USA	Canada
Sparine (Wyeth)	Intrazine (Organon)
	Promabec (Pharbec)
	Promanyl (Maney)
	Promazettes (Barlowe Cote)
	Promezerine (Barlowe Cote)
	Sparine (Wyeth)

Drug Family: Tranquilizer, Strong (Anti-psychotic) [Phenothiazines]
Antinausea (Anti-emetic)

Prescription Required: Yes

Available Dosage Forms and Strengths:
Tablets — 10 mg., 25 mg., 50 mg., 100 mg., 200 mg.
Syrup — 10 mg. per teaspoonful, 25 mg. per teaspoonful
Concentrate — 30 mg. per ml., 100 mg. per ml.
Injection — 25 mg. per ml., 50 mg. per ml.

How This Drug Works

Intended Therapeutic Effect(s):   Restoration of emotional calm. Relief of severe anxiety, agitation, and psychotic behavior.

Location of Drug Action(s):   Those nerve pathways in the brain that utilize the tissue chemical dopamine for the transmission of nerve impulses.

Method of Drug Action(s):   Not completely established. Present theory is that by inhibiting the action of dopamine, this drug acts to correct an imbalance of nerve impulse transmissions that is thought to be responsible for certain mental disorders.

THIS DRUG SHOULD NOT BE TAKEN IF
—you have had an allergic reaction to any dosage form of it previously.
—you have a disorder of the blood or bone marrow.

INFORM YOUR PHYSICIAN BEFORE TAKING THIS DRUG IF
—you are allergic or sensitive to any phenothiazine drug (see Drug Family, Section Four).
—you are taking sedatives, sleep-inducing drugs, tranquilizers, antidepressants, or narcotic drugs of any kind.
—you have epilepsy.
—you have a history of liver disease, heart disease, or lung disease, especially asthma or emphysema.
—you plan to have surgery under general or spinal anesthesia in the near future.

Time Required for Apparent Benefit
Approximately 1 to 2 hours. Maximal benefit may require regular use for several weeks.

Possible Side-Effects *(natural, expected, and unavoidable drug actions)*
Drowsiness (usually during the first 2 weeks), dryness of the mouth, nasal congestion, constipation, impaired urination.
Pink or purple coloration of the urine, of no significance.

Possible Adverse Effects *(unusual, unexpected, and infrequent reactions)*
IF ANY OF THE FOLLOWING DEVELOP, DISCONTINUE DRUG AND NOTIFY YOUR PHYSICIAN AS SOON AS POSSIBLE

Mild Adverse Effects
Allergic Reactions: Skin rashes (various kinds), hives, low-grade fever. Lowering of body temperature, especially in the elderly (over 60 years of age).
Lightheadedness or faintness in upright position (see orthostatic hypotension in Glossary), dizziness, heart palpitation.
Increased appetite and weight gain.
Breast fullness and tenderness, milk production.
Menstrual irregularity.
False positive pregnancy tests.

Serious Adverse Effects
Allergic Reactions: Hepatitis with jaundice (see Glossary), usually occurring between second and fourth week, high fever, asthma, anaphylactic reaction (see Glossary).
Bone marrow depression (see Glossary)—fatigue, weakness, fever, sore throat, unusual bleeding or bruising.
Parkinson-like disorders (see Glossary).
Muscle spasms affecting the jaw, neck, back, hands, or feet.
Eye-rolling, muscle twitching, convulsions.
Prolonged drop in blood pressure with weakness, perspiration, and fainting.

Advisability of Use During Pregnancy
Safety not established. Prudent use is best determined by the physician' evaluation.

Advisability of Use While Nursing Infant
Drug is known to be present in milk. Ask physician for guidance.

Habit-Forming Potential
None.

Effects of Overdosage
With Moderate Overdose: Marked drowsiness, weakness, tremor, impairment of stance and gait, agitation.
With Large Overdose: Stupor, deep sleep, coma, convulsions.

Possible Effects of Extended Use
Tardive dyskinesia (see Glossary).
Pigmentation of skin, gray to violet in color, usually in exposed areas, more common in women.
Eye changes: cataracts and pigmentation of retina with impairment of vision.

Recommended Periodic Examinations While Taking This Drug
Complete blood cell counts, especially between the fourth and tenth weeks of treatment.
Liver function tests.
Complete eye examinations, including eye structures and vision.
Careful inspection of the tongue for early evidence of fine, involuntary, wave-like movements that could indicate the beginning of tardive dyskinesia.
Periodic electrocardiograms.

While Taking This Drug, Observe the Following
Foods: No restrictions.
Beverages: No restrictions.
Alcohol: Use with extreme caution until combined effect has been determined. Alcohol can increase the sedative action of promazine and accentuate its depressant effects on brain function. Promazine can increase the intoxicating effects of alcohol.
Tobacco Smoking: No interactions expected.
Other Drugs
Promazine may *increase* the effects of
• all sedatives, sleep-inducing drugs, other tranquilizers, antihistamines, and narcotic drugs, and produce oversedation. Ask physician for guidance regarding dosage adjustment.
• all drugs containing atropine or having an atropine-like action (see Drug Family, Section Four).
• phenytoin (Dantoin, Dilantin, etc.).
• pargyline (Eutonyl), and cause excessive lowering of the blood pressure.
• reserpine (and related drugs), and cause excessive lowering of the blood pressure.
• methyldopa (Aldomet), and cause excessive lowering of the blood pressure.

Promazine may *decrease* the effects of
• guanethidine (Ismelin), and reduce its effectiveness in lowering blood pressure.
• oral anticoagulants, by hastening their destruction and elimination. Dosage adjustment of the anticoagulant may be necessary.
• oral anti-diabetic drugs and insulin, and reduce their effectiveness in regulating blood sugar.
• chlorphentermine (Pre-Sate), and reduce its effectiveness in controlling appetite.
• phenmetrazine (Preludin), and reduce its effectiveness in controlling appetite.

• levodopa (Dopar, Larodopa, etc.), and reduce its effectiveness in the treat ment of Parkinson's disease (shaking palsy).

Promazine *taken concurrently* with

• quinidine, may impair heart function. Avoid the combined use of these two drugs.

The following drugs may *increase* the effects of promazine

• oral contraceptives, by slowing the excretion of promazine.

Driving a Vehicle, Piloting a Plane, Operating Machinery: This drug car impair mental alertness, judgment, and physical coordination. Avoid haz ardous activities.

Exposure to Sun: Use caution until sensitivity has been determined. Thi drug can produce photosensitivity (see Glossary).

Exposure to Heat: Use caution and avoid excessive heat as much as possible This drug may impair the regulation of body temperature and increase the risk of heat stroke.

Heavy Exercise or Exertion: No restrictions.

Discontinuation: If it has been necessary to use this drug for an extended period of time, do not discontinue it suddenly. Ask physician for guidance regarding dosage reduction and withdrawal. Upon discontinuation of thi, drug, it may also be necessary to adjust the dosages of other drugs taken concurrently with it.

Special Storage Instructions
Keep in a tightly closed, light-resistant container.

PROMETHAZINE

Year Introduced: 1945

Brand Names

USA		Canada
Fellozine	Prosedin (Ulmer)	Histanil (ICN)
(Fellows-Testagar)	Provigan	Phenergan (Poulenc)
Ganphen (Tutag)	(Reid-Provident)	
K-Phen (Kay)	Remsed (Endo)	
Pentazine (Century)	Sigazine (Sig: Pharm.)	
Phenergan (Wyeth)	Synalgos [CD] (Ives)	
Phenerhist (Rocky	Synalgos-DC [CD]	
Mtn.)	(Ives)	
Prorex (Hyrex-Key)	ZiPan (Savage)	

Drug Family: Antihistamines [Phenothiazines]
Antinausea (Anti-emetic)

Prescription Required: Yes

Available Dosage Forms and Strengths

Tablets — 12.5 mg., 25 mg., 50 mg.

Syrup — 6.25 mg., 25 mg. per teaspoonful

Suppositories — 25 mg., 50 mg.

Injection — 25 mg. per ml., 50 mg. per ml.

Also available in cough preparations of various compositions (examine product labels)

How This Drug Works

Intended Therapeutic Effect(s)

• relief of symptoms associated with hayfever (allergic rhinitis) and with allergic reactions in the skin, such as itching, swelling, hives, and rash.

• prevention and management of the nausea, vomiting, and dizziness associated with motion sickness.

• the production of mild sedation and light sleep.

Location of Drug Action(s)

• those hypersensitive tissues that release excessive histamine as part of an allergic reaction. Principal tissue sites are the eyes, the nose, and the skin.

• the nerve pathways connecting the organ of equilibrium (the labyrinth) in the inner ear with the vomiting center in the brain.

• the site in the brain of this drug's action responsible for sedation and sleep is unknown.

Method of Drug Action(s)

This drug reduces the intensity of the allergic response by blocking the action of histamine after it has been released from sensitized tissue cells.

This drug also reduces the sensitivity of the nerve endings in the labyrinth and blocks the transmission of excessive nerve impulses to the vomiting center.

The way in which this drug produces sedation and light sleep is unknown.

THIS DRUG SHOULD NOT BE TAKEN IF

—you have had an allergic reaction to any dosage form of it previously.

—you have a blood or bone marrow disorder.

—you have glaucoma (narrow-angle type).

—it is prescribed for a newborn infant.

INFORM YOUR PHYSICIAN BEFORE TAKING THIS DRUG IF

—you are allergic or sensitive to any phenothiazine drug (see Drug Family, Section Four).

—you are taking any sedatives, sleep-inducing drugs, tranquilizers, other antihistamines, antidepressants, or narcotic drugs of any kind.

—you have a history of recurring peptic ulcer.

—you have a history of prostate gland enlargement.

—you plan to have surgery under general anesthesia in the near future.

Time Required for Apparent Benefit

Usually 1 to 2 hours when taken orally.

Possible Side-Effects *(natural, expected, and unavoidable drug actions)*

Drowsiness, blurred vision, dryness of the mouth, inability to concentrate.

CAUTION

Children with acute illness ("flu"-like infections, measles, chickenpox, etc.) are very susceptible to adverse effects involving muscular spasms of the face, neck, back, or extremities when this drug is used to control nausea and vomiting. Observe closely and notify physician if such reactions occur.

Possible Adverse Effects *(unusual, unexpected, and infrequent reactions)*

IF ANY OF THE FOLLOWING DEVELOP, DISCONTINUE DRUG AND NOTIFY YOUR PHYSICIAN AS SOON AS POSSIBLE

Mild Adverse Effects
  Allergic Reactions: None reported.
  Dizziness, weakness.

Serious Adverse Effects
  Paradoxical Reactions: hyperexcitability, abnormal movements of arms and legs, nightmares.
  Parkinson-like disorders (see Glossary).
  Muscle spasms of the face, neck, back, and extremities, causing rolling of the eyes, twisting of the neck, arching of the back, spasms of the hands and feet.
  Bone marrow depression (see Glossary), mild and very rare.
  Hepatitis with jaundice (see Glossary), very rare.

Advisability of Use During Pregnancy

Apparently safe; no reports of adverse effects to mother or fetus. However, use only when absolutely necessary and avoid large doses and prolonged use.

Advisability of Use While Nursing Infant

Apparently safe; ask physician for guidance regarding dosage. Observe infant for evidence of sedation.

Habit-Forming Potential

None.

Effects of Overdosage

With Moderate Overdose: Marked drowsiness, weakness, unsteady stance and gait, agitation, delirium.
With Large Overdose: Deep sleep, coma, convulsions.

Possible Effects of Extended Use

Bone marrow depression.

Recommended Periodic Examinations While Taking This Drug

Complete blood cell counts.

While Taking This Drug, Observe the Following

Foods: Take drug with or following food if it causes irritation of stomach.
Beverages: No restrictions.
Alcohol: Use with extreme caution until combined effect has been determined. Alcohol can increase the sedative action of promethazine and accentuate its depressant effects on brain function. Promethazine can increase the intoxicating action of alcohol.

Tobacco Smoking: No interactions expected.

Other Drugs

Promethazine may *increase* the effects of

- all sedatives, sleep-inducing drugs, pain-relieving drugs, other antihistamines, tranquilizers, and narcotic drugs, and cause oversedation. Ask physician for guidance regarding dosage adjustment.
- atropine and drugs with an atropine-like action (see Drug Family, Section Four).

Driving a Vehicle, Piloting a Plane, Operating Machinery: This drug can cause drowsiness and dizziness. Avoid hazardous activities until its effect has been determined.

Exposure to Sun: Use caution until sensitivity has been determined. This drug can cause photosensitivity (see Glossary).

Special Storage Instructions

Keep in a tightly closed container. Protect from light.

PROPANTHELINE

Year Introduced: 1953

Brand Names

USA	Canada
Norpanth (North Amer. Pharm.)	Banlin (Maney)
Pro-Banthine (Searle)	Novopropanthil (Novopharm)
Ropanth (Tutag)	Pro-Banthine (Searle)
Probital [CD] (Searle)	Propanthel (ICN)
	Probanthrax [CD] (Barlowe Cote)
	Probital [CD] (Searle)

Drug Family: Antispasmodic, Atropine-like Drug [Anticholinergics]

Prescription Required: Yes

Available Dosage Forms and Strengths

Tablets — 7.5 mg., 15 mg.
Prolonged Action Tablets — 30 mg.

How This Drug Works

Intended Therapeutic Effect(s):   Relief of discomfort resulting from excessive activity and spasm of the digestive tract (esophagus, stomach, intestine, and colon).

Location of Drug Action(s):   The terminal nerve fibers of the parasympathetic nervous system that control the activity of the gastrointestinal tract.

Method of Drug Action(s):   By blocking the action of the chemical (acetylcholine) that transmits impulses at parasympathetic nerve endings, this drug prevents stimulation of muscular contraction and glandular secretion within the organ involved. This results in reduced overall activity, including the prevention or relief of muscle spasm.

THIS DRUG SHOULD NOT BE TAKEN IF
—you have had an allergic reaction to any dosage form of it previously.
—your stomach cannot empty properly into the intestine (pyloric obstruction).
—you are unable to empty the urinary bladder completely.
—you have glaucoma (narrow-angle type).
—you have severe ulcerative colitis.

INFORM YOUR PHYSICIAN BEFORE TAKING THIS DRUG IF
—you have glaucoma (open-angle type).
—you have angina or coronary heart disease.
—you have chronic bronchitis.
—you have a hiatal hernia.
—you have enlargement of the prostate gland.
—you have myasthenia gravis.
—you have a history of peptic ulcer disease.
—you plan to have surgery under general anesthesia in the near future.

Time Required for Apparent Benefit
Drug action begins in 1 to 2 hours and persists for approximately 6 hours.

Possible Side-Effects *(natural, expected, and unavoidable drug actions)*
Blurring of vision (impairment of focus), dryness of the mouth and throat, constipation, hesitancy in urination. (Nature and degree of side-effects depend upon individual susceptibility and drug dosage.)

CAUTION
The elderly (over 60 years of age) may be more susceptible to all of the actions of this drug. Small doses are advisable until response has been determined.

Possible Adverse Effects *(unusual, unexpected, and infrequent reactions)*

IF ANY OF THE FOLLOWING DEVELOP, DISCONTINUE DRUG AND NOTIFY YOUR PHYSICIAN AS SOON AS POSSIBLE

Mild Adverse Effects
   Allergic Reactions: Skin rash, hives.
   Dilation of pupils, causing sensitivity to light.
   Flushing and dryness of the skin (reduced sweating).
   Rapid heart action.
   Lightheadedness, dizziness, unsteady gait.

Serious Adverse Effects
   Idiosyncratic Reactions: Acute confusion, delirium, erratic behavior.
   Development of acute glaucoma (in susceptible individuals).

Advisability of Use During Pregnancy
Safety not established. Prudent use is best determined by the physician's evaluation.

Advisability of Use While Nursing Infant
This drug may impair the formation of milk and make nursing difficult. It is reported not to be present in milk. Ask physician for guidance regarding nursing.

Habit-Forming Potential
None.

Effects of Overdosage
With Moderate Overdose: Marked dryness of the mouth, dilated pupils, blurring of near vision, rapid pulse, heart palpitation, headache, difficulty in urination.

With Large Overdose: Extremely dilated pupils, rapid pulse and breathing, hot skin, high fever, excitement, confusion, hallucinations, delirium, eventual loss of consciousness, convulsions, coma.

Possible Effects of Extended Use
Chronic constipation, severe enough to result in fecal impaction. (Constipation should be treated promptly with effective laxatives.)

Recommended Periodic Examinations While Taking This Drug
Measurement of internal eye pressure to detect any significant increase that could indicate developing glaucoma.

While Taking This Drug, Observe the Following
Foods: No interaction with drug. Effectiveness is greater if drug is taken one-half to 1 hour before eating. Follow diet prescribed for condition under treatment.

Beverages: No interactions. As allowed by prescribed diet.

Alcohol: No interactions expected with this drug. Follow physician's advice regarding use of alcohol (based upon its effect on the condition under treatment).

Tobacco Smoking: No interactions expected. Follow physician's advice regarding smoking.

Other Drugs

Propantheline may *increase* the effects of
• all other drugs having atropine-like actions (see Drug Family, Section Four).

Propantheline may *decrease* the effects of
• pilocarpine eye drops, and reduce their effectiveness in lowering internal eye pressure in the treatment of glaucoma.

Propantheline *taken concurrently* with
• mono-amine oxidase (MAO) inhibitor drugs (see Drug Family, Section Four), may cause an exaggerated response to normal doses of atropine-like drugs. It is best to avoid atropine-like drugs for 2 weeks after the last dose of any MAO inhibitor drug.
• haloperidol (Haldol), may significantly increase internal eye pressure (dangerous in glaucoma).

The following drugs may *increase* the effects of propantheline
- tricyclic antidepressants
- those antihistamines that have an atropine-like action
- meperidine (Demerol, pethidine)
- methylphenidate (Ritalin)
- orphenadrine (Disipal, Norflex)
- those phenothiazines that have an atropine-like action (see Drug Family, Section Four, for brand names)

Driving a Vehicle, Piloting a Plane, Operating Machinery: This drug may produce blurred vision, drowsiness, or dizziness. Avoid hazardous activities if these drug effects occur.

Exposure to Sun: No restrictions.

Exposure to Heat: Use extreme caution. The use of this drug in hot environments may significantly increase the risk of heat stroke.

Heavy Exercise or Exertion: Use caution in warm or hot environments. This drug may impair normal perspiration (heat loss) and interfere with the regulation of body temperature.

Special Storage Instructions
Keep in a tightly closed container. Protect from light.

PROPOXYPHENE

Year Introduced: 1955

Brand Names

USA	Canada
Darvon (Lilly)	Darvon-N (Lilly)
Darvon-N (Lilly)	Depronal-SA
Harmar (Zemmer)	(Warner/Chilcott)
Proproxychel (Rachelle)	Dymopoxyphene-65
SK-65 (Smith Kline &	(Dymond)
French)	Neo-Mal (Neo)
S-Pain-65 (Saron)	Progesic (A & H)
Darvocet-N [CD] (Lilly)	Pronalgic (Terapex)
Darvon Compound [CD]	Pro-65 (ICN)
(Lilly)	65P (Saunders)
Darvon With A.P.C. [CD]	642 (Frosst)
(Lilly)	
Wygesic [CD] (Wyeth)	

Drug Family: Analgesic, Mild

Prescription Required: Yes (Controlled Drug, U.S. Schedule 4)

Available Dosage Forms and Strengths
Tablets — 100 mg.
Capsules — 32 mg., 65 mg.
Oral Suspension — 50 mg. per teaspoonful

How This Drug Works
Intended Therapeutic Effect(s):   Relief of mild to moderate pain.
Location of Drug Action(s):   Those areas of the brain and spinal cord involved in the perception of pain.
Method of Drug Action(s):   Not completely established. It has been suggested that the resulting increase in chemicals that transmit nerve impulses somehow contributes to the analgesic effect of this drug.

THIS DRUG SHOULD NOT BE TAKEN IF
—you have had an allergic reaction to any dosage form of it previously. A combination drug [CD] should not be taken if you are allergic to *any* of its ingredients.
—it is prescribed for a child under 12 years of age.

INFORM YOUR PHYSICIAN BEFORE TAKING THIS DRUG IF
—you are taking sedatives, sleep-inducing drugs, tranquilizers, antidepressants, or narcotic drugs of any kind.

Time Required for Apparent Benefit
Usually 1 to 2 hours.

Possible Side-Effects *(natural, expected, and unavoidable drug actions)*
Drowsiness, lightheadedness, constipation.

Possible Adverse Effects *(unusual, unexpected, and infrequent reactions)*
IF ANY OF THE FOLLOWING DEVELOP, DISCONTINUE DRUG AND NOTIFY YOUR PHYSICIAN AS SOON AS POSSIBLE
Mild Adverse Effects
Allergic Reactions: Skin rashes.
Nausea, vomiting, abdominal discomfort.
Headache, dizziness, weakness, blurred vision, mild behavioral disturbances.

Serious Adverse Effects
Allergic Reactions: Hepatitis with jaundice (very rare).
Paradoxical excitement, agitation, and insomnia.

Advisability of Use During Pregnancy
Safety not established. Prudent use is best determined by the physician's evaluation.

Advisability of Use While Nursing Infant
Drug is known to be present in milk. Safety for infant not established. Ask physician for guidance.

Habit-Forming Potential
Can produce psychological and physical dependence (see Glossary) if used in large doses for an extended period of time.

Effects of Overdosage
With Moderate Overdose: Mental and behavioral disturbance, marked drowsiness progressing to stupor.
With Large Overdose: Coma, convulsions, depression of respiration.

Possible Effects of Extended Use
Psychological and physical dependence.

Recommended Periodic Examinations While Taking This Drug
None.

While Taking This Drug, Observe the Following
Foods: No restrictions.
Beverages: No restrictions.
Alcohol: Use with caution until combined effect is determined. Alcohol can increase this drug's depressant action on the brain. Propoxyphene may increase the intoxicating effects of alcohol.
Tobacco Smoking: Heavy smoking may reduce the effectiveness of propoxyphene.
Other Drugs
Propoxyphene may *increase* the effects of
  • sedatives, sleep-inducing drugs, tranquilizers, and narcotic drugs; dosage adjustment may be necessary to avoid excessive sedation.

Propoxyphene *taken concurrently* with
  • orphenadrine (Disipal, Norflex, Norgesic), may cause anxiety, confusion, or tremors (probably very rare).

The following drugs may *increase* the effects of propoxyphene
  • aspirin and related drugs; combined action increases effectiveness in relieving pain.
  • acetaminophen; combined action increases effectiveness in relieving pain.

Driving a Vehicle, Piloting a Plane, Operating Machinery: This drug can impair mental alertness, judgment, and physical coordination. Use caution until occurrence of drowsiness and/or dizziness is determined.
Exposure to Sun: No restrictions.

Special Storage Instructions
Keep in a dry, tightly closed container.

PROPRANOLOL

Year Introduced: 1965

Brand Names

USA	Canada
Inderal (Ayerst)	Inderal (Ayerst)

Drug Family: Anti-anginal; Anti-hypertensive (Hypotensive); Heart Rhythm Regulator (Anti-arrhythmic)

Prescription Required: Yes

Available Dosage Forms and Strengths
Tablets — 10 mg., 40 mg., 80 mg.
Injection — 1 mg. per ml.

How This Drug Works
Intended Therapeutic Effect(s)
- reduction in the frequency and intensity of pain associated with angina pectoris (coronary insufficiency).
- prevention and treatment of heart rhythm disorders (arrhythmias).
- reduction of high blood pressure.

Location of Drug Action(s):   Principal sites of therapeutic actions include:
- the heart pacemaker and tissues that comprise the electrical conduction system.
- the heart muscle.
- the vasomotor center in the brain that influences the control of the sympathetic nervous system over blood vessels (principally arterioles) throughout the body.
- sympathetic nerve terminals in blood vessel walls.

Method of Drug Action(s):   Not completely established. By blocking certain actions of the sympathetic nervous system, this drug
- reduces the rate and the contraction force of the heart, thus lowering the oxygen requirement of the heart muscle. This reduces the occurrence of angina.
- prolongs the conduction time of nerve impulses through the heart, of benefit in the management of rhythm disorders.
- reduces the degree of contraction of blood vessel walls, resulting in their relaxation and expansion and lowering of the blood pressure.

THIS DRUG SHOULD NOT BE TAKEN IF
—you have had an allergic reaction to any dosage form of it previously.
—you are subject to episodes of asthma.
—you are presently experiencing seasonal hay fever.
—you are taking, or have taken within the past 2 weeks, any mono-amine oxidase (MAO) inhibitor drug (see Drug Family, Section Four).

INFORM YOUR PHYSICIAN BEFORE TAKING THIS DRUG IF
—you have a history of serious heart disease, with or without episodes of heart failure.

—you have a history of hay fever (allergic rhinitis), asthma, chronic bronchitis, or emphysema.
—you have a history of overactive thyroid function (hyperthyroidism).
—you have a history of low blood sugar (hypoglycemia).
—you have a history of impaired liver or kidney function.
—you have diabetes.
—you are taking any form of digitalis or quinidine.
—you are taking any form of reserpine.
—you plan to have surgery under general anesthesia in the near future.

Time Required for Apparent Benefit
Drug action begins in 1 hour, reaches a maximum within 4 hours, and subsides in 6 to 8 hours. Full effectiveness can be determined only by continuous use on a regular schedule for several weeks, during which time dosage is carefully adjusted according to individual response (this can vary widely from person to person).

Possible Side-Effects *(natural, expected, and unavoidable drug actions)*
Lethargy and fatigability, cold hands and feet, lightheadedness in upright position (see orthostatic hypotension in Glossary).

CAUTION
Do not discontinue this drug suddenly if you have angina (coronary heart disease). Include a notation on your card of personal identification that you are taking this drug (see Table 14 and Section Seven).

Possible Adverse Effects *(unusual, unexpected, and infrequent reactions)*
IF ANY OF THE FOLLOWING DEVELOP, DISCONTINUE DRUG AND NOTIFY YOUR PHYSICIAN AS SOON AS POSSIBLE

Mild Adverse Effects
Allergic Reactions: Skin rashes, temporary loss of hair, drug fever.
Reduced appetite, nausea, vomiting, diarrhea.
Insomnia, vivid dreaming.

Serious Adverse Effects
Idiosyncratic Reactions: Acute behavioral disturbances: disorientation, confusion, hallucinations, amnesia.
Reduced heart muscle strength and reserve.
Increased risk of asthma.
Emotional depression.
Reduction of white blood cells resulting in fever and sore throat.
Reduction of blood platelets (see Glossary), resulting in unusual bleeding or bruising.

Advisability of Use During Pregnancy
Safety not established. Prudent use is best determined by the physician's evaluation.

Advisability of Use While Nursing Infant
Drug is present in milk in small amounts. Ask physician for guidance.

Habit-Forming Potential
None

Effects of Overdosage
With Moderate Overdose: General weakness, slow pulse, orthostatic hypotension.
With Large Overdose: Marked drop in blood pressure, fainting, weak and slow pulse, cold and sweaty skin.

Possible Effects of Extended Use
Reduced reserve of heart muscle strength, which may result from prolonged use of high doses.

Recommended Periodic Examinations While Taking This Drug
Complete blood cell counts, including platelet counts.
Evaluation of heart function.

While Taking This Drug, Observe the Following
Foods: No interactions with drug. Follow physician's advice regarding salt and total calorie intake. Drug is absorbed best when taken before eating.
Beverages: No restrictions.
Alcohol: Use with caution until combined effect has been determined. Alcohol may exaggerate this drug's ability to lower blood pressure and may increase its mild sedative action.
Tobacco Smoking: Follow physician's advice regarding use of tobacco. Nicotine may reduce this drug's effectiveness in treating angina, heart irregularities, and high blood pressure.
Other Drugs
Propranolol may *increase* the effects of
• oral anti-diabetic drugs and insulin, causing or prolonging hypoglycemia. Careful dosage adjustments are necessary.
• other anti-hypertensive drugs, and cause excessive lowering of the blood pressure. Careful dosage adjustments are necessary.
• barbiturates and narcotic drugs, and cause dangerous oversedation.
• reserpine, and cause excessive sedation and depression.

Propranolol may *decrease* the effects of
• antihistamines, and reduce their effectiveness in treating allergies.
• anti-inflammatory drugs, including aspirin, cortisone, phenylbutazone (Azolid, Butazolidin, etc.), oxyphenbutazone (Oxalid, Tandearil).

Propranolol *taken concurrently* with
• digitalis preparations (digitoxin, digoxin, etc.), may cause adverse interactions—excessive slowing of heart action and reduction of digitalis effectiveness in treating heart failure. Careful dosage adjustments are necessary.
• quinidine, may cause excessive slowing of the heart. Careful dosage adjustments are necessary.

The following drugs may *increase* the effects of propranolol
- phenytoin (Dantoin, Dilantin, etc.) may exaggerate its sedative action on the brain.

Driving a Vehicle, Piloting a Plane, Operating Machinery: Avoid hazardous activities until the full extent of drowsiness or lethargy has been determined.

Exposure to Sun: No restrictions.

Exposure to Heat: No restrictions.

Exposure to Cold: Use caution until combined effect has been determined. If you are subject to Raynaud's phenomenon, this drug may exaggerate further the impaired circulation in hands and feet.

Heavy Exercise or Exertion: Avoid levels of exertion which produced severe angina prior to the use of this drug. Ask physician for guidance regarding safe levels of exercise.

Occurrence of Unrelated Illness: If an illness causes vomiting and interrupts the regular use of this drug, notify your physician as soon as possible.

Discontinuation: This drug must not be discontinued abruptly. Gradual withdrawal over a period of 2 or more weeks is necessary to prevent serious increase of angina or risk of heart attack. Ask your physician for guidance.

Special Storage Instructions
Keep in a dry, tightly closed container.

PROTRIPTYLINE

Year Introduced: 1967

Brand Names

USA	Canada
Vivactil (Merck Sharp & Dohme)	Triptil (MSD)

Drug Family: Antidepressant, Tricyclic (Anti-psychotic)

Prescription Required: Yes

Available Dosage Forms and Strengths
Tablets — 5 mg., 10 mg.

How This Drug Works
Intended Therapeutic Effect(s):   Gradual improvement of mood and relief of emotional depression.

Location of Drug Action(s):   Those areas of the brain that determine mood and emotional stability.

Method of Drug Action(s):   Not established. Present thinking is that this drug slowly restores to normal levels certain constituents of brain tissue (such as norepinephrine) that transmit nerve impulses.

THIS DRUG SHOULD NOT BE TAKEN IF
—you have had an allergic reaction to any dosage form of it previously.
—you are taking or have taken within the past 14 days any mono-amine oxidase (MAO) inhibitor drug (see Drug Family, Section Four).
—you are recovering from a recent heart attack.
—you have glaucoma (narrow-angle type).
—it is prescribed for a child under 12 years of age.

INFORM YOUR PHYSICIAN BEFORE TAKING THIS DRUG IF
—you are allergic or sensitive to any other tricyclic antidepressant (see Drug Family, Section Four).
—you have a history of any of the following: diabetes, epilepsy, glaucoma, heart disease, prostate gland enlargement, or overactive thyroid function.
—you plan to have surgery under general anesthesia in the near future.

Time Required for Apparent Benefit
Some benefit may be apparent within the first 1 to 2 weeks. Adequate response may require continuous treatment for 4 to 6 weeks.

Possible Side-Effects *(natural, expected, and unavoidable drug actions)*
Drowsiness, blurring of vision, dryness of mouth, constipation, impaired urination.

CAUTION
The possibility of adverse effects from this drug is greater in the elderly (over 60 years of age). Small doses are advisable until tolerance has been determined.

Possible Adverse Effects *(unusual, unexpected, and infrequent reactions)*

IF ANY OF THE FOLLOWING DEVELOP, DISCONTINUE DRUG AND NOTIFY YOUR PHYSICIAN AS SOON AS POSSIBLE

Mild Adverse Effects
Allergic Reactions: Skin rash, hives, swelling of face or tongue, drug fever.
Nausea, indigestion, irritation of tongue or mouth, peculiar taste.
Headache, dizziness, weakness, fainting, unsteady gait, tremors.
Swelling of testicles, breast enlargement, milk formation.
Fluctuation of blood sugar levels.

Serious Adverse Effects
Allergic Reactions: Hepatitis with jaundice (see Glossary).
Confusion (especially in the elderly), hallucinations, agitation, restlessness, nightmares.
Heart palpitation and irregular rhythm.
Bone marrow depression (see Glossary)—fatigue, weakness, fever, sore throat, unusual bleeding or bruising.
Peripheral neuritis (see Glossary)—numbness, tingling, pain, loss of strength in arms and legs.
Parkinson-like disorders (see Glossary)—usually mild and infrequent; more likely to occur in the elderly (over 60 years of age).

Advisability of Use During Pregnancy
Safety not established. Prudent use is best determined by the physician's evaluation.

Advisability of Use While Nursing Infant
This drug may be present in milk in small quantities. Ask physician for guidance.

Habit-Forming Potential
Psychological or physical dependence is rare and unexpected.

Effects of Overdosage
With Moderate Overdose: Confusion, hallucinations, extreme drowsiness, drop in body temperature, heart palpitation, dilated pupils, tremors.
With Large Overdose: Stupor, deep sleep, coma, convulsions.

Possible Effects of Extended Use
None reported.

Recommended Periodic Examinations While Taking This Drug
Complete blood cell counts.
Liver function tests.
Serial blood pressure readings and electrocardiograms.

While Taking This Drug, Observe the Following
Foods: No restrictions.
Beverages: No restrictions.
Alcohol: Avoid completely. This drug can increase markedly the intoxicating effects of alcohol and accentuate its depressant action on brain function.
Tobacco Smoking: No interactions expected.
Other Drugs
Protriptyline may *increase* the effects of
• atropine and drugs with atropine-like actions (see Drug Family, Section Four).
• sedatives, sleep-inducing drugs, tranquilizers, antihistamines, and narcotic drugs, and cause oversedation. Dosage adjustments may be necessary.
• levodopa (Dopar, Larodopa, etc.), in its control of Parkinson's disease.

Protriptyline may *decrease* the effects of
• guanethidine, and reduce its effectiveness in lowering blood pressure.
• other commonly used anti-hypertensive drugs. Ask physician for guidance regarding the need to monitor blood pressure readings and to adjust dosage of anti-hypertensive medications. (The action of Aldomet is not decreased by tricyclic antidepressants.)

Protriptyline *taken concurrently* with
• thyroid preparations, may cause impairment of heart rhythm and function. Ask physician for guidance regarding thyroid dosage adjustment.
• ethchlorvynol (Placidyl), may cause delirium.

• quinidine, may impair heart rhythm and function. Avoid the combined use of these two drugs.

• mono-amine oxidase (MAO) inhibitor drugs (see Drug Family, Section Four), may cause high fever, delirium, and convulsions.

The following drugs may *increase* the effects of protriptyline

• thiazide diuretics (see Drug Family, Section Four) may slow its elimination from the body. Overdosage may result.

Driving a Vehicle, Piloting a Plane, Operating Machinery: This drug may impair mental alertness, judgment, physical coordination, and reaction time. Avoid hazardous activities.

Exposure to Sun: Use caution until sensitivity to sun has been determined. This drug may cause photosensitivity (see Glossary).

Discontinuation: If it has been necessary to use this drug for an extended period of time, do not discontinue it abruptly. Ask physician for guidance regarding dosage reduction and withdrawal. It may be necessary to adjust the dosage of other drugs taken concurrently.

Special Storage Instructions
Keep in a dry, tightly closed container.

PSEUDOEPHEDRINE
(ISOEPHEDRINE)

Year Introduced: 1957

Brand Names

USA		Canada
Cenafed (Century)	Fedahist [CD]	Sudafed (B.W. Ltd.)
D-Feda (Dooner)	(Dooner)	Actifed [CD] (B.W.
Novafed (Dow)	Fedrazil [CD]	Ltd.)
Ro-Fedrin (Robinson)	(Burroughs	
Sudafed (Burroughs	Wellcome)	
Wellcome)	Phenergan	
Actifed [CD]	Compound [CD]	
(Burroughs	(Wyeth)	
Wellcome)	(Other combination	
Dimacol [CD]	brand names)	
(Robins)		
Emprazil [CD]		
(Burroughs		
Wellcome)		

Drug Family: Decongestant [Sympathomimetics]

Prescription Required: For low-strength formulations—No
For high-strength formulations—Yes

Available Dosage Forms and Strengths
Tablets — 30 mg., 60 mg.
Prolonged Action Capsules — 120 mg.
Syrups — 30 mg. per teaspoonful

How This Drug Works
Intended Therapeutic Effect(s):   Relief of congestion of the nose, sinuses, and throat associated with allergic disorders and infections.

Location of Drug Action(s):   The small blood vessels (arterioles) in the tissues lining the nasal passages, the sinuses, and the throat.

Method of Drug Action(s):   By contracting the walls and thus reducing the size of the arterioles, this drug decreases the volume of blood in the tissues, resulting in shrinkage of tissue mass (decongestion). This expands the nasal airway and enlarges the openings into the sinuses and eustachian tubes.

THIS DRUG SHOULD NOT BE TAKEN IF
—you have had an allergic reaction to any dosage form of it previously.

INFORM YOUR PHYSICIAN BEFORE TAKING THIS DRUG IF
—you have high blood pressure or heart disease.
—you have an overactive thyroid gland (hyperthyroidism) or diabetes.
—you have difficulty emptying the urinary bladder.
—you are taking, or have taken during the past 2 weeks, any mono-amine oxidase (MAO) inhibitor drug (see Drug Family, Section Four).
—you are taking any form of digitalis (digitoxin, digoxin, etc.).
—you plan to have surgery under general anesthesia in the near future.

Time Required for Apparent Benefit
Drug action begins in 15 to 20 minutes, reaches a maximum in approximately 1 hour, and persists for 3 to 4 hours. (The prolonged action capsules may act for 12 hours.)

Possible Side-Effects *(natural, expected, and unavoidable drug actions)*
Nervousness, insomnia.

CAUTION
The elderly (over 60 years of age) are more likely to experience adverse effects from this drug. It is advisable to use small and short-acting doses until tolerance has been determined.

Possible Adverse Effects *(unusual, unexpected, and infrequent reactions)*
IF ANY OF THE FOLLOWING DEVELOP, DISCONTINUE DRUG AND NOTIFY YOUR PHYSICIAN AS SOON AS POSSIBLE
Mild Adverse Effects
Allergic Reactions: Skin rash (rare).
Headache, dizziness, heart palpitation, tremor (in sensitive individuals).
Serious Adverse Effects
None reported.

Advisability of Use During Pregnancy
No adverse effects on mother or fetus reported. However, it is advisable to use sparingly and in small doses. Ask physician for guidance.

Advisability of Use While Nursing Infant
Drug is known to be present in milk and to have adverse effects on the infant. Avoid drug or discontinue nursing. Ask physician for guidance.

Habit-Forming Potential
None.

Effects of Overdosage
With Moderate Overdose: Marked nervousness, restlessness, headache, rapid or irregular heart action, sweating, nausea, vomiting.

With Large Overdose: Anxiety, confusion, delirium, muscle tremors, rapid and irregular pulse.

Possible Effects of Extended Use
None reported.

Recommended Periodic Examinations While Taking This Drug
None required.

While Taking This Drug, Observe the Following
Foods: No restrictions.

Beverages: Excessive coffee or tea may increase the nervousness or insomnia caused by this drug in sensitive individuals.

Alcohol: No interactions expected.

Tobacco Smoking: No interactions expected. No restrictions unless advised otherwise by your physician.

Other Drugs

Pseudoephedrine may *increase* the effects of

• epinephrine (Adrenalin, Bronkaid Mist, Vaponefrin, etc.), and cause excessive stimulation of the heart and an increase in blood pressure. Use caution and avoid excessive dosage.

Pseudoephedrine may *decrease* the effects of

• anti-hypertensive drugs, and reduce their effectiveness in lowering blood pressure. Ask physician if any dosage adjustment is necessary to maintain proper blood pressure control.

Pseudoephedrine *taken concurrently* with

• digitalis preparations (digitoxin, digoxin, etc.), may cause serious disturbances of heart rhythm.
• ergot-related preparations (Cafergot, Ergotrate, Migral, Wigraine, etc.), may cause serious increase in blood pressure.
• guanethidine, may result in reduced effectiveness of both drugs.

The following drugs may *increase* the effects of pseudoephedrine

• mono-amine oxidase (MAO) inhibitor drugs (see Drug Family, Section Four). The combined effects may cause a dangerous increase in blood pressure.

• tricyclic antidepressants (see Drug Family, Section Four). The combined effects may cause excessive stimulation of the heart and/or elevation of blood pressure.

Driving a Vehicle, Piloting a Plane, Operating Machinery: No restrictions unless dizziness occurs.

Exposure to Sun: No restrictions.

Special Storage Instructions
Keep in a tightly closed, light-resistant container. Avoid excessive heat.

PYRILAMINE/MEPYRAMINE

Year Introduced: 1944

Brand Names

USA	Canada
Pyma [CD]	Neo-Antergan (Poulenc)
(Fellows-Testagar)	Triaminic [CD] (Anca)
Pyristan [CD] (Arcum)	Triaminicin [CD] (Anca)
Triaminic [CD] (Dorsey)	Triaminicol [CD] (Anca)
Triaminicin [CD]	
(Dorsey)	
Triaminicol [CD]	
(Dorsey)	

Drug Family: Antihistamines

Prescription Required: For low-strength formulations—No
For high-strength formulations—Yes

Available Dosage Forms and Strengths
Tablets — 25 mg., 50 mg.
Tablets — 12.5 mg., 25 mg. (in combination with other drugs)
Syrup — 6.25 mg. per teaspoonful (in combination with other drugs)
Pediatric Drops — 10 mg. per ml. (in combination with other drugs)

How This Drug Works
Intended Therapeutic Effect(s):   Relief of symptoms associated with hay-fever (allergic rhinitis) and with allergic reactions in the skin, such as itching, swelling, hives, and rash.

Location of Drug Action(s):   Those hypersensitive tissues that release excessive histamine as part of an allergic reaction. The principal tissue sites are the eyes, the nose, and the skin.

Method of Drug Action(s):   This drug reduces the intensity of the allergic response by blocking the action of histamine after it has been released from sensitized tissue cells.

THIS DRUG SHOULD NOT BE TAKEN IF
—you have had an allergic reaction to any dosage form of it previously.
—you are taking, or have taken during the past 2 weeks, any mono-amine oxidase (MAO) inhibitor drug (see Drug Family, Section Four).
—it has been prescribed for a newborn infant.

INFORM YOUR PHYSICIAN BEFORE TAKING THIS DRUG IF
—you have had an unfavorable reaction to any antihistamine drug in the past.
—you have glaucoma.
—you have a history of asthma, peptic ulcer disease, or impairment of urinary bladder function.
—you plan to have surgery under general anesthesia in the near future.

Time Required for Apparent Benefit
Drug action begins in approximately 30 minutes, reaches a maximum in 1 hour, and subsides in 4 to 6 hours.

Possible Side-Effects *(natural, expected, and unavoidable drug actions)*
Drowsiness, sense of weakness, dryness of nose, mouth, and throat, constipation.

CAUTION
The elderly (over 60 years of age) may be more susceptible to the adverse effects of this drug. Small doses are advisable until tolerance is determined.

Possible Adverse Effects *(unusual, unexpected, and infrequent reactions)*
IF ANY OF THE FOLLOWING DEVELOP, DISCONTINUE DRUG AND NOTIFY YOUR PHYSICIAN AS SOON AS POSSIBLE

Mild Adverse Effects
   Allergic Reactions: Skin rash, hives.
   Headache, dizziness, inability to concentrate, nervousness, blurring of vision, double vision, difficulty in urination.
   Nausea, vomiting, diarrhea.
Serious Adverse Effects
   Idiosyncratic Reactions: Emotional and behavioral disturbances—confusion, agitation, inappropriate actions.

Advisability of Use During Pregnancy
No reports of adverse effects on mother or fetus, but complete safety has not been established. It is advisable to limit use to small doses and for short periods of time.

Advisability of Use While Nursing Infant
This drug may impair milk formation and make nursing difficult. It is known to be present in milk. Avoid use or discontinue nursing. Ask physician for guidance.

Habit-Forming Potential
None.

Effects of Overdosage

With Moderate Overdose: Marked drowsiness, confusion, incoordination, unsteady gait, muscle tremors. In children: excitement, hallucinations, overactivity, convulsions.

With Large Overdose: Stupor progressing to coma, fever, flushed face, dilated pupils, weak pulse, shallow breathing.

Possible Effects of Extended Use

None.

Recommended Periodic Examinations While Taking This Drug

Complete blood cell counts.

While Taking This Drug, Observe the Following

Foods: No restrictions. Stomach irritation can be reduced if drug is taken after eating.

Beverages: Coffee and tea may help to reduce the drowsiness caused by most antihistamines.

Alcohol: Use with extreme caution until combined effect has been determined. The combination of alcohol and antihistamines can cause rapid and marked sedation.

Tobacco Smoking: No interactions expected.

Other Drugs

Pyrilamine may *increase* the effects of

- sedatives, sleep-inducing drugs, tranquilizers, antidepressants, pain relievers, and narcotic drugs, and cause oversedation. Careful dosage adjustments are necessary.
- atropine and drugs with atropine-like action (see Drug Family, Section Four).

The following drugs may *increase* the effects of pyrilamine

- all sedatives, sleep-inducing drugs, tranquilizers, pain relievers, and narcotic drugs may exaggerate its sedative action and cause oversedation.
- mono-amine oxidase (MAO) inhibitor drugs (see Drug Family, Section Four) may delay its elimination from the body, thus exaggerating and prolonging its action.

The following drugs may *decrease* the effects of pyrilamine

- amphetamines (Benzedrine, Dexedrine, Desoxyn, etc.) may reduce the drowsiness caused by most antihistamines.

Driving a Vehicle, Piloting a Plane, Operating Machinery: This drug may impair mental alertness, judgment, physical coordination, and reaction time. Avoid hazardous activities until full sedative effect has been determined.

Exposure to Sun: No restrictions.

Special Storage Instructions

Keep in a dry, tightly closed, light-resistant container.

QUINIDINE

Year Introduced: 1918

Brand Names

USA	Canada
Cardioquin (Purdue Frederick)	Biquin Durules (ASTRA)
Cin-Quin (Rowell)	Cardioquin (Purdue Frederick)
Quinaglute (Cooper)	Quinaglute (Cooper)
Quinidate (Thompson)	Quinate (Rougier)
Quinidex (Robins)	**Quinobarb [CD]
Quinora (Lakeside)	(Welcker-Lyster)
*Quinidine M.B. [CD] (Rowell)	

Drug Family: Heart Rhythm Regulator (Anti-arrhythmic)

Prescription Required: Yes

Available Dosage Forms and Strengths
Tablets — 100 mg., 130 mg., 200 mg., 325 mg., 330 mg.
Capsules — 100 mg., 200 mg., 300 mg.
Injection — 50 mg. per ml.

How This Drug Works

Intended Therapeutic Effect(s):   Correction of certain heart rhythm disorders.

Location of Drug Action(s):   The heart muscle and the tissues that comprise the electrical conduction system of the heart.

Method of Drug Action(s):   By slowing the activity of the pacemaker and delaying the transmission of electrical impulses through the conduction system and muscle of the heart, this drug assists in restoring normal heart rate and rhythm.

THIS DRUG SHOULD NOT BE TAKEN IF
—you have had an allergic reaction to any dosage form of it previously.
—you presently have an acute infection of any kind.

INFORM YOUR PHYSICIAN BEFORE TAKING THIS DRUG IF
—you are now taking, or have taken within the past 2 weeks, any digitalis preparation.
—you have a history of thyroid gland overactivity (hyperthyroidism).
—you have a history of angina or previous heart attack.
—you plan to have surgery under general anesthesia in the near future.

---

*Quinidine M.B. contains mephobarbital, a sedative of the barbiturate drug family.
**Quinobarb contains phenylethylbarbiturate, a sedative of the barbiturate drug family.

Time Required for Apparent Benefit
Drug action begins in 1 hour, reaches a maximum in 2 to 4 hours, and gradually subsides within 18 to 24 hours. On regular daily dosage, accumulation persists for 4 to 5 days.

Possible Side-Effects *(natural, expected, and unavoidable drug actions)*
Drop in blood pressure, resulting in lightheadedness in upright position (see orthostatic hypotension in Glossary).

CAUTION
1. The effects of this drug are very unpredictable because of the wide variation in response from person to person. Dosage adjustments must be based upon individual reaction. Notify your physician of any events that you suspect may be drug-related.
2. It is advisable to carry a card of personal identification that includes a notation that you are taking this drug (see Table 14 and Section Seven).
3. The elderly (over 60 years of age) may be more sensitive to this drug. Small doses are advisable until individual response has been determined.

Possible Adverse Effects *(unusual, unexpected, and infrequent reactions)*
IF ANY OF THE FOLLOWING DEVELOP, DISCONTINUE DRUG AND NOTIFY YOUR PHYSICIAN AS SOON AS POSSIBLE
Mild Adverse Effects
Allergic Reactions: Rash, hives, drug fever, skin eruption with peeling.
Loss of appetite, nausea, vomiting, diarrhea.
Dizziness, ringing in the ears.
Sudden fainting (due to drop in blood pressure).
Serious Adverse Effects
Allergic Reactions: Abnormal bruising due to allergic destruction of blood platelets (see Glossary).
Idiosyncratic Reactions: Confusion, delirium, and agitated behavior.
Hemolytic anemia (see Glossary).
Worsening of psoriasis (in sensitive individuals).
Bone marrow depression (see Glossary)—fatigue, weakness, fever, sore throat, abnormal bruising or bleeding.

Advisability of Use During Pregnancy
Safety not established. Prudent use is best determined by the physician's evaluation.

Advisability of Use While Nursing Infant
Drug is known to be present in milk. Safety for infant not established. Ask physician for guidance.

Habit-Forming Potential
None.

Effects of Overdosage
With Moderate Overdose: Headache, dizziness, blurred vision, ringing in the ears, nausea, vomiting, diarrhea, confusion.

With Large Overdose: Severe drop in blood pressure, difficulty in breathing, collapse of circulation.

Possible Effects of Extended Use
None reported.

Recommended Periodic Examinations While Taking This Drug
Complete blood cell counts.
Electrocardiograms.

While Taking This Drug, Observe the Following
Foods: No restrictions. Follow prescribed diet.

Beverages: Use caffeine-containing beverages (coffee, tea, cola) sparingly.

Alcohol: No interactions expected.

Tobacco Smoking: No interactions expected. However, nicotine can increase the irritability of the heart and can confuse interpretation of this drug's action. Follow physician's advice regarding smoking.

Other Drugs

Quinidine may *increase* the effects of

- anticoagulants, and cause abnormal bleeding or hemorrhage. Careful dosage adjustment is necessary.
- anti-hypertensive drugs, and cause excessive lowering of the blood pressure.
- atropine-like drugs (see Drug Family, Section Four).

Quinidine may *decrease* the effects of

- choline-like drugs such as Mestinon, Mytelase, pilocarpine, Prostigmin, and Urecholine, and reduce their effectiveness in the treatment of glaucoma and myasthenia gravis.

Quinidine *taken concurrently* with

- reserpine (and related drugs), may cause serious disturbances of heart rhythm.
- digitalis preparations, may cause excessive slowing of the heart. Dosage adjustment of both drugs is essential.
- propranolol (Inderal), may cause excessive slowing of the heart.

The following drugs may *increase* the effects of quinidine

- phenytoin (Dantoin, Dilantin, etc.)
- pyrimethamine (Daraprim)

Driving a Vehicle, Piloting a Plane, Operating Machinery: Usually no restrictions. Avoid hazardous activities if dizziness or lightheadedness occurs.

Exposure to Sun: No restrictions.

Special Storage Instructions
Keep in a tightly closed container. Protect from light.

RESERPINE

Year Introduced: 1953

Brand Names

USA		Canada
Alkarau (Ferndale)	Reserpaneed	Neo-Serp (Neo)
Arcum R-S (Arcum)	(Hanlon)	Resercrine (C & C)
Bonapene (Briar)	Reserpoid (Upjohn)	Reserfia (Medic)
Broserpine (Brothers)	Sandril (Lilly)	Reserpanca (Anca)
DeSerpa (de Leon)	Serp (Scrip)	Serpasil (CIBA)
Elserpine (Canright)	Serpalan (Lannett)	Serpax (Verdun)
Hiserpia (Bowman)	Serpaloid (Kay)	Sertina (Stickley)
Hyperine (Sutliff &	Serpanray (Panray)	
Case)	Serpasil (CIBA)	
Key-Serpine	Serpate (Vale)	
(Hyrex-Key)	Serpena (Haag)	
Lemiserp (Lemmon)	Sertabs (Table Rock)	
Lemiserp Ty-Med	Sertina	
(Lemmon)	(Fellows-Testagar)	
Rauloydin (Tutag)	Tensin (Standex)	
Rauraine	Tranquilsin (Sheryl)	
(Westerfield)	T-Serp (Tennessee)	
Rau-Sed (Squibb)	Vio-Serpine (Rowell)	
Rauserpin (Ferndale)	(Numerous	
Resercen (Central)	combination brand	
Reserjen (Jenkins)	names)	

Drug Family: Anti-hypertensive (Hypotensive)
Tranquilizer, Strong (Anti-psychotic)

Prescription Required: Yes

Available Dosage Forms and Strengths
Tablets — 0.1 mg., 0.25 mg., 0.5 mg., 1 mg.
Elixir — 0.2 mg. per teaspoonful

How This Drug Works
Intended Therapeutic Effect(s):   Reduction of high blood pressure.
Location of Drug Action(s):   The storage sites of norepinephrine in the nerve terminals of the sympathetic nervous system.
Method of Drug Action(s):   By displacing the nerve impulse transmitter norepinephrine from nerve terminals, this drug reduces the ability of the sympathetic nervous system to maintain the degree of blood vessel constriction responsible for high blood pressure. The reduced availability of norepinephrine results in relaxation of blood vessel walls and lowering of the blood pressure.

THIS DRUG SHOULD NOT BE TAKEN IF
—you have had an allergic reaction to any dosage form of it previously.

—you are emotionally depressed.
—you have an active peptic ulcer (stomach or duodenal).
—you have active ulcerative colitis.

INFORM YOUR PHYSICIAN BEFORE TAKING THIS DRUG IF
—you have a history of emotional depression.
—you have a history of peptic ulcer, ulcerative colitis, or gall stones.
—you have epilepsy.
—you are taking oral anticoagulants.
—you are taking any form of digitalis, quinidine, or any mono-amine oxidase (MAO) inhibitor drug (see Drug Family, Section Four).
—you plan to have surgery under general anesthesia in the near future.

Time Required for Apparent Benefit
Continuous use on a regular schedule for 3 weeks is usually necessary to determine this drug's full effectiveness in lowering the blood pressure.

Possible Side-Effects *(natural, expected, and unavoidable drug actions)*
Drowsiness and lethargy (especially during first few weeks), reddening of the eyes, nasal stuffiness (frequent), dryness of the mouth, increased hunger contractions, acid indigestion, intestinal cramping, diarrhea, water retention.

CAUTION
It is advisable to discontinue this drug at the first sign of despondency, loss of appetite, early morning awakening (insomnia), or impaired sex drive or performance. Notify your physician of this action promptly.

Possible Adverse Effects *(unusual, unexpected, and infrequent reactions)*
IF ANY OF THE FOLLOWING DEVELOP, DISCONTINUE DRUG AND NOTIFY YOUR PHYSICIAN AS SOON AS POSSIBLE

Mild Adverse Effects
Allergic Reactions: Skin rash, itching, spontaneous bruising.
Nausea, vomiting, diarrhea.
Headache, dizziness, nasal congestion, nosebleeds.
Breast enlargement, milk production, change in menstrual pattern.

Serious Adverse Effects
Idiosyncratic Reactions: Paradoxical nervousness, agitation, nightmares, confusion, hallucinations.
Parkinson-like disorders (see Glossary).
Mental depression.
Activation of stomach or duodenal ulcer.
Impaired sex drive, potency, and performance.

Advisability of Use During Pregnancy
Safety not established. This drug is known to have adverse effects on the fetus. Avoid use during entire pregnancy.

Advisability of Use While Nursing Infant
This drug is known to be present in milk. Avoid use or discontinue nursing. Ask physician for guidance.

Habit-Forming Potential
None.

Effects of Overdosage
With Moderate Overdose: Marked drowsiness, slow and weak pulse, slow and shallow breathing, diarrhea.

With Large Overdose: Stupor progressing to deep sleep or coma, flushing of skin, decreased body temperature, severe depression of breathing and heart action.

Recommended Periodic Examinations While Taking This Drug
Complete blood cell counts.
Eye examinations for impaired vision.

While Taking This Drug, Observe the Following
Foods: Avoid highly spiced foods. Ask physician for guidance if you are subject to acid indigestion or have a history of peptic ulcer.

Beverages: Avoid heavy use of carbonated drinks.

Alcohol: Use with extreme caution until combined effect has been determined. This drug can increase the intoxicating effect of alcohol.

Tobacco Smoking: No interactions expected. Follow physician's advice regarding smoking.

Other Drugs

Reserpine may *increase* the effects of

• other anti-hypertensive drugs, and cause excessive lowering of blood pressure. Careful dosage adjustments are necessary.

• sedatives, sleep-inducing drugs, tranquilizers, antihistamines, pain relievers, and narcotic drugs, and cause oversedation.

Reserpine may *decrease* the effects of

• levodopa (Dopar, Larodopa, etc.), and reduce its effectiveness in the treatment of Parkinson's disease.

• aspirin, and reduce its pain-relieving action.

Reserpine *taken concurrently* with

• oral anticoagulants, may cause unpredictable fluctuations in coagulation control. Ask physician for guidance regarding prothrombin time testing and dosage adjustment.

• anti-convulsants, may cause a serious change in the pattern of epileptic seizures. Some individuals may require an increase in the dose of anti-convulsants.

• digitalis preparations and quinidine, may cause serious disturbances of heart rhythm. Careful dosage adjustments are necessary.

• mono-amine oxidase (MAO) inhibitor drugs, may cause severe emotional depression, cramping, and diarrhea.

The following drugs may *increase* the effects of reserpine

• propranolol (Inderal) may increase its sedative effect and cause oversedation.

• members of the phenothiazine family (see Drug Family, Section Four) may increase both the sedative effect and the blood pressure-lowering action.

Driving a Vehicle, Piloting a Plane, Operating Machinery: This drug can impair mental alertness, judgment, physical coordination, and reaction time. Avoid hazardous activities if you experience drowsiness, lethargy, or dizziness.

Exposure to Sun: No restrictions.

Heavy Exercise or Exertion: No restrictions.

Discontinuation: Upon stopping this drug, careful readjustments of dosages will be necessary for the following drugs if taken concurrently with reserpine: other anti-hypertensives, oral anticoagulants, anti-convulsants.

Special Storage Instructions
Keep in a dry, tightly closed container.

RIFAMPIN

Year Introduced: 1967 (Europe); 1971 (USA)

Brand Names

USA	Canada
Rifadin (Dow)	Rifadin (Dow)
Rifomycin (Various Manufacturers)	Rimactane (CIBA)
Rimactane (CIBA)	

Drug Family: Antibiotic (Anti-infective) [Rifamycins]

Prescription Required: Yes

Available Dosage Forms and Strengths
Capsules—150 mg., 300 mg.

How This Drug Works
Intended Therapeutic Effect(s):   The treatment of active tuberculosis, in conjunction with other drugs.

Location of Drug Action(s):   Those body tissues and fluids in which adequate concentration of the drug can be achieved. The principal site of therapeutic action is the lung.

Method of Drug Action(s):   This drug prevents the growth and multiplication of susceptible tuberculosis organisms by interfering with enzyme systems involved in the formation of essential proteins.

THIS DRUG SHOULD NOT BE TAKEN IF
—you are allergic to any of the drugs bearing the brand names listed above or to any rifamycin drug.

—you have active liver disease.

—it is prescribed for a child under 5 years of age.

INFORM YOUR PHYSICIAN BEFORE TAKING THIS DRUG IF
—you are pregnant.
—you have a history of liver disease or impaired liver function.
—you are taking oral contraceptives (any form of "the pill").
—you are taking anticoagulants.

Time Required for Apparent Benefit
Varies with nature of infection under treatment; may be from 4 to 6 weeks.

Possible Side-Effects *(natural, expected, and unavoidable drug actions)*
Red, orange, or brown discoloration of tears, sweat, saliva, sputum, urine, or stool.
Yellow discoloration of skin (not jaundice).
Note: In the absence of symptoms indicating illness, any discoloration is a harmless drug effect and does not indicate toxicity.
Superinfections (see Glossary).

Possible Adverse Effects *(unusual, unexpected, and infrequent reactions)*
IF ANY OF THE FOLLOWING DEVELOP, DISCONTINUE DRUG AND NOTIFY YOUR PHYSICIAN AS SOON AS POSSIBLE
Mild Adverse Effects
    Allergic Reactions: Skin rash (various kinds), hives, itching, irritation of mouth or tongue, fever.
    Loss of appetite, heartburn, nausea, vomiting, abdominal cramps, diarrhea.
    Headache, drowsiness, dizziness, disturbed vision, impaired hearing, vague numbness or tingling.
    Mild menstrual irregularity.
Serious Adverse Effects
    Liver damage, causing jaundice (see Glossary).
    Abnormally low blood platelets (see Glossary)—unusual bleeding or bruising.

Advisability of Use During Pregnancy
Safety not established. Prudent use is best determined by the physician's evaluation.

Advisability of Use While Nursing Infant
Safety for infant not established. Ask physician for guidance.

Habit-Forming Potential
None.

Effects of Overdosage
Nausea, vomiting, drowsiness, unconsciousness, severe liver damage, jaundice.

Possible Effects of Extended Use
Superinfections (see Glossary).

Recommended Periodic Examinations While Taking This Drug
Complete blood cell counts.
Liver and kidney function tests.
Hearing acuity tests if hearing loss is suspected.

While Taking This Drug, Observe the Following
Foods: No restrictions of food selection. Most effective when taken 1 hour before or 2 hours after eating.

Beverages: No restrictions.

Alcohol: Avoid while taking this drug if you have a history of liver disease.

Tobacco Smoking: No interactions expected.

Other Drugs

Rifampin may *decrease* the effects of

- oral contraceptives, and impair their effectiveness in preventing pregnancy.

Rifampin *taken concurrently* with

- oral anticoagulants, may cause unpredictable changes in blood coagulation. Monitor blood prothrombin time closely and adjust dosage accordingly.

The following drugs may *decrease* the effects of rifampin

- para-aminosalicylic acid (PAS) may interfere with its absorption. Take each drug separately, 6 to 8 hours apart.

Driving a Vehicle, Piloting a Plane, Operating Machinery: Restricted only if you experience dizziness, impaired balance, or impaired vision.

Exposure to Sun: No restrictions.

Discontinuation: It is advisable not to interrupt or discontinue this drug without consulting your physician. Interrupted or intermittent administration can increase the possibility of allergic reactions.

Special Storage Instructions
Keep in a dry, tightly closed, light-resistant container.

SECOBARBITAL

Year Introduced: 1936

Brand Names

USA	Canada
Seco-8 (Fleming)	Secocaps (M.T.C.)
Seconal (Lilly)	Secogen (Maney)
Tuinal [CD] (Lilly)	Seconal (Lilly)
	Seral (Medic)

Drug Family: Sedative, Mild; Sleep Inducer (Hypnotic) [Barbiturates]

Prescription Required: Yes (Controlled Drug, U.S. Schedule 2)

Available Dosage Forms and Strengths
Tablets — 100 mg.
Capsules — 30 mg., 50 mg., 100 mg.
Elixir — 22 mg. per teaspoonful
Suppositories — 30 mg., 60 mg., 120 mg., 200 mg.

How This Drug Works
Intended Therapeutic Effect(s)
- with low dosage, relief of mild to moderate anxiety or tension (sedative effect).
- with higher dosage taken at bedtime, sedation sufficient to induce sleep (hypnotic effect).

Location of Drug Action(s):   The connecting points (synapses) in the nerve pathways that transmit impulses between the wake-sleep centers of the brain.

Method of Drug Action(s):   Not completely established. Present thinking is that this drug selectively blocks the transmission of nerve impulses by reducing the amount of available norepinephrine, one of the chemicals responsible for impulse transmission. '

THIS DRUG SHOULD NOT BE TAKEN IF
—you have had an allergic reaction to any dosage form of it previously.
—you have a history of porphyria.

INFORM YOUR PHYSICIAN BEFORE TAKING THIS DRUG IF
—you are allergic or sensitive to any barbiturate drug.
—you are taking any sedative, sleep-inducing drugs, tranquilizers, antihistamines, pain relievers, or narcotic drugs of any kind.
—you have epilepsy.
—you have a history of liver or kidney disease.
—you plan to have surgery under general anesthesia in the near future.

Time Required for Apparent Benefit
Approximately 30 minutes.

Possible Side-Effects *(natural, expected, and unavoidable drug actions)*
Drowsiness, lethargy, and sense of mental or physical sluggishness as "hangover" effects.

CAUTION
The elderly (over 60 years of age) and the debilitated may experience agitation, excitement, confusion, and delirium with standard doses. Small doses are advisable until tolerance has been determined.

Possible Adverse Effects *(unusual, unexpected, and infrequent reactions)*

IF ANY OF THE FOLLOWING DEVELOP, DISCONTINUE DRUG AND NOTIFY YOUR PHYSICIAN AS SOON AS POSSIBLE

Mild Adverse Effects
Allergic Reactions: Skin rash (various kinds), hives, localized swellings of eyelids, face, or lips, drug fever.
"Hangover" effect, dizziness, unsteadiness.

Nausea, vomiting, diarrhea.
Joint and muscle pains, most often in the neck, shoulder, and arms.
Serious Adverse Effects
Allergic Reactions: Hepatitis with jaundice (see Glossary), severe skin reactions.
Idiosyncratic Reactions: Paradoxical excitement and delirium (rather than sedation).
Anemia—weakness and fatigue.
Abnormally low blood platelets (see Glossary)—unusual bleeding or bruising.

Advisability of Use During Pregnancy
Safety not established. Prudent use is best determined by the physician's evaluation.

Advisability of Use While Nursing Infant
Drug is known to be present in milk. Ask physician for guidance.

Habit-Forming Potential
This drug can cause both psychological and physical dependence (see Glossary).

Effects of Overdosage
With Moderate Overdose: Behavior similar to alcoholic intoxication: confusion, slurred speech, physical incoordination, staggering gait, drowsiness.
With Large Overdose: Deepening sleep, coma, slow and shallow breathing, weak and rapid pulse, cold and sweaty skin.

Possible Effects of Extended Use
Psychological and/or physical dependence.
Anemia.
If dose is excessive, a form of chronic drug intoxication can occur: headache, impaired vision, slurred speech, and depression.

Recommended Periodic Examinations While Taking This Drug
Complete blood cell counts.
Liver function tests.

While Taking This Drug, Observe the Following
Foods: No restrictions.
Beverages: No restrictions.
Alcohol: Avoid completely. Alcohol can increase greatly the sedative and depressant actions of this drug on brain function.
Tobacco Smoking: No interactions expected.
Other Drugs
Secobarbital may *increase* the effects of
• other sedatives, sleep-inducing drugs, tranquilizers, antihistamines, pain relievers, and narcotic drugs, and cause oversedation. Ask your physician for guidance regarding dosage adjustments.

Secobarbital may *decrease* the effects of
- oral anticoagulants of the coumarin drug family. Ask physician for guidance regarding prothrombin time testing and adjustments of the anticoagulant dosage.
- aspirin, and reduce its pain-relieving action.
- cortisone and related drugs, by hastening their elimination from the body.
- oral contraceptives, by hastening their elimination from the body.
- griseofulvin (Fulvicin, Grisactin, etc.), and reduce its effectiveness in treating fungus infections.
- phenylbutazone (Azolid, Butazolidin, etc.), and reduce its effectiveness in treating inflammation and pain.

Secobarbital *taken concurrently* with
- anti-convulsants, may cause a change in the pattern of epileptic seizures. Careful dosage adjustments are necessary to achieve a balance of actions that will give the best protection from seizures.

The following drugs may *increase* the effects of secobarbital
- both mild and strong tranquilizers may increase the sedative and sleep-inducing actions and cause oversedation.
- isoniazid (INH, Isozide, etc.) may prolong the action of barbiturate drugs.
- antihistamines may increase the sedative effects of barbiturate drugs.
- oral anti-diabetic drugs of the sulfonylurea type may prolong the sedative effect of barbiturate drugs.
- mono-amine oxidase (MAO) inhibitor drugs may prolong the sedative effect of barbiturate drugs.

Driving a Vehicle, Piloting a Plane, Operating Machinery: This drug can produce drowsiness and can impair mental alertness, judgment, physical coordination, and reaction time. Avoid hazardous activities.

Exposure to Sun: Use caution until sensitivity has been determined. Some barbiturates can cause photosensitivity (see Glossary).

Exposure to Cold: The elderly may experience excessive lowering of body temperature while taking this drug. Keep dosage to a minimum during winter and dress warmly.

Discontinuation: If it has been necessary to use this drug for an extended period of time, do not discontinue it abruptly. Ask physician for guidance regarding dosage adjustment and withdrawal. It may also be necessary to adjust the doses of other drugs taken concurrently with it.

Special Storage Instructions
Keep tablets and capsules in a dry, tightly closed container. Keep elixir in a tightly closed, amber glass bottle. Keep suppositories refrigerated.

SPIRONOLACTONE

Year Introduced: 1962

Brand Names

USA	Canada
Aldactone (Searle)	Aldactone (Searle)
Aldactazide [CD] (Searle)	Aldactazide [CD] (Searle)

Drug Family: Anti-hypertensive (Hypotensive); Diuretic

Prescription Required: Yes

Available Dosage Forms and Strengths
Tablets — 25 mg.

How This Drug Works
Intended Therapeutic Effect(s)
- elimination of excessive fluid retention (edema) without loss of potassium from the body.
- reduction of high blood pressure.

Location of Drug Action(s):   The tubular systems of the kidney that determine the final composition of the urine.

Method of Drug Action(s):   By increasing the elimination of salt and water but not potassium from the body (through increased urine production), this drug reduces the volume of fluid in the blood and body tissues and lowers the sodium content throughout the body. These changes may produce a lowering of the blood pressure.

THIS DRUG SHOULD NOT BE TAKEN IF
—you have had an allergic reaction to any dosage form of it previously.
—you have seriously impaired kidney function.

INFORM YOUR PHYSICIAN BEFORE TAKING THIS DRUG IF
—you have a history of kidney or liver disease.
—you are taking anticoagulant drugs or any form of digitalis.
—you plan to have surgery under general anesthesia in the near future.

Time Required for Apparent Benefit
Maximal diuretic effect requires continuous use for 3 to 5 days. Continuous use on a regular schedule for 2 or more weeks may be necessary to determine this drug's effectiveness in lowering your blood pressure.

Possible Side-Effects *(natural, expected, and unavoidable drug actions)*
Usually none, unless there is excessive loss of salt and water from the body or excessive retention of potassium (see Effects of Overdosage, below).

CAUTION
It is advisable not to use potassium supplements or deliberately to increase your intake of potassium-rich foods while using this diuretic drug.

Possible Adverse Effects *(unusual, unexpected, and infrequent reactions)*

IF ANY OF THE FOLLOWING DEVELOP, DISCONTINUE DRUG AND NOTIFY YOUR PHYSICIAN AS SOON AS POSSIBLE

Mild Adverse Effects
Allergic Reactions: Skin rashes (various kinds), hives, drug fever.
Headache, drowsiness, lethargy, confusion.
Indigestion, nausea, vomiting, diarrhea.
Enlargement and sensitivity of the male breasts.
Menstrual irregularities, deepening of the female voice.

Serious Adverse Effects
None reported.

Advisability of Use During Pregnancy
Safety not established. Prudent use is best determined by the physician's evaluation.

Advisability of Use While Nursing Infant
Presence of this drug in milk is not known. Ask physician for guidance.

Habit-Forming Potential
None.

Effects of Overdosage
With Moderate Overdose: Imbalance of body water, salt, and potassium, causing thirst, drowsiness, fatigue, weakness, nausea, vomiting.
With Large Overdose: Marked lethargy, irregular heart action, excessive drop in blood pressure.

Possible Effects of Extended Use
Retention of potassium in the body, resulting in blood potassium levels above the normal range. This can have an adverse effect on the regulation of heart rhythm and performance.

Recommended Periodic Examinations While Taking This Drug
Kidney function tests.
Measurements of blood sodium, chloride, and potassium levels.

While Taking This Drug, Observe the Following
Foods: Do not restrict the intake of salt (or salted foods) unless directed to do so by your physician.
Beverages: No restrictions.
Alcohol: No interactions expected.
Tobacco Smoking: No interactions expected.
Other Drugs
Spironolactone may *increase* the effects of
• other anti-hypertensive drugs, and cause excessive lowering of the blood pressure. Dosage adjustments are necessary.

Spironolactone may *decrease* the effects of
- oral anticoagulants, and reduce their protective action. Ask physician for guidance regarding prothrombin time testing and dosage adjustments.
- digitalis preparations, if excessive potassium is retained in the body.

Spironolactone *taken concurrently* with
- triamterene, may cause excessive (dangerous) retention of potassium in the body. Avoid the simultaneous use of these two drugs.

The following drugs may *decrease* the effects of spironolactone
- aspirin (in large doses)

Driving a Vehicle, Piloting a Plane, Operating Machinery: No restrictions unless drowsiness or confusion occurs.

Exposure to Sun: No restrictions.

Heavy Exercise or Exertion: No restrictions.

Discontinuation: Consult physician for guidance regarding the need to readjust the dosage schedule of the following drugs taken concurrently with spironolactone: anticoagulants, anti-hypertensives, digitalis.

Special Storage Instructions
Keep in a dry, tightly closed, light-resistant container.

SULFAMETHOXAZOLE

Year Introduced: 1961

Brand Names

USA	Canada
Gantanol (Roche)	Gantanol (Roche)
Azo Gantanol [CD] (Roche)	Bactrim [CD] (Roche)
Bactrim [CD] (Roche)	Septra [CD] (B.W. Ltd.)
Septra [CD] (Burroughs Wellcome)	

Drug Family: Antimicrobial (Anti-infective) [Sulfonamides]

Prescription Required: Yes

Available Dosage Forms and Strengths
Tablets — 500 mg.
Oral Suspension — 500 mg. per teaspoonful

How This Drug Works
Intended Therapeutic Effect(s):   The elimination of infections responsive to the action of this drug.

Location of Drug Action(s):   Any body tissue or fluid in which sufficient concentration of the drug can be achieved.

Method of Drug Action(s):   This drug prevents the growth and multiplication of susceptible bacteria by interfering with their formation of folic acid, an essential nutrient.

THIS DRUG SHOULD NOT BE TAKEN IF

—you are allergic to any sulfonamide ("sulfa") drug (see Drug Family, Section Four).

—you are in the ninth month of pregnancy.

—it is prescribed for an infant under 2 months of age.

INFORM YOUR PHYSICIAN BEFORE TAKING THIS DRUG IF

—you are allergic to any of the drugs chemically related to the sulfonamide ("sulfa") drugs: acetazolamide (Diamox), oral anti-diabetics, and thiazide diuretics (see Drug Family, Section Four).

—you are allergic by nature and have a history of hayfever, asthma, hives or eczema.

—you have a history of serious liver or kidney disease.

—you have a history of acute intermittent porphyria.

—you have ever had anemia caused by a drug.

—you are now taking any of the following drugs:

oral anticoagulants

oral anti-diabetic preparations

methotrexate

oxyphenbutazone (Oxalid, Tandearil)

phenylbutazone (Azolid, Butazolidin, etc.)

phenytoin (Dantoin, Dilantin, etc.)

probenecid (Benemid)

—you plan to have surgery under pentothal anesthesia while taking this drug.

Time Required for Apparent Benefit

Varies with nature of infection under treatment; usually 2 to 5 days.

Possible Side-Effects *(natural, expected, and unavoidable drug actions)*

Brownish discoloration of urine, of no significance.

Superinfections (see Glossary).

Possible Adverse Effects *(unusual, unexpected, and infrequent reactions)*

IF ANY OF THE FOLLOWING DEVELOP, DISCONTINUE DRUG AND NOTIFY YOUR PHYSICIAN AS SOON AS POSSIBLE

Mild Adverse Effects

Allergic Reactions: Skin rashes (various kinds), hives, itching, swelling of face, redness of eyes.

Reduced appetite, nausea, vomiting, abdominal pain, diarrhea, irritation of mouth.

Headache, impaired balance, dizziness, ringing in ears, numbness and tingling of extremities, acute mental or behavioral disturbance.

Serious Adverse Effects

Allergic Reactions: Anaphylactic reaction (see Glossary), fever, swollen glands, swollen painful joints.

Idiosyncratic Reactions: Hemolytic anemia (see Glossary).

Bone marrow depression (see Glossary)—fatigue, weakness, fever, sore throat, unusual bleeding or bruising.
Hepatitis with or without jaundice (see Glossary).
Kidney damage with reduction of urine formation.

Advisability of Use During Pregnancy
Safety not established. Prudent use during first 8 months is best determined by the physician's evaluation. Definitely avoid during ninth month.

Advisability of Use While Nursing Infant
Drug known to be present in milk and known to have adverse effects on infant. Avoid use. Ask physician for guidance.

Habit-Forming Potential
None.

Effects of Overdosage
With Moderate Overdose: Nausea, vomiting, abdominal pain, possibly diarrhea.
With Large Overdose: Blood in urine, reduced urine formation.

Possible Effects of Extended Use
Development of thyroid gland enlargement (goiter) with or without reduced thyroid function (hypothyroidism).
Superinfections.

Recommended Periodic Examinations While Taking This Drug
Complete blood cell counts, weekly for the first 8 weeks.
Liver and kidney function tests.

While Taking This Drug, Observe the Following
Foods: No restrictions of food selection. Drug may be taken immediately after eating to minimize irritation of stomach.
Beverages: No restriction of beverage selection. However, total liquid intake should be no less than 4 pints every 24 hours while taking a sulfonamide.
Alcohol: Use with caution until combined effect is determined. Sulfonamide drugs can increase the intoxicating effects of alcohol.
Tobacco Smoking: No interactions expected.
Other Drugs
Sulfamethoxazole may *increase* the effects of
• oral anticoagulants (see Drug Family, Section Four). Dosage adjustments may be necessary to prevent abnormal bleeding or hemorrhage.
• oral anti-diabetic preparations (see Drug Family, Section Four). Dosage adjustments may be necessary to prevent hypoglycemia (see Glossary).
• methotrexate.
• phenytoin (Dantoin, Dilantin, etc.). Dosage adjustments may be necessary to prevent toxic effects on the brain.

Sulfamethoxazole may *decrease* the effects of
• penicillin.

Sulfamethoxazole *taken concurrently* with
• methenamine, may cause crystal formation and kidney blockage.
• isoniazid, may cause hemolytic anemia (see Glossary).

The following drugs may *increase* the effects of sulfamethoxazole
• aspirin
• oxyphenbutazone (Oxalid, Tandearil)
• phenylbutazone (Azolid, Butazolidin, etc.)
• probenecid (Benemid)
• promethazine (Phenergan, etc.)
• sulfinpyrazone (Anturane)
• trimethoprim (Syraprim)

The following drugs may *decrease* the effects of sulfamethoxazole
• paraldehyde (Paral)
• para-aminosalicylic acid (PAS)

Driving a Vehicle, Piloting a Plane, Operating Machinery: No restriction unless dizziness or disturbance of balance occurs.

Exposure to Sun: Use caution until sensitivity is determined. Some sulfona mide drugs can cause photosensitivity (see Glossary).

Discontinuation: Dosage adjustment may be necessary for the followin drugs if taken concurrently with sulfamethoxazole: oral anticoagulants, ora anti-diabetic preparations, phenytoin.

After (not during) treatment with a sulfonamide drug, ask physician fo guidance regarding the need for supplemental Vitamin C to correct an deficiency due to therapy.

Special Storage Instructions
Keep in a tightly closed, light-resistant container.

SULFASALAZINE

Year Introduced: 1949

Brand Names

USA	Canada
Azulfidine (Pharmacia)	Salazopyrin (Pharmacia)
SAS-500 (Rowell)	SAS-500 (ICN)
Sulcolon (Lederle)	

Drug Family: Antimicrobial (Anti-infective) [Sulfonamides]

Prescription Required: Yes

Available Dosage Forms and Strengths
Tablets — 500 mg.

How This Drug Works

Intended Therapeutic Effect(s)

- the reduction of inflammation, ulceration and bleeding associated with the active form of chronic ulcerative colitis.
- the prevention of recurrence of active ulcerative colitis.

Location of Drug Action(s):   The inflamed and ulcerated tissues in the diseased areas of the colon.

Method of Drug Action(s):   Not completely established. Possible beneficial effects include:

- an anti-infective action which prevents the growth and multiplication of certain bacteria in the colon by interfering with their formation of folic acid, an essential nutrient.
- an anti-inflammatory action which reduces the formation of prostaglandins, tissue chemicals that induce inflammation, tissue destruction and diarrhea.

THIS DRUG SHOULD NOT BE TAKEN IF

—you are allergic to any sulfonamide ("sulfa") drug (see Drug Family, Section Four).
—you are allergic to salicylates: aspirin, choline salicylate, sodium salicylate.
—you are in the ninth month of pregnancy.
—it is prescribed for an infant under 2 months of age.

INFORM YOUR PHYSICIAN BEFORE TAKING THIS DRUG IF

—you are allergic to any of the drugs chemically related to the sulfonamide ("sulfa") drugs: acetazolamide (Diamox), oral anti-diabetics, and thiazide diuretics (see Drug Family, Section Four).
—you are allergic by nature and have a history of hayfever, asthma, hives or eczema.
—you have a history of serious liver or kidney disease.
—you have a history of acute intermittent porphyria.
—you have ever had anemia caused by a drug.
—you are now taking any of the following drugs:
  oral anticoagulants
  oral anti-diabetic preparations
  methotrexate
  oxyphenbutazone (Oxalid, Tandearil)
  phenylbutazone (Azolid, Butazolidin, etc.)
  phenytoin (Dantoin, Dilantin, etc.)
  probenecid (Benemid)
—you plan to have surgery under pentothal anesthesia while taking this drug.

Time Required for Apparent Benefit

Varies with severity and duration of colitis; usually from 1 to 3 weeks.

Possible Side-Effects *(natural, expected, and unavoidable drug actions)*

Orange-yellow discoloration of urine, of no significance.

Possible Adverse Effects *(unusual, unexpected, and infrequent reactions)*

IF ANY OF THE FOLLOWING DEVELOP, DISCONTINUE DRUG AND NOTIFY YOUR PHYSICIAN AS SOON AS POSSIBLE

Mild Adverse Effects

Allergic Reactions: Skin rashes (various kinds), hives, itching, swelling of face, redness of eyes.

Reduced appetite, nausea, vomiting, abdominal pain, diarrhea, irritation of mouth.

Headache, impaired balance, dizziness, ringing in ears, numbness and tingling of extremities, acute mental or behavioral disturbance.

Serious Adverse Effects

Allergic Reactions: Anaphylactic reaction (see Glossary), fever, swollen glands, swollen painful joints.

Idiosyncratic Reactions: Hemolytic anemia (see Glossary).

Bone marrow depression (see Glossary)—fatigue, weakness, fever, sore throat, unusual bleeding or bruising.

Hepatitis with or without jaundice (see Glossary).

Kidney damage with reduction of urine formation.

Peripheral Neuritis (see Glossary).

Pancreatitis—severe abdominal pain, nausea and vomiting.

Pneumonitis—inflammatory reaction within the lung.

Advisability of Use During Pregnancy

Safety not established. Prudent use during first 8 months is best determined by the physician's evaluation. Definitely avoid during ninth month.

Advisability of Use While Nursing Infant

Drug known to be present in milk and known to have adverse effects on infant. Avoid use. Ask physician for guidance.

Habit-Forming Potential

None.

Effects of Overdosage

With Moderate Overdose: Nausea, vomiting, abdominal pain, possibly diarrhea.

With Large Overdose: Blood in urine, reduced urine formation.

Possible Effects of Extended Use

Development of thyroid gland enlargement (goiter) with or without reduced thyroid function (hypothyroidism).

An orange-yellow discoloration of the skin has been reported. This is not jaundice.

Recommended Periodic Examinations While Taking This Drug

Complete blood cell counts, weekly for the first 8 weeks.

Liver and kidney function tests.

While Taking This Drug, Observe the Following

Foods: Follow prescribed diet. Sulfasalazine does not require any specific food restriction. Drug may be taken immediately after eating to minimize irritation of stomach.

Beverages: Ask physician for guidance regarding the intake of milk. Sulfasalazine does not require any specific beverage restriction. Total liquid intake should be no less than 3 pints every 24 hours.

Alcohol: Use with caution until combined effect is determined. Some sulfonamide drugs can *increase* the intoxicating effects of alcohol. Colitis may react unfavorably to alcohol.

Tobacco Smoking: No interactions expected.

Other Drugs

Sulfasalazine may *increase* the effects of

- oral anticoagulants (see Drug Family, Section Four). Dosage adjustments may be necessary to prevent abnormal bleeding or hemorrhage.
- oral anti-diabetic preparations (see Drug Family, Section Four). Dosage adjustments may be necessary to prevent hypoglycemia (see Glossary).
- methotrexate.
- phenytoin (Dantoin, Dilantin, etc.). Dosage adjustments may be necessary to prevent toxic effects on the brain.

Sulfasalazine may *decrease* the effects of
- penicillin.

Sulfasalazine *taken concurrently* with
- methenamine, may cause crystal formation and kidney blockage.
- isoniazid, may cause hemolytic anemia (see Glossary).

The following drugs may *increase* the effects of sulfasalazine
- aspirin
- oxyphenbutazone (Oxalid, Tandearil)
- phenylbutazone (Azolid, Butazolidin, etc.)
- probenecid (Benemid)
- promethazine (Phenergan, etc.)
- sulfinpyrazone (Anturane)
- trimethoprim (Syraprim)

The following drugs may *decrease* the effects of sulfasalazine
- antibiotic drugs
- iron preparations
- paraldehyde (Paral)
- para-aminosalicylic acid (PAS)

Driving a Vehicle, Piloting a Plane, Operating Machinery: No restrictions unless dizziness or disturbance of balance occurs.

Exposure to Sun: Use caution until sensitivity is determined. Some sulfonamide drugs can cause photosensitivity (see Glossary).

Discontinuation: Dosage adjustment may be necessary for the following drugs if taken concurrently with sulfasalazine: oral anticoagulants, oral anti-diabetic preparations, phenytoin.

After (not during) treatment with a sulfonamide drug, ask physician for guidance regarding the need for supplemental Vitamin C to correct any deficiency due to therapy.

Special Storage Instructions
Keep in a tightly closed, light-resistant container.

SULFISOXAZOLE

Year Introduced: 1949

Brand Names

USA	Canada
Barazole (Barry Martin)	Gantrisin (Roche)
Chemovag (Fellows)	Novosoxazole
Gantrisin (Roche)	(Novopharm)
G-Sox (Scrip)	Sulfagen (Verdun)
SK-Soxazole (Smith Kline & French)	Sulfizole (ICN)
	U.S.-67 (Saunders)
Sodizole (First Texas)	Azo Gantrisin [CD]
Sosol (McKesson)	(Roche)
Soxa (Vita Elixir)	
Soxomide (Upjohn)	
Sulfalar (Parke-Davis)	
Sulfium (Alcon)	
Sulfizin (Tutag)	
Urisoxin (Blaine)	
Azo Gantrisin [CD] (Roche)	

Drug Family: Antimicrobial (Anti-infective) [Sulfonamides]·

Prescription Required: Yes

Available Dosage Forms and Strengths

Tablets — 500 mg.
Syrup — 500 mg. per teaspoonful
Pediatric Suspension — 500 mg. per teaspoonful
Emulsion — 1 Gm. per teaspoonful
Suppositories — 500 mg.

How This Drug Works
Intended Therapeutic Effect(s):   The elimination of infections responsive to the action of this drug.

Location of Drug Action(s):   Any body tissue or fluid in which sufficient concentration of the drug can be achieved.

Method of Drug Action(s):   This drug prevents the growth and multiplication of susceptible bacteria by interfering with their formation of folic acid, an essential nutrient.

THIS DRUG SHOULD NOT BE TAKEN IF
—you are allergic to any sulfonamide ("sulfa") drug (see Drug Family, Section Four).
—you are in the ninth month of pregnancy.
—it is prescribed for an infant under 2 months of age.

INFORM YOUR PHYSICIAN BEFORE TAKING THIS DRUG IF
—you are allergic to any of the drugs chemically related to the sulfonamide ("sulfa") drugs: acetazolamide (Diamox), oral anti-diabetics, and thiazide diuretics (see Drug Families, Section Four).
—you are allergic by nature and have a history of hayfever, asthma, hives or eczema.
—you have a history of serious liver or kidney disease.
—you have a history of acute intermittent porphyria.
—you have ever had anemia caused by a drug.
—you are now taking any of the following drugs:
  oral anticoagulants
  oral anti-diabetic preparations
  methotrexate
  oxyphenbutazone (Oxalid, Tandearil)
  phenylbutazone (Azolid, Butazolidin, etc.)
  phenytoin (Dantoin, Dilantin, etc.)
  probenecid (Benemid)
—you plan to have surgery under pentothal anesthesia while taking this drug.

Time Required for Apparent Benefit
Varies with nature of infection under treatment; usually 2 to 5 days.

Possible Side-Effects *(natural, expected, and unavoidable drug actions)*
Brownish discoloration of urine, of no significance.
Superinfections (see Glossary).

Possible Adverse Effects *(unusual, unexpected, and infrequent reactions)*
IF ANY OF THE FOLLOWING DEVELOP, DISCONTINUE DRUG AND NOTIFY YOUR PHYSICIAN AS SOON AS POSSIBLE
Mild Adverse Effects
  Allergic Reactions: Skin rashes (various kinds), hives, itching, swelling of face, redness of eyes.
  Reduced appetite, nausea, vomiting, abdominal pain, diarrhea, irritation of mouth.
  Headache, impaired balance, dizziness, ringing in ears, numbness and tingling of extremities, acute mental or behavioral disturbance.
Serious Adverse Effects
  Allergic Reactions: Anaphylactic reaction (see Glossary), fever, swollen glands, swollen painful joints.
  Idiosyncratic Reactions: Hemolytic anemia (see Glossary).

Bone marrow depression (see Glossary)—fatigue, weakness, fever, sore throat, unusual bleeding or bruising.
Hepatitis with or without jaundice (see Glossary).
Kidney damage with reduction of urine formation.

Advisability of Use During Pregnancy

Safety not established. Prudent use during first 8 months is best determined by the physician's evaluation. Definitely avoid during ninth month.

Advisability of Use While Nursing Infant

Drug known to be present in milk and known to have adverse effects on infant. Avoid use. Ask physician for guidance.

Habit-Forming Potential

None.

Effects of Overdosage

With Moderate Overdose: Nausea, vomiting, abdominal pain, possibly diarrhea.
With Large Overdose: Blood in urine, reduced urine formation.

Possible Effects of Extended Use

Development of thyroid gland enlargement (goiter) with or without reduced thyroid function (hypothyroidism).
Superinfections.

Recommended Periodic Examinations While Taking This Drug

Complete blood cell counts, weekly for the first 8 weeks.
Liver and kidney function tests.

While Taking This Drug, Observe the Following

Foods: No restrictions of food selection. Drug may be taken immediately after eating to minimize irritation of stomach.

Beverages: No restriction of beverage selection. However, total liquid intake should be no less than 4 pints every 24 hours while taking a sulfonamide.

Alcohol: Use with caution until combined effect is determined. Sulfonamide drugs can *increase* the intoxicating effects of alcohol.

Tobacco Smoking: No interactions expected.

Other Drugs

Sulfisoxazole may *increase* the effects of

- oral anticoagulants (see Drug Family, Section Four). Dosage adjustments may be necessary to prevent abnormal bleeding or hemorrhage.
- oral anti-diabetic preparations (see Drug Family, Section Four). Dosage adjustment may be necessary to prevent hypoglycemia (see Glossary).
- methotrexate.
- phenytoin (Dantoin, Dilantin, etc.). Dosage adjustments may be necessary to prevent toxic effects on the brain.

Sulfisoxazole may *decrease* the effects of

- penicillin.

Sulfisoxazole *taken concurrently* with
- methenamine, may cause crystal formation and kidney blockage.
- isoniazid, may cause hemolytic anemia (see Glossary).

The following drugs may *increase* the effects of sulfisoxazole
- aspirin
- oxyphenbutazone (Oxalid, Tandearil)
- phenylbutazone (Azolid, Butazolidin, etc.)
- probenecid (Benemid)
- promethazine (Phenergan, etc.)
- sulfinpyrazone (Anturane)
- trimethoprim (Syraprim)

The following drugs may *decrease* the effects of sulfisoxazole
- paraldehyde (Paral)
- para-aminosalicylic acid (PAS)

Driving a Vehicle, Piloting a Plane, Operating Machinery: No restrictions unless dizziness or disturbance of balance occurs.

Exposure to Sun: Use caution until sensitivity is determined. Some sulfonamide drugs can cause photosensitivity (see Glossary).

Discontinuation: Dosage adjustment may be necessary for the following drugs if taken concurrently with sulfisoxazole: oral anticoagulants, oral anti-diabetic preparations, phenytoin.

After (not during) treatment with a sulfonamide drug, ask physician for guidance regarding the need for supplemental Vitamin C to correct any deficiency due to therapy.

Special Storage Instructions
Keep in a tightly closed, light-resistant container.

TETRACYCLINE

Year Introduced: 1953

Brand Names

USA

Achromycin (Lederle)
Achromycin V
  (Lederle)
Amtet (Amid)
Bicycline (Knight)
Bristacycline (Bristol)
Centet (Central)
Cycline-250 (Scrip)
Cyclopar
  (Parke-Davis)
Desamycin
  (Pharmics)
Duratet (Meyer)
Fed-Mycin (Fed.
  Pharm.)
G-Mycin (Coast)
Kesso-Tetra
  (McKesson)
Maytrex (Mayrand)
Mericycline (Merit)
Nor-Tet (North Amer.
  Pharm.)
Paltet (Palmedico)
Panmycin (Upjohn)
Piracaps (Tutag)
QIDtet (Mallinckrodt)
Retet
  (Reid-Provident)
Retet-S
  (Reid-Provident)
Robitet (Robins)
Ro-Cycline (Rowell)

Sarocycline (Saron)
Scotrex (Scott/Cord)
SK-Tetracycline
  (Smith Kline &
  French)
Sumycin (Squibb)
T-125 (Elder)
T-250 (Elder)
Tet-Cy (Metro)
Tetra-C (Century)
Tetrachel (Rachelle)
Tetrachlor (Kenyon)
Tetra-Co (Coastal)
Tetracyn (Pfizer)
Tetra-500 (Ulmer)
Tetralan (Lannett)
Tetram (Dunhall)
Tetramax (Rand)
Tetrex (Bristol)
Trexin (A.V.P.
  Pharm.)
Achrostatin V [CD]
  (Lederle)
Comycin [CD]
  (Upjohn)
Mysteclin-F [CD]
  (Squibb)
Tetrastatin [CD]
  (Pfizer)

Canada

Achromycin
  (Lederle)
Achromycin V
  (Lederle)
Cefracycline (Frosst)
Chemcycline
  (Chemo)
Decycline
  (Desbergers)
Gene-cycline
  (Franca)
GT-250 (Horner)
GT-500 (Horner)
Medicycline (Medic)
Muracine (Nadeau)
Neo-Tetrine (Neo)
Novotetra
  (Novopharm)
Pexobiotic (Terapex)
Sumycin (Squibb)
Tetrabiotic (Nordic)
Tetracaps (M & M)
Tetracrine (C & C)
Tetracyn (Pfizer)
Tetral (Verdun)
Tetralean (Harris)
Tetrex (Bristol)
Tetrosol (Horner)
Triacycline (Trianon)
T-250 (Saunders)
T-Caps (ICN)
T-Liquid (ICN)
T-Tabs (ICN)
Wintracin (ICN)

Drug Family: Antibiotic (Anti-infective) [Tetracyclines]

Prescription Required: Yes

Available Dosage Forms and Strengths
Tablets — 250 mg.
Capsules — 100 mg., 125 mg., 250 mg., 500 mg.
Oral Suspension — 250 mg. per teaspoonful
Syrup — 125 mg. per teaspoonful
Pediatric Drops — 100 mg. per ml.
Eye Suspension — 1%

How This Drug Works
Intended Therapeutic Effect(s):   The elimination of infections responsive to the action of this drug.

Location of Drug Action(s):   Any body tissue or fluid in which sufficient concentration of the drug can be achieved.

Method of Drug Action(s):   This drug prevents the growth and multiplication of susceptible bacteria by interfering with their formation of essential proteins.

THIS DRUG SHOULD NOT BE TAKEN IF
—you are allergic to any tetracycline drug (see Drug Family, Section Four).
—you are pregnant or breast feeding.
—it is prescribed for a child under 9 years of age.

INFORM YOUR PHYSICIAN BEFORE TAKING THIS DRUG IF
—you have a history of liver or kidney disease.
—you have systemic lupus erythematosus.
—you are taking any penicillin drug.
—you are taking any anticoagulant drug.
—you plan to have surgery under general anesthesia in the near future.

Time Required for Apparent Benefit
Varies with nature of infection under treatment; usually 2 to 5 days.

Possible Side-Effects *(natural, expected, and unavoidable drug actions)*
Superinfections (see Glossary), often due to yeast organisms. These can occur in the mouth, intestinal tract, rectum, and/or vagina, resulting in rectal and vaginal itching.

Possible Adverse Effects *(unusual, unexpected, and infrequent reactions)*
IF ANY OF THE FOLLOWING DEVELOP, DISCONTINUE DRUG AND NOTIFY YOUR PHYSICIAN AS SOON AS POSSIBLE
Mild Adverse Effects
Allergic Reactions: Skin rash (various kinds), hives, itching of hands and feet, swelling of face or extremities.
Photosensitivity Reactions: Exaggerated sunburn or skin irritation occurs commonly with some tetracyclines (see Glossary).
Loss of appetite, nausea, vomiting, diarrhea.
Irritation of mouth or tongue, "black tongue," sore throat, abdominal pain or cramping.
Serious Adverse Effects
Allergic Reactions: Anaphylactic reaction (see Glossary), asthma, fever,

600   Tetracycline

painful swollen joints, unusual bleeding or bruising, jaundice (see Glossary).

Permanent discoloration and/or malformation of teeth when taken under 9 years of age, including unborn child and infant.

Advisability of Use During Pregnancy

Tetracyclines can have adverse effects on mother and fetus. Avoid use.

Advisability of Use While Nursing Infant

Tetracyclines can be present in milk and can have adverse effects on infant. Avoid use.

Habit-Forming Potential

None.

Effects of Overdosage

Possible nausea, vomiting, diarrhea.

Acute liver damage (rare).

Possible Effects of Extended Use

Impairment of bone marrow, liver, or kidney function (all rare).

Superinfections.

Recommended Periodic Examinations While Taking This Drug

Complete blood cell counts.

Liver and kidney function tests.

During extended use, sputum and stool examinations may detect early superinfections due to yeast organisms.

While Taking This Drug, Observe the Following

Foods: Dairy products can interfere with absorption. Tetracyclines should be taken 1 hour before or 2 hours after eating.

Beverages: Avoid milk for 1 hour before and after each dose of a tetracycline.

Alcohol: Avoid while taking a tetracycline if you have a history of liver disease.

Tobacco Smoking: No interactions expected.

Other Drugs

Tetracyclines may *increase* the effects of

• oral anticoagulants, and make it necessary to reduce their dosage.

Tetracyclines may *decrease* the effects of

• the penicillins, and impair their effectiveness in treating infections.

The following drugs may *decrease* the effects of tetracyclines

• antacids may reduce drug absorption.

• iron and mineral preparations may reduce drug absorption.

Driving a Vehicle, Piloting a Plane, Operating Machinery: No restrictions.

Exposure to Sun: Avoid as much as possible. Photosensitivity (see Glossary) is common with some tetracyclines.

Special Storage Instructions
Keep in a tightly closed, light-resistant container.

THEOPHYLLINE
(Aminophylline, Oxtriphylline)

Year Introduced: 1930

Brand Names

USA

Amesec [CD] (Lilly)
Aminodur (Cooper)
Aminophylline +
    Amytal [CD] (Lilly)
Amodrine [CD]
    (Searle)
Brondecon [CD]
    (Warner/Chilcott)
Bronkaid [CD]
    (Drew)
Bronkolixir [CD]
    (Breon)
Bronkotabs [CD]
    (Breon)
Choledyl
    (Warner/Chilcott)
Elixophyllin (Cooper)

Isuprel Compound
    [CD] (Winthrop)
Kiophyllin [CD]
    (Searle)
Marax [CD] (Roerig)
Mudrane [CD]
    (Poythress)
Quadrinal [CD]
    (Knoll)
Quibron [CD] (Mead
    Johnson)
Quibron Plus [CD]
    (Mead Johnson)
Slo-Phyllin (Dooner)
Somophyllin (Fisons)
Tedral [CD]
    (Warner/Chilcott)

Verequad [CD]
    (Knoll)
(Numerous other
    combination brand
    names)

Canada

Aminophyl (Eddé)
Asthmophylline
    (C.P.F.)
Choledyl
    (Warner/Chilcott)
Corivin (M & M)
Corophyllin (M & M)
Elixophyllin (Cooper)
Theocyne (Nordic)
Theolixir (Dymond)

Drug Family: Anti-asthmatic (Bronchodilator)

Prescription Required: For low-strength formulations—No
For high-strength formulations—Yes

Available Dosage Forms and Strengths

Tablets — 100 mg., 200 mg.
Prolonged Action Tablets — 300 mg.
Capsules — 60 mg., 100 mg., 125 mg., 200 mg., 250 mg.
Elixir — 27 mg., 86 mg., 100 mg. per teaspoonful
Suppositories — 25 mg., 100 mg., 250 mg., 500 mg.
Also marketed in a variety of tablets, cap-
sules, and liquids in combination with other
drugs.
Syrup — 80 mg. per tablespoonful.

How This Drug Works

Intended Therapeutic Effect(s):   Symptomatic relief in the management of
bronchial asthma.

Location of Drug Action(s):   The muscles of the bronchial tubes.

Method of Drug Action(s):   This drug increases the activity of the chemical system within the muscle cell that causes relaxation and expansion of the bronchial tube, thus reversing the constriction responsible for asthma.

THIS DRUG SHOULD NOT BE TAKEN IF

—you have had an allergic reaction to any dosage form of it previously.

—you have an active peptic ulcer.

INFORM YOUR PHYSICIAN BEFORE TAKING THIS DRUG IF

—you have a history of kidney disease or impaired kidney function.

—you have a history of gastritis or peptic ulcer.

—you have high blood pressure or heart disease.

—you are taking any medication for gout.

Time Required for Apparent Benefit

Drug action begins in 15 to 30 minutes, reaches a maximum in 1 to 2 hours, and subsides in 7 to 10 hours (depending upon dosage form and size of dose).

Possible Side-Effects *(natural, expected, and unavoidable drug actions)*

Nervousness, insomnia.

CAUTION

This drug should not be taken concurrently with other anti-asthmatic drugs unless you are directed to do so by your physician. Serious overdosage could result.

Possible Adverse Effects *(unusual, unexpected, and infrequent reactions)*

IF ANY OF THE FOLLOWING DEVELOP, DISCONTINUE DRUG AND NOTIFY YOUR PHYSICIAN AS SOON AS POSSIBLE

Mild Adverse Effects

Allergic Reactions: Skin rash.

Stomach irritation, nausea, vomiting, diarrhea.

Headache, dizziness, rapid or irregular heart action.

Serious Adverse Effects

Idiosyncratic Reactions: Severe anxiety, confusion, behavioral disturbances.

Advisability of Use During Pregnancy

Safety not established. Prudent use is best determined by the physician's evaluation.

Advisability of Use While Nursing Infant

Drug is present in milk in small amounts. Ask physician for guidance.

Habit-Forming Potential

None.

Effects of Overdosage

With Moderate Overdose: Nausea, vomiting, restlessness, irritability, confusion, thirst, increased urination.

With Large Overdose: Delirium, convulsions, high fever, weak and rapid pulse, collapse of circulation.

Possible Effects of Extended Use
Stomach irritation.

Recommended Periodic Examinations While Taking This Drug
None required.

While Taking This Drug, Observe the Following
Foods: No restrictions. Drug is more effective if taken on empty stomach, but antacids may be necessary to reduce stomach irritation.
Beverages: Large intake of coffee or tea may increase the nervousness and insomnia caused by this drug in sensitive individuals.
Alcohol: No interactions expected.
Tobacco Smoking: No interactions expected with this drug. However, smoking may aggravate asthma, bronchitis, or emphysema. Follow physician's advice.
Other Drugs
Theophylline may *increase* the effects of
• other drugs used to treat asthma, especially epinephrine (Adrenalin) and ephedrine. The combined effects are beneficial when dosages are adjusted properly.

Theophylline may *decrease* the effects of
• drugs commonly used to treat gout; these include allopurinol (Zyloprim), probenecid (Benemid), sulfinpyrazone (Anturan). Consult physician regarding tests of uric acid blood levels and adjustment of dosage schedules for control of gout.
• lithium (Eskalith, Lithane, etc.), by hastening its elimination in the urine.
Driving a Vehicle, Piloting a Plane, Operating Machinery: No restrictions unless lightheadedness or dizziness occurs.
Exposure to Sun: No restrictions.

Special Storage Instructions
Keep in a dry, tightly closed container.

THIORIDAZINE

Year Introduced: 1959

Brand Names

USA	Canada
Mellaril (Sandoz)	Mellaril (Sandoz)
	Novoridazine
	(Novopharm)
	Thioril (ICN)

Drug Family: Tranquilizer, Strong (Anti-psychotic) [Phenothiazines]

Prescription Required: Yes

Available Dosage Forms and Strengths
Tablets — 10 mg., 15 mg., 25 mg., 50 mg., 100 mg., 150 mg., 200 mg.
Concentrate — 30 mg. per ml., 100 mg. per ml.

How This Drug Works
Intended Therapeutic Effect(s):   Restoration of emotional calm. Relief of severe anxiety, agitation, and psychotic behavior.
Location of Drug Action(s):   Those nerve pathways in the brain that utilize the tissue chemical dopamine for the transmission of nerve impulses.
Method of Drug Action(s):   Not completely established. Present theory is that by inhibiting the action of dopamine, this drug acts to correct an imbalance of nerve impulse transmissions that is thought to be responsible for certain mental disorders.

THIS DRUG SHOULD NOT BE TAKEN IF
—you have had an allergic reaction to any dosage form of it previously.
—you have severe heart disease.
—it is prescribed for a child under 2 years of age.

INFORM YOUR PHYSICIAN BEFORE TAKING THIS DRUG IF
—you are allergic or sensitive to any phenothiazine drug (see Drug Family, Section Four).
—you are taking any sedatives, sleep-inducing drugs, other tranquilizers, antidepressants, antihistamines, or narcotic drugs of any kind.
—you have epilepsy.
—you plan to have surgery under general or spinal anesthesia in the near future.

Time Required for Apparent Benefit
Some benefit usually apparent in first week. Maximal benefit may require regular dosage for several weeks.

Possible Side-Effects *(natural, expected, and unavoidable drug actions)*
Drowsiness, lethargy, blurred vision, nasal congestion, dryness of the mouth, constipation, impaired urination.

Possible Adverse Effects *(unusual, unexpected, and infrequent reactions)*
IF ANY OF THE FOLLOWING DEVELOP, DISCONTINUE DRUG AND NOTIFY YOUR PHYSICIAN AS SOON AS POSSIBLE
Mild Adverse Effects
Allergic Reactions: Skin rash (various kinds), hives, swelling of the salivary glands, fever.
Headache, lightheadedness and faintness in upright position (see orthostatic hypotension in Glossary).
Confusion, agitation, restlessness.
Breast congestion, milk formation, menstrual irregularity.
Nausea, vomiting, loss of appetite.

Serious Adverse Effects

Allergic Reactions: Hepatitis with jaundice (see Glossary), very rare with this drug.

Bone marrow depression (see Glossary), usually mild.

Convulsions.

Parkinson-like disorders (see Glossary), less frequent than with other phenothiazines.

Advisability of Use During Pregnancy

Safety not established. Prudent use is best determined by the physician's evaluation.

Advisability of Use While Nursing Infant

Safety not established. Ask physician for guidance.

Habit-Forming Potential

None.

Effects of Overdosage

With Moderate Overdose: Marked drowsiness, confusion, disorientation, blurred vision, nasal congestion, marked dryness of mouth, weakness.

With Large Overdose: Deep sleep, coma, convulsions, drop in body temperature, shallow breathing.

Possible Effects of Extended Use

Pigmentation of the retina of the eye, causing impairment of vision, brownish coloration of vision, reduced night vision.

Tardive dyskinesia (see Glossary).

Recommended Periodic Examinations While Taking This Drug

Complete eye examinations for changes in vision and pigment deposits in the retina.

Complete blood cell counts and liver function tests.

Periodic electrocardiograms.

Periodic examination of the tongue for the appearance of fine, involuntary, wave-like movements that could indicate the development of tardive dyskinesia.

While Taking This Drug, Observe the Following

Foods: No restrictions.

Beverages: No restrictions.

Alcohol: Use extreme caution until combined effects have been determined. Alcohol can increase the sedative action of thioridazine and accentuate its depressant effects on brain function. Thioridazine can increase the intoxicating effects of alcohol.

Tobacco Smoking: No interactions expected.

Other Drugs

Thioridazine may *increase* the effects of

• all sedatives, sleep-inducing drugs, other tranquilizers, antidepressants, antihistamines, and narcotic drugs, and produce oversedation. Ask physician for guidance regarding dosage adjustments.

• all drugs containing atropine or having atropine-like actions (see Drug Family, Section Four).

Thioridazine may *decrease* the effects of

• levodopa (Dopar, Larodopa, etc.), and reduce its effectiveness in the treatment of Parkinson's disease (shaking palsy).
• appetite suppressant drugs (Pre-Sate, Preludin, Benzedrine, Dexedrine, etc.).

Thioridazine *taken concurrently* with

• quinidine, may impair heart function. Avoid the use of these two drugs at the same time.

The following drugs may *increase* the effects of thioridazine

• tricyclic antidepressants (see Drug Family, Section Four).

Driving a Vehicle, Piloting a Plane, Operating Machinery: This drug can impair mental alertness, judgment, and physical coordination. Avoid hazardous activities.

Exposure to Sun: Use caution until sensitivity has been determined. This drug may produce photosensitivity (see Glossary).

Exposure to Heat: Use caution and avoid excessive heat. This drug may impair the regulation of body temperature and increase the risk of heat stroke.

Heavy Exercise or Exertion: Use caution and follow your physician's instructions if you have any form of heart disease.

Discontinuation: If it has been necessary to use this drug for an extended period of time, do not discontinue it suddenly. Ask physician for guidance regarding dosage reduction and withdrawal. Upon discontinuation of this drug, it may also be necessary to adjust the dosages of other drugs taken concurrently with it.

Special Storage Instructions

Store liquid concentrate in a tightly closed, amber glass container, at temperatures below 86°F. (30°C.).

THIOTHIXENE

Year Introduced: 1967

Brand Names

USA	Canada
Navane (Roerig)	Navane (Pfizer)

Drug Family: Tranquilizer, Strong (Anti-psychotic) [Thioxanthines]

Prescription Required: Yes

Available Dosage Forms and Strengths
Capsules — 1 mg., 2 mg., 5 mg., 10 mg., 20 mg.
Concentrate — 5 mg. per ml.
Injection — 2 mg. per ml.

How This Drug Works
Intended Therapeutic Effect(s):   Restoration of emotional calm. Relief of severe anxiety, agitation, and psychotic behavior.

Location of Drug Action(s):   Those nerve pathways in the mesolimbic area of the brain that utilize the tissue chemical dopamine for the transmission of nerve impulses.

Method of Drug Action(s):   Not completely established. Present theory is that by inhibiting the action of dopamine, this drug acts to correct an imbalance of nerve impulse transmissions that is thought to be responsible for certain mental disorders.

THIS DRUG SHOULD NOT BE TAKEN IF
—you have had an allergic reaction to any dosage form of it previously.
—you have a serious blood disorder.
—you have any form of Parkinson's disease.
—it is prescribed for a child under 12 years of age.

INFORM YOUR PHYSICIAN BEFORE TAKING THIS DRUG IF
—you have had an allergic reaction to any phenothiazine drug in the past (see Drug Family, Section Four).
—you have a history of liver or kidney disease, or impaired liver or kidney function.
—you have epilepsy.
—you have glaucoma.
—you have any form of heart disease, especially angina (coronary insufficiency).
—you have high blood pressure.
—you drink alcoholic beverages daily.
—you are taking sedatives, sleep-inducing drugs, tranquilizers, antidepressants, antihistamines, or narcotic drugs of any kind.
—you plan to have surgery under general or spinal anesthesia in the near future.

Time Required for Apparent Benefit
Significant benefit may occur within 3 weeks. However, maximal benefit may require continuous use on a regular basis for several months.

Possible Side-Effects *(natural, expected, and unavoidable drug actions)*
Drowsiness, lethargy, blurred vision, dryness of the mouth, impaired urination, constipation, transient drop in blood pressure.

CAUTION
1. The elderly (over 60 years of age) and the debilitated are more sensitive to standard doses. Small doses are advisable until the full effects have been determined.
2. Dosage must be carefully individualized. The maintenance dose should be the lowest effective dose.

Possible Adverse Effects *(unusual, unexpected, and infrequent reactions)*

IF ANY OF THE FOLLOWING DEVELOP, DISCONTINUE DRUG AND NOTIFY YOUR PHYSICIAN AS SOON AS POSSIBLE

Mild Adverse Effects
Allergic Reactions: Itching, skin rash, hives, drug fever (see Glossary).
Lightheadedness, fainting, rapid heart rate.
Insomnia, restlessness, agitation.
Nausea, vomiting, diarrhea.
Increased appetite, gain in weight.
Change in menstrual pattern.
Breast fullness, tenderness, and milk production.

Serious Adverse Effects
Allergic Reactions: Anaphylactic reaction (see Glossary).
Parkinson-like disorders (see Glossary).
Muscle spasms affecting the jaw, neck, back, hands, or feet.
Eye-rolling, muscle twitching, convulsions.
Sexual impotence.
Fluctuations in number of white blood cells.

Advisability of Use During Pregnancy
Safety not established. Definitely avoid use during the first 3 months. Prudent use during the last 6 months is best determined by the physician's evaluation.

Advisability of Use While Nursing Infant
The presence of this drug in milk is not known. Ask your physician for guidance.

Habit-Forming Potential
None.

Effects of Overdosage
With Moderate Overdose: Marked drowsiness, dizziness, weakness, muscle rigidity and twitching, tremors, confusion, dryness of mouth, blurred or double vision.
With Large Overdose: Deep sleep progressing to coma, weak and rapid pulse, shallow and slow breathing, very low blood pressure, convulsions.

Possible Effects of Extended Use
Eye changes, such as pigment deposits in the lens and retina.
Tardive dyskinesia (see Glossary).

Recommended Periodic Examinations While Taking This Drug
Complete blood cell counts.
Liver function tests.
Complete eye examinations, including eye structures and visual acuity.
Careful inspection of the tongue for early evidence of fine, involuntary, wave-like movements that could indicate the beginning of tardive dyskinesia.

While Taking This Drug, Observe the Following
Foods: No restrictions.

Beverages: No restrictions. The liquid concentrate form of this drug may be taken in water, in fruit or vegetable juices, or in milk.

Alcohol: Avoid completely. Alcohol can increase this drug's sedative action and accentuate its depressant effects on brain function. Thiothixene can increase the intoxicating effects of alcohol.

Tobacco Smoking: No interactions expected.

Other Drugs

Thiothixene may *increase* the effects of
- atropine-like drugs, and cause an increase in internal eye pressure in the presence of glaucoma (see Drug Family, Section Four).
- sedatives, sleep-inducing drugs, other tranquilizers, antihistamines, and narcotic drugs, and cause excessive sedation.

Thiothixene may *decrease* the effects of
- bethanidine.
- guanethidine.
- levodopa.

Thiothixene *taken concurrently* with
- anti-convulsant drugs, may cause a change in the pattern of seizures. Dosage adjustment of the anti-convulsant may be necessary.
- anti-hypertensive drugs (some), may cause excessive lowering of the blood pressure.

The following drugs may *increase* the effects of thiothixene
- barbiturates may cause excessive sedation.
- other tranquilizers may cause excessive sedation.
- tricyclic antidepressants may cause excessive sedation.

Driving a Vehicle, Piloting a Plane, Operating Machinery: This drug can impair mental alertness, judgment, and physical coordination. Avoid all hazardous activities if you experience such drug effects.

Exposure to Sun: Use caution until full effect is known. This drug can cause photosensitivity.

Exposure to Heat: Use caution in hot environments. This drug may contribute to the development of heat stroke.

Heavy Exercise or Exertion: Use caution until tolerance for physical activity and exercise are determined. This drug may alter normal adaptive responses in perspiration and blood pressure adjustment.

Special Storage Instructions
Keep all forms of this drug in airtight containers. Protect from light.

THYROID
(Thyroid Preparations)

Year Introduced: 1896

Brand Names

USA	Canada
Armour Thyroid	Chemthyroid (Chemo)
(Armour)	Proloid (Warner/Chilcott)
Proloid (Warner/Chilcott)	
S-P-T (Fleming)	
Thyrobrom (Mills)	

Drug Family: Thyroid Hormones

Prescription Required: Yes

Available Dosage Forms and Strengths:
   Tablets — 15 mg. (0.25 gr.), 30 mg. (0.5 gr.), 65 mg. (1 gr.), 100 mg. (1.5 gr),
              130 mg. (2 gr.), 200 mg. (3 gr.), 260 mg. (4 gr.), 325 mg. (5 gr.)
   Capsules — 65 mg. (1 gr.), 130 mg. (2 gr.), 200 mg. (3 gr.), 325 mg. (5 gr.)

How This Drug Works
   Intended Therapeutic Effect(s):   Correction of thyroid hormone deficiency
   (hypothyroidism) by replacement therapy.
   Location of Drug Action(s):   Affects the biochemical activity of all tissues
   throughout the body.
   Method of Drug Action(s):   By altering the processes of cellular chemistry
   that store energy in an inactive (reserve) form, this drug makes more
   energy available for biochemical activity and increases the rate of cellular
   metabolism.

THIS DRUG SHOULD NOT BE TAKEN IF
—you have had an allergic reaction to any dosage form of it previously.
—you are recovering from a recent heart attack (ask physician for guidance).
—you are using it to lose weight and you do not have a thyroid deficiency (your
   thyroid function is normal).

INFORM YOUR PHYSICIAN BEFORE TAKING THIS DRUG IF
—you have any form of heart disease.
—you have high blood pressure.
—you have diabetes.
—you have Addison's disease or a history of adrenal gland deficiency.
—you are using Adrenalin, ephedrin, or isoproterenol to treat asthma.
—you are taking any anticoagulant drugs.

Time Required for Apparent Benefit
   Drug action begins within 48 hours and reaches a maximum in 8 to 10 days.
   Full effectiveness requires continuous use on a regular schedule for several
   weeks.

Possible Side-Effects *(natural, expected, and unavoidable drug actions)*
None if dosage is adjusted correctly.

CAUTION

1. Thyroid hormones are used to correct conditions due to thyroid deficiency and to treat thyroid gland enlargement (goiter) and thyroid cancer. They should not be used to treat obesity if diagnostic studies indicate that there is no thyroid deficiency contributing to the obesity.
2. The need for and response to thyroid hormone treatment varies greatly from person to person. Careful supervision of individual response is necessary to determine correct dosage. Do not change your dosage schedule without consulting your physician.
3. The elderly (over 60 years of age) are usually more sensitive to thyroid hormone action. Small doses are advisable until nature of response has been determined.

Possible Adverse Effects *(unusual, unexpected, and infrequent reactions)*

IF ANY OF THE FOLLOWING DEVELOP, DISCONTINUE DRUG AND NOTIFY YOUR PHYSICIAN AS SOON AS POSSIBLE

Mild Adverse Effects
  Allergic Reactions: Skin rash, hives.
  Headache in sensitive individuals, even with proper dosage adjustment.
  Changes in menstrual pattern, during dosage adjustments.

Serious Adverse Effects
  Increased frequency or intensity of angina in the presence of coronary artery disease.

Advisability of Use During Pregnancy
Thyroid hormones do not reach the fetus (cross the placenta) in significant amounts. This drug is safe to use in pregnancy but *only* if given to correct a true thyroid deficiency, and with properly adjusted dosage.

Advisability of Use While Nursing Infant
Thyroid hormones are present in milk. Nursing is safe when the mother's dose of thyroid hormones is correctly adjusted to maintain normal thyroid activity.

Habit-Forming Potential
None.

Effects of Overdosage
  With Moderate Overdose: Sense of increased body heat, heart palpitation, nervousness, increased sweating, hand tremors, insomnia.
  With Large Overdose: Rapid and irregular pulse, fever, headache, marked nervousness and irritability, diarrhea, weight loss, muscle spasm and cramping.

Possible Effects of Extended Use
None with correct dosage adjustment.

Recommended Periodic Examinations While Taking This Drug
Physician's assessment of response to treatment, with evaluation of subjective and objective changes due to thyroid hormone activity. Measurement of thyroid hormone levels in the blood.

While Taking This Drug, Observe the Following
Foods: To improve absorption this drug should be taken on arising and before eating. Avoid heavy use of soybean preparations because of their ability to interfere with thyroid function.

Beverages: No restrictions.

Alcohol: No interactions expected.

Tobacco Smoking: No interactions expected.

Other Drugs

Thyroid may *increase* the effects of

- stimulants such as Adrenalin, ephedrine, the amphetamines (Dexedrine), methylphenidate (Ritalin), etc., and cause excessive stimulation. Dosage adjustment may be necessary.
- oral anticoagulants of the coumarin family (see Drug Family, Section Four), and cause bleeding or hemorrhage. Reduction in dosage of the anticoagulant is usually necessary.
- tricyclic antidepressants (see Drug Family, Section Four).
- digitalis preparations. Careful dosage adjustment is necessary to prevent digitalis toxicity.

Thyroid may *decrease* the effects of

- barbiturates, making larger doses necessary for effective sedation.

Thyroid *taken concurrently* with

- all anti-diabetic drugs (insulin and oral anti-diabetic medications), may require an increase in the dosage of the anti-diabetic agent to obtain proper control of blood sugar levels. After correct doses of both drugs have been determined, a reduction in the dose of thyroid will require a simultaneous reduction in the dose of the anti-diabetic drug to prevent hypoglycemia.
- cortisone-like drugs, requires careful dosage adjustment to prevent the development of cortisone deficiency.

The following drugs may *increase* the effects of thyroid

- aspirin (in large doses and with continuous use)
- phenytoin (Dantoin, Dilantin, etc.)

The following drugs may *decrease* the effects of thyroid

- cholestyramine (Cuemid, Questran) may reduce its absorption. Intake of the two drugs should be 5 hours apart.

Driving a Vehicle, Piloting a Plane, Operating Machinery: No restrictions or precautions.

Exposure to Sun: No restrictions.

Exposure to Heat: This drug may decrease individual tolerance to warm environments, increasing the discomfort due to heat. Avoid excessive sweating.

Exposure to Cold: This drug may increase individual tolerance to cold, decreasing the discomfort due to cold.

Heavy Exercise or Exertion: Use caution in the presence of angina and known coronary artery disease. This drug may increase the frequency of angina during physical activity.

Discontinuation: This drug must be taken continuously on a regular schedule to correct thyroid deficiency. Do not discontinue it without consulting your physician.

Special Storage Instructions
Keep in a dry, tightly closed container at room temperature. Protect from light.

THYROXINE
(T–4)
Year Introduced: 1953

Brand Names

USA	Canada
Cytolen (Len-Tag)	Eltroxin (Glaxo)
Letter (Armour)	Synthroid (Flint)
Levoid (Nutrition Control)	Thyrolar [CD] (Harris)
Synthroid (Flint)	
Euthyroid [CD] (Warner/Chilcott)	
Thyrolar [CD] (Armour)	

Drug Family: Thyroid Hormones

Prescription Required: Yes

Available Dosage Forms and Strengths
Tablets — 0.025 mg., 0.05 mg., 0.1 mg., 0.15 mg., 0.2 mg., 0.3 mg., 0.5 mg.
Injection — 0.05 mg. per ml., 0.1 mg. per ml.

How This Drug Works
Intended Therapeutic Effect(s):   Correction of thyroid hormone deficiency (hypothyroidism) by replacement therapy.

Location of Drug Action(s):   Affects the biochemical activity of all tissues throughout the body.

Method of Drug Action(s):   By altering the processes of cellular chemistry that store energy in an inactive (reserve) form, this drug makes more energy available for biochemical activity and increases the rate of cellular metabolism.

THIS DRUG SHOULD NOT BE TAKEN IF
—you have had an allergic reaction to any dosage form of it previously.
—you are recovering from a recent heart attack (ask physician for guidance).
—you are using it to lose weight and you do not have a thyroid deficiency (your thyroid function is normal).

INFORM YOUR PHYSICIAN BEFORE TAKING THIS DRUG IF
—you have any form of heart disease.
—you have high blood pressure.
—you have diabetes.
—you have Addison's disease or a history of adrenal gland deficiency.
—you are using Adrenalin, ephedrin, or isoproterenol to treat asthma.
—you are taking any anticoagulant drugs.

Time Required for Apparent Benefit
Drug action begins within 48 hours and reaches a maximum in 8 to 10 days. Full effectiveness requires continuous use on a regular schedule for several weeks.

Possible Side-Effects *(natural, expected, and unavoidable drug actions)*
None if dosage is adjusted correctly.

CAUTION
1. Thyroid hormones are used to correct conditions due to thyroid deficiency and to treat thyroid gland enlargement (goiter) and thyroid cancer. They should not be used to treat obesity if diagnostic studies indicate that there is no thyroid deficiency contributing to the obesity.
2. The need for and response to thyroid hormone treatment varies greatly from person to person. Careful supervision of individual response is necessary to determine correct dosage. Do not change your dosage schedule without consulting your physician.
3. The elderly (over 60 years of age) are usually more sensitive to thyroid hormone action. Small doses are advisable until nature of response has been determined.

Possible Adverse Effects *(unusual, unexpected, and infrequent reactions)*

IF ANY OF THE FOLLOWING DEVELOP, DISCONTINUE DRUG AND NOTIFY YOUR PHYSICIAN AS SOON AS POSSIBLE

Mild Adverse Effects
Allergic Reactions: Skin rash, hives.
Headache in sensitive individuals, even with proper dosage adjustment.
Changes in menstrual pattern, during dosage adjustments.

Serious Adverse Effects
Increased frequency or intensity of angina in the presence of coronary artery disease.

Advisability of Use During Pregnancy
Thyroid hormones do not reach the fetus (cross the placenta) in significant amounts. This drug is safe to use in pregnancy but only if given to correct a true thyroid deficiency and with properly adjusted dosage.

Advisability of Use While Nursing Infant
Thyroid hormones are present in milk. Nursing is safe when the mother's dose of thyroid hormones is correctly adjusted to maintain normal thyroid activity.

Habit-Forming Potential
None.

Effects of Overdosage
With Moderate Overdose: Sense of increased body heat, heart palpitation, nervousness, increased sweating, hand tremors, insomnia.

With Large Overdose: Rapid and irregular pulse, fever, headache, marked nervousness and irritability, diarrhea, weight loss, muscle spasm and cramping.

Possible Effects of Extended Use
None with correct dosage adjustment.

Recommended Periodic Examinations While Taking This Drug
Physician's assessment of response to treatment, with evaluation of subjective and objective changes due to thyroid hormone activity.

Measurement of thyroid hormone levels in the blood.

While Taking This Drug, Observe the Following
Foods: To improve absorption this drug should be taken on arising and before eating. Avoid heavy use of soybean preparations because of their ability to interfere with thyroid function.

Beverages: No restrictions.

Alcohol: No interactions expected.

Tobacco Smoking: No interactions expected.

Other Drugs

Thyroxine may *increase* the effects of

• stimulants such as Adrenalin, ephedrine, the amphetamines (Dexedrine), methylphenidate (Ritalin), etc., and cause excessive stimulation. Dosage adjustments may be necessary.

• oral anticoagulants of the coumarin family (see Drug Family, Section Four), and cause bleeding or hemorrhage. Reduction in dosage of the anticoagulant is usually necessary.

• tricyclic antidepressants (see Drug Family, Section Four).

• digitalis preparations. Careful dosage adjustment is necessary to prevent digitalis toxicity.

Thyroxine may *decrease* the effects of

• barbiturates, making larger doses necessary for effective sedation.

Thyroxine *taken concurrently* with

• all anti-diabetic drugs (insulin and oral anti-diabetic medications), may require an increase in the dosage of the anti-diabetic agent to obtain proper control of blood sugar levels. After correct doses of both drugs have been determined, a reduction in the dose of thyroid will require a simultaneous reduction in the dose of the anti-diabetic drug to prevent hypoglycemia.

• cortisone-like drugs, requires careful dosage adjustment to prevent the development of cortisone deficiency.

The following drugs may *increase* the effects of thyroxine

• aspirin (in large doses and with continuous use)
• phenytoin (Dantoin, Dilantin, etc.)

The following drugs may *decrease* the effects of thyroxine

• cholestyramine (Cuemid, Questran) may reduce its absorption. Intake of the two drugs should be 5 hours apart.

Driving a Vehicle, Piloting a Plane, Operating Machinery: No restrictions or precautions.

Exposure to Sun: No restrictions.

Exposure to Heat: This drug may decrease individual tolerance to warm environments, increasing discomfort due to heat. Avoid excessive sweating.

Exposure to Cold: This drug may increase individual tolerance to cold, decreasing the discomfort due to cold.

Heavy Exercise or Exertion: Use caution in the presence of angina and known coronary artery disease. This drug may increase the frequency of angina during physical activity.

Discontinuation: This drug must be taken continuously on a regular schedule to correct thyroid deficiency. Do not discontinue it without consulting your physician.

Special Storage Instructions
Keep in a dry, tightly closed container at room temperature. Protect from light.

TOLAZAMIDE

Year Introduced: 1966

Brand Names

USA	Canada
Tolinase (Upjohn)	None

Drug Family: Anti-diabetic, Oral (Hypoglycemic) [Sulfonylureas]

Prescription Required: Yes

Available Dosage Forms and Strengths
Tablets — 100 mg., 250 mg., 500 mg.

How This Drug Works

Intended Therapeutic Effect(s):   The correction of insulin deficiency in adult (maturity-onset) diabetes of moderate severity.

Location of Drug Action(s):   The insulin-producing tissues of the pancreas.

Method of Drug Action(s):   It is well established that sulfonylurea drugs stimulate the secretion of insulin (by a pancreas capable of responding to stimulation). Therapeutic doses may increase the amount of available insulin.

THIS DRUG SHOULD NOT BE TAKEN IF

—you have had an allergic reaction to any dosage form of it previously.

—you have a history of impaired liver function or kidney function.

INFORM YOUR PHYSICIAN BEFORE TAKING THIS DRUG IF

—your diabetes has been difficult to control in the past ("brittle type").

—you have a history of peptic ulcer of the stomach or duodenum.

—you have a history of porphyria.

—you do not know how to recognize or treat hypoglycemia (see Glossary).

Time Required for Apparent Benefit

A single dose may lower the blood sugar within 4 to 6 hours. Regular use for 1 to 2 weeks may be needed to determine this drug's effectiveness in controlling your diabetes.

Possible Side-Effects *(natural, expected, and unavoidable drug actions)*

Usually none. If drug dosage is excessive or food intake is inadequate, abnormally low blood sugar (hypoglycemia) will occur as a predictable drug effect.

CAUTION

The elderly (over 60 years of age) require smaller doses and are more likely to experience episodes of *prolonged* hypoglycemia when taking this drug.

Possible Adverse Effects *(unusual, unexpected, and infrequent reactions)*

IF ANY OF THE FOLLOWING DEVELOP, DISCONTINUE DRUG AND NOTIFY YOUR PHYSICIAN AS SOON AS POSSIBLE

Mild Adverse Effects

Allergic Reactions: Skin rashes (various kinds), hives, itching, drug fever. Headache, ringing in ears.

Indigestion, heartburn, nausea, diarrhea.

Serious Adverse Effects

Allergic Reactions: Hepatitis with jaundice (see Glossary).

Idiosyncratic Reactions: Hemolytic anemia in susceptible individuals (see Glossary).

Bone marrow depression (see Glossary)—fatigue, weakness, fever, sore throat, unusual bleeding or bruising.

Advisability of Use During Pregnancy

Safety not established. Prudent use is best determined by the physician's evaluation.

Advisability of Use While Nursing Infant
Drug is known to be present in milk. Ask physician for guidance.

Habit-Forming Potential
None.

Effects of Overdosage
With Moderate Overdose: Symptoms of mild to moderate hypoglycemia: headache, lightheadedness, faintness, nervousness, confusion, tremor, sweating, heart palpitation, weakness, and hunger.
With Large Overdose: Hypoglycemic coma (see Glossary).

Possible Effects of Extended Use
Reduced function of the thyroid gland (hypothyroidism), resulting in lowered metabolism.
Reports of increased frequency and severity of heart and blood vessel diseases associated with long-term use of the members of this drug family are highly controversial and inconclusive. A direct cause-and-effect relationship (see Glossary) has not been established to date. Ask your physician for guidance regarding extended use.

Recommended Periodic Examinations While Taking This Drug
Complete blood cell counts.
Liver function tests.
Thyroid function tests.
Periodic evaluation of heart and circulatory system.

While Taking This Drug, Observe the Following
Foods: Follow the diabetic diet prescribed by your physician.
Beverages: As directed in the diabetic diet prescribed by your physician.
Alcohol: Use with extreme caution until the combined effect has been determined. This drug can cause a marked intolerance to alcohol resulting in a disulfiram-like reaction (see Glossary).
Tobacco Smoking: No interactions expected. No restrictions unless imposed as part of your overall treatment program. Ask physician for guidance.
Other Drugs
Tolazamide may *increase* the effects of
• sedatives and sleep-inducing drugs, by slowing their elimination from the body.
• "sulfa" drugs, by slowing their elimination from the body.

Tolazamide *taken concurrently* with
• oral anticoagulants, may cause unpredictable changes in anticoagulant drug actions. Ask physician for guidance regarding prothrombin blood tests and dosage adjustment.
• propranolol (Inderal), may allow hypoglycemia to develop without adequate warning. Follow diet and dosage schedules very carefully.

The following drugs may *increase* the effects of tolazamide
• bishydroxycoumarin (Dicumarol, Dufalone)
• chloramphenicol (Chloromycetin, etc.)

• clofibrate (Atromid-S)
• mono-amine oxidase (MAO) inhibitors (see Drug Family, Section Four)
• oxyphenbutazone (Tandearil)
• phenformin (DBI)
• phenylbutazone (Azolid, Butazolidin, etc.)
• phenyramidol (Analexin)
• probenecid (Bememid)
• propranolol (Inderal)
• salicylates (aspirin, sodium salicylate)
• sulfaphenazole (Orisul, Sulfabid)
• sulfisoxazole (Gantrisin, Novosoxazole, etc.)

The following drugs may *decrease* the effects of tolazamide
• chlorpromazine (Thorazine, Largactil, etc.)
• cortisone and related drugs (see Drug Family, Section Four)
• estrogens (Premarin, Menotrol, Ogen, etc.)
• isoniazid (INH, Isozide, etc.)
• nicotinic acid (Niacin, etc.)
• oral contraceptives
• pyrazinamide (Aldinamide)
• thiazide diuretics (see Drug Family, Section Four)
• thyroid preparations (see Drug Family, Section Four)

Driving a Vehicle, Piloting a Plane, Operating Machinery: Regulate your dosage schedule, eating schedule and physical activities very carefully to prevent hypoglycemia. Be able to recognize the early symptoms of hypo- glycemia and avoid hazardous activities if you suspect that hypoglycemia is developing.

Exposure to Sun: Use caution until sensitivity has been determined. This drug can cause photosensitivity (see Glossary).

Exposure to Heat: No restrictions.

Exposure to Cold: No restrictions.

Heavy Exercise or Exertion: Use caution. Excessive exercise may result in hypoglycemia.

Occurrence of Unrelated Illness: Acute infections, illnesses causing vomit- ing or diarrhea, serious injuries, and the need for surgery can interfere with diabetic control and may require a change in medication. If any of these conditions occur, ask your physician for guidance regarding the continued use of this drug.

Discontinuation: If you find it necessary to discontinue this drug for any reason, notify your physician and ask for guidance regarding necessary changes in your treatment program for diabetic control.

Special Storage Instructions
Keep in a dry, tightly closed container.

TOLBUTAMIDE

Year Introduced: 1956

Brand Names

USA	Canada
Orinase (Upjohn)	Chembutamide (Chemo)
	Mellitol (Nordic)
	Mobenol (Horner)
	Neo-Dibetic (Neo)
	Novobutamide
	(Novopharm)
	Oramide (ICN)
	Orinase (Hoechst)
	Tolbutone (Maney)
	Wescotol (Saunders)

Drug Family: Anti-diabetic, Oral (Hypoglycemic) [Sulfonylureas]

Prescription Required: Yes

Available Dosage Forms and Strengths
Tablets — 500 mg.

How This Drug Works
Intended Therapeutic Effect(s): The correction of insulin deficiency in adult (maturity-onset) diabetes of moderate severity.
Location of Drug Action(s): The insulin-producing tissues of the pancreas.
Method of Drug Action(s): It is well established that sulfonylurea drugs stimulate the secretion of insulin (by a pancreas capable of responding to stimulation). Therapeutic doses may increase the amount of available insulin.

THIS DRUG SHOULD NOT BE TAKEN IF
—you are allergic to any of the drugs bearing the brand names listed above.
—you have severe impairment of liver function or kidney function.

INFORM YOUR PHYSICIAN BEFORE TAKING THIS DRUG IF
—your diabetes has been difficult to control in the past ("brittle type").
—you have a history of peptic ulcer of the stomach or duodenum.
—you have a history of porphyria.
—you do not know how to recognize or treat hypoglycemia (see Glossary).

Time Required For Apparent Benefit
A single dose may lower the blood sugar within 3 to 6 hours. Regular use for 1 to 2 weeks may be needed to determine this drug's effectiveness in controlling your diabetes.

Possible Side-Effects (natural, expected, and unavoidable drug actions)
Usually none. If drug dosage is excessive or food intake is inadequate, abnormally low blood sugar (hypoglycemia) will occur as a predictable drug effect (see Glossary).

CAUTION
The elderly (over 60 years of age) require smaller doses and are more likely to experience episodes of prolonged hypoglycemia when taking this drug.

Possible Adverse Effects *(unusual, unexpected, and infrequent reactions)*

IF ANY OF THE FOLLOWING DEVELOP, DISCONTINUE DRUG AND NOTIFY YOUR PHYSICIAN AS SOON AS POSSIBLE

Mild Adverse Effects
Allergic Reactions: Skin rashes (various kinds), hives, itching, drug fever.
Headache, ringing in ears.
Indigestion, heartburn, nausea, diarrhea.

Serious Adverse Effects
Allergic Reactions: Hepatitis with jaundice (see Glossary).
Idiosyncratic Reactions: Hemolytic anemia (see Glossary).
Bone marrow depression (see Glossary)—fatigue, weakness, fever, sore throat, unusual bleeding or bruising.

Advisability of Use During Pregnancy
Safety not established. Prudent use is best determined by the physician's evaluation.

Advisability of Use While Nursing Infant
Drug is known to be present in milk. Ask physician for guidance.

Habit-Forming Potential
None.

Effects of Overdosage
With Moderate Overdose: Symptoms of mild to moderate hypoglycemia: headache, lightheadedness, faintness, nervousness, confusion, tremor, sweating, heart palpitation, weakness and hunger.
With Large Overdose: Hypoglycemic coma (see Glossary).

Possible Effects of Extended Use
Reduced function of the thyroid gland (hypothyroidism), resulting in lowered metabolism.
Reports of increased frequency and severity of heart and blood vessel diseases associated with long-term use of the members of this drug family are highly controversial and inconclusive. A direct cause-and-effect relationship (see Glossary) has not been established to date. Ask your physician for guidance regarding extended use.

Recommended Periodic Examinations While Taking This Drug
Complete blood cell counts.
Liver function tests.
Thyroid function tests.
Periodic evaluation of heart and circulatory system.

While Taking This Drug, Observe the Following
Foods: Follow the diabetic diet prescribed by your physician.
Beverages: As directed in the diabetic diet prescribed by your physician.

Alcohol: Use with extreme caution until the combined effect has been determined. This drug can cause a marked intolerance to alcohol, resulting in a disulfiram-like reaction (see Glossary).

Tobacco Smoking: No restrictions unless imposed as part of your overall treatment program. Ask physician for guidance.

Other Drugs

Tolbutamide may *increase* the effects of

- sedatives and sleep-inducing drugs, by slowing their elimination from the body.
- "sulfa" drugs, by slowing their elimination from the body.

Tolbutamide *taken concurrently* with

- oral anticoagulants, may cause unpredictable changes in anticoagulant drug actions. Ask physician for guidance regarding prothrombin blood tests and dosage adjustments.
- propranolol (Inderal), may allow hypoglycemia to develop without adequate warning. Follow diet and dosage schedules very carefully.

The following drugs may *increase* the effects of tolbutamide

- anabolic drugs (Adroyd, Anavar, Dianabol, etc.)
- oral anticoagulants of the coumarin type (see Drug Family, Section Four)
- chloramphenicol (Chloromycetin, etc.)
- clofibrate (Atromid-S)
- fenfluramine (Pondimin)
- guanethidine (Ismelin)
- mono-amine oxidase (MAO) inhibitors (see Drug Family, Section Four)
- oxyphenbutazone (Oxalid, Tandearil)
- phenformin (DBI)
- phenylbutazone (Azolid, Butazolidin, etc.)
- phenyramidol (Analexin)
- probenecid (Bememid)
- propranolol (Inderal)
- salicylates (aspirin, sodium salicylate)
- sulfaphenazole (Orisul, Sulfabid)
- sulfinpyrazone (Anturane)
- sulfisoxazole (Gantrisin, Novosoxazole, etc.)

The following drugs may *decrease* the effects of tolbutamide

- chlorpromazine (Thorazine, Largactil, etc.)
- cortisone and related drugs (see Drug Family, Section Four)
- ethacrynic acid (Edecrin)
- estrogens (Premarin, Menotrol, Ogen, etc.)
- furosemide (Lasix)
- isoniazid (INH, Isozide, etc.)
- nicotinic acid (Niacin, etc.)
- oral contraceptives
- pyrazinamide (Aldinamide)
- thiazide diuretics (see Drug Family, Section Four)
- thyroid preparations (see Drug Family, Section Four)

Driving a Vehicle, Piloting a Plane, Operating Machinery: Regulate your dosage schedule, eating schedule, and physical activities very carefully to prevent hypoglycemia. Be able to recognize the early symptoms of hypoglycemia and avoid hazardous activities if you suspect that hypoglycemia is developing.

Exposure to Sun: Use caution until sensitivity has been determined. This drug can cause photosensitivity (see Glossary).

Heavy Exercise or Exertion: Use caution. Excessive exercise may result in hypoglycemia.

Occurrence of Unrelated Illness: Acute infections, illnesses causing vomiting or diarrhea, serious injuries, and the need for surgery can interfere with diabetic control and may require a change in medication. If any of these conditions occur, ask your physician for guidance regarding the continued use of this drug.

Discontinuation: If you find it necessary to discontinue this drug for any reason, notify your physician and ask for guidance regarding necessary changes in your treatment program for diabetic control.

Special Storage Instructions
Keep in a dry, tightly closed container.

TRIAMCINOLONE

Year Introduced: 1958

Brand Names

USA	Canada
Aristocort (Lederle)	Aristocort (Lederle)
Kenacort (Squibb)	Kenacort (Squibb)

Drug Family: Cortisone-like Drug [Adrenocortical Steroids (Glucocorticoids)]

Prescription Required: Yes

Available Dosage Forms and Strengths
Tablets — 1 mg., 2 mg., 4 mg., 8 mg., 16 mg.
Syrup — 2 mg. and 4 mg. per teaspoonful
Cream — 0.025%, 0.1%, 0.5%
Ointment — 0.1%, 0.5%

How This Drug Works
Intended Therapeutic Effect(s): The symptomatic relief of inflammation (swelling, redness, heat and pain) in any tissue, and from many causes. (Cortisone-like drugs do not correct the underlying disease process).

Location of Drug Action(s):   Significant biological effects occur in most tissues throughout the body. The principal actions of therapeutic doses occur at sites of inflammation and/or allergic reaction, regardless of the nature of the causative injury or illness.

Method of Drug Action(s):   Not completely established. Present thinking is that cortisone-like drugs probably inhibit several mechanisms within the tissues that induce inflammation. Well-regulated dosage aids the body in restoring normal stability. However, prolonged use or excessive dosage can impair the body's defense mechanisms against infectious disease.

THIS DRUG SHOULD NOT BE TAKEN IF

—you have had an allergic reaction to any dosage form of it previously.

—you have an active peptic ulcer (stomach or duodenum).

—you have an active infection of the eye caused by the herpes simplex virus (ask your eye doctor for guidance).

—you have active tuberculosis.

INFORM YOUR PHYSICIAN BEFORE TAKING THIS DRUG IF

—you have had an unfavorable reaction to any cortisone-like drug in the past.

—you have a history of tuberculosis.

—you have diabetes or a tendency to diabetes.

—you have a history of peptic ulcer disease.

—you have glaucoma or a tendency to glaucoma.

—you have a deficiency of thyroid function (hypothyroidism).

—you have high blood pressure.

—you have myasthenia gravis.

—you have a history of thrombophlebitis.

—you plan to have surgery of any kind in the near future, especially if under general anesthesia.

Time Required for Apparent Benefit

Evidence of beneficial drug action is usually apparent in 24 to 48 hours. Dosage must be individualized to give reasonable improvement. This is usually accomplished in 4 to 10 days. It is unwise to demand complete relief of all symptoms. The effective dose varies with the nature of the disease and with the patient. During long-term use it is essential that the smallest effective dose be determined and maintained.

Possible Side-Effects *(natural, expected, and unavoidable drug actions)*

Flushing of the face, increased sweating, increased susceptibility to infection.

CAUTION

1. It is advisable to carry a card of personal identification with a notation that you are taking this drug if your course of treatment is to exceed 1 week (see Table 14 and Section Seven).
2. Do not discontinue this drug abruptly.
3. While taking this drug, immunization procedures should be given with caution. If vaccination against measles, smallpox, rabies, or yellow fever is required, discontinue this drug 72 hours before vaccination and do not resume for at least 14 days after vaccination.

Possible Adverse Effects *(unusual, unexpected, and infrequent reactions)*

IF ANY OF THE FOLLOWING DEVELOP, DISCONTINUE DRUG AND NOTIFY
YOUR PHYSICIAN AS SOON AS POSSIBLE

Mild Adverse Effects
Allergic Reactions: Skin rash.
Headache, dizziness, insomnia.
Acid indigestion, abdominal distention.
Muscle cramping and weakness.
Irregular menstrual periods.
Acne, excessive growth of facial hair.

Serious Adverse Effects
Mental and emotional disturbances of serious magnitude.
Reactivation of latent tuberculosis.
Development of peptic ulcer.
Increased blood pressure.
Development of inflammation of the pancreas.
Thrombophlebitis (inflammation of a vein with the formation of blood clot)
—pain or tenderness in thigh or leg, with or without swelling of the foot,
ankle, or leg.
Pulmonary embolism (movement of blood clot to the lung)—sudden short-
ness of breath, pain in the chest, coughing, bloody sputum.

Advisability of Use During Pregnancy
Safety has not been established. If possible, avoid completely. If use of this
drug is considered necessary, limit dosage and duration of use as much as
possible. Following birth, the infant should be examined for possible defective function of the adrenal glands (deficiency of adrenal cortical hormones).

Advisability of Use While Nursing Infant
Drug is known to be present in milk. Ask physician for guidance.

Habit-Forming Potential
Use of this drug to suppress symptoms over an extended period of time may
produce a state of functional dependence (see Glossary). In the treatment of
conditions like rheumatoid arthritis and asthma, it is advisable to try alternate-day drug administration to keep the daily dose as small as possible, and
to attempt drug withdrawal after periods of reasonable improvement. Such
procedures may reduce the degree of "steroid rebound"—the return of
symptoms as the drug is withdrawn.

Effects of Overdosage
With Moderate Overdose: Fatigue, muscle weakness, stomach irritation,
acid indigestion, excessive sweating.
With Large Overdose: Marked flushing of the face, muscle cramping, emotional depression, erratic behavior.

Possible Effects of Extended Use
Development of increased blood sugar, possibly diabetes.
Increased fat deposits on the trunk of the body ("buffalo hump"), rounding
of the face ("moon face"), and thinning of the arms and legs.

Thinning and fragility of the skin, easy bruising.
Loss of texture and strength of the bones, resulting in spontaneous fractures.
Development of increased internal eye pressure, possibly glaucoma.
Development of cataracts.
Retarded growth and development in children.

Recommended Periodic Examinations While Taking This Drug
Measurement of blood potassium levels.
Measurement of blood sugar levels 2 hours after eating.
Measurement of blood pressure at regular intervals.
Complete eye examination at regular intervals.
Chest X-ray if history of previous tuberculosis.
Determination of the rate of development of the growing child to detect retardation of normal growth.

While Taking This Drug, Observe the Following
Foods: No interactions. Consult physician regarding need to restrict salt intake or to eat potassium-rich foods. During long-term use of this drug it is advisable to have a high protein diet.

Beverages: No restrictions.

Alcohol: No interactions expected.

Tobacco Smoking: Nicotine increases the blood levels of naturally-produced cortisone and related hormones. Heavy smoking may add to the expected actions of this drug and requires close observation for excessive effects.

Other Drugs
Triamcinolone may *increase* the effects of
- barbiturates and other sedatives and sleep-inducing drugs, causing over-sedation.

Triamcinolone may *decrease* the effects of
- insulin and oral anti-diabetic drugs, by raising the level of blood sugar. Doses of anti-diabetic drugs may have to be raised.
- anticoagulants of the coumarin family. Monitor prothrombin times closely and adjust dosage accordingly.
- choline-like drugs (Mestinon, pilocarpine, Prostigmin), and reduce their effectiveness in treating glaucoma and myasthenia gravis.

Triamcinolone *taken concurrently* with
- thiazide diuretics, may cause excessive loss of potassium. Monitor blood levels of potassium on physician's advice.
- atropine-like drugs, may cause increased internal eye pressure and initiate or aggravate glaucoma (see Drug Family, Section Four).
- digitalis preparations, requires close monitoring of body potassium stores to prevent digitalis toxicity.
- stimulant drugs (Adrenalin, amphetamines, ephedrine, etc.), may increase internal eye pressure and initiate or aggravate glaucoma.

The following drugs may *increase* the effects of triamcinolone:
- indomethacin (Indocin, Indocid)
- aspirin

The following drugs may *decrease* the effects of triamcinolone:
- barbiturates
- phenytoin (Dantoin, Dilantin, etc.)
- antihistamines
- chloral hydrate (Noctec, Somnos)
- glutethimide (Doriden)
- phenylbutazone (Azolid, Butazolidin, etc.) may reduce its effectiveness following a brief, initial increase in effectiveness.
- propranolol (Inderal)

Driving a Vehicle, Piloting a Plane, Operating Machinery: No restrictions or precautions.

Exposure to Sun: No restrictions.

Occurrence of Unrelated Illness

This drug may decrease natural resistance to infection. Notify your physician if you develop an infection of any kind.

This drug may reduce your body's ability to respond appropriately to the stress of acute illness, injury, or surgery. Keep your physician fully informed of any significant changes in your state of health.

Discontinuation

If you have been taking this drug for an extended period of time, do not discontinue it abruptly. Ask physician for guidance regarding gradual withdrawal.

For a period of 2 years after discontinuing this drug, it is essential in the event of illness, injury, or surgery that you inform attending medical personnel that you used this drug in the past. The period of inadequate response to stress following the use of cortisone-like drugs may last for 1 to 2 years.

Special Storage Instructions

Keep in a tightly closed container. Protect from light.

TRIAMTERENE

Year Introduced: 1964

Brand Names

USA	Canada
Dyrenium (Smith Kline & French)	Dyrenium (SK&F)
Dyazide [CD] (Smith Kline & French)	Dyazide [CD] (SK&F)

Drug Family: Anti-hypertensive (Hypotensive); Diuretic

Prescription Required: Yes

Available Dosage Forms and Strengths
Capsules — 100 mg.

How This Drug Works
Intended Therapeutic Effect(s):   Elimination of excessive fluid retention (edema) without loss of potassium from the body.

Location of Drug Action(s):   The tubular systems of the kidney that determine the final composition of the urine.

Method of Drug Action(s):   By increasing the elimination of salt and water but not potassium from the body (through increased urine production), this drug reduces the volume of fluid in the blood and body tissues and lowers the sodium content throughout the body.

THIS DRUG SHOULD NOT BE TAKEN IF
—you have had an allergic reaction to any dosage form of it previously.
—you have a history of severe liver or kidney disease with impaired function of either.

INFORM YOUR PHYSICIAN BEFORE TAKING THIS DRUG IF
—you have a history of gout.
—you have diabetes.
—you are taking any form of digitalis.

Time Required for Apparent Benefit
Increased volume of urine begins in 2 hours and persists for 8 to 12 hours. Maximal effectiveness in removing fluid from the body may require 2 to 3 days. Usefulness in treatment of high blood pressure may require regular use for 2 to 3 weeks.

Possible Side-Effects *(natural, expected, and unavoidable drug actions)*
Blue coloration of the urine, of no significance. Usually no other side effects, unless there is *excessive* loss of salt and water from the body or *excessive* retention of potassium (see Effects of Overdosage, below).

CAUTION
It is not advisable to use potassium supplements or to deliberately increase your intake of potassium-rich foods while using this diuretic drug.

Possible Adverse Effects *(unusual, unexpected, and infrequent reactions)*

IF ANY OF THE FOLLOWING DEVELOP, DISCONTINUE DRUG AND NOTIFY YOUR PHYSICIAN AS SOON AS POSSIBLE

Mild Adverse Effects
Allergic Reactions: Skin rash.
Nausea, vomiting, diarrhea, dryness of mouth.
Headache, weakness, dizziness.

Serious Adverse Effects
Allergic Reactions: Anaphylactic reaction (see Glossary).
Bone marrow depression (see Glossary), resulting in anemia.

Advisability of Use During Pregnancy
Safety not established. Prudent use is best determined by the physician's evaluation.

Advisability of Use While Nursing Infant
Drug is known to be present in milk. Ask physician for guidance.

Habit-Forming Potential
None.

Effects of Overdosage
With Moderate Overdose: Imbalance of body water, salt, and potassium, causing drowsiness, fatigue, weakness, nausea, vomiting, thirst.
With Large Overdose: Marked lethargy, irregular heart action.

Possible Effects of Extended Use
Retention of potassium in the body, resulting in blood potassium levels above the normal range. This can have an adverse effect on the regulation of heart rhythm and performance.

Recommended Periodic Examinations While Taking This Drug
Complete blood cell counts.
Liver function tests.
Kidney function tests.
Measurement of blood sodium, chloride, and potassium levels.

While Taking This Drug, Observe the Following
Foods: Do not restrict the intake of salt (or salted foods) unless directed to do so by your physician.
Beverages: No restrictions.
Alcohol: No interactions expected.
Tobacco Smoking: No interactions expected.
Other Drugs
Triamterene may *increase* the effects of
• other anti-hypertensive drugs. Dosage adjustments are necessary to avoid excessive lowering of blood pressure.

Triamterene may *decrease* the effects of
• oral anti-diabetic drugs. Ask for guidance regarding dosage adjustments to insure proper diabetic control.
• digitalis preparations, if excessive potassium is retained in the body.

Triamterene *taken concurrently* with
• spironolactone, may cause excessive (dangerous) retention of potassium in the body. Concurrent use of these two drugs should be avoided.
Driving a Vehicle, Piloting a Plane, Operating Machinery: No restrictions unless drowsiness or dizziness occurs.
Exposure to Sun: Use caution until sensitivity has been determined. This drug may cause photosensitivity (see Glossary).
Heavy Exercise or Exertion: No restrictions.

Discontinuation: This drug should be discontinued gradually to prevent a rapid loss of potassium from the body that could occur with sudden discontinuation. Consult physician for guidance regarding the need to adjust the dosage schedule of the following drugs taken concurrently with triamterene: anti-diabetic drugs, anti-hypertensives, digitalis preparations.

Special Storage Instructions
Keep in a dry, tightly closed, light-resistant container.

TRIDIHEXETHYL

Year Introduced: 1955

Brand Names

USA	Canada
Pathilon (Lederle)	Pathibamate [CD]
Milpath [CD] (Wallace)	(Lederle)
Pathibamate [CD]	
(Lederle)	

Drug Family: Antispasmodic, Atropine-like Drug [Anticholinergics]

Prescription Required: Yes

Available Dosage Forms and Strengths
Tablets — 25 mg.
Prolonged Action Capsules — 75 mg.
Injection — 10 mg. per ml.

How This Drug Works
Intended Therapeutic Effect(s):   Relief of discomfort resulting from excessive activity and spasm of the digestive tract (esophagus, stomach, intestine, and colon).

Location of Drug Action(s):   The terminal nerve fibers of the parasympathetic nervous system that control the activity of the gastrointestinal tract.

Method of Drug Action(s):   By blocking the action of the chemical (acetylcholine) that transmits impulses at parasympathetic nerve endings, this drug prevents stimulation of muscular contraction and glandular secretion within the organ involved. This results in reduced overall activity, including the prevention or relief of muscle spasms.

THIS DRUG SHOULD NOT BE TAKEN IF
—you have had an allergic reaction to any dosage form of it previously.
—your stomach cannot empty properly into the intestine (pyloric obstruction).
—you are unable to empty the urinary bladder completely.
—you have glaucoma (narrow-angle type).
—you have severe ulcerative colitis.

INFORM YOUR PHYSICIAN BEFORE TAKING THIS DRUG IF
—you have glaucoma (open-angle type).
—you have angina or coronary heart disease.
—you have chronic bronchitis.
—you have a hiatal hernia.
—you have enlargement of the prostate gland.
—you have myasthenia gravis.
—you have a history of peptic ulcer disease.
—you plan to have surgery under general anesthesia in the near future.

Time Required for Apparent Benefit
Drug action begins in 1 to 2 hours and persists for approximately 4 hours.

Possible Side-Effects *(natural, expected, and unavoidable drug actions)*
Blurring of vision (impairment of focus), dryness of the mouth and throat, constipation, hesitancy in urination. (Nature and degree of side effects depend upon individual susceptibility and drug dosage.)

CAUTION
The elderly (over 60 years of age) may be more susceptible to all of the actions of this drug. Small doses are advisable until response has been determined.

Possible Adverse Effects *(unusual, unexpected, and infrequent reactions)*

IF ANY OF THE FOLLOWING DEVELOP, DISCONTINUE DRUG AND NOTIFY YOUR PHYSICIAN AS SOON AS POSSIBLE

Mild Adverse Effects
  Allergic Reactions: Skin rash, hives.
  Dilation of pupils, causing sensitivity to light.
  Flushing and dryness of the skin (reduced sweating).
  Rapid heart action.
  Lightheadedness, dizziness, unsteady gait.
Serious Adverse Effects
  Idiosyncratic Reactions: Acute confusion, delirium, and erratic behavior.
  Development of acute glaucoma (in susceptible individuals).

Advisability of Use During Pregnancy
Safety not established. Prudent use is best determined by the physician's evaluation.

Advisability of Use While Nursing Infant
This drug may impair the formation of milk and make nursing difficult. It is known to be present in milk. Ask physician for guidance.

Habit-Forming Potential
None.

Effects of Overdosage
  With Moderate Overdose: Marked dryness of the mouth, dilated pupils, blurring of near vision, rapid pulse, heart palpitation, headache, difficulty in urination.

With Large Overdose: Extremely dilated pupils, rapid pulse and breathing, hot skin, high fever, excitement, confusion, hallucinations, delirium, eventual loss of consciousness, convulsions, and coma.

Possible Effects of Extended Use
Chronic constipation, severe enough to result in fecal impaction. (Constipation should be treated promptly with effective laxatives.)

Recommended Periodic Examinations While Taking This Drug
Measurement of internal eye pressure to detect any significant increase that could indicate developing glaucoma.

While Taking This Drug, Observe the Following
Foods: No interaction with drug. Effectiveness is greater if drug is taken one-half to 1 hour before eating. Follow diet prescribed for condition under treatment.

Beverages: No interactions. As allowed by prescribed diet.

Alcohol: No interactions expected with this drug. Follow physician's advice regarding use of alcohol (based upon its effect on the condition under treatment).

Tobacco Smoking: No interactions expected. Follow physician's advice regarding smoking.

Other Drugs

Tridihexethyl may *increase* the effects of

• all other drugs having atropine-like actions (see Drug Family, Section Four).

Tridihexethyl may *decrease* the effects of

• pilocarpine eye drops, and reduce their effectiveness in lowering internal eye pressure in the treatment of glaucoma.

Tridihexethyl *taken concurrently* with

• mono-amine oxidase (MAO) inhibitor drugs (see Drug Family, Section Four), may cause an exaggerated response to normal doses of atropine-like drugs. It is best to avoid atropine-like drugs for 2 weeks after the last dose of any MAO inhibitor drug.

• haloperidol (Haldol), may significantly increase internal eye pressure, dangerous in glaucoma.

The following drugs may *increase* the effects of tridihexethyl:

• tricyclic antidepressants
• those antihistamines that have an atropine-like action
• meperidine (Demerol, pethidine)
• methylphenidate (Ritalin)
• orphenadrine (Disipal, Norflex)
• those phenothiazines that have an atropine-like action
(see Drug Family, Section Four, for specific brand names)

Driving a Vehicle, Piloting a Plane, Operating Machinery: This drug may produce blurred vision, drowsiness, or dizziness. Avoid hazardous activities if these drug effects occur.

Exposure to Sun: No restrictions.

Exposure to Heat: Use extreme caution. The use of this drug in hot environments may significantly increase the risk of heat stroke.

Heavy Exercise or Exertion: Use caution in warm or hot environments. This drug may impair normal perspiration (heat loss) and interfere with the regulation of body temperature.

Special Storage Instructions
Keep in a tightly closed container. Protect from light.

TRIFLUOPERAZINE

Year Introduced: 1958

Brand Names

USA	Canada
Stelazine (Smith Kline & French)	Chemflurazine (Chemo)
	Clinazine (M & M)
	Dymoperazine (Dymond)
	Novoflurazine (Novopharm)
	Pentazine (Pentagone)
	Solazine (Horner)
	Stelazine (SK&F)
	Terfluzine (ICN)
	Trifluoper-Ez-Ets (Barlowe Cote)
	Triflurin (Maney)

Drug Family: Tranquilizer, Strong (Anti-psychotic) [Phenothiazines]

Prescription Required: Yes

Available Dosage Forms and Strengths
Tablets — 1 mg., 2 mg., 5 mg., 10 mg.
Concentrate — 10 mg. per ml.
Injection — 2 mg. per ml.

How This Drug Works
Intended Therapeutic Effect(s):   Restoration of emotional calm. Relief of severe anxiety, agitation, and psychotic behavior.

Location of Drug Action(s):   Those nerve pathways in the brain that utilize the tissue chemical dopamine for the transmission of nerve impulses.

Method of Drug Action(s):   Not completely established. Present theory is that by inhibiting the action of dopamine, this drug acts to correct an imbalance of nerve impulse transmissions that is thought to be responsible for certain mental disorders.

THIS DRUG SHOULD NOT BE TAKEN IF
—you have had an allergic reaction to any dosage form of it previously.
—you have a blood or bone marrow disorder.
—you have impaired liver function.

INFORM YOUR PHYSICIAN BEFORE TAKING THIS DRUG IF
—you are allergic or sensitive to any phenothiazine drug (see Drug Family, Section Four).
—you are taking any sedatives, sleep-inducing drugs, other tranquilizers, antidepressants, antihistamines, or narcotic drugs of any kind.
—you have angina (coronary heart disease).
—you have epilepsy.
—you have glaucoma.
—you have a lung disorder, especially asthma or emphysema.
—you plan to have surgery under general or spinal anesthesia in the near future.

Time Required for Apparent Benefit
Approximately 1 to 2 hours. In treating nervous and mental disorders, maximal benefit may require regular use for several weeks.

Possible Side-Effects *(natural, expected, and unavoidable drug actions)*
Drowsiness, blurring of vision, nasal congestion, dryness of mouth, constipation, impaired urination.

Possible Adverse Effects *(unusual, unexpected, and infrequent reactions)*
IF ANY OF THE FOLLOWING DEVELOP, DISCONTINUE DRUG AND NOTIFY YOUR PHYSICIAN AS SOON AS POSSIBLE

Mild Adverse Effects
Allergic Reactions: Skin rashes (various kinds), hives, low-grade fever.
Dizziness, fatigue, weakness.
Agitation, restlessness, insomnia.
Menstrual irregularity, breast congestion, milk formation.

Serious Adverse Effects
Parkinson-like disorders (see Glossary).
Spasms of the muscles of the face, neck, back, and extremities, causing rolling of the eyes, grimacing, clamping of the jaw, protrusion of the tongue, difficulty in swallowing, arching of the back, cramping of the hands and feet.

Advisability of Use During Pregnancy
Safety not established. Prudent is best determined by the physician's evaluation.

Advisability of Use While Nursing Infant
Drug is known to be present in milk. Ask physician for guidance.

Habit-Forming Potential
None.

Effects of Overdosage
With Moderate Overdose: Marked drowsiness, weakness, tremor, restlessness, agitation.

With Large Overdose: Stupor, deep sleep, coma, convulsions.

Possible Effects of Extended Use
Tardive dyskinesia (see Glossary).

Recommended Periodic Examinations While Taking This Drug
Complete blood cell counts, especially during first 3 months of treatment.

Careful inspection of the tongue for early evidence of fine, involuntary, wave-like movements that could indicate the beginning of tardive dyskinesia.

While Taking This Drug, Observe the Following
Foods: No restrictions.

Beverages: No restrictions.

Alcohol: Use with extreme caution until combined effect has been determined. Alcohol can increase the sedative action of trifluoperazine and accentuate its depressant effects on brain function. Trifluoperazine may increase the intoxicating effects of alcohol.

Tobacco Smoking: No interactions expected.

Other Drugs

Trifluoperazine may *increase* the effects of
• all sedatives, sleep-inducing drugs, other tranquilizers, antihistamines, and narcotic drugs, and produce oversedation. Ask physician for guidance regarding dosage adjustment.
• all drugs containing atropine or having an atropine-like action (see Drug Family, Section Four).
• phenytoin (Dantoin, Dilantin, etc.).

Trifluoperazine may *decrease* the effects of
• levodopa (Dopar, Larodopa, etc.), and reduce its effectiveness in the treatment of Parkinson's disease (shaking palsy).
• appetite suppressant drugs (Pre-Sate, Preludin, Benzedrine, Dexedrine, etc.).

Trifluoperazine *taken concurrently* with
• quinidine, may impair heart function. Avoid the combined use of these two drugs.

The following drugs may *increase* the effects of trifluoperazine
• tricyclic antidepressants (see Drug Family, Section Four)

Driving a Vehicle, Piloting a Plane, Operating Machinery: This drug can impair mental alertness, judgment, and physical coordination. Avoid hazardous activities.

Exposure to Sun: Use caution. Drugs closely related to trifluoperazine are known to produce photosensitivity (see Glossary).

Exposure to Heat: Use caution and avoid excessive heat. This drug may impair the regulation of body temperature and increase the risk of heat stroke.

Heavy Exercise or Exertion: Use caution and follow your physician's instructions if you have angina.

Discontinuation: If it has been necessary to use this drug for an extended period of time, do not discontinue it suddenly. Ask physician for guidance regarding dosage reduction and withdrawal. Upon discontinuation of this drug, it may also be necessary to adjust the dosages of other drugs taken concurrently with it.

Special Storage Instructions
Keep in a tightly closed, light-resistant container.

TRIHEXYPHENIDYL

Year Introduced: 1949

Brand Names

USA	Canada
Artane (Lederle)	Aparkane (ICN)
Pipanol (Winthrop)	Artane (Lederle)
Tremin (Schering)	Novohexidyl
	(Novopharm)
	Trihexy (Barlowe Cote)
	Trixyl (Maney)

Drug Family: Anti-parkinsonism; Atropine-like drug [Anticholinergics]

Prescription Required: Yes

Available Dosage Forms and Strengths
Tablets — 2 mg., 5 mg.
Prolonged Action Capsules — 5 mg.
Elixir — 2 mg. per teaspoonful

How This Drug Works
Intended Therapeutic Effect(s):   Relief of the rigidity, tremor, sluggish movement, and impaired gait associated with Parkinson's disease.

Location of Drug Action(s):   The principal site of the desired therapeutic action is the regulating center in the brain (the basal ganglia) which governs the coordination and efficiency of bodily movements.

Method of Drug Action(s):   The improvement in Parkinson's disease results from the restoration of a more normal balance of the chemical activities responsible for the transmission of nerve impulses within the basal ganglia.

THIS DRUG SHOULD NOT BE TAKEN IF
—you have had an allergic reaction to any dosage form of it previously.
—it is prescribed for a child under 3 years of age.

INFORM YOUR PHYSICIAN BEFORE TAKING THIS DRUG IF
—you have experienced an unfavorable response to atropine or atropine-like drugs in the past.
—you have glaucoma.
—you have high blood pressure or heart disease.
—you have a history of liver or kidney disease.
—you have difficulty emptying the urinary bladder.

Time Required for Apparent Benefit
Drug action begins in approximately 1 hour and persists for 3 to 6 hours. Adjustment of dosage according to individual response is necessary. Regular use for several weeks may be necessary to determine the most satisfactory dosage schedule.

Possible Side-Effects *(natural, expected, and unavoidable drug actions)*
Nervousness, blurring of vision, dryness of the mouth, constipation. (These often subside as drug use continues.)

CAUTION
The elderly (over 60 years of age) are often more sensitive to the actions of this drug. Small doses are advisable until tolerance has been determined.

Possible Adverse Effects *(unusual, unexpected, and infrequent reactions)*

IF ANY OF THE FOLLOWING DEVELOP, DISCONTINUE DRUG AND NOTIFY YOUR PHYSICIAN AS SOON AS POSSIBLE

Mild Adverse Effects
    Allergic Reactions: Skin rashes.
    Drowsiness, dizziness, headache.
    Nausea, vomiting.
    Urinary hesitancy, difficulty emptying bladder.
Serious Adverse Effects
    Idiosyncratic Reactions: Confusion, delusions, hallucinations, agitation, erratic behavior.

Advisability of Use During Pregnancy
Safety not established. Prudent use is best determined by the physician's evaluation.

Advisability of Use While Nursing Infant
Drug is present in milk in small quantities. Safety for infant not established. Ask physician for guidance.

Habit-Forming Potential
Extended use of large doses can produce euphoria in some individuals. It is advisable to keep the dose at the smallest effective level (see dependence, psychological, in Glossary).

Effects of Overdosage
    With Moderate Overdose: Drowsiness, stupor, weakness, impaired vision, rapid pulse.
    With Large Overdose: Excitement, confusion, agitation, hallucinations, dry and hot skin, generalized skin rash, markedly dilated pupils.

Possible Effects of Extended Use
Increased internal eye pressure, possibly glaucoma.

Recommended Periodic Examinations While Taking This Drug
Measurement of internal eye pressure (glaucoma detection) at regular intervals.

While Taking This Drug, Observe the Following
Foods: No restrictions. Drug may be taken after food if it causes indigestion.

Beverages: No restrictions.

Alcohol: No interactions expected.

Tobacco Smoking: No interactions expected.

Other Drugs

Trihexyphenidyl may *increase* the effects of
- levodopa (Dopar, Larodopa, etc.), and improve its effectiveness in the treatment of parkinsonism.
- mild and strong tranquilizers, and cause excessive sedation.

Trihexyphenidyl *taken concurrently* with
- cortisone (and related drugs) on an extended basis, may cause an increase in internal eye pressure, possibly glaucoma.
- primidone (Mysoline), may cause excessive sedation.
- phenothiazine drugs, may cause (in sensitive individuals) severe behavioral disturbances (toxic psychosis).

The following drugs may *increase* the effects of trihexyphenidyl
- antihistamines may increase the dryness of mouth and throat.
- tricyclic antidepressants may increase internal eye pressure, dangerous in glaucoma.
- mono-amine oxidase (MAO) inhibitor drugs (see Drug Family, Section Four) may increase all effects of this drug.
- meperidine (Demerol)
- methylphenidate (Ritalin)
- orphenadrine (Disipal, Norflex)
- quinidine

Driving a Vehicle, Piloting a Plane, Operating Machinery: Drowsiness and dizziness may occur in sensitive individuals. Avoid hazardous activities until full effects and tolerance have been determined.

Exposure to Sun: No restrictions.

Exposure to Heat: Use caution. This drug may reduce sweating, cause an increase in body temperature, and contribute to the development of heat stroke.

Heavy Exercise or Exertion: Avoid in hot environments.

Discontinuation: Do not discontinue this drug suddenly. Ask physician for guidance in reducing dose gradually.

Special Storage Instructions
Keep in a dry, tightly closed container. Protect from light.

TRIMEPRAZINE

Year Introduced: 1958

Brand Names

USA	Canada
Temaril (Smith Kline & French)	Panectyl (Poulenc)

Drug Family: Anti-itching (Antipruritic) [Phenothiazines]

Prescription Required: Yes

Available Dosage Forms and Strengths
Tablets — 2.5 mg., 5 mg., 10 mg.
Prolonged Action Capsules — 5 mg.
Syrup — 2.5 mg. per teaspoonful

How This Drug Works
Intended Therapeutic Effect(s):   Relief of itching associated with hives, allergic dermatitis, chicken pox, and other skin disorders.
Location of Drug Action(s):   Those hypersensitive areas of the skin that release excessive histamine as part of an allergic reaction.
Method of Drug Action(s):   This drug reduces the intensity of the allergic response by blocking the action of histamine after it has been released from sensitized tissue cells. In addition, it produces a mild sedative effect.

THIS DRUG SHOULD NOT BE TAKEN IF
—you have had an allergic reaction to any dosage form of it previously.
—you have a blood or bone marrow disorder.
—it is prescribed for an infant under 6 months of age.
—the prolonged action capsule is prescribed for a child under 6 years of age.

INFORM YOUR PHYSICIAN BEFORE TAKING THIS DRUG IF
—you are allergic or sensitive to any phenothiazine drug (see Drug Family, Section Four).
—you are taking any sedatives, sleep-inducing drugs, tranquilizers, other antihistamines, antidepressants, or narcotic drugs of any kind.
—you have a history of recurring peptic ulcer.
—you have a history of prostate gland enlargement.
—you plan to have surgery under general anesthesia in the near future.

Time Required for Apparent Benefit
Usually 1 to 2 hours.

Possible Side-Effects *(natural, expected, and unavoidable drug actions)*
Drowsiness, blurred vision, dryness of the mouth, inability to concentrate.

CAUTION
Children with acute illness ("flu"-like infections, measles, chickenpox, etc.) are very susceptible to adverse effects, involving muscular spasms of the face, neck, back, or extremities, when this drug is used in the presence of nausea, vomiting, and dehydration. Observe closely and notify the physician if such reactions occur.

Possible Adverse Effects *(unusual, unexpected, and infrequent reactions)*

IF ANY OF THE FOLLOWING DEVELOP, DISCONTINUE DRUG AND NOTIFY YOUR PHYSICIAN AS SOON AS POSSIBLE

Mild Adverse Effects
Allergic Reactions: Skin rash (very rare).
Dizziness, weakness.

Serious Adverse Effects
Paradoxical Reactions: hyperexcitability, abnormal movements of arms and legs, nightmares.
Parkinson-like disorders (see Glossary).
Muscle spasms of the face, neck, back, and extremities, causing rolling of the eyes, twisting of the neck, arching of the back, spasms of the hands and feet.
Bone marrow depression (see Glossary), mild and very rare.
Hepatitis with jaundice (see Glossary), very rare.

Advisability of Use During Pregnancy
Apparently safe. No reports of adverse effects to mother or fetus. However, it is advisable to use this drug only when absolutely necessary and to avoid large doses and prolonged use.

Advisability of Use While Nursing Infant
Apparently safe; ask physician for guidance regarding dosage schedule. Observe infant for evidence of sedation.

Habit-Forming Potential
None.

Effects of Overdosage
With Moderate Overdose: Marked drowsiness, weakness, unsteady stance and gait, agitation, delirium.
With Large Overdose: Deep sleep, coma, convulsions.

Possible Effects of Extended Use
Bone marrow depression (see Glossary).

Recommended Periodic Examinations While Taking This Drug
Complete blood cell counts.

While Taking This Drug, Observe the Following

Foods: Drug may be taken with or following food if it causes stomach irritation.

Beverages: No restrictions.

Alcohol: Use with caution until combined effect has been determined. Alcohol can increase the sedative action of trimeprazine. Trimeprazine can increase the intoxicating action of alcohol.

Tobacco Smoking: No interactions expected.

Other Drugs

Trimeprazine may *increase* the effects of

• all sedatives, sleep-inducing drugs, pain-relieving drugs, other antihistamines, tranquilizers, and narcotic drugs, and cause oversedation. Ask physician for guidance regarding dosage adjustment.

• atropine and drugs with an atropine-like action (see Drug Family, Section Four).

Driving a Vehicle, Piloting a Plane, Operating Machinery: This drug can cause drowsiness and dizziness. Avoid hazardous activities until its full effect has been determined.

Exposure to Sun: Use caution until sensitivity has been determined. This drug can cause photosensitivity (see Glossary).

Special Storage Instructions

Keep in a tightly closed container. Protect from light.

TRIMETHOBENZAMIDE

Year Introduced: 1959

Brand Names

USA	Canada
Tigan (Beecham)	Tigan (Roche)

Drug Family: Antinausea (Anti-emetic)

Prescription Required: Yes

Available Dosage Forms and Strengths
Capsules — 100 mg., 250 mg.
Suppositories — 200 mg.
Injection — 100 mg. per ml.

How This Drug Works
Intended Therapeutic Effect(s): Relief of nausea and vomiting.
Location of Drug Action(s): Those nerve pathways within the brain that activate the vomiting centers.

Method of Drug Action(s):   Not completely established. It is thought that this drug relieves nausea and prevents vomiting by blocking the action of the tissue chemicals that transmit nerve impulses to the vomiting centers.

THIS DRUG SHOULD NOT BE TAKEN IF

—you have had an allergic reaction to any dosage form of it previously (Note: The suppositories contain benzocaine).

INFORM YOUR PHYSICIAN BEFORE TAKING THIS DRUG IF

—you have had any unfavorable reaction to antihistamine drugs in the past. (This drug resembles antihistamines in its pharmacological actions.)

Time Required for Apparent Benefit

Drug action begins in 20 to 40 minutes and persists for approximately 3 to 4 hours.

Possible Side-Effects *(natural, expected, and unavoidable drug actions)*

Drowsiness.

Temporary drop in blood pressure, when given by injection.

CAUTION

Use with extreme caution in children with acute infections characterized by fever, vomiting, and dehydration. Such children may be very susceptible to the adverse effects of this drug.

Possible Adverse Effects *(unusual, unexpected, and infrequent reactions)*

IF ANY OF THE FOLLOWING DEVELOP, DISCONTINUE DRUG AND NOTIFY YOUR PHYSICIAN AS SOON AS POSSIBLE

Mild Adverse Effects

Allergic Reactions: Skin rash.

Headache, dizziness, blurring of vision, muscle spasm, and cramping.

Serious Adverse Effects

Parkinson-like disorders (see Glossary).

Liver damage with jaundice (see Glossary).

Advisability of Use During Pregnancy

Safety not established. Prudent use is best determined by the physician's evaluation.

Advisability of Use While Nursing Infant

Presence of drug in milk is not known. Safety for infant not established. Ask physician for guidance.

Habit-Forming Potential

None.

Effects of Overdosage

With Moderate Overdose: Drowsiness, weakness, incoordination, muscle spasms in neck and extremities.

With Large Overdose: Confusion, disorientation, convulsions, coma.

Possible Effects of Extended Use
None reported.

Recommended Periodic Examinations While Taking This Drug
Liver function tests.

While Taking This Drug, Observe the Following
Foods: No restrictions. Follow prescribed diet.

Beverages: No restrictions. As allowed by prescribed diet.

Alcohol: Best avoided. Alcohol may increase the sedative response which some individuals experience with this drug.

Tobacco Smoking: No interactions expected.

Other Drugs

Trimethobenzamide may *increase* the effects of
- all other drugs with sedative effects, and cause oversedation. Dosage adjustments may be necessary.

Driving a Vehicle, Piloting a Plane, Operating Machinery: This drug may cause drowsiness. Avoid hazardous activities until full effect has been determined.

Exposure to Sun: No restrictions.

Special Storage Instructions
Keep in a dry, tightly closed container. Keep suppositories refrigerated.

TRIMETHOPRIM

Year Introduced: 1967

Brand Names

USA	Canada
Syraprim (Burroughs Wellcome)	Bactrim [CD] (Roche)
	Septra [CD] (B.W. Ltd.)
Bactrim [CD] (Roche)	
Septra [CD] (Burroughs Wellcome)	

Drug Family: Antimicrobial (Anti-infective)

Prescription Required: Yes

Available Dosage Forms and Strengths
Tablets — 80 mg. (+ 400 mg. sulfamethoxazole)*
— 160 mg. (+ 800 mg. sulfamethoxazole)
Oral Suspension — 40 mg. (+ 200 mg. sulfamethoxazole) per teaspoonful

*In some countries the generic name co-trimoxazole is used to designate the combination of trimethoprim and sulfamethoxazole in a single drug product.

How This Drug Works

Intended Therapeutic Effect(s):   The elimination of infections responsive to the action of this drug.

Location of Drug Action(s):   Those body tissues and fluids in which adequate concentration of the drug can be achieved.

Method of Drug Action(s):   This drug prevents the growth and multiplication of susceptible infecting organisms by interfering with the enzyme systems essential to the formation of proteins.

THIS DRUG SHOULD NOT BE TAKEN IF

—you have had an allergic reaction to any dosage form of it previously (see also the SULFAMETHOXAZOLE Drug Profile).

INFORM YOUR PHYSICIAN BEFORE TAKING THIS DRUG IF

—you are pregnant or nursing an infant.
—you have a history of liver or kidney disease.

Time Required for Apparent Benefit

Varies with nature of infection under treatment; usually 2 to 5 days.

Possible Side-Effects *(natural, expected, and unavoidable drug actions)*

None.

Possible Adverse Effects *(unusual, unexpected, and infrequent reactions)*

IF ANY OF THE FOLLOWING DEVELOP, DISCONTINUE DRUG AND NOTIFY YOUR PHYSICIAN AS SOON AS POSSIBLE

Mild Adverse Effects

Allergic Reactions: Skin rashes (various kinds), nausea, vomiting.

Serious Adverse Effects

Idiosyncratic Reactions: Interference with red blood cell production.

Advisability of Use During Pregnancy

Safety not established. Prudent use is best determined by the physician's evaluation.

Advisability of Use While Nursing Infant

Safety for infant not established. Avoid use if possible. Ask physician for guidance. (See also the SULFAMETHOXAZOLE Drug Profile.)

Habit-Forming Potential

None.

Effects of Overdosage

With Moderate Overdose: Nausea, vomiting, diarrhea.

Possible Effects of Extended Use

Bone marrow depression (see Glossary), with impaired red blood cell production resulting in anemia.

Recommended Periodic Examinations While Taking This Drug

Complete blood cell counts.

While Taking This Drug, Observe the Following
Foods: No restrictions of food selection. May be taken with food to minimize stomach irritation.

Beverages: No restrictions.

Alcohol: No interactions expected with trimethoprim. However, see SULFAMETHOXAZOLE Drug Profile if you are taking a combination of these two drugs.

Tobacco Smoking: No interactions expected.

Other Drugs

Trimethoprim may *increase* the effects of
- sulfamethoxazole, making it more effective in the treatment of certain infections.

Trimethoprim *taken concurrently* with
- thiazide diuretics, may cause unusual bleeding or bruising (see Drug Family, Section Four). This is more likely to occur in the elderly.

Driving a Vehicle, Piloting a Plane, Operating Machinery: No restrictions regarding trimethoprim. However, see SULFAMETHOXAZOLE Drug Profile if you are taking a combination of these two drugs.

Exposure to Sun: No restrictions regarding trimethoprim (see SULFAMETHOXAZOLE Drug Profile).

Special Storage Instructions
Keep in a dry, tightly closed, light-resistant container.

TRIPELENNAMINE
Year Introduced: 1945

Brand Names

USA	Canada
Pyribenzamine (CIBA)	Pyribenzamine (CIBA)
Ro-Hist (Robinson)	

Drug Family: Antihistamines

Prescription Required: Yes

Available Dosage Forms and Strengths

Tablets — 25 mg., 50 mg.

Prolonged Action Tablets — 50 mg., 100 mg.

Elixir — 25 mg. per teaspoonful

Injection — 25 mg. per ml.

How This Drug Works
Intended Therapeutic Effect(s):   Relief of symptoms associated with hayfever (allergic rhinitis) and with allergic reactions in the skin, such as itching, swelling, hives, and rash.

Location of Drug Action(s):   Those hypersensitive tissues that release excessive histamine as part of an allergic reaction. The principal tissue sites are the eyes, the nose, and the skin.

Method of Drug Action(s):   This drug reduces the intensity of the allergic response by blocking the action of histamine after it has been released from sensitized tissue cells.

THIS DRUG SHOULD NOT BE TAKEN IF
—you have had an allergic reaction to any dosage form of it previously.
—you are subject to acute attacks of asthma.
—you have glaucoma (narrow-angle type).
—you have difficulty emptying the urinary bladder.
—you are taking, or have taken during the past 2 weeks, any mono-amine oxidase (MAO) inhibitor drug (see Drug Family, Section Four).
—it has been prescribed for a newborn infant.

INFORM YOUR PHYSICIAN BEFORE TAKING THIS DRUG IF
—you have had an unfavorable reaction to any antihistamine drug in the past.
—you have a history of peptic ulcer disease.
—you plan to have surgery under general anesthesia in the near future.

Time Required for Apparent Benefit
Drug action begins in approximately 30 minutes, reaches a maximum in 1 hour, and subsides in 4 to 6 hours.

Possible Side-Effects *(natural, expected, and unavoidable drug actions)*
Drowsiness, sense of weakness, dryness of nose, mouth, and throat, constipation.

CAUTION
The elderly (over 60 years of age) may be more susceptible to the adverse effects of this drug. Small doses are advisable until tolerance is determined.

Possible Adverse Effects *(unusual, unexpected, and infrequent reactions)*

IF ANY OF THE FOLLOWING DEVELOP, DISCONTINUE DRUG AND NOTIFY YOUR PHYSICIAN AS SOON AS POSSIBLE

Mild Adverse Effects
   Allergic Reactions: Skin rash, hives.
   Headache, dizziness, inability to concentrate, nervousness, blurring of vision, double vision, difficulty in urination.
   Nausea, vomiting, diarrhea.
   Reduced tolerance for contact lenses.

Serious Adverse Effects
   Allergic Reactions: Anaphylactic reaction (see Glossary).
   Idiosyncratic Reactions: Acute behavioral disturbances—excitement, confusion, hallucinations, insomnia (more common in children).
   Hemolytic anemia (see Glossary).
   Bone marrow depression (see Glossary)—fatigue, weakness, fever, sore throat, unusual bleeding or bruising.

Advisability of Use During Pregnancy
No reports of adverse effects on mother or fetus, but complete safety has not been established. Prudent use is best determined by the physician's evaluation.

Advisability of Use While Nursing Infant
This drug may impair milk formation and make nursing difficult. The drug is thought to be present in milk. Ask physician for guidance.

Habit-Forming Potential
None.

Effects of Overdosage
With Moderate Overdose: Marked drowsiness, confusion, incoordination, unsteady gait, muscle tremors. In children: excitement, hallucinations, overactivity, convulsions.

With Large Overdose: Stupor progressing to coma, fever, flushed face, dilated pupils, weak pulse, shallow breathing.

Possible Effects of Extended Use
Bone marrow depression.
Emotional and behavioral abnormalities.

Recommended Periodic Examinations While Taking This Drug
Complete blood cell counts.

While Taking This Drug, Observe the Following
Foods: No restrictions. Stomach irritation can be reduced if drug is taken after eating.

Beverages: Coffee and tea may help to reduce the drowsiness caused by most antihistamines.

Alcohol: Use with extreme caution until combined effect has been determined. The combination of alcohol and antihistamines can cause rapid and marked sedation.

Tobacco Smoking: No interactions expected.

Other Drugs

Tripelennamine may *increase* the effects of

- sedatives, sleep-inducing drugs, tranquilizers, antidepressants, pain relievers, and narcotic drugs, and result in oversedation. Careful dosage adjustments are necessary.
- atropine and drugs with atropine-like action (see Drug Family, Section Four).

The following drugs may *increase* the effects of tripelennamine

- all sedatives, sleep-inducing drugs, tranquilizers, pain relievers, and narcotic drugs may exaggerate its sedative action and cause oversedation.
- mono-amine oxidase (MAO) inhibitor drugs (see Drug Family, Section Four) may delay its elimination from the body, thus exaggerating and prolonging its action.

The following drugs may *decrease* the effects of tripelennamine
• amphetamines (Benzedrine, Dexedrine, Desoxyn, etc.) may reduce the drowsiness caused by most antihistamines.

Driving a Vehicle, Piloting a Plane, Operating Machinery: This drug may impair mental alertness, judgment, physical coordination, and reaction time. Avoid hazardous activities until full sedative effect has been determined.

Exposure to Sun: No restrictions.

Special Storage Instructions
Keep in a dry, tightly closed, light-resistant container.

TRIPROLIDINE

Year Introduced: 1958

Brand Names

USA	Canada
Actidil (Burroughs Wellcome)	Actidil (B.W. Ltd.)
Actifed [CD] (Burroughs Wellcome)	Actifed [CD] (B.W. Ltd.)
Actifed-C [CD] (Burroughs Wellcome)	Actifed-A [CD] (B.W. Ltd.)
	Actifed-Plus [CD] (B.W. Ltd.)

Drug Family: Antihistamines

Prescription Required: Yes (Actifed-C is a Controlled Drug, U.S. Schedule 5)

Available Dosage Forms and Strengths
Tablets — 2.5 mg.
Syrup — 1.25 mg. per teaspoonful

How This Drug Works
Intended Therapeutic Effect(s):   Relief of symptoms associated with hayfever (allergic rhinitis) and with allergic reactions in the skin, such as itching, swelling, hives, and rash.

Location of Drug Action(s):   Those hypersensitive tissues that release excessive histamine as part of an allergic reaction. The principal tissue sites are the eyes, the nose, and the skin.

Method of Drug Action(s):   This drug reduces the intensity of the allergic response by blocking the action of histamine after it has been released from sensitized tissue cells.

THIS DRUG SHOULD NOT BE TAKEN IF
—you have had an allergic reaction to any dosage form of it previously.
—you are taking, or have taken within the past 2 weeks, any mono-amine oxidase (MAO) inhibitor drug (see Drug Family, Section Four).
—it has been prescribed for a newborn infant.

INFORM YOUR PHYSICIAN BEFORE TAKING THIS DRUG IF
—you have had an unfavorable reaction to any antihistamine in the past.
—you have glaucoma (narrow-angle type).
—you have difficulty emptying the urinary bladder.
—you plan to have surgery under general anesthesia in the near future.

Time Required for Apparent Benefit
Drug action begins in approximately 30 minutes, reaches a maximum in 3 and one-half hours, and subsides in 12 hours.

Possible Side-Effects *(natural, expected, and unavoidable drug actions)*
Drowsiness, lassitude, dryness of nose, mouth and throat.

Possible Adverse Effects *(unusual, unexpected, and infrequent reactions)*

IF ANY OF THE FOLLOWING DEVELOP, DISCONTINUE DRUG AND NOTIFY YOUR PHYSICIAN AS SOON AS POSSIBLE

Mild Adverse Effects
  Allergic Reactions: Skin rash (rare).
  Dizziness, incoordination, unsteadiness, inability to concentrate.
  Indigestion, nausea.
Serious Adverse Effects
  Idiosyncratic Reactions: Acute behavioral disturbances—excitement, irritability, insomnia.

Advisability of Use During Pregnancy
Safety not established. Prudent use is best determined by the physician's evaluation.

Advisability of Use While Nursing Infant
Presence of drug in milk is not known. Other antihistamine drugs are known to be present in milk. Ask physician for guidance.

Habit-Forming Potential
None.

Effects of Overdosage
With Moderate Overdose: Marked drowsiness, confusion, delirium, excitement and agitation; in the young, hallucinations, muscle tremors.
With Large Overdose: Stupor progressing to coma, convulsions.

Possible Effects of Extended Use
None reported.

Recommended Periodic Examinations While Taking This Drug
Complete blood cell counts. Some antihistamines have caused bone marrow depression and hemolytic anemia (see Glossary) with extended use.

While Taking This Drug, Observe the Following
Foods: No restrictions.
Beverages: Coffee and tea may offset the drowsiness caused by some antihistamines.

Alcohol: Use with extreme caution until combined effect has been determined. The combination of alcohol and antihistamines can produce rapid and marked sedation.

Tobacco Smoking: No interactions expected.

Other Drugs

Triprolidine may *increase* the effects of

- all sedatives, sleep-inducing drugs, tranquilizers, antidepressants, pain relievers, and narcotic drugs, and cause oversedation. Dosage adjustments may be necessary.

The following drugs may *increase* the effects of triprolidine

- all sedatives, sleep-inducing drugs, tranquilizers, antidepressants, pain relievers, and narcotic drugs. Dosage adjustments may be necessary to prevent oversedation.

Driving a Vehicle, Piloting a Plane, Operating Machinery: This drug may impair mental alertness, judgment, physical coordination, and reaction time. Avoid hazardous activities until its full sedative effect has been determined.

Exposure to Sun: Use caution until sensitivity has been determined. This drug has caused photosensitivity (see Glossary).

Special Storage Instructions

Keep in a dry, tightly closed, light-resistant container.

TRISULFAPYRIMIDINES
(SULFADIAZINE, SULFAMERAZINE, SULFAMETHAZINE)

Year Introduced: 1945

Brand Names

USA	Canada
Meth-Dia-Mer	None
Sulfonamides (Various	
Manufacturers)	
Neotrizine (Lilly)	
Terfonyl (Squibb)	
Triple Sulfa (Various	
Mfrs.)	
Tri-Sulfa (Columbia)	
Trisulfazine (Central)	
Trisureid	
(Reid-Provident)	

Drug Family: Antimicrobial (Anti-infective) [Sulfonamides]

Prescription Required: Yes

Available Dosage Forms and Strengths
Tablets — 250 mg., 500 mg.
Oral Suspension — 500 mg. per teaspoonful

How This Drug Works
Intended Therapeutic Effect(s):   The elimination of infections responsive to the action of this drug.
Location of Drug Action(s):   Any body tissue or fluid in which sufficient concentration of the drug can be achieved.
Method of Drug Action(s):   This drug prevents the growth and multiplication of susceptible bacteria by interfering with their formation of folic acid, an essential nutrient.

THIS DRUG SHOULD NOT BE TAKEN IF
—you are allergic to any sulfonamide ("sulfa") drug (see Drug Family, Section Four).
—you are in the ninth month of pregnancy.
—it is prescribed for an infant under 2 months of age.

INFORM YOUR PHYSICIAN BEFORE TAKING THIS DRUG IF
—you are allergic to any of the drugs chemically related to the sulfonamide ("sulfa") drugs: acetazolamide (Diamox), oral anti-diabetics, and thiazide diuretics (see Drug Families, Section Four).
—you are allergic by nature and have a history of hayfever, asthma, hives or eczema.
—you have a history of serious liver or kidney disease.
—you have a history of acute intermittent porphyria.
—you have ever had anemia caused by a drug.
—you are now taking any of the following drugs
oral anticoagulants
oral anti-diabetic preparations
methotrexate
oxyphenbutazone (Oxalid, Tandearil)
phenylbutazone (Azolid, Butazolidin, etc.)
phenytoin (Dantoin, Dilantin, etc.)
probenecid (Benemid)
—you plan to have surgery under pentothal anesthesia while taking this drug.

Time Required for Apparent Benefit
Varies with nature of infection under treatment; usually 2 to 5 days.

Possible Side-Effects *(natural, expected, and unavoidable drug actions)*
Brownish discoloration of urine, of no significance.
Superinfections (see Glossary).

Possible Adverse Effects *(unusual, unexpected, and infrequent reactions)*

IF ANY OF THE FOLLOWING DEVELOP, DISCONTINUE DRUG AND NOTIFY YOUR PHYSICIAN AS SOON AS POSSIBLE

Mild Adverse Effects

Allergic Reactions: Skin rashes (various kinds), hives, itching, swelling of face, redness of eyes.

Reduced appetite, nausea, vomiting, abdominal pain, diarrhea, irritation of mouth.

Headache, impaired balance, dizziness, ringing in ears, numbness and tingling of extremities, acute mental or behavioral disturbance.

Serious Adverse Effects

Allergic Reactions: Anaphylactic reaction (see Glossary), fever, swollen glands, swollen painful joints.

Idiosyncratic Reactions: Hemolytic anemia (see Glossary).

Bone marrow depression (see Glossary)—fatigue, weakness, fever, sore throat, unusual bleeding or bruising.

Hepatitis with or without jaundice (see Glossary).

Kidney damage with reduction of urine formation.

Advisability of Use During Pregnancy

Safety not established. Prudent use during the first 8 months is best determined by the physician's evaluation. Definitely avoid during ninth month.

Advisability of Use While Nursing Infant

Drug is known to be present in milk and known to have adverse effects on infant. Avoid use. Ask physician for guidance.

Habit-Forming Potential

None.

Effects of Overdosage

With Moderate Overdose: Nausea, vomiting, abdominal pain, possibly diarrhea.

With Large Overdose: Blood in urine, reduced urine formation.

Possible Effects of Extended Use

Development of thyroid gland enlargement (goiter) with or without reduced thyroid function (hypothyroidism).

Superinfections.

Recommended Periodic Examinations While Taking This Drug

Complete blood cell counts, weekly for the first 8 weeks.

Liver and kidney function tests.

While Taking This Drug, Observe the Following

Foods: No restrictions of food selection. Drug may be taken immediately after eating to minimize irritation of stomach.

Beverages: No restriction of beverage selection. However, total liquid intake should be no less than 4 pints every 24 hours while taking a sulfonamide.

Alcohol: Use with caution until combined effect is determined. Sulfonamide drugs can increase the intoxicating effects of alcohol.

Tobacco Smoking: No interactions expected.

Other Drugs

Trisulfapyrimidines may *increase* the effects of
- oral anticoagulants (see Drug Family, Section Four). Dosage adjustments may be necessary to prevent abnormal bleeding or hemorrhage.
- oral anti-diabetic preparations (see Drug Family, Section Four). Dosage adjustments may be necessary to prevent hypoglycemia (see Glossary).
- methotrexate.
- phenytoin (Dantoin, Dilantin, etc.). Dosage adjustments may be necessary to prevent toxic effects on the brain.

Trisulfapyrimidines may *decrease* the effects of
- penicillin.

Trisulfapyrimidines *taken concurrently* with
- methenamine, may cause crystal formation and kidney blockage.
- isoniazid, may cause hemolytic anemia (see Glossary).

The following drugs may *increase* the effects of trisulfapyrimidines
- aspirin
- oxyphenbutazone (Oxalid, Tandearil)
- phenylbutazone (Azolid, Butazolidin, etc.)
- probenecid (Benemid)
- promethazine (Phenergan, etc.)
- sulfinpyrazone (Anturane)
- trimethoprim (Syraprim)

The following drugs may *decrease* the effects of trisulfapyrimidines
- paraldehyde (Paral)
- para-aminosalicylic acid (PAS)

Driving a Vehicle, Piloting a Plane, Operating Machinery: No restrictions unless dizziness or disturbance of balance occurs.

Exposure to Sun: Use caution until sensitivity is determined. Some sulfonamide drugs can cause photosensitivity (see Glossary).

Discontinuation: Dosage adjustment may be necessary for the following drugs if taken concurrently with trisulfapyrimidines: oral anticoagulants, oral anti-diabetic preparations, phenytoin.

After (not during) treatment with a sulfonamide drug, ask physician for guidance regarding the need for supplemental Vitamin C to correct any deficiency due to therapy.

Special Storage Instructions

Keep in a tightly closed, light-resistant container.

TYBAMATE

Year Introduced: 1967

Brand Names

USA	Canada
Tybatran (Robins)	None

Drug Family: Tranquilizer, Mild (Anti-anxiety)

Prescription Required: Yes

Available Dosage Forms and Strengths
Capsules — 125 mg., 250 mg., 350 mg.

How This Drug Works
Intended Therapeutic Effect(s)
- relief of mild to moderate anxiety and tension (sedative effect).
- relief of insomnia due to anxiety and tension (hypnotic effect).

Location of Drug Action(s):   Not completely established. It is thought that this drug acts on multiple sites in the brain, including the thalamus and limbic systems.

Method of Drug Action(s):   Not known.

THIS DRUG SHOULD NOT BE TAKEN IF
—you are allergic or sensitive to tybamate or to any chemically related drugs: carisoprodol, meprobamate (see Drug Profiles for brand names).
—you have a history of acute intermittent porphyria.
—it is prescribed for a child under 6 years of age.

INFORM YOUR PHYSICIAN BEFORE TAKING THIS DRUG IF
—you have epilepsy or a history of convulsions.
—you have impaired liver or kidney function.
—you are taking sedatives, sleep-inducing drugs, tranquilizers (especially phenothiazines), antidepressants, narcotic drugs, or anti-convulsants.

Time Required for Apparent Benefit
Approximately 1 to 2 hours. For severe symptoms of some duration, benefit may require regular medication for several days.

Possible Side-Effects *(natural, expected, and unavoidable drug actions)*
Drowsiness, lethargy, unsteadiness in stance and gait.
In the elderly (over 60 years of age) and debilitated: lightheadedness, confusion, weakness. (The elderly are very susceptible to standard doses. Small doses are advisable until tolerance has been determined.)

Possible Adverse Effects *(unusual, unexpected, and infrequent reactions)*

IF ANY OF THE FOLLOWING DEVELOP, DISCONTINUE DRUG AND NOTIFY YOUR PHYSICIAN AS SOON AS POSSIBLE

Mild Adverse Effects
Allergic Reactions: Skin rashes (various kinds), hives, itching, swelling of face, hands, or feet, low-grade fever.

Dizziness, slurred speech, headache, blurred vision, nausea, flushing of face, heart palpitation, fainting.

Serious Adverse Effects

Allergic Reactions: Anaphylactic reaction (see Glossary), high fever, asthmatic breathing.

Paradoxical Reactions: Excitement, panic reaction. (See lists of Adverse Effects in the CARISOPRODOL and MEPROBAMATE Drug Profiles.)

Advisability of Use During Pregnancy

The findings of some recent studies suggest a possible association between the use of a drug closely related to tybamate during early pregnancy and the occurrence of birth defects, such as cleft lip. It is advisable to avoid this drug completely during the first 3 months of pregnancy.

Advisability of Use While Nursing Infant

Safety not established. Avoid use if possible. Ask physician for guidance.

Habit-Forming Potential

Neither psychological nor physical dependence has been reported. However, high dosage and/or prolonged use should be avoided.

Effects of Overdosage

With **Moderate Overdose:**   Dizziness, slurred speech, impaired stance, staggering.

With **Large Overdose:**   Stupor progressing to deep sleep and coma, depression of breathing and heart function.

Possible Effects of Extended Use

None reported.

Recommended Periodic Examinations While Taking This Drug

Complete blood cell counts during long-term use.

While Taking This Drug, Observe the Following

Foods: No restrictions.

Beverages: Large intake of coffee, tea, or cola drinks (because of their caffeine content) may reduce the calming action of this drug.

Alcohol: Use with extreme caution until combined effect is determined. Alcohol combined with tybamate can cause severe impairment of mental and physical functions.

Tobacco Smoking: No interactions expected.

Other Drugs

Tybamate may *increase* the effects of

- other sedatives, sleep-inducing drugs, tranquilizers, antidepressants, and narcotic drugs, and cause oversedation. Use such drugs with caution until combined effect has been determined. Ask physician for guidance regarding dosage adjustments.

Tybamate *taken concurrently* with

- phenothiazines, may cause convulsions and seizures resembling epilepsy.

The following drugs may *increase* the effects of tybamate
- mono-amine oxidase (MAO) inhibitor drugs (see Drug Family, Section Four) can increase the sedative and brain-depressant effects of tybamate. Ask physician for guidance regarding dosage adjustments.

Driving a Vehicle, Piloting a Plane, Operating Machinery: This drug can impair mental alertness, judgment, and physical coordination. Avoid hazardous activities.

Exposure to Sun: No restrictions.

Discontinuation: If it has been necessary to use this drug for an extended period of time, do not discontinue it suddenly. Ask physician for guidance regarding dosage reduction and withdrawal.

Special Storage Instructions
Keep in a dry, tightly closed container.

VITAMIN C
(Ascorbic Acid)

Year Introduced: 1933 (Chemical identity established)

Brand Names

USA	Canada
Ascorbajen (Jenkins)	Adenex (ICN)
Ascorbicap (ICN)	Chem C (Chemo)
Cetane (Fellows)	C-Vita (Nordic)
Cevalin (Lilly)	C-Vite (Stickley)
Cevi-Bid (Geriatric)	Erivit C (Eri)
Synchro-C (Carnrick)	Redoxon (Roche)
(Numerous others)	(Numerous others)

Drug Family: Vitamins

Prescription Required: No

Available Dosage Forms and Strengths
Tablets — 25 mg., 50 mg., 100 mg., 250 mg., 500 mg., 1000 mg.
Capsules — 25 mg., 100 mg., 250 mg., 500 mg.
Oral Drops — 100 mg. per ml.
Syrup — 500 mg. per teaspoonful (5 ml.)
Injection — 100 mg. per ml., 200 mg. per ml., 250 mg. per ml., 500 mg. per ml.

How This Drug Works
Intended Therapeutic Effect(s)
- prevention and treatment of scurvy, a disease resulting from deficiency of Vitamin C.
- treatment of some types of anemia.
- maintenance of an acid urine (using a dose of 1 gram every 6 hours).

Location of Drug Action(s)

- tissues throughout the body that require Vitamin C for the formation of collagen, a principal structural protein of skin, tendon, bone, teeth, cartilage, and connective tissue.
- the intestinal tract and bone marrow.
- the kidneys, ureters, and bladder.

Method of Drug Action(s)

Not established. It is thought that Vitamin C plays an essential role in the enzyme activity involved in the formation of collagen.

Vitamin C increases the absorption of iron from the intestine and contributes to the formation of hemoglobin and red blood cells in the bone marrow.

By acidifying the urine, Vitamin C (ascorbic acid) creates an environment which is unfavorable to the growth of certain bacteria that commonly infect the urinary tract. This action also enhances the therapeutic effects of some widely used anti-infective drugs.

Note: There is insufficient scientific evidence to establish that Vitamin C is significantly beneficial in the prevention or treatment of the common cold. Individual experience varies greatly. For those who find that the benefits of using Vitamin C in large doses clearly outweigh the small risks involved, no significant toxicity is anticipated.

THIS DRUG SHOULD NOT BE TAKEN IF

—you have had an allergic reaction to a Vitamin C drug product previously. (Ask physician for guidance.)

INFORM YOUR PHYSICIAN BEFORE TAKING THIS DRUG IF

—you have sickle cell anemia.
—you have a history of kidney stones.
—you are taking an oral anticoagulant drug.

Time Required for Apparent Benefit

In the treatment of Vitamin C deficiency, significant improvement is apparent within 1 week.

Possible Side-Effects *(natural, expected, and unavoidable drug actions)*

None.

CAUTION

1. Some Vitamin C preparations for oral use contain sodium ascorbate as the principal component. For individuals on a low-sodium diet, the intake of sodium could be significant, depending upon daily dosage. Consult your physician.
2. It is advisable to avoid large doses of Vitamin C while taking any sulfonamide ("sulfa") drug.
3. Large doses of Vitamin C may give a *false positive* test result for urine sugar when testing with Benedict's solution, and a *false negative* test result when testing with Clinistix or Tes-Tape.

Possible Adverse Effects *(unusual, unexpected, and infrequent reactions)*

IF ANY OF THE FOLLOWING DEVELOP, DISCONTINUE DRUG AND NOTIFY YOUR PHYSICIAN AS SOON AS POSSIBLE

Mild Adverse Effects
Diarrhea, with large doses.

Serious Adverse Effects
Idiosyncratic Reactions: Hemolytic anemia (see Glossary).
Formation of kidney stones, with large doses.
Precipitation of crisis in individuals with sickle cell anemia.

Advisability of Use During Pregnancy
Adhere to recommended dose of 100 mg. daily. Avoid large doses.

Advisability of Use While Nursing Infant
Adhere to recommended dose of 150 mg. daily. Avoid large doses.

Habit-Forming Potential
None.

Effects of Overdosage
With Moderate Overdose: Diarrhea.
With Large Overdose: No toxic effects reported.

Possible Effects of Extended Use
Formation of kidney stones, when taken in large doses.

Recommended Periodic Examinations While Taking This Drug
Urine analyses.

While Taking This Drug, Observe the Following
Foods: No restrictions.
Beverages: No restrictions.
Alcohol: No interactions expected.
Tobacco Smoking: Smoking appears to increase the requirement for Vitamin C. The reasons for this are not known.
Other Drugs
Vitamin C (in large doses) may *increase* the effects of
• aspirin.
• barbiturates (see Drug Family, Section Four).
• iron preparations.
• sulfonamide ("sulfa") drugs (see Drug Family, Section Four).

Vitamin C (in large doses) may *decrease* the effects of
• oral anticoagulants (see Drug Family, Section Four).
• atropine and atropine-like drugs (see Drug Family, Section Four).
• quinidine.

Vitamin C (in large doses) *taken concurrently* with
• sulfonamide drugs, may cause crystal formation in the kidneys, resulting in kidney damage and impaired kidney function.

The following drugs may *decrease* the effects of Vitamin C
- barbiturates
- mineral oil
- salicylates (principally aspirin)
- sulfonamide drugs

Exposure to Sun: No restrictions.

Occurrence of Unrelated Illness: Vitamin C requirements are increased during pregnancy, nursing, peptic ulcer, infections, and overactive thyroid states; also following surgery, injuries, and burns.

Special Storage Instructions
Keep all forms of Vitamin C in tightly closed, nonmetallic containers. Protect from light.

WARFARIN
(and other* Coumarin Anticoagulants)
Year Introduced: 1954

Brand Names

USA	Canada
Athrombin-K (Purdue Frederick)	Athrombin-K (Purdue Frederick)
Coumadin (Endo)	Coumadin (Endo)
Panwarfin (Abbott)	Warfilone (Frosst)
	Warnerin (Warner/Chilcott)

Drug Family: Anticoagulant [Coumarins]

Prescription Required: Yes

Available Dosage Forms and Strengths
Tablets — 2 mg., 2.5 mg., 5 mg., 7.5 mg., 10 mg., 25 mg.
Injection — 50 mg. per vial, 75 mg. per vial

How This Drug Works
Intended Therapeutic Effect(s):   A deliberate reduction in the ability of the blood to clot. This effect is often beneficial in the management of stroke, heart attack, abnormal clotting in arteries and veins (thrombosis), and the movement of a blood clot from vein to lung (pulmonary embolism).

Location of Drug Action(s):   Those tissues in the liver that use Vitamin K to produce prothrombin (and other factors) essential to the clotting of blood.

---

*Other members of the coumarin anticoagulant drug family available in the United States are Dicumarol, Liquamar, Sintrom, and Tromexan. Dicumarol and Sintrom are also available in Canada. The major characteristics of warfarin are shared by all coumarin anticoagulants.

Method of Drug Action(s):   The coumarin anticoagulants interfere with the production of four essential blood-clotting factors by blocking the action of Vitamin K. This leads to a deficiency of these clotting factors in circulating blood and inhibits blood-clotting mechanisms.

THIS DRUG SHOULD NOT BE TAKEN IF
—you are allergic to any of the drugs bearing the brand names listed above.
—you have a history of a bleeding disorder.
—you have an active peptic ulcer.
—you have ulcerative colitis.

INFORM YOUR PHYSICIAN BEFORE TAKING THIS DRUG IF
—you are now taking *any other drugs*—either drugs prescribed by another physician or non-prescription drugs you purchased over-the-counter (see OTC drugs in Glossary).
—you have high blood pressure.
—you have abnormally heavy or prolonged menstrual bleeding.
—you have diabetes.
—you are using an indwelling catheter.
—you have a history of serious liver or kidney disease, or impaired liver or kidney function.
—you plan to have a surgical or dental procedure in the near future.

Time Required for Apparent Benefit
Drug action begins in 24 to 36 hours, produces desired effects within 36 to 72 hours, and persists for 4 to 5 days. Continuous use on a regular schedule for up to 2 weeks (with daily prothrombin testing and dosage adjustment) is needed to determine the correct maintenance dose for each individual.

Possible Side-Effects *(natural, expected, and unavoidable drug actions)*
Minor episodes of bleeding may occur even when dosage is well within the recommended range. If in doubt regarding its significance, consult your physician regarding the need for prothrombin testing.

CAUTION
1. Always carry with you a card of personal identification that includes a statement indicating that *you are using an anticoagulant* (see Table 14 and Section Seven).
2. While you are taking an anticoagulant drug, always consult your physician *before* starting any new drug, changing the dosage schedule of any drug, or discontinuing any drug.

Possible Adverse Effects *(unusual, unexpected, and infrequent reactions)*

IF ANY OF THE FOLLOWING DEVELOP, DISCONTINUE DRUG AND NOTIFY YOUR PHYSICIAN AS SOON AS POSSIBLE
Mild Adverse Effects
    Allergic Reactions: Skin rash, hives, loss of scalp hair, drug fever.
    Nausea, vomiting, diarrhea.
Serious Adverse Effects
    Abnormal bruising, major bleeding, or hemorrhage. Notify physician of

nosebleeds, bleeding gums, bloody sputum, blood-tinged urine, bloody
or tarry stools. (The incidence of significant bleeding is 2% to 4%.)

Advisability of Use During Pregnancy
This drug can cause hemorrhage in the fetus. Avoid use completely if possible.

Advisability of Use While Nursing Infant
This drug is present in milk and may cause bleeding or hemorrhage in the
nursing infant. Ask physician for guidance.

Habit-Forming Potential
None.

Effects of Overdosage
With Moderate Overdose: Episodes of minor bleeding: blood spots in white
portion of eye, nosebleeds, gum bleeding, small bruises, prolonged bleeding from minor cuts received while shaving or from other small lacerations.
With Large Overdose: Episodes of major internal bleeding: vomiting of
blood, grossly bloody urine or stools.

Possible Effects of Extended Use
None reported.

Recommended Periodic Examinations While Taking This Drug
Regular determination of prothrombin time is essential to safe dosage and
proper control.
Occasional urine analysis for red blood cells.

While Taking This Drug, Observe the Following
Foods: A larger intake than usual of foods high in Vitamin K may reduce
the effectiveness of this drug and make larger doses necessary. Foods rich
in Vitamin K include: cabbage, cauliflower, fish, kale, liver, spinach.
Beverages: No restrictions.
Alcohol: Use with caution until combined effect has been determined. Alcohol can either increase or decrease the effect of this drug. It is advisable
to use alcohol sparingly while taking anticoagulants.
(Note: Heavy users of alcohol with liver damage may be very sensitive to
anticoagulants and require smaller than usual doses.)
Tobacco Smoking: No interactions expected. Follow physician's advice regarding smoking (based upon condition under treatment).
Other Drugs: Refer to individual Drug Profiles and to Drug Families (Section Four) for brand names of the drugs listed below.
Warfarin may *increase the* effects of
• insulin.
• phenytoin (Dantoin, Dilantin, etc.).
• sulfonylureas (Diabinese, Dymelor, Orinase, Tolinase).

The following drugs *taken concurrently* with warfarin may cause *either an
increase or a decrease* in anticoagulant effect
• antihistamines
• benzodiazepines (Dalmane, Librium, Serax, Valium)

- chloral hydrate (Noctec, Somnos, Chloralixir, etc.)
- cholestramine (Cuemid, Questran)
- clofibrate (Atromid-S)
- cortisone and related drugs
- oral contraceptives
- reserpine (Ser-Ap-Es, Serpasil, Neo-Serp, etc.)

The following drugs may *increase* the effects of warfarin
- acetaminophen (Tempra, Tylenol, etc.)
- allopurinol (Zyloprim)
- anabolic drugs (Adroyd, Anavar, Dianabol, etc.)
- androgens (Android, Metandren, Oreton, etc.)
- antibiotics (Kantrex, the penicillins, tetracyclines, etc.)
- chloramphenicol (Chloromycetin, etc.)
- disulfiram (Antabuse)
- ethacrynic acid (Edecrin)
- glucagon
- guanethidine (Ismelin)
- hydroxyzine (Atarax, Vistaril)
- indomethacin (Indocin, Indocid)
- isoniazid (INH, Isozide, Niconyl, etc.)
- mefenamic acid (Ponstel, Ponstan)
- mercaptopurine (Purinethol)
- methyldopa (Aldomet, Dopamet)
- methylphenidate (Ritalin, Methidate)
- nalidixic acid (NegGram)
- nortriptyline (Aventyl)
- oxyphenbutazone (Oxalid, Tandearil)
- para-aminosalycylic acid (P.A.S., Pamisyl, etc.)
- phenylbutazone (Butazolidin, Phenbutazone, etc.)—increase with initial use only
- phenyramidol (Analexin)
- probenecid (Benemid)
- propylthiouracil (Propacil, Propyl-Thyracil)
- quinidine (Quinidex, Cardioquin)
- salicylates (aspirin, aspirin combinations)
- sulfinpyrazone (Anturane)
- sulfonamides (certain short- and long-acting "sulfa" drugs)
- sulfonylureas (Diabinese, Dymelor, Orinase, Tolinase)
- thyroid preparations (Cytomel, Proloid, Synthroid, Thyroxine, etc.)
- tricylic antidepressants (Elavil, Sinequan, Tofranil)

The following drugs may *decrease* the effects of warfarin
- antacids (when used in large doses)
- barbiturates (Amytal, Butisol, Seconal, etc.)
- carbamazepine (Tegretol)
- chlorpromazine (Thorazine, Largactil, etc.)
- digitalis preparations

- estrogens (Premarin, Milprem, Formatrix, etc.)
- ethchlorvynol (Placidyl)
- furosemide (Lasix)
- glutethimide (Doriden, Somide)
- griseofulvin (Fulvicin, Grisactin, Grifulvin)
- haloperidol (Haldol)
- meprobamate (Equanil, Miltown, etc.)
- oral contraceptives
- phenylbutazone (Butazolidin, Phenbutazone, etc.)—subsequent decrease following initial increase
- phenylpropanolamine (Propadrine, Allerest, Naldecon, Triaminic, etc.)
- phenytoin (Dantoin, Dilantin, etc.)
- Vitamin C (when used in large doses)

Driving a Vehicle, Piloting a Plane, Operating Machinery: No restrictions. Avoid unnecessary hazardous activities that could cause injury and result in excessive bleeding.

Exposure to Sun: No restrictions.

Exposure to Heat: Prolonged hot weather may increase the prothrombin time and make it advisable to reduce anticoagulant dosage. Ask physician for guidance.

Occurrence of Unrelated Illness: Any acute illness that causes fever, vomiting, or diarrhea can alter your response to this drug. Notify your physician so corrective action can be taken.

Discontinuation: Do not discontinue this drug abruptly unless abnormal bleeding occurs. Ask physician for guidance regarding gradual reduction of dosage over a period of 3 to 4 weeks.

Special Storage Instructions
Keep in a dry, tightly closed container. Protect from light.

SECTION FOUR

Drug Families

Drug Families

Throughout the Drug Profiles in Section Three reference is made to various drug families. The reader may be advised to consult Section Four to become familiar with the drugs that belong to a particular family (or class) of drugs that share important characteristics in their chemical composition or in their actions within the body. Often it is important to know that *any* drug (or *all* drugs) within a given family can be expected to behave in a particular way. Such information may be useful in preventing interactions that could reduce the effectiveness of the drugs in use or result in unanticipated and sometimes hazardous adverse effects.

Each Drug Family listing consists of two columns. The left-hand column contains the more widely recognized brand names of the drugs within the family; the right-hand column contains the generic names of the family members. In some instances the number of brand names in use is so large that a complete listing is not possible. In such cases, to be certain that you are consulting the correct drug family, determine the generic name of the drug that concerns you and consult the right-hand column to see whether it is listed there. The generic name listing is sufficiently complete to serve the scope of this book.

The names in both listings are arranged alphabetically for easier searching. Names which appear opposite each other in the two columns are not necessarily related and are not to be interpreted as representing the brand and generic names of the same drug. For correct identification of corresponding brand and generic names, see the brand name-generic name cross-index in Section Two.

AMPHETAMINE-LIKE DRUGS

BRAND NAMES (alphabetical)		GENERIC NAMES (alphabetical)
Amodril	Ionamin	amphetamine
Bamadex	Obotan	benzphetamine
Benzedrine	Plegine	dextroamphetamine
Biphetamine	Preludin	diethylpropion
Desoxyn	Ritalin	levamphetamine
Dexedrine	Tenuate	methamphetamine
Didrex	Tepanil	methylphenidate
Eskatrol	Tora	phendimetrazine
Fastin	Wilpo	phenmetrazine
Fetamin		phentermine

ANALGESICS, MILD

BRAND NAMES (alphabetical)	GENERIC NAMES (alphabetical)
A.P.C. Compound	acetaminophen
A.S.A. Preparations	aspirin
Darvocet	codeine
Darvon	oxycodone
Datril	paregoric
Nebs	pentazocine
Percodan	phenacetin
Talwin	propoxyphene
Taper	
Tempra	
Tylenol	
Valadol	

ANALGESICS, STRONG (NARCOTIC DRUGS)

BRAND NAMES (alphabetical)	GENERIC NAMES (alphabetical)
Demerol	anileridine
Dilaudid	hydromorphone
Dolophine	meperidine
Leritine	methadone
	morphine

ANTICOAGULANTS

Coumarin Family

BRAND NAMES (alphabetical)	GENERIC NAMES (alphabetical)
Coumadin	acenocoumarol
Dicumarol	dicumarol
Liquamar	phenprocoumon
Panwarfin	warfarin
Sintrom	
Tromexan	

Indandione Family

BRAND NAMES (alphabetical)	GENERIC NAMES (alphabetical)
Danilone	anisindione
Dipaxin	diphenadione
Eridione	phenindione
Hedulin	
Miradon	

ANTIDEPRESSANTS, TRICYCLIC

BRAND NAMES (alphabetical)	GENERIC NAMES (alphabetical)
Anafranil	amitriptyline
Aventyl	clomipramine
Elavil	desipramine
Ensidon	doxepin
Norpramin	imipramine
Pertofrane	nortriptyline
Presamine	opipramol
Sinequan	protriptyline
Surmontil	trimipramine
Tofranil	
Vivactil	

ANTI-DIABETICS, ORAL

Sulfonylurea Family

BRAND NAMES (alphabetical)	GENERIC NAMES (alphabetical)
Chloronase	acetohexamide
Diabeta	chlorpropamide
Diabinese	glyburide
Dimelor	tolazamide
Dymelor	tolbutamide
Euglucon	
Mobenol	
Orinase	
Stabinol	
Tolinase	

Biguanide Family

BRAND NAMES (alphabetical)	GENERIC NAMES (alphabetical)
DBI	metformin
Glucophage	phenformin

ANTIHISTAMINES

BRAND NAMES (alphabetical)	GENERIC NAMES (alphabetical)
Actidil	brompheniramine
Atarax	carbinoxamine
Benadryl	chlorpheniramine
Bonine	cyclizine
Chlor-Trimeton	cyproheptadine
Clistin	dimenhydrinate
Decapryn	diphenhydramine
Dimetane	diphenylpyraline
Dramamine	doxylamine
Hispril	hydroxyzine
Histadyl	meclizine
Histalon	methapyrilene
Inhiston	orphenadrine

Marezine
Neo-Antergan
Norflex
Periactin
Phenergan
Pyribenzamine
Trimeton
Vistaril

pheniramine
promethazine
pyrilamine
tripelennamine
triprolidine

ANTI-HYPERTENSIVES

BRAND NAMES
(alphabetical)

GENERIC NAMES
(alphabetical)

Aldomet
Anhydron
Apresoline
Catapres
Diuril
Enduron
Esbaloid
Esidrix
Eutonyl
Exna
HydroDiuril
Hygroton
Inderal
Inversine
Ismelin
Lasix
Naqua
Naturetin
Renese
Saluron
Serpasil

bendroflumethiazide
benzthiazide
bethanidine
chlorothiazide
chlorthalidone
clonidine
cyclothiazide
furosemide
guanethidine
hydralazine
hydrochlorothiazide
hydroflumethiazide
mecamylamine
methyclothiazide
methyldopa
pargyline
polythiazide
propranolol
reserpine
trichlormethiazide

ANTI-PARKINSONISM DRUGS

BRAND NAMES (alphabetical)	GENERIC NAMES (alphabetical)
Akineton	benztropine
Artane	biperiden
Bendopa	chlorphenoxamine
Biodopa	cycrimine
Cogentin	ethopropazine
Disipal	levodopa
Dopar	orphenadrine
Kemadrin	procyclidine
Larodopa	trihexyphenidyl
Levodopa	
Norflex	
Pagitane	
Parda	
Parsidol	
Phenoxene	
Pipanol	
Tremin	

ANTISPASMODICS, SYNTHETIC

BRAND NAMES (alphabetical)	GENERIC NAMES (alphabetical)
Antrenyl	clidinium
Banthine	dicyclomine
Bentyl	diphemanil
Cantil	glycopyrrolate
Darbid	hexocyclium
Nacton	isopropamide
Pamine	mepenzolate
Pathilon	methantheline
Prantal	methscopolamine
Pro-Banthine	oxyphenonium
Quarzan	poldine
Robinul	propantheline
Tral	tridihexethyl
Trocinate	thiphenamil

ATROPINE-LIKE DRUGS

The drugs included in the following groups may exhibit atropine-like (anticholinergic) action. This can be important in the management of certain diseases and in potential interactions with other drugs used concurrently.

All drugs containing

atropine

belladonna

hyoscyamine

scopalamine

Antidepressants, Tricyclic

Antihistamines (some)

Anti-parkinsonism Drugs

Antispasmodics, Synthetic

Muscle Relaxants (some)

BARBITURATES

BRAND NAMES (alphabetical)	GENERIC NAMES (alphabetical)
Alurate	amobarbital
Amytal	aprobarbital
Butisol	butabarbital
Lotusate	butalbital
Luminal	hexobarbital
Mebaral	mephobarbital
Nembutal	pentobarbital
Seconal	phenobarbital
Sombulex	secobarbital

CORTISONE-LIKE DRUGS
(Adrenocortical Steroids)

BRAND NAMES (alphabetical)		GENERIC NAMES (alphabetical)
Aristocort	Hydrocortone	betamethasone
Colisone	Inflamase	cortisone
Cortef	Kenacort	dexamethasone
Cortril	Maxidex	hydrocortisone
Decadron	Medrol	methylprednisolone
Delta-Cortef	Meticorten	prednisolone
Deltasone	Novadex	prednisone
Deltra	Novapred	triamcinolone
Deronil	Paracort	
Dexameth	Prednis	
Dexamethadrone	Servisone	
Dexasone	Sterane	
Gammacorten	Valisone	
Hexadrol	Wescopred	
Hydeltra		

DECONGESTANTS

BRAND NAMES (alphabetical)	GENERIC NAMES (alphabetical)
Afrin	ephedrine
Gluco-Fedrin	naphazoline
Neo-Synephrine	oxymetazoline
Novafed	phenylephrine
Otrivin	phenylpropanolamine
Privine	pseudoephedrine
Propadrine	tetrahydrozoline
Sudafed	xylometazoline
Tyzine	

DIURETICS

BRAND NAMES (alphabetical)	GENERIC NAMES (alphabetical)
Aldactone	acetazolamide
Diamox	chlorthalidone
Dyrenium	ethacrynic acid
Edecrin	furosemide
Hygroton	spironolactone
Lasix	triamterene
(See Thiazide Brand Names)	thiazides (see Drug Family)

MONO-AMINE OXIDASE (MAO) INHIBITOR DRUGS

BRAND NAMES (alphabetical)	GENERIC NAMES (alphabetical)
Actomol	furazolidone
Catron	iproniazid
Drazine	isocarboxazid
Eutonyl	mebanazine
Furoxone	nialamide
Marplan	pargyline
Marsilid	phenelzine
Nardil	pheniprazine
Niamid	phenoxypropazine
Parnate	piohydrazine
Tersavid	tranylcypromine

NITRATES

BRAND NAMES (alphabetical)	GENERIC NAMES (alphabetical)
Cardilate	erythrityl tetranitrate
Isordil	isosorbide dinitrate
Laserdil	nitroglycerin
Neo-Corovas	pentaerythritol tetranitrate
Nitro-Bid	
Nitroglyn	
Nitrospan	
Nitrostat	
Peritrate	
SK-Petn	
Sorbide	
Sorbitrate	

PENICILLINS

Alpen	Penbritin	amoxicillin
Amcill	Pentids	ampicillin
Amoxil	Pen-Vee K	carbenicillin
Bactocil	Polycillin	cloxacillin
Dynapen	Polymox	dicloxacillin
Geocillin	Principen	nafcillin
Geopen	Prostaphlin	oxacillin
Larotid	Tegopen	penicillin G
Omnipen	Unipen	penicillin V
Orbenin	V-Cillin K	
Pathocil	Veracillin	

PHENOTHIAZINES

Chlor-PZ	Repoise	acetophenazine	piperacetazine
Compazine	Sparine	butaperazine	prochlorperazine
Largon	Serentil	carphenazine	promazine
Levoprome	Stelazine	chlorpromazine	promethazine
Mellaril	Tacaryl	ethopropazine	propiomazine
Parsidol	Temaril	fluphenazine	thiethylperazine
Permitil	Thorazine	mesoridazine	thioridazine
Phenergan	Tindal	methdilazine	trifluoperazine
Proketazine	Torecan	methotrimeprazine	triflupromazine
Prolixin	Trilafon	perphenazine	trimeprazine
Promatar	Vesprin		
Quide			

SEDATIVES/SLEEP INDUCERS (HYPNOTICS), NON-BARBITURATE

BRAND NAMES (alphabetical)	GENERIC NAMES (alphabetical)
Carbrital	carbromal
Dalmane	chloral hydrate
Doriden	ethchlorvynol
Dorimide	ethinamate
Felsules	flurazepam
Noctec	glutethimide
Noludar	methaqualone
Parest	methyprylon
Placidyl	
Quaalude	
Somnafac	
Somnos	
Sopor	
Valmid	

SULFONAMIDES ("SULFA" DRUGS)

BRAND NAMES (alphabetical)	GENERIC NAMES (alphabetical)
Azulfidine	acetazolamide
Coco-Diazine	sulfachlorpyridazine
Cosulfa	sulfadiazine
Dagenan	sulfadimethoxine
Diamox	sulfamerazine
Elkosin	sulfamethazine
Gantanol	sulfamethizole
Gantrisin	sulfamethoxazole
Kynex	sulfamethoxypyridazine
Madribon	sulfapyridine
Midicel	sulfasalazine
Neotrizine	sulfisomidine
Sonilyn	sulfisoxazole
Suladyne	trisulfapyrimidines
Thiosulfil	
Triple Sulfas	
Urobiotic	

TETRACYCLINES

BRAND NAMES (alphabetical)	GENERIC NAMES (alphabetical)
Achromycin	chlortetracycline
Aureomycin	demeclocycline
Declomycin	doxycycline
Minocin	methacycline
Panmycin	minocycline
Rondomycin	oxytetracycline
Steclin	rolitetracycline
Sumycin	tetracycline
Terramycin	
Tetrachel	
Tetracyn	
Vectrin	
Velacycline	
Vibramycin	

THIAZIDE DIURETICS

BRAND NAMES (alphabetical)		GENERIC NAMES (alphabetical)
Anhydron	Hydrodiuretex	bendroflumethiazide
Chemhydrazide	HydroDiuril	benzthiazide
Diucardin	Hydrosaluret	chlorothiazide
Diuchlor	Hydrozide	cyclothiazide
Diuril	Metahydrin	hydrochlorothiazide
Duretic	Naqua	hydroflumethiazide
Edemol	Naturetin	methyclothiazide
Enduron	Neocodema	polythiazide
Esidrix	Novohydrazide	trichlormethiazide
Exna	Oretic	
Hydrazide	Renese	
Hydrid	Saluron	
Hydrite	Thiuretic	
Hydro-Aquil	Urozide	

TRANQUILIZERS, MILD

BRAND NAMES (alphabetical)	GENERIC NAMES (alphabetical)
Atarax	benactyzine
Deprol	chlordiazepoxide
Equanil	chlormezanone
Fenarol	clorazepate
Librium	diazepam
Miltown	hydroxyzine
Serax	meprobamate
Trancopal	oxazepam
Tranxene	phenaglycodol
Tybatran	tybamate
Ultran	
Valium	
Vistaril	

TRANQUILIZERS, STRONG

BRAND NAMES (alphabetical)	GENERIC NAMES (alphabetical)
Carbolith	chlorprothixene
Eskalith	haloperidol
Haldol	lithium
Lithane	phenothiazines (see Drug Family)
Lithonate	reserpine
Lithotabs	thiothixene
Navane	
Sandril	
Serpasil	
Taractan	
(See Phenothiazines, Brand Names)	

A Glossary of Drug-Related Terms

Glossary

Addiction The traditional term used to identify the irresistible craving for and compulsive use of habit-forming drugs. The more recent preference for the term *dependence* has served to clarify the distinction between habituation and addiction. Drugs capable of producing addiction do so by interacting with the biochemistry of the brain in such a way that they assume a working role. This physical incorporation of the drug into the fundamental processes of brain tissue function is responsible for the agony of the "withdrawal syndrome"—the intense mental and physical pain experienced by the addict when intake of the drug is stopped abruptly. Thus addiction is a *physical dependence.* (See DEPENDENCE for a further account of physical and psychological dependence.)

    Example: The sedative and pain-relieving derivatives of opium—heroin, morphine, codeine—and their synthetic substitutes are all capable of producing addiction through physical dependence.

Adverse Effect or Reaction An abnormal, unexpected, infrequent and usually unpredictable injurious response to a drug. Used in this restrictive sense, the term adverse reaction does *not* include effects of a drug which are normally a part of its pharmacological action, even though such effects may be undesirable and unintended. (See SIDE-EFFECT). Adverse reactions are of three basic types: those due to drug *allergy,* those caused by individual *idiosyncrasy,* and those representing *toxic* effects of drugs on tissue structure and function (see ALLERGY, IDIOSYNCRASY, and TOXICITY).

    Example: The possible interference with normal bone marrow function by phenylbutazone (Butazolidin), resulting in a serious reduction in formation of blood cells, is an adverse effect of a toxic nature. (See BONE MARROW DEPRESSION.)

Allergy (Drug) An abnormal mechanism of drug response that occurs in individuals who produce injurious antibodies* that react with foreign substances—in this instance, a drug. The person who is allergic by nature and has a history of hayfever, asthma, hives, or eczema is more likely to develop drug allergies. Allergic reactions to drugs take many forms: skin eruptions of various kinds, fever, swollen glands, painful joints, jaundice, interference with breathing, acute collapse of circulation, etc. Drug allergies can develop gradually over a long period of time, or they can appear with dramatic suddenness and require life-saving intervention.

---

*Antibodies are special tissue proteins that combine with substances foreign to the body. Protective antibodies destroy bacteria and neutralize toxins. Injurious antibodies, reacting with foreign substances, cause the release of histamine, the principal chemical responsible for allergic reactions.

Example: A 70-year-old woman developed a measles-like rash over her entire body. All diagnostic studies were normal. She left the city to attend a wedding and forgot her phenobarbital, which she had taken for epilepsy since she was in her late teens. The rash disappeared. Upon returning home she resumed the phenobarbital and the rash promptly reappeared. Her allergy to phenobarbital had developed after 50 years of continuous use.

Example: An 18-year-old girl developed a severe sore throat the day before her senior prom. She had taken penicillin once previously with no unfavorable effects. She was given an injection of penicillin to treat her infected throat. Within five minutes she complained of shortness of breath and shortly thereafter collapsed to the floor unconscious. Emergency resuscitation saved her life. She had experienced an acute reaction to penicillin, to which she had become allergic after a single exposure several years before (see ANAPHYLACTIC REACTION).

Anaphylactic (Anaphylactoid) Reaction A group of symptoms which represent (or resemble) a sometimes overwhelming and dangerous allergic reaction due to extreme hypersensitivity to a drug. Anaphylactic reactions, whether mild, moderate, or severe, often involve several body systems. Mild symptoms consist of itching, hives, nasal congestion, nausea, abdominal cramping, and/or diarrhea. Sometimes these precede more severe symptoms such as choking, shortness of breath, and sudden loss of consciousness (usually referred to as anaphylactic shock).

Characteristic features of anaphylactic reaction must be kept in mind. It can result from a very small dose of drug; it develops suddenly, usually within a few minutes after taking the drug; it can be rapidly progressive and can lead to fatal collapse in a short time if not reversed by appropriate treatment. A developing anaphylactic reaction is a true medical emergency. Any adverse effect that appears within 20 minutes after taking a drug should be considered the early manifestations of a possible anaphylactic reaction. Obtain medical attention immediately! (see ALLERGY and HYPERSENSITIVITY).

Example: A 40-year-old lawyer consulted his dentist (whose office was in the same building) for treatment of a gum abscess. Following surgical drainage of the abscess, the lawyer was given a prescription for penicillin tablets and instructed to begin medication immediately. The lawyer obtained the penicillin, returned to his office, and took the first tablet. Within 10 minutes his hands and feet began to itch, his face became swollen, and a choking sensation made it difficult to breathe. He rushed to his dentist's office, where he was given emergency treatment (Adrenalin and oxygen) to reverse the anaphylactic reaction to penicillin.

Anti-hypertensive A drug used to lower the blood pressure. The term "hypertension" denotes blood pressure above the normal range. It does not refer to excessive nervous or emotional tension. The term "anti-hypertensive" is sometimes used erroneously as if it had the same meaning as anti-anxiety (or tranquilizing) drug action.

Today there are more than 100 drug products in use for treating hypertension. Those most frequently prescribed for long-term use fall into three major groups:

drugs that increase urine production (the diuretics)
drugs that relax blood vessel walls
drugs that reduce the activity of the sympathetic nervous system.

Regardless of their mode of action, all these drugs share an ability to lower the blood pressure. It is important to remember that many other drugs can interact with anti-hypertensive drugs: some add to their effect and cause excessive reduction in blood pressure; others interfere with their action and reduce their effectiveness. Anyone who is taking medications for hypertension should consult with his or her physician whenever drugs are prescribed for the treatment of other conditions as well.

Example: A 45-year-old personnel officer was found to have a blood pressure of 185/115 during a routine examination by his company physician. Repeated examinations over the following week confirmed that his blood pressure was remaining unacceptably high. Although he felt well and had no symptoms indicative of hypertension, he followed his physician's urging and began a trial of chlorothiazide. Over the following 4 weeks his blood pressure gradually decreased to an average of 160/100, but it remained in this range in spite of maximal doses of chlorothiazide. By increasing the elimination of salt and water from the body through increased urine production, this thiazide diuretic had achieved a beneficial response but was unable to lower the pressure to the desired level. The physician then added methyldopa to the treatment program. Appropriate dosage adjustments of both drugs were made over the following 6 weeks. By reducing the activity of the sympathetic nervous system, the methyldopa provided additional anti-hypertensive effect. Through the combined actions of both drugs, the patient's blood pressure was maintained consistently below 145/95. Combining drugs with different actions made it possible to achieve satisfactory blood pressure control with reduced dosage of each drug and with fewer undesirable side effects.

Example: Some of the phenothiazine drugs (such as Compazine, Phenergan, and Thorazine) are used widely to treat nausea and vomiting. In some individuals these drugs are capable of causing a significant drop in blood pressure. In treating nausea and vomiting in a person on medication for high blood pressure, the selection of an antinausea (anti-emetic) drug should exclude those that could produce sudden and excessive reductions in blood pressure.

Example: The action of guanethidine (Ismelin) is significantly impaired by the oral contraceptives. In approximately 80% of hypertensive women taking guanethidine while they are using oral contraceptives concurrently, the dose of guanethidine has to be raised substantially to control their blood pressure.

Aplastic Anemia A form of bone marrow failure in which the production of all 3 types of blood cells is seriously impaired (also known as pancytopenia). Aplastic anemia can occur spontaneously from unknown causes, but about one-half of reported cases are induced by certain drugs or chemicals. The symptoms reflect the consequences of inadequate supplies of all 3 blood cell types: deficiency of red blood cells (anemia) results in fatigue, weakness, and pallor; deficiency of white blood cells (leukopenia) predisposes to infections; deficiency of blood platelets (thrombocytopenia) leads to spontaneous bruising and hemorrhage. Treatment is difficult and the outcome unpredictable. Even with the best of care, approximately 50% of cases end fatally.

These drugs and chemicals are known to be capable of inducing aplastic anemia:

acetazolamide	meprobamate
anti-cancer drugs	methimazole
aspirin	oxyphenbutazone
benzene (solvent)	penicillin
carbamazepine	phenacetin
carbon tetrachloride (solvent)	phenylbutazone
chlordane (insecticide)	phenytoin
chlordiazepoxide	primidone
chloromycetin	promazine
chlorothiazide	quinacrine
chlorpheniramine	sulfonamides
chlorpromazine	tetracyclines
chlorpropamide	thiouracil
colchicine	tolbutamide
DDT (insecticide)	triflupromazine
indomethacin	trimethadione
lithium	tripelennamine
mephenytoin	

Although aplastic anemia is a rare consequence of drug treatment (3 in 100,000 users of quinacrine, for example), anyone taking a drug capable of inducing it should have complete blood cell counts periodically if the drug is to be used over an extended period of time.

Blood Platelets The smallest of the three types of blood cells produced by the bone marrow. Platelets are normally present in very large numbers. Their primary function is to assist the process of normal blood clotting so as to prevent excessive bruising and bleeding in the event of injury. When present in proper numbers and functioning normally, platelets preserve the retaining power of the walls of the smaller blood vessels. By initiating appropriate clotting processes in the blood, platelets seal small points of leakage in the vessel walls, thereby preventing spontaneous bruising or bleeding (that which is unprovoked by trauma).

Certain drugs and chemicals may reduce the number of available blood platelets to abnormally low levels. Some of these drugs act by suppressing platelet formation; other drugs hasten their destruction. When the number of functioning platelets falls below a critical level, blood begins to leak through the thin walls of smaller vessels. The outward evidence of this leakage is the spontaneous appearance of scattered bruises in the skin of the thighs and legs. This is referred to as purpura. Bleeding may occur anywhere in the body, internally as well as superficially into the tissues immediately beneath the skin.

Example: A woman in her early forties developed a persistent bursitis in her shoulder. A popular form of buffered aspirin provided reasonable relief of pain. Certain that the bursitis would eventually disappear, she continued to use the aspirin in doses of 4 to 6 tablets daily over a period of 9 months. While bathing she noticed the appearance of a few small painless bruises scattered over her thighs. She could recall no injury to account for the bruising, so she dismissed the discovery as unimportant. As her recurrent bursitis required, she continued the intermittent use of aspirin. The areas of bruising became more numerous and extensive. On examination by her physician, blood studies revealed "a very low blood platelet count." She was advised to discontinue all drugs and was scheduled for bone marrow examination. Within a few days after discontinuing the use of aspirin, the bruises began to fade and no new bruising occurred. Bone marrow studies were normal and repeated examinations of the blood revealed that the blood platelets had returned to a normal level. She had experienced an allergic destruction of her blood platelets, a well-known adverse reaction to aspirin in sensitive individuals.

Bone Marrow Depression A serious reduction in the ability of the bone marrow to carry on its normal production of blood cells. This can occur as an adverse reaction to the toxic effect of certain drugs and chemicals on bone marrow components. When functioning normally, the bone marrow produces the majority of the body's blood cells. These consist of three types: the red blood cells (erythrocytes), the white blood cells (leukocytes), and the blood platelets (thrombocytes). Each type of cell performs one or more specific functions, all of which are indispensable to the maintenance of life and health.

Drugs that are capable of depressing bone marrow activity can impair the production of all types of blood cells simultaneously or of only one type selectively. Periodic examinations of the blood can reveal significant changes in the structure and number of the blood cells that indicate a possible drug effect on bone marrow activity.

Impairment of the production of red blood cells leads to anemia, a condition of abnormally low red cells and hemoglobin. This causes weakness, loss of energy and stamina, intolerance to cold environments, and shortness of breath on physical exertion. A reduction in the formation of white blood cells can impair the body's immunity and lower its resistance to infection. These changes may result in the development of fever, sore throat, or pneumonia. When the formation of blood platelets is suppressed to abnormally low levels, the blood loses its ability to quickly seal small points of leakage in blood vessel walls. This may lead to episodes of unusual and abnormal spontaneous bruising or to prolonged bleeding in the event of injury.

Any of these symptoms can occur in the presence of bone marrow depression. They should alert both patient and physician to the need for prompt studies of blood and bone marrow.

Example: A 10-year-old boy developed pneumonia while on a winter camping trip. He responded promptly to a course of chloramphenicol (Chloromycetin) and recovered without complication. Within a few weeks he began to experience a series of head and chest colds. Anxious to keep his absence from school to a minimum, and remembering how promptly he responded to earlier treatment for pneumonia, the boy's mother began to administer chloramphenicol whenever a head cold or chest cold began to develop. After several short courses of the drug over a period of 3 months, the boy's health began to fail noticeably. Concerned by his loss of weight, persistent fever, paleness, and fatigue, the mother arranged for medical evaluation. Routine blood studies disclosed a significant reduction of all three series of blood cells. A bone marrow examination confirmed the diagnosis of aplastic anemia due to the repeated use of chloramphenicol (see APLASTIC ANEMIA).

Brand Name The registered trade name given to a drug product by its manufacturer. Many drugs are marketed by more than one manufacturer or distributor. Each company adopts a distinctive trade name to identify its brand of the generic drug from that of its competitors. Thus a brand name designates a proprietary drug—one that is protected by patent or copyright. Generally brand names are shorter, easier to pronounce, and more readily remembered than their generic counterparts.

Example: The generic drug hydrochlorothiazide is marketed in the U.S. and Canada by sixteen manufacturers under the following *brand names:*

Chemhydrazide	Hydrodiuretex
Diuchlor H	HydroDiuril
Edemol	Hydrosaluret
Esidrix	Hydrozide
Hydrazide	Neo-Codema
Hydrid	Novohydrazide
Hydrite	Oretic
Hydro-Aquil	Urozide

Cause-and-Effect Relationship A possible causative association between a drug and an observed biologic event—most commonly a side-effect or an adverse effect. Knowledge of a drug's full spectrum of effects (wanted and unwanted) is highly desirable when weighing its benefits and risks in any treatment situation. However, it is often impossible to establish with certainty that a particular drug is the primary agent responsible for a suspected adverse effect. In the evaluation of every cause-and-effect relationship, therefore, meticulous consideration must be given to such factors as the time sequence of drug administration and possible reaction, the use of multiple drugs, possible interactions among these drugs, the effects of the disease under treatment, the physiological and psychological characteristics of the patient, and the possible influence of unrecognized disorders and malfunctions.

The majority of adverse drug reactions occur sporadically, unpredictably, and infrequently in the general population. A *definite* cause-and-effect relationship between drug and reaction is established when (1) the adverse effect immediately follows administration of the drug; or (2) the adverse effect disappears after the drug is discontinued (dechallenge) and promptly reappears when the drug is used again (rechallenge); or (3) the adverse effects are clearly the expected and predictable toxic consequences of drug overdosage.

In contrast to the obvious "causative" (definite) relationship, there exists a large gray area of "probable," "possible," and "coincidental" associations that are clouded by varying degrees of uncertainty. These classifications usually apply to alleged drug reactions that require a relatively long time to develop, are of low incidence, and for which there are no clear-cut objective means of demonstrating a causal mechanism that links drug and reaction. Clarification of cause-and-effect relationships in these uncertain groups requires carefully designed observation over a long period of time, followed by sophisticated statistical analysis. Occasionally the public is alerted to a newly found "relationship" based upon suggestive but incomplete data. Though early warning is clearly in the public interest, such announcements should make clear whether the presumed relationship is based upon definitive criteria or is simply inferred because the use of a drug and an observed event were found to occur together within an appropriate time frame.

The most competent techniques for evaluating cause-and-effect relationships of adverse drug reactions have been devised by the Division of Tissue Reactions to Drugs, a research unit of the Armed Forces Institute of Pathology. Based upon a highly critical examination of all available evidence, the Division's study of 2800 drug-related deaths yielded the following levels of certainty regarding cause-and-effect relationship:

No association	5.0%
Coincidental	14.5%
Possible	33.0%
Probable	30.0%
Causative	17.5%

It is significant that expert evaluation of 2800 drug-related cases concluded that only 47.5% could be substantiated as definitely or probably causative.

Example: A 48-year-old man went into anaphylactic shock within a few minutes after the administration of penicillin given to treat a large abscess on his neck. The almost immediate development of this overwhelming allergic reaction established a "causative" association between drug and adverse effect.

Example: A 50-year-old woman developed jaundice during the fourth week of chlorpromazine (Thorazine) treatment for chronic anxiety, raising the question of a possible drug reaction. A liver biopsy (tissue examination) and appropriate laboratory tests of liver function revealed a familiar pattern of results consistent with the type of liver disorder and jaundice generally associated with use of phenothiazine tranquilizers in sensitive individuals. The cause-and-effect relationship in this case was judged to be "probable."

Example: A 53-year-old man with a history of peptic ulcer (a stomach ulcer which bled 10 years earlier) was given phenylbutazone (Butazolidin) to treat acute bursitis of the shoulder. He took the drug after meals to reduce the possibility of indigestion. On the fifth day of treatment he awoke in the middle of the night acutely nauseated and vomiting blood. He required emergency hospitalization and blood transfusion. Subsequent X-ray studies revealed a prominent ulcer of the stomach. Although the mechanism of drug-induced peptic ulcer (in the stomach or duodenum) is not well understood, the association of ulcer reactivation with the use of certain drugs is well recognized. In the absence of definitive tests that could link his drug to stomach ulceration, the cause-and-effect relationship in this case was judged to be "possible."

Example: A husband and wife attended a community church supper and ate liberally of most foods served. Earlier the same day the husband had begun taking chlorthalidone (Hygroton), which had just been prescribed for his high blood pressure. Shortly after retiring, the husband developed abdominal cramping and diarrhea. He immediately concluded that he was probably experiencing a "reaction to the new medicine." An hour later his wife developed cramping and diarrhea. They learned the next day that most of their neighbors who ate chicken salad at the church supper also experienced cramping and diarrhea. The cause-and-effect relationship between drug and "reaction" in this case was judged to be "coincidental." Continued use of chlorthalidone was not accompanied by cramps or diarrhea.

Contraindication   A condition or disease that precludes the use of a particular drug. Some contraindications are *absolute,* meaning that the use of the drug would expose the patient to extreme hazard and therefore cannot be justified. Other contraindications are *relative,* meaning that the condition or disease does not entirely bar the use of the drug but requires that, before the decision to use the drug is made, special consideration be given to factors which could aggravate existing disease, interfere with current treatment, or produce new injury.

Example: Severe allergy to penicillin is an *absolute contraindication* to its use for any reason.

Example: Reduced kidney function (such as that which results from chronic kidney disease) is a *relative contraindication* to the use of kanamycin (Kantrex) because the potential toxicity of kanamycin can be enhanced if kidney function is impaired.

Dependence   The preferred term used to identify the drug-dependent states of *psychological dependence* (or *habituation*), and *physical dependence* (or *addiction*). In addition, a third kind of drug-dependence can be included under this term. This might be called *functional dependence*—the need to use a drug continuously in order to sustain a particular body function, the impairment of which causes annoying symptoms of varying degree and significance.

Psychological dependence is a form of neurotic behavior. Its principal characteristic is an obsession to satisfy a particular desire, be it one of self-gratification or one of escape from some real or imagined distress. Psychological dependence is a very human trait that is seen often in many socially acceptable patterns and practices such as entertainment, gambling, sports, and collecting. A common form of this dependence in today's culture is the increasing reliance upon drugs to help in coping with the every-day problems of living: pills for frustration, disappointment, nervous stom-ach, tension headache, and insomnia. The 20 million smokers of marijuana have found it to be a drug that eases their stress, one whose effectiveness fosters habit (psychological dependence) but not addiction.

Physical dependence, which is true addiction, includes two elements: habituation and tolerance. Addicting drugs provide relief from anguish and pain swiftly and effectively; they also induce a physiological tolerance that requires increasing dosage on repeated use if they are to remain effective. These two features foster the continued need for the drug and lead to its becoming a functioning component in the biochemistry of the brain. As this occurs, the drug assumes an "essential" role in ongoing chemical pro-cesses. (Thus some authorities prefer the term *chemical dependence.*) Sud-den removal of the drug from the system causes a major upheaval in body chemistry and provokes a withdrawal syndrome—the intense mental and physical pain experienced by the addict when intake of the drug is stopped abruptly—that is the hallmark of addiction.

Functional dependence differs significantly from both psychological and physical dependence. It occurs when a drug effectively relieves an annoying or distressing condition and the particular body function in-volved becomes increasingly dependent upon the action of the drug to provide a sense of well-being. Drugs which are capable of inducing func-tional dependence are used primarily for the relief of symptoms. They do not act on the brain to produce alteration of mood or consciousness as do those drugs with potential for either psychological or physical dependence. The most familiar example of functional dependence is the "laxative habit." Some types of constipation are made worse by the wrong choice of laxative, and natural function gradually fades as the colon becomes more and more dependent upon the action of certain laxative drugs.

Disulfiram-Like (Antabuse-Like) Reaction The symptoms that result from the interaction of alcohol and any drug that is capable of provoking the pattern of response typical of the "Antabuse effect." The interacting drug inter-rupts the normal decomposition of alcohol by the liver and thereby permits the accumulation of a toxic by-product that enters the bloodstream. When sufficient levels of both alcohol and drug are present in the blood the reaction occurs. It consists of intense flushing and warming of the face, a severe throbbing headache, shortness of breath, chest pains, nausea, re-peated vomiting, sweating, and weakness. If the amount of alcohol ingested has been large enough, the reaction may progress to blurred vision, vertigo, confusion, marked drop in blood pressure, and loss of consciousness. Severe reactions may lead to convulsions and death. The reaction can last from 30 minutes to several hours, depending upon the amount of alcohol in the body. As the symptoms subside, the individual is exhausted and usually sleeps for several hours.

Example: A 52-year-old business executive was found to have diabe-tes during his annual physical examination. His blood sugar levels re-mained above the normal range in spite of his careful adherence to a prescribed diet. To obtain better control of the blood sugar, his physician started him on a trial of chlorpropamide (Diabinese) but failed to mention that some individuals taking anti-diabetic drugs of the sulfonylurea family experience a disulfiram-like reaction following the use of alcohol. On the third day after starting his medication, the executive invited an associate to join him for a business lunch. As was his custom on such occasions, he drank two cocktails before starting to eat. Ten minutes later he began to experience a sense of warmth and fullness in his head. This was soon followed by pounding of his heart, shortness of breath, and profuse sweating. Alarmed and puzzled by this sudden development, he asked his associate to take him to the nearest hospital emergency room. When the attending physician obtained a history of current chlorpropamide therapy and luncheon cocktails, he readily identified the resulting disulfiram-like reaction.

Dosage Forms and Strengths This information category in the individual Drug Profiles (Section Three) uses several abbreviations to designate measurements of weight and volume. These are:

mcg. = microgram = 1,000,000th of a gram (weight)
mg. = milligram   = 1000th of a gram (weight)
ml. = milliliter = 1000th of a liter (volume)
gm. = gram   = 1000 milligrams (weight)

There are approximately 65 mg. in 1 grain.
There are approximately 5 ml. in 1 teaspoonful.
There are approximately 15 ml. in 1 tablespoonful.
There are approximately 30 ml. in 1 ounce.
1 milliliter of water weighs 1 gram.
There are approximately 454 grams in 1 pound.

Drug, Drug Product Terms often used interchangeably to designate a medicine (in any of its dosage forms) used in medical practice. Strictly speaking, the term *drug* refers to the single chemical entity that provokes a specific response when placed within a biological system—the "active" ingredient. A *drug product* is the manufactured dosage form—tablet, capsule, elixir, etc.—that contains the active drug intermixed with inactive ingredients to provide for convenient administration.

Drug products which contain only one active ingredient are referred to as single entity drugs. Drug products with two or more active ingredients are called combination drugs (designated [CD] in the lists of brand names in the Drug Profiles, Section Three).

Examples: Tylenol Elixir is a single entity *drug product;* acetaminophen is its only active *drug* ingredient.

Ser-Ap-Es is a combination *drug product;* it contains three active *drug* ingredients:

Serpasil (a brand name for reserpine)
Apresoline (a brand name for hydralazine)
Esidrix (a brand name for hydrochlorothiazide)

Drug Family A group or class of drugs that are similar in chemistry, method of action, and use in treatment. Because of their common characteristics, many drugs within a family will produce the same side-effects and have similar potential for provoking related adverse reactions and interactions. However, significant variations among members within a drug family can occur. This sometimes allows the physician an important degree of selectivity in choosing a drug if certain beneficial actions are desired or particular side-effects are to be minimized.

Examples: Antihistamines, oral contraceptives, phenothiazines, tetracyclines (see Section Four).

Drug Fever The elevation of body temperature that occurs as an unwanted manifestation of drug action. Drugs can induce fever by several mechanisms; these include allergic reactions, drug-induced tissue damage, acceleration of tissue metabolism, constriction of blood vessels in the skin with resulting decrease in loss of body heat, and direct action on the temperature-regulating center in the brain.

The most common form of drug fever is that associated with allergic reactions. It may be the only allergic manifestation apparent, or it may be part of a complex of allergic symptoms that can include skin rash, hives, joint swelling and pain, enlarged lymph glands, hemolytic anemia, or hepatitis. The fever usually appears about 7 to 10 days after starting the drug and may vary from low-grade to alarmingly high levels. It may be sustained or intermittent, but it usually persists for as long as the drug is taken. In previously sensitized individuals drug fever may occur within one or two hours after taking the first dose of medication.

While many drugs are capable of producing fever, the following are more commonly responsible:

allopurinol	para-aminosalicylic acid
antihistamines	penicillin
atropine-like drugs	pentazocine
barbiturates	phenytoin
coumarin anticoagulants	procainamide
hydralazine	propylthiouracil
iodides	quinidine
isoniazid	rifampin
methyldopa	sulfonamides
novobiocin	

Example: A 56-year-old man under treatment for high blood pressure was found to have an inadequate response to a trial of thiazide drugs used alone. His physician added methyldopa to his treatment routine and asked him to return for evaluation in 2 weeks. After 1 week of taking methyldopa daily, the patient experienced an abrupt onset of fever, chills, and fatigue. Believing he had the "flu," he stayed in bed, took aspirin and increased his intake of fluids. After 3 days of persistent fever (to levels of 103°), he discontinued all medication. Within 48 hours all symptoms disappeared. He called his physician, reported what had happened, and requested instructions regarding the resumption of medications for his high blood pressure. He was advised to resume the same medications he was taking before the episode of "flu." Within a few hours after restarting methyldopa, the patient experienced a sudden rise in temperature to 104°. By discontinuing the drug initially (dechallenge) and later resuming it (rechallenge), he inadvertently established the cause-and-effect relationship between methyldopa and his drug fever.

Extension Effect An unwanted but predictable drug response that is a logical consequence of mild to moderate overdosage. An extension effect is an exaggeration of the drug's normal pharmacological action; it can be thought of as a mild form of dose-related toxicity (see OVERDOSAGE and TOXICITY).

Example: The continued "hangover" of drowsiness and mental sluggishness that persists after arising in the morning is a common extension effect of a long-acting sleep inducing drug (hypnotic) taken the night before.

Example: The persistent intestinal cramping and diarrhea that result from too generous a dose of laxative are extension effects of the drug's anticipated action.

Generic Name The official, common, or public name used to designate an active drug entity, whether in pure form or in dosage form. Generic names are coined by committees of officially appointed drug experts and are approved by governmental agencies for national and international use. Thus they are non-proprietary. Many drug products are marketed under the generic name of the principal active ingredient and bear no brand name of the manufacturer.

Though the total number of prescriptions written in the United States in 1975 declined by 1%, prescriptions specifying the *generic name* of the drug increased by 3.2%. Generically written prescriptions now account for 11.1% of all new prescriptions written in the United States. The drugs most commonly prescribed by generic name are listed below, ranked in descending order of the number of new prescriptions issued.

ampicillin	phenobarbital
tetracycline	penicillin G
erythromycin	meprobamate
penicillin V	digoxin
prednisone	thyroid

Example: Meprobamate is the generic name designating the active drug ingredient of two trademarked brands, Equanil and Miltown. *Diazepam* is the generic name that identifies the active drug entity of the widely used mild tranquilizer marketed as Valium.

Habituation A form of drug dependence based upon strong psychological gratification rather than the physical (chemical) dependence of addiction. The habitual use of drugs that alter mood or relieve minor discomforts results from a compulsive need to feel pleasure and satisfaction or to escape the manifestations of emotional distress. The abrupt cessation of habituating drugs does not produce the withdrawal syndrome seen in addiction. Thus habituation is a *psychological dependence.* (See DEPENDENCE for a further account of psychological and physical dependence.)

Example: Amphetamines (Benezedrine, Dexedrine) are capable of producing extreme psychological dependence but are not addicting. Many over-the-counter drugs used to relieve headaches, minor pains, nervous tension and insomnia can lead to psychological dependence if taken excessively. Regardless of the drug taken, its abusive use is a form of neurotic behavior.

Hemolytic Anemia A form of anemia (deficient red blood cells and hemoglobin) resulting from the premature destruction (hemolysis) of circulating red blood cells. Several mechanisms can be responsible for the development of hemolytic anemia; among these is the action of certain drugs and chemicals. Some individuals are susceptible to hemolytic anemia because of a genetic deficiency in the makeup of their red blood cells. If such people are given certain antimalarial drugs, sulfa drugs, or numerous other drugs, some of their red cells will disintegrate on contact with the drug. (About 10% of American blacks have this genetic trait.)

Another type of drug-induced hemolytic anemia is a form of drug allergy. Many drugs in wide use (including quinidine, methyldopa, levodopa, and chlorpromazine) are known to cause hemolytic destruction of red cells as a hypersensitivity (allergic) reaction.

Hemolytic anemia can occur abruptly (with evident symptoms) or silently. The acute form lasts about 7 days and is characterized by fever, pallor, weakness, dark-colored urine, and varying degrees of jaundice (yellow coloration of eyes and skin). When drug-induced hemolytic anemia is mild, involving the destruction of only a small number of red blood cells, there may be no symptoms to indicate its presence. Such episodes are detected only by means of laboratory studies (see IDIOSYNCRASY and ALLERGY, DRUG).

Hepatitis-Like Reaction Changes in the liver, induced by certain drugs, which closely resemble those produced by viral hepatitis. The symptoms of drug-induced hepatitis and virus-induced hepatitis are often so similar that the correct cause cannot be established without precise laboratory studies.

Hepatitis due to drugs may be a form of drug allergy (as in reaction to many of the phenothiazines), or it may represent a toxic adverse effect (as in reaction to some of the mono-amine oxidase inhibitor drugs). Liver reactions of significance usually result in jaundice and represent serious adverse effects (see JAUNDICE; see also Table 4 in Section Six).

Hypersensitivity A term subject to varying usages for many years. One common use has been to identify the trait of overresponsiveness to drug action, that is, an intolerance to even small doses. Used in this sense, the term indicates that the nature of the response is appropriate but the degree of response is exaggerated.

The term is more widely used today to identify a state of allergy. To have a *hypersensitivity* to a drug is to be *allergic* to it (see ALLERGY, DRUG).

Some individuals develop cross-hypersensitivity. This means that once a person has developed an allergy to a certain drug, that person will experience an allergic reaction to other drugs which are closely related in chemical composition.

Example: The patient was known to be *hypersensitive* by nature, having a history of seasonal hay fever and asthma since childhood. His *allergy* to tetracycline developed after his third course of treatment. This drug *hypersensitivity* manifested itself as a diffuse, measles-like rash.

Hypoglycemia A condition in which the amount of glucose (a sugar) in the blood is below the normal range. Since normal brain function is dependent upon an adequate supply of glucose, reducing the level of glucose in the blood below a critical point will cause serious impairment of brain activity. The resulting symptoms are characteristic of the hypoglycemic state. Early indications are headache, a sensation resembling mild drunkenness, and an inability to think clearly. These may be accompanied by hunger. As the level of blood glucose continues to fall, nervousness and confusion develop. Varying degrees of weakness, numbness, trembling, sweating, and rapid heart action follow. If sugar is not provided at this point and the blood glucose level drops further, impaired speech, incoordination, and unconsciousness, with or without convulsions, will follow.

Hypoglycemia in any stage requires prompt recognition and treatment. Because of the potential for injury to the brain, the mechanisms and management of hypoglycemia should be understood by all who use drugs capable of producing it.

Example: A 24-year-old traveling salesman required a morning dose of 65 units of an intermediate-acting insulin to control his diabetes. Late one afternoon, while driving between cities, he had a flat tire. During the process of changing wheels, he began to experience lightheadedness, weakness, trembling, and excessive perspiring. He felt flushed and noted rapid pounding of his heart. Recognizing these symptoms to be the early manifestations of an "insulin reaction," he immediately swallowed the cubes of table sugar he always carried with him for such an emergency. The concurrent effects of emotional stress, unusual physical exertion, a delayed evening meal, and unopposed insulin action had combined to induce a state of hypoglycemia; his prompt recognition of glucose deficiency and his timely corrective action prevented progression of his situation to a state of helplessness and coma.

Example: Upon returning home late one evening, a woman found her 61-year-old diabetic mother unconscious on the living room sofa. The family physician was summoned, and he promptly restored her to consciousness with an intravenous injection of glucose solution. She related that during her daughter's absence she had developed a headache, had taken two aspirin tablets along with her evening dose of tolbutamide (Orinase), and had lain down to rest before dinner. Apparently she fell asleep and slipped into hypoglycemia coma. The headache was probably an early manifestation of impending hypoglycemia. The interaction of aspirin with tolbutamide increased its ability to lower the blood glucose still further. Sleep prevented the intake of food that could have relieved the hypoglycemia.

(NOTE: The elderly are more susceptible to hypoglycemia from the use of oral anti-diabetic drugs.)

Idiosyncrasy An abnormal mechanism of drug response that occurs in individuals who have a peculiar defect in their body chemistry (often hereditary) which produces an effect totally unrelated to the drug's normal pharmacological action. Idiosyncrasy is not a form of allergy. The actual chemical defects responsible for certain idiosyncratic drug reactions are well understood; others are not.

Example: Approximately 100 million people in the world (including 10% of American blacks) have a specific enzyme deficiency in their red blood cells that causes these cells to disintegrate when exposed to drugs such as sulfonamides (Gantrisin, Kynex), nitrofurantoin (Furadantin, Macrodantin), probenecid (Benemid), quinine, and quinidine. As a result of this reaction, these drugs (and others) can cause a significant anemia in susceptible individuals.

Example: Approximately 5% of the population of the United States is susceptible to the development of glaucoma on prolonged use of cortisone-related drugs (see Cortisone Drug Family in Section Four).

Interaction An unwanted change in the body's response to a drug that results when a second drug that is capable of altering the action of the first is administered at the same time. Some drug interactions can enhance the effect of either drug, producing an overresponse similar to overdosage. Other interactions may reduce drug effectiveness and cause inadequate response. A third type of interaction can produce a seemingly unrelated toxic response with no associated increase or decrease in the pharmacological actions of the interacting drugs.

Theoretically, many drugs can interact with one another, but in reality drug interactions are comparatively infrequent. Many interactions can be anticipated, and the physician can make appropriate adjustments in dosage to prevent or minimize unintended fluctuations in drug response.

Examples: Aspirin can *interact* with anticoagulant drugs (such as warfarin and dicumarol) to increase the anticoagulant effect. This may lead to abnormal bleeding, ranging from mild nose or gum bleeding to severe hemorrhage.

Barbiturates (such as phenobarbital) can *interact* with anticoagulants to decrease the anticoagulant effect. Larger than usual doses of the anticoagulant are then required to produce the desired response. Withdrawal of the barbiturate, without an appropriate reduction in the anticoagulant dose, may result in abnormal bleeding due to excessive (unopposed) anticoagulant effect.

A tricyclic antidepressant (amitriptyline, imipramine, etc.) given inadvertently to someone taking a mono-amine oxidase (MAO) inhibitor drug (furazolidone, pargyline, phenelzine, etc.) can produce a severe toxic reaction consisting of agitation, tremor, high fever, and coma.

Jaundice A yellow coloration of the skin (and the white portion of the eyes) that occurs when excessive bile pigments accumulate in the blood as a result of impaired liver function. Jaundice can be produced by several mechanisms. It may occur as a manifestation of a wide variety of diseases, or it may represent an adverse reaction to a particular drug. At times it is difficult to distinguish between disease-induced jaundice and drug-induced jaundice.

Jaundice due to a drug is always a serious adverse effect. Anyone taking a drug that is capable of causing jaundice should watch closely for any significant change in the color of urine or feces. Dark discoloration of the urine and paleness (lack of color) of the stool may be early indications of a developing jaundice. Should either of these symptoms occur, it is advisable to discontinue the drug and notify the prescribing physician promptly. Diagnostic tests are available to clarify the nature of the jaundice.

Example: A 30-year-old man was found to have converted from a negative to a positive tuberculin skin test after a fellow worker was hospitalized for active tuberculosis. As a preventive measure he was started on a one-year course of isoniazid (INH, Nydrazid). During the third week of treatment he began to feel ill. He lost his appetite and became aware of vague nausea. Within a few days he began to itch. His wife detected a yellowish tint in his eyes. The following day the skin of his chest and abdomen was found to be turning yellow when examined in daylight. Blood tests for viral hepatitis were negative. His physician discontinued the isoniazid and the jaundice cleared within 3 weeks. This type of drug-induced jaundice closely resembles viral hepatitis (an infection of the liver). It is thought to be allergic in nature and to represent a hypersensitivity reaction to the drug.

Lupus Erythematosus A serious disease of unknown cause that occurs in two forms, one limited to the skin (discoid LE) and the other involving several body systems (systemic LE). Both forms occur predominantly in young women. About 5% of cases of the discoid form convert to the systemic form. Basically, systemic LE is a disorder of the body's immune system which may result in chronic, progressive inflammation and destruction of the connective tissue framework of the skin, blood vessels, joints, brain, heart muscle, lungs, and kidneys. Altered proteins in the blood lead to the formation of antibodies which react with certain organ tissues to produce the inflammation and destruction characteristic of the disease. A reduction in the number of white blood cells and blood platelets often occurs. The course of systemic LE is usually quite protracted and unpredictable. While no cure is known, satisfactory management may be achieved in some cases by the judicious use of cortisone-like drugs.

Several drugs in wide use are capable of initiating a form of systemic LE quite similar to that which occurs spontaneously. (More than 100 cases due to the use of procainamide have been reported.) Suggestive symptoms may appear as early as 2 weeks or as late as 8 years after starting the responsible drug. The initial symptoms usually consist of low-grade fever, skin rashes of various kinds, aching muscles, and multiple joint pains. Chest pains (pleurisy) are fairly common. Enlargement of the lymph glands occurs less frequently. Symptoms usually subside following discontinuation of the responsible drug, but laboratory evidence of the reaction may persist for many months.

Drugs known to induce systemic LE include:

chlorpromazine	phenothiazines (some)
clofibrate	phenylbutazone
hydralazine	phenytoin
isoniazid	practolol
oral contraceptives	procainamide
penicillamine	thiouracil
phenolphthalein	

Example: A 48-year-old registered nurse with a history of premature heart beats since 18 years of age consulted her physician because of heart palpitation of increasing severity. As a result of multiple stresses, she had increased her cigarette consumption to 50 a day. She was found to have high blood pressure and a serious disorder of heart rhythm. She responded well to chlorothiazide and procainamide, and she resumed her professional activities. After 23 months of continuous use of procainamide she began to notice stiffness of her fingers on arising. This was soon followed by joint pain and tenderness in both hands and both elbows. A temperature of 99° to 99.4° was noted on several occasions. She interpreted her symptoms to be due to early rheumatoid arthritis (which her mother had quite severely) and treated herself for the next 3 months. When her hands became so painful she was unable to sleep, she was referred to a rheumatologist. Laboratory studies confirmed his suspicion of drug-induced systemic LE. The procainamide was discontinued and prednisone was started to treat the LE manifestations. Significant improvement occurred within 2 weeks, but complete clearance of all symptoms required 6 months of continuous treatment.

Orthostatic Hypotension A type of low blood pressure that is related to body position or posture (also called postural hypotension). The individual who is subject to orthostatic hypotension may have a normal blood pressure while lying down, but on sitting upright or standing he will experience sudden sensations of lightheadedness, dizziness, and a feeling of impending faint that compel him to return quickly to a lying position. These symptoms are manifestations of inadequate blood flow (oxygen supply) to the brain due to an abnormal delay in the rise in blood pressure that always occurs as the body adjusts the circulation to the erect position.

Many drugs (especially the stronger anti-hypertensives) may cause orthostatic hypotension. Individuals who experience this drug effect should report it to their physician so that appropriate dosage adjustment can be made to minimize it. Failure to correct or to compensate for these sudden drops in blood pressure can lead to severe falls and injury.

The tendency to orthostatic hypotension can be reduced by avoiding sudden standing, prolonged standing, vigorous exercise, and exposure to hot environments. Alcoholic beverages should be used cautiously until their combined effect with the drug in use has been determined.

Overdosage The meaning of this term should not be limited to the concept of doses that clearly exceed the normal dosage range recommended by the manufacturer. The optimal dose of many drugs (that amount which gives the greatest benefit with least distress) varies greatly from person to person. What may be an average dose for the majority of individuals will be an overdose for some and an underdose for others. Numerous factors, such as age, body size, nutritional status, and liver and kidney function, have significant influence on dosage requirements. Drugs with narrow safety margins often produce indications of overdosage if something delays the regular elimination of the customary daily dose. In this instance, overdosage results from accumulation of prescribed daily doses. Massive overdosage—as occurs with accidental ingestion of drugs by children or with suicidal intention by adults—is referred to as poisoning.

Example: The proper use of digitalis is based upon achieving a correct maintenance dose, one that provides a relatively stable level of the drug in blood and body tissues. The maintenance of this "steady state" requires a daily dose that very closely replaces the amount of the drug eliminated from the body each day in the urine and stool. The patient who is properly digitalized with digoxin (that is, on the correct maintenance dose) may develop manifestations of overdosage if his regular intake of liquids drops to a level that does not provide for adequate urine production.

Over-the-Counter (OTC) Drugs Drug products that can be purchased without prescription. Many are available in food stores, variety stores, and newsstands as well as in conventional drug stores. Because of the unrestricted availability of these drugs, many people do not look upon OTC medicines as drugs. But drugs they are! And like the more potent drug products that are sold only on prescription, they are chemicals that are capable of a wide variety of actions on biological systems. Within the last 30 years, many OTC drugs have assumed greater importance because of their ability to interact unfavorably with some widely used prescription drugs. Serious problems in drug management can arise when (1) the patient fails to inform the physician of the OTC drug(s) he is taking ("because they really aren't drugs") and (2) the physician fails to specify that his question about what medicines are being taken currently *includes all OTC drugs.* During any course of treatment, whether medical or surgical, the patient should consult with the physician regarding any OTC drug that he wishes to take.

The major classes of OTC drugs for internal use include:

allergy medicines (antihistamines)	laxatives
antacids	menstrual aids
anti-worm medicines	motion sickness remedies
aspirin and aspirin combinations	pain relievers
aspirin substitutes	reducing aids
asthma aids	salt substitutes
cold medicines (decongestants)	sedatives and tranquilizers
cough medicines	sleeping pills
diarrhea remedies	stimulants (caffeine)
digestion aids	sugar substitutes (saccharin)
diuretics	tonics
iron preparations	vitamins

Example: An insurance adjuster with a history of stress-induced indigestion used antacids occasionally during the day and always at bedtime in liberal amounts. During a period of chronic insomnia, his physician prescribed pentobarbital to be taken at bedtime. The habitual use of antacids at bedtime was never discussed by patient or physician. After a trial of pentobarbital for several nights, the patient reported no significant sedative effect. He was unaware that antacids can retard the absorption of pentobarbital and prevent the attainment of an effective blood level.

Example: A 42-year-old housewife was advised that she needed a hysterectomy (surgical removal of the womb). For the previous year she had been consuming large quantities of a popular aspirin-containing OTC preparation promoted to relieve headaches and nervous tension. When asked by her surgeon to name "the drugs" she was taking, she said she was not using any drugs. Since she did not consider an OTC preparation to be a "drug," her regular use of aspirin went undetected. During the course of her operation, the surgical team had considerable difficulty controlling her bleeding. She required a blood transfusion and intravenous Vitamin K to correct her impairment of normal blood clotting. The patient was unaware that large doses of aspirin can affect some of the clotting factors in the blood and predispose to abnormal bleeding.

Paradoxical Reaction An unexpected drug response that is not consistent with the known pharmacology of the drug and may in fact be the opposite of the intended and anticipated response. Such reactions are due to individual sensitivity or variability and can occur in any age group. They are seen more commonly, however, in children and the elderly.

Example: An 80-year-old man was admitted to a nursing home following the death of his wife. He had difficulty adjusting to his new environment and was restless, agitated, and irritable. He was given a trial of the tranquilizer diazepam (Valium) to relax him, starting with small doses. On the second day of medication he became confused and erratic in behavior. The dose of diazepam was increased. On the third day he began to wander aimlessly, talked incessantly in a loud voice, and displayed anger and hostility when attempts were made to help him. Suspecting the possibility of a paradoxical reaction, the diazepam was discontinued. All behavioral disturbances gradually subsided within 3 days.

Parkinson-Like Disorders (Parkinsonism) A group of symptoms that resembles those caused by Parkinson's disease, a chronic disorder of the nervous system also known as shaking palsy. The characteristic features of parkinsonism include a fixed, emotionless facial expression (mask-like in appearance), a prominent trembling of the hands, arms, or legs, and stiffness of the extremities that limits movement and produces a rigid posture and gait.

Parkinsonism is a fairly common adverse effect that occurs in about 15% of all patients who take large doses of strong tranquilizers (notably the phenothiazines) or use them over an extended period of time. If recognized early, the parkinson-like features will lessen or disappear with reduced dosage or change in medication. In some instances, however, parkinson-like changes may become permanent, requiring appropriate medication for their control.

Example: A 58-year-old woman was hospitalized for extreme agitation and depression following attempted suicide. She experienced remarkable improvement in the third week of treatment with high doses of chlorpromazine (Thorazine). To stabilize her condition, medication was continued at the same dosage. After 6 weeks of treatment she developed a constant shaking of her head and hands, a rigid, forward-bending posture, and a blank, apathetic expression. The dose of chlorpromazine was reduced by one-half, and an appropriate anti-parkinsonism drug was started. All parkinson-like features gradually disappeared and the anti-parkinsonism drug was withdrawn. Parkinsonism did not reappear with a smaller maintenance dose of chlorpromazine.

Peripheral Neuritis (Peripheral Neuropathy) A group of symptoms that results from injury to nerve tissue in the extremities. A variety of drugs and chemicals are capable of inducing changes in nerve structure or function. The characteristic pattern consists of a sensation of numbness and tingling that usually begins in the fingers and toes and is accompanied by an altered sensation to touch and vague discomfort ranging from aching sensations to burning pain. Severe forms of peripheral neuritis may include loss of muscular strength and coordination.

A relatively common form of peripheral neuritis is that seen with the long-term use of isoniazid in the treatment of tuberculosis. If Vitamin B-6 (pyridoxine) is not given concurrently with isoniazid, peripheral neuritis may occur in sensitive individuals. Vitamin B-6 can be both preventive and curative in this form of drug-induced peripheral neuritis.

Since peripheral neuritis can also occur as a late complication following many viral infections, care must be taken to avoid assigning a cause-and-effect relationship to a drug which is not responsible for the nerve injury (see CAUSE-AND-EFFECT RELATIONSHIP).

Pharmacology The medical science that relates to the development and use of medicinal drugs, their composition and action in animals and man. Used in its broadest sense, pharmacology embraces the related sciences of medicinal chemistry, experimental therapeutics, and toxicology.

Example: The widely used sulfonylurea drugs (Diabinese, Dymelor, Orinase, Tolinase) are effective in the treatment of some forms of diabetes because of the accidental discovery that some of their parent "sulfa" drugs produced hypoglycemia (low blood sugar) during their early therapeutic trials as anti-infectives. Subsequent investigation of the mechanisms of action *(pharmacology)* of these drugs revealed that they are capable of stimulating the pancreas to produce more insulin.

Pharmacological studies on another group of "sulfa" related drugs—the thiazide diuretics—revealed that they could induce the kidney to excrete more water and salt in the urine. This drug action is of great value in treating high blood pressure and heart failure.

Photosensitivity A drug-induced change in the skin that results in the development of a rash or exaggerated sunburn on exposure to the sun or ultraviolet lamps. The reaction is confined to uncovered areas of skin, providing a clue to the nature of its cause. (See Table 6.)

Example: A patient receiving demeclocycline (Declomycin) for viral pneumonia decided to hasten his convalescence by sunbathing. Within 24 hours after his first sunbath, all exposed skin areas developed a severe sunburn far out of proportion to the intensity of the sun or the duration of the exposure.

Secondary Effect A by-product or complication of drug use which does not occur as part of the drug's primary pharmacological activity. Secondary effects are unwanted consequences and may therefore be classified as adverse effects.

Example: The reactivation of dormant tuberculosis can be a *secondary effect* of long-term cortisone administration for arthritis. Cortisone and related drugs (see Drug Family, Section Four) suppress natural immunity and lower resistance to infection.

Example: The cramping of leg muscles can be a *secondary effect* of diuretic (urine-producing) drug treatment for high blood pressure. Excessive loss of potassium through increased urination renders the muscle vulnerable to painful spasm during exercise.

Side-Effect A normal, expected, and predictable response to a drug that accompanies the principal (intended) response sought in treatment. Side-effects are part of a drug's pharmacological activity and thus are unavoidable. Most side-effects are undesirable. The majority cause minor annoyance and inconvenience; some may cause serious problems in managing certain diseases; a few can be hazardous.

Example: The drug propantheline (Pro-Banthine) is used to treat peptic ulcer because one of the consequences of its pharmacological action is the reduction of acid formation in the stomach (an intended effect). Other consequences can include blurring of near vision, dryness of the mouth, and constipation. These are *side-effects.*

Superinfection (Suprainfection) The development of a second infection that is superimposed upon an initial infection currently under treatment. The superinfection is caused by organisms that are not susceptible to the killing action of the drug(s) used to treat the original (primary) infection. Superinfections usually occur during or immediately following treatment with a broad spectrum antibiotic—one that is capable of altering the customary balance of bacterial populations in various parts of the body. The disturbance of this balance permits the overgrowth of organisms that normally exist in numbers too small to cause disease. The superinfection may also require treatment, using those drugs that are effective against the offending organism.

Example: Recurrent infections of the kidney and bladder often require repeated courses of treatment with a variety of anti-infective drugs. When these are taken by mouth they can suppress the normally dominant types of bacteria present in the colon and rectum, encouraging the overgrowth of yeast organisms which are capable of causing *colitis.* When this occurs, colitis is a *superinfection.*

Tardive Dyskinesia A late-developing, drug-induced disorder of the nervous system characterized by involuntary bizarre movements of the jaws, lips, and tongue. It occurs after long-term treatment with the more potent drugs used in the management of serious mental illness. While it may occur in any age group, it is more common in the middle-aged and the elderly. Older, chronically ill women are particularly susceptible to this adverse drug effect. Once developed, the pattern of uncontrollable chewing, lip puckering, and repetitive tongue protruding (fly-catching movement) appears to be irreversible. No consistently satisfactory treatment or cure is available. To date, there is no way of identifying beforehand the individual who may develop this distressing reaction to drug treatment, and there is no known prevention. Fortunately, the persistent dyskinesia (abnormal movement) is not accompanied by further impairment of mental function or deterioration of intelligence. It is ironic, however, that the patient who shows significant improvement in his mental illness but is unfortunate enough to develop tardive dyskinesia may have to remain hospitalized because of a reaction to a drug that was given to make it possible for him to leave the hospital.

Example: A 39-year-old man with a diagnosis of schizophrenia developed a typical pattern of tardive dyskinesia in his third year of continuous treatment with a series of potent tranquilizing drugs. By actual count, he averaged 31 tongue protrusions, 32 chewing motions, and 24 lip-puckering movements per minute. Separate trials of treatment using four different drugs produced only a temporary reduction in the frequency of abnormal mouth and jaw movements. The patient is now in his fourth year of tardive dyskinesia and shows no indication of spontaneous recovery.

Tolerance An adaptation by the body that lessens responsiveness to a drug on continuous administration. Body tissues become accustomed to the drug's presence and react to it less vigorously. Tolerance can be beneficial or harmful in treatment.

Examples: Beneficial tolerance occurs when the hay fever sufferer finds that the side effect of drowsiness gradually disappears after four or five days of continuous use of antihistamines.

Harmful tolerance occurs when the patient with "shingles" (herpes zoster) finds that the usual dose of codeine is no longer sufficient to relieve pain and that the need for increasing dosage creates a risk of physical dependence or addiction.

Toxicity The capacity of a drug to dangerously impair body functions or to damage body tissues. Most drug toxicity is related to total dosage: the larger the overdose, the greater the toxic effects. Some drugs, however, can produce toxic reactions when used in normal doses. Such adverse effects are not due to allergy or idiosyncrasy; in many instances their mechanisms are not fully understood. Toxic effects due to overdosage are generally a harmful extension of the drug's normal pharmacological actions and—to some extent—are predictable and preventable. Toxic reactions which occur with normal dosage are unrelated to the drug's known pharmacology and for the most part are unpredictable and unexplainable.

Examples: Dose-related toxicity is seen quite commonly in the coma and death resulting from an overdose of "sleeping pills."

Toxicity unrelated to dosage is seen with some frequency in the occurrence of peptic ulcers (stomach and duodenum) shortly after starting treatment with indomethacin (Indocid, Indocin) or phenylbutazone (Butazolidin).

Tyramine A chemical present in many common foods and beverages that causes no difficulties to body functioning under normal circumstances. The main pharmacological action of tyramine is to raise the blood pressure. Normally, enzymes present in many body tissues neutralize this action of tyramine in the quantities in which it is consumed in the average diet. The principal enzyme responsible for neutralizing the blood-pressure-elevating action of tyramine (and chemicals related to it) is mono-amine oxidase (MAO). Mono-amine oxidase provides an important regulatory function that helps to balance several of the chemical processes in the body that control certain activities of the nervous system. Stabilization of the blood pressure is one of these activities. If the action of mono-amine oxidase is blocked, chemical substances like tyramine function unopposed, and relatively small amounts can cause alarming and dangerous elevations of blood pressure.

Several drugs in use today are capable of blocking the action of mono-amine oxidase. These drugs are commonly referred to as mono-amine oxidase inhibitors (see Drug Family, Section Four). If an individual is taking one of these drugs and his diet includes foods or beverages that contain a significant amount of tyramine, he may experience a sudden increase in blood pressure. Before this interaction of food and drug was understood, several deaths due to brain hemorrhage occurred in persons taking MAO inhibitor drugs as a result of an extreme elevation of blood pressure following a meal of tyramine-rich foods.

It should be noted also that MAO inhibitor drugs can interact with many other drugs and cause serious adverse effects. Consult your physician before taking *any* drug concurrently with one that can inhibit the action of mono-amine oxidase.

Any protein-containing food that has undergone partial decomposition may present a hazard because of its increased tyramine content. The following foods and beverages have been reported to contain varying amounts of tyramine. Unless their tyramine content is known to be insignificant, they should be avoided altogether while taking a MAO inhibitor drug (see Drug Family, Section Four). Consult your physician about the advisability of using any of the foods or beverages on these lists if you are taking such drugs.

FOODS	BEVERAGES
Aged cheeses of all kinds	Chianti wines
Beef liver (improperly stored)	Vermouth
Chicken liver (improperly stored)	Beer (unpasteurized)
Salted dried fish	Sour cream
Pickled herring	
Meat extracts	
"Marmite" and "Bovril" extracts	
Yeast extracts	
Broad bean pods	
Banana skins	
Raspberries	
Avocado	

SECTION SIX

Tables of Drug Information

TABLE 1

A Checklist of Health Conditions That Can Influence the Choice of Drugs

Inform your physician if you have or have had any of the following health conditions. They could influence his or her choice of drugs, or the dosages of drugs, in planning any treatment you may require. In some instances these conditions may be *contraindications* to the use of certain drugs.

Addison's disease
Alcoholism
Allergies (hay fever, asthma, hives, eczema)
Allergies to specific drugs
Anemia (any type), especially
  Hemolytic anemia
  Sickle cell anemia
Angina
Arthritis (any type)
Asthma
Bleeding disorder
Bone marrow disorder
Bronchiectasis
Bronchitis, chronic
Cancer (any type)
Cataracts
Cirrhosis
Colitis
Constipation, chronic
Cystic breast disease
Diabetes
Drug dependence
Emotional depression
Epilepsy
Fibroid tumors of the uterus
Gall bladder disease, gall stones
Gastritis
Glaucoma
Gout
Headaches (any type), especially
  Histamine headache
  Migraine headache
  Vascular headache
Hearing loss
Heart disease (any type)
Heart rhythm disorder
Hepatitis
Hiatal hernia

High blood pressure
Hypoglycemia
Jaundice
Kidney disease, kidney stone
Liver disease
Low blood pressure
Lung disease (any type)
Lung embolism
Lupus erythematosus
Malabsorption disorder
Manic type of mental disorder
Meniere's disease
Menstrual disorder
Multiple Sclerosis
Myasthenia gravis
Nervous tension (anxiety)
Neuritis (any type)
Pancreatitis
Parkinson's disease
Peptic ulcer disease
Phlebitis
Porphyria
Pregnancy
Prostate gland enlargement
Raynaud's phenomenon
Red blood cell disorder:
  Glucose-6-phosphate
  dehydrogenase deficiency
Schizophrenia
Sprue
Stroke
Sun sensitivity
Thyroid disorder
  Hyperthyroidism
  Hypothyroidism
Tuberculosis (any type)
Urinary tract infection (chronic or recurrent)

TABLE 2

Your Drugs, Your Anesthetic, and Your Surgery

Many drugs can affect the body's response to anesthetics and surgical procedures. If you are taking, or have taken recently, any of the drugs listed below, and you plan to have an operation in the near future, consult your physician regarding the need to modify your drug treatment *before* surgery.* It is essential that your anesthesiologist and surgeon be made aware of any of the listed drugs you are taking. For some drugs, it may be advisable to adjust the dosage; for others, it may be necessary to discontinue them altogether. The timing and nature of such changes must be determined on an individual basis. Ask for guidance at least one month before planned surgery. If it is necessary to have emergency surgery, it is most important that your anesthesiologist and surgeon be informed of any medications you are taking.

anticoagulants**
antidepressants, tricyclic**
antihistamines**
aspirin
atropine-like drugs**
barbiturates**
bethanidine
clindamycin
clonidine
codeine
colistin
cortisone-like drugs**
cyclophosphamide
decongestants**
digitalis preparations
disulfiram
diuretics**
ecothiopate
emetine
ergotamine
guanethidine
haloperidol
hydralazine
hypnotics (see Sedatives/Sleep
   Inducers)**
isoniazid
kanamycin

levodopa
lincomycin
meperidine
methadone
methyldopa
mono-amine oxidase inhibitor
   drugs**
neomycin
neostigmine
oral contraceptives
pentazocine
phenothiazines**
phenytoin
primidone
procainamide
propranolol
quinidine
reserpine
sodium salicylate
streptomycin
tetracyclines**
thiazides**
thiothixene
tranquilizers, mild**
tranquilizers, strong**
viomycin

*Consult the appropriate Drug Profile in Section Three to learn the family designation of the drug you are taking.
**See Drug Family, Section Four.

TABLE 3

Specific Diseases and the Drugs That Can Interfere with Their Management

The management of most chronic diseases includes the use of drugs for an extended period of time. During such long-term treatment, a patient may develop other illnesses that require the use of additional drugs. The introduction of new medicines into a well-established treatment program may (1) adversely affect the course of the chronic disease, and/or (2) create a potential for interaction with the drugs already in use. The success of drug therapy is significantly greater when the patient realizes such treatment situations can be complex and shares with his or her physician the responsibility for monitoring the course of illnesses and evaluating responses to the drugs he or she is using.

If you are on drug therapy for a chronic disease, always consult your physician for specific guidance when a new drug is prescribed or if you intend to use a non-prescription drug. The Drug Profiles in Section Three will help you identify the effects drugs may have on certain diseases, as well as their possible interactions with foods, alcohol, and other drugs you may be taking.

If you have **DIABETES** and you intend to use any of the drugs listed below, it may be necessary to modify your treatment program in one or more of the following ways:

- increase the frequency of urine sugar testing to detect any change in the pattern of your diabetes.
- adjust the dosage of anti-diabetic drugs (insulin and/or oral medications) as directed to maintain proper control of blood sugar levels.
- adjust your diet and eating schedule as necessary to maintain proper control of blood sugar levels.
- adjust periodically the dosage schedule of the newly added drug, as your physician directs, to assure effectiveness, to prevent overdosage, and to avoid toxicity.

acenocoumarol	furosemide
amitriptyline	haloperidol
amphetamines	hydrocortisone
anisindione	imipramine
aspirin	isoniazid
chlordiazepoxide	isoproterenol
chlorthalidone	levodopa
clofibrate	liothyronine
desipramine	lithium
dexamethasone	medroxyprogesterone
diazepam	methylprednisolone
dicumarol	nicotinic acid
disulfiram	nortriptyline
doxepin	oral contraceptives
estrogen	oxymetazoline

phenindione
phenoxybenzamine
phenylephrine
phenylpropanolamine
potassium
prednisolone
prednisone
propranolol

protriptyline
pseudoephedrine
thiazides
thyroid
thyroxine
triamcinolone
triamterene
trimipramine

If you have **EPILEPSY** and you intend to use any of the drugs listed below, it may be necessary to modify your treatment program in one or more of the following ways:

- be alert for any increase in the frequency of seizures (reduced anti-convulsant effect) and for any toxic symptoms (excessive anti-convulsant effect).
- adjust the dosage schedule of anti-convulsant(s) as directed to increase protection or to decrease possible toxicity from overdosage.
- adjust periodically the dosage schedule of the newly added drug, as your physician directs, to assure effectiveness, to prevent overdosage, and to avoid toxicity.

amitriptyline
amobarbital
butabarbital
butalbital
caffeine
chlordiazepoxide
chlorpromazine
clorazepate
desipramine
diazepam
diethylpropion
disulfiram
doxepin
estrogen
fluphenazine
flurazepam
haloperidol
hydroxyzine
imipramine
indomethacin
isoniazid
levodopa
lithium
medroxyprogesterone

meperidine
meprobamate
mesoridazine
methylphenidate
nalidixic acid
nortriptyline
oral contraceptives
oxazepam
para-aminosalicylic acid
pentazocine
pentobarbital
perphenazine
pethidine
phenobarbital/phenobarbitone
prochlorperazine
promazine
protriptyline
reserpine
secobarbital
thioridazine
thiothixene
trifluoperazine
trimipramine
tybamate

If you have **GLAUCOMA** and you intend to use any of the drugs listed below, it may be necessary to modify your treatment program in one or more of the following ways:

• obtain measurement of internal eye pressures regularly to detect any significant increase.
• adjust the dosage schedule of anti-glaucoma medications as directed to maintain normal internal eye pressures.
• adjust periodically the dosage schedule of the newly added drug, as your physician directs, to assure effectiveness, to prevent overdosage, and to avoid toxicity.

amitriptyline
amphetamines
anisotropine
atropine
benztropine
biperiden
brompheniramine
chlorpheniramine
chlorpromazine
clidinium
clorazepate
cyclandelate
cyproheptadine
desipramine
dexamethasone
diazepam
dicyclomine
diethylpropion
diphenhydramine
doxepin
doxylamine
erythrityl tetranitrate
haloperidol
hydrocortisone
imipramine
isopropamide
isosorbide dinitrate
levodopa

meperidine
methscopolamine
methylphenidate
methylprednisolone
mepyramine
nitroglycerin
nortriptyline
orphenadrine
papaverine
pentaerythritol tetranitrate
pheniramine
phentermine
prednisolone
prednisone
prochlorperazine
procyclidine
promethazine
propantheline
protriptyline
pyrilamine
thiothixene
triamcinolone
tridihexethyl
trifluoperazine
trihexiphenidyl
trimipramine
tripelennamine
triprolidine

If you have **GOUT** and you intend to use any of the drugs listed below, it may be necessary to modify your treatment program in one or more of the following ways:

• obtain measurement of blood uric acid levels periodically to detect any significant change that could require adjustment of anti-gout medications.

• report attacks of acute gout so that all drug therapy can be reviewed and corrective adjustments can be made.

acetazolamide	nicotinic acid
aspirin	theophylline
chlorthalidone	thiazides
furosemide	triamterene
ibuprofen	

If you have **HEART DISEASE** and you intend to use any of the drugs listed below, it may be necessary to modify your treatment program in one or more of the following ways:

• obtain periodic evaluation of heart performance to detect significant changes in rate, rhythm, and functional capacity that may be attributable to a newly added drug.

• adjust your intake of sodium and/or potassium, as your physician directs, to correct abnormalities produced by newly added drugs.

• report promptly the development of new and unexpected symptoms that could indicate derangement of heart function, such as chest pain, rapid or forceful heart action, irregular heart rhythm, shortness of breath (especially on exertion), and episodes of lightheadedness, weakness, or sense of impending faint.

• adjust periodically the dosage of newly added drugs, as your physician directs, to assure effectiveness, to prevent overdosage, and to avoid toxicity.

amitriptyline	imipramine
amphetamines	isopropamide
anisotropine	isoproterenol
antacids (high sodium)	levodopa
atropine	liothyronine
benztropine	lithium
biperiden	mesoridazine
caffeine	methscopolamine
chlorpromazine	methysergide
clidinium	nortriptyline
clonidine	oral contraceptives
cyclandelate	orphenadrine
desipramine	oxymetazoline
diethylpropion	papaverine
disulfiram	phenoxybenzamine
doxepin	phentermine
ephedrine	phenylbutazone
ergotamine	phenylephrine
estrogen	phenylpropanolamine
guanethidine	potassium
haloperidol	prochlorperazine
hydralazine	procyclidine

promazine
propantheline
propanolol
pseudoephedrine
theophylline
thioridazine
thiothixene

thyroid
thyroxine
tridihexethyl
trifluoperazine
trihexiphenidyl
trimipramine

If you have **HIGH BLOOD PRESSURE** and you intend to use any of the drugs listed below, it may be necessary to modify your treatment program in one or more of the following ways:

• obtain measurement of blood pressure regularly to detect significant increases or decreases (without symptoms) that may be attributable to a newly added drug.
• adjust your intake of sodium and/or potassium, as your physician directs, to correct abnormalities produced by newly added drugs.
• report promptly the development of new and unexpected symptoms that could indicate excessive drop in blood pressure, such as lightheadedness, weakness, and faintness (see orthostatic hypotension in Glossary), or excessive rise in blood pressure, indicated by such symptoms as recurring headaches, forceful heart action, restlessness, and agitation.
• adjust periodically the dosage of newly added drugs, as your physician directs, to assure effectiveness, to prevent overdosage, and to avoid toxicity.

acenocoumarol
amphetamines
anisindione
antacids (high sodium)
benztropine
biperiden
dexamethasone
dicumarol
diethylpropion
ephedrine
ergotamine
estrogen
haloperidol
hydrocortisone
isoproterenol
isoxsuprine
levodopa
liothyronine
methylphenidate
methylprednisolone

methysergide
oral contraceptives
oxymetazoline
oxyphenbutazone
phenindione
phentermine
phenylbutazone
phenylephrine
phenypropanolamine
prednisolone
prednisone
procyclidine
protriptyline
pseudoephedrine
theophylline
thiothixene
thyroid
thyroxine
triamcinolone
trihexyphenidyl

If you have **PEPTIC ULCER DISEASE** and you intend to use any of the drugs listed below, it may be necessary to modify your treatment program in one or more of the following ways:

- consult your physician regarding the ulcer-producing potential of any new drug you intend to use.
- report, during the course of treatment for active peptic ulcer, any indications of continued or increased ulcer activity (possible delayed healing) that may be attributable to a newly added drug.
- be alert, during the quiescent phase of peptic ulcer disease (history of a "previous ulcer" or a "healed ulcer"), for symptoms that could indicate the development ("reactivation") of a new ulcer that may be attributable to a drug started recently for another condition.
- observe your stools regularly, if you have a history of peptic ulcer disease (currently active or inactive), for evidence of gastro-intestinal bleeding while taking any drug. Bleeding is indicated by dark coloration (gray to black) of the stool.
- consult your physician regarding the ability of any drug to cause obstruction if this condition is present:
  When repeated ulceration and healing of the stomach outlet result in scar tissue and narrowing (pyloric obstruction), the ability of the stomach to empty may be seriously impaired. Some of the drugs listed below can intensify this impairment.
- adjust periodically the dosage of newly added drugs, as your physician directs, to assure effectiveness, to prevent overdosage, and to avoid toxicity.

acenocoumarol	indomethacin
acetohexamide	isopropamide
anisindione	levodopa
anisotropine	mepyramine
aspirin	methscopolamine
atropine	methylprednisolone
benztropine	methysergide
caffeine	naproxen
chlorpromazine	nicotinic acid
chlorpropamide	orphenadrine
clidinium	oxyphenbutazone
clofibrate	para-aminosalicylic acid
cyproheptadine	phenindione
dexamethasone	pheniramine
dicumarol	phenylbutazone
dicyclomine	potassium (wax matrix)
diphenhydramine	prednisolone
doxylamine	prednisone
fluphenazine	probenecid
glyburide	prochlorperazine
guanethidine	promethazine
hydrocortisone	propantheline
ibuprofen	pyrilamine

reserpine
theophylline
tolazamide
tolbutamide
triamcinolone

tridihexethyl
trihexyphenidyl
trimeprazine
tripelennamine
warfarin

TABLE 4

Symptoms That May Warn of Serious Adverse Effects

Symptoms that occur during a course of drug treatment may or may not be related to the drug(s) being taken. Occasionally, symptoms may appear that suggest the development of a serious adverse effect. On those occasions when a drug *is* responsible for the symptoms observed, early recognition of this association is essential. Often the drug can be discontinued before the harmful effect becomes irreversible. Therefore, whenever the symptoms listed below appear, it is advisable for you to discontinue the drug(s) in question and inform your physician promptly. He or she will be able to make a careful evaluation of the situation.

If you experience any of these symptoms:	And you are taking (generic names*):	It may indicate the development of:
Increased frequency or severity of headaches Throbbing or pulsating headaches Headaches more intense when lying down Awareness of forceful heart action	amphetamine-like drugs cortisone-like drugs levodopa medroxyprogesterone mono-amine oxidase inhibitor drugs oral contraceptives	A significant increase in blood pressure
Pattern of sudden headaches Increased frequency or severity of migraine headaches Sudden dizziness Sudden changes in vision or hearing Difficulty in speaking Sudden weakness of any part of the body Sudden numbness, tingling, or loss of feeling of any part of the body	estrogens oral contraceptives progestins	A stroke—a blood clot in the brain (cerebral thrombosis)

*Some drugs are represented by their Drug Family designation.

If you experience any of these symptoms:	And you are taking (generic names*):	It may indicate the development of:
Abrupt changes in vision in one or both eyes, without pain. "Spots" in front of the eyes Blank areas in the field of vision Flashes of light Reduced clarity of vision Poor vision in dim light	carisoprodol ibuprofen indomethacin isoniazid naproxen nicotinic acid (large doses) oral contraceptives oxyphenbutazone phenylbutazone thiothixene	Eye damage—retinal impairment, optic nerve impairment
Pain, discomfort, sense of pressure in the eyes Headache adjacent to the eyes Reduced clarity of vision Difficulty in focusing Loss of side vision "Halo" effect on looking at lights	antidepressants, tricyclic anti-parkinsonism drugs chlordiazepoxide clorazepate cortisone-like drugs cyproheptadine dextroamphetamine diazepam haloperidol oral contraceptives orphenadrine thiothixene	Glaucoma—increasing internal eye pressure
Sudden pain or pressure in heart region, neck, jaws, shoulders, arms Shortness of breath, weakness, nausea, sweating, or sense of impending faint	estrogens oral contraceptives	A heart attack (coronary thrombosis)
Soreness and tenderness of leg veins Swelling of foot, ankle or leg Sudden pain in the chest, worse with breathing Shortness of breath, with or without pain Cough, with or without bloody sputum	cortisone-like drugs estrogens medroxyprogesterone oral contraceptives	Phlebitis—vein inflammation, vein thrombosis, lung embolism

If you experience any of these symptoms:	And you are taking (generic names*):	It may indicate the development of:
Acid indigestion Upper abdominal pain or distress Vomiting of blood ("coffee grounds" vomitus) Blood in stools (dark-colored or "tarry" stools) Progressive weakness due to "silent" blood loss from the stomach	aspirin caffeine cortisone-like drugs ethacrynic acid guanethidine ibuprofen indomethacin levodopa naproxen nicotinic acid oxyphenbutazone para-aminosalicylic acid phenylbutazone potassium (wax matrix) reserpine	Peptic ulcer—stomach ulcer, duodenal ulcer, and/or Stomach/intestinal bleeding
Loss of appetite Nausea, with or without vomiting Fever, weakness, exhaustion Yellow coloration of eyes and skin Dark-colored urine Light-colored stools Itching	acetazolamide acetohexamide allopurinol anisindione antidepressants, tricyclic aspirin barbiturates chloramphenicol chlordiazepoxide chlorpromazine chlorpropamide chlorthalidone chlorzoxazone clindamycin clorazepate diazepam erythromycin (estolate) ethchlorvynol flurazepam griseofulvin haloperidol hydralazine indomethacin isoniazid medroxyprogesterone methyldopa	Drug-induced hepatitis with jaundice

*Some drugs are represented by their Drug Family designation.

If you experience any of these symptoms:	And you are taking (generic names*):	It may indicate the development of:
Loss of appetite Nausea, with or without vomiting Fever, weakness, exhaustion Yellow coloration of eyes and skin Dark-colored urine Light-colored stools Itching	nalidixic acid naproxen nicotinic acid nitrofurantoin oral contraceptives oxazepam oxyphenbutazone papaverine para-aminosalicylic acid phenazopyridine phenindione phenobarbital phenothiazines phenylbutazone phenytoin promethazine propoxyphene sulfonamides tetracyclines thiazides tolazamide tolbutamide trimethobenzamide	Drug-induced hepatitis with jaundice
Pain or discomfort in upper right side of abdomen Swelling or enlargement in upper right side of abdomen (liver) Sudden abdominal pain, intense and persistent (internal bleeding)	oral contraceptives	Liver tumor, with threat of internal bleeding
Progressive fatigue and weakness Paleness Susceptibility to infection Fever Sore throat	acetaminophen acetazolamide acetohexamide allopurinol amitriptyline amoxicillin ampicillin	Bone marrow depression—low red blood cells (anemia), low white blood cells, low blood platelets (these can occur singly or in any combination)

*Some drugs are represented by their Drug Family designation.

If you experience any of these symptoms:	And you are taking (generic names*):	It may indicate the development of:
(continued) Unusual, abnormal bleeding or bruising, nosebleeds, gum bleeding, bloody urine, extensive bruising unprovoked by trauma	anisindione aspirin brompheniramine carbenicillin cephalexin cephaloglycin cephradine chloramphenicol chlordiazepoxide chlorpheniramine chlorpromazine chlorpropamide chlorthalidone clofibrate clorazepate cloxacillin desipramine diazepam dicloxacillin diethylpropion doxepin fluphenazine furosemide glutethimide glyburide guanethidine haloperidol hydralazine ibuprofen imipramine indomethacin isoniazid levodopa lincomycin meprobamate mesoridazine methaqualone methyldopa methylphenidate methyprylon methysergide metronidazole	Bone marrow depression—low red blood cells (anemia), low white blood cells, low blood platelets (these can occur singly or in any combination)

*Some drugs are represented by their Drug Family designation.

If you experience any of these symptoms:	And you are taking (generic names*):	It may indicate the development of:
Progressive fatigue and weakness Paleness Susceptibility to infection Fever Sore throat Unusual, abnormal bleeding or bruising, nosebleeds, gum bleeding, bloody urine, extensive bruising unprovoked by trauma	nafcillin nalidixic acid naproxen nortriptyline oxacillin oxazepam oxyphenbutazone para-aminosalicylic acid penicillin G penicillin V pentazocine perphenazine phenacetin phenindione phenylbutazone phenytoin primidone probenecid procainamide prochlorperazine promazine promethazine propranolol protriptyline quinidine sulfonamides thiazides thioridazine tolazamide tolbutamide triamterene trimeprazine trimethoprim trimipramine tripelennamine tybamate	Bone marrow depression
Unusual and abnormal bleeding or bruising, without other symptoms Evidence of bleeding from any part of the body without apparent cause	acenocoumarol acetaminophen acetohexamide acetazolamide amitriptyline amoxicillin ampicillin anisindione	Impairment of normal blood coagulation, low prothrombin, low blood platelets

*Some drugs are represented by their Drug Family designation.

If you experience any of these symptoms:	And you are taking (generic names*):	It may indicate the development of:
Unusual and abnormal bleeding or bruising, without other symptoms Evidence of bleeding from any part of the body without apparent cause	aspirin barbiturates bethanidine carbenicillin chloramphenicol chlordiazepoxide chlorpromazine chlorpropamide chlortetracycline chlorthalidone chlorzoxazone cloxacillin demeclocycline desipramine dicloxacillin dicumarol digitoxin diphenhydramine doxepin doxycycline ethchlorvynol ethinamate fluphenazine furosemide glutethimide glyburide guanethidine hydralazine imipramine indomethacin isoniazid lincomycin meprobamate methacycline methaqualone methyldopa methylphenidate methyprylon minocycline nafcillin nortriptyline oxacillin oxyphenbutazone oxytetracycline	Impairment of normal blood coagulation, low prothrombin, low blood platelets

*Some drugs are represented by their Drug Family designation.

If you experience any of these symptoms:	And you are taking (generic names*):	It may indicate the development of:
Unusual and abnormal bleeding or bruising, without other symptoms Evidence of bleeding from any part of the body without apparent cause	para-aminosalicylic acid penicillin G penicillin V phenacetin phenindione phenylbutazone phenytoin procainamide probenecid promazine propranolol protriptyline quinidine rifampin sulfonamides tetracycline thiazides tolazamide tolbutamide trimipramine tripelennamine tybamate warfarin	Impairment of normal blood coagulation, low prothrombin, low blood platelets
Fever, chills, fatigue, weakness, dark-colored urine, mild jaundice	acetazolamide acetohexamide aspirin chlorpropamide diphenhydramine furazolidone levodopa methyldopa methysergide nalidixic acid nitrofurantoin phenacetin phenazopyridine phenytoin procainamide probenecid quinidine sulfonamides tolazamide tolbutamide tripelennamine	Hemolytic anemia—destruction of red blood cells

*Some drugs are represented by their Drug Family designation.

TABLE 5

Your Drugs and Alcohol

Beverages containing alcohol may interact unfavorably with a wide variety of drugs. The most important (and most familiar) interaction occurs when the depressant action on the brain of sedatives, sleep-inducing drugs, tranquilizers, and narcotic drugs is intensified by alcohol. Alcohol may also reduce the effectiveness of some drugs, and it can interact with certain other drugs to produce toxic effects. Some drugs may increase the intoxicating effects of alcohol, producing further impairment of mental alertness, judgment, physical coordination, and reaction time.

While drug interactions with alcohol are generally predictable, the intensity and significance of these interactions can vary greatly from one individual to another and from one occasion to another. This is because many factors influence what happens when drugs and alcohol interact. These factors include individual variations in sensitivity to drugs (including alcohol), the chemistry and quantity of the drug, the type and amount of alcohol consumed, and the sequence in which drug and alcohol are taken. If you need to use any of the drugs listed in the following tables, you should ask your physician for guidance concerning the use of alcohol.

Drugs with which it is advisable to avoid alcohol completely

Drug name or family	Possible interaction with alcohol
amphetamines	excessive rise in blood pressure with alcoholic beverages containing tyramine**
barbiturates*	excessive sedation
bromides	confusion, delirium, increased intoxication
calcium carbimide	disulfiram-like reaction**
carbamazepine	excessive sedation
chlorprothixene	excessive sedation
chlorzoxazone	excessive sedation
disulfiram	disulfiram reaction**
ergotamine	reduced effectiveness of ergotamine
fenfluramine	excessive stimulation of nervous system with some beers and wines
furazolidone	disulfiram-like reaction**
haloperidol	excessive sedation
MAO inhibitor drugs*	excessive rise in blood pressure with alcoholic beverages containing tyramine**
meperidine	excessive sedation
meprobamate	excessive sedation

*See Drug Family, Section Four.
**See Glossary.

Drug name or family	Possible interaction with alcohol
metformin	increased lactic acidosis
methotrexate	increased liver toxicity and excessive sedation
metronidazole	disulfiram-like reaction**
narcotic drugs	excessive sedation
oxyphenbutazone	increased stomach irritation and/or bleeding
pentazocine	excessive sedation
pethidine	excessive sedation
phenformin	increased lactic acidosis
phenothiazines*	excessive sedation
phenylbutazone	increased stomach irritation and/or bleeding
procarbazine	disulfiram-like reaction**
propoxyphene	excessive sedation
reserpine	excessive sedation, orthostatic hypotension**

sleep-inducing drugs (hypnotics)
  carbromal
  chloral hydrate
  ethchlorvynol
  ethinamate
  glutethimide
  flurazepam
  methaqualone
  methyprylon
	excessive sedation

thiothixene	excessive sedation
tricyclic antidepressants*	excessive sedation, increased intoxication
trimethobenzamide	excessive sedation

Drugs with which alcohol should be used only in small amounts (use cautiously until combined effects have been determined)

Drug name or family	Possible interaction with alcohol
anticoagulants (coumarins)*	increased anticoagulant effect
anti-diabetic drugs (sulfonylureas)*	increased anti-diabetic effect, excessive hypoglycemia**
antihistamines*	excessive sedation
anti-hypertensives*	excessive orthostatic hypotension**
aspirin (large doses or continuous use)	increased stomach irritation and/or bleeding
carisoprodol	increased alcoholic intoxication

*See Drug Family, Section Four.
**See Glossary.

Drug name or family	Possible interaction with alcohol
diethylpropion	excessive nervous system stimulation with alcoholic beverages containing tyramine**
dihydroergotoxine	excessive lowering of blood pressure
diphenoxylate	excessive sedation
diuretics*	excessive orthostatic hypotension**
ethionamide	confusion, delirium, psychotic behavior
griseofulvin	flushing and rapid heart action
ibuprofen	increased stomach irritation and/or bleeding
insulin	excessive hypoglycemia**
isoniazid	decreased effectiveness of isoniazid
lithium	increased confusion and delirium (avoid all alcohol if any indication of lithium overdosage)
methotrimeprazine	excessive sedation
methylphenidate	excessive nervous system stimulation with alcoholic beverages containing tyramine**
nalidixic acid	increased alcoholic intoxication
naproxen	increased stomach irritation and/or bleeding
nicotinic acid	possible orthostatic hypotension**
nitrates* (vasodilators)	possible orthostatic hypotension**
orphenadrine	excessive sedation
phenoxybenzamine	possible orthostatic hypotension**
phentermine	excessive nervous system stimulation with alcoholic beverages containing tyramine**
phenytoin	decreased effect of phenytoin
pilocarpine	prolongation of alcohol effect
primidone	excessive sedation
propranolol	excessive orthostatic hypotension**
sulfonamides*	increased alcoholic intoxication
tranquilizers (mild)	excessive sedation
chlordiazepoxide	
clorazepate	
diazepam	
hydroxyzine	
meprobamate	
oxazepam	
phenaglycodol	
tybamate	

*See Drug Family, Section Four.
**See Glossary.

Drugs capable of producing a disulfiram-like reaction** when used concurrently with alcohol

anti-diabetic drugs (sulfonylureas)*
calcium carbimide
chloral hydrate
chloramphenicol
disulfiram
furazolidone
metronidazole

nifuroxine
nitrofurantoin
procarbazine
quinacrine
sulfonamides*
tinidazole
tolazoline

*See Drug Family, Section Four.
**See Glossary.

TABLE 6

Photosensitivity: Your Drugs and the Sun

Some drugs are capable of sensitizing the skin of some individuals to the action of ultraviolet light. This can cause uncovered areas of the skin to react with a rash or exaggerated burn on exposure to sun or ultraviolet lamps. If you are taking any of the following drugs, ask your physician for guidance and use caution with regard to sun exposure.

acetohexamide
amitriptyline
barbiturates
bendroflumethiazide
chlordiazepoxide
chloroquine
chlorothiazide
chlorpromazine
chlorpropamide
chlortetracycline
chlorthalidone
clindamycin
cyproheptadine
demeclocycline
desipramine
diphenhydramine
doxepin
doxycycline
estrogen
fluphenazine
gold preparations
glyburide
griseofulvin
hydrochlorothiazide
hydroflumethiazide
imipramine
lincomycin

mesoridazine
methacycline
nalidixic acid
nortriptyline
oral contraceptives
oxyphenbutazone
oxytetracycline
perphenazine
phenobarbital
phenylbutazone
phenytoin
prochlorperazine
promazine
promethazine
protriptyline
pyrazinamide
sulfonamides
tetracycline
thioridazine
tolazamide
tolbutamide
triamterene
trifluoperazine
trimeprazine
trimipramine
triprolidine

TABLES 7-11

Drugs and the Fetus, Infant, and Child*

Our present knowledge of drug effects during the earliest periods of life is very limited. Recent research has established that the actions of drugs in the developing child (both before and after birth) differ significantly from the usual patterns seen in the older child and the adult. In these early periods of life, the growing tissues are extremely sensitive to the presence of such foreign chemicals as drugs, and interactions are more rapid and more unpredictable. The unborn child's mechanisms for neutralizing drugs and eliminating them from its body are immature and deficient, and they remain so for at least four weeks following full-term birth.

These factors make it essential that any drugs taken by the mother during pregnancy be selected with great care and given only when the benefit to the mother outweighs the possible harm to the fetus. It is now known that most drugs cross the placenta and enter the bloodstream of the developing fetus. While the risk of injury to the unborn child from most prescription and non-prescription drugs appears to be small, it is advisable to avoid **all** drugs during pregnancy unless there is unquestionable need and the effectiveness of the drug to be used is well established. When drug treatment during pregnancy is considered necessary, every attempt should be made to limit its use to the smallest effective dose and to the briefest possible period of time.

The successive periods of child development are defined as follows:

Embryo	from the second through the eighth weeks after conception
Fetus	from the ninth week after conception until birth
Premature Infant	one born from the 27th to the 38th weeks (full term) after conception
Newborn Infant	from the first through the fourth weeks following full-term birth
Infant	from birth to two years of age
Child	from two through eleven years of age

*See also Section Seven.

TABLE 7

Drug Use During the First Trimester (First Three Months) of Pregnancy

The greatest risk of injury to the unborn child from exposure to drugs occurs during the first three months of pregnancy. The critical period of major organ development in the embryo occurs from the fourth through the eighth weeks. Drugs acting adversely upon the embryo during this period may cause permanent birth defects. For this reason, the use of any drug during early pregnancy must be considered hazardous. Based upon our present knowledge, it is advisable to observe the following guidelines.

Drugs to avoid completely (definitely harmful)	Drugs to use only if essential to mother's health (potentially harmful)	Drugs to avoid if possible or to use sparingly (may be harmful)
sex hormones	amphetamines	antacids
estrogens	anti-cancer drugs	aspirin
diethylstilbesterol	anticoagulants (oral)*	iron
oral contraceptives	barbiturates*	lithium
anabolic drugs (male	cortisone-like drugs*	nicotinamide
sex hormone-like	haloperidol	oral anti-diabetics
drugs used to	metronidazole	(sulfonylureas)*
stimulate appetite	nalidixic acid	sulfamethoxazole**
and weight gain)	phenytoin	tranquilizers (mild)*
tetracyclines*	primidone	trimethoprim**
nicotine (tobacco)	thiazide diuretics*	Vitamin C (large doses)
	thiothixene	Vitamin D (large doses)

*See Drug Family, Section Four.

**In some countries these two drugs in combination are designated generically as co-trimoxazole.

TABLE 8

Drug Use During the Second and Third Trimesters (Fourth Through Ninth Months) of Pregnancy

The developing fetus continues to be vulnerable to the adverse effects of drugs in various ways. Drugs may impair the normal development of the brain, the nervous system, and the external genital organs. The mother's use of drugs during the final weeks of pregnancy is of major concern because certain drugs within the fetus at the time of birth may have serious adverse effects. When the fetus becomes the newborn infant it must assume the full burden of drug metabolism and elimination. At that time, however, its incompletely developed metabolism is unable to process and eliminate drugs rapidly and effectively, and thus drugs may accumulate within the infant and produce manifestations of overdosage. For the premature infant, whose metabolism is even more immature, the hazards are proportionately greater.

Drugs to avoid completely	Drugs to use only on physician's orders
anabolic drugs (male sex hormone-like drugs used to stimulate appetite and weight gain)	amphetamines
	analgesics (strong)
	anesthetics
	antacids (containing sodium)
anticoagulants (oral)*	anti-thyroid drugs
aspirin (in large doses or for an extended period of time)	barbiturates*
	bromides
chloramphenicol	chloroquine
iodides	cortisone-like drugs*
nicotine (tobacco)	ergotamine
nitrofurantoin	laxatives
oral anti-diabetics (sulfonylureas)* after 33 weeks	lithium
	nalidixic acid
sex hormones of any kind	narcotic drugs
sulfonamides* (sulfa drugs)	phenothiazines*
tetracyclines*	phenytoin
	primidone
	propranolol
	quinine
	reserpine
	thiazide diuretics*
	tranquilizers (mild)*
	Vitamin C (large doses)
	Vitamin K (synthetic form)

*See Drug Family, Section Four.

TABLE 9

Drug Use While Nursing an Infant

Most drugs taken by the nursing mother will be present to some degree in her milk. The amount of the drug in the milk and its effect on the nursing infant will vary greatly, depending on the chemical characteristics of the drug, the dosage, and the duration of use. The value of breast feeding is well established and it should not be compromised by the unwise or unnecessary use of drugs. Many drugs can be taken by the nursing mother without adverse effects on the infant, but it is advisable to consult your physician about the use of any drug while nursing an infant. It is important that the nursing infant be observed carefully and continuously for possible unwanted effects due to the presence of drugs in the milk.

Drugs to avoid completely	Drugs to use only on physician's orders (observing infant closely)
anti-cancer drugs	amphetamines
anticoagulants (oral)*	antacids (containing sodium)
carisprodol	aspirin (in large doses)
chloramphenicol	atropine
ergotamine	barbiturates*
erythromycin estolate	bromides
heroin	caffeine
iodine (radioactive)	carbamazepine
isoniazid	chloral hydrate
meprobamate	chlorpromazine
metronidazole	cortisone-like drugs*
nicotine (tobacco)	diazepam
oral contraceptives*	diphenhydramine
penicillins*	imipramine
propranolol	iodides
sulfonamides*	laxatives
tetracyclines*	lithium
thiouracil	nalidixic acid
	naproxen
	oxyphenbutazone
	phenytoin
	primidone
	pyrimethamine
	reserpine
	thiazide diuretics*

*See Drug Family, Section Four.

TABLE 10

Drug Use During Infancy (Birth to Two Years of Age)

This period includes the premature and newborn infant, to whom the special considerations on page 731 apply. Among the characteristics of infancy are the relative ease with which drugs enter the tissues of the brain and the fact that drugs applied to the skin (in the form of lotions and ointments) are absorbed more rapidly and to a greater degree than in older children, sometimes causing generalized (systemic) effects though they are intended only for local use. During infancy and childhood all drug use requires careful observation for possible impairment of normal growth and development.

Drugs to avoid completely if possible	Drugs to use with caution and under physician's close supervision
chloramphenicol	anti-worm drugs containing
diphenoxylate	piperazine
erythromycin estolate	aspirin
isoniazid	colistin
nalidixic acid, under 3 months of	cortisone-like drugs*
age	nalidixic acid, over 3 months of age
nitrofurantoin	phenacetin
sulfonamides* (sulfa drugs), under 2	phenothiazines*
months of age	sulfonamides* (sulfa drugs), over 2
tetracyclines*	months of age
	Vitamin A (in large doses)

*See Drug Family, Section Four.

TABLE 11

Drug Use During Childhood (Two to Twelve Years of Age)

The child's ability to neutralize and eliminate drugs is significantly greater than the infant's, but it does not yet equal that of the adult. It is important that the selection and dosage of each drug be matched carefully to the individual child's age, weight, and sensitivity to medications. Accurate measurement of liquid doses can be greatly improved by shaking the bottle to ensure uniform mixing of drug components and by using a standard measuring device. (The common household "teaspoon" can vary in size from 2.5 to 9 milliliters.) It is important to follow exactly the physician's instructions concerning the duration of drug therapy and not to discontinue the drug as soon as symptoms subside. Children are susceptible to certain infections which can produce serious complications if drug therapy is stopped too soon.

Drugs to avoid completely if possible	Drugs to use with caution and under physician's close supervision
anabolic steroids (male sex hormone-like drugs used to stimulate appetite and weight gain)	anti-worm drugs containing piperazine
dextroamphetamine, under 3 years of age	aspirin
	cortisone-like drugs* (long-term use)
	imipramine
methylphenidate, under 6 years of age	methylphenidate, over 6 years of age
oxyphenbutazone	nalidixic acid
phenylbutazone	para-aminosalicylic acid
tetracyclines,* under 9 years of age	phenacetin
	phenothiazines*
	phenytoin
	reserpine
	sulfonamides* (sulfa drugs)

*See Drug Family, Section Four.

TABLE 12

Drugs and the Elderly (over 60 Years of Age)*

Advancing age brings changes in body structure and function that may alter significantly the action of drugs. An impaired digestive system may interfere with drug absorption. Reduced capacity of the liver and kidneys to metabolize and eliminate drugs may result in the accumulation of drugs in the body to toxic levels. By impairing the body's ability to maintain a "steady state" (homeostasis), the aging process may increase the sensitivity of many tissues to the actions of drugs, thereby altering greatly the responsiveness of the nervous and circulatory systems to standard drug doses. If aging should cause deterioration of understanding, memory, vision, or physical coordination, people with such impairments may not always use drugs safely and effectively.

Adverse reactions to drugs occur three times more frequently in the older population. An unwanted drug response can render a functioning and independent older person, whose health and reserves are at marginal levels, confused, incompetent, or helpless. For these reasons, drug treatment in the elderly must always be accompanied by the most careful consideration of the individual's health and tolerances, the selection of drugs and dosage schedules, and the possible need for assistance in treatment routines.

Guidelines for the use of drugs by the elderly

• Be certain that drug treatment is necessary. Many health problems of the elderly can be managed without the use of drugs.

• Avoid if possible the use of many drugs at one time. It is advisable to use not more than three drugs concurrently.

• Dosage schedules should be as uncomplicated as possible. When feasible, a single daily dose of each drug is preferable.

• In order to establish individual tolerance, treatment with most drugs is usually best begun by using smaller than standard doses. Maintenance doses should also be determined carefully. A maintenance dose is often smaller for persons over 60 years of age than for younger persons.

• Avoid large tablets and capsules if other dosage forms are available. Liquid preparations are easier for the elderly or debilitated to swallow.

• Have all drug containers labeled with the drug name and directions for use in large, easy-to-read letters.

• Ask the pharmacist to package drugs in easy-to-open containers.

• Do not take any drug in the dark. Identify each dose of medicine carefully in adequate light to be certain you are taking the drug intended.

• To avoid taking the wrong drug or an extra dose, do not keep drugs on a bedside table. Drugs for emergency use, such as nitroglycerin, are an exception. It is advisable to have only one such drug at the bedside for use during the night.

• Drug use by older persons may require supervision. Observe drug effects continuously to ensure safe and effective use.

*See also Table 13, Your Drugs and Sexual Activity.

Drugs best avoided by the elderly because of increased possibility of adverse reactions

antacids (high sodium)*
barbiturates*
indomethacin
oxyphenbutazone

phenacetin
phenylbutazone
tetracyclines*

Drugs that should be used by the elderly in reduced dosages until full effect has been determined

anticoagulants (oral)*
anti-diabetic drugs*
antihistamines*
anti-hypertensives*
barbiturates*
cortisone-like drugs*
digitalis preparations
diuretics* (all types)
ephedrine

haloperidol
nalidixic acid
naproxen
narcotic drugs
pseudoephedrine
quinidine
sleep inducers (hypnotics)*
thyroid preparations
tricyclic antidepressants*

Drugs that may cause confusion and behavioral disturbances in the elderly

amantadine
anti-diabetic drugs*
antihistamines*
atropine* (and drugs
    containing belladonna)
barbiturates*
digitalis preparations
dihydroergotoxine
diuretics*
levodopa
meprobamate
methyldopa

narcotic drugs
pentazocine
phenytoin
primidone
reserpine
sedatives
sleep inducers (hypnotics)*
thiothixene
tranquilizers (mild)*
tricyclic antidepressants*
trihexyphenidyl

Drugs that may cause orthostatic hypotension** in the elderly

anti-hypertensives*
diuretics* (all types)
phenothiazines*
sedatives

tranquilizers (mild)*
tricyclic antidepressants*
vasodilators

Drugs that may cause constipation and retention of urine in the elderly

anti-parkinsonism drugs*
atropine-like drugs*
dihydroergotoxine

narcotic drugs
phenothiazines*
tricyclic antidepressants*

Drugs that may cause loss of bladder control (urinary incontinence) in the elderly

diuretics* (all types)
sedatives

sleep inducers (hypnotics)*
tranquilizers (mild)*

*See Drug Family, Section Four.

TABLE 13

Your Drugs and Sexual Activity

The drugs listed below are capable of affecting some aspects of sexuality. As would be expected, the principal therapeutic effect of all of them is on the nervous or circulatory systems. As with any drug effect, the nature and degree of altered sexual function will vary greatly from one individual to another. While such effects may occur at any age, they are usually more frequent and more troublesome after the age of 50. If you suspect the possibility of such a drug response, consult your physician regarding the advisability of modifying your treatment program.

Drug name or family	Possible effects
alcohol	reduced potency in men, delayed orgasm in women
amphetamine	reduced libido and potency
bethanidine	impaired ejaculation
clonidine	reduced libido
debrisoquine	reduced potency, impaired ejaculation
dextroamphetamine	reduced libido and potency
disulfiram	reduced potency
guanethidine	reduced potency, impaired ejaculation
haloperidol	reduced potency
levodopa	increased libido (in some men and women)
lithium	reduced potency
methyldopa	reduced libido and potency
oral contraceptives	reduced libido (in some women)
phenothiazines*	reduced libido and potency, impaired ejaculation (occasionally)
phenoxybenzamine	impaired ejaculation
primidone	reduced libido and potency
reserpine	reduced libido and potency
sedative and sleep-inducing drugs (hypnotics)* when used on a regular basis	reduced libido and potency
thiazide diuretics*	reduced libido (occasionally, in some men)
tranquilizers (mild)*	reduced libido and potency
tricyclic antidepressants*	reduced libido and potency

*See Drug Family, Section Four.

TABLE 14

Your Drugs and Personal Identification

Should you require emergency medical care, it is essential that those attending you be aware of certain health conditions that may warrant special attention. You are urged to carry with you (in wallet or purse) a card of personal identification that includes a statement of significant conditions and the names and dosages of the drugs you are taking. A model form for such a card will be found in Section Seven. Listed below are those health conditions and drugs which should be noted on your identification card.

Significant Health Conditions

Addison's disease
Alcoholism
Allergic disorders
Allergies to drugs
Bleeding disorders
Cancer (any type)
Coronary heart disease
Depression
Diabetes
Epilepsy
Hemolytic anemia
Hemophilia
Hypertension (high blood pressure)

Kidney disease (chronic)
Lupus erythematosus
Manic disorder
Myasthenia gravis
Parkinson's disease
Peptic ulcer disease
Pernicious anemia
Phlebitis
Porphyria
Pregnancy
Rheumatic heart disease
Schizophrenia

Significant Medications

ambenonium
anti-cancer drugs
anticoagulant drugs*
antidepressants, tricyclic*
anti-diabetic drugs (oral)*
anti-hypertensive drugs*
anti-parkinsonism drugs*
carbamazepine
clonidine
cortisone-like drugs*
digitalis
digitoxin
digoxin
disulfiram
haloperidol
insulin

lithium
mono-amine oxidase inhibitor drugs*
mephenytoin
neostigmine
penicillin (any type)*
phenacemide
phenobarbital (as an anti-convulsant)
phenothiazines*
phenytoin
primidone
procainamide
propranolol
pyridostigmine
quinidine
reserpine
thiothixene
Vitamin B-12

*See Drug Family, Section Four.

SECTION SEVEN

Personal Drug Histories

A written account of significant drug experiences is an important part of your family's medical record. This section provides the following forms to assist you in maintaining a file of appropriate drug information:

- Drugs Taken During Pregnancy
- Drugs Taken During Infancy and Childhood
- Drugs Taken by Adults
- Medical Alert

Drugs Taken During Pregnancy
(Record all prescription and non-prescription drugs)

Mother: _____
Residence: _____

Attending Physician: _____
Physician's Address: _____

Hospital: _____

Pregnancy Number: _____   Mother's Age: _____   Father's Age: _____
Estimated Date of Conception: _____
Estimated Date of Delivery: _____
Actual Date of Delivery: _____
Condition of Infant: _____

Complications During Pregnancy: _____

Drug Name, Dosage Form & Strength	Prescribing Physician	Indication for Drug	Date Started	Date Stopped	Daily Dose	Drug Experience

Additional Notes: _____

Drugs Taken During Infancy and Childhood
(That Require Documentation)

Child's Name: _____ Date of Birth: _____

Residence: _____

Attending Physician: _____

Physician's Address: _____

Pharmacies Used: _____

Prescription #: _____

Drug Name Dosage Form & Strength	Prescribing Physician	Indication for Drug	Date Started	Date Stopped	Daily Dose	Drug Experience

Additional Notes:

Drugs Taken by Adults
(That Require Documentation)

Name: _____ Date of Birth: _____

Residence: _____

Attending Physician: _____

Physician's Address: _____

Pharmacies Used: _____

Prescription #: _____

Drug Name Dosage Form & Strength	Prescribing Physician	Indication for Drug	Date Started	Date Stopped	Daily Dose	Drug Experience

Additional Notes:

743

Card for Wallet or Purse

MEDICAL ALERT

Patient's Name:_____ Date of Birth: _____
   Address:_____
   Telephone: (Home) _____(Business) _____
In Emergency Please Notify: (Name) _____
         (Telephone) _____   _____
Physician:_____ Employer: _____
(Telephone)_____ (Telephone) _____

Medical Conditions	Present Medications	Known Drug Allergies

(A copy of this form should be carried in wallet or purse at all times.)

Sources

The following sources were consulted in the compilation of this book:

Adverse Drug Reaction Bulletin. Edited by D. M. Davies. Newcastle upon Tyne, England: Regional Postgraduate Institute for Medicine and Dentistry.

AMA Department of Drugs, *American Medical Association Drug Evaluations.* 2nd ed. Acton, Mass.: Publishing Sciences Group, Inc., 1973.

American Pharmaceutical Association, *Evaluations of Drug Interactions.* Washington, D.C.: American Pharmaceutical Association, 1973.

Avery, Graeme S., ed., *Drug Treatment.* Acton, Mass.: Publishing Sciences Group, Inc. Sydney, Australia: ADIS Press, 1976.

Azarnoff, Daniel L. *Steroid Therapy.* Philadelphia: W. B. Saunders Company, 1975.

Blacow, Norman W., ed., *Martindale, The Extra Pharmacopoeia.* 26th ed. London: The Pharmaceutical Press, 1973.

Casarett, Louis, J., and Doull, John, eds., *Toxicology, The Basic Science of Poisons.* New York: Macmillan, 1975.

Clin-Alert. Louisville, Kentucky: Science Editors, Inc.

Clinical Pharmacology and Therapeutics. Edited by Walter Modell. St. Louis: The C. V. Mosby Co.

Cluff, Leighton E.; Caranasos, George J.; and Stewart, Ronald B., *Clinical Problems With Drugs.* Philadelphia: W. B. Saunders Company, 1975.

Cluff, L. E., and Petrie, J. C., eds., *Clinical Effects of Interaction Between Drugs.* New York: American Elsevier Publishing Co., Inc., 1974.

Deichmann, William B., and Gerarde, Horace W., *Toxicology of Drugs and Chemicals.* New York: Academic Press, 1969.

Drug and Therapeutics Bulletin. Edited by Andrew Herxheimer. London: Consumers' Association.

Drug Intelligence and Clinical Pharmacy. Edited by Donald E. Francke. Hamilton, Illinois: Hamilton Press.

Facts and Comparisons. Edited by Erwin K. Kastrup and Gene H. Schwach. St. Louis: Facts and Comparisons, Inc.

F.D.A. Clinical Experience Abstracts. Edited by Elizabeth C. Kelly. Rockville, Maryland: Department of Health, Education and Welfare, Food and Drug Administration.

F.D.A. Drug Bulletin. Edited by Eric W. Martin. Rockville, Maryland: Department of Health, Education and Welfare, Food and Drug Administration.

Fraunfelder, F. T., *Drug-Induced Ocular Side Effects and Drug Interactions.* Philadelphia: Lea & Febiger, 1976.

Giffenhagen, George B., and Hawkins, Linda L., eds., *Handbook of Non-Pre-*

scription Drugs. Washington, D.C.: American Pharmaceutical Association, 1973.

Gleason, Marion N.; Gosselin, Robert E.; Hodge, Howard C.; and Smith, Roger P., *Clinical Toxicology of Commercial Products.* 3rd ed. Baltimore: The Williams & Wilkins Co., 1969.

Goodman, Louis S., and Gilman, Alfred, *The Pharmacological Basis of Therapeutics.* 5th ed. New York: Macmillan, 1975.

Hantsen, Philip D., *Drug Interactions.* Philadelphia: Lea & Febiger, 1972.

Hollister, Leo E., *Clinical Use of Psychotherapeutic Drugs.* Springfield, Illinois: Charles C. Thomas, 1973.

Huff, Barbara B., ed., *The Physicians' Desk Reference.* 30th ed. Oradell, New Jersey: Medical Economics Company, 1976.

International Drug Therapy Newsletter. Edited by Frank J. Ayd, Jr. Baltimore: Ayd Medical Communications.

Journal of the American Medical Association. Edited by William R. Barclay. Chicago: American Medical Association.

Kagan, Benjamin M., *Antimicrobial Therapy.* 2nd ed. Philadelphia: W. B. Saunders Company, 1974.

Lewis, Arthur J., ed. *The Modern Drug Encyclopedia and Therapeutic Index.* 13th ed. Yorke Medical Books. New York: Dun-Donnelley Publishing Corp., 1975.

Martin, Eric W., *Hazards of Medication.* Philadelphia: J. B. Lippincott Co., 1971.

The Medical Clinics of North America, *Symposium on Individualization of Drug Therapy.* Vol. 58, No. 5. Philadelphia: W. B. Saunders Company, 1974.

The Medical Letter on Drugs and Therapeutics. Edited by Harold Aaron. New Rochelle, N.Y.: The Medical Letter, Inc.

Melmon, Kenneth L., and Morrelli, Howard F., *Clinical Pharmacology.* New York: Macmillan, 1972.

Meyler, L., and Herxheimer, A., eds., *Side Effects of Drugs.* Vol. 8. Amsterdam: Excerpta Medica, 1975.

Meyler, L., and Peck, H. M., eds., *Drug-Induced Diseases.* Vol. 4. Amsterdam: Excerpta Medica, 1972.

Miller, Russell R., and Greenblatt, David J., eds., *Drug Effects in Hospitalized Patients.* New York: John Wiley & Sons, 1976.

Modell, Walter; Schild, Heinz O.; and Wilson, Andrew, *Applied Pharmacology.* Philadelphia: W. B. Saunders Company, 1976.

Moss, Arthur J., and Patton, Robert D., *Antiarrhythmic Agents.* Springfield, Illinois: Charles C. Thomas, 1973.

The New England Journal of Medicine. Edited by F. J. Ingelfinger. Boston: Massachusetts Medical Society.

Nishumura, Hideo, and Tanimura, Takashi, *Clinical Aspects of the Teratogenicity of Drugs.* New York: American Elsevier Publishing Co., Inc., 1976.

Osol, Arthur, and Pratt, Robertson, *The United States Dispensatory.* 27th ed. Philadelphia: J. B. Lippincott Co., 1973.

The Pediatric Clinics of North America, *Symposium on Pediatric Pharmacology.* Vol. 19, No. 1. Philadelphia: W. B. Saunders Company, 1972.

Reilly, Mary Jo, ed., *American Hospital Formulary Service.* Bethesda, Maryland: American Society of Hospital Pharmacists, 1976.

Rotenberg, Gerald N., ed., *Compendium of Pharmaceuticals and Specialties.* 11th ed. Toronto: Canadian Pharmaceutical Association, 1976.

Siegelman, Stanley, ed., *American Druggist Blue Book.* New York: Hearst Corporation, 1976.

Stockley, Ivan, *Drug Interactions and Their Mechanisms.* London: The Pharmaceutical Press, 1974.

The United States Pharmacopeia XIX. 19th rev. Rockville, Maryland: United States Pharmacopeial Convention, Inc., 1975.

Wade, O. L., *Adverse Reactions to Drugs.* London: William Heinemann Medical Books, Ltd., 1970.

Wilson, Charles O., and Jones, Tony E., *American Drug Index.* Philadelphia: J. B. Lippincott Co., 1976.

Index of Generic Names

Index of Brand Names

ABOUT THE AUTHOR

James W. Long, M.D., was born in Allentown, Pennsylvania. He received his pre-medical education from the University of Maryland and his medical degree from the George Washington University School of Medicine in Washington, D.C. For twenty years he was in the private practice of internal medicine in the Washington metropolitan area, and for over twenty-five years he has been a member of the faculty of the George Washington University School of Medicine. He has served with the Food and Drug Administration, the National Library of Medicine, and the Bureau of Health Manpower of the National Institutes of Health. Dr. Long is now director of Health Services for the National Science Foundation in Washington. He lives in Rockville, Maryland.

Dr. Long's involvement in drug information activities includes service on the H.E.W. Task Force on Prescription Drugs, on the F.D.A. Task Force on Adverse Drug Reactions, as a delegate-at-large to the U.S. Pharmacopeial Convention, as Editorial Consultant for *Hospital Formulary,* as a director of the Drug Information Association, and as a member of the Toxicology Information Program Committee of the National Research Council/National Academy of Sciences. He is the author of numerous articles in professional journals. *The Essential Guide to Prescription Drugs* is an outgrowth of his conviction that the general public needs and is entitled to practical drug information which is the equivalent of the professional "package insert." He believes the patient can be reasonably certain of using medications with the least risk and the greatest benefit only when the patient has all the relevant information about the drugs he or she is taking.

Placidyl

p- 2 83